PROGRESS IN
NATURAL RESOURCE
ECONOMICS

PROGRESS IN NATURAL RESOURCE ECONOMICS

Essays in Resource
Analysis by Members of the
Programme in Natural Resource
Economics (PNRE) at the University
of British Columbia

Edited by
ANTHONY SCOTT

with the assistance of
John Helliwell, Tracy Lewis, and Philip Neher

CLARENDON PRESS · OXFORD
1985

Oxford University Press, Walton Street, Oxford OX2 6DP

Oxford New York Toronto
Delhi Bombay Calcutta Madras Karachi
Kuala Lumpur Singapore Hong Kong Tokyo
Nairobi Dar es Salaam Cape Town
Melbourne Auckland
and associated companies in
Beirut Berlin Ibadan Mexico City Nicosia

Oxford is a trade mark of Oxford University Press

Published in the United States
by Oxford University Press, New York

© Anthony Scott 1985

British Library Cataloguing in Publication Data
Progress in natural resource economics.
1. Natural resources—Mathematical models
I. Scott, Anthony
333.7'0724   HC55
ISBN 0-19-828460-8

Library of Congress Cataloging in Publication Data
Main entry under title:
Progress in natural resource economics.
Bibliography: p.
Includes index.
1. Natural resources—Addresses, essays, lectures.
2. Natural resources—Canada—Addresses, essays, lectures.
I. Scott, Anthony.   II. Helliwell, John F.   III. Lewis,
Tracy R.   IV. Neher, Philip A., 1934- V. University
of British Columbia. Programme in Natural Resource
Economics.
HC59.P685   1984   333.7   84-17447
ISBN 0-19-828460-8

Set by Joshua Associates Limited, Oxford
Printed in Great Britain by
The Alden Press, Oxford

CONTENTS

PART VI INSTITUTIONS AND IDEOLOGIES

PART I
PROGRESS IN NATURAL RESOURCE ECONOMICS

1. INTRODUCTION

Anthony Scott

NOTES ON THE EMERGENCE OF NATURAL RESOURCE ECONOMICS

The papers in this volume all stem from work done by members of the University of British Columbia's Programme in Natural Resource Economics (PNRE), which in the mid-1970s was awarded a Canada Council 'programme grant'. This group's original proposal, negotiated with the Council during the period 1974-6, stemmed from a convergence of three circumstances: an obvious need for intensive research on resource topics; a growing demand for graduate students versed in natural resource economics; and, on the supply side, an opportunity to utilize existing faculty capital in the form of familiarity with resource economics, which had almost accidentally been accumulated at the University of British Columbia.

The first of these—an obvious need for intensive economic research on natural resources—had two origins. One was a professionally perceived lag in the application of standard theoretical developments to routine resource situations; the other was a demand for economic analysis of new resource policies. That there had been a serious delay between the refinement of economic theories and their application to the worlds of natural resource harvesting and management was all too obvious. There was much to be done if the field was to catch up. And catching up would bring obvious benefits to the whole field of economics—for example, if the care and attention that had gradually shaped such sub-disciplines as labour economics and industrial organization were also devoted to land and resources, not only might the economics of resource decisions be improved, but there would also be a nutritious feedback to the main body of economic analysis.

To bring the main body of economics to bear on natural resource questions would be something like diverting the flow from a large river to irrigate a neglected field. Like others, we reckoned that the soil might be fertile enough to repay the cost of diversion; furthermore, the associated tender care might trigger new, unsuspected, growths with exciting fruit. And this was not all. Much water diverted through a field eventually flows back to nourish the main stream itself, so the main body of economics might be enriched by what had been bestowed on natural resources. Indeed, this had already happened once. In the eighteenth century, economics had lavished analytical attention on farming, land, and the extensive margin. That time the flow-back—the concept of rent—had been sufficient to keep the mainstream of classical economic theory going for more than a century. Since then, however, there had been little attention from professional economics to the natural resources, and little flow-back. As a consequence, resource economics in the 1960s was not recognized as a field awaiting a new diversion from the now-swollen stream of analytical economics. It was not even recognized as such by its best-known pioneers, men like Faustmann, Jevons, Pigou, Gray, and Hotelling. By the mid-1970s, however, almost-forgotten contributions of these forerunners did suggest that there was a field waiting to be developed, and that such development might yield a rich flow-back for economics as a whole.

The second origin of a 'need' for progress in natural resource economics was policy analysis. To apply new concepts to unfamiliar problems was justification enough, but from many points of view it was less important than that connected with economic policy. But what policy? The apparent irrelevance for policy of the contributions by the four pioneering economists mentioned above may help explain the neglect of the whole field for so many decades. To understand their irrelevance, consider the following. Faustmann (1849) prescribed rules for forest renewal just as the world was opening up the mature forests of Russia and the new world: his optimum rotation remained a redundant concept for a century. Then Jevons (1866) considered coal shortage just as petroleum discoveries made energy a drug on the market everywhere. Finally, Pigou (1932) analysed briefly the economizing of atmospheric capacity to receive smoke, and Gray (1913) and Hotelling (1931) the mineral capacity to sustain future consumption, just as world depression was removing these matters from policy agendas. Their analyses were forgotten all the faster because in the 1930s there were other, more urgent, resource policy issues demanding keen legislative attention. And economists of the 1930s were not oblivious to these urgent problems. In the field of energy, for example, Keynes and many of his contemporaries had struggled to suggest how to revive declining coal mining districts; in fisheries, Harold Innis's analysis of the cod fishery had attempted to explain the decline of the salt fish industry; and in the extractive industries a generation of economists had, while trying to explain the changing terms of trade between raw materials and manufacturers, emerged with ideas about gold mining (Earl Hamilton and Frank Paish, for example) and about booms in the staple industries (Innis and Lower, 1936, for example). Their approaches were often helpful. They were perhaps too loose to enable analysts confidently to predict that, if a resource policy involved a tax (or tariff or subsidy), it was *ipso facto* inefficient; or even that the tax would prolong or shorten production (see Paish, 1938, however). For that kind of sharpness the 1930s policy-maker would have been forced to refine the Faustmann, Hotelling, or Pigou models. But with the interesting exception of benefit-cost analysis of water resource projects, the elegance of static, partial analyses was not needed for policies devised as rescue measures for resource industries.

In other words, the field of resource economics had not in the 1930s been cultivated in such a way as to develop a set of generally applicably analytical ideas. Instead, growths had sprouted here and there that tended to obscure whatever consistencies and uniformities there might be.

The events of the Second World War and the decade after did little to change this. Vast studies of possible world material and energy shortages were undertaken, on very slender analytical foundations. A few economists applied simplified versions of the interwar models of capital and investment to the conservation issue. Others made a start on common property analysis of fishery questions. And a larger group of competent economists devoted themselves to water resource problems concerned with investments in flood protection, irrigation, and electricity generation. But only the last of these activities had any impetus of its own, the others developing spasmodically as individual economists carried particular analyses a step or so further.

The low tide of resource studies was finally reversed in the 1960s. Where the study of durable resources had been little more than a textbook example (along with wine-ageing) of allocation over time in the presence of an interest rate, new studies revived enthusiasm for the questions addressed by Faustmann, Jevons, and Hotelling. Two analytical innovations were seen to cast light on these questions: the new body of aggregative dynamic growth models developed by such figures as Baumol, Solow, and Swann, and the broadened understanding of both mathematical programming and later of the techniques of optimum control theory stemming from L. S. Pontryagin. These approaches turned questions about natural resource use over time into questions susceptible of genuinely dynamic analysis.

By the end of the 1960s the need for economists to meet resource problems with full-scale analyses was becoming apparent. Demand studies were obviously needed to replace the primitive projection methods used by energy councils and public utility boards. On the production side, econometrics, computer simulation, and linear programming had all been used sporadically, in particular instances; but much more was needed if economics was to contribute more to sorting out the new environmental and energy issues. In other words, there was not just an opportunity to turn economics on and let it 'find its own level' in natural resource topography; there was also a challenge to adapt its methods to assist with new resource policy questions that lay outside the known faculty of economics.

We were also aware of a second need: for better opportunities for training graduate students in the economic analysis of natural resources problems. In comparison with those in the natural and applied sciences relating to natural resources, such opportunities had been meagre in spite of the increasing emphasis placed on the 'economic and social aspects' of resource development projects. It seemed clear to us that training should be provided by supplementing a conventional graduate programme with arrangements for students to work closely with established researchers on actual research projects.

Training to be what? The demand for graduate students was clear enough. Specialist government departments and businesses had almost no staff analysts who were even aware that an economic literature on resources existed and was growing. Consequently they exerted a steady if imprecise demand for 'mineral economists' and the like. We thought we could respond to this demand. Our graduates should not be too specialized; they should be able to keep in touch with the wider concerns and approaches of the central core of the profession. This professionalism would arm them against unsound theory and poor econometric technique in a field notorious for fuzzy 'inter-disciplinary' thinking. But they must accumulate special resource knowledge as well.

A third circumstance was that, since the later 1950s, there had been emerging at the University of British Columbia (UBC) a considerable group of economists with research interests in natural resource questions. Natural resources had become something of a teaching specialty within the Department of Economics, and increasing size had enabled the department gradually to expand this teaching at various student levels. This was before the days of the economics of the ecology–environmental movement or, of course, of the energy crisis. The usual fare offered had been a strong and plentiful shot of welfare economics as a cocktail; water, fisheries, and other common-property resource as starters; and forests, minerals, and their conservation as main dishes. This had been a very suitable diet for Western students whose governments were struggling with the access, investment, and tax policy problems of just these resources. But similar problems were evidently of concern elsewhere, for the new resource studies being published (for example, by the emerging Resources for the Future group in Washington) were all welcome course reading matter. It seemed at that time that what the new field of resource studies lacked was a coherent, robust, theoretical framework. True, some models used in agricultural economics were suitable for resource economics as far as they went, but that was not very far from the farming sector of the economy. The industrial organization analyses of oil and coal were also helpful, but they were written with the basic aim of illuminating anti-trust policy. Thus, much exposition at the outset had taken the form of adapting available theory: capital theory to resource exhaustion, Knight's views on common-property theory to fisheries and water, and 'potential' welfare economics to benefit–cost analysis. Consequently, the research output of this period, though vigorous enough, was clearly the product of a group spread very thin. Supplying rather imprecise models for new policy problems, members of the group darted from resource to resource. Their papers were often in response to a demand for conference papers, conferences where the main running would be made by specialists from strong technical and scientific programmes (concerned especially with fisheries and water research).

This undermanning of resource economics appeared even more serious when two new policy problems raised their own research questions. First, the birth of the environmental movement in the 1960s placed a severe strain on existing concepts and knowledge. Second, the petroleum crisis of the 1970s showed just how undeveloped were methods of predicting the supply and demand of any mineral product. These two events brought new economists into a broadened field, some of whom spread out beyond pollution or petroleum studies. Nevertheless, the few old-style resource specialists, including a few at UBC (like the single-taxers and institutional land economists of earlier decades), appeared somewhat overwhelmed by the new and major issues, and unequipped to deal with the new challenges.

PNRE: A MAJOR RESEARCH GRANT, 1976

These three circumstances combined in the mid-1970s to bring us together to apply for a type of grant new to Canada, a social science negotiated programmed grant. Application for it gave us an opportunity to test our understanding of these three circumstances in debate with expert and helpful consultants to the financing agency, the Social Science and Humanities Research Council of Canada (SSHRCC). After several iterations, all profitable, ten of us obtained a research grant to support us and our research assistant graduate students in a loosely co-ordinated Programme in Natural Resources Economics (PNRE). The university administration and the Department of Economics helped generously as well.

The Research Council suggested that we should plan to wind up our programme by holding an academic conference to measure the road we had travelled. This volume records that such a conference did take place. It is an incomplete measure of our progress in resource analysis, for two reasons. First, although our group was vigorous, it must not seek credit for the enormous strides made in natural resource analysis throughout the whole discipline. In the event, we were only one cog in a very large and productive machine. Others had seen the needs and opportunities when we had. Second, because the impetus is by no means over, it is not yet profitable to stop to assess the final results. All members of our group, our visitors, and our former students and colleagues who also contributed are still engaged in resource economics. The grant did develop our group, and our subject, and we are still at work.

PROGRESS IN NATURAL RESOURCE ECONOMICS
SINCE THE MID-1970s

Nevertheless, it is possible to trace progress since the mid-1970s by making comparisons.

One possible comparison is that between the state of resource-economic theory in 1976, sketched in the first section of this chapter, and today. In earlier times an economist well versed in welfare economics could have mastered, and criticized, almost the whole of resource economic literature in a few months; he or she could probably have written a publishable addition to it in a few months more. That day is past, the literature having been filled in and extended. The literature has consolidated, so that an increasing number of researchers are teaching standard courses that bring the various fragments together; but it has also sprawled, to include analysis of land markets and property rights, open-access industries, systems of regulation, taxation, and so on. Furthermore, there has been obvious success in attaching to macroeconomics and to industrial organization additions that take account of exploration problems, uncertainty about scarcity, exhaustibility, and irreversibility. The results are very evident, not only in the four or five international journals wholey devoted to natural resource or energy economics, but also in the ten or so leading general journals.

Another revealing comparison is that between our own original 1975 appreciation of the task for resource studies, and what the profession actually did. This can be done by consulting our research grant application. In an appreciation of the field in 1975 (drafted for us by Jim Wilen), we suggested the following conclusion:

In view of the rapid change which Natural Resource Economics has experienced during the past decade, it is difficult to pinpoint exactly where the core is 'going', but as we have tried to suggest, it appears to be developing around a focus of dynamic welfare economics. The next few years will probably witness a solidifying of such a core and an extension into some frontier area employing uncertainty and information theory, second-best problems of restricted policy choice, and analyses of alternative institutional design. In addition, of course, there is an important need for empirical work which tests the validity of the theoretical propositions and employs such results in the analysis of alternative policies. . . .

This prediction of the coming of what we referred to as research that would firm up the core turned out to be only partly accurate.

We had presented a four-fold classification of recent research into renewable, non-renewable, common-property, and macro-problems, a classification that has had some staying power. For example, Peterson and Fisher (1977) and Fisher and Peterson (1976) had devoted one survey to literature on renewable and non-renewable resources, mostly dynamic, and mostly concerned with welfare; and another to externalities and environmental common-property problems of the environment. They showed uncertainty about how to deal with the fourth category, macro-models, and in the event scattered partial surveys of that approach throughout their two main articles. Textbooks, too, have tended to use this four-fold classification, at least if they made claim to dealing with all natural resources. For example, Herfindahl and Kneese (1974), Howe (1979) and Fisher (1981) all reveal a similar understanding of the four main divisions into which their subject falls and also of the research or theorizing available to be transmitted to students. And these are the major divisions into which our volume is also divided.

Most of them, however, provide a fifth and a sixth sub-division. The fifth of these is also represented here: economic ideology. The field of natural resources was a target of the land tax movement almost from the dawn of classical economics. This connection became strongest in the Henry George days, and survives in various schemes for mineral and forest taxation. Even more influential was the later conservation movement, noticed by Jevons and Pigou, Gray and Hotelling. The single word 'conservation', like the word 'environment', described a bundle of disciplinary approaches to resource problems, especially in connection with the management of the public lands. In Chapter 12 below Ernst Berndt discusses a rather specialized ideological approach to energy resource problems: technocracy.

The surveys under discussion usually also contain a sixth aspect: benefit–cost analysis. A holdover from the 1930-40 preoccupation with river development, this analytical approach has apparently gained a more permanent foothold in resource economics than in other applied fields. In our group Pearse, Scott and Campbell have all made contributions to benefit–cost literature, although it is not represented explicitly in this volume. In the textbook and survey literature, benefit–cost analysis is elaborated so it can serve as a general utilitarian rationalistic framework for discussions of issues as disparate as public land management, energy pricing policy, conservation of scarce materials, and quasi-ideological questions. They add important chapters dealing with uses of public lands, with property rights, and with public choice, all in a style that reveals their descent from the benefit–cost resource.

Of course, these five or six groupings of resource economics research are the result, not the cause, of individual decisions by economists planning their own activities. When we look at the results of their research, their articles are found to draw on branches of economic theory other than those suggested by our original appreciation and deal with applied problems that do not fit neatly into our four or five classifications. They are also distributed among the four headings very unevenly, so that some classifications have so far remained empty research boxes. Let us examine these three assertions.

Consider, first, contributions to abstract analysis and theory. The following generalizations may be suggested. We were right that the literature of the 1970s would be heavily dominated by dynamics, much of it cashing in on a widening professional understanding of capital theory as illuminated by new techniques of dynamic programming and control theory. This was particularly the case in analysing exhaustible resource extraction; but no applied field of resource analysis was left untouched. On the other hand, much progress has been made in applying to the analysis of resource extraction some barely dynamic models of industrial organization and of production theory (i.e., theory of the firm using duality relationships), and this non-normative body of analysis seems to us to have made greater headway than we foresaw in the mid-1970s. Furthermore, our confidence that theorizing about 'uncertainty and information theory' would progress because of new ways in which uncertainty cropped up in policy analysis (in the energy crisis and in ecological and biological models) appears to have been excessive. Although the analysis of oil exploration and the related behavioural models did put the resources of mathematical statistics at the service of economics to an extent that went beyond econometrics as usually defined, it must be concluded that in no other respect has resource economics done more than adapt well-known approaches to risk and uncertainty to resource questions.

Of course, the need to deal with uncertainty in applied studies dealing with policy choices has been reduced by two general innovations in economics: the new emphasis on investment in information rather than on the strategic reaction to uncertainty (the oil exploration models may be typical here); and the capacity of simulation methods to make sensitivity analyses of alternative assumptions about the real world to an extent that actually dispels a decision-maker's uncertainty. The generalizations about theorizing in research in economics of natural resources as a whole are represented within the group that finally wrote the papers in this volume. Neher, Munro, Lewis, Campbell, and later Eswaran, Slade, and Lasserre ventured into dynamic theorizing to a major extent. Several of these also introduced elements from industrial organization theorizing, mostly as applied to minerals and fisheries. Over the whole period, only a couple of theoretical forest economics papers were written, involving Neher along with Colin Clark and Terry Heaps; and one dealing with pollution of the environment in a theoretical fashion, by Neher. Several of these also introduced elements from industrial organization. Uhler offered statistical approaches to exploration and to fisheries stock estimation.

The second generalization offered above was that in the period surveyed economists' studies of applied resource problems, especially of policy problems, did not exploit the available methods fully or consistently. We can illustrate the generalization only by reference to the work done within our group. To begin with, many were 'applied' but many, perhaps most, were non-quantitive. Among those that did deal in numbers, four distinct methods could be seen. First, as already mentioned, Uhler, almost unique in the economics profession, mined his Alberta data to obtain models of the firm's exploratory behaviour. Second, Helliwell undertook an extensive series of simulation studies, mostly employing the same model of energy sector of the economy, but some purpose-built to deal with mining taxation, pipeline costs, and other partial problems. Third, Helliwell, used a mining model, worked out with Bradley (and Campbell too developed a mining model), using what are usually described as engineering, rather than econometric, estimates of cost functions. Fourth, more familiar econometric methods were developed by Berndt in numerous studies of consumer and of firm demand, the latter fully exploiting the duality approach to input demands; while Wilen, in papers with Pearse and with Donald Paterson on fishery and sealing topics, adapted econometric methods for production analysis. The distinction between these four methods is often artificial. Berndt in particular has contributed articles to the literature reconciling engineering and econometric approaches to analysis; Helliwell, with McRae and Bradley, has combined econometric and deterministic modelling; and most would probably deny that any boundary exists between Uhler's statistical analyses and the main body of econometrics.

Another smaller set of applied projects by members of the group was strictly non-quantitative. Here one might mention Pearse, whose extensive policy analyses of forest and fishery regulation and tenure problems are for the most part in the tradition of applied static welfare economics, overlapping public finance, public choice, and industrial organization. His work on regulation has been paralleled by numerous companion studies by Munro, Neher, Campbell, Wilen, and Scott on alternative methods of fishery regulation and by Bradley on petroleum industry regulation and pricing. These studies in turn shade off into an area in which economists have studied the economic effects of various institutions (such as types of common-property tenure; accounting principles for pipeline regulation; alternative tax methods for minerals and energy; constitutional studies on the assignment of powers over resource revenues by alternative levels of government; the usefulness of public hearings; energy unit economics; international resource management alternatives, and many more).

Indeed, when confronted with policy problems in the natural resource industries, we like other economists seem most frequently to have responded with suggestions for inventing or installing new procedures and property rights. This recourse to new institutions is not surprising, for until recently the resource industries as a group have been remarkably free of regulation, taxes, and other instruments of government intervention. In spite of the power or obligation of government to manage the public lands and to control common property, and in spite of administrative processes concerned with safety and with public utility pricing, many natural resource activities became the preserve of the no-nonsense, free-enterprise, cut-and-run, fish-or-cut-bait miner, logger, and fisherman. Perhaps the export orientation of these raw material enclaves freed them from much interference. Those days are gone for ever. In the developed nations at least a dense underbrush of controls and charges, and of supervised subsidies and tax gimmicks as well, has accumulated around the resource industries. These policy instruments have become a natural target for controversy and research. Economists have not been slow to enter the fray, especially in criticizing and proposing particular institutional arrangements.

In retrospect, it cannot be said that this work was uniform or systematic. This is my third generalization. Much remains to be done, even if it only fills in obvious gaps. The econometric work on energy demand has not yet been matched by corresponding econometric work on supply; the painstaking theoretical emphasis on competition versus monopoly in mineral and energy studies is largely absent in the forestry and fisheries studies—indeed, our work on forestry by any technique seems to have lagged well behind that in fisheries or mining. Most surprising of all, perhaps, is our slowness to exploit fully the massive simulation models of the fishery, surprising because such fishery models are already used extensively outside economics by ecologists and biologists. These continue to present many opportunities for genuine inter-disciplinary research at a relatively profound level. Spulber's comments on fisheries research at the end of Chapter 3 below are worth reading in this connection. A third way to obtain evidence on the contrast between 1976 and 1982, however, is to examine the following papers, with an eye specially cocked for evidence of changes since the earlier period. This is the business of the parts making up the bulk of the book.

The volume is arranged into parts similar to those used by the surveys of natural resource economics and the textbooks, mentioned above. Part II deals with 'macroeconomics', Part III with renewable resources, Part IV with the theory of exhaustible resources, Part V with the empirical analysis of exhaustible resources, and Part VI with institutions and ideologies. Each part contains an Introductory Note to the papers within it, describing their connection with recent progress in natural resource economics. Most obvious omissions from our contents are the economics of the forest as a unit of management, and the economics of the environment and recreation. As the list of our contributions to the literature (see pp. 426-31) will suggest, members of our group have worked in these two fields, but were not actively doing so in 1981-2. However, the paper by Neher does deal in abstract fashion with planning the use of a resource that can be enjoyed as a stock or as a flow, the first an amenity and the second a consumable good. And a series of papers and public reports by P. H. Pearse, the latest of which prevented his representation in this volume, though not at the conference, deals with renewable resources and includes whole chapters on sport and recreation.

The introductions were written by the editors: John Helliwell on macro-economics and on the empirical papers on exhaustible resources; Philip Neher on renewable resources (an essay in itself); Tracy Lewis on the theoretical papers on exhaustible resources, and Anthony Scott on institutions and ideologies.

ACKNOWLEDGEMENTS

As for the Programme in Natural Resource Economics, so with the Conference in which these papers were presented: our basic source of finance was the Social Science and Humanities Research Council of Canada. We are grateful for its support and also for the helpful intervention at various times in our programme's career of members of the Council, the President, the Director, and of several gracious grants officers whose problems we had become. We also benfited from the suggestions of several visiting teams of academic appraisers.

At the University of British Columbia this conference, like the Programme before it, had considerable help at crucial stages from President Douglas Kenny, Dean Robert Will, Dr Richard Spratly, our colleagues Ronald Shearer and John Cragg, and the co-operative indulgence of our other department colleagues and of Susan Eldrige, departmental administrative assistant.

At least six generations of academic visitors, assistants, and graduate students were represented at the Conference or contributed to this volume, or both. Among those who helped and whose names do not appear elsewhere are Tim Padmore, who helped at the conference as well as being an author; André Plourde, and Jim Johnston. The indexer was Elizabeth Paterson.

Throughout the six years PNRE depended heavily on the secretaries who undertook to see to its organization and budgeting and to the production and circulation of its papers. Two of them were directly concerned with this volume and with the conference from which it originated. Susan McLintock assisted in setting up the conference and saw it through. As PNRE was phased out, she was succeeded in administration by Kate Birkinshaw, who with Laurel Slaney worked with Shelley Phipps and the editors to arrange the present volume. We are much indebted to them.

Naturally, everyone in a collective enterprise is grateful to the other members. But there were some outsiders whose help we welcomed warmly. Some of the most useful and provocative pages in the volume were contributed by our commentators. Most of them were friends, but few of them were previously connected with PNRE. The quality of their constructive work speaks for itself; the editors wish only to thank them, especially those whose pieces expanded from bare discussions to full-blown essays in the topics to which they were asked to contribute.

REFERENCES

Faustmann, M. (1849), 'On the Determination of the Value which Forest Lands and Immature Stands Possess for Forestry', translated in M. Game (ed.), *Oxford Institute Paper*, 42, 1968.

Fisher, A. C. (1981), *Resource and Environmental Economics*, Cambridge, Cambridge University Press.

Fisher, A. C. and Peterson, T. M. (1976), 'The Environment in Economics', *Journal of Economic Literature*, 14, 1-33.

Gray, L. C. (1913), 'The Economic Possibilities of Conservation', *Quarterly Journal of Economics*, 27, 497-519.

Herfindahl, O. C. and Kneese, A. V. (1974), *Economic Theory of Natural Resources* Columbus, Ohio, Charles E. Merrill.

Howe, C. W. (1979), *Natural Resource Economics*, New York, John Wiley.

Hotelling, Harold (1931), 'The Economics of Exhaustible Resources', *Journal of Political Economy*, 39, 137-75.

Innis, H. A. and Lower, A. R. M. (1936), *Settlement and the Forest and Mining Frontiers*, Toronto, Macmillan.

Jevons, W. S. (1866), *The Coal Question*, London, Macmillan.

Paish, F. W. (1938), 'Courses of Changes in Gold Supply', *Economica*, 5, 379-409; reprinted in *The Post-War Financial Problem*, London, Macmillan.

Pigou, A. C. (1932), *The Economics of Welfare 4th edn.*, London, Macmillan.

Pearse, P. H. (1982), *Turning the Tide: A New Policy for Canada's Pacific Fisheries*, Ottawa, Department of Fisheries and Oceans.

Peterson, F. M. and Fisher, A. C. (1977), 'The Exploitation of Extractive Resources', *Economic Journal*, 87, 687-721.

PART II
MACROECONOMIC ANALYSIS OF NATURAL RESOURCES

Introductory Note

John F. Helliwell

The paper by Helliwell and associates, and the comment by Lawrence Klein, describe the latest PNRE research on the macroeconomic effects of the investment, financing, output, taxation, and pricing of major natural resource projects. The paper provides the main description of the MACE model's structure, along with references to earlier work and application to a number of important issues, such as the effects of changes in world oil prices, changes in the volume of natural gas exports, and the construction and operation of large oil sands projects. Since the MACE model contains detailed treatment of the costs, pricing, and taxation of crude oil and natural gas, a consistent disaggregation of energy demand by fuel and by region, and a macroeconomic structure that is suitable for both short-run and long-run simulations, it is now possible to use the same model for both macroeconomic assessment and evaluation of the size and distribution of costs and benefits.

2. Energy and the National Economy: An Overview of the MACE Model*

John F. Helliwell, Robert N. McRae, Paul Boothe,
Ardo Hansson, Michael Margolick, Tim Padmore,
André Plourde, and Reg Plummer

1. BACKGROUND

What role did higher energy prices play in creating national and world stagflation in the 1970s and 1980s? What are the direct and indirect effects of domestic energy prices on energy demand, energy supply, national output, inflation, and the exchange rate? What are the macroeconomic effects of alternative rates of development and exploitation of new energy sources? These are among the most important and difficult of the questions that have faced economists and policy-makers over the past decade. They are especially complicated for countries like Canada, with open economies and important supplies of both renewable and non-renewable energy sources.

In this paper, we outline the structure and make some use of a new model that we have developed to focus on these and similar questions about the Canadian economy. The MACE model (for MACro and Energy) is in many respects a natural evolution of model-building efforts by ourselves and others over the past fifteen years, although the decision to highlight the role of energy, as distinct from other Canadian natural resources, reflects the impact that the world oil price shocks of 1973-4 and 1979-80 had on Canadian issues and events. However, the earliest versions of the University of British Columbia (UBC) energy model were constructed in 1972-3, before the oil price shocks, to evaluate the macroeconomic impacts [M6, M7, M8, M9], and the costs and benefits [M45], of a then-proposed natural gas pipeline to carry Alaskan and Canadian natural gas along the Mackenzie Valley to markets in southern Canada and the United States. Two versions of the pipeline model were built: a quarterly version, which was linked to the macroeconomic model RDX2 to show the macroeconomic impacts, and an annual version, which was run well into the next century to assess the distribution of the costs and benefits of the pipeline and related production of natural gas. A similar twinning of quarterly and annual models was used for the assessment, in 1975 and 1976, of the Syncrude synthetic oil sands project [M40, M41, M53].

* The current version of MACE is the culmination of many years of modelling energy and the national economy. The authors of the current paper are thus building on the work of many others. Rather than acknowledge their efforts here, we have included a list of the main papers and documents relating to MACE and its predecessor models (see pp. 82-5). Throughout the paper, references to these documents will be by the letter M, followed by the document's number on the list.

The earlier work on the pipeline project revealed that the key economic issues turned on the costs and timing of the energy production more than on the macroeconomic effects of the projects. Between 1973 and 1976 the energy model was further developed to include an integrated set of energy demand equations by fuel and by region [M55], and extensive modelling of the production, costs, and taxation of non-frontier crude oil and natural gas [M54]. The supply and demand sectors were linked with each other, and integrated with the oil sands and Arctic pipelines sectors, by equations showing the costs and energy losses in the oil and gas transport system. Exports of western crude oil and natural gas were, and are, generally treated as exogenous policy variables. Oil requirements in eastern Canada (to the extent not provided for by the oil pipeline extended to Montreal in the mid-1970s) are met by imports.

As the 1970s progressed, the model was extended to include estimates of the efficiency effects of alternative energy pricing policies [M50], and the effects of oil and gas revenues on federal equalization payments [M46]. Both of these issues came to the fore at the end of the decade, when the 1979–80 jump in world oil prices destroyed the fragile federal–provincial compromises on the pricing, taxation, and revenue-sharing arrangements for crude oil and natural gas.

The magnitude of the required adjustments in Canadian energy prices raised important questions about their macroeconomic impacts. The annual flow of potential economic rents from energy was approching almost 10 per cent of GNP. The uneven distribution of energy resources (more than 85 per cent in Alberta for oil and natural gas, with a somewhat less uneven distribution for hydroelectricity) and rents was exaggerating the already substantial regional differences in the growth of income and fiscal capacity. Existing macro-econometric models for Canada were not very suitable for analysing the output and inflation consequences of energy prices, as they did not treat energy as a separate factor of production, and hence were not able to assess fully the effects of energy prices on production costs, profitability, and potential output. Thus we decided to build a new two-sector macro-model that would provide a fairly complete and consistent analysis of the linkages between the energy-producing and energy-using sectors of the national economy. Our plan was to keep the energy model's capability for analysing in some detail the short- and long-term consequences of energy supply and demand, while maintaining a high level of aggregation in the modelling of the energy-using sector. Given the annual nature of the main energy data, and our wish to use the model over both short and long forecast periods, we decided to use annual data throughout. This decision was also consistent with our desire to keep to a minimum the difficulties of maintaining and updating our data and equations. If the model was to be of maximum use to ourselves and others, it would have to be kept as simple and small-scale as possible. We also had in mind that, if the macro-sectors could be kept sufficiently small, it might be possible in the future to estimate similar models for other countries. We might thereby hope to extend the empirical basis for comparative macroeconomics, and perhaps to pool cross-country and time-series data to extend the sample of post-OPEC experience.

Thus far, our estimation and results relate entirely to the Canadian economy. In the remainder of this paper we shall first outline the structure and properties of the model and then put it to use in examining some major issues that illustrate the important linkages between the energy and non-energy sectors. In our description, we shall start first with our interrelated treatment of the production and factor demand behaviour of the energy-using sector. We then deal with our somewhat more conventional handling of final demand, wages, prices, and domestic and international financial linkages.

Two subsequent sectors outline the modelling of disaggregated energy demands and supplies, while the final five sections put the model to use, and outline some avenues for future development.

In an earlier paper we used the MACE model to illustrate the macroeconomic effects of alternative energy pricing policies for Canada [M27]. For this paper we have chosen first to highlight the effect of changes in world oil prices, and then to consider two other aspects of the linkage between the energy and non-energy sectors. In the first of these experiments, we analyse the effects of the possible construction and operation of one additional large new oil sands plant during the 1980s. These simulations highlight, as did our earlier analysis of Arctic pipelines and oil sands projects, the impacts of additional energy investment on domestic employment, inflation, and inflows of foreign goods and capital. The final experiment assesses the effects of natural gas exports associated with the early construction of the southern Canadian legs of the proposed Alaska Highway natural gas pipeline. Since the gas in question was already discovered, and had only modest investment requirements in any case, the primary impact of the increased exports is on the balance of payments and the exchange rate, with induced effects on natural gas exploration, development, and revenues. The macroeconomic issues therefore relate to the extent to which energy exports lessen the competitiveness, profitability, and hence output of the non-energy sector.

An appendix contains all of the equations and variables in the macroeconomic sectors of the model. We are also preparing a model-users' manual, which will give a more complete description of the entire model.

2. BASIC STRUCTURE OF THE MACE MODEL

There are two main industries in the model, one using capital and natural resources to produce, transport, refine, and distribute energy (the energy-producing industry), and the other using labour, capital, and energy to produce everything else (the energy-using industry). The output (q) of the energy-using sector is therefore equal to gross domestic product plus energy imports minus energy exports. Canadian GDP is modelled to be imperfectly substitutable for non-energy imports but to an equal extent for all final demands (including investment in the energy supply sectors). There is a different estimated elasticity of sub-stitution between Canadian GDP and foreign output in world markets, as mea-sured by the price elasticity of the world demand for Canadian non-energy exports. The equations for the non-energy sector, and for the aggregate eco-nomy, are all contained in an appendix, divided among the following five groups.

1. The *supply sector* deals with output and factor demands (including the total demand for energy) making use of a vintage Constant Elasticity (CES) bund-ling of capital and energy nested within a Cobb–Douglas function for gross output based on capital-plus-energy and efficiency units of labour. This production function, given the current levels of measured inputs of capital, labour, and energy, determines the level of output that would be forthcoming at normal rates of factor utilization. The actual production level is set as a utilization rate, which is estimated to depend on current sales, the current ratio of operating costs to output price, and the discrepancy between actual and target inventory stocks. Inventory increases are then determined residu-ally as production plus imports minus sales. Non-energy imports are also determined as part of this sector, as explained in section 3.
2. The *absorption sector* models domestic consumption and non-energy exports.
3. The *price–wage block* explains the determination of the output price, the absorption price, annual earnings per employed worker, the price of non-energy exports, and various national income identities. National income is obtained from q by subtracting net energy imports and net interest and dividend payments to foreigners.
4. The *international finance sector* has equations for the foreign ownership ratio for Canadian business assets, foreign demand for Canadian financial assets, the exchange rate, and various accounting relationships for the balances of trade and payments.
5. The *domestic finance sector* has equations for the demand for money, for the market value of domestic business assets, for direct and indirect taxes, and for government transfer payments. Identities then determine net govern-ment liabilities and net private sector wealth.

The energy sector has six main blocks of equations:

1. The demand block spreads national energy expenditure, in billions of constant dollars, among regions and fuels. The major split is among oil products, natural gas, and electricity, but there is also a subsystem explaining the choice of fuels (among natural gas, coal, and oil) in the generation of any electricity demanded in excess of the exogenous supplies of hydro and nuclear power. This block also contains the equations transforming the demands from trillion output btu back into physical units, and modelling the often complicated procedures and policies for converting regulated or internationally-set prices for crude oil and natural gas to the prices paid by

users and the (rather different) prices received by producers. For each region there are estimated equations explaining the refining, distribution, and excise tax margin on oil products, and for the distributor's margin on natural gas.
2. The arctic pipeline block (not used in this paper) models the proposed Alaska Highway natural gas pipeline [M33] and the possible associated production of gas from the Mackenzie Delta.
3. The non-frontier natural gas supply sector, described in section 7.
4. The non-frontier crude oil supply sector, as described in section 7.
5. The oil sands supply sector, described in section 7.
6. A final block of equations modelling energy transportation and losses, along with alternative models showing the effects of different systems for linking energy revenues to equalization payments.

There is also a partially completed set of equations for the regional costs and production of hydroelectricity, and plans are being developed for a sub-model of oil production from the Hibernia field off the coast of Newfoundland.

Finally, there are two blocks of equations containing the links between the energy and non-energy sectors. One block contains the linkages from the energy to the non-energy sector, and the other contains the linkages in the reverse direction. Either type of feedback can be suppressed by exogenizing either or both of these blocks of equations. We turn now to consider the structure and properties of the model in more detail.

3. OUTPUTS, FACTOR DEMANDS, AND PRODUCTIVITY

MACE is an unusually supply-oriented macro-model, so the supply sector is a logical place to start our detailed description of the model. At the core of the model is a nested production function $q = \{(k, e), n\}$, where capital and energy are combined in a vintage CES function, and this vintage bundle is combined with labour in an outer function taking a Cobb–Douglas form. We did not choose to estimate this function directly, since it is our view that all factors are costly to adjust, and that substantial variations in output take the form of changes in the rates of utilization of employed factors. Thus the production function must hold on an average basis but not on a year-by-year basis. We therefore followed the RDX2 [M47] strategy of using sample averages to determine as many parameters as possible. In our current model, with its more complicated production structure, there are too many parameters to be identified by sample averages, so we also made use of the derived factor demand equations.

To keep the number of parameters as low as possible, we assume that all technical progress is Harrod-neutral and that there are constant returns to scale. This gives us seven parameters to estimate: (1) the rate of decay (delta 1) of the fixity of the energy–capital bundle; (2) the elasticity of substitution (sigma) between energy and capital in the energy–capital bundle; (3) and (4) two constants in the CES function; (5) the exponent on the energy–capital bundle in the Cobb-Douglas outer function; (6) the rate of Harrod-neutral technical progress; and (7) the constant in the Cobb-Douglas function.

For given sigma, the optimal average energy/capital ratio can be derived. If we assume that the actual energy/capital ratio equals the cost-minimizing ratio on average over the twenty-nine-year data period, and scale the energy-capital bundle so that it has the same mean as the capital stock (hence making the CES price index for capita plus energy equal to the cost of renting and powering a unit of capital equipment), it is possible to identify the two CES constants. If we then further assume a value for the decay coefficient delta 1, it is possible to construct a series for the vintage energy–capital bundle (equation (1.3)). Given this series, and using the average share of payments to capital and energy (0.356) to determine the Cobb-Douglas exponent, we can then follow the RDX2 procedure for determining the Cobb-Douglas constant and the rate of technical progress by the condition that, over the twenty-nine-year period, the synthetic bundle of factors should have the same mean and the same trend rate of growth as the actual output series.

Thus, for any pair of values for delta 1 and sigma it is possible to use sample averages to determine all of the remaining parameters of the production system. How should we determine delta 1 and sigma? Many vintage models assume that the putty becomes clay as soon as the capital is put in place, and that no further adjustments in factor proportions are possible until the capital is replaced. If we were willing to accept this assumption, then we could use the depreciation rate for capital to define the vintage bundle, and only sigma would be left to be estimated. However, the possibilities for retrofitting and for otherwise altering the energy use of a given stock of buildings and equipment seemed to be great enough that we should free up delta 1 to be estimated. Since a number of complicated nonlinear transformations are required to derive the other parameters, for given values of delta 1 and sigma, the most practical and efficient form of estimation was a maximum-likelihood grid-search technique.

This leaves the issue of whether to use a single factor demand equation or the whole set of equations as a basis for choosing the best pair of values for delta 1 and sigma. Originally we had some preference for using all of the factor demand equations as a group, with their forecasts being combined in the production function itself to give the best possible explanation of either synthetic output qsv or, by adding the additional required variables, of actual output q. However, we found that only the fit of the energy demand equation was materially affected by the parameter choice, so our final selection was based entirely on the energy demand equation.

We considered two different versions of the energy demand equation in our final tests. In both equations the coefficient on the synthetic energy demand variable was constrained to be 1.0. One of the equations, which we have chosen to use and present as appendix equation (1.8), also includes a time trend, and the other does not. Neither form rejects the constraint that the coefficient be 1.0 on the synthetic energy variable, but the version with the time trend has a much lower standard error even when each form is allowed to have its most likely set of parameters.

The preferred values for delta 1 and sigma are 0.72 and 0.60, respectively. After this selection was made, an even finer grid search suggested small increases in the likelihood from further increases in delta 1, but not by enough to affect materially the model's properties. The likelihood surface is fairly flat as delta 1 is varied but fairly steep if sigma differs by more than 0.1 or so on either side of 0.6.

There are two slightly disturbing features of these results. The speed of lagged response (i.e., the size of delta 1) is rather high, and the significant time trend suggests either that the lagged responses have not been properly identified or that technical progress over the period has on average been energy-using rather than Harrod-neutral. To test the idea that the time trend is merely a rough way of capturing the lagged effects of the long downward trend of energy prices from the early 1950s to 1973, we tried splitting the sample period at the end of 1973. The trend remained the same in each period, as might have been suspected from the fact that the original equation had errors of less than 1 per cent in each of the last four years of the sample, and was less than 0.1 per cent off in 1980. We expect that the apparent energy-using bias of past technological change will turn out to have been in part a lagged response to the past downward trend in energy prices, and in part an increase in the relative energy intensity of Canada's mix of output in the face of lower energy prices in Canada than elsewhere. These possibilities remain to be investigated.

The synthetic vintage energy demand series (equation 4) is essentially a decaying-weighted sum of past investment multiplied by desired energy/capital ratios, where the latter are functions of relative prices and the parameters of the production function. Energy demand thus tracks output growth more rapidly than does the capital stock (because delta 1 is greater than zero) but less rapidly than current investment (because delta 1 is less than 1.0). In our original theoretical development of the MACE production structure, we supposed that energy use might also provide an index of the degree of capital utilization, and hence that the ratio of actual to synthetic vintage output (q/qsv) should also appear in the energy demand equation. We found that neither this ratio, nor current output in any other form, contributed to our capital-based vintage explanation of energy demand.

What about the changes of capital and labour in response to changes in expected output and factor costs? Our general approach is to model an expected target level of output and then to derive consistent cost-minimizing target demands for all three factors. As with RDX2, we have considered both 'short-term' and 'long-term' desired demands. In RDX2, we found the best results with a hierarchical structure, with the demand for capital driven by a 'long-term' gap with forward-looking output expectations and relative costs, and labour demand based on a 'short-term' gap obtained by inverting the Cobb–Douglas production function with the existing level of the capital stocks. We also considered this hierarchical structure for MACE, but found that the annual data prefer a more symmetric structure in which the target stocks of employment and capital each depend on a desired value of future output and the cost-minimizing factor proportions.

We retained a possible element of the capital–labour hierarchy by permitting different parameters in the expectations processes for expected output. In both cases, the expected level of profitable future output was specified as a weighted average of trend output adjusted for expected labour force growth two years hence and the current level of output adjusted for expected output growth, for unintended inventory accumulation, and for the lagged effects of changes in international competitiveness. The parameters of the expected output functions were fixed by tests of maximum likelihood on equations (1.1) and (1.6). We found, as in earlier work by ourselves and others, that there are considerable empirical difficulties in disentangling expectations processes from adjustment lags, and that the data prefer (as shown in equations (1.16) and (1.19) for the expected output (1.1) for investment, and (1.6) for employment) fairly extrapolative output expectations combined with fairly slow closure of the indicated gaps between actual and target stocks of capital and labour. Looking at the expected output equations by themselves, it would appear that output expectations are more cyclical for capital demands than for labour demands, thus reversing the normal hierarchical response. However, the estimated proportional response to the indicated gaps is sufficiently higher for labour than for capital (0.16 as opposed to an initial 0.05), so that the net effect is for employment to respond substantially more quickly than the capital stock in response to changes in desired future output.

The gap between labour demand and labour supply determines the unemployment rate, an important driving variable in the model. Labour supply is driven by capacity utilization, the ratio of the natural to the actual rate of unemployment and a wage term. A separate term models the social phenomenon of a greatly increased women's participation in the labour force. The equation is constrained so that, when the driving variables have their normal values, the rate of change of the labour force is given solely by the term modelling women's participation.

The investment equation is estimated as a ratio of investment to the capital stock, with the lagged ratio entering to enrich the distributed lag response. The labour equation needs no such complicated lag structure, and follows a simple adaptive adjustment, with the coefficients on the desired and lagged levels of employment constrained (easily) to sum to 1.0. Fairly early in our research, we discovered that all of the derived factor demand equations fit better if the expected rental price of capital was taken to be constant (as a fraction of the replacement cost of capital goods) rather than to vary with either the RDX2 measure of the supply price of capital or any standard measure of real (or nominal) interest rates. Since monetary stringency has no impact on the desired long-term factor proportions, we wished to consider the possibility that some measure of financial market conditions, or of current profitability, should influence the rate at which investment takes place. We first considered using 'Tobin's q', the ratio of the sharemarket value to the replacement cost of the business capital stock. If the average and marginal values of this variable are correlated, then higher values should increase the profitability and hence the pace of new capital spending. In earlier versions of MACE this variable appeared significantly, but extending the data period through 1980 and re-calculating our market values to exclude energy shares led the variable to drop out. An alternative that performs somewhat the same function is the cost variable cq, which is the ratio of current unit operating costs to the current output price. It is therefore equal to 1.0 minus the current rate of 'abnormal' profits. This measure of operating costs (equation (1.10)) includes a rental charge on capital along with the costs of the current levels of employment and energy. To reflect the cost effects of changes in nominal interest rates, we have used average debt/equity ratios to establish the rental charge as a weighted average of a constant and the long-term interest rate, on the assumption that changes in equity prices have no impact on current costs.

The cost variable cq provides an important channel for monetary policy to influence both investment and output, since the impact of the long-term interest rate on total costs, in the numerator of cq, is greater than its impact on the output price, in the denominator of cq. Taking account of both these effects, we find that the net eleasticity of cq with respect to the long-term interest rate is 0.07.

The output equation (1.11) is central to the operation of the model. Since the elasticity of output with respect to synthetic output is constrained to be 1.0, the output decision can equally well be interpreted as a factor utilization decision. The partial elasticities are estimated to be -0.22 for relative operating costs, 0.59 for final sales, and 0.05 for the proportionate gap between desired and actual inventory stocks. Once the fundamental decision has been made to tie the output level to the production-function-based bundle of employed factors, on average but not at all times, it need not matter much whether one estimates a production equation, as we have done, or an inventory change equation, as was done in RDX2. In either case, one hopes to identify a reasonable buffer-stock role for inventories and a suitable production response to any growing gap between actual and target levels of inventory stocks. In MACE, we have been able to achieve this and also to find an important role for profitability, in the form of the cq variable. This gives monetary policy a further influence on inventory investment, which is determined by subtracting sales from production. The net effect of interest rates on inventory investment is approximately 55 per cent ($100\% - 60\%$* output/sales) of the impact of interest rates on the components of final spending. This 55 per cent of buffer-stock change in inventory in the first year then later feeds back to production, prices, and exports via the inventory gap.

The cost impact on the production decision, in the context of a vintage model of production, also helps to show how a rise in energy prices, for which the initial impact on operating costs is larger than the final impact after all substitution effects are worked out, can lead to output reductions as producers find it unprofitable to maintain previous production levels. This variable also provides an important channel whereby world prices influence domestic activity. Through the direct competition of domestic output with foreign goods, a rise in the world price level leads to an increase in the domestic output price. This increases profitability, and hence output. Inventories build up, and excess inventories have a direct effect on export sales (as shown in equation (2.2)).

How important is it to model the output decision directly, rather than to take the level of output directly from the production function? We did a test of this by using $q = qsv$ as a predictor of output. That equation had a standard error of 2 per cent and highly autocorrelated residuals, compared to a standard error of 0.73 per cent for our equation.

A final issue about the production structure is whether there has been a drop in aggregate productivity growth in the latter part of the 1970s. The issue is of special importance for a model, like ours, that is to be used for projections of a decade or more into the future. Other modellers and commentators have identified a post-1973 drop in productivity growth, measured in one or more ways, so we decided to see whether such a break appeared in our production structure after accounting for the effects of slower energy demand growth. We did this by introducing a second technical progress (or regress) term in our production function. We did a sequence of tests, using secondary technical progress terms staring in each year from 1971 to 1978. The differential technical progress term was slightly positive if it started in 1971, 1972, or 1973, and slightly negative if it started in any later year. The estimate of the drop in trend output growth (relative to a synthetic bundle of factors with no allowance for technical progress) grew slightly larger if the differential started later in the decade, but the break never became either large or significant.

We also discovered that even this small apparent drop in output was generally better explained by demand and profitability factors than by a change in the trend rate of productivity growth. This test was done by taking each of the split-trend models in turn, using them to construct new measures of qsv, and then re-estimating our production equation. The equation with a split in 1977 fitted as well as our basic equation and all of the others fitted less well. The implied drop in overall annual productivity growth was from 1.33 per cent until end 1976 to 1.31 per cent thereafter. This difference would not cumulate to as much as 1 per cent of output over a twenty-five-year horizon. Thus it would appear that our separation of energy and non-energy sectors, along with the inclusion of energy in the production function of the non-energy sector, eliminates any significant 1970s drop in total factor productivity at the aggregate level.

It may be useful to disentangle the reasons for the model's ability to explain the apparent decline in aggregate labour productivity. If gross output q is regressed on employment, the actual level of output is 3.4 per cent above the regression line in 1973 and 6.6 per cent below in 1980. Thus there was a 10 per cent drop in output per employed person between 1973 and 1980, relative to what it would have been at the average labour productivity increase of 3.2 per cent per annum. If instead we look at the ratio of actual output to the synthetic output measure $q$sv, the actual level of output is 3.1 per cent above $q$sv in 1973 and 4.3 per cent below in 1980. Thus, about one-third of the 1973–80 drop in output per efficiency unit of labour was due to the reduced relative size of the capital-plus-energy bundle.

If we then turn to equation (1.11) for the production decision, we find that output was 0.2 per cent below its predicted value in 1973, 0.1 per cent below in 1979, and 0.7 per cent below in 1980. Thus the model leaves unexplained only a 0.5 per cent drop in output between 1973 and 1980. According to the output equation, the 7 per cent drop between 1973 and 1980 in the amount of output per unit of employed factors was more than two-thirds due to the 8 per cent drop in the final sales and one-third due to the 10 per cent increase in the relative cost variable. Offsetting these two influences was a slight increase in production to partially make up the 5 per cent drop in actual relative to desired inventories (where the latter are measured as a fraction of the stock of fixed capital).

Putting all of these elements together, the MACE equations suggest that, of the 10 per cent drop in output per efficiency unit of labour between 1973 and 1980, 5 per cent (or half) was due to reduction of demand, 3 per cent was due to reductions in energy use, and 2 per cent was due to a decline in current profitability.

The final key equation in the supply sector is that for non-energy imports. Conceptually, we treat non-energy imports and domestic output as inputs into an implicit CES function for the utility of final sales. We can thus derive the equilibrium ratio of non-energy imports to synthetic domestic output $q$sv as a function of their relative prices. We can thereby estimate the elasticity of substitution between imports and domestic output, and find it to be (in equation (1.12)) 0.34 in the first year and 1.03 at the end of three years, when all of the lagged effects are worked out. There is an additional (but not statistically significant) effect from capacity utilization, with a 1 per cent increase in capacity utilization leading to a 1.22 per cent increase in non-energy imports.

4. FINAL DEMANDS, WAGES, AND PRICES

Per capita personal consumption expenditure is explained (in equation (2.1)) by means of a life-cycle model based on after-tax wage and transfer income and the real value of household wealth. The marginal propensity to spend disposable wage and transfer income is 0.8, and the coefficient on per capita wealth is 0.021. To compute the equivalent spending and savings propensities for non-wage income, it is necessary to have some idea of the real rate of return on wealth. If that return is above 2.6 per cent, then the marginal savings rate is higher out of non-wage income than out of wage and transfer income. Monetary policy has an impact on consumption through the wealth term. According to equation (5.6), explaining the market value of business assets, a one percentage point increase in the short-term interest rate leads to a drop of about 10 per cent in the market value of business assets (excluding the housing stock). After adjusting for housing, government bonds, and foreign assets and liabilities, this amounts to a drop of about 5 per cent in the market value of wealth, and a drop of one-quarter per cent in consumption spending. (This does not include any effects on residential construction, which is treated as part of non-energy capital investment.)

The non-energy export equation, like the equation for non-energy imports, excludes cars and parts as well as interest and dividends. Interest and dividends must be treated separately because they are needed to make the distinction between domestic product and national income. Cars and parts are treated separately because of rapid growth of two-way trade following the United States–Canada Auto Pact in the mid-1960s. The export trade flow has an elasticity of 1.16 with respect to growth of real income in the OECD, and a price elasticity of −0.13 in the first year and about −0.40 after three years. A new feature in this version of MACE (suggested to us by Patrick Artus of the OECD) is the inclusion of the ratio of actual to desired inventories in the non-energy export equation. Export markets are, to this extent, regarded as a vent for surplus domestic production. Since inventory stocks and non-energy exports (net of cars) are of roughly equal size, the coefficient implies that almost half of any excess inventory accumulation will go into export markets.

The wage–price sector involves several features of special importance to an open economy. First, an important distinction is made between the real wage as seen by workers, which is defined in terms of the absorption price, and the real wage as seen by producers, which is defined in terms of the output price. The key difference between these two prices relates to the terms of trade. The second feature is the direct role of world prices in the determination of the output price. A third feature, of equal interest in closed and open economies, is the inclusion of an excess inventory term in the output price equation.

In our modelling of the wage bargaining process (equation (3.1), best interpreted as a quasi-reduced-form reflecting both supply and demand factors), we explain the proportionate annual wage change in terms of the ratio of the 'natural' to the actual unemployment rates and the proportionate changes in the absorption price, the terms of trade, capacity utilization, and the lagged wage. To reflect absence of money illusion on the part of labour suppliers, the coefficients on the changes in the lagged wage and the absorption price are constrained (easily) to sum to 1.0. The terms-of-trade effect is statistically weak but empirically substantial. The coefficient of 0.09, coupled with the coefficient of about 0.5 on the lagged wage change, implies that a change in the terms of trade will alter the product real wage by about half as much as the absorption real wage (bearing in mind that non-energy exports are about 25 per cent of the gross output of the non-energy sector). The coefficient on the unemployment term indicates that a one percentage point increase in the unemployment rate will reduce the initial annual rate of wage inflation by 0.4 per cent if the unemployment rate is at its natural level, by 0.8 per cent if the unemployment rate is at half its natural level, and by 0.2 per cent if the unemployment rate is twice its natural level. The longer-run effects are about twice as large. This is not the whole link between real activity and wage inflation, however, as any change in the rate of capacity utilization also changes the rate of wage increase, by just under half (0.46) in the short run and just under 1.0 when the lags are worked out. The capacity utilization variable also captures any effects of cyclical variations in factor productivity, since it represents changes in the ratio of output to the synthetic bundle of factor inputs at normal utilization rates and with trend growth in labour productivity. When utilization, absorption prices, and the terms of trade are all unchanging, the steady-state rate of wage increase, in the absence of wage and price controls, and with the actual rate of unemployment equal to its natural value, is just under 4 per cent, or almost twice the estimated rate of labour-embodied technical progress. The implied tendency towards secular inflation is countered somewhat by the estimated price equations, but also tends to lead, for any given rate of monetary growth, to an equilibrium rate of unemployment that is higher than the natural rate.

Finally, the wage equation shows important direct effects from the 1976-8 system of wage and price controls. Since our data relate to earnings rather than settlements, they do not show any effect in 1976, but if lags are taken into account the cumulative direct effect of the controls on the 1980 level of wages is over 10 per cent. Simulations of the wage–price sector as a whole, ignoring other macroeconomic feedbacks, suggest that the 1980 wage level would have been 21 per cent higher and prices 11 per cent higher without the controls. Whole-model simulations suggest a range of 23-27 per cent, depending on monetary and exchange rate policy in the absence of controls. The largest nominal increase in wages, and the smallest real increase, is seen with a rigid monetary policy and a fixed exchange rate.

The rate of output price inflation (equation (3.2)) depends on the rate of increase in domestic costs, the rate of increase in the price of competing world products, and the difference between actual and desired inventory stocks. The coefficients on the first two variables are constrained (easily) to sum to 1.0. The domestic cost variable is the CES bundle of energy and capital rental prices combined in a Cobb–Douglas function with the wages per efficiency unit of labour. By using the production function form and parameters to set the relative effects of the cost components. we obtained an improvement in the fit of the price equation as well as greater consistency with our underlying supply framework. The effects of direct foreign competition are shown by the world price term, while the impact of imbalance between supply and demand for domestic output is captured by the excess inventory term. Energy prices, long-term interest rates and wages influence inflation through the domestic cost variable approximately as follows: a 1 per cent increase in wages increases the price level by 0.7 per cent; 1 per cent on energy prices increases the price level by 0.16 per cent; and one percentage point on interest rates increases the price level by 1 per cent. The coefficient on the inventory term is such that the inflation rate drops by 1.2 per cent for each 10 per cent that the stock of inventories is above its normal value. If world prices and domestic costs are growing at a constant rate, the domestic output price will grow at the same rate if the stock of inventories is about 5 per cent less than its historical average, measured relative to the stock of fixed capital.

The prices of non-energy exports (which are a sub-category of total output) depend on the total output price, the exchange rate, the price of world exports of goods, and the inventory disequilibrium term used in the output price and export equations. The coefficients on the exchange rate and the world price are constrained to be equal to each other, and to be 1.0 minus the coefficient on the price of domestic output. These constraints are easily accepted, and show the export price to have an elasticity of 0.3 with respect to the exchange rate and the world price, 0.7 with respect to the domestic output price, and -0.2 with respect to the proportionate inventory stock discrepancy. The absorption price is just a weighted average of the prices of domestic output and non-energy imports.

5. THE BALANCE OF PAYMENTS, EXCHANGE RATES, AND FINANCIAL PORTFOLIOS

In modelling the net foreign demand for Canadian assets, we separate the foreign demand for ownership of Canadian non-energy business from the net demand for all other Canadian assets. For the former we have equation (4.8), which explains movements of the foreign ownership ratio in terms of current earnings yields in Canada and the United States. A 10 per cent drop of share prices in Canada, with corporate earnings and the US earnings yield held constant, would increase the foreign ownership ratio by over 5 per cent in the short run, and several times as much if the gap were maintained for a number of years. Since the Canadian earnings yield is linked closely to Canadian interest rates (in equation (5.6)), foreign investment in Canadian businesses (which can take the form of shares, bonds, or direct ownership of physical assets) is an important source of interest elasticity of foreign capital movements.

The remaining equation explains net foreign liabilities (excluding business assets) as a fraction of total OECD income (as a proxy for wealth), measured in US dollars and multiplied by the price of foreign exchange raised to the 0.25 power. This latter adjustment is to bring into line the currency mix of the numerator and denominator, and reflects the fact that about one-quarter of portfolio debt to foreigners is denominated in Canadian dollars. We have also tested alternative versions of this equation, in which all or none of the denominator was converted to Canadian dollars, and found the resulting equations to be rather similar in fit and simulation properties. This portfolio share is explained by its lagged value, the difference between Canadian and US short-term interest rates, and 'temporary' deficits or surpluses in the current account of the balance of payments. Based on the 1980 size of OECD income, an increase of one percentage point in Canadian short-term interest rates would increase net capital inflows by $3.8 billion in the first year, by $2.7 billion in the second, and by declining amounts thereafter. Ignoring subsequent growth in OECD wealth, the one percentage point increase in the interest differential shifts a cumulative total of $12.9 billion into Canada. If OECD wealth is growing by 10 per cent per year, there is an additional 'continuing flow' effect from the interest rate change of $380 million net annual inflow, once again measured in terms of 1980 prices and portfolio sizes.

The role of exchange rate expectations as a determinant of capital movements is rather important for any model, such as MACE, where the current account effects of exchange rate changes are modest. In the first year, a 10 per cent increase in the price of foreign exchange leads to a slight worsening of the current account, so that some exchange-rate-smoothing capital flows are required if the foreign exchange market is to be stable. We have addressed this issue in a number of ways.

The first approach was to model directly the effects of exchange rate expectations on capital movements. Although earlier versions of MACE included either changes in the exchange rate, or, in some versions, changes of the expected exchange rate, as a determinant of capital movements, we have found these effects to be generally small, difficult to identify, and varying with data revisions and changes in the sample period.

A second approach, which we have used in the current version of the equation, is to take account of portfolio balance effects of changes in the exchange rate, making use of the estimated extent of Canadian pay securities among the Canadian financial assets held by foreigners. A decrease in the price of the Canadian dollar thus leads to a drop in the value share of Canadian-denominated securities in foreign portfolios, and, for given expected rates of return at home and abroad, lead to an increased demand for Canadian securities. This effect provides for only temporary capital flows, since it stops when portfolio balance is restored, but it can help to stabilize the exchange market while trade responses to relative prices are working themselves out.

Third, we have set the model up to permit official capital movements to supplement private capital flows in providing short-term stabilization to the exchange rate. We model the authorities as 'leaning into the wind' and using official reserves to cushion changes in the exchange rate, while always letting the exchange rate move in the direction indicated by the current state of the balance of payments.

Finally, in an attempt to employ the structure of the model to provide a more explicit modelling of forward-looking rational expectations, we developed the concept of expected or permanent imports and exports, based on the estimated equations but with all capacity utilization terms set at their average values and with all lagged relative price effects fully worked out. The difference between the current and the permanent trade balance can be used as a measure of a temporary imbalance that ought to trigger offsetting capital flows by far-sighted speculators. Included in our equation (4.4) for capital movements, the temporary trade imbalance variable has a coefficient of 0.39, implying that about two-fifths of any J-curve effects are financed by private capital movements. If the Marshall–Lerner conditions are easily met in the long run, then a 39 per cent financing of the gap may provide a stable foreign exchange market. In the current version of MACE, the sum of the long-term price elasticities is about 1.4, with the first-year some one-third as great. Taking account only of the responses of export prices and quantities of non-energy imports and exports, including trade in cars and exports in the form of interest and dividends, the first-year current account effect of a change in exchange rate is close to zero. (The effect is 0.32 on export prices plus 0.29 on export quantity plus 0.45 on import quantity for a total of 1.06, compared with 1.00 for neutrality.) The full effects are more complicated than this, since there are important changes in export and domestic prices, domestic absorption, energy trade prices and quantities, trade in cars and parts, and debt service payments.

To complete our portfolio modelling, we need an equation that converts our estimates of changes in market values back to the balance of payments measures of net capital inflows. This link is provided by our equation (4.7) for retained earnings and valuation adjustments, which depends on changes in market values and in the foreign ownership ratio.

To reveal clearly the effects of exchange rate flexibility, we also model a fixed exchange rate system, which makes use of all of the model's trade and capital account equations and uses the balance of payments identity to determine the change in foreign exchange reserves required to maintain the fixed value for the price of foreign exchange.

To supplement our portfolio modelling of flexibile exchange rates, we have also developed a number of alternative models of the exchange rate, and use some of them in the simulations reported in this paper and elsewhere. In an earlier paper [M26] we presented and tested a number of alternative simple models for determining the exchange rate. If we use the purchasing power parity (PPP) model, which emphasizes the tight international linkage of goods markets, then we continue to employ our usual equations for international capital movements, use the PPP equation to determine the exchange rate, and use the balance of payments identity to determine the level of non-energy exports, thus overriding the estimated equation (2.2).

If we use a nominal interest parity relationship to determine the exchange rate, we use it to replace equation (4.4), and use the balance of payments identity to determine net capital inflows. We think that our procedures represent the most logical way to implement PPP and interest parity models, since the former implies a perfectly elastic world demand for Canadian output of tradable goods, and the latter implies an equally perfect linkage of capital markets. When we use the interest parity model, it is necessary to tie down the expected future exchange rate in order that interest parity can be used to determine the level of the spot rate. We do this by applying a weaker form of PPP, in which the lagged exchange rate and the projected ratio of domestic and foreign price levels are used to predict the future exchange rate expected by speculators. Implicit in this formulation is the assumption that arbitrageurs remove any covered interest differential and speculators stop any gap appearing between the (implicit) forward exchange rate and the PPP-based expectation of the future value of the spot exchange rate.

The domestic financial sector is modelled by equations for the demands for business assets and for high-powered money. In simulation, these two equations serve to determine the market value of the business capital stock and the level of the short-term interest rate. The estimated interest elasticity of the demand for high-powered money is quite low (-0.13), implying that fairly small changes in the money supply have large impacts on the short-term interest rate. Government bonds are the residual asset in domestic private sector portfolios. The long-term interest rate is determined by equation (5.7), involving a lagged response to Canadian and US short-term interest rates.

We have a number of ways of modelling monetary policy. If we treat the supply of high-powered money as an exogenous policy vairable, then the demand-for-money equation is inverted to determine the short-term interest rate. If the short-term interest rate is treated as an exogenous policy variable, then government debt-management policy becomes endogenous, with high-powered money issued in the quantity demanded at the chosen interest rate, and all other financial requirements met by new debt. For most of the experiments reported in this paper, we follow a middle course, and use an endogenous policy that falls part-way between a constant money supply and constant interest rate policy. This is done by starting with a monetary growth target, and permitting departures from the path only to cushion changes in the real interest rate. The domestic financial sector is completed by equations for indirect and direct taxes, and balance sheet identities for the government and private sectors. The direct and indirect tax equations exclude, so far as possible, the indirect taxes paid on energy products and the taxes and royalties paid by energy producers. These latter flows are modelled explictly in the energy supply sectors, although there are some further accounting refinements still to be made, especially in the modelling of indirect taxes on oil products. The aggregate indirect tax equation is fitted as an identity determining implicitly the average rate of indirect tax. This rate is then held fixed for simulation purposes, and projected forward at its 1980 value. The direct tax equation contains one term representing wage and transfer income (multiplied by an average rate of personal tax on disposable income) and another term approximating non-wage income.

6. ENERGY PRICES AND DEMANDS BY REGION AND FUEL

For our model description to be at all complete, there is no escaping the complexities of Canadian energy pricing. For the historical period, our data for final energy prices were based on estimates of actual user prices for each of the three main final energy sources (electricity, natural gas, and oil products) in each region. The model contains a number of possible ways of determining these prices. For this paper, it will be sufficient to describe how these prices are determined under the 1981–6 energy pricing and revenue-sharing agreements signed in late 1981 between the federal government and the governments of the three western producing provinces.

The well-head price of 'old oil' (produced from pools discovered before 1 January 1981) is scheduled to move up fairly rapidly towards a ceiling of 75 per cent of the price of imported oil. All synthetic oil, oil from post-1980 discoveries, and oil from most new enhanced recovery projects receive a 'New Oil Reference Price' (NORP), which in general cannot exceed (and is likely to be equal to) the landed price of imported oil. The refinery gate price of crude oil in each province is based on the delivered price of old oil plus a compensation charge and a Canadian ownership charge. The compensation charge is a per-barrel levy that is periodically adjusted to raise enough money to cover the additional payments to producers of synthetic oil, producers of new oil, and purchasers of imported oil. The Canadian ownership charge, which is currently $1.15 per barrel for crude oil and $0.15 per thousand cubic feet (m.c.f.) for natural gas, and is assumed to remain at that level, was introduced to finance Petro-Canada's purchase of Petrofina. The refinery gate crude oil price is thus very much an endogenous variable, depending on world oil prices, oil demand by region, oil exports, and the supplies of oil from various sources. Exports of crude oil and products are set by federal policy and are priced at world levels, with the difference between these prices and the old oil price collected as an export tax and split evenly between the federal government and the governments of the exporting provinces.

User prices for oil products are determined by adding a per-barrel refining, distribution, and excise tax margin that is separate for each region. These margins depend principally on the rate of general price inflation, with some impact from the refinery gate crude oil price.

Natural gas well-head prices for Alberta gas used in Canada but outside Alberta have scheduled annual increases of $0.50 per m.c.f. over the life of the agreement. The average Alberta well-head price is a weighted average of this price, the (lower) price of gas sold for Alberta use, and the higher price of gas sold in export markets. Its level therefore depends on the average degree of gas price discounting in Alberta and the rates of growth of natural gas sales in Alberta, in the rest of Canada, and in export markets. There is also an impact from world oil prices, since the Canada–US agreement links natural gas export prices to world oil prices, although there is now a discount from that price which is modelled to continue, although in diminishing degree, through the forecast period.

The natural gas price paid by Canadian users outside Alberta and British Columbia is linked, by federal policy, to the refinery gate crude oil price, including all taxes and levies. The Toronto city-gate natural gas price is to be set at 65 per cent of the price of a b.t.u.-equivalent quantity of crude oil. The federal plan, as embodied in our model, is to alter the rate of the Natural Gas and Natural Gas Liquids Tax to absorb the increasing difference between this price and the regulated Alberta border price for natural gas used elsewhere in Canada. The natural gas price in the prairies is assumed to continue to be discounted relative to the Toronto city-gate price. Following the intent expressed in the letters of agreement between British Columbia (BC) and the federal government, the royalty-free well-head price of gas in British Columbia is set equal to the after-royalty well-head price in Alberta. Following past BC pricing policy, the city-gate price of natural gas for BC users is set equal to the well-head price plus transmission costs.

The distribution margin for natural gas is modelled to depend on the rate of inflation of the absorption price, an expansion of the natural gas distribution system, and a time trend. As with oil products, the proportionate margin becomes smaller as city-gate prices rise. In the case of natural gas, this effect is increased by the negative time trend, which reflects the 'front-end loading' of utility tariffs, whereby charges are higher in the early years of the system than they are later on. This front-end loading also explains why in most regions the natural gas distribution charge is significantly increased by the proportionate expansion in the number of kilometres of distribution pipeline.

Electric utilities in Canada are largely owned and regulated by provincial governments. In the current version of MACE, electricity prices are assumed to grow in the future at the general rate of inflation. The observed prices are those paid by final users, so no distribution margin can be estimated.

Appendix 2 contains the latest equations for energy demands by region and fuel. As mentioned earlier, the total national demand for energy is taken from the integrated set of national factor demands. The distribution across regions is done by a set of regional demand equations based on national energy use, regional real domestic product relative to the national value, and regional energy prices relative to national energy prices. The elasticity with respect to relative energy prices is constrained (easily) to have the same value and lag pattern as in the national equation. To the small extent that the predicted values from these equations do not sum to national energy demand (the difference is usually much less than 1 per cent), the discrepancy is distributed according to the ratio of predicted values.

We have estimated the fuel share equations both as value shares and as quantity shares. For the quantity shares, as for aggregate energy expenditure, the physical units of each fuel are converted into output b.t.u. by multiplying by national average conversion efficiencies. The oil product prices for each region are calculated using national average product proportions. In some earlier versions of the energy model we used regional b.t.u. conversion factors and oil product prices based on the regonal product mix. This had the anomalous result of making average oil product prices, in terms of dollars per million output b.t.u., higher in Alberta than in Quebec, even though the price of each separate product was lower in Alberta. The result came about because Alberta used much more gasoline, with a relatively high price per gallon and a low average conversion efficiency (because of being used in internal combustion engines), while Quebec used much more residual oil, with a low price per gallon and a fairly high efficiency of conversion to heat. Using national averages makes the prices comparable across regions and improves the regional demand and fuel share equations.

Value share equations could not easily be made consistent with the vintage specification for national and regional demands for total energy. We have therefore decided, in the latest version, to use quantity share equations. These equations show all of the price effects to be significant, with all of the own-price effects negative and all of the cross-price effects positive.

We can best summarize the properties of the demand system by combining the national, regional, and interfuel substitution models to obtain national average effects of changes in the city-gate and user prices of each fuel separately. Appendix 2 contains two tables of simulated own-price and cross-price effects for changes in city-gate and user prices of energy. It should be noted that the elasticities for natural gas and crude oil are lower for the city-gate prices than for the user prices. This is because the refining and distribution charges do not increase with city-gate prices (except to a small extent in the case of oil products). Thus any increases in the prices of crude oil or natural gas have much larger proportionate impacts on the city-gate prices than on the user prices.

Because the elasticities in the fuel share equations are small relative to the 0.60 price elasticity of the demand for total energy, some of the net cross-price effects for electricity are negative in the combined results.

Towards the end of the 1970s, several provinces changed their per-unit excise taxes on petroleum products to ad valorem taxes. We plan to build the excise taxes explicitly into future versions of our margin equations for oil products, as these tax changes will increase the extent to which user prices respond when refinery-gate prices change.

A final element of the disaggregated demand equations is the submodel for determining the shares of thermally generated electricity that come from coal, oil, and natural gas. As in earlier versions of the model, we subtract exogenous estimates of hydro and nuclear electricity supply from total regional electricity demand, and add exogenous estimates of exports, in order to derive the amount of thermally generated electricity. We are still using the system of thermal fuel share equations estimated by McRae. Because of rapidly rising crude oil and natural gas prices, the equations have predicted negative oil and gas use in some regions. We naturally bound these estimates at zero, and assume the use of coal for all thermal generation when oil and gas become uneconomic. Over the 1980s, most provinces plan to phase out crude oil and natural gas from base-load electricity generation, so there is not much need to revise and update our thermal generation submodel. From the point of view of the model as a whole, it will be more important to complete our preliminary modelling of hydroelectricity costs and expenditures, and to consider nuclear electricity investment as well, because electricity investment comprises more than half of projected energy investment over the 1980s. In the meantime, we continue to use exogenous official forecasts of the quantities and costs of new electricity supplies.

Economic rents accruing to purchasers of oil products and natural gas at less than their opportunity values are calculated by integrating under the compensated derived demand curves, for each of the two fuels, between the actual price paid and the opportunity values, evaluated using the simulated quantities purchased at the new prices. The reduced-form demand elasticities (which are used to allow for income effects) have not yet been recomputed using our latest parameter estimates for the demand system.

7. ENERGY SUPPLY: INVESTMENT, PRODUCTION, TAXATION, AND ALLOCATION OF REVENUES

As mentioned above, most of electricity supply is exogenous in the current version of MACE. The same is true of coal, most of which is exported for metallurgical and, more recently, for thermal uses in overseas markets. Thus the energy supply sectors in MACE are for non-frontier natural gas, conventional crude oil, synthetic oil from oil sands plants, and natural gas from the Mackenzie Delta. We shall briefly describe the first three in turn. The current versions of the Arctic gas pipeline and production sectors have been described elsewhere.

Total demand for Canadian natural gas is obtained by adding domestic demand to policy-determined export series (although the latter are adjusted downwards in the early 1980s to reflect weak US markets), estimates of fuel and losses, and net petrochemical feedstock demands to obtain total field production. If this demand exceeds the normal production capacity of already-connected reserves, then the model connects enough new reserves, drawn from the existing stock of discovered but unconnected gas, to meet the demand. If current production capacity should exceed demand, the unproduced gas is used to extend the future production life of the currently connected reserves.

The stock of unconnected reserves is augmented by reserve additions, which are triggered by exploration and development drilling. We do not distinguish between exploration and development drilling, nor between new discoveries, revisions, and extensions. The level of drilling (and hence of reserve additions) is driven by the ratio of the net-of-tax-and-royalty netback (discounted to form a present value) relative to the marginal cost of new gas. The assumed elasticity of drilling response is 1.0. The marginal cost of gas is obtained from an estimated cost function that shows real costs increasing as the accumulated stock of discoveries approaches the ultimate geologic potential. The level of discoveries becomes zero when it reaches the model's time-varying estimate of the ultimate economic potential. The latter is based initially on National Energy Board and provincial estimates, adjusted (with an elasticity of 0.10) by the ratio of the current after-tax well-head price, in real terms, relative to its value in a base period. Total investment expenditures (which include the costs of gas processing plants) are obtained by multiplying the new discoveries by marginal cost.

Total gross producer revenues from natural gas are obtained by mutliplying production by the well-head price described earlier. An allowance is also made for average revenues from natural gas liquids. These revenues are estimated to continue at about 20 per cent of natural gas well-head revenues. Royalties are calculated using average Alberta values, adjusted for investment incentive payments and including provisions of the April 1982 Alberta Oil and Gas Activity programme, with production from freehold lands distinguished from that from Crown lands. Federal and provincial corporation income taxes are separately calculated, since the provincial governments treat royalties as a deductible expense and the federal government does not. The Alberta government's indemnification of federal taxes paid on deemed royalties is also modelled. Depletion allowances are modelled for the historic period, and petroleum incentive payments for the future. The Petroleum and Gas Revenue Tax (PGRT) is levied at a rate of 12 per cent (after allowing for a 25 per cent resource allowance) on revenues net of operating costs. The June 1982 NEP update, which modified the PGRT, the IORT, and the well-head price of crude oil, has been incorporated in the coding of this section. Revenues are based on estimated equations, updated by industry data and government forecasts. Land payments are estimated to depend on the ratio of well-head price to marginal cost, multiplied by the estimated remaining stock of economic but undiscovered reserves.

Economic rents to each level of government, and to the producing firms, are calculated by cumulating revenues and subtracting costs. Kick-off values for cumulated rents were obtained from model runs starting back in the 1950s, when western Canadian oil and gas investment and production were becoming large. In calculating economic rents we make a distinction between the social opportunity cost of capital and the rate of social time preference. The social opportunity cost of capital is a pre-tax rental cost, which we calculate to be 10 per cent, 7 per cent of which is an after-tax supply price of capital to business (based on the RDX2 data) and 3 per cent of which is the average corporation tax yield in the economy as a whole, measured as a percentage of the replacement cost of business capital. Real investment expenditures are accumulated as they are undertaken, and are written off on a per-unit-of-production basis.

This accumulated cost of reserves is multiplied by the general price index to provide the basis for opportunity cost calculations. The 7 per cent after-tax cost is charged against the rents accruing to the producing firms, while the 3 per cent tax opportunity cost is split between the federal and provincial governments, about two-thirds being charged to the federal government. All accumulation and discounting is done using the 7 per cent real after-tax rate, on the assumption that it is also roughly equal to the rate of social time preference. Since all revenues and costs are in nominal terms, all accumulation and discounting is done using the nominal social time preference factor $STPNOM = (1.07) (1 + PDOT)$, where $PDOT$ is the current rate of inflation. The product of all the future annual values of $STPNOM$ is used as a discount factor to obtain present values.

Economic rents to the industry are equal, on an annual basis, to well-head revenues plus government subsidies minus operating costs, royalties, taxes, land payments, and the rental price of capital. Rents to the provincial governments are based on land payments, royalties, and taxes, less royalty abatements, incentive payments, and the tax opportunity cost. Rents to the federal government come, in the case of natural gas, from the Natural Gas and Gas Liquids Tax, the Petroleum and Gas Revenue Tax, and the corporation income tax, less the Petroleum Incentive Payments and the tax opportunity cost.

The non-frontier oil supply sector is similar in its basic structure, so only the major differences need be noted. Exports of western Canadian oil are set exogenously, and in the 1980s comprise mainly heavy oils, for which refining facilities are not readily available. Domestic production of crude and synthetic oil is used first to meet the exogenous export series and all domestic demands west of the Ottawa Valley. If there is surplus production capacity (from connected or available unconnected reserves) it is used to meet demands in Quebec and the Maritimes, up to the exogenously set limit to the capacity of the pipeline to Montreal. The exploration and development behaviour, the cost functions, and the taxation regimes are modelled analogously with those for natural gas. There is an additional complication posed by the Incremental Oil Revenue Tax (IORT), which siphons off the revenue from the post-NEP price increases for old oil into a separate category which is subject to a special 50 per cent tax but not to the corporation income tax. Economic rents are calculated the same way as for natural gas.

The oil sands sector is based on a detailed modelling of the timing and costs of the Syncrude plant. The earlier Suncor plant revenues and costs are modelled in a more rudimentary way. Subsequent plants are invoked automatically by specifying a starting date for production, and this then triggers a series of investment expenditures over the five preceding years. Our control solution supposes the construction of no oil sands plants during the 1980s.

Before returning to our analysis of the macroeconomic effects of oil sands projects, we shall first present a summary of the main properties of the current version of MACE.

8. SOME DYNAMIC PROPERTIES OF MACE

To give some idea of the error properties of the model as a whole, table 2.1 shows the year-by-year errors and the root-mean-square errors for a seven-year dynamic simulation from 1974 to 1980. In these calculations, the exchange rate is determined by the structural model, and the nominal interest rate is treated as the exogenous monetary policy variable. Results are shown for the major macroeconomic variables, whose names are fully defined in the attached list of variables. We are fairly well satisfied with the tracking power of the model, as the errors are typically rather small, and show little tendency to diverge increasingly from history as the simulation proceeds.

To provide some background to our later analysis of various energy-related shocks in the 1980s, table 2.2 shows the 1982-91 control solution for the model, and tables 2.3-2.5 show the effects of fiscal and monetary shocks applied over the forecast period. The $1 billion increase in government spending, maintained constant thereafter in real terms, is just over 1 per cent of total government spending in 1982, or just under 0.25 per cent of GNP. The contractionary monetary policy shown in table 2.4 is a reduction of 1 per cent per year in the growth rate of the supply of high-powered money. This policy experiment, and the fiscal policy experiment preceding it, were selected from the various experiments that were run in conjunction with the cross-model comparison seminar of July 1982. Table 2.5 helps to display the non-linearities of the model. It shows the result of an expansionary monetary policy that increases the rate of monetary growth by 1 per cent per annum.

The sustained government expenditure increase is accompanied by the partially accommodating monetary policy described earlier. The supply of high-powered money is above its control solution value, but there are also increases in both nominal and real interest rates relative to their control solution values. A more accommodating monetary policy would increase the GNP and inflation effects of the spending increase, and vice versa. Even with some monetary accommodation, there are substantial crowding-out effects, and the real multiplier follows a cyclical decline from its initial peak of 0.88. There is an induced trade deficit throughout the simulation period, but the higher nominal and real interest rates draw in enough additional capital that the price of foreign exchange is down slightly during the first three years of the simulation. Later on, as the induced inflationary effects continue to accumulate and as stock reallocation effects on foreign capital are completed, the currency starts to weaken. By the end of the ten-year simulation, the domestic output price is 1.1 per cent higher, and the price of foreign exchange 1.0 per cent higher, than in the control solution, thus roughly maintaining relative purchasing power parity over the ten-year horizon.

As can be seen from tables 2.4 and 2.5, monetary policy has substantial effects in the MACE model, and the model shows significant nonlinearity of response even under a control solution involving substantial excess capacity.

For example, after ten years of slower monetary growth, nominal GNP is reduced by 8.0 per cent, of which 2.7 per cent is real and the rest price. Ten years of faster monetary growth increases nominal GNP by 8.4 per cent, with only 2.3 per cent real and the rest price. At the end of the ten years of slower monetary growth, the inflation rate is down by 0.8 per cent, while it is 0.9 per cent higher with the faster monetary growth. The split between the real and the inflationary effects of expansionary or contractionary policies shifts away from real effects and towards price effects as the utilization rates increase, especially as the unemployment rate approaches the so-called natural rate.

The exchange rate effects of the monetary policies are substantially greater than the price effects over the first few years of the policy, and even after several more years the change in the exchange rate is about one-quarter greater than the change in the domestic output price. This is because the monetary policies have substantial continuing effects on both nominal and real interest rates. The interest rate effects have portfolio reallocation effects that substantially alter exchange rates in the short run, and have continuing influence on the international allocation of new savings, and hence on the real exchange rate, even over a period of several years. Simulations of a once-and-for-all expansion of the money supply by 1 per cent show the exchange rate moving by 1 per cent in the first year, while the domestic price effects gradually accumulate over a period of several years. Thus an unexpected monetary expansion or contraction causes an immediate change in the real exchange rate, but the change in the nominal exchange rate does not, in our current portfolio model, overshoot its long-term change.

In the sections that follow, we shall make primary use of the flexibile exchange rate version analysed in this section, although we shall also report results from a fixed exchange rate version to illustrate more clearly the effects of exchange rate flexibility in determining the macroeconomic responses to the shocks considered.

9. THE EFFECTS OF CHANGES IN WORLD OIL PRICES

World oil prices affect the world economy in complicated ways. Since they affect output, inflation, and trade flows all over the world, one must use world models (e.g. Klein, 1978) to assess their overall effects. However, we think that it is useful, given the complexities of Canadian energy policy, to take a partial view of the direct linkages between world oil prices and the Canadian economy. We shall thus ignore the effects coming through world output and inflation, and conduct our experiment as though Canada were the only country trading energy at the different world oil price.

In the MACE model, there are many energy prices linked to the world oil price. These include coal import and export prices, natural gas export prices, and, to a greater or lesser extent, most domestic oil and gas prices. In this section we examine the effects of world oil prices being 10 per cent below their control solution path in 1981 and each subsequent year.

TABLE 2.1

Simulated minus actual values and root-mean-square (RMS) errors for dynamic simulation, 1974–80.
(Short-term interest rates are exogenous.)

	E RMS (%)	INE RMS (%)	KNE RMS (%)	KINV RMS (%)	NL RMS (%)	NE RMS (%)	Q RMS (%)	QSV RMS (%)	UGNP RMS (%)	UGNPDOT RMS (LEV)
1974	-0.756	-1.619	-0.155	-2.545	-0.013	-0.433	-0.275	-0.298	-0.198	-0.205
1975	3.410	-0.290	0.167	-2.214	0.090	0.915	0.030	0.542	-0.077	0.123
1976	1.103	-3.831	-0.500	-0.252	0.194	1.261	-0.469	0.686	-0.817	-0.782
1977	-1.258	2.672	-0.231	7.984	0.434	2.189	1.137	1.254	1.096	1.970
1978	-0.654	12.921	0.796	8.955	0.598	2.381	1.170	1.582	1.519	0.433
1979	-0.322	3.299	1.000	-1.931	0.410	1.411	0.399	1.146	0.601	-0.931
1980	-0.410	-8.817	0.213	-6.282	0.019	0.054	-0.057	0.169	-0.094	-0.691
	1.498	6.326	0.539	5.326	0.330	1.467	0.668	0.946	0.810	0.932

	YGNP$ RMS (%)	C RMS (%)	XNE RMS (%)	MNE RMS (%)	W RMS (%)	WDOT RMS (LEV)	PA RMS (%)	PADOT RMS (LEV)	PQ RMS (%)	PFX RMS (%)
1974	-0.070	-0.529	-1.298	-4.747	-0.553	-0.637	0.583	0.661	0.111	-0.122
1975	0.814	-1.102	4.808	2.053	-1.109	-0.640	0.066	-0.575	0.943	-0.243
1976	0.136	-1.433	2.406	0.645	-1.557	-0.514	-0.417	-0.525	0.978	-0.039
1977	2.290	-0.637	2.043	5.381	-1.432	0.138	-0.678	-0.283	1.167	-0.235
1978	1.598	0.044	-0.682	3.138	-1.580	-0.159	-2.076	-1.516	0.071	-0.623
1979	-0.521	0.616	0.021	-6.483	-1.097	0.529	-2.087	-0.013	-1.133	0.413
1980	-0.113	0.093	-5.035	-12.334	-0.055	1.148	-1.158	1.050	-0.038	-0.595
	1.119	0.788	2.942	6.096	1.178	0.623	1.253	0.804	0.803	0.386

	BOT RMS (LEV)	FI RMS (LEV)	LF RMS (%)	HPM RMS (%)	RL RMS (LEV)	LB RMS (%)	V RMS (%)	TI RMS (%)	TDP RMS (%)	TCNE RMS (%)
1974	1.383	−0.870	−1.332	1.601	−0.416	7.189	2.086	0.160	0.151	−11.357
1975	1.765	−0.704	−0.642	0.004	−0.325	8.990	6.552	−1.277	−0.988	−5.332
1976	1.895	−1.739	6.066	2.908	−0.294	1.400	13.196	−2.226	−1.632	8.060
1977	1.013	0.056	2.114	3.343	−0.010	−4.543	7.307	−0.550	0.369	20.586
1978	1.778	1.273	−3.960	−1.396	0.095	−2.975	−7.073	−0.271	−1.318	10.107
1979	4.374	−6.451	−4.595	−2.169	0.438	−8.215	−1.209	−1.310	0.040	0.641
1980	4.262	−1.244	−5.367	−3.487	−0.211	−2.494	0.981	−2.475	0.123	−2.688
	2.675	2.647	3.947	2.420	0.295	5.827	6.837	1.455	0.891	10.392

Guide to the variables

E Energy expenditure (1971 $ billion)
INE Business fixed investment, excluding energy investment (1971 $ billion)
KNE Business fixed capital stock, excluding energy sector (1971 $ billion)
$IINV$ Value of physical change in inventories (1971 $ billion)
$KINV$ Stock of inventories (1971 $ billion)
NE Total employed persons, excluding armed forces (millions)
Q Gross output at factor cost of non-energy sector (equals real GDP plus net energy imports) (1971 $ billion)
QSV Vintage-based synthetic supply (1971 $ billion)
$UGNP$ Real gross national product (1971 $ billion)
$UGNPDOT$ Rate of change of UGNP (per cent per year)
$YGNP\$$ Nominal gross national product ($ billion)
C Personal consumption expenditures (1971 $ billion)
XNE Exports of goods and services, excluding energy (1971 $ billion)
MNE Imports of goods and services, excluding energy (1971 $ billion)
W Wage rate (thousands of dollars per year per employed person)
$WDOT$ Wage inflation (per cent increase in W per year)
PA Implicit price of absorption (1971 = 1.0)
$PADOT$ Price inflation (per cent increase in PA per year)
PQ Implicit price for gross domestic output, including net energy imports (1971 = 1.0)
PFX Spot price of foreign exchange (Can $ per US $)
BOT Current account of the balance of payments ($ billion)
FI Net capital inflows, excluding official monetary movements ($ billion)

TABLE 2.1 *Continued*

LF	Net liabilities to non-residents, excluding official reserves ($ billion)
HPM	High-powered money ($ billion)
RS	Average yield on Government of Canada bonds, 1–3 years (per cent)
RL	Average yield on Government of Canada bonds, 10 years and over (per cent)
LB	Net stock of government non-monetary liabilities ($ billion)
V	Market value of private sector wealth ($ billion)
TI	Indirect taxes net of subsidies ($ billion)
TDP	Total direct taxes on persons ($ billion)
TCNE	Total corporate taxes in the non-energy sector ($ billion)
PE	Price of primary energy (1971 = 0)
PO•CA	User price of oil for Canada ($ per million output b.t.u.)
PG•CA	User price of natural gas for Canada ($ per million output b.t.u.)
PCGO•CA	City-gate price of oil for Canada ($ per barrel)
PCGG•CA	City-gate price of natural gas for Canada ($ per mcf)
DOIL•CAN	Canadian demand for crude oil (thousand barrels per day)
DGAS•CAN	Canadian demand for natural gas (t.c.f. per year)
QELEC	Canadian demand for electricity (billion kWh per year)
IE	Energy investment (1971 $ billion)
BOTE	Balance of trade in energy ($ billion)

During the 1980s, Canada is forecast to have a balance of trade surplus in energy trade, and most of these products have prices that are linked to the world oil price. Thus, the lower world oil price imposes a terms of trade loss. However, the lower domestic price index for total energy (down by about 3 per cent in 1982, and by 5 per cent in 1985, when all domestic oil and gas user prices start to move proportionately with world oil prices) cuts the aggregate 1982 inflation rate by 0.6 per cent under flexible exchange rates and 0.9 per cent under fixed exchange rates. The cost reduction leads to lower nominal and real interest rates, higher profitability, and higher domestic output and national income. Figures 2.1 and 2.2 show the results for real GNP and the rate of increase in the absorption price under both fixed and flexible exchange rates. Note that the lower world oil prices give greater real GNP growth and less inflation under both exchange rate systems, but both effects are less under flexible exchange rates. The reason for this difference is Canada's position as a net energy exporter, with most energy imports and exports being sold at prices that move with world oil prices. The 10 per cent drop in world oil prices reduces Canada's current dollar balance on energy trade by $500 million in 1982, and by three times as much in 1985. Under flexibile exchange rates, this leads to an increase in the price of foreign exchange that exceeds 1 per cent in 1983. The higher price of foreign exchange increases the domestic price level and thus limits the extent to which the lower world oil price cuts the overall domestic rate of inflation. The reduced impact on the domestic inflation rate then leads to slightly smaller expansionary effects on real GNP. The impact on real GNP might have been bigger under flexible than under fixed exchange rates if the depreciating exchange rate had led to substantial increases in the demand for domestic output. However, in the MACE model, a currency devaluation has little or no expansionary effect on real output unless it is accompanied by an expansionary monetary policy that offsets the depressive effects of increases in real interest rates and price levels caused by the depreciation.

The 10 per cent reduction in oil prices is relative to a control solution that supposes the OPEC oil price to remain fixed in nominal terms at US $34 per barrel until the end of 1983, and thereafter to rise at 10 per cent per annum, once again in terms of US dollars. This 10 per cent change is not very large in terms of the sort of changes that have taken place recently in actual and expected world oil prices. For example, our control solution world oil prices are themselves about 25 per cent lower than the world oil prices that were assumed by the federal and provincial governments in their energy agreements in September and October 1981.

There is an intersectoral shift of income and activity that is not apparent in the aggregate results reported in figures 2.1 and 2.2. For example, 1983 fixed investment in the energy-using industry is up by 2.3 per cent, while it is down by less than 0.5 per cent in the energy-producing industry (assuming that the lower world oil price has no effect on investment in oil sands, coal,

TABLE 2.2
Control solution with flexibile exchange rates and endogenous monetary policy

	E	INE	KNE	IINV	KINV	NE	Q	QSV	UGNP	UGNPDOT
1982	10.367	17.544	250.362	0.353	27.672	10.970	122.519	133.185	133.862	-0.043
1983	10.439	15.949	254.393	0.360	28.032	11.022	125.510	135.811	136.743	2.152
1984	10.650	16.181	258.463	1.005	29.037	11.130	130.185	139.029	142.118	3.930
1985	10.952	17.158	263.317	1.403	30.440	11.290	135.419	142.954	148.079	4.194
1986	11.309	8.301	269.082	1.556	31.996	11.483	140.863	147.444	154.272	4.182
1987	11.703	19.341	275.614	1.509	33.505	11.690	146.065	152.309	160.345	3.937
1988	12.105	20.382	282.875	1.080	34.586	11.916	151.604	157.574	166.761	4.001
1989	12.527	21.338	290.746	0.696	35.282	12.159	157.194	163.191	173.120	3.814
1990	12.983	22.090	298.995	0.545	35.827	12.399	162.906	169.003	179.465	3.665
1991	13.497	22.669	307.430	0.755	36.583	12.626	168.734	174.923	185.662	3.453

	YGNP$	C	XNE	MNE	W	WDOT	PA	PADOT	PQ	PFX
1982	365.995	85.765	30.751	31.104	18.757	11.010	2.689	10.160	2.716	1.202
1983	416.457	89.310	30.921	30.893	20.937	11.621	2.958	9.986	3.010	1.203
1984	472.030	94.051	31.115	32.222	23.396	11.745	3.208	8.459	3.284	1.186
1985	537.113	98.992	31.908	34.120	26.216	12.052	3.486	8.674	3.592	1.173
1986	608.994	104.129	32.848	36.136	29.388	12.098	3.791	8.739	3.925	1.170
1987	687.703	109.205	33.878	37.919	32.851	11.785	4.112	8.473	4.272	1.177
1988	775.547	114.283	34.919	39.377	36.649	11.561	4.461	8.494	4.644	1.194
1989	875.366	119.313	35.834	40.627	40.956	11.752	4.859	8.918	5.069	1.218
1990	995.841	124.489	36.538	42.006	46.032	12.395	5.325	9.598	5.580	1.237
1991	1142.066	130.039	37.093	43.845	52.193	13.383	5.879	10.394	6.203	1.252

	BOT	FI	LF	RS	HPM	LB	V	TI	TDP	TCNE
1982	-3.674	6.630	202.574	13.227	21.174	73.854	650.025	41.443	58.812	9.814
1983	2.017	-0.260	227.849	13.139	23.831	85.470	807.468	46.347	66.091	11.948
1984	2.090	6.736	253.442	12.089	27.049	105.109	940.334	52.452	74.575	14.153
1985	1.355	5.522	283.196	11.957	30.572	122.785	1102.411	59.729	84.565	16.632
1986	-2.418	4.699	313.860	11.804	34.466	136.313	1274.576	68.081	95.940	19.109
1987	-4.827	2.560	342.056	11.407	38.826	145.337	1454.493	76.915	108.449	21.072
1988	-8.598	2.121	370.762	11.177	43.611	150.777	1650.040	86.938	122.543	23.165
1989	-14.864	5.315	403.938	11.349	48.808	154.192	1862.492	98.412	138.633	25.497
1990	-22.422	14.363	449.938	12.174	54.651	159.718	2100.181	122.119	157.756	28.710
1991	-34.001	28.174	517.014	13.473	61.420	167.926	2374.705	128.833	180.905	33.123

	PE	PO•CA	PG•CA	PCGO•CA	PCGG•CA	DOIL•CAN	DGAS•CAN	QELEC	IE	BOTE
1982	4.051	18.563	4.514	34.642	3.032	1525.637	1.954	327.191	6.587	3.505
1983	4.524	20.823	5.134	39.611	3.480	1513.558	2.006	332.387	6.759	6.495
1984	4.913	22.687	5.640	43.639	3.847	1522.323	2.064	339.523	6.930	6.973
1985	5.328	24.762	6.207	48.150	4.256	1540.867	2.160	349.617	7.137	7.106
1986	5.785	27.163	6.853	53.456	4.725	1562.400	2.235	362.343	7.414	5.061
1987	6.275	29.692	7.632	59.070	5.299	1590.314	2.338	377.287	7.364	4.678
1988	6.844	32.760	8.475	66.054	5.919	1611.383	2.426	392.331	7.703	2.915
1989	7.498	36.398	9.490	74.428	6.667	1629.502	2.510	408.722	8.056	-0.805
1990	8.244	40.430	10.619	83.655	7.499	1664.117	2.605	426.643	8.718	-4.437
1991	9.067	44.828	11.869	93.627	8.399	1714.528	2.689	446.997	9.584	-8.814

TABLE 2.3
Sustained increase in real government spending: G up by (1982) $1 billion

	E (S−C)/C(%)	INE (S−C)/C(%)	KNE (S−C)/C(%)	IINV S−C	KINV (S−C)/C(%)	NE (S−C)/C(%)	Q (S−C)/C(%)	QSV (S−C)/C(%)	UGNP (S−C)/C(%)	UGNPDOT S−C
1982	0.080	0.461	0.032	−0.054	−0.195	0.069	0.214	0.053	0.206	0.207
1983	0.197	0.675	0.073	0.039	−0.055	0.128	0.259	0.111	0.205	−0.001
1984	0.277	0.522	0.101	0.088	0.249	0.139	0.247	0.137	0.167	−0.040
1985	0.290	0.419	0.121	0.073	0.476	0.142	0.231	0.150	0.148	−0.020
1986	0.265	0.434	0.143	0.008	0.478	0.158	0.225	0.165	0.151	0.003
1987	0.230	0.446	0.164	−0.054	0.295	0.183	0.222	0.183	0.157	0.006
1988	0.211	0.360	0.178	−0.081	0.053	0.199	0.209	0.194	0.145	−0.013
1989	0.214	0.183	0.178	−0.060	−0.119	0.194	0.183	0.192	0.114	−0.032
1990	0.241	−0.003	0.165	−0.016	−0.162	0.171	0.154	0.177	0.070	−0.045
1991	0.265	−0.154	0.141	0.028	−0.083	0.139	0.122	0.155	0.016	−0.055

	YGNP$ (S−C)/C(%)	C (S−C)/C(%)	XNE (S−C)/C(%)	MNE (S−C)/C(%)	W (S−C)/C(%)	WDOT S−C	PA (S−C)/C(%)	PADOT S−C	PQ (S−C)/C(%)	PFX (S−C)/C(%)
1982	0.326	0.100	−0.076	0.254	0.098	0.108	0.084	0.092	0.125	−0.137
1983	0.486	0.179	−0.127	0.572	0.265	0.186	0.209	0.137	0.296	−0.231
1984	0.549	0.208	−0.136	0.736	0.392	0.142	0.303	0.102	0.406	−0.171
1985	0.577	0.212	−0.079	0.738	0.464	0.081	0.360	0.061	0.452	0.003
1986	0.593	0.199	−0.031	0.582	0.495	0.034	0.394	0.037	0.457	0.256
1987	0.628	0.174	−0.044	0.360	0.521	0.029	0.445	0.056	0.483	0.513
1988	0.701	0.142	−0.166	0.160	0.575	0.060	0.535	0.097	0.567	0.711
1989	0.810	0.115	−0.220	0.054	0.671	0.107	0.663	0.138	0.709	0.835
1990	0.944	0.098	−0.314	0.045	0.804	0.148	0.815	0.166	0.889	0.918
1991	1.089	0.085	−0.366	0.099	0.958	0.174	0.984	0.185	1.087	1.009

	BOT S−C	FI S−C	LF (S−C)/C(%)	RS S−C	HPM (S−C)/C(%)	LB (S−C)/C(%)	V (S−C)/C(%)	TI (S−C)/C(%)	TDP (S−C)/C(%)	TCNE (S−C)/C(%)
1982	−0.257	0.965	0.749	0.216	0.102	1.867	0.244	0.472	0.209	1.624
1983	−0.674	1.158	1.416	0.269	0.201	2.967	0.291	0.674	0.382	1.842
1984	−1.079	0.766	1.805	0.217	0.291	2.862	0.344	0.761	0.486	1.687
1985	−1.302	0.423	1.928	0.158	0.378	2.515	0.344	0.790	0.546	1.377
1986	−1.430	0.159	1.904	0.107	0.446	2.141	0.345	0.801	0.581	1.056
1987	−1.521	0.216	1.884	0.100	0.482	1.969	0.349	0.825	0.619	0.865
1988	−1.615	0.567	1.976	0.137	0.508	2.132	0.380	0.870	0.683	0.881
1989	−1.823	1.072	2.227	0.195	0.549	2.652	0.467	0.951	0.779	1.118
1990	−2.225	1.662	2.603	0.261	0.622	3.386	0.603	1.066	0.904	1.510
1991	−2.900	2.343	3.018	0.327	0.723	4.229	0.763	1.204	1.043	1.938

	PE (S−C)/C(%)	PO·CA (S−C)/C(%)	PG·CA (S−C)/C(%)	PCGO·CA (S−C)/C(%)	PCGG·CA (S−C)/C(%)	DOIL·CAN (S−C)/C(%)	DGAS·CAN (S−C)/C(%)	QELEC (S−C)/C(%)	IE (S−C)/C(%)	BOTE S−C
1982	−0.029	−0.039	−0.042	−0.078	−0.078	0.083	0.080	0.071	−0.033	−0.014
1983	−0.048	−0.065	−0.074	−0.145	−0.153	0.203	0.192	0.180	−0.066	−0.039
1984	−0.025	−0.034	−0.036	−0.124	−0.133	0.288	0.261	0.272	−0.067	−0.100
1985	0.085	0.104	0.128	0.052	0.042	0.297	0.244	0.320	−0.057	−0.096
1986	0.218	0.281	0.321	0.283	0.264	0.254	0.190	0.337	−0.040	−0.085
1987	0.371	0.477	0.557	0.530	0.524	0.210	0.113	0.360	−0.003	−0.081
1988	0.502	0.643	0.757	0.726	0.732	0.183	0.056	0.394	0.006	−0.086
1989	0.601	0.755	0.895	0.840	0.858	0.183	0.033	0.437	0.005	−0.130
1990	0.661	0.843	0.989	0.921	0.928	0.193	0.030	0.483	−0.007	−0.192
1991	0.745	0.952	1.121	1.023	1.036	0.217	0.037	0.543	−0.023	−0.285

TABLE 2.4
Reduce money supply growth rate by 1 percentage point

	E (S−C)/C(%)	INE (S−C)/C(%)	KNE (S−C)/C(%)	IINV S−C	KINV (S−C)/C(%)	NE (S−C)/C(%)	Q (S−C)/C(%)	QSV (S−C)/C(%)	UGNP (S−C)/C(%)	UGNPDOT S−C
1982	0.052	−0.937	−0.066	0.065	0.234	−0.092	−0.176	−0.064	−0.311	−0.310
1983	0.072	−2.622	−0.226	0.134	0.708	−0.279	−0.410	−0.209	−0.803	−0.504
1984	0.093	−3.817	−0.451	0.200	1.371	−0.493	−0.647	−0.392	−1.235	−0.453
1985	−0.117	−4.284	−0.701	0.148	1.795	−0.667	−0.827	−0.573	−1.547	−0.329
1986	−0.471	−4.217	−0.940	−0.038	1.588	−0.753	−0.943	−0.719	−1.739	−0.204
1987	−0.896	−3.978	−1.153	−0.257	0.749	−0.755	−1.022	−0.820	−1.848	−0.115
1988	−1.300	−3.925	−1.353	−0.408	−0.453	−0.725	−1.104	−0.897	−1.945	−0.103
1989	−1.622	−4.310	−1.570	−0.392	−1.556	−0.728	−1.230	−0.990	−2.109	−0.174
1990	−1.850	−5.115	−1.832	−0.209	−2.117	−0.808	−1.414	−1.131	−2.380	−0.287
1991	−2.068	−6.067	−2.144	0.033	−1.983	−0.956	−1.638	−1.323	−2.734	−0.376

	YGNP$ (S−C)/C(%)	C (S−C)/C(%)	XNE (S−C)/C(%)	MNE (S−C)/C(%)	W (S−C)/C(%)	WDOT S−C	PA (S−C)/C(%)	PADOT S−C	PQ (S−C)/C(%)	PFX (S−C)/C(%)
1982	−0.152	−0.055	0.052	0.317	0.047	0.052	0.049	0.054	0.167	−0.720
1983	−0.645	−0.156	0.528	0.891	0.013	−0.038	−0.065	−0.126	0.183	−1.803
1984	−1.464	−0.261	0.893	1.481	−0.248	−0.292	−0.467	−0.436	−0.194	−2.669
1985	−2.384	−0.382	1.430	1.826	−0.735	−0.547	−1.053	−0.640	−0.822	−3.410
1986	−3.405	−0.518	1.921	1.743	−1.434	−0.790	−1.810	−0.831	−1.692	−3.960
1987	−4.421	−0.684	2.210	1.347	−2.264	−0.941	−2.607	−0.881	−2.641	−4.338
1988	−5.336	−0.881	2.232	0.831	−3.108	−0.963	−3.340	−0.817	−3.500	−4.773
1989	−6.167	−1.080	2.034	0.474	−3.882	−0.893	−3.983	−0.724	−4.201	−5.485
1990	−7.009	−1.251	1.760	0.462	−4.589	−0.827	−4.597	−0.701	−4.810	−6.557
1991	−7.982	−1.404	1.646	0.721	−5.307	−0.854	−5.272	−0.781	−5.471	−7.780

Year	BOT S-C	FI S-C	LF (S-C)/C(%)	RS S-C	HPM (S-C)/C(%)	LB (S-C)/C(%)	V (S-C)/C(%)	TI (S-C)/C(%)	TDP (S-C)/C(%)	TCNE (S-C)/C(%)
1982	-0.158	3.872	1.585	0.926	-1.000	5.425	-0.671	-0.118	-0.105	0.315
1983	-0.638	6.225	3.602	1.525	-1.990	11.844	-1.799	-0.484	-0.452	0.320
1984	-1.757	6.023	5.214	1.640	-2.970	14.446	-2.724	-1.022	-1.061	-0.702
1985	-2.620	6.191	6.058	1.747	-3.940	16.190	-4.070	-1.737	-1.804	-2.126
1986	-3.165	5.878	6.361	1.735	-4.901	17.547	-5.436	-2.575	-2.669	-3.998
1987	-3.576	5.595	6.366	1.681	-5.852	18.882	-6.733	-3.463	-3.574	-6.017
1988	-3.722	6.256	6.390	1.743	-6.794	20.935	-7.939	-4.321	-4.443	-7.657
1989	-3.794	7.966	6.730	1.946	-7.726	24.298	-9.007	-5.129	-5.253	-8.726
1990	-4.287	10.438	7.331	2.259	-8.648	28.620	-9.990	-5.916	-6.052	-9.345
1991	-5.250	12.215	7.684	2.512	-9.562	33.056	-10.990	-6.754	-6.924	-10.033

Year	PE (S-C)/C(%)	PO·CA (S-C)/C(%)	PG·CA (S-C)/C(%)	PCGO·CA (S-C)/C(%)	PCGG·CA (S-C)/C(%)	DOIL·CAN (S-C)/C(%)	DGAS·CAN (S-C)/C(%)	QELEC (S-C)/C(%)	IE (S-C)/C(%)	BOTE (S-C)/C(%)
1982	-0.223	-0.288	-0.337	-0.418	-0.421	0.066	0.109	-0.017	-0.082	-0.854
1983	-0.678	-0.867	-1.032	-1.178	-1.207	0.109	0.256	-0.153	-0.152	-1.941
1984	-1.523	-1.970	-2.290	-2.568	-2.566	0.194	0.499	-0.423	-0.131	-3.804
1985	-2.042	-2.640	-3.055	-3.309	-3.286	0.028	0.461	-0.864	-0.084	-4.053
1986	-2.510	-3.233	-3.725	-3.896	-3.844	-0.300	0.256	-1.425	-0.004	-2.916
1987	-2.900	-3.725	-4.305	-4.340	-4.293	-0.705	-0.014	-2.014	-0.055	0.045
1988	-3.302	-4.231	-4.892	-4.814	-4.777	-1.084	-0.289	-2.572	-0.029	9.085
1989	-3.834	-4.932	-5.676	-5.555	-5.518	-1.353	-0.457	-3.080	-0.027	81.460
1990	-4.589	-5.895	-6.790	-6.636	-6.638	-1.523	-0.474	-3.575	-0.033	25.180
1991	-5.453	-6.984	-8.047	-7.860	-7.905	-1.671	-0.440	-4.099	-0.026	19.713

TABLE 2.5
Increase money supply growth rate by 1 percentage point

	E (S−C)/C(%)	INE (S−C)/C(%)	KNE (S−C)/C(%)	IINV S−C	KINV (S−C)/C(%)	NE (S−C)/C(%)	QSV (S−C)/C(%)	Q (S−C)/C(%)	UGNP (S−C)/C(%)	UGNPDOT S−C
1982	−0.049	0.875	0.061	−0.059	−0.214	0.086	0.060	0.165	0.289	0.289
1983	−0.056	2.441	0.210	−0.114	−0.620	0.261	0.196	0.385	0.735	0.455
1984	−0.106	3.566	0.421	−0.170	−1.185	0.464	0.367	0.609	1.117	0.394
1985	0.046	4.066	0.658	−0.135	−1.575	0.637	0.539	0.783	1.399	0.291
1986	0.350	4.157	0.896	−0.004	−1.509	0.746	0.693	0.919	1.591	0.197
1987	0.738	4.041	1.117	0.171	−0.930	0.782	0.811	1.016	1.704	0.115
1988	1.147	3.958	1.321	0.322	0.032	0.771	0.901	1.100	1.779	0.076
1989	1.503	4.152	1.529	0.372	1.086	0.763	0.988	1.203	1.881	0.105
1990	1.771	4.731	1.766	0.273	1.831	0.806	1.104	1.347	2.054	0.176
1991	1.979	5.550	2.045	0.076	2.002	0.912	1.262	1.527	2.298	0.247

	YGNP$ (S−C)/C(%)	C (S−C)/C(%)	XNE (S−C)/C(%)	MNE (S−C)/C(%)	W (S−C)/C(%)	WDOT S−C	PA (S−C)/C(%)	PADOT S−C	PQ (S−C)/C(%)	PFX (S−C)/C(%)
1982	0.139	0.053	−0.048	−0.297	−0.043	−0.048	−0.045	−0.050	−0.156	0.680
1983	0.566	0.153	−0.483	−0.838	−0.018	0.028	0.047	0.102	−0.191	1.716
1984	1.304	0.245	−0.800	−1.411	0.218	0.264	0.418	0.402	0.146	2.608
1985	2.152	0.351	−1.272	−1.803	0.664	0.499	0.964	0.591	0.710	3.454
1986	3.152	0.480	−1.725	−1.857	1.325	0.736	1.697	0.789	1.524	4.189
1987	4.238	0.634	−2.043	−1.620	2.162	0.924	2.538	0.897	2.502	4.747
1988	5.300	0.816	−2.160	−1.204	3.085	1.008	3.387	0.898	3.493	5.290
1989	6.304	1.006	−2.085	−0.817	4.002	0.994	4.189	0.845	4.395	6.040
1990	7.303	1.165	−1.885	−0.692	4.878	0.947	4.971	0.823	5.212	7.191
1991	8.419	1.280	−1.725	−0.878	5.762	0.955	5.821	0.984	6.063	8.703

	BOT S−C	FI S−C	LF (S−C)/C(%)	RS S−C	HPM (S−C)/C(%)	LB (S−C)/C(%)	V (S−C)/C(%)	TI (S−C)/C(%)	TDP (S−C)/C(%)	TCNE (S−C)/C(%)
1982	0.139	−3.640	−1.465	−0.867	1.000	−5.136	0.673	0.112	0.097	−0.300
1983	0.517	−5.858	−3.300	−1.419	2.010	−11.306	1.862	0.448	0.399	−0.370
1984	1.471	−5.886	−4.901	−1.559	3.030	−14.157	2.804	0.938	0.945	0.488
1985	2.193	−6.312	−5.823	−1.710	4.060	−16.383	4.266	1.612	1.629	1.692
1986	2.605	−6.256	−6.274	−1.745	5.101	−18.484	5.790	2.452	2.472	3.447
1987	2.904	−5.865	−6.360	−1.690	6.151	−20.560	7.261	3.404	3.424	5.557
1988	2.880	−6.007	−6.246	−1.682	7.213	−23.160	8.689	4.387	4.408	7.583
1989	2.546	−7.022	−6.211	−1.781	8.285	−26.894	10.015	5.356	5.371	9.196
1990	2.296	−8.943	−6.323	−1.998	9.368	−31.649	11.265	6.315	6.326	10.322
1991	2.251	−10.778	−6.310	−2.225	10.461	−37.042	12.529	7.324	7.345	11.340

	PE (S−C)/C(%)	PO·CA (S−C)/C(%)	PG·CA (S−C)/C(%)	PCGO·CA (S−C)/C(%)	PCGG·CA (S−C)/C(%)	DOIL·CAN (S−C)/C(%)	DGAS·CAN (S−C)/C(%)	QELEC (S−C)/C(%)	IE (S−C)/C(%)	BOTE (S−C)/C(%)
1982	0.211	0.272	0.319	0.395	0.397	−0.063	−0.012	0.016	0.077	0.811
1983	0.593	0.766	0.910	1.044	1.067	−0.093	−0.220	0.138	0.149	1.864
1984	1.470	1.910	2.224	2.501	2.501	−0.202	−0.489	0.383	0.138	3.802
1985	2.052	2.659	3.091	3.358	3.347	−0.089	−0.512	0.785	0.100	4.440
1986	2.580	3.369	3.868	4.108	4.035	0.152	−0.386	1.296	0.036	4.087
1987	3.073	3.997	4.611	4.723	4.653	0.503	−0.171	1.875	0.087	1.640
1988	3.553	4.618	5.350	5.320	5.270	0.884	0.072	2.480	0.059	−6.654
1989	4.139	5.370	6.223	6.092	6.060	1.199	0.264	3.050	0.045	−79.158
1990	4.942	6.422	7.443	7.255	7.249	1.398	0.311	3.590	0.033	−26.237
1991	5.979	7.772	9.034	8.780	8.837	1.536	0.238	4.160	0.023	−21.288

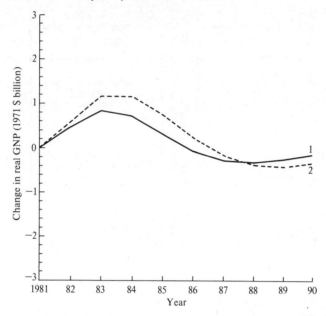

FIG. 2.1 Change in gross national product owing to cut in world oil price: 1, flexible exchange rate; 2, fixed exchange rate

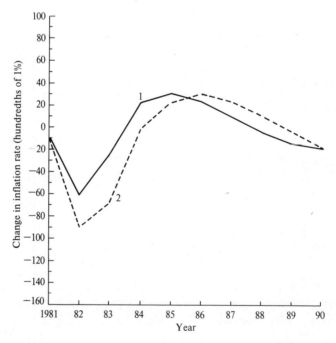

FIG. 2.2   Change in rate of inflation owing to cut in world oil price: 1, flexible exchange rate; 2, fixed exchange rate

and electricity). Government revenues are sharply down, since most of the marginal effects of the energy price changes are felt by government revenues, and this tax reduction is part of the reason for the expansion in domestic spending and income.

10. THE MACROECONOMIC IMPACT OF OIL SANDS PROJECTS

In this section we consider the impact on the aggregate economy if the recently cancelled Alsands oil sands project had gone ahead as planned. The approximate impact on energy investment is shown in figure 2.3. We assume a 1987 start of production and construction accumulating to over $13 billion, as recently forecast by the project sponsors. After adjusting for changes in the aggregate GNP price deflator between the mid-1970s (when the predecessor Syncrude plant was constructed) and the mid-1980s, the projected Alsands costs were about twice as high as the Syncrude costs. Some of this was apparently due to some design and scale changes, but most was due to abnormally high rates of inflation in oil industry costs, no doubt arising in large measure from the unusually rapid growth in the Alberta petroleum industry since 1975. Using the

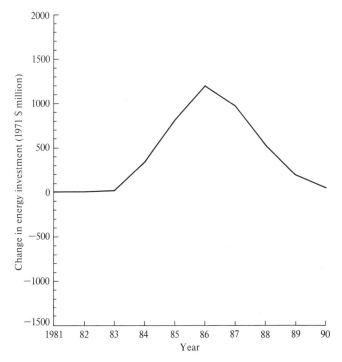

FIG. 2.3 Change in energy investment from resurrection of Alsands plant (flexible exchange rate)

aggregate absorption price index to deflate the projected costs of the Alsands plant, resurrection of the project would increase total energy investment by about 13 per cent during the three peak years of construction. This is equivalent to an increase of about 4 per cent of economy-wide investment; energy investment is projected to be almost one-half as large as non-energy investment during these years.

Figures 2.4 and 2.5 show the effects of the Alsands project on real GNP and the aggregate rate of inflation. In both figures, the results are reported for both fixed and flexible exchange rate systems. Until 1987, the effects are from the impact of Alsands construction, but thereafter the primary impact comes from the effects of the oil sands production on net energy imports (down about $2.6 billion annually at the end of the decade), offset by the increased interest and dividend payments (up $1 billion under flexible exchange rates) on the stock of foreign debt.

Construction of the plant would increase real GNP by about 1 per cent, with somewhat smaller effects on the inflation rate, during the peak years of construction. The effects on the unemployment rate are of about the same size as for the inflation rate, but of course of the opposite sign. The real GNP effects of the construction are larger, and the inflationary effects smaller, under flexible than under fixed exchange rates. Although the current account of the balance of payments is in substantial additional deficit during the construction phase (up by about $4 billion, or 0.6 per cent of nominal GNP in

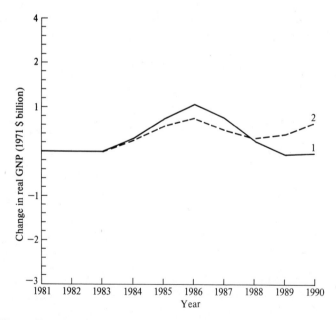

FIG 2.4 Change in gross national product from resurrection of Alsands plant: 1, flexible exchange rate; 2, fixed exchange rate

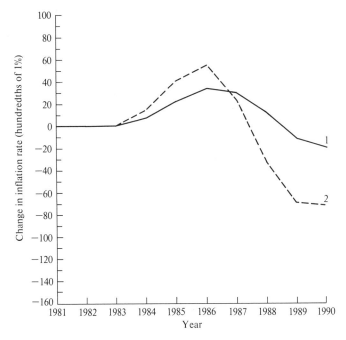

FIG. 2.5 Change in inflation rate from resurrection of Alsands plant: 1, flexible exchange
rate; 2, fixed exchange rate

1987), short-term nominal interest rates are up by almost 0.7 per cent, and real
interest rates by half as much, drawing in foreign capital in sufficient quantities
to drive down the price of foreign exchange during the peak construction years.
This means that induced inflation and induced monetary tightness are lower
under flexible rates, thus permitting a larger expansion of real GNP.

As the construction phase winds down at the end of the decade, there is an
induced slump caused by investment accelerator effects in the non-energy industry. Under flexible exchange rates the original boom is greater, and so,
therefore, is the post-boom hangover.

The simulation does not run long enough to show the subsequent effects of
the reduction in oil imports, as the Alsands production is still building up in
1990. During the operations phase, the oil sands plant is rather like any other
natural resource project with its capital already in place. To explain the impact
of this phase on the macroeconomics of the energy and non-energy sectors, we
can equally well use the results of a change in natural gas exports.

11. THE IMPACT OF ENERGY EXPORTS: THE CASE
OF NATURAL GAS

The National Energy Board has authorized a large temporary expansion of
natural gas exports linked to the early construction of the southern Canadian

branches (to export points in British Columbia and Saskatchewan) of the Alaska Highway natural gas pipeline. This construction is now largely completed, and the so-called pre-build exports have started to flow through the western leg of the system. In the simulations for this section of the paper, we take as given the investment in new pipeline facilities (about $1 billion for the pre-build sections) and examine the macroeconomic effects of the natural gas exports themselves. Neither the control solution nor the shock solution includes the construction expenditures on the northern Canadian legs of the Alaska Highway Pipeline, since these expenditures have recently been deferred by a further two years, and remain rather indefinite.

Our control solution involves reductions in all gas exports by amounts ranging from 30 per cent to 5 per cent below their approved limits between 1980 and 1985, to reflect the current softness in US markets for Canadian natural gas. Thus, when we remove the pre-build exports, we are removing slightly less than their approved amounts.

The macroeconomic issues posed by incremental exports of natural resources, especially where, as in this case, the marginal production costs are almost zero, are the same as those posed in the question, 'Oil or Industry?' (Barker and Brailovsky, 1981) faced by countries deciding how fast to exploit and export their stocks of natural resources. (There is a more complicated form of the disease, in which the resource industry also attracts capital and labour away from the other sector. These issues were the focus of our section on oil sands investment, and do not arise in this section, since the gas is already discovered and production and transportation facilities are in place.) We and others have considered elsewhere the microeconomics of this question, wherein the resource owner must compare future increases in the expected shadow value of the resource against the rate of return available on alternative investments, and against the relative utility of increased consumption expenditures now and in the future. In this section we shall consider instead the macroeconomic implications, or the possibilities of a Canadian manifestation of the celebrated 'Dutch disease' (Ellman, 1981). The symptoms of the Dutch disease are that increased resource exports raise the value of the domestic currency, or perhaps the domestic price level, and render the manufacturing sector uncompetitive in world markets. In this section we examine not the onset of the Dutch disease but the effects of a 'Norwegian solution', with energy exports held well below their technically feasible levels.

Figure 2.6 shows the projected level of Canadian energy exports both with and without the pre-build gas exports. The pre-build exports do not appear large when measured in 1971 dollars, since the price of natural gas exported then was only 5 per cent of its current level. However, the quantities of gas are large—up to about 0.7 trillion cubic feet (t.c.f.) per year—and the effects on the current account are substantial. Removing the pre-build gas exports would reduce nominal energy exports by $5 billion per year in 1985. This is about 1 per cent of nominal GNP, or 3 per cent of total export revenues.

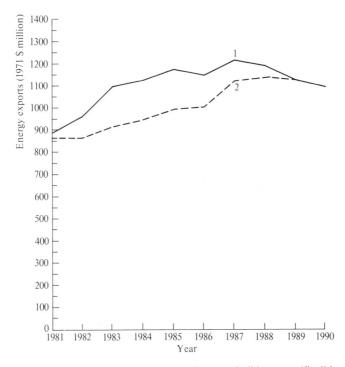

FIG. 2.6 Energy exports with and without natural gas pre-build exports (flexible exchange rate): 1, with pre-build; 2, without pre-build

Figures 2.7 and 2.8 show the real GNP and inflation effects of the reduction in gas exports. Since real government spending is taken to be exogenous, the government share of revenues is assumed to be saved. Thus, under fixed exchange rates there are few direct spending effects from the cutback in natural gas exports, since they lead, in the first instance, to a drop in foreign exchange reserves. These drops are so substantial ($5 to $6 billion per year in the mid-1980s) as to threaten the credibility of the fixed exchange rate and the almost unchanged supply of high-powered money, which is down by 1.8 per cent in 1985.

Even under fixed exchange rates, the drop in gas export revenues has depressing effects in the long run on real income and spending. In 1985, for example, real wealth is down by almost 0.7 per cent and real consumption down by 0.3 per cent. We should note that our current version of MACE treats V_e, the market value of the remaining stocks of energy resources, as an exogenous component of wealth. When this link between the energy and non-energy sectors is properly established, the higher value of V_e in the reduced-export case would serve partly to offset the drop in the market value of total wealth and hence in real consumer spending. It is true that the reduced domestic demand and prices improve the competitive position of Canada's non-energy

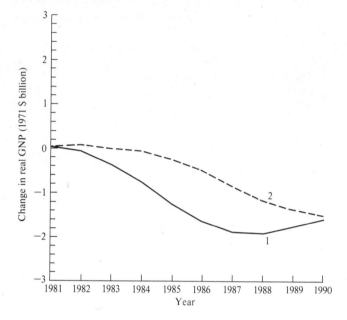

FIG. 2.7 Change in gross national product owing to cancellation of pre-build exports: 1, flexible exchange rate; 2, fixed exchange rate

importers and exporters, but the net effects on non-energy trade flows are very small. Thus MACE does not exhibit one of the main symptoms of the Dutch disease.

In the flexible exchange rate version, the weakening current account pushes up the price of foreign exchange (although there is a continuing severe loss of foreign reserves) with induced effects on the domestic price level and a larger squeeze on real income and wealth. For example, in 1985 real wealth is down by 3 per cent and real consumption by 0.9 per cent. The higher price of foreign exchange does improve the international trading position of firms in the non-energy industry. The real 1985 non-energy trade balance is improved by (1971) $350 million—and the difference would be closer $1 billion but for the loss of interest on the plundered foreign exchange account. But this is not enough to offset the stagflationary effects of the higher absorption price (up by 1.2 per cent in 1985). It is possible to choose a combination of exchange rate and monetary policy to produce long-run income gains, but the gains are always less than would be obtained without the gas export cuts. Thus the flexible exchange rate version of MACE follows the fixed exchange rate version in minimizing the effects of competition between the energy and non-energy sectors at the export phase of natural resource projects.

Our results reveal that large temporary changes in energy exports may impose substantial swings of activity and investment in the non-energy sector. These swings in the non-energy sector cause sympathetic movements in the main macro-

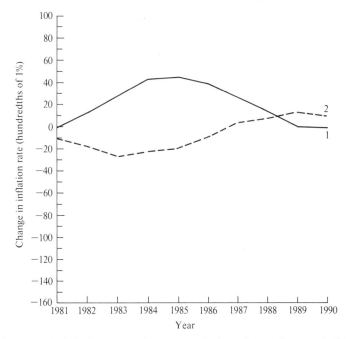

FIG. 2.8 Change in inflation rate owing to cancellation of natural gas pre-build exports: 1, flexible exchange rate; 2, fixed exchange rate

economic variables in cases, like the one analysed in this section, where the changes in energy exports do not change markedly the amounts of factors used by the resource industry itself. The cut in natural gas exports does lower the well-head price of gas (because of the 'flow-back' mechanism for export revenues), and this does reduce the incentive to discover and develop new deposits. Non-frontier natural gas investment is lower by as much as 6 per cent in some years. However, this is well under 1 per cent of total energy investment, and much smaller in absolute size than the late-1980s reductions in non-energy capital spending.

12. FUTURE PROSPECTS

The latest version of MACE is a flexible tool for examining a broad range of linkages between energy and the national economy. We are able to do all of what one would normally expect to do with a macroeconometric model, and to examine a large range of energy issues in considerable detail, including the assessment of their costs and benefits over several decades. In order to achieve this diversity and flexibility, we have had to limit, at least for now, the detail and sophistication of many of the individual elements of the model. Although we realize that this is a necessary cost if the model is to remain integrated, up-to-date, and applicable to real-world issues, we are always planning revisions and extensions that will, we hope, make the model richer, more interesting, and more informative. Among the many issues that are ripe for renewed or further research, we might mention:

1. the specification and estimation of cost functions, and industry responses, for conventional onshore oil and natural gas;
2. the separate treatment of the costs and potential for extracting and upgrading of heavy oils;
3. further research on the longer-term trends in energy demand by region and by fuel;
4. possible inclusionof a coal supply sector;
5. more precise accounting for condensate and liquid petroleum gases in the oil and gas supply sectors;
6. integrated modelling of the electricity supply sector, including hydroelectricity, nuclear, conventional thermal, industrial cogeneration (building on the hog fuel modelling), and alternate sources;
7. further emphasis on the determination of flexible exchange rates, with an eye to limiting the range of alternative models to be used;
8. more explicit modelling of the causes and consequences of interregional variations in growth rates;
9. modelling Hibernia and other potential offshore oil and gas deposits.

This list could be extended almost without limit. We choose to keep it short enough to appear feasible, but long enough to show that we still have much to do. We ought also to record our general conclusion that we have found the progress thus far to be satisfying and interesting enough to lead us to carry on.

ACKNOWLEDGEMENTS

The chief financial support for the MACE model has come from the SSHRCC, primarily through its support of UBC's Programme in Natural Resource Economics, but also from previous and subsequent research grants. We gratefully acknowledge this support, and also the assistance of the Bank of Canada, the University of British Columbia, the University of Calgary, Energy Mines and Resources Canada, and the British Columbia Science Council. We also wish to thank Ken White (1978) for the magic of SHAZAM, and for his help in response to our requests for new options and tests. We are grateful to Lawrence Klein and others for helpful comments and suggestions on an earlier version of this paper presented to the PNRE research conference at UBC in February 1982.

Appendix 1: The list of variables

CONVENTIONS

* denotes desired value, e.g., k_{inv}^{*}

~ denotes quatntity given by a CES bundle, e.g., $\tilde{k}_e$

— denotes a two-period average, e.g., $\bar{k}_{ne} = \frac{1}{2}k_{ne} + k_{ne-1}$

$-t$ denotes a lag of t years, e.g., q_{-1}

^ denotes equilibrium value at full capacity utilization after lags are worked out, e.g., $\hat{m}_{ne}$

• denotes one-period proportionate change; e.g.,

$$\dot{p}_a = (p_a - p_{a-1})/p_{a-1}$$

Variable	Equation no.	Description
a	(2.3)	Real absorption, 1971 \$ billion
a_2	exogenous	Real US absorption, 1975 US \$ billion
B	(4.6)	Current account of the balance of payments, \$ billion
B_e	(4.9)	The balance of trade in energy, \$ billion
c	(2.1)	Personal consumption expenditures, 1971 \$ billion
C_{ca}	(5.8)	Capital consumption allowance, \$ billion
c_q	(1.10)	Production costs relative to output price for q
D_{aib}		Dummy variable in labour force equation, equal to 1 in 1976 and -1 in 1978, to account for effects of anti-inflation board policies
D_{77}, D_{78}		Dummy variables in wage equation to account for effects of anti-inflation board in 1977 and 1978
e	(1.8)	Energy expenditure, 1971 \$ billion
e_v	(1.4)	Vintage-based energy requirement, 1971 \$ billion
F_i	(4.1)	Net capital inflows excluding official monetary movements, \$ billion
F_{ireva}	(4.7)	Retained earnings and revaluation on foreign-held domestic assets, \$ billion
F_{xo}	(4.2)	Official purchases of foreign exchange, US \$ billion
g	exogenous	Real government current and capital expenditures on goods and services, 1971 \$ billion
G_{misc}	exogenous	Balancing item to link government National Accounts Balances to changes in government money and debt outstanding, \$ billion

Variable	Equation no.	Description
G_t	(5.9)	Government transfers to persons, $ billion
H	(5.4)	High-powered money, $ billion
i_e	link	Energy investment, 1971 $ billion
i_{inv}	(1.13)	Value of physical change in inventories 1971 $ billion
i_{ne}	(1.1)	Business fixed investment (excluding energy investment), 1971 $ billion
i_{new}	(1.3)	Re-investment with energy use malleable if the current year, 1971 $ billion
$\tilde{k}_{ev}$	(1.3)	Vintage measure of capital and energy 1971 $ billion
k_{inv}	(1.14)	Stock of inventories, 1971 $ billion
k_{ne}	(1.2)	Business fixed capital stock (excluding energy), 1971 $ billion
L_b	(5.3)	Net stock of government non-monetary liabilities, $ billion
L_f	(4.4)	Net liabilities to non-residents (excluding official reserves), $ billion
m_e	link	Canadian imports of energy fuels, 1971 $ billion
M_{id}	(4.5)	Interest and dividend payments to foreigners, $ billion
m_{ne}	(1.12)	Imports of goods and services (excluding energy, interest, and dividends), 1971 $ billion
N_e	(1.6)	Total employed (excluding armed forces), millions of persons
N_ϱ	(1.5)	Total civilian labour force, millions of persons
N_p	exogenous	Average population in each period, millions of persons
$N_{p\varrho}$	exogenous	Population of labour force age, millions of persons
p_a	(3.4)	Implicit price of absorption, 1971 = 1.0
p_c	(2.1)	Implicit consumption price index, 1971 = 1.0
p_e	link	Price of energy, 1971 = 1.0
p_{fx}	(4.3)	Spot price of foreign exchange, CDN $ per US $
p_g	(5.3)	Implicit price index for government spending, 1971 = 1.0
p_{me}	link	Price index for imported energy, 1971 = 1.0
p_{mne}	(3.5)	Price of imports of goods and services (excluding energy), 1971 = 1.0

Variable	Equation no.	Description
p_{mw}	exogenous	Index of world price of Canadian imports (excluding energy), $p_{mw} = p_{mne}/p_{fx}$
p_q	(3.2)	Implicit price for gross domestic output, including imported energy, $1971 = 1.0$
p_w	exogenous	OECD real output deflator, $1971 = 1.0$
p_{wxg}	exogenous	Price index of world exports of goods, $1971 = 1.0$
p_{xe}	link	Price of energy exports, $1971 = 1.0$
p_{xne}	(3.3)	Price of exports of goods and services (excluding energy), $1971 = 1.0$
q	(1.11)	Gross output (at factor cost) of the non-energy sector, 1971 \$ billion (equals real GDP plus net energy imports)
q_a	(1.15)	Aggregate demand (output less unintended inventory accumulation), 1971 \$ billion
q_s	(1.9)	Synthetic supply variable, 1971 \$ billion
q^*	(1.16)	Desired level of profitable future output for investment demand, 1971 \$ billion
q_ℓ^*	(1.19)	Desired level of profitable future output for labour demand, 1971 \$ billion
q_{sv}	(1.17)	Vintage-based synthetic supply, 1971 \$ billion
r_d	exogenous	Ratio of Canadian bonds held by foreigners to total net liabilities to foreigners
r_{ep2}	exogenous	Earnings/price ratio for US equities, per cent
r_ℓ	(5.7)	Average yield on Government of Canada bonds, 10 years and over, per cent
r_{m2}	exogenous	Average yield on US government bonds, 3-5 years, per cent
r_{nat}	exogenous	Natural rate of unemployment, per cent
r_{nu}	(1.7)	Unemployment rate, per cent
r_{part}	exogenous	Participation rate in labour force
r_s	(5.5)	Average yield on Government of Canada bonds, 1-3 years, per cent
r_{tb2}	exogenous	Yield on 91-day US Treasury bills converted to Canadian equivalence, per cent
r_{tp}	exogenous	Total personal income tax rate
r_{ti}	exogenous	Indirect tax rate yielding taxes in non-energy sector
r_{vbe}	exogenous	Proportion of energy sector capital stock owned by foreigners

Variable	Equation no.	Description
r_{vb}	(4.8)	Proportion of non-energy business capital owned by foreigners
t		Time (1952 = 1, 1953 = 2, etc.)
T_{cne}	(5.45)	Total corporate taxes in the non-energy sector, $ billion
T_{cog}	link	Direct taxes on oil and gas industry, $ billion
T_{dp}	(5.2)	Total direct taxes on persons, $ billion
T_i	(5.1)	Indirect taxes less subsidies, $ billion
T_{iog}	link	Indirect taxes, less subsidies, on oil and gas industry, $ billion
U_{res}	(4.0)	Stock of foreign reserves, US $ billion
V	(5.10)	Market value of private sector wealth, $ billion
V_e	exogenous	Market value of year-end stock of energy sector fixed capital and inventories, $ billion
V_{kb}	(5.6)	Market value of year-end stock of business fixed capital and inventories in Canada, excluding energy sector, $ billion
W	(3.1)	Wage rate, thousands of dollars per year per employed person
x_e	link	Exports of primary energy, 1971 $ billion
X_{id}	(2.10)	Interest and dividend receipts from non-residents, $ billion
x_{ne}	(2.2)	Exports of goods and services (excluding energy), 1971 $ billion
X_{tr}	exogenous	Net transfers plus miscellaneous other items required to satisfy the balance of payments identity, $ billion
y	(3.6)	Real gross national product, 1971 $ billion
y_{res}	exogenous	Residual error of estimate, 1971 $ billion
Y	(3.7)	Nominal gross national product, $ billion
y_w	exogenous	Real output in major OECD economies, 1975 US $ billion
δ_1	estimated parameter	Annual rate at which energy/capital proportions become malleable in k_{ev}. $\delta_1 = 0.72$
δ_2	exogenous	Depreciation rate for non-energy capital stock (including housing): $\delta_2 = 0.05$
Π	estimated	Labour productivity index for Harrod-neutral technical progress in Cobb–Douglas function for q. The annual growth rate is 1.99 per cent

Variable	Equation no.	Description
ρ_r	exogenous	Real supply price of capital, per cent: $\rho_r = 7.0$
$\alpha, \beta,$ γ, σ	estimated parameters	Parameters for nested production functions: $\alpha = 0.356; \beta = 0.70584; \gamma = 0.10831; \sigma = 0.6$

MACE MODEL STRUCTURE

1. Supply and factor demands
Fixed business investment

$$i_{ne}/\bar{k}_{ne} = 0.38258\, i_{ne-1}/\bar{k}_{ne-1} + 0.052500\,(k^* - \bar{k}_{ne})/\bar{k}_{ne}$$
$$(3.70) \qquad\qquad (6.96)$$
$$- 0.079159\, c_q + 0.12167 \qquad\qquad (1.1)$$
$$(5.87) \qquad (7.42)$$

2SLS 1954–1980: s.e.e $= 0.00296$; $\bar{R}^2 = 0.823$; Durbin-$h = 1.11$

Business fixed capital stock

$$k_{ne} = (1 - \delta_2)k_{ne-1} + i_{ne} \qquad (1.2)$$

Vintage bundle of capital and energy ('energized capital')

$$\bar{k}_{ev} = (1 - \delta_1 - \delta_2)\bar{k}_{ev-1} + i_{new}\left\{\beta + \gamma\left(\frac{\gamma p_k}{\beta p_e}\right)^{\sigma-1}\right\}^{\sigma/(\sigma-1)} \qquad (1.3)$$

where

$$i_{new} = i_{ne} + \delta_1 k_{ne-1}$$

is re-investment with energy use malleable in the current year.

Vintage-based energy requirement

$$e_v = (1 - \delta_1 - \delta_2)e_{v-1} + \left(\frac{\gamma p_k}{\beta p_e}\right)^{\sigma} i_{new} \qquad (1.4)$$

Labour force

$$(N_\varrho/N_{p\varrho}) = 0.19526(q/q_{sv}) + 0.011779(r_{nat}/r_{n\dot{u}})$$
$$(3.48) \qquad\qquad (2.34)$$
$$+ 0.015185\, \text{sech}^2\{(t - 29)/15\}$$
$$(6.86)$$
$$- 0.051421\, W/(6.0209\Pi P_a)$$
$$(2.86)$$

$$+ 0.0083121\, D_{aib} - 0.15562$$
$$(3.12) \qquad\qquad (3.10)$$

2SLS 1956–1980; s.e.e. $= 0.00377$; $R^2 = 0.650$; $DW = 1.66$; F-test on con-straint that constant plus coefficients on the first, second, and fourth terms sum to zero $= 1.03$

Employment

$$N_e = 0.83757\, N_{e-1} + 0.16243\, \frac{1}{\Pi}\left(\frac{q_\varrho^* \bar{k}_{ev}^{-\alpha}}{3.5196}\right)^{1/(1-\alpha)} \tag{1.6}$$
$$(95.76)\qquad\quad (18.57)$$

2SLS 1954–1980; s.e.e. $= 0.0595$; $\bar{R}^2 = 0.9987$; Durbin-$h = 2.23$; F-test on constraint $= 1.06$

Unemployment rate

$$r_{nu} = 100\,\frac{N_\varrho - N_e}{N_\varrho} \tag{1.7}$$

Energy demand

$$\ln e = \ln e_v + 0.010024t - 0.69028 \tag{1.8}$$
$$(23.22)\qquad (23.54)$$

2SLS 1954–1980; s.e.e. $= 0.0165$; $\bar{R}^2 = 0.9987$; $DW = 1.29$; F-test on con-straint $= 0.007$

Optimal capital stock

$$k^* = \frac{q^*}{3.5196}\left\{\beta + \gamma^\sigma\left(\beta\frac{p_e}{p_k}\right)^{1-\sigma}\right\}^{\sigma/(1-\sigma)}\left\{\frac{\alpha W/\Pi}{(1-\alpha)(\beta^\sigma p_k^{1-\sigma} + \gamma^\sigma p_e^{1-\sigma})^{1/(1-\sigma)}}\right\}^{1-\alpha} \tag{1.9}$$

where $p_k = (\delta_2 + 0.01\rho_r)p_a$ is the price of capital services.

Average unit cost, relative to output price, for producing gross output of the non-energy sector

$$c_q = \frac{ep_e + \bar{k}_{ne}(\delta_2 + 0.023354 + 0.0071\,r_\varrho)p_a + N_e W}{qp_q} \tag{1.10}$$

Output equation

$$\ln q = -0.19840 + \ln q_{sv} - 0.21787\ln c_q$$
$$(9.69)\qquad\qquad (7.40)$$

$$+ 0.59121\ln\frac{a + x_{ne}}{q_{sv}} + 0.048907\ln\frac{k_{inv}^*}{\bar{k}_{inv}} \tag{1.11}$$
$$(9.52)\qquad\qquad (1.02)$$

2SLS 1954–1980; s.e.e. $= 0.00727$; $\bar{R}^2 = 0.9996$; $DW = 1.29$; F-test for constraint on $q_{sv} = 7.1$

where $k^*_{inv} = 0.12423\,\bar{k}_{ne}$.

Non-energy imports

$$\ln(m_{ne} - m_{car2}) = -1.5850 + \ln q_{sv}$$
$$(96.5)$$

$$- 1.0302 \ln\left(\tfrac{1}{3}\sum_{i=0}^{2}\frac{p_{mne-i}}{p_{q-i}}\right) + 1.2170 \ln\left(\overline{\frac{q}{q_{sv}}}\right) \quad (1.12)$$
$$(4.18) \qquad\qquad\qquad\qquad (1.43)$$

2SLS 1955–1980; s.e.e. $= 0.0549$; $\bar{R}^2 = 0.9826$; $DW = 0.83$; F-test on constraint on $q_{sv} = 0.853$

where imports of cars from the United States is given by

$$\ln m_{car2} = -7.3935 - 1.0388 \ln(p_{mne}/p_q)$$
$$(10.76) \qquad (1.81)$$

$$+ 1.2659 \ln\left\{(0.9656\,a_2 + a)\ \tanh\left|\frac{t-12}{5}\right|\right\}$$
$$(12.96)$$

OLS 1966–1980: s.e.e. $= 0.140$; $\bar{R}^2 = 0.936$; $DW = 1.15$

Change in business inventories

$$i_{inv} = q + T_i/p_q - a - x_{ne} + m_{ne} - M_{id}/p_q + M_{id}/p_{mne} - y_{res} \quad (1.13)$$

Stock of non-farm business inventories

$$k_{inv} = k_{inv-1} + i_{inv} \quad (1.14)$$

Aggregate demand

$$q_a = q - \{i_{inv} - 0.08\,(k^*_{inv} - \bar{k}_{inv})\} \quad (1.15)$$

Desired level of future output for investment demand

$$q^* = q_a\{1 + 2.5(m_{ne} - \hat{m}_{ne})/q\}q/q_{-2} \quad (1.16)$$

where m_{ne} is the equilibrium level of imports at full capacity with lags worked out

$$\ln(\hat{m}_{ne} - m_{car2}) = -1.5850 + \ln q_{sv} - 1.0302 \ln\frac{p_{mne}}{p_q}$$

Vintage based synthetic supply

$$q_{sv} = 3.5196\,(\bar{k}_{ev})^\alpha (\Pi\,N_e)^{1-\alpha} \quad (1.17)$$

Desired level of future output for labour demands

$$q_\ell^* = 0.65 \, q_a\{1 + 1.3(m_{ne} - \dot{m}_{ne})/q\}q/q_{-2}$$

$$+ (1 - 0.65)9.5153(\Pi N_\ell)^2/(\Pi_{-2}N_{\ell-2}) \qquad (1.19)$$

2. Personal and foreign expenditure on goods and services

Personal expenditure

$$c/N_p = 0.82233(N_e W + G_t)(1 - r_{tp})/(p_c N_p)$$
$$(95.78)$$

$$+ \, 0.021237 \, \overline{\left(\frac{V}{p_c N_p}\right)} + 0.42639 \qquad (2.1)$$
$$(3.86) \qquad\qquad (16.99)$$

2SLS 1954–1980: s.e.e. $= 0.0144; \bar{R}^2 = 0.9995; DW = 1.41$

where

$$\ln p_c = -\,0.0058406 + 0.68719 \ln p_q + 0.19119 \ln p_{mne}$$
$$(2.78) \qquad\quad (23.92) \qquad\qquad (6.17)$$

OLS 1954–1980: s.e.e. $= 0.00763; \bar{R}^2 = 0.9995; DW = 0.91$

Non-energy exports

$$\ln\,(x_{ne} - x_{car2} - X_{id}/p_{xne}) = -\,6.0823$$
$$(24.6)$$

$$+ \, 1.1592 \ln y_w - 0.39802 \ln \left(\tfrac{1}{3}\sum_{i=0}^{2}\frac{p_{xne-i}}{p_{fx-i}p_{wxg-i}}\right)$$
$$(34.1) \qquad\qquad (4.28)$$

$$+ \, 0.48326 \ln\,(\bar{k}_{inv}/k_{inv}^*) \qquad (2.2)$$
$$(2.18)$$

2SLS 1955–1980: s.e.e. $= 0.0355; \bar{R}^2 = 0.9928; DW = 1.03$

where exports of cars to the United States is given by

$$\ln x_{car2} = -10.450 - 2.1977 \ln \frac{p_{xne}}{p_{fx}p_{a2}}$$
$$(12.06) \quad (3.65)$$

$$+ \, 1.7080 \ln \left\{ (0.96756 \, a_2 + a) \tanh \frac{t-12}{5} \right\}$$
$$(13.36)$$

OLS 1966–1980: s.e.e. $= 0.128; \bar{R}^2 = 0.929; DW = 0.87$

Real absorption

$$a = c + g + i_{ne} + i_e \qquad (2.3)$$

Exports in the form of interest and dividends

$$X_{id} = 0.081525 + 0.012109 \, p_{fx} r_{tb2} \bar{U}_{res}$$
$$\phantom{X_{id} = }(4.66) \qquad (8.85)$$

$$+ \, 0.000039457 \, p_{fx} r_{m2} a_2 \qquad\qquad (2.10)$$
$$(25.38)$$

2SLS 1955–1980: s.e.e. $= 0.055; \bar{R}^2 = 0.982; DW = 1.85$

3. *Prices, wages and national income*

Proportionate annual wage change

$$\dot{W} = -0.0011861 + 0.49260 \, \dot{W}_{-1} + 0.50740 \dot{p}_a + 0.094350 \, \frac{p_{xne}}{p_{mne}}$$
$$\phantom{\dot{W} = }(0.13) \qquad\quad (5.69) \qquad\qquad (5.86) \qquad\qquad (0.92)$$

$$+ \, 0.45638 \, \overline{\left(\frac{q}{q_{sv}}\right)} + 0.021407 \, r_{nat}/r_{nu} \qquad\qquad (3.1)$$
$$(2.96) \qquad\qquad\quad (3.22)$$

$$- \, 0.030377 \, D_{77} - 0.028767 \, D_{78}$$
$$(3.87) \qquad\qquad (3.22)$$

with coefficients on $\dot{W}_{-1}$ and $\dot{p}_a$ constrained to sum to unity.

2SLS 1955–1980; s.e.e. $= 0.0069$; $\bar{R}^2 = 0.957$; Durbin-h $= 0.29$; *F*-statistic for constraint $= 0.060$

Proportionate change in implicit price index for output

$$\dot{p}_q = -0.00574 + 0.95009 \, \dot{c}_{kew} + 0.049905 \, \dot{p}_{\bar{w}}$$
$$\phantom{\dot{p}_q = }(0.13) \quad (24.02) \qquad\qquad (1.26)$$

$$- \, 0.11900 \, (\bar{k}_{inv} - k^*_{inv})/k^*_{inv} \qquad\qquad (3.2)$$
$$(2.77)$$

with cost and world price shares constrained to add to unity.

2SLS 1955–1980: s.e.e. $= 0.0073$; $\bar{R}^2 = 0.964$; $DW = 1.97$; *F*-statistic for constraint $= 0.460$

where

$$p_{\bar{w}} = p_{fx}(\tfrac{1}{3} \, p_{wxg} + \tfrac{2}{3} \, p_{a2})$$
$$c_{kew} = p_{ke}^{\alpha}(W/\Pi)^{1-\alpha}$$

and

$$p_{ke} = \{\beta^{\sigma}(\delta_2 + 0.023354 + 0.071 \, r_\varrho)^{1-\sigma} p_a^{1-\sigma} + \gamma^{\sigma} p_e^{1-\sigma}\}^{1/(1-\sigma)}$$

Price of non-energy exports

$$\dot{p}_{xne} = -0.00364 + 0.68165\,\dot{p}_q + 0.31835\,\dot{p}_{fx}$$
$$\phantom{\dot{p}_{xne} =} (1.03) \qquad (13.13) \qquad\quad (6.13)$$

$$+\ 0.31835\,\dot{p}_{wxg} - 0.14627\,(\bar{k}_{inv} - k^*_{inv})/k^*_{inv} \qquad (3.3)$$
$$(6.13) \qquad\qquad (1.50)$$

Coefficients on $\dot{p}_q$ and $\dot{p}_{fx}$ constrained to sum to 1.
Coefficients on $\dot{p}_q$ and $\dot{p}_{wxg}$ constrained to sum to 1.
2SLS 1954–1980: s.e.e. $= 0.0180$; $\bar{R}^2 = 0.905$; $DW = 1.54$; F-test on constraints $= 0.681$

Proportionate change in absorption price index

$$\dot{p}_a = 0.0047457 + 0.79032\,\dot{p}_q + 0.11875\,\dot{p}_{mne} \qquad (3.4)$$
$$(2.68) \qquad\quad (16.78) \qquad\quad (3.35)$$

OLS 1955–1980: s.e.e. $= 0.0064$; $\bar{R}^2 = 0.967$; $DW = 1.75$

Price of non-energy imports

$$p_{mne} = p_{fx}\,p_{mw} \qquad (3.5)$$

Real GNP

$$y = a + i_{inv} + x_{ne} + x_e - m_{ne} - m_e - M_{id}/p_{mne} + y_{res} \qquad (3.6)$$

Nominal GNP

$$Y = qp_q - M_{id} + x_e p_{xe} - m_e p_{me} + T_i \qquad (3.7)$$

4. *Balance of payments, capital movements*

Stock of foreign reserves

$$U_{res} = U_{res-1} + F_{xo} \qquad (4.0)$$

Capital inflows, changes in official reserves, price of foreign exchange and liabilities to non-residents

(a) *Portfolio model with limited intervention*

$$F_i = L_f - L_{f-1} - F_{ireva} \qquad (4.1)$$
$$F_{xo} = (X_{tr} + B + F_i)/p_{fx} \qquad (4.2)$$
$$p_{fx} = (1 - 0.3)\,\{p_{fx} - 0.001(X_{tr} + B + F_i)\} + 0.3 p_{fxe} \qquad (4.3)$$

$$\frac{L_f - r_{vb}V_{kb} - r_{vbe}V_e}{p_{fx}^{0.25}\,p_w Y_w} = 0.000040366 + 0.71049 \left(\frac{L_f - r_{vb}V_{kb} - r_{vbe}V_e}{p_{fx}^{0.25}\,p_w Y_w}\right)_{-1}$$
$$(0.17) \qquad\qquad (6.15)$$

$$+ 0.00055710\,(r_s - r_{tb2})$$
$$(3.90)$$
$$+ 0.38694\,\{p_{xne}(\hat{x}_{ne} - x_{ne}) - p_{mne}(\hat{m}_{ne} - m_{ne})\}/(p_{fx}^{0.25} p_w Y_w) \qquad (4.4)$$
$$(2.18)$$

2SLS 1954–1980: s.e.e. = 0.000380; $\bar{R}^2 = 0.813$; Durbin-$h = 1.54$

and where

$$\hat{x}_{ne} = -6.0823 + 1.1592\ln y_w - 0.39802\ln\frac{p_{xne}}{p_{fx}p_{wxg}}$$

(b) *Fixed exchange rate*

$$F_i = L_f - L_{f-1} - F_{ireva} \qquad (4.1)$$
$$F_{xo} = (X_{tr} + B + F_i)/p_{fx} \qquad (4.2)$$
$$p_{fx} \text{ is exogenous} \qquad (4.3)$$

$$\frac{L_f - r_{vb}V_{kb} - r_{vbe}V_e}{p_{fx}^{0.25}p_w Y_w} = 0.000040366 + 0.71049\left(\frac{L_f - r_{vb}V_{kb} - r_{vbe}V_e}{p_{fx}^{0.25}p_w Y_w}\right)_{-1}$$
$$+ 0.00055710\,(r_s - r_{tb2})$$
$$+ 0.38694\,\{p_{xne}(\hat{x}_{ne} - x_{ne}) - p_{mne}(\hat{m}_{ne} - m_{ne})\}/(p_{fx}^{0.25} p_w y_w) \qquad (4.4)$$

(c) *Nominal interest parity*

$$F_i = -X_{tr} - B + p_{fx}F_{xo} \qquad (4.1)$$
$$F_{xo} \text{ is exogenous} \qquad (4.2)$$
$$\ln p_{fx} = 0.010882 + \ln\left(\frac{1 + r_{m2}/100}{1 + r_s/100}p_{fxe}\right) \qquad (4.3)$$

OLS 1953–1961, 1971–1980: s.e.e. = 0.0316; $\bar{R}^2 = 0758$; $DW = 1.51$; F-test on constraint = 0.36

where the expected exchange rate is given by

$$\ln p_{fxe} = -0.023333 + 0.46359\ln\frac{p_q(1 + \dot{p}_q)}{p_{a2}(1 + \dot{p}_{a2})} + 0.53541\ln p_{fx-1}$$
$$(1.09) \qquad (2.36) \qquad\qquad (2.73)$$

OLS 1953–1961, 1971–1980: s.e.e. = 0.0433; $\bar{R}^2 = 0.669$; $DW = 1.13$

$$L_f = L_{f-1} + F_i + F_{ireva} \qquad (4.4)$$

(d) *Purchasing power parity*

$$F_i = L_f - L_{f-1} - F_{ireva} \qquad (4.1)$$
$$F_{xo} \text{ is exogenous} \qquad (4.2)$$

$$\ln p_{fx} = -0.087342 + \ln (p_q/p_{a2}) \tag{4.3}$$
$$(9.68)$$

OLS 1952–1961, 1971–1980: s.e.e. $= 0.0403; \bar{R}^2 = 0.591; DW = 0.85; F$-test on constraint $= 0.15$

$$\frac{L_f - r_{vb} V_{kb} - r_{vbe} V_e}{p_{fx}^{0.25} p_w Y_w} = 0.000040366 + 0.71049 \left(\frac{L_f - r_{vb} V_{kb} - r_{vbe} V_e}{p_{fx}^{0.25} p_w Y_w} \right)_{-1}$$

$$+ 0.00055710 \, (r_s - r_{tb2})$$

$$+ 0.38694 \, \{ p_{xne}(\hat{x}_{ne} - x_{ne}) - p_{mne}(\hat{m}_{ne} - m_{ne}) \} / p_{fx}^{0.25} p_w Y_w \tag{4.4}$$

and where the export equation is modified to

$$x_{ne} = (-X_{tr} + M_{id} + m_{ne} p_{mne} - F_i + p_{fx} F_{xo} - B_e)/p_{xne} \tag{2.2}$$

and

$$\hat{x}_{ne} = x_{ne}$$

Interest and dividend payments to foreigners (BOP definition)

$$M_{id} = -0.23211 + 0.010736 \, r_{\varrho} \overline{(L_f - r_{vb} V_{kb} - r_{vbe} V_e)}$$
$$(1.77) \qquad (6.27)$$

$$+ 0.037424 \, \overline{(r_{vb} V_{kb} + r_{vbe} V_e)} \tag{4.5}$$
$$(9.88)$$

OLS 1954–1980: s.e.e. $= 0.269; \bar{R}^2 = 0.980; DW = 1.28$

Balance of trade

$$B = -M_{id} + x_{ne} p_{xne} - m_{ne} p_{mne} + B_e \tag{4.6}$$

Retained earnings and revaluation adjustments increasing liabilities to foreigners

$$F_{ireva} = 0.66328 + 0.99319 \, \bar{r}_{vb}(V_{kb} - V_{kb-1})$$
$$(5.08) \qquad (48.62)$$

$$+ 0.95063 \, \bar{V}_{kb}(r_{vb} - r_{vb-1}) + 0.95061 \, \bar{r}_{vbe}(V_e - V_{e-1})$$
$$(14.58) \qquad\qquad\qquad (38.93)$$

$$+ 0.90259 \, \bar{V}_e(r_{vbe} - r_{vbe-1}) - 0.0034168 \, (\bar{V}_{kb} + \bar{V}_e) \tag{4.7}$$
$$(3.66) \qquad\qquad\qquad (3.97)$$

OLS 1954–1980: s.e.e. $= 0.360; \bar{R}^2 = 0.997; DW = 1.08$

Return to non-residents on Canadian non-energy business assets, as a fraction of the total return

$$r_{vb} = 0.87722 \, r_{vb-1} + 0.56779 \, Y_{corp}/V_{kb} - 0.0018465 \, r_{ep2} + 0.0034048 \tag{4.8}$$
$$(6.00) \qquad\qquad (2.71) \qquad\qquad (1.86) \qquad\qquad (0.10)$$

2SLS 1954-1980: s.e.e. $= 0.00434; \bar{R}^2 = 0.957$, Durbin-$h = 1.29$

where

$$Y_{\text{corp}} = q \, p_q - N_e W - e \, p_e - C_{\text{ca}} - T_{\text{cne}}$$

Balance of trade in energy

$$B_e = x_e p_{xe} - m_e p_{me} \tag{4.9}$$

5. *Government and private finance*

Corporate income taxes in the non-energy sector

$$T_{\text{cne}} = 0.10576 + 0.22219 \, (qp_q - ep_e - C_{\text{ca}} - N_e W) \tag{5.0}$$
$$\quad (0.90) \quad (34.69)$$

2SLS 1955-1980: s.e.e. $= 0.340; \bar{R}^2 = 0.979; DW = 0.59$

Indirect taxes

$$T_i = r_{ti}(ap_a - ep_e) + T_{iog} \tag{5.1}$$

Direct taxes

$$T_{\text{dp}} = 0.080038 + 0.062852 \, (Y - C_{\text{ca}} - T_i - WN_e - T_{\text{cne}} - T_{\text{cog}})$$
$$\quad (0.54) \quad\quad (2.21)$$
$$+ 1.5904 \, r_{tp}(WN_e + G_t) \tag{5.2}$$
$$(30.89)$$

2SLS 1954-1980: s.e.e. $= 0.246; \bar{R}^2 = 0.9996; DW = 1.02$

Government bonds

$$L_b = L_{b-1} + gp_g + G_t - T_i - T_{\text{dp}} - T_{\text{cne}} - T_{\text{cog}} + p_{fx}F_{xo} + G_{\text{misc}} - H + H_{-1}$$
$$\tag{5.3}$$

where the implicit price of government spending

$$\ln p_g = -0.70864 + 0.78366 \ln p_a + 0.34374 \ln W + 0.023800 \ln t$$
$$(19.43) \quad (22.55) \quad\quad (12.98) \quad\quad (5.18)$$

OLS 1952-1980: s.e.e. $= 0.0074; \bar{R}^2 = 0.9998; DW = 1.79$

High-powered money supply

$$H = (H^* \hat{H})^{0.5} \tag{5.4}$$

where

$$H^* = 1.1 H_{-1}$$

and

$$\hat{H} = -2.2157 + 0.94658 \ln Y - 0.12730 \ln \{100(\dot{p}_a + 0.0099)\}$$

Short-term interest rate, calculated from the demand for high-powered money

$$\ln H = -2.2157 + 0.94658 \ln Y - 0.12730 \ln r_s \tag{5.5}$$
$$(20.15) \quad (31.65) \qquad\qquad (4.58)$$

Cochrane-Orcutt 1954–1980: s.e.e. $= 0.0242; \bar{R}^2 = 0.969; \rho = 0.826$

Business capital at market value, exlcuding the energy sector

$$100 Y_{corp}/(V_{kb} - V_{res}) = 8.3868 + r_s + 1.1420\,(r_{ep2} - r_{m2}) \tag{5.6}$$
$$(8.46) \qquad\qquad (4.14)$$

2SLS 1955–1980; s.e.e. $= 3.10; \bar{R}^2 = 0.025; DW = 1.49$

where the market value of residential housing is given by

$$\ln V_{res} = -0.51297 + 1.3480 \ln p_a + 1.0927 \ln k_{ne} - 0.19638 \ln t$$
$$(0.66) \qquad (16.15) \qquad\qquad (5.83) \qquad\qquad (3.16)$$

OLS 1954–1980: s.e.e. $= 0.0223; \bar{R}^2 = 0.9991; DW = 0.80$

Long-term interest rate

$$r_\varrho = 0.21418 + 0.51350\,r_{\varrho-1} + 0.30180\,r_s + 0.25440\,r_{m2} \tag{5.7}$$
$$(1.45) \qquad (8.93) \qquad\qquad (1.92) \qquad\qquad (1.40)$$

2SLS 1954–1980: s.e.e. $= 0.209; \bar{R}^2 = 0.992; \text{Durbin-}h = 0.197$

Capital consumption allowance

$$\ln C_{ca} = -2.7123 + 0.9977 \ln (k_{ne} p_a) \tag{5.8}$$
$$(65.96) \quad (119.51)$$

OLS 1954–1980; s.e.e. $= 0.0301; \bar{R}^2 = 0.9982; DW = 0.69$

Government transfers to persons

$$\ln (G_t/N_{popt}) = -3.8794 + 1.6091 \ln (y/N_{popt}) + 0.35546 \ln r_{nu} + 0.82588 \ln p_a$$
$$(14.61) \quad (12.22) \qquad\qquad (5.01) \qquad\qquad (8.01)$$

$$\tag{5.9}$$

2SLS 1954–1980: s.e.e. $= 0.0447; \bar{R}^2 = 0.996; DW = 1.42$

Private sector wealth

$$V = V_{kb} + V_e + L_b + H - L_f \tag{5.10}$$

Appendix 2

INTRODUCTION

The demand sector of the energy model has at its core two sets of demand equations. The first splits aggregate energy demand into five regional total energy demands. The regions are the Atlantic provinces, Quebec, Ontario, the Prairies and British Columbia. This is accomplished by equations apportioning the total demand according to the region's share of gross domestic product, the ratio of the price of energy in the region to the price of energy in Canada as whole, and total Canadian energy demand. Each region's total energy demand is divided into fuel shares according to the weighted price of each fuel, and on the number of gas distribution pipeline kilometres in the region. The quantities of each fuel so determined are used to determine the price indices of energy (which are ratios of quantity-weighted sums of prices) used in the first set of demand equations.

SYSTEM OF REGIONAL DEMAND EQUATIONS

$\ln QE \cdot AT = a1 + b1 * \ln QE + c1 * \ln SRDP \cdot AT + d * \ln \{ew(PE \cdot AT/PE)\}$

$\ln QE \cdot QU = a2 + b2 * \ln QE + c2 * \ln SRDP \cdot QU + d * \ln \{ew(PE \cdot QU/PE)\}$

$\ln QE \cdot ON = a3 + b3 * \ln QE + c3 * \ln SRDP \cdot ON + d * \ln \{ew(PE \cdot ON/PE)\}$

$\ln QE \cdot PR = a4 + b4 * \ln QE + c4 * \ln SRDP \cdot PR + d * \ln \{ew(PE \cdot PR/PE)\}$

$\ln QE \cdot BC = a5 + b5 * \ln QE + c5 * \ln SRDP \cdot BC + d * \ln \{ew(PE \cdot BC/PE)\}$

where $QE \cdot AT$ is the quantity of energy demanded in the Atlantic, trillions output b.t.u.;

$QE \cdot QU$ is the quantity of energy demanded in Quebec, trillions output b.t.u.;

$QE \cdot ON$ is the quantity of energy demanded in Ontario, trillions output b.t.u.;

$QE \cdot PR$ is the quantity of energy demanded in the Prairies, trillions output b.t.u.;

$QE \cdot BC$ is the quantity of energy demanded in BC, trillions output b.t.u.;

QE is the quantity of energy demanded in Canada, trillions output b.t.u.;

$SRDP \cdot AT$ is the Atlantic's share of national real (1971$) domestic product;

$SRDP \cdot QU$ is Quebec's share of national real (1971$) domestic product;

$SRDP \cdot ON$ is Ontario's share of national real (1971$) domestic product;

$SRDP \cdot PR$ is the Prairies' share of national real (1971$) domestic product;

$SRDP \cdot BC$ is BC's share of national real (1971$) domestic product;

$PE \cdot AT$ is the user price of energy in the Atlantic, current $ per million output b.t.u.;

PE·QU is the user price of energy in Quebec, current $ per million output b.t.u.;

PE·ON is the user price of energy in Ontario, current $ per million output b.t.u.;

PE·PR is the user price of energy in the Prairies, current $ per million output b.t.u.;

PE·BC is the user price of energy in BC, current $ per million output b.t.u.;

PE is the price of energy in Canada, current $ per million output b.t.u.;

ew represents a set of exponential weights (*w*1, *w*2, *w*3, *w*4)* derived as follows:

$$R1 = 0.72$$
$$R1TOT = (1.-R1) + \{(1.-R1)^{**}2.\} + \{(1.-R1)^{**}3.\}$$
$$+ \{(1.-R1)^{**}4.\}$$
$$w1 = (1.-R1)/R1TOT$$
$$w2 = (1.-R1)^{**}2./R1TOT$$
$$w3 = (1.-R1)^{**}3./R1TOT$$
$$w4 = (1.-R1)^{**}4./R1TOT$$

The parameter estimates, with *t*-statistics in parenthesis, and equation statistics are as follows:

$$\log L = 317.71$$
estimation period: 1961–1980
estimation procedure: iterative Zellner
nobs: 20 for each equation

*a*1	−2.2426	(−10.892)	the *QE·AT* equation statistics:
*a*2	0.09014	(0.47798)	$R^2 = 0.9948$
*a*3	−0.47210	(−6.3414)	$DW = 0.9469$
*a*4	−0.14567	(−0.68233)	s.e.e. = 0.023637
*a*5	0.21591	(0.66388)	
*b*1	1.1554	(67.916)	the *QE·QU* equation statistics:
*b*2	0.95017	(41.660)	$R^2 = 0.9857$
*b*3	1.0278	(166.87)	$DW = 0.3196$
*b*4	0.96891	(43.352)	s.e.e. = 0.032640
*b*5	0.92358	(43.287)	
*c*1	0.52753	(7.2056)	the *QE·ON* equation statistics:
*c*2	0.76760	(10.183)	$R^2 = 0.9993$
*c*3	0.89426	(12.345)	$DW = 1.5538$
*c*4	0.73816	(12.789)	s.e.e. = 0.0085529

* When reporting weights, the following convention will be used: the first mnemonic refers to the weight for the current year, the second for the preceding year, and so on.

c5	0.81578	(9.6914)	
d	−0.60000	(imposed)	

the QE · PR equation statistics:
$R^2 = 0.9916$
$DW = 0.3894$
s.e.e. = 0.032413

the $QE \cdot BC$ equation statistics:
$R^2 = 0.9967$
$DW = 1.7931$
s.e.e. = 0.021856

SYSTEM OF QUANTITY SHARE EQUATIONS

(a) *Atlantic region*

$SO = ao1*DUMAT + boo*\ln\{ew(PO)\} + bol*\ln\{ew(PL)\}$

$SL = a1*DUMAT + blo*\ln\{ew(PO)\} + b1*\ln\{ew(PL)\}$

where SO is the quantity share of crude oil;
   SL is the quantity share of electricity;
   DUMAT is the regional dummy variable for the Atlantic;
   PO is the user price of crude oil, current $ per million output b.t.u.;
   PL is the user price of electricity, current $ per million output b.t.u.;
   ew represents a set of exponential weights (w1, w2, w3, w4) derived
   as follows:
   $R1 = 0.72$
   $R1TOT = (1.-R1) + \{(1.-R1)**2.\} + \{(1.-R1)**3.\}$
     $+ \{(1.-R1)**4.\}$
   $w1 = (1.-R1)/R1TOT$
   $w2 = \{(1.-R2)**2.\}/R1TOT$
   $w3 = \{(1.-R3)**3.\}/R1TOT$
   $w4 = \{(1.-R4)**4.\}/R1TOT$

The parameter estimates including parameters from the dropped *SL* equation (with *t*-statistics in parenthesis) and equation statistics are as follows:

ao1	0.72365	(153.65)	$R^2 = 0.8973$
al1 = 1.−aol	0.27635		$DW = 0.3332$
boo = bill	0.15553	(12.539)	s.e.e. = 0.013495
bol = blo = −boo	−0.15553		nobs: 20

estimation period: 1961–1980
estimation procedure: OLS

(b) *Quebec, Ontario, Prairies, and BC regions*

$SG = ag2*DUMOU + ag3*DUMON + ag4*DUMPR + ag5*DUMBC$
   $+ bgo*\ln\{ew(PO)\} + bgg*\ln\{ew(PG)\} + bgl*\ln\{ew(PL)\} + dg*GPKM$

$$SO = ao2*DUMOU + ao3*DUMON + ao4*DUMPR + ao5*DUMBC$$
$$+ boo*\ln\{ew(PO)\} + boq*\ln\{ew(PG)\} + bol*\ln\{ew(PL)\} + do*GPKM$$

$$SL = al2*DUMOU + al3*DUMON + al4*DUMPR + al5*DUMBC$$
$$+ blo*\ln\{ew(PO)\} + blg*\ln\{ew(PG)\} + bll*\ln\{ew(PL)\} + dl*GPKM$$

where SG is the quantity share of natural gas;
   SO is the quantity share of crude oil;
   SL is the quantity share of electricity;
   $DUMQU, DUMON, DUMPR, DUMBC$ are the regional dummy variables;
   $GPKM$ is the kilometres of natural gas distribution pipeline;
   PG is the price of natural gas, current $ per million output b.t.u.;
   PO is the price of crude oil, current $ per million output b.t.u.;
   PL is the price of electricity, current $ per million output b.t.u.;
   ew represents a set of exponential weights ($w1, w2, w3, w4$) derived as
   follows:
   $$R1 = 0.72$$
   $$R1TOT = (1. -R1) + \{(1. -R1)**2.\} + \{(1. -R1)**3.\}$$
   $$+ \{(1. -R1)**4.\}$$
   $$w1 = (1. -R1)/R1TOT$$
   $$w2 = \{(1. -R2)**2.\}/R1TOT$$
   $$w3 = \{(1. -R3)**3.\}/R1TOT$$
   $$w4 = \{(1. -R4)**4.\}/R1TOT$$

The parameter estimates including parameters from the dropped SL equation (with t-statistics in parenthesis) and equation statistics are as follows:

log L = 420.28
estimation period: 1961–1980
estimation procedure: iterative Zellner
nobs: 80

$ag2$	−0.090561	(−6.2630)	the SG equation statistics
$ag3$	−0.022151	(−0.91935)	$R^2 = 0.9830$
$ag4$	0.037787	(1.0759)	$DW = 0.6135$
$ag5$	−0.029586	(−1.3823)	s.e.e. = 0.021242
$ao2$	0.69846	(48.183)	
$ao3$	0.73757	(33.499)	the SO equation statistics
$ao4$	0.72046	(22.996)	$R^2 = 0.9290$
$ao5$	0.64020	(33.469)	$DW = 0.7038$
$al2 = 1. -ag2 - a02$	0.392101	s.e.e. = 0.023972	
$al3 = 1. -ag3 - a03$	0.284581		
$al4 = 1. -ag4 - a04$	0.241753		
$al5 = 1. -ag5 - a05$	0.385660		
$bgo = bog$	0.12172	(8.5232)	

$bgl = blg$	0.049909	(4.9794)
$bgg = 0. -bgo - bgl$	-0.17163	(-11.032)
$boo = 0. -bog - bol$	-0.15270	(-8.5020)
$bol = blo$	0.030975	(2.9349)
dl	0.0	(imposed)
dg	$0.56460*10E-5$	(12.940)
$do = 0. -dg - dl$	$-0.56460*10E-5$	

TABLE A2.1
Estimated five-year city-gate price elasticities
for fuels in Canada

	Quantity		
	Oil	Gas	Electricity
P_{oil}	-0.506	0.0490	-0.119
R			
I_{gas}	0.135	-0.615	-0.0033
C			
E_{elec}	-0.0640	-0.0203	-0.426

TABLE A.2.2
Estimated five-year user price elasticities
for fuels in Canada

	Quantity		
	Oil	Gas	Electricity
P_{oil}	-0.656	0.0635	-0.154
R			
I_{gas}	0.153	-0.699	-0.0037
C			
E_{elec}	-0.0640	-0.0203	-0.426

REFERENCES

Barker, T. and Brailovsky, V. (eds) (1981), Oil or Industry? Energy, Industrialization and Economic Policy in Canada, Mexico, the Netherlands, Norway and the United Kingdom. London, Academic Press.

Bjerkholt, O., Lorentsen, L., and Strom, S. (1981), 'Using the Oil and Gas Revenues: The Norwegian Case', in T. Barker and V. Brailovsky (eds), *Oil or Industry? Energy, Industrialization and Economic Policy in Canada, Mexico, the Netherlands, Norway and the United Kingdom*. London, Academic Press, pp. 171-84.

Branson, W. H. (1979) 'Exchange Rate Dynamics and Monetary Policy', in A. Lindbeck (ed.), *Inflation and Employment in Open Economies*. Amsterdam, North Holland, pp. 189-224.

Ellman, M. (1981), 'Natural Gas, Restructuring and Re-industralization: The Dutch Experience of Industrial Policy', in Barker and Brailovsky, op. cit. pp. 149-66.

Klein, L. R. (1978), 'Disturbances to the International Economy', in *After the Phillips Curve: Persistence of High Inflation and High Unemployment*. Conference Series no. 19, Federal Reserve Bank of Boston, pp. 84-103.

White, K. J. (1978), 'A General Computer Program for Econometric Methods—SHAZAM', *Econometrica*, 46, 239-40.

PAPERS DESCRIBING OR USING MACE AND EARLIER RELATED MODELS

[M1] Battle, E. (1982), 'The Economic Rents from Canadian Hydroelectric Power', MA Extended Essay, University of British Columbia.

[M2] Bernard, J. T., Bridges, G. E., and Scott, A. D. (1982), 'An Evaluation of Potential Ricardian Hydro Electric Rents', Programme in Natural Resource Economics, University of British Columbia.

[M3] Duncan, B. (1977), 'An Econometric Model for Forecasting Investment in the Exploration, Development and Extraction Phases of the British Columbia Natural Gas Supply Sector', MA Extended Essay, University of British Columbia.

[M4] Duncan, B. (1977), 'A Model for Assessing the Costs and Benefits of the British Columbia Natural Gas Supply Sector', MA Extended Essay, University of British Columbia.

[M5] Fortin, P. and Newton, K. (1981), 'Labour Market Tightness and Wage Inflation in Canada', *Cahier*, 81-04, Groupe de Recherche en Politique Economique, Université Laval, Quebec.

[M6] Helliwell, J. F. (1973), 'More on the National Economic Effects of Arctic Energy Developments', *Proceedings of the House of Commons Standing Committee on Natural Resources and Public Works*, 5 June 1973 (Issue 22). Ottawa: Queen's Printer, pp. 41-80.

[M7] Helliwell, J. F. (1973), 'Estimating the National Economic Effects of Arctic Energy Developments', *Proceedings of the Royal Society of Canada Conference on Energy Resources*, October 1973.

[M8] Helliwell, J. F. (1974), 'Economic Consequences of Developing Canada's Arctic Gas', in E. Erickson and L. Waverman (eds), *The Energy Question: Failures of Multinational Policies*. University of Toronto Press, pp. 267-89.

[M9] Helliwell, J. F. (1974), 'Impact of a Mackenzie Pipeline on the National Economy', in P. Pearse (ed.), *The Mackenzie Pipeline: Arctic Gas and Canadian Energy Policy*. Toronto, McClelland and Stewart, pp. 143-82.

[M10] Helliwell, J. F. (1974), 'A Model for Calculating Costs and Benefits of Alternative Uses of Canada's Arctic Gas', UBC Department of Economics Discussion Paper 74-02, January 1974.

[M11] Helliwell, J. F. (1974), 'Policy Alternatives for Arctic Gas', in *Gas From the Mackenzie Delta: Now or Later?* Ottawa, Canadian Arctic Resources Committee, pp. 1-15.

[M12] Helliwell, J. F. (1975), 'The National Energy Board's 1974–1975 Natural Gas Supply Hearings', *Canadian Public Policy*, 1, 415–25.

[M13] Helliwell, J. F. (1975), 'Trade, Capital Flows, and Migration as Channels for the International Transmission of Stabilization Policies', in A. Ando *et al.* (eds), *International Aspects of Stabilization Policies*. Boston, Federal Reserve Bank of Boston, pp. 241–78.

[M14] Helliwell, J. F. (1977), 'Arctic Pipelines in the Context of Canadian Energy Requirements', *Canadian Public Policy*, 3, 344–54.

[M15] Helliwell, J. F. (1977), 'The Distribution of Economic Benefits from a Pipeline', in M. H. Watkins (ed.), *Dene Nation: The Colony Within*, University of Toronto Press, pp. 75–83.

[M16] Helliwell, J. F. (1979), 'Canadian Energy Policy', *Annual Review of Energy*, 4, 175–229.

[M17] Helliwell, J. F. (1979), 'Taxation and Energy Policy', *Report of Proceedings of the 31st Tax Conference*, November 1979. Toronto, Canadian Tax Foundation, pp. 7–20.

[M18] Helliwell, J. F. (1980), 'Can Canada Be Insulated from Developments Abroad?' in *Developments Abroad and the Domestic Economy*. Toronto, Ontario Economic Council, pp. 79–101.

[M19] Helliwell, J. F. (1980), 'The Distribution of Energy Revenues Within Canada: Functional or Factional Federalism?' Resources Paper no. 48, Programme in Natural Resource Economics, University of British Columbia.

[M20] Helliwell, J. F. (1980), 'Trade Policies for Natural Gas and Electricity', in *Energy Policies for the 1980s: An Economic Analysis*. Toronto, Ontario Economic Council, pp. 1–53.

[M21] Helliwell, J. F. (1981), 'Canadian Energy Pricing', *Canadian Journal of Economics*, 14, 579–95.

[M22] Helliwell, J. F. (1981), 'An Economic Evaluation of the National Energy Program', *Report of Proceedings of the 32nd Tax Conference*, November 1980. Toronto, Canadian Tax Foundation.

[M23] Helliwell, J. F. (1981), 'The Stagflationary Effects of Higher Energy Prices in an Open Economy', *Canadian Public Policy* 7, Supplement, April 1981, 155–64.

[M24] Helliwell, J. F. (1981), 'Using Canadian Oil and Gas Revenues in the 1980s: Provincial and Federal Perspectives', in T. Barker and V. Brailovsky (eds), *Oil or Industry?: Energy, Industrialization and Economic Policy in Canada, Mexico, the Netherlands, Norway and the United Kingdom*. London, Academic Press.

[M25] Helliwell, J.F.(1982),'Canadian Oil and Gas Taxation',*The Energy Journal*, April, 1982.

[M26] Helliwell, J. F. and Boothe, P. M. (1981), 'Macroeconomic Implications of Alternative Exchange Rate Models', presented at the International Workshop on 'Exchange Rates in Multicountry Econometric Models', University of Leuven, Belgium, 26–28 November 1981.

[M27] Helliwell, J. F., Boothe, P. M., and McRae, R. N. (1982), 'Stabilization, Allocation, and the 1970s Oil Price Shocks', *Scandinavian Journal of Economics*, 84, 259–88.

[M28] Helliwell, J. F., Christofides, L. N., and Lester, J. M. (1976), 'The Conversion Loan of 1958: A Simulation Study of Its Macroeconomic Consequences', *Canadian Journal of Economics*, 9, 425–41.

[M29] Helliwell, J. F., Duncan, B. C. E., Hendricks, K., McRae, R. N., May, G., and Williams, D. B. C. (1979), 'An Integrated Simulation Approach to the Analysis of Canadian Energy Policies', in P. Nemetz (ed.), *Energy Policy: The Global Challenge*. Montreal, Institute for Research on Public Policy, pp. 283–93; reprinted in a special issue of the *Journal of Business Administration*, 10, Fall 1978/Spring 1979.

[M30] Helliwell, J. F. *et al.* (1976), 'An Integrated Model for Energy Policy Analysis', Resources Paper no. 7, Programme in Natural Resource Economics, University of British Columbia.

[M31] Helliwell, J. F. and Glorieux G. (1970), 'Forward-looking Investment Behavior', *Review of Economic Studies*, 37, 499–516.

[M32] Helliwell, J. F., Gorbet, F., Sparks, G., and Stewart I. (1973), 'Comprehensive Linkage of Large Models: Canada and the United States', in R. J. Ball (ed.), *International Linkage of National Economic Models*. Amsterdam, North Holland, pp. 395–426.

[M33] Helliwell, J. F., Hendricks, K., and Williams, D. B. C. (1979). 'Canadian Perspectives on the Alaska Highway Pipeline: Modelling the Alternatives', in W. T. Ziemba *et al.* (eds), *Energy Policy Modelling: Canadian and U.S. Experiences.* Hingham, Mass.: Martinus Nijhoff, pp. 279–317.

[M34] Helliwell, J. F. and Higgins, C. I. (1976), 'Macroeconomic Adjustment Processes', *European Economic Review*, 7, 221–38.

[M35] Helliwell, J. F. and Lester, J. M. (1975), 'A New Approach to Price Setting for Regulated Pipelines', *Logistics and Transportation Review*, 11, 320–37.

[M36] Helliwell, J. F. and Lester, J. M. (1976), 'External Linkages of the Canadian Monetary System', *Canadian Journal of Economics*, 9, 648–69.

[M37] Helliwell, J. F. and Margolick, M. (1982), 'The Link Between Energy Prices and the Need for New Dams in British Columbia', prepared for the British Columbia Energy Commission Site C Dam Hearings.

[M38] Helliwell, J. F. and Maxwell, T. (1972), 'Short-term Capital Flows and the Foreign Exchange Market', *Canadian Journal of Economics*, 5, 199–214.

[M39] Helliwell, J. F. and Maxwell, T. (1974), 'Monetary Interdependence of Canada and the United States Under Alternative Exchange Rate Systems', in R. Z. Aliber (ed.), National Monetary Policies and the International System. University of Chicago Press, pp. 82–108.

[M40] Helliwell, J. F. and May, G. (1975), 'A Model for Assessing the Economic Costs and Benefits of Athabaska Oil Sands Projects', UBC Department of Economics Discussion Paper 75–29, October 1975.

[M41] Helliwell, J. F. and May G. (1976), 'Taxes, Royalties and Equity Participation as Alternative Methods of Dividing Resource Revenues: The Syncrude Example', in A. D. Scott (ed.), *Natural Resource Revenues: A Test of Federalism.* Vancouver: University of British Columbia Press.

[M42] Helliwell, J. F. and McRae, R. N. (1981), 'An Economic Evaluation of the September Energy Agreement', in *Tax Treatment of the Petroleum Industry Under the National Energy Program—A Technical Analysis,* proceedings of a conference held 21-22 September 1981 in Calgary, Alberta. Toronto: Canadian Tax Foundation.

[M43] Helliwell, J. F. and McRae, R. N. (1981), 'The National Energy Conflict', *Canadian Public Policy,* 7, 15–23.

[M44] Helliwell, J. F. and McRae, R. N. (1982), 'Resolving the National Energy Conflict: From the National Energy Program to the Energy Agreements', *Canadian Public Policy,* 8, 14–23.

[M45] Helliwell, J. F., Pearse, P., Sanderson, C., and Scott, A. (1974), 'Where Does Canada's National Interest Lie? A Quantitative Appraisal', in Pearse, op. cit., pp. 197–227.

[M46] Helliwell, J. F. and Scott, A. D. (1981), *Canada in Fiscal Conflict: Resources and the West.* Vancouver: Pemberton Securities.

[M47] Helliwell, J. F., Shapiro, H., Sparks, G., Stewart, I., Gorbert, F., and Stephenson, D. (1971), *The Structure of RDX2.* Bank of Canada Staff Research Studies no. 7 (2 vols).

[M48] Helliwell, J. F., Sparks, G., and Frisch, J. (1973), 'The Supply Price of Capital in Macroeconomic Models', in A. A. Powell and R. A. Williams (eds), *Econometric Studies of Macro and Monetary Relations.* Amsterdam, North Holland, pp. 262–83.

[M49] Hendricks, K. (1977), 'Costs Models for Natural Gas and Oil Pipelines', unpublished MA Extended Essay, University of British Columbia.

[M50] Hendricks, K. (1977), 'Consumer Surplus Measures and the Case of Natural Gas', unpublished MA Extended Essay, University of British Columbia.

[M51] MacGregor, M. E. (1980), 'Estimates and Analysis of Foreign Ownership Changes in Canadian Oil and Gas Production: 1972-1979', unpublished MA Extended Essay, University of British Columbia.

[M52] Margolick, M., Hansson, A. H., and Helliwell, J. F. (1981), 'Competing Energy Uses for Wood Wastes in British Columbia', Resources Paper no. 65, Programme in Natural Resource Economics, University of British Columbia.

[M53] May, G. (1976), 'Syncrude and the Oil Sands: An Economic Evaluation', MA thesis, University of British Columbia.

[M54] McRae, R. N. (1977), 'A Quantitative Analysis of Some Policy Alternatives Affecting Canadian Natural Gas and Crude Oil Demand and Supply', unpublished PhD thesis, University of British Columbia.

[M55] McRae, R. N. (1979), 'Primary Energy Demand in Canada', *Energy Economics,* October, 203–210.

[M56] Osler, S. L. (1977), 'An Application of Marginal Cost Pricing Principles to B. C. Hydro', Resources Paper no. 12, Programme in Natural Resource Economics, University of British Columbia.

[M57] Ross, A. (1977), 'The Production of and Revenues From Natural Gas Liquids in the Province of Alberta: 1947–2020', unpublished MA Extended Essay, University of British Columbia.

[M58] Smith, M. (1975), 'The Impact of Alternative Fiscal Regimes: The Natural Gas Sector in British Columbia', unpublished MA thesis, University of British Columbia.

[M59] Weisbeck, D. (1976), 'A Methodological and Cost Comparison of Alternative Analyses of Exploiting Canadian and US Frontier Natural Gas Resources', unpublished MA thesis, University of British Columbia.

Comment   Lawrence Klein

It is a pleasure to have the opportunity to review the MACE model and to examine its application to specific problems. It is an admirable example of careful econometric research, based on state-of-the-art model-building, with applications of contemporary relevance. The publication record of the whole project based on this model is very impressive.

The paper begins on an attractive note: 'What role did higher energy prices play in creating national and world stagflation in the 1970s and 1980s?' The reason why this is the appropriate question and why its answer is important is that the answer sets the pattern of economic policy. It guides the use of overall monetary/fiscal policy in coping with stagflation in relation to the case of true supply-side energy or resource policy.

After the first oil shock of the 1970s (the 1973 embargo, followed by high OPEC price rises in 1974–5), there was much discussion about the applicability of strict monetary policy as a suitable response. It was important to assess to what extent prices were rising, in general, because of the oil price rise and to what extent they were rising because of lax monetary policy.

In an interesting research paper, economists at Washington University, St Louis, have found that a multiple regression of percentage price change in the United States on rate of growth of money supply and an indicator of oil supply disruption shows a point estimate for the coefficient of the latter variable of about 0.04; thus, 400 basis points in an inflation rate of about 10–15 per cent can be accounted for by the energy supply interruption. This is a substantial and significant finding for the net contribution of the external supply shock, but it is a crude and suggestive result. What John Helliwell and associates are doing in the MACE model research project is to uncover the structural aspects of the answer to the question being posed.

THE MACE MODEL

The paper explains the overall structure of MACE and lists the whole equation set. First, I want to examine some particular properties of this system. As I indicated already, I find this model to be a state-of-the-art system based on received long-term growth properties, neoclassical optimization relationships, variable exchange rates, monetary factors, rational expectations, and separate treatment of energy.

Energy enters the system in an extension of the conventional value-added production function to one that can be written as

$$X = F\{(K, E), L\}.$$

It is a nested function that uses a CES bundle for capital and energy (*KE*), and labour (*L*), put together is a final Cobb–Douglas bundle. Gross output is represented by X. I would prefer, personally, to use

$$X = F\{(K, E), L\}, M.$$

Energy is not the only intermediate input of strategic importance. It has unusual significance at the present time, but there will likely be future occasions when other intermediate inputs will be strategic.

As a result of work done on US production functions by some of my associates, I conclude that straightforward CES specification of nested functions including both energy and material inputs is feasible and preferable. These estimates are not difficult to obtain and seem to me to be better than mixed CES, Cobb–Douglas specifications. It is best, of course, to estimate these on a more detailed sector split than is found in the MACE model. In our large-scale Wharton model, which includes both an input–output (I-O) system and a macro-system of final demand and income generation, production functions for each sector are estimated, where the columns of the I-O table are used to obtain both the intermediate (*EM*) and value-added (*KL*) inputs.

In the study of energy prices and their effects on the economy as a whole this extension can be important. Consider the case of steel, an industry that is presently in trouble. Because of high energy prices, much less steel is used in the manufacture of fuel-efficient cars than was previously the case (before 1973). Energy prices affect not only the direct use of energy inputs, but also other intermediate inputs, such as steel, in the production process. The best way of capture these subtle effects is to use a model containing a complete input–output system. That is the way that we have interpreted energy shortfalls in the United States. We first worked out results with the large-scale model, *cum* input–output system; we then adjusted the macro-model (Wharton short-term model) to agree with this result through corrections to inventory flows. I would feel more comfortable with the MACE results, which are by no means implausible by themselves, if they were checked out against similar results with CANDIDE.

I am pleased to see the use of a Phillips curve explanation, in part at least, for the generation of wage rate changes. Many people have commented on the demise of the Phillips curve, but it has a clear role to play in the explanation of Canadian wage changes and occurs in the MACE model through the un-employment term in the wage equation. We are presently seeing, throughout the world, a rise in unemployment and a weakening of the rate of wage increases. The reaction coefficients of MACE that describe this relationship seem to be quite reasonable—a reduction of wage inflation by two percentage points for each percentage point increase of the unemployment rate, in the neighbourhood of its natural rate. That degree of wage restraint seems to be what is taking place now, in the industrial world.

In the text of the manuscript, there is a remark that exports should be looked upon as a means of shipping surplus goods not required for use at home. This is good classical economics, but can it be done irrespective of the foreign market situation? Will partner countries buy the goods, and if so, at what price? An eonomic analysis of external market prospects is required, beyond what is already included in the MACE Model.

Do capital flows stabilize exchange rates? The answer to this question is uncertain. Maybe they do, maybe they do not; but one result does seem to be apparent in the MACE model, namely, that they respond quite strongly to interest rate differentials.

Finally, as far as specific comments on the paper are concerned, I find the elasticity coefficients (along the diagonal) for energy use, in appendix 2, to be quite reasonable. They vary from -0.4 to -0.7. At the beginning of the oil crisis, in 1973, most analysts thought that the relevant own-price elasticities were about -0.1 or -0.2. As the process has passed through time, the build-up of long-term elasticities has shown through in the rise of conservation (fall of the b.t.u./GDP ratio). It is now generally accepted that the medium-term elasti-cities are in the range from -0.5 to -1.0.

SOME CONSIDERATIONS FOR MODEL APPRAISAL

The simulation results with error analysis and response to change in policy instruments (table 2.1) are plausible and not unusual. MACE model perform-ance thus measures up well within these respects with other national or inter-national models.

One of the best ways of checking reliability is to compare results with other studies of Canadian sensitivity to oil price changes. The MACE model results suggest that Canada responds like any other OECD country. When world oil prices rise, there is a tendency for domestic inflation to increase and for pro-duction to fall. The quantitative magnitudes are close to those found for the United States and for the OECD area as a whole in Project LINK, but I want to raise the question: Is there any reason to expect Canada to be different? The principal characteristic that would differentiate Canada from other OECD

TABLE C2.1
Dynamic elasticities
(with respect to oil price changes)

		1979	1980	1981	1982	1983	1984	1985
$\dfrac{\Delta \ln \text{GDP}}{\Delta \ln P_{\text{oil}}} *100$	post-	−0.7	−0.2	−0.4	0.9	1.7	2.3	2.4
	pre-	(−0.3)	(−0.5)	(−0.3)	(−0.3)	(−0.2)	(−0.2)	(1.4)
$\dfrac{\Delta \ln \text{PC}}{\Delta \ln P_{\text{oil}}} *100$	post-	3.4	6.6	6.3	7.8	9.1	10.0	10.0
	pre-	(4.6)	(1.8)	(1.8)	(1.4)	(0.9)	(0.8)	(0.5)

countries is the fact that Canada is a net energy exporter. In various oil price or shortfall scenarios with Project LINK, I find that countries that are net or major exporters—the UK, Netherlands, Norway, Canada—react in a particular way. When world oil prices rise, and other energy prices also rise sympathetically inflation rates go up (as in the OECD area generally), but overall production also goes up, although not necessarily immediately, because terms of trade become favourable and because there is increased supply-side activity. The favourable turn in the terms of trade enables net exporting countries to continue to maintain import flows of goods that contribute to production such as materials and real fixed capital. There is no immediate need to restrain imports and shift into the 'stop' phase of 'stop–go' economic dynamics. As energy prices rise, there should be an increase in exploring, drilling, and transporting of energy, together with capital expansion to deliver an increased supply.

The Canadian model in Project LINK has been the TRACE model, but recently there has been a shift towards incorporation of the FOCUS model, also from Toronto. When these models are simulated within the LINK system, the economic relations with a whole spectrum of trading partners are activated and taken into account. This makes the full linked simulations essentially different, in a qualitative sense, from those in the paper by Professor Helliwell and associates.

Some results from project LINK, in which an increase (ten percentage points in 1979) of the world oil price has been imposed with unchanged exogenous growth rates for this variable for the six-year period after 1979, are compared with a baseline simulation. In table C2.1 I present dynamic system elasticities for GDP and consumer price deflator with respect to world oil price change. These system elasticities show the total effect of national and international effects when world prices change. They are expressed as the ratio of percentage deviation from the baseline simulation paths (GDP and PC) to the percentage point increase in the growth path of P_{oil}. The results are for Canada alone. The figures in parentheses are pre-linkage; they are obtained from simulations of the TRACE model alone, without putting it in to the context of world economy adjustment. In the fully linked case, inflation sensitivity is larger and always positive. The effect of the price change on GDP reverses from negative (the conventional result for an energy importer) to positive after three years. The same reversal occurs without international linkage but takes longer to appear.

I have looked at pre-link simulations of FOCUS, initialized in 1981. There is a slight tendency for domestic inflation to rise, in response to a world price increase for oil, but it is not uniform; similarly, there is a tendency for GDP to rise above the baseline path, but the changes are not large enough to be considered significant.

These brief references to and examinations of other Canadian macro-models are only exploratory and indicative. They are not definitive. They have been examined only for oil price increases, but should have enough symmetry to hold, with signs reversed, for oil price declines.

(Pure model results are symmetric for oil price increases or decreases, but recent (summer–autumn 1982) developments indicate that oil price decreases can be so serious for major oil exporters that have undertaken large debt burdens that serious financial disturbances on a world scale can have some of the large adverse effects that oil price increases had in the 1970s. These disturbances emanate from Mexico, Nigeria, Venezuela, and some other oil exporting countries.)

There are several different Canadian models, and the questions of sign of response should be investigated in a larger variety of experiments. Given the complicated nature of energy sector interactions with other sectors, I would place great importance on an examination of results with CANDIDE.

PART III
ANALYSIS OF RENEWABLE RESOURCES

Introductory Note

Philip A. Neher

Replenishable resources have two properties that distinguish them as a special category for economic investigation. First, they involve natural production functions, the properties of which are often obscure. They are the object of sometimes intense but always expensive research, and current knowledge of them is changing almost from day to day. Pelagic production functions provide a prime example. Airsheds provide another.

Second, while the natural capital is the object of exploitation and conservation, institutions are often not in place to assure that the resources are managed in socially desirable ways. Neither property rights nor political control are naturally exercised either at all or in ways that inspire confidence that the job is being done. So-called 'common property' problems are endemic.

Since natural resources are natural capital, the Clark, Munro, and Charles paper, followed by Neher's, naturally take a capital-theoretic approach to the question of how these resources *ought* to be managed. These are followed by Wilen's study of how a resource *is* managed.

The first two papers share the same capital-theoretic structure, but turn it to different purposes.

The structure is simply put. Let $\pi(x, b)$ represent a 'payoff' or 'profit' function where b is a natural capital *stock* and x is a flow rate of output. In Clark, Munro, and Charles (CMC), $\pi = p \cdot x - w \cdot a$ where p and w are parametric prices of output (x) and fishing effort (a). However, fish are caught with effort (a) and the co-operation of the fish stock itself (b). In symbols, the production function for fishing is $x = F(a, b)$, which can be written as $a = a(x, b)$ by virtue of the implicit function theorem. Substituting, $\pi = \pi(x, b) = p \cdot x - w \cdot a(x, b)$. CMC use a special form of a ($\cdot$) such that $a = a(x, b) = b^{-\beta} \cdot x$. Neher employs a social utility function $U(\cdot)$ in which the consumption flow of the natural asset (x) and the asset itself (b) contribute together to the commonwealth: $\pi = \pi(x, b) = u(x, b)$. The economic problem in both models is to maximize an additively separable *objective functional* in the form $J = \int D \cdot \pi dt$ where D is a discount factor that weights the π being generated at each moment of time (t). The limits of integration are determined in the context of the problem.

Maximizing J is subject to nature's own budget constraint, which allows net growth of (investment in) the natural asset ($db/dt = \dot{b}$) to be its own natural rate of growth $G(b)$ minus the rate at which it is consumed (harvested or exploited), x. That is, $\dot{b} = G(b) - x$ is the *dynamic constraint* (DC).

As CMC emphasize, it has been the casting of resource problems into this framework that has dominated natural resource economics over the past two decades. The values of endogenous variables (x, a, b) typically take on different values in the course of time. In this sense, the problem is truly dynamic. Solutions are *paths* through time, or trajectories. These replace the maximizing *points* which were sought as solutions to static problems for so many years.

The dominance of the capital-theoretic approach may be due partly to the development and diffusion of solution algorithms since the Second World War. Both dynamic programming (DP) and the maximum principle (MP) have become widely accessible to investigators. CMC and Neher employ the latter using continuous time, but the former could have been used (but not so conveniently) if discrete time had been chosen.

The maximum principle (MP) is congenial to economists for two reasons. First, Ramsey (1928) and Hotelling (1932) had used the classical calculus of variations (C of V) to solve dynamic economic problems before, and the MP is an elaboration of the C of V, which itself was developed in the seventeenth century.

Ramsey asked, 'how much of its income should a nation save?' In skeleton form his problem was to maximize $J = \int D \cdot \pi dt$ where π was a social utility function in the form $u(x)$, where x is consumption. The dynamic constraint was imposed by industrial, not natural, technology. But otherwise the structure was similar. For Ramsey, $\dot{b} = G(b) - x$ where b is industrial capital and $\dot{b}$ is its rate of growth (saving).

Hotelling enquired how quickly a homogeneous ore supply of known size S should be depleted. Again, the problem was to maximize $J = \int D \cdot \pi dt$. If the costs of extraction are put aside, π is extraction revenues equal to $p(x) \cdot x$ for the industry. Since the mineral does not grow, $\dot{b} = -x$, so a non-trivial steady state is impossible. However, an iso-parametric constraint must be observed. It is

$$-\int \dot{b} dt \equiv \int x dt \leqslant S.$$

Neither Ramsey's work nor Hotelling's made a large contemporary impact. But when economists turned to dynamic problems of growth, development, and resource depletion after the Second World War, these early works served as models of what could be done with DP and MP. Old puzzles in capital theory were seen to have more transparent solutions. New problems were suggested by the economic concerns of the times, and economists were encouraged to investigate them because the new algorithms had rendered them more tractable.

The second reason economists have found the MP so congenial is that it appeals to concepts that were already well developed in the prevailing oral and discussive literature. The concept of GNP or NNP as a 'performance indicator' consisting of 'consumption' plus 'investment' components was well imbedded. Application of MP begins with this fundamental concept: $H = (\pi + \lambda \cdot \dot{b})$.

Here, H is called the 'Hamiltonian' after the Irish mathematician Hamilton (1805-65). The 'consumption' component of H is $\pi(x, b) = p \cdot x - w \cdot a(x, b)$ in (CMC); it is $u(x, b)$ in Neher, $u(x)$ in Ramsey, and $p \cdot x$ or $p(x) \cdot x$ in Hotelling. Physical investment is $\dot{b} = G(b) - x$ in all of these examples $(G(b) = 0$ in Hotelling). The price of $\dot{b}$ is λ, which is the price of 'investment' measured in terms of 'consumption'.

Once H is formed, the algorithm for finding necessary conditions for maximizing J is eminently appealing, and by now rather well known. Briefly, MP requires that a 'controller', or maximizer, vary that which he can, at every point in time, to maximize H. The *flow* variable is x, so it becomes the *control* variable, and MP requires $\max_{\{x\}} H$. In CMC, H happens to be linear in x, so

$x = x_{max}, x = x_{min}$ or $x \epsilon (x_{min}, x_{max})$ according as the net value of the marginal product of a exceeds, falls short of, or equals the price of the fishing effort. The *net* price is $(p - \lambda)$, the price of 'fish on the quay' *minus* the price of the 'fish in the sea'. The marginal physical product of a is b^{β}. So the net value of the marginal product is $(p - \lambda) \cdot b^{\beta}$. When this equals w, x is free to be chosen on the *control set* (x_{min}, x_{max}). Otherwise, there is a 'most rapid approach' towards an equilibrium stock (b^*). This 'bang-bang' control is common in engineering problems, where the control is either 'on' or 'off'. It does not occur so often in economics, where the nature of the problem suggests a sufficient degree of concavity so that the desired control can be found within the limits of the control set (x_{min}, x_{max}).

In Neher, MP is applied by $\max_{\{x\}} H$ where $H = u(x, b) + \lambda \cdot \dot{b}$. The dynamic constraint, $\dot{b} = G(b) - x$ is shared with CMC. The appropriate algorithm is $H_x = 0$ or $\lambda = u_x$. The value of the resource is its opportunity cost in consumption.

After applying the maximum principle, the condition for *portfolio balance* (PB) is evoked to ensure that the marginal efficiency of investment in the resource is competitive with the aggregate or representative asset in the economy which pays a positive rate of interest, r. The marginal benefits must just balance the marginal opportunity cost of holding the natural asset. The condition is well known: capital gains *plus* the net value of the marginal product *minus* the value of physical depreciation (plus the value of physical depreciation) equals the rental rate of the asset. In CMC,

$$\dot{\lambda} + (p - \lambda)\beta ab^{-(\beta-1)} - \{-G'(b)\} \cdot \lambda = r\lambda.$$

Similarly, in Neher, $\dot{\lambda} + u_b - \{-G'(b)\} \cdot \lambda = r\lambda$.

To sum up the algorithm, form $H = \pi + \lambda \cdot \dot{b}$, then apply

(MP) $\max_{\{a\}} H$

(PB) $\dot{\lambda} = r\lambda - H_b$

(DC) $\dot{b} = H_\lambda.$

These are necessary (not sufficient) conditions for a maximum of *J*. They describe the *motions* of *a, b,* and λ. More information in the form of initial states, terminal states, transversality conditions, and the like are furnished in the context of individual problems to provide the constants of integration and complete the solution.

The steady state is particularly easy to characterize, however. This is where $\dot{a} = \dot{b} = \dot{\lambda} = 0$, and the solution conditions will be most familiar.

In CMC

(MP) $$(p - \lambda)b^{\beta} = w$$

(PB) $$(p - \lambda)\beta ab^{-(\beta-1)} - \{-G\,'(b)\} \cdot \lambda = r \cdot \lambda$$

(DC) $$G(b) = ab^{\beta}.$$

In Neher,

(MP) $$\lambda = u_c$$

(PB) $$u_b - \{-G'(b)\} \cdot \lambda = r \cdot \lambda$$

(DC) $$G(b) = x.$$

These are variants of the familiar static problem for a profit-maximizing firm in the form of

$$\max \pi = p \cdot F(a, b) - w \cdot a - rP_b b - \delta b \cdot \lambda$$

where parametric prices are p, w, rP_b (the rental rate of capital goods) and P_b (the supply price of capital goods). The rate of depreciation is δ. Necessary conditions for a maximum are

$$pF_a = w$$
$$pF_b - \delta \cdot \lambda = r \cdot \lambda.$$

A comparison of these results with MP and DC derived by CMC and Neher reveals that the only conceptual difference is that the price of (natural) capital is endogenous and perhaps not observed (a 'shadow price') in CMC and Neher. The price of (industrial) capital is exogenous to the competitive firm. This is because a resource firm normally owns (or controls) its (natural) capital stock for which there may not be a well-organized market. The paradigmatic competitive firm is free to rent its (industrial) capital stock at the going market price.

Having noted the structural similarity of the CMC and Neher models, it is interesting to see how they turn their models to different purposes.

CMC (chapter 3) are concerned that it may be the case in some large and specialized fisheries that second-hand markets for vessels, gear, navigation equipment, processing facilities and the like are non-existent or very poor. Moreover, specialized skills of fishermen may not be easily transferred to other occupations. Theirs is a putty-clay model with no market for clay. The capital is, in this sense, 'non-malleable'. There is no upper bound on the rate at which capital can be added, but subtractions are limited to depreciations (at an exogenous, physical, exponential decay rate). In this case, fishing requires *two* capital stocks: natural and industrial. So a complete solution requires that optimal trajectories be found for *four* variables: the two capitals and the associated (shadow) prices for each. CMC present a *synthesized* solution of the problem which 'solves out' the prices and shows how the two capitals evolve over time (figure 3.3). It should be remarked, however, that the production function is of a particular Cobb–Douglas form $x = ab$ (equation (3.15)), which imparts substantial tractability to the problem with some loss of generality. The important point is that simple models which assume perfect second-hand markets can suggest misleading advice. The accidents of history *do* matter. Bygones are *not* strictly bygone when investments are not easily reversible in historical time.

Their next step is to introduce stochastic fluctuations in the fish stock and to allow for a delay in the delivery of new vessels, gear, and trained crews. This moves the enquiry in the direction of greater realism. The entailed cost is to force the investigators to employ DP and numerical methods of solution. Robust qualitative results are still obtainable, however. For example, if the cost of (non-malleable) capital is small, then the expected value of the programme may be maximized by employing more vessels in the steady state than in a deterministic optimum. This is particularly true for fast-growing stocks (prawns) which offer greater opportunity to make particularly large catches in 'good' years. Conclusions like this suggest some rethinking of commonly held views that certain fisheries are characterized by 'excess capacity' to catch and process fish *owing to* open-access, common-property problems. Can the awesome catching power of the North Pacific salmon fleet be justified in terms of having the capacity to catch unexpectedly large runs (Bristol Bay, Alaska, 1980)? Can previously presumed 'stay-out' capacity to process North Atlantic catches, especially cod, in Newfoundland be explained as optimal reserve capacity for the good years?

Spulber, in his Comment on chapter 3, discusses some of the related uncertainty literature that has appeared in recent years. While there has been a great deal of research, it has centred on models where random disturbances are drawn from known probability distributions, and much has been learned.

At another level, and as any fisherman will tell you, experience is a teacher. Probability distributions of fish stocks, prices, and the like are not immutable facts imposed by nature. Rather, people 'learn by doing'. Knowledge of stochastic structures is a product of experience. This observation suggests that learning models, perhaps constructed along Bayesian lines, can fruitfully be investigated.

Neher pursues a different line of investigation in chapter 4. Undeterred by a lack of evidence, he takes the basic fisheries model as a paradigm of (almost) all economic activity, either large or small. Neher reminds the reader that natural resource stocks can yield direct benefits through amenity values which they are alleged to offer. Clean air and sylvan scenes are part of the commonwealth. But common consumption is obtained by gross degradation of the wealth. How should a 'multiple-use' economy like this be managed? A long-range plan in the tradition of Ramsey is investigated first.

A second kind of intertemporal allocation is then investigated. Suppose the proper objective of a social policy is to manage the resource on behalf of the citizens who *are currently alive* instead of, as in the Ramsey conception, on behalf of all the citizens who *will ever be alive*? If it is the former, then the allocation is generated by a sequence of rolling plans. Each momentary rolling plan is constructed with a time horizon equal to the median life expectancy of extant citizens of different ages. In this sense, the momentary plan is democratic since these citizens would vote for that time horizon given pairwise alternatives.

Can these plans 'mimic' observed intertemporal allocations of a natural resource? If so, then one can begin with an observed plan and 'solve back' to find a 'phantom plan' that would give rise to the observed allocation if it were implemented. Characteristics of the plantom plan could then be used for the purpose of evaluating the 'goodness' of the observed plan from a social point of view.

Not surprisingly, it turns out that sequences of these rolling plans are less 'draconian' during an accumulation phase than the corresponding Ramsey plan. The intertemporal distribution of income is more even. In terms of the corresponding phantom plan, the phantom utility function is imputed to be more concave than the Ramsey counterpart. This leads the phantom planner to be more 'inequality-adverse'.

In his Comments, Dasgupta complains that this imputation procedure is unnecessarily indirect. Why not regard the Ramsey allocation as the 'right thing to do'? Then one can *compute* the shortfall of additive social welfare promised by alternative plans; observed or democratic.

Dasgupta's procedure is clearly complementary to Neher's in evaluating observed allocations. But its merit is less clear in the case of democratic plans. Dasgupta is on firm ground if one believes that the relevant constituency is everyone in an ongoing, perpetual society in which everyone who ever lives is to matter. But if one believes that the relevant constituency is persons currently alive, then the rolling plan allocation is the 'right' one in the first place.

While the CMC and Neher contributions are in the direction of greater realism and implementability at the public policy level, Wilen's central concern in chapter 5 is to help regulators implement management plans by developing descriptive models of managed fisheries. This attempt is in the tradition of 'positive economics' to explain the behaviour of the regulated fishery. The task is indeed formidable, entailing as it does a theory of how regulating bodies (institutions) react with fishermen, individually and in groups, in a regulated 'common property' setting.

With few exceptions, this problem has not attracted much attention. This is surprising in view of the policy orientation of most fishery economists. They are interested in *policy* questions, but they have made little progress in devising a *theory* of policy.

The theory of the regulated industry has been oriented towards the understanding of public control of 'natural monopolies' (electricity and gas utilities, municipal transportation firms), and of other areas of economic activity where the public interest is thought to be particularly at stake (banking, communication, transportation).

There are theories of how firms react to different modes of regulation (the 'rate-of-return' criterion for public utilities) and 'quantitative performance criteria' (which give weight to branching service to remote areas, to public service content, to abatement of undesirable byproducts, and the like). These theories evoke more or less conventional views of the regulated firm maximizing conventionally defined profits subject to market forces *and* the constraint(s) of regulation.

There are other theories of how regulated firms react with their regulators. These range from reductionist theories, which predict that regulators will be captured by regulatees, to complex interactive theories of bilateral bureaucracies, each reflecting a multitude of internally generated objectives.

Wilen's contribution employs the more conventional method of exploring how the regulated fishing firm responds to a rigorously enforced total allowable catch (TAC) set for a single-species industry. The number of firms is 'small' so that each takes into account the harvesting decision of the others when making its own: 'expected profits depend upon rivals' behaviour'. Thus, a game-theoretic problem is posed and Wilen evokes the Cournot-Nash concept of equilibrium to obtain a solution. This is done separately for 'schooling fisheries' (where adequate escapement is paramount) and for 'search fisheries' (where yields are regulated to maintain a biomass). In each case, the specific nature of the regulation(s) is chosen by the authority taking into account the relevant biology of the fish and the technology of the fishermen. The choice is (presumably) based on cost–benefit calculations, so that the desired objective is obtained at least cost. Wilen does not model this choice of technique problem explicitly, however. Hence, there is no solution for the optimal *level* of enforcement in each of several modes ('net set restrictions, shortened seasons, area closures, etc.').

Wilen suggests that regulators (presumably in North America, Europe, Australasia) are not *capable* of such calculations as they rush from one crisis to another, responding *ex post* to breakouts of fishing power by sequentially alternating more stringent gear restrictions with shorter seasons. The plodding bureaucrat is always thwarted in his intent by the wily, profit-oriented fishermen. Notwithstanding this, however, Wilen hypothesizes that 'regulators will be effective in causing no more than the targeted levels to be caught'. While being pessimistic about the regulatory process, Wilen is optimistic about its outcome. But he warns us that these are observations on the actual state of the world, and no normative judgements are being made. For example, the enforcement cost of ensuring adequate escapement may far outweigh the benefits of protecting the stock.

Since Wilen raises many questions, it is not surprising that he answers few of them. One is struck, for example, by the explicit omission of uncertainty in his analysis. A fisherman may be uncertain of his colleagues' plans to go fishing, but that uncertainty washes out in the Nash–Cournot equilibrium. The regulator may be uncertain that a season closure will have the desired effect of preserving a stock, but that uncertainty is swamped by yet another crisis as the intent of the closure is subverted by more powerful boats. These uncertainties can be added to the list already discussed by CMC and by Spulber.

Clark, in discussing Wilen's contribution, worries that Wilen pays too little attention to the dynamics of a regulatory process. But Wilen is breaking new ground, and experience suggests that simple, familiar, if blunt, tools are best used first. For example, the understanding of fishery dynamics by CMC in this volume grew from the static analysis that began developing a quarter of a century ago.

REFERENCES

Hotelling, H. (1932), 'The Economics of Exhaustible Resources', *Journal of Political Economy,* 39, 137–75.
Ramsey, F. P. (1928), 'A Mathematical Theory of Saving', *The Economic Journal*, 38, 543–59.

3. Fisheries, Dynamics, and Uncertainty

Colin W. Clark, Gordon R. Munro, and Anthony T. Charles

Introduction

Fisheries economics, along with other branches of natural resource economics, has enjoyed a rapid growth since the late 1960s. This growth can be attributed to general concerns about the state of the environment, but also, and more importantly, to interest in fisheries matters arising out of the Third United Nations Law of the Sea Conference. Although the Conference may not produce a treaty, it has led to a revolutionary change in the management of many of the world's fishery resources, in that they have been changed in status from international common property to the property of individual coastal states. Several fishery resources off the Atlantic and Pacific coasts of Canada and the United States provide examples.

In this paper we attempt to review some of the major theoretical developments in fisheries economics over the past decade and a half which point to the directions that future theoretical developments are likely to take. We argue that the major development of the late 1960s and early to mid-1970s was the shift away from static or timeless to dynamic or capital-theoretic analysis. The shift to dynamic analysis, in turn, has led naturally to considerations of uncertainty. Much of the current theoretical work in fisheries economics is in this area.

STATIC V. DYNAMIC MODELS OF THE FISHERY

The economist's static analysis of the fishery owes its origins to the seminal 1954 article of H. Scott Gordon (1954). The central point of the Gordon article is that the readily observed ills of many of the world's fisheries can be ascribed to the fact that the resources upon which they are based are common property. Open access, common-property fisheries inevitably result in economic, if not biological, overfishing.

The Gordon model, sometimes referred to as the Gordon–Schaefer model because of its close link to the biologist M. B. Schaefer's (1957) model of the fishery, can be described in terms of figure 3.1, which is to be found extensively in the literature on static fisheries economics (see Anderson, 1977).

Fishing effort in figure 3.1 refers to the flow of labour plus capital services devoted to harvesting. In the Gordon model the supply of fishing effort is assumed to be perfectly elastic, as is the demand for harvested fish.

Since the resource is renewable, it can, like other renewable resources, be exploited on a sustainable yield basis. The curve TR pictures sustainable revenue as a function of effort E, multiplied by the price of harvested fish, p. The curve TC is self-explanatory.

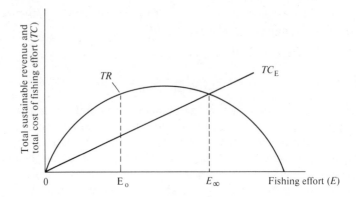

FIG. 3.1 Bionomic equilibrium and sustainable rent maximization: a static approach

Left to its own devices, an open-access, common-property fishery will expand to E_∞. Since the resource is common property, all resource rent (i.e. $TR - TC$) that is forthcoming will accrue to the labour and capital employed in the fishery. But if labour and capital in the fishery are enjoying returns in excess of their opportunity costs, the fishery will expand. Thus the fishery can be in equilibrium only when $TC = TR$, $E = E_\infty$, a situation described by Gordon as 'bionomic' equilibrium. The optimal level of fishing effort is, however, at E_0, at which *sustainable* resource rent is maximized. At this level of fishing effort, the value of the marginal product of fishing effort (VMP_E) is equal to the marginal cost of fishing effort (MC_E)—or so the argument goes (Gordon, 1954).

For want of a better term, let us call this a Class I common-property problem. There exists as well a different variant of the common-property problem (Class II), which is commonly found in many fisheries. A Class II problem arises when the authorities do not permit unchecked depletion of the resource, but rather attempt to maintain the stock by imposing global restrictions on the harvest on a yearly or seasonal basis. The authorities do not, however, attempt to control the size of the fleet or number of fishermen. In this case resource rent will be dissipated through the emergence of excessive labour and capital in the fishery. The British Columbia salmon and herring fisheries are obvious cases in point.

Let us return to our example of a Class I common-property problem in which resource depletion is a central aspect of the problem. In his book, *Mathematical Bioeconomics*, Clark (1976) points out that to argue that the optimal level of fishing effort is as shown by E_0 in figure 3.1. serves to ignore 'the dynamics of both economic and biological processes'. Suppose, for example, that we commence at $E = E_\infty$; that the authorities intervene to control the fishery and have as their object the maximization of sustainable resource rent. In order to reach the goal, the resource must be rebuilt by restricting harvests.

As we observe in the real world, the rebuilding of a fishery resource can be a slow and painful process. Once the cost of rebuilding the resource is recognized, it is not at all obvious that it is worth society's while to rebuild the resource to the extent that sustainable resource rent is maximized.

The question we are really asking is the extent to which it is appropriate for society to invest/disinvest in the resource. Hence a capital-theoretic approach is called for.

The desirability of employing capital-theoretic models in fisheries economics was recognized at the inception of the field. Anthony Scott's (1955) article was a first attempt to re-cast the Gordon model in a dynamic framework. Gordon himself, in a 1956 paper, spoke forcefully of the need for a capital-theoretic approach to fisheries economics (Gordon, 1956).

Be that as it may, although there were a few attempts to develop dynamic models of the fisheries in the early 1960s (e.g. Crutchfield and Zellner, 1962), the static analysis remained dominant throughout. The first truly successful attempts to develop a dynamic optimization approach to fisheries appeared in the early 1970s with the pioneering work of Plourde (1970, 1971), Quirk and Smith (1970), and others. These models were characterized by the extensive application of optimal control theory.

A particularly simple version of the new dynamic optimization model is provided by the following model (Clark and Munro, 1975; Clark, 1976), in which the harvest rate (the 'control variable') enters linearly. The model is deterministic.[1]

The model, like the static Gordon model, is one of a fishery in which a single stock of fish is exploited. The model rests upon the standard 'general production' fishery model associated with Schaefer (1957), Pella and Tomlinson (1969) and others. The several influences upon the natural growth rate of the stock or biomass are lumped together and the aquatic environment is assumed to be constant. Thus the rate of growth of the stock through time can be expressed simply as

$$\dot{x} = F(x) - h(t) \tag{1}$$

where $x(t)$ denotes the biomass at time t, $F(x)$ the natural growth rate of the resource, and $h(t)$ the harvest rate at time t. It is assumed that

$$F(x) > 0 \quad \text{for } 0 < x < K, \; F(0) = F(K) = 0$$

and

$$F''(x) < 0 \quad \text{for all } x > 0 \tag{2}$$

where K denotes the natural equilibrium level of x; i.e., if $h(t) = 0$, then

$$\lim_{t \to \infty} x(t) = K.$$

The harvest production function is given by

$$h(t) = qE^{\alpha}(t)x^{\beta}(t) \tag{3}$$

where $E(t)$ is the rate of fishing effort (labour plus capital services devoted to harvesting) at time (t); q, a constant, is the catchability coefficient; and α and β are constants. It is assumed that $\alpha = 1$ and that $\beta \geq 0$.[2] Finally, we have the feasibility constraints:

$$x(t) \geq 0, \quad E(t) \geq 0. \tag{4}$$

We next introduce prices and costs. We assume that the price of fish, p, is a constant and suppose that the total cost of fishing effort, $C(E)$, is given by

$$C(E) = aE \tag{5}$$

where a, a constant, is the unit cost of effort. From equations (3) and (4) we can easily derive a harvest cost function:

$$C(h, x) = \frac{ah}{qx^\beta}$$

where $C(h, x)$ denotes total harvest costs. Harvest costs, given our assumptions, are thus linear in h and are a decreasing function of x, given $\beta \geq 0$.

We abstract from second-best conditions and assume that p adequately measures the marginal social benefit of fish to society and that a adequately measures the marginal social cost of effort. Thus society's objective can be seen as maximizing the present value of the resource rent from the fishery. The resource rent flow from the fishery at a given time t can be expressed simply as

$$\pi(x, h) = \{p - c(x)\}h \tag{7}$$

where

$$c(x) = \frac{a}{qx^\beta}$$

Society's problem can be viewed as an optimal control problem. The biomass $x(t)$ is the state variable, or variable to be controlled, while $h(t)$ is the control variable. Society's objective functional can be expressed as:

$$PV = \int_0^\infty e^{-\delta t} \pi\{x(t), h(t)\}dt \tag{8}$$

where δ is the social rate of discount. The problem is to determine the optimal control $h(t) = h^*(t)$, $t \geq 0$ and the corresponding optimal biomass $x(t) = x^*(t)$, $t \geq 0$, subject to equation (1), which we now term the state equation, and subject to equation (4).

Since the objective functional is linear in the control variable, the optimal control problem is linear. It is routinely handled by means of the maximum principle. The Hamiltonian of the problem is:

$$H = \pi\{x(t), h(t)\} + \lambda(t)\{F(x) - h(t)\} \tag{9}$$

where $\lambda(t)$ is the adjoint or costate variable at time t. This variable can be interpreted as the shadow price of the resource.

We are particularly interested in the optimal equilibrium biomass level $x = x^*$. This is determined in the steady state by

$$\frac{\partial H}{\partial h} = 0; \quad \frac{d\lambda}{dt} = \delta\lambda - \frac{\partial H}{\partial x} = 0.$$

A straightforward calculation yields the following equations for the determination of x^*:

$$\frac{\langle(d/dx^*)[\pi\{x^*, F(x^*)\}]\rangle}{\{\partial\pi(x^*, h)/\partial h\}_{h=F(x^*)}} = \delta \tag{10}$$

The LHS of (10) is the marginal sustainable resource rent divided by the 'cost' of the incremental investment in the resource stock—the return from current harvesting sacrificed in making the investment. As such it is simply the 'own rate of interest' of the resource. Thus, x^* is that biomass level at which the own rate of interest of the resource is equal to the social rate of discount.

If we carry out the differentiation in the numerator of the LHS of (10) the equation becomes

$$F'(x^*) + \frac{\partial\pi/\partial x^*}{\partial\pi/\partial h}\bigg|_{h=F(x^*)} = \delta. \tag{11}$$

The 'own rate of interest' of the resource is thus seen to consist of two components: the instantaneous marginal product of the resource and what has come to be known as the 'marginal stock effect' (Clark and Munro, 1975). The marginal stock effect is a measure of the marginal influence of stock abundance upon net revenue or rent flows, $\pi(x, h)$. It will be recalled from (6) that harvesting costs are a decreasing function of x (given that $\beta > 0$).

The optimal harvest rate once x^* has been achieved is given by

$$h^*(t) = F(x^*) \tag{12}$$

i.e., the resource is to be exploited on a sustained yield basis. The optimal effort rate in equilibrium, $E^*(t)$, is in turn given by

$$E^*(t) = \frac{F(x^*)}{qx^{*\beta}}. \tag{13}$$

Since the optimal control problem is linear the optimal approach path to x^* from the initial stock level is the most rapid, or the 'bang-bang', one; i.e.,

$$h^*(t) = h_{max} \text{ whenever } x(t) > x^*$$

$$= h_{min} \text{ whenever } x(t) < x^*. \tag{14}$$

Several comments are now in order. First, the use of optimal control theory terminology should not be allowed to disguise the essential and rather elementary capital-theoretic nature of the problem. In fact, for this specific problem optimal control theory is not required and a more elementary solution (integration by parts) exists.[3] In determining x^* we determine the extent to which it is worth society's while to invest/disinvest in the resource. Equation (11) can be seen to be a 'modified golden rule' equation. Indeed, it can be observed that, if the marginal stock effect is negligible, as appears to be the case in certain fisheries, then (11) reduces to

$$F'(x^*) = \delta.$$

In determining the optimal approach path, one is determining the optimal resource investment policy until x^* is achieved. If $h(t) < F(x)$, then investment in the resource is occurring; if $h(t) > F(x)$ the reverse is occurring; i.e., one is literally eating one's capital. The only fundamental difference between fisheries economics (or any other branch of natural resource economics, for that matter) as capital theory and standard capital theory is that nature presents society with an initial endowment of resource capital.

The second set of comments concerns comparisons between the static and capital-theoretic models. We make the comparison with the aid of figure 3.2, in which sustainable yield is viewed as a function of the biomass, x. In the figure TC should be interpreted as the minimum total cost of harvesting the sustainable yield. The biomass levels x_0 and x_∞ are the levels associated with maximum sustainable resource rent and bionomic equilibrium, respectively.

If we return to equation (10), it can be seen that maximizing sustainable resource rent would be optimal, i.e., $x^* = x_0$, only if $\delta = 0$. If $\delta > 0$, as assuredly it must be, then the static model prescribes an over-investment in the resource. Conversely, bionomic equilibrium would be optimal only if $\delta = \infty$. This does, of course, indicate the essence of the common property problem, namely that the exploiters view the resource as having a negligible future value.

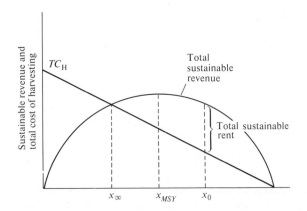

FIG. 3.2. Sustainable revenue and rent as functions of the biomass

In figure 3.2 we have deliberately not shown x^*. All that we can say, *a priori*, is that, if $0 < \delta < \infty$, then $x_0 < x^* < x_\infty$, and that as δ increases from 0 to $+\infty$ the biomass x^* decreases from x_0 to x_∞.

The chief benefit of the dynamic model is not that it allows us to correct the static model's mis-specification of the optimal biomass level; it is rather that it compels us to recognize what we noted earlier, namely that achieving the optimum may well require a lengthy and difficult period of adjustment. It is not merely a matter of restricting the level of fishing effort as is implied by figure 3.1. We return to this theme at many points in the paper.

The third set of comments pertain to extensions to the simple linear, deterministic model. Many have now been made. We shall do no more than list some of the major ones. At an early stage the model was extended to allow for non-linearities, e.g., by relaxing the assumptions that the demand for fish and supply of fishing effort are perfectly elastic, and to allow for the possibility of continuous parameter shifts through time (Clark and Munro, 1975). The most important conclusion forthcoming from models allowing for continuous parameter shifts over time—non-autonomous models—is that the fisheries manager does not need to project the time-path of the time-dependent parameters far into the future. 'Myopic' or near-myopic resource investment decision rules are appropriate.

At a later point cognizance was taken of the fact that fishery resources are often subject to joint ownership of two or more states. The issue of transboundary or shared stocks has become particularly important with the advent of UN Law of the Sea inspired Extended Fisheries Jurisdiction (Gulland, 1980). The model was extended to address the problem of optimal management of jointly owned resources, assuming that the joint owners have divergent goals and interests (Munro, 1979[4]).

The final extension of the deterministic dynamic model that we wish to discuss pertains to the relaxation of an implicit, but important and restrictive, assumption used in all of the dynamic models discussed to this point. This is the assumption that capital in the form of vessels and gear, processing plants, and human capital is perfectly malleable. That is to say, the capital can easily and costlessly be shifted to other uses or, alternatively, can be sold (except human capital, of course) without danger of capital loss. The concept is analogous to the financial concept of liquidity.

The use of this assumption offers immense analytical advantages. It can be shown that, if this assumption is adopted, non-resource capital can be treated as a flow variable. Consequently, one has only one investment or asset management problem to address, namely investment in the resource itself. In terms of optimal control theory, we have a relatively tractable, one-state-variable, one-control-variable problem.

The disadvantage of the assumption is that in real-world fisheries it is, more often than not, invalid. One can point to innumerable examples of non-malleable capital in fisheries (see in particular Baker, 1980). The large excess fleet capacity

experienced by many distant water nations following the widespread implementation of Extended Fisheries Jurisdiction is but one case in point. Indeed
one can argue that non-malleability of capital is ubiquitous among fisheries.

If the assumption of perfect malleability of capital is relaxed, the analysis
becomes substantially more demanding. Moreover, we discover that the implications for the adjustment phase of the resource management programmes
are profound.[5] So profound are they, and so well do they serve to illustrate
the value of dynamic models in permitting us to analyse the adjustment phase
of fisheries management, that we wish to examine the issue of capital non-
malleability in detail.

NON-MALLEABILITY OF CAPITAL AND FISHERIES MANAGEMENT

Our basic model of non-malleability (or irreversible investment) is the following
(Clark, Clarke, and Munro, 1979):

$$\frac{dx}{dt} = F(x) - qEx, \quad x(0) = x_0 \tag{15}$$

$$0 \leqslant E \leqslant E_{max} = K \tag{16}$$

$$\frac{dK}{dt} = I - \gamma K, \quad K(0) = K_0 \tag{17}$$

$$I \geqslant 0 \tag{18}$$

$$PV = \int_0^\infty e^{-\delta t}\{(pqx - c)E - c_f I\}dt. \tag{19}$$

where K is capital invested in effort capacity, E_{max} (e.g. number of vessels),
I is the rate of gross investment, γ is the depreciation rate ($\gamma > 0$), and c_f is
the price of capital.

The non-malleability assumption is incorporated in equation (18); a less
extreme form, in which disinvestment is allowed, but at a price $c_s < c_f$, is
discussed in Clark, Clarke, and Munro (1979, section 6).

In contrast to the models discussed in the previous section, there are two
investment problems, which must be addressed simultaneously. Correspondingly,
our model contains two state variables, x and K, and two control variables,
E and I.[6]

To commence, however, let us first justify the assertion made above that, if
capital is perfectly malleable, the number of state variables is reduced from two
to one, as is the number of control variables. If capital is perfectly malleable,
condition (18) is omitted. Thus we can write

$$\int_0^\infty e^{-\delta t}I dt = \int_0^\infty e^{-\delta t}\left(\frac{dK}{dt} + \gamma K\right)dt$$

$$= (\delta + \gamma) \int_0^\infty e^{-\delta t} K dt - K_0.$$

Since obviously $E(t) \equiv K(t)$ in this case, we obtain

$$PV = \int_0^\infty e^{-\delta t} \{pqx - c - c_f(\delta + \gamma)\} E dt + c_f K_0 \qquad (20)$$

i.e., the investment control I drops out and we revert to the simpler model of the previous section with unit effort cost given by[7]

$$c_{total} = c + (\delta + \gamma) c_f. \qquad (21)$$

Note that c_{total} consists of unit variable effort cost c plus interest and depreciation on (perfectly malleable) capital.

Let x^* denote the optimal equilibrium biomass for this model, with unit effort cost c_{total}. It turns out that x^* is also the long-run equilibrium for the non-malleable case (provided $\gamma \neq 0$), but the optimal approach path now takes a more complicated and interesting form. To describe the approach path, define $\tilde{x}$ as the optimal biomass of the previous section for the case where the rental cost of capital is irrelevant; i.e., unit cost of effort $= c$. (For the technically minded, both x^* and $\tilde{x}$ turn out to be 'singular solutions' to the optimal control problem (15)–(19).)

The fully 'synthesized' (or feedback) solution to our control problem has been obtained, and is illustrated in figure 3.3. The x, K-state space is divided by certain curves into three regions R_1, R_2, and R_3. The figure specifies the optimal values of I and K for points (x, K) in these regions. Gross investment ($I = +\infty$) occurs only in R_3, and the optimal level of such investment is specified by the curve labelled σ_2. Note that positive gross investment *never* occurs if $x < x^*$; for $x_0 > x^*$ the optimal initial investment is an increasing function of the initial biomass, x_0.

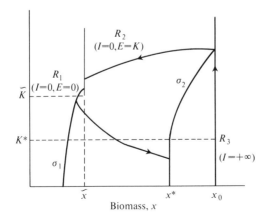

Fig. 3.3 Feedback control: optimal harvest and investment policies

Consider now the following example of optimal fishery management policy. Let it be supposed that the fishery had hitherto been unexploited.[8] Hence x_0 corresponds to the natural equilibrium level. Exploitation now takes place, but under the direction of a social manager.

The optimal level of investment (gross) in the fleet, K, is given by the switching curve, σ_2. Once the fleet investment has been undertaken, the cost of acquisition of the vessels ceases to be relevant. Hence the optimal biomass level is now $\tilde{x}$. It will be seen, however, that $\tilde{x}$ will prove to be a short-run equilibrium biomass.

In any event, the appropriate policy is to reduce the resource, utilizing the fleet to capacity ($E = K$). Indeed, optimality calls for setting $E = K$ for all points in R_2. While full utilization of the fleet will occur, it is also true that, for all points in R_2, $I = 0$. Hence during this phase in the management programme optimal resource and fleet investment policy calls for the maximum rate of disinvestment in the resource permitted by fleet capacity combined with net disinvestment in the fleet proceeding at a rate equal to γK.

In our particular example, the initial investment in fleet capacity is sufficient to allow the resource to be reduced to $\tilde{x}$. Once $\tilde{x}$ is reached, the policy of harvesting at maximum capacity ceases to be optimal. The appropriate harvest policy is to harvest at $\tilde{x}$ on a sustained yield basis, even though this results in apparent fleet redundancy.

Optimal fleet investment policy is still to set $I = 0$, with the consequence that the fleet will continue to diminish in size. Ultimately it will no longer be feasible to harvest at $\tilde{x}$ on a sustained yield basis. We then enter a new phase of the management programme in which positive investment in the resource occurs. Note, however, that investment in the resource will be gradual, since it will now be optimal to utilize the diminishing fleet capacity.

The resource recovery phase will continue until $x = x^*$. At that point, it will be optimal to harvest the resource on a sustained yield basis. The biomass level, x^*, thus constitutes a long-run equilibrium. In order to harvest at x^* on a sustained yield basis it will be necessary to reinvest in fleet capacity such that $K = K^*$ and then to set the rate of net investment in the fleet equal to zero thereafter; i.e., $I^* = \gamma K^*$.[9]

As an alternative example, we might suppose that the fishery had hitherto been subject to severe over-exploitation and that we commence at a point in R_3. The appropriate policy at the beginning of the management programme will be to declare a harvest moratorium, i.e., maximum rate of investment in the resource. This policy will continue to be optimal until we reach the switching curve σ_1 (this is a 'blocked-interval' switch—cf. Arrow, 1968). The fishery is then reopened using the existing fleet to capacity, but setting $I = 0$. The resource will continue to recover until $x = x^*$, at which point it will, as in our previous example, be optimal to harvest on a sustained yield basis.

One should note the difference in the resource recovery programme described here and the one implied by our linear model in the previous section. If capital is perfectly malleable and if the resource is to be rebuilt, then the appropriate policy is to maintain a harvest moratorium until x has recovered to x^*. If, on the other hand, capital is non-malleable, then at most a short harvest moratorium will be appropriate. For the rest of the recovery programme it will be optimal to keep the fishery open and to use the existing fleet to capacity.

The above model has been fitted to data from the Antarctic baleen whale fishery (Clark and Lamberson, 1982). Biomass is measured in blue whale units (BWU), and capital in factory units (= one floating factory with associated fleet of catcher vessels). The model (with $\delta = 10$ per cent per annum) produces a long-run equilibrium involving approximately one unit of capital (and 110,000 BWU). From an unexploited biomass level of 400,000 BWU, the optimal initial capital investment is 13.5 factory units. The cycle from initial investment to equilibrium takes 31 years.[10] The actual development of this fishery (1925-81) is discussed in the reference. The fishery is currently under an IWC moratorium.

UNCERTAINTY IN FISHERIES ECONOMICS

The irreversible investment model described above, while indicating clearly the importance of fishery dynamics to the management problem, maintains a deterministic approach. It has long been observed, however, that fisheries, perhaps as much as any natural resource, exhibit remarkably high levels of uncertainty, arising from both economics and biological factors, and affecting not only the participants in the fishery but the resource managers as well. Hence it has seemed obvious that attempts should be made to incorporate uncertainty into fishery management models.

In this section we present a brief review of the literature on uncertainty in fisheries economics, and proceed to an examination of one particular example in this area, namely a stochastic version of the irreversible investment model outlined in the previous section.

Walters and Hilborn (1978) distinguish three general classes of uncertainty in fisheries management:

1. random effects, whose future frequency of occurrence can be determined from past experience;
2. parameter uncertainty, which can be reduced by research and acquisition of information through future experience;
3. ignorance about the appropriate variables to consider and the appropriate form of the model.

Most studies of the optimal management of fisheries under uncertainty have concentrated on the first type of uncertainty. Typically, the corresponding deterministic dynamics of the fishery are transformed to a stochastic analogue, and the resulting stochastic optimization problem is analysed using dynamic programming.

In a realistic multi-species, multi-cohort, multi-parameter fishery, stochastic effects can enter in a number of ways. Typically, the source of uncertainty is taken to be environmental fluctuations affecting the population dynamics of the fish stocks, although Lewis (1975) and Andersen (1982) allow for price variability as well. Dudley and Waugh (1980) study a simulation–optimization model in which yearly recruitment, mortality rate, and catchability fluctuate simultaneously. While fluctuations are usually taken to be independent from one point in time to another, they may in fact form a Markov process (Spulber, 1982). Each species or each age-cohort may respond to randomness differently (Mendelssohn, 1978, 1980; Spulber, 1982). Non-convexities and risk aversion can affect substantially the role of uncertainty (Lewis, 1981).

Andersen (1981) reviews research on the behaviour of competitive firms under uncertainty, and applies these results to optimal management of fishing firms faced with stock and price uncertainties. Pindyck (1982) examines the interaction of ecological uncertainty, demand elasticity, and the biomass growth function in the context of renewable resource markets, extending the analysis of the exhaustible resource case in Pindyck (1980). Optimal allocation of a randomly fluctuating fish stock between two fishing fleets is considered by Beddington and Clark (1984) and by McKelvey (1983).

Methods of solving stochastic optimization problems in fisheries management have also varied considerably. Jaquette (1972, 1974) and Reed (1974, 1978, 1982) used analytic approaches to study the effects of uncertainty on discrete-time dynamic programming models of fisheries. Walters (1975) and Walters and Hilborn (1976), using a dynamic programming approach with Kalman filter techniques, examined both stochastic effects and problems of parameter uncertainty. Beddington and May (1977) studied the effect of uncertainty on Maximum Sustainable Yield policies using characteristic return times and the coefficient of variation in fisheries yields. Ludwig (1979) formulated a continuous-time stochastic control model to which he applied perturbation techniques, while Ludwig and Varah (1979) used numerical methods to study the same model. Smith (1978) looked at continuous-time models where the optimal policy was not a bang-bang control. Mendelssohn and Sobel (1980) placed the fisheries problem in the context of capital accumulation and used discrete-time dynamic programming techniques to obtain theoretical results for a fairly general fisheries model. Both May *et al.* (1978) and Spulber (1982) have emphasized the role of steady-state probability distributions for optimally harvested fish stocks. Aron (1979) formulated and analysed a compromise harvesting policy which performed well according to a number of indicators and which in addition was robust to lack of knowledge of yearly biomass levels.

The above research has concentrated for the most part on normative optimization approaches. There is also a growing body of work in the areas of behavioural modelling with uncertainty (see, for example, Bockstael and Opaluch, 1983) and predictive modelling (Eswaran and Wilen, 1977). In addition, several researchers have begun to attack problems of parameter uncertainty in fisheries; this work is described at the end of this section. For more detailed surveys of the literature on fisheries under uncertainty, see Andersen and Sutinen (1984).

To provide a flavour for the problems involved in managing fisheries under uncertainty, we turn now to an examination of one particular stochastic fisheries model. This model, studied in detail by Charles (1982, 1983a, 1983b) extends the deterministic investment model of the previous section by incorporating stochastic fluctuations in the fish stock. In addition, the stochastic model is based on a seasonal (discrete-time) fishery, and allows for delays in bringing new investment on-line.

The population dynamics of a simple stochastic seasonal fishery can be described by a stock-recruitment relationship, where the biomass at the start of year n, R_n (the recruitment) is assumed to follow a probability distribution with mean $F(S_{n-1})$, where S_{n-1} is the biomass at the end of the previous year (the escapement) and $F(\cdot)$ is the underlying deterministic reproduction function. Apart from incorporation of a one-year delay in bringing investment on-line, the treatment of the capital stock is similar to that of Clark, Clarke, and Munro (1979); in particular, the irreversibility assumption is maintained. Capital investment remains a decision variable, but the second control is now taken to be end-of-year escapement.

The model can be summarized as follows:

Biomass dynamics: $R_n = F(S_{n-1}) \cdot Z_n$

Capital stock dynamics: $K_n = (1 - \gamma)K_{n-1} + I_n$

Escapement constraint: $R_n e^{-qTK_n} \leqslant S_n \leqslant R_n$

Investment constraint: $I_n \geqslant 0$

Rent function: $\pi(R_n, K_n, S_n, I_{n+1}) = p(R_n - S_n) - \dfrac{c}{q} \ln\left(\dfrac{R_n}{S_n}\right) - c_f I_{n+1}$

Objective: $\underset{(S_1, I_2, S_2, \ldots)}{\max.} \ \left[\Sigma_{n=1}^{\infty} \ \alpha^{n-1} \tilde{E}\{\pi(R_n, K_n, S_n, I_{n+1})\}\right].$

The random variables (Z_n) are assumed to be independent and identically distributed. For our purposes, they will be assumed to follow a lognormal distribution with mean 1 and known variance. The parameters p, c, q, c_f and γ are as defined in the preceding section. The discount factor α is given by $\alpha = 1/(1 + \delta)$, and T is the maximum feasible season length. The expectation operator is E. There is an implicit assumption in the model that during the course of the nth fishing season the biomass is governed by $dx/dt = -qE(t)x(t)$, with $x(0) = R_n$ and the instantaneous fishing effort $E(t)$ subject to $0 \leqslant E(t) \leqslant K_n$.

This model can be solved numerically using a dynamic programming approach. To understand the effects of introducing randomness, it is first necessary to examine the corresponding deterministic model. This is done in Charles (1982, 1983a), where the numerical method is described and comparative dynamics results obtained for the cases of instantaneous and delayed investment.

The instantaneous case differs from that of Clark, Clarke, and Munro (1979) solely in the use of discrete time. The primary result is that a sudden impulse investment at x^* is no longer optimal; instead, a more gradual approach to the long-run equilibrium is desired, reflecting the possibility of harvesting for part of the season in years when investment in the resource stock is occurring.

The introduction of delays in investment necessitates advance planning of the investment, so that the decision regarding new vessels desired for next year must be made this year. This tends to increase the uncertainty in capital investment planning (but is only a change in accounting procedure for the deterministic case). Figure 3.4 (from Charles, 1982) illustrates the optimal policies for a discrete-time fishery with delayed investment; sample trajectories are also shown. Note that, as in Clark, Clarke and Munro, there are three regions to consider. In regions R_3 and R_2 harvesting takes place, driving the resource stock down towards the target $s(K)$, while in R_1 no harvesting takes place. Investment occurs only for escapements lying in R_3, with $h(S)$ representing the optimal capacity for next year's fleet given escapement S this season.

The effect of delayed investment is in fact more noticeable for fast-growing resource stocks, where a fourth management regime is possible, in which the resource stock is too low to warrant harvesting, but is expected to recover sufficiently over the 'investment delay' period to make investment desirable given a low current capital stock.

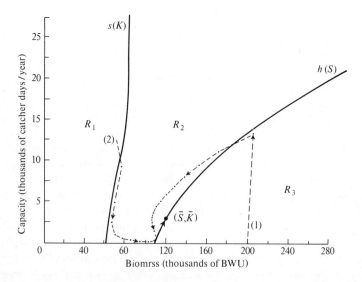

FIG. 3.4 The optimal fleet capacity $h(S)$, as a function of escapement S, and the target escapement $s(K)$, as a function of fleet capacity K, are shown for a (slow-growing) whale fishery with delayed investment. The long-run equilibrium and two sample trajectories are also indicated. In trajectory (1) investment occurs initially in the resource as well as in the capital stock, so that at the outset the trajectory moves upwards and to the right.

The introduction of uncertainty, in the form of random fluctuations, changes the position but not the structure of the optimal policy functions shown in figure 3.4. The optimal policy curves for a fast-growing stochastic fishery are shown in figure 3.5. The point marked on the optimal capacity curve $h(S)$ represents the location of the long-run equilibrium *if* the fishery were deterministic. In the stochastic case, however, the fishery will not rest in equilibrium. Figure 3.5 indicates a sample fifteen-year outcome for this *optimally managed* fishery; the four processes of investment, depreciation, harvesting, and stochastic recruitment combine to determine the fishery dynamics, governed by the policy curves $s(K)$ and $h(S)$. The end-points of each arrow represent end-of-season escapement and fleet capacity values. Clearly, both the resource stock and the capital stock can be expected to fluctuate considerably.

The qualitative effect of randomness on the optimal management of a fishery depends very much on the growth rate of the resource stock, and on the ratio of unit capital (fixed) costs to variable costs. It can be shown analytically (Charles, 1982) that, for a sufficiently fast-growing stock, the optimal fleet capacity increases with the level of uncertainty, decreases with the unit cost

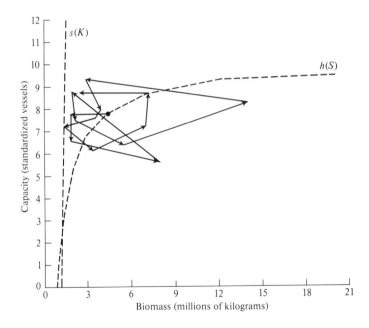

FIG. 3.5 The effect of stochastic fluctuations on the optimal management of the base-case prawn fishery is shown for a sample fifteen-year outcome, governed by the policy curves indicated. End-points of arrows represent end-of-season escapement and capital stock values (*S, K*). While deterministic trajectories converge upon a long-run equilibrium point, in the stochastic case it appears that a two-dimensional steady-state distribution is eventually approached. (From Charles, 1983b.)

of capital (for fixed unit variable cost), but is always greater than the deterministic optimum. On the other hand, the optimal fleet capacity for a slow-growing fishery with a high ratio of fixed costs to variable costs is lower with uncertainty than without. These results are summarized in table 3.1.

TABLE 3.1

	Low cost of capital	*High cost of capital*
Slow-growing resource	Stochastic optimal capacity $\geq$ deterministic optimum	Stochastic optimal capacity $<$ deterministic optimum
Fast-growing resource	Stochastic optimal capacity $>$ deterministic optimum	Stochastic optimal capacity $\geq$ deterministic optimum

The variations in optimal fleet capacity under uncertainty relative to optimal capacity under certainty, as summarized in the table, have a straightforward explanation. The advantage of a large fleet capacity in an uncertain world lies in the fact that it permits one to take advantage of exceptionally large recruitments. The disadvantage, however, is that during periods of low recruitment a significant portion of the fleet will lie idle.

For a given ratio of fixed to variable costs, the advantages of a large fleet capacity are particularly great when both the harvest opportunities provided by exceptionally large recruitments and the harvest consequences of exceptionally low recruitments are short-lived. This will be true when the resource is fast growing. In fact, for sufficiently fast growing resources the optimal capacity under uncertainty will *never be less* than the optimal capacity under certainty, even if the ratio of fixed to variable costs is high.

For a given rate of resource growth, the greater will be the penalty for having idle capacity, the greater is the ratio of fixed (or unavoidable) to variable (avoidable) costs. Thus, for relatively slow-growing resources, the optimal capacity under uncertainty will be less than that under certainty, when the ratio of fixed to variable costs is sufficiently high.

Using data drawn from the Australian Gulf of Carpenteria prawn fishery (Clark and Kirkwood, 1979), it was found that, for the prawn fishery's moderately high level of variability, the relative difference between the stochastic and deterministic optimal capacity curves could reach 30–40 per cent. Use of deterministic policies, which neglect the stochastic nature of the resource, can therefore result in substantial over- or under-investment in fleet capacity, particularly for initial investments in developing fisheries. Target escapements, on the other hand, tend to be less sensitive to the level of uncertainty in the fishery: this is in agreement with previous results. Examples of optimal investment and escapement policies, comparing the deterministic and stochastic cases, are shown in figure 3.6.

While these results indicate that optimal stochastic and deterministic investment

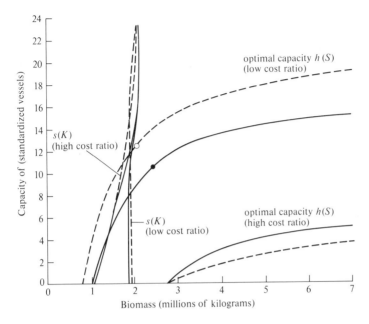

FIG. 3.6 For a fixed (moderate) biomass growth rate, and for each of two capital cost–operating cost ratios, optimal fleet capacity and optimal escapement target curves are shown for deterministic ($\sigma = 0$, solid lines) and stochastic ($\sigma = 0.58$, broken lines) cases. Long-run equilibrium points (or, in stochastic cases, points where such equilibrium would occur in the absence of fluctuations) are also shown. Note that, when capital is relatively cheap, the optimal capacity is higher under uncertainty, while the reverse is true with relatively expensive capital. The optimal escapement curves, while appearing to be rather complicated, differ little between the deterministic and stochastic cases.

policies can differ considerably, it is also of interest to examine the extent to which stochastic strategies actually out-perform their deterministic counterparts. This is bound to depend on such factors as the degree of randomness in the fishery, the fishing cost function, and the management objectives. In particular, it has been shown that use of stochastic strategies can be particularly important given decreasing marginal fishing costs (Lewis, 1981), risk aversion, or the desire to avoid low resource stock sizes (Walters and Hilborn, 1978, and references therein). However, numerical results for the above model (Charles, 1983b) indicate that use of the deterministic strategy rather than the stochastic strategy reduces the expected present value of economic rents by only a few percentage points. This may be the norm for models that are 'not too nonlinear' and that use an expected rent maximization objective— see Ludwig (1980). In such cases, economic optimization is 'forgiving', in the sense that investment policies can be altered (within limits) to achieve secondary objectives without substantial loss of economic rents. Considerable research remains to be done in order properly to characterize those situations where stochastic effects are most important to fisheries management.

While less research has been undertaken on the other two areas of uncertainty, those of parameter uncertainty and 'basic ignorance', they may prove to be even more significant in managing our fisheries.

Optimization models in these areas involve both random fluctuations and subjective probability distributions for unknown parameters. The role of 'passive' or 'inactive' learning must also be considered, since inherent lack of knowledge can be cured partially through fishing experience. The reader should consult Walters and Hilborn (1978), Charles (1983c), Ludwig and Walters (1982), Mangel and Clark (1983), and references therein for detailed discussion and results on the question of parameter uncertainty. The problem of 'basic ignorance' has been subject to less study, but the resilience concept of Holling (1973) and the robust optimization model of Aron (1979) are of interest in this area.

Certainly the problem of uncertainty is central to fisheries management and fisheries regulation. Research in this field will undoubtedly provide new, important insights in the future.

CONCLUSIONS

We have argued that the major development in fisheries economics at the beginning of the 1970s was the decisive shift away from static to dynamic analysis. Perhaps the major benefit of this shift was that it placed economists in a position to analyse effectively what might be termed adjustment or disequilibrium phases of fisheries management programmes.

Considerations of dynamics lead naturally to a consideration of the problems raised by uncertainty. We would predict that much of the work in fisheries economics during the coming decade will be in the realm of uncertainty.

A major omission from our discussion has been the economics of fisheries regulations. This reflects not our lack of interest in the subject, but rather our desire not to overlap with other papers in this volume which will be addressing the subject in detail.

NOTES

1. There are now a large number of different treatments of deterministic dynamic fisheries models: see, for example: Brown (1974), Dasgupta and Heal (1979), Levhari *et al.* (1981), Long (1976), Neher (1974), Peterson and Fisher (1977), V. L. Smith (1977).
2. If $\alpha \neq 1$, the model would not be linear.
3. Let
$$Z(x) = \int_{x_\infty}^{x} \{p - c(y)\} dy,$$
where x_∞ is the solution of $c(x) = p$, and let
$$V(x) = \{p - c(x)\} F(x) - \delta Z(x).$$
Then, noting that $h = F(x) - \dot{x}$ and integrating by parts, the objective becomes

$$\max \int_0^\infty e^{-\delta t} V\{x(t)\}\mathrm{d}t.$$

Suppose $V(x)$ has a unique maximum at x^*; then it can be shown that x^* is the target biomass and that equation (14) follows by differentiation.

4. Another example of joint exploitation of a fishery arises in the case of a fishery shared by commercial and sports fishermen. See Bishop and Samples (1980) and McConnell and Sutinen (1979).
5. See the following section.
6. Fishing effort, E is used as a control variable as an alternative to h.
7. Note that unit harvest cost as defined in earlier parts of the paper, $c(x)$, is equal to $c_{\text{total}}/(qx)$.
8. We might suppose, for example, that a once-for-all change in the landed price of fish transforms a commercially unexploitable fishery into an exploitable one.
9. In our example the initial investment in fleet capacity was sufficient to reduce the stock to $\bar{x}$. There is, of course, no necessary reason why this should be so.
10. The switching curves σ_1 and σ_2 are obtained numerically; a computer program for this calculation is on file at the UBC Computing Centre.

REFERENCES

Andersen, P. (1981), 'Selected Aspects of the Behavior of the Competitive Firm under Uncertainty with Application to the Fishing Firm and Comments on the Competitive Industry', paper presented to the Workshop on Uncertainty and Fisheries Economics, University of Rhode Island.

Andersen, P. (1982), 'Commercial Fisheries under Price Uncertainty', *Journal of Environmental Economics and Management,* 9, 11–28.

Andersen, P. and Sutinen, J. G. (1984), 'A Survey of Stochastic Bioeconomics: Methods and Results', Marine Resource Economics, 1, 117–36.

Anderson, L. G. (1977), *The Economics of Fisheries Management,* Baltimore: Johns Hopkins University Press.

Aron, J. L. (1979), 'Harvesting a Protected Population in an Uncertain Environment', *Mathematical Biosciences,* 47, 197–205.

Arrow, K. J. (1968), 'Optimal Capital Policy with Irreversible Investment', in J. N. Wolfe (ed.), *Value, Capital and Growth: Papers in Honour of Sir John Hicks.* Edinburgh University Press.

Baker, D. M. (1980), 'The Capital Development Fund: A Capital Assistant Plan for Fishermen', Report prepared for the Government of Canada Department of Fisheries and Oceans, Halifax.

Beddington, J. R. and Clark, C. W. (1984), 'Allocation Problems between National and Foreign Fisheries with a Fluctuating Fish Resource', Marine Resource Economics, 1, 137–54.

Beddington, J. R. and May, R. M. (1977), 'Harvesting Natural Populations in a Randomly Fluctuating Environment', *Science,* 197, 463–5.

Bishop, R. C. and Samples, K. C. (1980), 'Sport and Commerical Fishing Conflicts: A Theoretical Analysis', *Journal of Environmental Economics and Management,* 7, 220–33.

Bockstael, N. E. and Opaluch, J. J. (1983), 'Discrete modelling of supply response under uncertainty: The case of the fishery', *Journal of Environmental Economics and Management,* 10, 125–37.

Brown, G. Jr. (1974), 'An Optimal Program for Managing Common Property Resources with Congestion Externalities', *Journal of Political Economy*, 82, 163–74.

Charles, A. T. (1982), 'Optimal fisheries investment', PhD dissertation, University of British Columbia, Vancouver.

Charles, A. T. (1983a), 'Optimal Fisheries Investment: Comparative Dynamics for a

Deterministic Seasonal Fisher', *Canadian Journal of Fisheries and Aquatic Sciences*, 40, 2069–79.

Charles, A. T. (1983b), 'Optimal Fisheries Investment under Uncertainty', *Canadian Journal of Fisheries and Aquatic Sciences,* 40, 2080–91.

Charles, A. T. (1983c), 'Effects of Parameter Uncertainty and Bayesian Updating on Fisheries Investment', University of British Columbia Institute of Applied Mathematics and Statistics, Report no. 83-2.

Charles, A. T. and Munro, G. R. (1981), 'Irreversible Investment and Optimal Fisheries Management: A Stochastic Analysis', presented to the Workshop on Uncertainty and Fisheries Economics, University of Rhode Island, November 1981.

Clark, C. W. (1976), *Mathematical Bioeconomics: The Optimal Management of Renewable Resources.* New York: Wiley-Interscience.

Clark, C. W., Clarke, F. H., and Munro, G. R. (1979), 'The Optimal Exploitation of Renewable Resource Stocks: Problems of Irreversible Investment', *Econometrica,* 47, 25–47.

Clark, C. W. and Kirkwood, G. P. (1979), 'Bioeconomic Model of the Gulf of Carpenteria Prawn Fishery', *Journal of the Fisheries Research Board of Canada*, 36, 1304–12.

Clark, C. W. and Lamberson, R. H. (1982), 'An Economic History and Analysis of Pelagic Whaling', *Marine Policy.*

Clark, C. W. and Munro, G. R. (1975), 'The Economics of Fishing and Modern Capital Theory: A Simplified Approach', *Journal of Environmental Economics and Management,* 2, 92–106.

Crutchfield, J. and Zellner, A. (1962), 'Economic Aspects of the Pacific Halibut Fishery', US Department of the Interior, *Fishery Industrial Research*, 1:1.

Dasgupta, P. S. and Heal, G. M. (1979), *Economic Theory and Exhaustible Resources.* Cambridge University Press.

Dudley, N. and Waugh, G. (1980), 'Exploitation of a Single-cohort Fishery under Risk: A Simulation–Optimization Approach', *Journal of Environmental Economics and Management,* 7, 234–55.

Eswaran, M. and Wilen, J. E. (1977), 'Expectations and Adjustment in Open Access Resource Use', University of British Columbia, PNRE Paper no. 10.

Gordon, H. S. (1954), 'The Economic Theory of a Common-property Resource: The Fishery', *Journal of Political Economy,* 62, 124–42.

Gordon, H. S. (1956), 'Obstacles to Agreement on Control in the Fishing Industry', in R. Turvey and J. Wiseman (eds), *The Economics of Fisheries,* Rome: FAO, 65–72.

Gulland, J. A. (1980), 'Some Problems of the Management of Shared Stocks', *FAO Fisheries Technical Paper,* 206.

Holling, C. W. (1973), 'Resilience and Stability of Ecological Systems', *Annual Review of Ecology and Systemetics,* 4, 1–23.

Jaquette, D. L. (1972), 'A Discrete Time Population Control Model', *Mathematical Biosciences,* 15, 231–52.

Jaquette, D. L. (1974), 'A Discrete Time Population Control Model with Setup Cost', *Operations Research,* 22, 298–303.

Levhari, D., Michener, R., and Mirman, L. J. (1981), 'Dynamic Programming Models of Fisheries', *American Economic Review,* 71, 649–61.

Lewis, T. R. (1975), 'Optimal Resource Management under Conditions of Uncertainty: The Case of an Ocean Fishery', PhD dissertation, University of California at San Diego.

Lewis, T. R. (1981), 'Exploitation of a Renewable Resource under Uncertainty', *Canadian Journal of Economics,* 14, 422–39.

Long, N. V. (1976), 'Optimal Exploitation and Replenishment of a Natural Resource', in J. Pitchford and S. Turnovsky (eds), *Applications of Control Theory to Economic Analysis*, Amsterdam: North Holland, 81–106.

Ludwig, D. (1979), 'Optimal Harvesting of a Randomly Fluctuating Resource, I: Application of Perturbation Methods', *SIAM Journal of Applied Mathematics,* 37, 166–84.

Ludgwig, D. (1980), 'Harvesting Strategies for a Randomly Fluctuating Population', *Journal du Conseil International pour l'exploration de la Mer,* 39, 168–74.

Ludwig, D. and Varah, J. M. (1979), 'Optimal Harvesting of a Randomly Fluctuating Resource, II: Numerical Methods and Results', *SIAM Journal of Applied Mathematics,* 37, 185–205.

Ludwig, D. and Walters, C. J. (1982), 'Optimal Harvesting with Imprecise Parameter Estimates', *Ecological Modelling*, 14, 273–92.

Mangel, M. and Clark (1983), 'Uncertainty, search and information in fisheries', *Journal du Conseil International pour l'Exploration de la Mer*, 41, 98–103.

May, R. M., Beddington, J. R., Horwood, J. W. and Shepherd, J. G. (1978), 'Exploiting Natural Populations in an Uncertain World', *Mathematical Biosciences*, 42, 219–52.

McConnell, K. E. and Sutinen, J. G. (1979), 'Bioeconomic Models of Marine Recreational Fisheries', *Journal of Environmental Economics and Management*, 6, 125–39.

McKelvey, R. (1983), 'The Fishery in a Fluctuating Environment: Optimal Co-existence of Specialist and Generalist Fishing Vessels in a Multi-purpose Fleet', *Journal of Environmental Economics and Management* 10, 287–309.

Mendelssohn, R. (1978), 'Optimal Harvesting Strategies for Stochastic Single-species, Multi-age Class Models', *Mathematical Biosciences*, 41, 159–74.

Mendelssohn, R. (1980), 'Managing Stochastic Multispecies Models', *Mathematical Biosciences*, 49, 249–61.

Mendelssohn, R. and Sobel, M. J. (1980), 'Capital Accumulation and the Optimization of Renewable Resource Models', *Journal of Economic Theory*, 23, 243–60.

Munro, G. R. (1979), 'Optimal Management of Transboundary Renewable Resources', *Canadian Journal of Economics*, 12, 355–76.

Neher, P. A. (1974), 'Notes on the Volterra Quadratic Fishery', *Journal of Economic Theory*, 6, 39–49.

Pella, J. J. and Tomlinson, P. K. (1969), 'A Generalized Stock Production Model', *Bulletin of the Inter-American Tropical Tuna Commission*, 13, 421–96.

Peterson, F. M. and Fisher, A. C. (1977), 'The Exploitation of Extractive Resources: A Survey', *Economic Journal*, 87, 681–721.

Pindyck, R. S. (1980), 'Uncertainty and Exhaustible Resource Markets', *Journal of Political Economy*, 88, 1203–25.

Pindyck, R. S. (1982), 'Uncertainty in the Theory of Renewable Resource Markets', Review of Economic Studies, 51, 289–303.

Plourde, G. C. (1970), 'A Simple Model of a Replenishable Resource Exploitation, *American Economic Review*, 60, 518–22.

Plourde, G. C. (1971), 'Exploitation of a Common-property Replenishable Resource', *Western Economic Journal*, 9, 256–66.

Quirk, J. P. and Smith, V. L. (1970), 'Dynamic Economic Models of Fishing', in A. D. Scott (ed.), *Economics of Fisheries Management: A Symposium*, University of British Columbia Institute for Animal Resource Ecology, Report no. 3-32.

Reed, W. J. (1974), 'A Stochastic Model for the Economic Management of a Renewable Resource', *Mathematical Biosciences*, 22, 313–37.

Reed, W. J. (1978), 'The Steady State of a Stochastic Harvesting Model', *Mathematical Biosciences*, 41, 273–307.

Reed, W. J. (1982), 'Sex-selective Harvesting of Pacific Salmon: a Theoretically Optimal Solution', *Ecological Modelling*, 14, 261–71.

Schaefer, M. B. (1957), 'Some Considerations of Population Dynamics and Economics in Relation to the Management of Marine Fisheries', *Journal of Fisheries Research Board of Canada*, 14, 669–81.

Scott, A. D. (1955), 'The Fishery: The Objectives of Sole-ownership', *Journal of Political Economy*, 63, 116–24.

Smith, J. B. (1978), 'An Analysis of Optimal Replenishable Resource Management under Uncertainty', PhD dissertation, University of Western Ontario.

Smith, V. L. (1977), 'Control Theory Applied to Natural and Environmental Resources: An Exposition', *Journal of Environmental Economics and Management*, 4, 1–24.

Spulber, D. F. (1982), 'Adaptive Harvesting of a Renewable Resource and Stable Equilibrium', in L. J. Mirman and D. F. Spulber (eds), *Essays in the Economics of Renewable Resources*, Amsterdam: North-Holland, 117–39.

Walters, C. J. (1975), 'Optimal Harvest Strategies for Salmon in Relation to Environmental Variability and Uncertain Production Parameters', *Journal of the Fisheries Research Board of Canada*, 32, 1777–85.

Walters, C. J. and Hilborn, R. (1976), 'Adaptive Control of Fishing Systems', *Journal of the Fisheries Research Board of Canada*, 33, 145–59.
Walters, C. J. and Hilborn, R. (1978), 'Ecological Optimization and Adaptive Management', *Annual Review of Ecology and Systematics*, 9, 157–88.

Comment   Daniel F. Spulber

INTRODUCTION

Random environmental disturbances such as variation in climate, ocean currents, water temperature, available food supply, predators, and the presence of competing species have significant effects on the growth of fish populations. In a dynamic optimization framework, these disturbances affect optimal harvesting policies as well as the long-run state of the natural population. If we let x_t describe the natural population at date t and w_t represent the environmental disturbance at date t, the growth of the natural population may be represented in discrete time by a growth function g:

$$x_{t+1} = g(x_t, w_{t+1}). \tag{1}$$

The stock x_t and disturbance w_{t+1} may be vectors. As noted by Clark, Munro, and Charles above, 'most studies of the optimal management of fisheries under uncertainty' have concentrated on random effects with a known probability distribution. We will examine some of these studies.

In a dynamic optimization problem, the focus of the analysis is upon whether the system approaches a steady state and, if a steady state is attained, upon what the characteristics of the steady state are. In deterministic models, characterizing the steady state involves a complete description of the resource stock. While there may be multiple steady states, the characteristics of the stock at a steady state remain invariant over time. For a resource not subject to harvesting, the population may attain a natural equilibrium. For various harvesting strategies, stable yields and resource stock levels may or may not be attained. In population biology, the effect of uncertainty on natural populations has been widely studied. There, the equilibrium concept is a time-independent probability distribution on population size. This is the analogue in a stochastic setting of the steady-state or equilibrium population level. As May (1974, p. 110) emphasizes, '[The] equilibrium probability distribution is to the stochastic environment as the stable equilibrium point is to the deterministic one.'

The time-independent probability distribution on population size may also be examined in a model of a natural population subject to harvesting. For harvested fish populations, deterministic models have focused upon the equilibrium concepts of maximal sustained yield and optimal sustained yield. *In economic models of resource harvesting, the stochastic analogue of the sustained yield equilibrium is the time-invariant probability distribution on harvest levels.*

To examine the existence, stability, and characteristics of the steady-state probability distribution on harvests and population size, the properties of the harvesting rule, of the biological growth function, and of the distribution of environmental disturbances must be studied. The harvesting rule need not be the outcome of an optimization procedure; it may simply be a description of behaviour resulting from market forces affecting free access, regulation, or simple rules of thumb. In what follows we focus on rules that are chosen to maximize the expected present discounted value of the resource.

LUMPED PARAMETER MODELS UNDER UNCERTAINTY

Stochastic growth

A large literature on one-sector growth with a stochastic production function like (1) examines optimal consumption and investment decisions and the steady state of the economy. The discrete-time formulation is considered by Brock and Mirman (1972), Mirman (1972, 1973), Mirman and Zilcha (1975), Schechtman (1976), and Schechtman and Escudero (1977). In these models, a social planner maximizes utility of the consumption of the stock in each period. The concave utility function u is easily reinterpreted as a net consumer's surplus measure for a planner managing a renewable resource stock in a partial equilibrium setting. Let h_t denote the harvest at date t, let $p(\cdot)$ denote the market inverse demand, and let $c'(\cdot)$ denote marginal harvesting costs when costs are not stock-dependent. The objective function is then

$$u(h_t) = \int_0^{h_t} \{p(s) - c'(s)\} ds. \tag{2}$$

If harvests are the result of effort e_t devoted to fishing at date t, $k(e_t)$ is the effort cost function, and

$$h_t = f(e_t, x_t) \tag{3}$$

describes the yield–effort relation, then harvesting costs will be stock-dependent. Assuming that f is invertible in e_t for all x_t, then

$$e_t = f^{-1}(\cdot, x_t)(h_t)$$

so that harvesting costs are defined by

$$c(h_t, x_t) \equiv k\{f^{-1}(\cdot, x_t)(h_t)\}. \tag{4}$$

Let $c_1(h_t, x_t) = \partial c(h_t, x_t)/\partial h_t$. Then the stochastic growth problem is easily generalized to allow stock-dependent harvesting costs:

$$u(h_t, x_t) = \int_0^{h_t} \{p(s) - c_h(s, x_t)\} ds. \tag{5}$$

A utility function that depends upon the decision-maker's action as well as on the state of the system and the random disturbance is examined in an infinite-horizon dynamic programming formulation by Easley and Spulber (1981). All of the analyses discussed above obtain optimal stock-dependent policy functions. Mendelssohn and Sobel (1980) bring together much of the literature on capital accumulation and renewable resource management under uncertainty in a unified framework. To permit renewable resource applications, they allow a stock-dependent single-period utility function, and avoid imposing strict concavity on the utility function. In addition, they do not impose Inada-type conditions on the growth or stock transition equation permitting linear or quadratic forms, and they consider the possibility of corner solutions at which resource constraints become effective. This approach allows analysis in a unified framework of stock-dependent harvesting policies, which may resemble either optimal growth rules or inventory-type stock adjustment functions.

Dynamic capital theory with growth uncertainty in a continuous-time formulation has been examined by Bourguignon (1974), Merton (1975), Bismut (1975), and others. Similar analyses have been performed for renewable resource models of Gleit (1978) and Ludwig (1979) employing stochastic calculus. As with the discrete-time models, these models obtain state-dependent or 'closed-loop' harvesting policies.

For a different approach, where the regulating authority may control variance in the producer price, see Andersen (1982). He assumes that the biological growth function is deterministic and focuses attention on comparative static effects of price uncertainty.

Consider now a discrete-time formulation under uncertainty. Let the disturbance w be distributed on the positive real line with Lebesque measure. This is permitted by the general form of the growth function $g(x, w)$ but can easily be generalized to an arbitrary cumulative distribution function. Here (w_t) is taken as a sequence of independent and identically distributed disturbances, but the discussion may be easily generalized to allow for Markovian disturbances. Employing the recursive equation of stochastic dynamic programming, the value of the current stock of fish x is given by

$$V(x) = \max_{h} \left[\int_0^h \{p(s) - c(s, x)\}ds + \left(\frac{1}{1+r}\right)\int_{\mathbb{R}} V\{g(x-h, w)\}dw \right]. \tag{6}$$

The first-order condition for the harvesting problem in (6) is

$$p(h) - c_h(h, w) = \frac{1}{1+r}\int_{\mathbb{R}} V'\{g(x-h, w)\}g_x(x-h, w)dw \tag{7}$$

where $h = h(x)$ solves (7) and defines the optimal harvesting policy. Applying (7) and the envelope theorem to (6), we obtain the marginal valuation of the current stock,

$$V'(x) = p(h) - c_h(h, x) - c_x(h, x). \tag{8}$$

Let $\check{x} = g(x - h, w)$ and $\bar{h} = h(\check{x})$. Then, employing (7) and (8) and rearranging terms, we obtain

$$\int_{\mathbb{R}} g_x(x-h, w)dw$$
$$+ \frac{\int_{\mathbb{R}} g_x\left[\bar{p}(\tilde{h}) - c_h(\tilde{h}, \tilde{x}) - c_x(\tilde{h}, \tilde{x}) - \{p(h) - c_h(h, x)\}\right] g_x(x-h, w)dw}{p(h) - c_h(h, x)}$$

$$= 1 + r. \tag{9}$$

This is the stochastic analogue of the fundamental deterministic equation (see Clark, Munro, and Charles above, eqn (11) and Clark, 1976, eqn (7.60), p. 245). The first term is the *expected marginal growth* of the resource given the escapement $x - h$ and the range of environmental disturbances w. The second term is the stochastic equivalent of the marginal stock effect, (see Clark, Munro and Charles above), that is, the *expected rate of return to conservation of the resource*. Suppose the decision-maker takes the market price p as given. Then (9) becomes

$$\int_{\mathbb{R}} g_x(x-h, w)dw$$
$$+ \frac{\int_{\mathbb{R}} \{-c_h(\tilde{h}, \tilde{x}) - c_x(\tilde{h}, \tilde{x}) + c_h(h, x)\}g_x(x-h, w)dw}{p - c_h(h, x)} = 1 + r \tag{10}$$

which is similar to the deterministic discrete-time model in Clark (1976). The term $c_x(h, x)$ is essentially a *user cost* of the resource, similar to that observed in non-renewable resource problems. Thus, the marginal stock effect is a rate of return corrected for user costs.

The nonlinearity of the growth function, market inverse demand, and harvesting cost function will introduce significant effects of uncertainty on the resource policy $h(x)$ that solves (9). In addition, uncertainty will have significant effects on resource growth, where the dynamic growth process is given by the Markov process (x_t),

$$x_{t+1} = g\{x_t - h(x_t), w_t\} \tag{11}$$

for (w_t) independent and identically distributed. For (w_t) Markovian, (x_t, w_t) together form a Markov process where the sequence (x_t) follows the dynamic equation

$$x_{t+1} = g\{x_t - h(x_t, w_t), w_{t+1}\}. \tag{12}$$

Inventory adjustment

Many analyses of renewable resource management problems are extensions of the stock adjustment or inventory models in economics and operations research. The origins of the large field of study of inventory adjustment may be examined in Arrow, Karlin, and Scarf (1958), Arrow, Karlin, and Suppes (1960) and

Scarf, Gilford, and Shelly (1963). A stochastic dynamic programming formulation in discrete time is employed by Jaquette (1972b, 1974) and Reed (1974,
1978, 1979). See Jaquette (1972a) for an early survey of control models for
biological populations under uncertainty. In the analyses of Jaquette and of
Reed, harvesting costs are linear in harvesting, and a fixed set-up harvesting
cost is incurred in each period in which harvesting is positive. This framework
is used to obtain (S, s) policies where S is the optimal unconstrained escapement and s is the minimum population required for harvesting to be profitable.
The minimum population that must be exceeded for harvesting to be profitable equals the optimal escapement S (an S policy) when set-up costs are zero.
With a linear objective and zero fixed costs, Mendelssohn and Sobel (1980)
generalize the conditions under which an S policy is optimal. In particular,
the growth relation may be pseudo-concave and continuous if additional restrictions are placed upon the form of the distribution of the independent
and identically distributed disturbances.

Spulber (1982) generalizes the stock adjustment model to allow for Markovian
environmental disturbances and shows the existence of a state-dependent (S, s)
harvesting policy which is referred to as pulse-fishing. Given a disturbance w_t
and a current resource stock $y_t = g(x_{t-1}, w_t)$, the harvesting policy has the form

$$h_t = \begin{cases} 0 & \text{if} \quad y_t \leqslant s(w_t) \\ \\ y_t - S(w_t) & \text{if} \quad y_t > s(w_t) \end{cases} \tag{13}$$

where $0 \leqslant S(w_t) \leqslant s(w_t) \leqslant \bar{x}$ and $\bar{x}$ is the maximum population size.

Steady-state distributions on the population level

In models of growth and of renewable resource management, the question of
primary importance is the nature of the long-run behaviour of the stock subject
to consumption or harvesting policies. The models of growth under uncertainty
of Brock and Mirman (1972), Mirman (1972) and Mirman and Zilcha (1975)
demonstrate convergence of the transition probability on capital stock levels
to a unique steady-state probability distribution, given optimal consumption
and investment decisions. Mirman (1973) considers a set of 'positive' models
of economic growth under uncertainty and defines a set of admissible consumption policies associated with these models which will result in the existence,
uniqueness, and stability of a steady-state probability distribution on capital
stocks. The analysis in Mirman (1973) focuses upon Doeblin's condition as
stated in Doob (1953) and demonstrates convergence to a unique steady-state
distribution for a very wide class of consumption policies. Mirman's framework
should allow examination of the ergodic properties of transition probabilities
on fishery stocks when managers apply various rules of thumb in a consistent
manner over time.

On the steady state of a stochastic harvesting model see Reed (1978).
Mendelssohn and Sobel (1980) also consider convergence to a steady state when

stationary consumption policies are followed by examining the properties of the stochastic kernel describing the probability of being within a set of states in the next period, given the decision-maker's action in the current period. Easley and Spulber (1981) consider an ϵ-optimal rolling plan and show convergence to a stochastic equilibrium for a more general constraint correspondence and transition equation by employing the differentiability of the rolling plan. Their approach involves a demonstration that the stochastic process on the states of the system can be restricted to a collection of disjoint, invariant sets. The rolling plan approach of Easley and Spulber might yield interesting insights if applied to renewable resource management models. The fishery regulator may face legal constraints or high planning expenses, which may force him to adopt a rolling planning horizon.

All of the models discussed above assume independent and identically distributed environmental disturbances when examining the stationary state of the system. Spulber (1982) introduces Markovian environmental disturbances and demonstrates that pulse-fishing or (S, s) harvesting policies imply convergence to a unique steady-state probability distribution on the population size. (See also Spulber, 1981a, b for the multi-cohort problem.) When pulse-fishing harvesting policies are employed the fish population periodically exceeds the optimal size for harvesting, and is then harvested down to the optimal escapement. Pulse-fishing thus ensures that the optimal escapement level is a *recurrent state* for the stochastic process of escapement levels. This result may be used to demonstrate convergence to a steady-state distribution on the size of the fish population when the sequence of environmental disturbances exhibits a recurrent state. Spulber then considers how biological and economic parameters affect the form of the steady-state probability distribution. A logistic growth equation is examined for the cases of a random intrinsic growth rate and a random environmental carrying capacity. The effects of the interest rate and the parameters of the distribution of environmental disturbances on expected harvests and on the optimal escapement are analysed.

Empirical and numerical simulation studies

Any survey of renewable resources harvesting under uncertainty must include the important analyses of Lewis (1975, 1981). Lewis (1981) presents a dynamic programming decision model in which the population dynamics are represented by a finite-state Markov process. The model is fitted to data from the Eastern Pacific yellowfin tuna fishery. The effect of uncertainty on optimal strategies and on the performance of certainty-equivalent strategies is analysed.

There is a large literature on the biological effects of harvesting under uncertainty that must be emphasized; see Beddington and May (1977) and May *et al.* (1978, 1979) for extensive references. Fishery dynamics under uncertainty are examined for the North Atlantic Cod fishery by Hannesson (1975). Hanneson carries out an empirical investigation in a stochastic dynamic framework.

J. B. Smith (1980) presents a stochastic differential model of the growth process for the US northern lobster fishery. This paper is of special interest because of its characterization of the stochastic steady-state distribution on stock sizes. Smith's paper comments on the methodology and results of Bell (1972) and, using data similar to Bell's, estimates the stochastic growth equation of the population subject to harvesting. While Smith's and Bell's estimates differ, they both find excessive fishing effort at the steady state.

MULTIPLE PARAMETER MODELS

Economic growth

If a fishery manager may selectively harvest each cohort in a multi-cohort harvesting problem, the structure of the problem is similar to a multi-sector model of economic growth. Brock and Majumdar (1978) present a stochastic turnpike theorem for a multi-sector growth model which depends upon a stochastic version of deterministic curvature conditions discussed by McKenzie (1976) using value loss techniques and by Cass and Shell (1976) in a Hamiltonian framework. The curvature condition (assumption A4, Brock and Majumdar, 1978, p. 234) involves conditions applied jointly to the utility function, production function and discount rate. This condition may not be satisfied by harvesting profit functions and biological growth functions. The multi-sector growth model is not applicable to multi-parameter renewable resource management problems when selective harvesting is not possible.

Renewable resource models

There are many renewable resource management problems that require a multi-dimensional description of the natural population. For age-structured populations a multi-cohort description is required where the population is represented by a vector of cohort biomass levels. For some populations, variation in the ratio of males to females is significant in analysing growth and reproduction. Finally, some populations interact with other species either in competition for food sources or as predator and prey.

A harvesting rule for a natural population where males and females are distinguished for the population growth function and where each sex may be harvested separately is presented by Mann (1970) in an inventory adjustment framework. Mann delineates four regions in the space of male and female biomass levels such that the harvesting rule is to harvest both males and females to optimal unconstrained biomass levels, to not harvest at all or to harvest either only males or only females to a stock-dependent biomass level.

Spulber (1981a, b) examines the optimal management of a multi-cohort fishery under uncertainty for the cases where cohorts may be harvested selectively and where only a proportion of the total population may be harvested. He allows Markov environmental disturbances and shows that, when selective harvesting is possible and the current return to fishing is a linear function, there will be a recurrent state in escapement levels if there is a positive probability of harvesting all cohorts at the same time within a finite number of time periods. Without selective harvesting, there will be a recurrent state in escapement levels if recruitment is random, if there are no interactions among adult cohorts, and if harvesting involves taking all of the fish above the age of liability to capture. Thus, under some conditions of pulse-fishing the multi-cohort fishery implies that there is a stable invariant probability distribution. These conditions are verifiable for models of actual fisheries. The steady-state probability distribution on cohort escapement levels can be used to derive steady-state distributions on total population biomass, preharvest cohort biomass levels, and the value of the resouce stock to the fishery managers. Additional references on multi-cohort models are given in Spulber (1981a, b).

The selective harvesting problem may be solved as in the lumped parameter problem. Let $R(\Sigma_{i=1}^{n} h^i)$ and $C(h^1, \ldots, h^n)$ represent the firm's revenue and cost functions respectively. Further, let the growth function be given by

$$x_{t+1} = g(x_t, w_{t+1}) = \{g^1(x_t, w_{t+1}), \ldots, g^n(x_t, w_{t+1})\} \tag{14}$$

where x_{t+1} represents a vector of n cohort biomass levels. The dynamic programming problem yields n simultaneous Euler equations,

$$R'\left(\sum_{i=1}^{n} h^i\right) - C_i(h^1, \ldots, h^n)$$

$$= \frac{1}{1+r} \int_{\mathbb{R}} \sum_{j=1}^{n} \left\{ R'\left(\sum_{\ell=1}^{n} \tilde{h}_\ell\right) - C_j(\tilde{h}^1, \ldots, \tilde{h}^n) \right\} g_i^j(x - h, w) \, dw. \tag{15}$$

These equations imply that the marginal return to harvesting cohort i should be equated to the discounted marginal returns arising from recruitment, own-cohort growth, and intercohort effects. Environmental uncertainty may have significant effects on harvesting through recruitment and inter-cohort interaction.

ACKNOWLEDGEMENTS

I thank Tracy Lewis for helpful suggestions.

REFERENCES

Andersen, P. (1982), 'Commercial Fisheries Under Price Uncertainty', *Journal of Environmental Economics and Management,* 9, 11–28.

Arrow, K. J., Karlin, S., and Scarf, H. (1958), *Studies in the Mathematical Theory of Inventory and Production,* Stanford, California: Stanford University Press.

Arrow, K. J., Karlin, S., and Suppes, P. (1960), *Mathematical Methods in the Social Sciences,* Standford, California: Stanford University Press.

Beddington, J. R. and May, R. M. (1977), 'Harvesting Natural Populations in a Randomly Fluctuating Environment', *Science,* 29 July, 463–5.

Bell, F. W. (1972), 'Technological Externalities and Common Property Resources: An Empirical Study of the US Northern Fishery', *Journal of Political Economy,* 80, 148–58.

Bismut, J. M. (1975), 'Growth and Optimal Intertemporal Allocation of Risks', *Journal of Economic Theory,* 10, 239–57.

Brock, W. A. and Majumdar, M. (1978), 'Global Asymptotic Stability Results for Multi-sector Models of Optimal Growth under Uncertainty When Future Utilities are Discounted', *Journal of Economic Theory,* 18, 225–43.

Brock, W. A. and Mirman, L. J. (1972), 'Optimal Economic Growth and Uncertainty: The Discounted Case', *Journal of Economic Theory,* 4, 479–513.

Bourguignon, F. (1974), 'A Particular Class of Continuous-time Stochastic Growth Models', *Journal of Economic Theory,* 9, 141–58.

Cass, D. and Shell, K. (1976), 'The Structure and Stability of Competitive Dynamical Systems', *Journal of Economic Theory,* 12, 31–70.

Clark, C. W. (1976), *Mathematical Bioeconomics, The Optimal Management of Renewable Resources,* London: John Wiley.

Clark, C. W., Clarke, F. H., and Munro, G. R. (1979), 'The Optimal Exploitation of Renewable Resource Stocks: Problems of Irreversible Investments', *Econometrica,* 47, 25–47.

Doob, J. (1953), *Stochastic Processes,* New York: John Wiley.

Easley, D. and Spulber, D. F. (1981), 'Stochastic Equilibrium and Optimality with Rolling Plans', *International Economic Review,* 22, 79–103.

Gleit, A. (1978), 'Optimal Harvesting in Continuous Time with Stochastic Growth', *Mathematical Biosciences,* 41, 111–23.

Hannesson, R. (1975), 'Fishery Dynamics: A North Atlantic Cod Fishery', *Canadian Journal of Economics,* 8, 151–73.

Jaquette, L. (1972a), 'Mathematical Models for the Control of Growing Biological Populations: A Survey', *Operations Research,* 20, 1142–51.

Jaquette, L. (1972b), 'A Discrete-time Population-control Model', *Mathematical Biosciences,* 15, 231–52.

Jaquette, L. (1974), 'A Discrete-time Population Control Model with Setup Cost', *Operations Research,* 22, 298–303.

Levhari, D., Michener, R. and Mirman, L. (1982), 'Nonconcave Dynamic Programming: An Example', in L. J. Mirman and D. F. Spulber (eds), *Essays in the Economics of Renewable Resources,* Amsterdam: North-Holland, 79–93.

Lewis, T. R. (1975), 'Optimal Resource Management Under Conditions of Uncertainty: The Case of an Ocean Fishery', PhD dissertation, University of California at San Diego.

Lewis, T. R. (1981), 'Exploitation of a Renewable Resource Under Uncertainty', *Canadian Journal of Economics,* 14, 422–39.

Ludwig, D. (1979), 'Optimal Harvesting of a Randomly Fluctuating Resource, I. Application of Perturbation Methods', *SIAM Journal of Applied Mathematics,* 37, 166–84.

Mann, S. H. (1970), 'A Mathematical Theory for the Harvest of Natural Animal Populations when Birth Rates are Dependent on Total Population Size', *Mathematical Biosciences,* 7, 97–110.

May, R. M. (1974), *Stability and Complexity in Model Ecosystems,* 2nd ed., Princeton University Press.

May. R. M., Beddington, J. R., Clark, C. W., Holt, S. J., and Laws, R. M. (1979), 'Management of Multispecies Fisheries', *Science,* 205, 267–77.

May, R. M. Beddington, J. R., Horwood, J. W. and Shepherd, J. G. (1978), 'Exploiting Natural Populations in an Uncertain World', *Mathematical Biosciences,* 42, 219–52.

McKenzie, L. W. (1976), 'Turnpike Theory', *Econometrica,* 44, 851–66.

Mendelssohn, R. and Sobel, M. J. (1980), 'Capital Accumulation and the Optimization of Renewable Resource Models', *Journal of Economic Theory,* 23, 243–60.

Merton, R. C. (1975), 'An Asymptotic Theory of Growth Under Uncertainty', *Review of Economic Studies,* 42, 375–93.

Mirman, L. J. (1972), 'On the Existence of Steady-state Measures for One-sector Growth Models with Uncertain Technology', *International Economic Review*, 13, 271–86.

Mirman, L. J. (1973), 'The Steady-state Behavior of a Class of One-sector Growth Models with Uncertain Technology', *Journal of Economic Theory*, 6, 219–42.

Mirman, L. J. and Zilcha, I. (1975), 'On Optimal Growth under Uncertainty', *Journal of Economic Theory*, 11, 329–39.

Reed, W. J. (1974), 'A Stochastic Model for the Economic Management of a Renewable Animal Resource', *Mathematical Biosciences*, 22, 313–37.

Reed, W. J. (1978), 'The Steady-state of a Stochastic Harvesting Model', *Mathematical Biosciences*, 41, 273–307.

Reed, W. J. (1979), 'Optimal Escapement Levels in Stochastic and Deterministic Models', *Journal of Environmental Economics and Management*, 6, 350–63.

Scarf, H., Gilford, D. M., and Shelly, M. W. (1963), *Multistage Inventory Models and Techniques*, Stanford, California: Stanford University Press.

Schechtman, J. (1976), 'An Income Fluctuation Problem', *Journal of Economic Theory*, 12, 218–41.

Schechtman, J. and Escudero, V. (1977), 'Some Results on "An Income Fluctuation Problem" ', *Journal of Economic Theory*, 16, 151–66.

Smith, J. B. (1980), 'Replenishable Resource Management under Uncertainty: A Re-examination of the US Northern Fishery', *Journal of Environmental Economics and Management*, 7, 209–19.

Spulber, D. F. (1981a), 'Pulse Fishing and Stochastic Equilibrium in the Multicohort Fishery', *Journal of Economic Dynamics and Control*, 6, 309–32.

Spulber, D. F. (1981b), 'Pulse Fishing the Multicohort Fishery Under Uncertainty', paper presented at the Workshop on Uncertainty and Fisheries Economics, University of Rhode Island.

4. Resource Allocation Rules and Long-Range Planning

Philip A. Neher

INTRODUCTION

It is common that natural resources are valued for their amenity benefits, which augment the quality of human life. At the same time, the gross depletion of these resources contributes to the production of ordinary economic goods, which are also valued. Forests and wilderness areas provide particular examples of 'multiple-use' resources in the sense that sylvan scenes compete with saw logs and slag heaps. In a more general way, natural surroundings such as air and water have amenity value when pristine, but are also valuable dumps for by-products of ordinary production and consumption.

A stylized representation of this multiple-use characteristic distinguishes amenity benefits yielded directly by the *stock* of the natural capital (A) and those derived from the gross *flow* of its depletion (C). An ordinary social benefit function $U(C, A)$ can be defined on these two arguments.

The public interest in the allocation of multiple-use resources is well established, based on alleged public good properties of natural amenities, and upon the impossibility or impracticality of establishing exclusive private property rights in the amenity, with entailed rights of exclusion against third parties. But while the public interest is well established, it is not often clearly articulated in well defined public policy objectives.

This paper attempts to clarify a general resource allocation problem as a guide to practical cost–benefit evaluations in specific instances. While incomplete, the analysis is sufficiently general to encompass global considerations put in the context of 'space ship earth' models (Boulding, 1966) as well as those raised at the micro-level having to do with the day-to-day management of public forests, seashores, wilderness areas, and the like.[1]

After exploring in some detail the primitive allocation problem, two public policy questions are taken up.

First, casual observation suggests certain empirical regularities in allocation decisions actually made by elected officials in social democracies, along with their supporting civil services. While governments are of the day, the civil service contributes some intertemporal continuity to interactive decision-making processes. The outcomes are solutions to intertemporal allocation problems. If regularities can be discerned, how can they be characterized in terms of objective characteristics of abstract planning models: implicit discount rates, implied intertemporal distributions of income, and the like?

Second, for whom should resources be managed by officials responsible to sovereign citizens who are currently alive? This imposes a rather different perspective than the one usually taken to be that of a sovereign state supposed to represent an on-going, immortal society (Ramsey, 1928). This question is related to the first, but is posed in a more normative way. If elected officials are responsible to citizens who are currently alive, what intertemporal allocation patterns should they advocate? If civil servants have professional obligations to a continuing society, which includes future citizens, what intertemporal allocations should they advocate?

Related issues have been investigated in earlier papers (Neher, 1976; Lewis and Neher, 1982) employing more primitive and tractable analytical frameworks. Here the model is significantly generalized, and it is more specifically directed towards these issues of public policy.

THE MODEL

Factories, refineries, and warehouses are reproducible forms of capital which, however productive of goods and services, are not particularly valued for their direct contribution to the quality of life. For this reason, they are not naturally included in social benefit functions along with the final products they generate. (For a notable exception, see Kurtz, 1968.)

Forests, foreshores, and wilderness areas are natural and replenishable resources that do yield amenities. These are naturally included in performance indicators for micro-units (a forest) and larger aggregates (a national economy). Performance is computed as the sum of benefits generated by current economic activity plus the value of current investment. Benefits are represented by a social utility function ($u(\cdot)$) defined on amenities generated by natural capital (A) and by ordinary consumption (C). Investment is defined as the increase in natural capital ($dA/dt \equiv \dot{A}$). It is valued at its accounting, or 'shadow', price (q). Consumption is computed net of extraction and processing costs. Taking these considerations together, the current value performance indicator is

$$H = \{u(c, A) + q \cdot \dot{A}\}. \tag{1}$$

This looks like an expression for net national product along lines suggested for net economic welfare (NEW) calculations (Nordhaus and Tobin, 1972). Any net depletion of natural assets ($\dot{A} < 0$) counts directly against the current performance of the micro- or macro-economy in question through the investment term. At the same time, natural amenity augments NEW through the direct enjoyment of it.

The social utility, or benefit, function $U(\cdot)$ is restricted in usual ways. Having more C and A is preferred to hving less (U_C, $U_A > 0$) but at a decreasing rate in each case (U_{CC}, $U_{AA} < 0$). Complementary associations of C and A are indicated by the 'cross-partial' derivatives being positive ($U_{CA} = U_{AC} > 0$. Otherwise, ($U_{CA} = U_{AC} < 0$) indicates that they are substitutes. But $U_{CA} = U_{AC}$ may be zero, indicating 'independence'. However, assuming concavity of $U(\cdot)$, $U_{CC}U_{AA} - U_{CA}^2$ is positive.

There is no strong presumption on the sign of $U_{CA} = U_{AC}$. Does one enjoy an additional hamburger more or less on a more or less polluted beach? It is clear that this is an empirical question.

But two theoretical points should be made. First, $U_{CA} = U_{AC} < 0$ is a necessary condition for either C or A to be 'inferior' goods. Define the marginal rate of substitution (MRS_{AC}) as the ratio of marginal utilities (U_A/U_C) along a social indifference curve. If C is inferior, then a rise in C may reduce the MRS_{AC}.

$$\frac{\partial}{\partial C}\left(\frac{U_A}{U_C}\right) = \frac{U_C \cdot U_{AC} - U_A U_{CC}}{U_C^2}.$$

This may be negative if $U_{AC} < 0$. Likewise,

$$\frac{\partial}{\partial A}\left(\frac{U_A}{U_C}\right) = \frac{U_C \cdot U_{AA} - U_A U_{CA}}{U_C^2}.$$

This may be positive if $U_{CA} < 0$.

The second point comes up in connection with homothetic utility functions. These are positive transforms of homogeneous aggregator functions nested within. For example, let

$$U(C, A) = V(Y) = V\{F(C, A)\}; \qquad V' > 0, V'' < 0$$

where Y is an expression for 'consumption' derived from its components (C and A) through a constant returns to scale (CRTS) aggregator: $F(\cdot)$ is homogeneous of the first degree. In this case,

$$U_A = V' \cdot F_A$$

$$U_{AC} = V' \cdot F_{AC} + F_A V'' \cdot F_C$$

$$= V' F_{AC}\left(1 + \frac{V'' F}{V'} \cdot \frac{F_A F_C}{F \cdot F_{AC}}\right)$$

$$= V' \cdot F_{AC}(1 - \sigma_V \sigma_F)$$

where $\sigma_V \equiv - V'' F/V'$ and $\sigma_F \equiv F_A F_C/F_{AC} F$. Here, V' is positive (more Y yields more utility); F_{AC} is positive (the 'inputs' are complements in the CRTS case); σ_V is the (positive) elasticity of the marginal utility function with respect to income; and σ_F is the (positive) elasticity of substitution in the CRTS aggregator (Allen, 1960, p. 343). Looked at this way, C and A are complements if both elasticities are 'small'. In terms of curvature of V and F, complementarity is favoured if the utility function has little curvature (V'' is 'small') and the Y indifference curves bend substantially inward towards the origin. As a special case, let both σ_V and σ_F equal unity; then U_{AC} is zero and the marginal utility of either good is unaffected by the quantity of the other one (independence). It will be seen that the sign of U_{AC} can be crucial in shaping the qualitative properties of intertemporal allocation profiles.

While the value of performance (H) is augmented by more ordinary consumption (C), more amenity (A) and by more investment ($\dot{A}$), nature throws up an inviolable constraint in the form

$$\dot{A} = G(A) - C; \qquad G' = ?, G'' < 0. \tag{2}$$

Natural replenishment of the natural asset is represented by $G(A)$. The *growth* of the asset depends upon its level. It may be at first increasing and then decreasing in A (a biomass fishery (Schaeffer, 1959)). Or it may be everywhere increasing but at a decreasing rate (an airshed (Donaldson and Victor, 1976)). A non-replenishable asset is modelled with $G(A) = 0$.

With (2) as the dynamic constraint, the objective is to maximize the (possibly discounted) sum of social benefits or utilities (J).

$$J = \int_0^T D \cdot U(C, A) dt. \tag{3}$$

The discount factor $(D \equiv \exp(-rt))$ is used to weight social benefits over the planning interval, which extends from time zero to an as-yet unspecified terminal time (T). The social discount rate (r) is presumably non-negative, and is included for completeness.

Formally, the problem is to maximize (3) subject to (2) and side constraints, which will be appropriately introduced later in different contexts.

The first step towards a solution is to find the necessary conditions for a maximum in the form of the equations of motion.

Intuition suggests, and the maximum principle (MP) requires (Pontryagin *et al.* 1964), that the planner should 'do the best he can with what he has got' by maximizing the current value performance indicator (H) at every point in time with respect to those events that he can control. In this case the *control variable* is consumption (C).

(MP) $$\max_{\{C\}} H = [U(C, A) + q \cdot \{G(A) - C\}].$$

It is appropriate to assume an interior maximum, so the algorithm is

$$\frac{\partial H}{\partial C} = 0$$

which yields

$$U_C = q.$$

This is a 'marginal benefit equals marginal cost' rule. The 'marginal benefit' of consumption is U_C. The marginal cost is the 'user cost' of accumulating more of the resource for the purpose of future consumption and additional growth of the asset.

Figure 4.1 illustrates the application of the MP. At every point in time, the state of the world is momentarily immutable and represented by A. As shown in the upper panel, the value of H is augmented by C, but at a decreasing rate along the $U(\cdot)$ benefit line. The cost of C is charged off against H at the conceptually constant rate q along the $q \cdot C$ cost line. The value of H is maximized

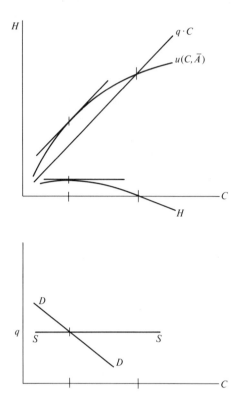

FIG. 4.1

where the slopes of the benefit and cost lines are the same. These slopes are translated to the lower planel of the figure where marginal benefits of C are interpreted as representing demand (DD). The supply of $C(SS)$ is valued at cost of forgone investment (q).

Geometrically, the maximizing problem has a formal analogue in the profit-maximizing calculus of a constant-cost monopolist for whom SS would represent marginal $(=$ average$)$ cost and DD would represent marginal revenue.

Having introduced q, it is required to find another equation to help account for it. The Zero Net Profit (ZNP) condition is a step in that direction. As an asset, A is a *state variable* and must earn a rate of return that is competitive with society's rate of time preference (r) except in so far as it makes a (marginal) contribution to the value of the performance indicator (H). Falling short of this return, A is liable to be entirely consumed on the spot. A higher return would induce indefinite postponement of its consumption. Since neither of these extreme outcomes could characterize the maximizing of (3), a condition of indifference must be found. Reasoning along lines just suggested, suppose at first that A made no (marginal) contribution to H at all ($H_A = 0$). Then to be competitive with the desire to eat it, A must increase in value at the rate $(\dot{q}/q) = r$. That is, capital gains must equal the rental rate ($\dot{q} = rq$). Next, suppose the value of A were stationary ($\dot{q} = 0$); then A's (marginal) contribution to H must justify the cost of renting it ($H_A = rq$). Taking these considerations together, marginal benefits ($\dot{q} + H_A$) must equal the rental cost (rq). Or, as it is usually put,

(ZNP) $$\dot{q} = rq - H_A.$$

Calculating,

$$\dot{q} = rq - \{U_A + q \cdot G'(A)\}. \tag{5}$$

Figure 4.2 illustrates the application of the ZNP. Again, A represents the immutable state of the momentary world. However, A is conceptually variable. Also, C is conceptually held constant. So what is free to be adjusted in order to satisfy (5)? Clearly, both the *level* of q and its rate of change ($\dot{q}$) are candidates. It will be clear that choosing q itself must be done in a larger context with sufficient scope to encompass such global issues as where the system should begin its development and where it should end. So for now, q is taken as conceptually given. This clears the way to concentrate first on the *equations of motion*, which include an expression for the changes in q from moment to moment. So the problem at hand is to *choose the rate of capital gains* to satisfy (5).

The upper panel of figure 4.2 shows how H varies with A, holding all other variables constant. There are two additive components: A contributes to H directly through $U(\bar{C}, A)$ in the usual way; A also affects the gross rate of investment in A through $G(A)$. The net rate of investment is $G(A) - C$ and this is valued at the price q. The vertical addition of $U(C, A)$ and $q \cdot \{G(A) - C\}$ yields H. The slope of the H curve is H_A in (5). It shows the marginal contribution to H that can justify the rental (rq) of A when added to capital gains ($\dot{q}$).

This computation is illustrated in the lower panel of the figure. The marginal contribution of A to H (that is, H_A) is labelled *DD*, and is analogous to *DD* in figure 4.1. The supply rental price of A is *rq*, and it is represented by the *SS* curve. The gap between the supply price (rq) and the demand price (H_A) is filled by assigning capital gains or losses ($\dot{q}$). If the demand price (H_A) exceeds the supply price (rq), then there is 'excess demand', the price is 'too high', so q is falling ($\dot{q} < 0$), and vice versa. (It is perhaps trivial, but nevertheless interesting, to note that, if H_A is zero, as in the case of an underground mineral deposit, then *DD* is congruent with the horizontal axis so that q is positive and equal to rq (Hotelling, 1931). This is the case of 'excess supply'. That is, all minerals being exploited are in excess supply. If there is 'increasing scarcity' of these minerals, it means that excess supply is being worked off.)

The assignment of capital gains according to (5) completes the dynamic system, when taken along with the maximum principle and with the dynamic

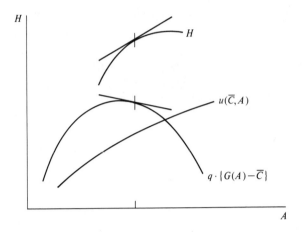

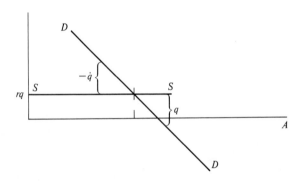

FIG. 4.2

constraint (DC):

$$\text{(DC)} \qquad \dot{A} = H_q$$
$$\dot{A} = G(A) - C. \qquad (2)$$

To sum up, the system reads

(MP)	$U_C = q$	(4)
(ZNP)	$\dot{q} = rq - \{U_A + q \cdot (G')\}$	(5)
(DC)	$\dot{A} = G(A) - C$	(2)

where it is understood that $U_C = U_C(C, A)$ and $U_A = U_A(C, A)$. The variables are, in order of appearance,

(MP) C, A, q

(ZNP) $C, A, q; \dot{q}$

(DC) $C, A; \dot{A}.$

The motions of the system can be illustrated by *phase diagrams* relating the development of the natural asset (A) along with its price (q) and the rate of consumption (C). Since Kurtz (1968), it has been known that in systems like this these relationships can be complex indeed.

Sources of the complexity are most easily seen by solving the system for the motions of q and A in the neighbourhood of a (possibly more than one) singularity where $\dot{q} = \dot{A} = 0$. This is done by totally differentiating MP, ZNP, and DC with respect to their arguments, solving for dC in MP, and then using this to 'substitute out' dC in ZNP and DC. With $\dot{q} = \dot{A} = 0$, this procedure yields

$$\begin{bmatrix} d\dot{q} \\ d\dot{A} \end{bmatrix} = \begin{bmatrix} \dfrac{U_{CC}U_A - U_A - U_{AC}U_C}{U_{CC}U_C} + U_C\left(\dfrac{U_{CA}U_{AC} - U_{CC}U_{AA}}{U_{CC}U_C} - G''\right) & \dfrac{dq}{} \\ \dfrac{1}{U_{CC}} + \left(G' + \dfrac{U_{CA}}{U_{CC}}\right) & dA \end{bmatrix}$$

and for this characteristic matrix [ ],

$$DET [\ ] = | \ | = \frac{U_{CC}U_A - U_{AC}U_C}{U_{CC}U_C} G' - \frac{1}{U_{CC}}G'' + \frac{U_{CA}U_A - U_{AA}U_C}{U_{CC}U_C}.$$

The relevant phase diagrams can be drawn if there is knowledge of the algebraic sign, and sometimes the magnitude, of each element of [ ]. Clearly, there are not yet sufficient restrictions on the system to get very far. It has already been assumed that: U_C, $U_A > 0$ (marginal utility is positive); U_{CC}, $U_{AA} < 0$ (but declining); $U_{CA}U_{AC} - U_{CC}U_{AA} < 0$ (concavity); $G'' < 0$. However, $U_{CA} = (?)$ and $G' = (?)$. So one can conclude

$$\begin{bmatrix} (?) & (+) \\ (+) & (?) \end{bmatrix}$$

and that $DET [\ ] = (?)$, but no more. Even the local stability property of a singularity is not clear, and there may be more than one singularity. For example, multiple saddlepoints may be separated by unstable modes (Kurtz, 1968). This observation is a discouragement for the tasks at hand. For these, it will help if optimal paths of C and A display robust uniformities which can be compared with the observed ones. Stronger assumptions, which one would prefer not to make, are required to make progress.

Some ambiguities in [ ] can be resolved if one is prepared to assume that neither C nor A are inferior goods. In that case,

$$
\begin{array}{cc}
(+) & (+) \\
(+) & (?)
\end{array}
$$

and *DET* [   ] is

$$
\frac{U_{CC}U_A - U_{AC}U_C}{U_{CC}U_C} \cdot G' - \frac{G''}{U_{CC}} + \frac{U_{CA}U_A - U_{AA}U_C}{U_{CC}U_C} = | \quad |.
$$

$$
\begin{array}{cccc}
(+) & (?) & & (-) & \qquad (?)
\end{array}
$$

There are two cases to examine.

Case I: $G' < 0$. A sufficient condition for this, from ZNP, is that $r = 0$. In turn, $G' < 0$ is a sufficient condition for

$$
\begin{bmatrix}
(+) & (+) \\
(+) & (-)
\end{bmatrix}
$$

and *DET* [   ] is (−). This case is illustrated in the lower panel of figure 4.3. A regular saddlepoint is indicated with q and A being inversely correlated during both accumulation and decumulation toward the (q^*, A^*) equilibrium.
  However, from MP,

$$
\dot{C} = \frac{1}{U_{CC}}\dot{q} - \frac{1}{U_{CA}} \cdot \dot{A}
$$

and it is easy to see that a positive correlation between C and A during these phases is not guaranteed unless $U_{CA} \geqslant 0$. This result differs from the usual Ramsey (1928) outcome because the asset (A) enters the benefits (utility) function directly. Hence, if C and A are substitutes $(U_{CA} < 0)$, then (say) accumulation of the asset (A), and a fall in its price (q), may induce a substitution towards A and away from C, so that C may actually decline.

Case II: $G' > 0$. This can occur if $r > 0$. If the social rate of discount is high enough, the steady-state society may require that the assets' 'own (marginal) rate of return' (G') be positive, notwithstanding that A makes a direct contribution to $U(\cdot)$. In this case, singularities are saddlepoints (the upper left-hand panel of figure 4.3) or are unstable modes (the upper right-hand panel of the figure). In both cases, one has

$$
\begin{array}{cc}
(+) & (+) \\
(+) & (?)
\end{array}
$$

but *DET* [   ] < 0 for the saddlepoint and *DET* [   ] > 0 for the node. As in Kurtz (1968), saddlepoints equilibria may be separated by unstable nodes so that the optimal steady state is not unique, but is chosen according to the initial value of A. However, q and A are negatively correlated, regardless of

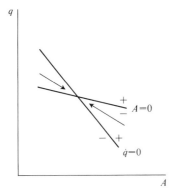

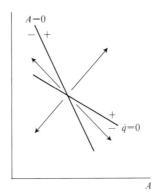

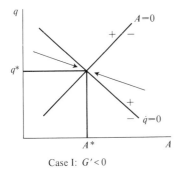

Case I: $G' < 0$

FIG. 4.3

the steady state that is being approached. Nevertheless, ambiguities are still attached to the characteristic motions of C and A as before.

RULES OF THUMB

Casual observation suggests that a variety of resource management programmes can be characterized by apparently simple, closed-loop, state-dependent harvesting policies. Loosely put, the current 'rate of use' of the resource is positively correlated to its 'abundance', so that a flow is positively related to the stock.

The great American conservation movement was motivated at the turn of this century by a perception of material prosperity and a concern that the western frontier had been closed in the decades following the Civil War. More recently, alleged affluence has brought with it a demand for public intervention to improve the quality of air and water, and to provide more park and wilderness areas. In a smaller way, management policies generally permit a larger cut from a more extensive forest; more fish may be harvested from more abundant stocks.

While the positive correlation seems pervasive over long periods of time and in many contexts, it is seldom overtly supported by even rudimentary economic calculation or argument. So it is of some interest to ask if an observed allocator rule can be derived as the reduced-form, synthesized, solution of one or more primitive constrained maximum or minimum problems. If so, the inverse optimal problem will have certain imputed (revealed) parameters that are ideally unique to a particular allocator rule. One can judge better the outcome of a rule if it can be understood as the solution of a well understood problem.

For example, a certain allocator rule may be construed as the solution to a problem posed in the last section with a systematic interest rate equal to 40 per cent. Is such a rate reasonable? Could advocates of the rule support the underlying rate of discount? Perhaps a mistake has been made.

While imputations like this are not common in economics, they are done in the revealed preference approach in consumer theory, and they have been applied to the understanding of central banks' behaviour by investigators interested in how these institutions 'trade off' inflation and unemployment. Maximum sustained yield forestry practices are understood to imply that managers have solved a Faustman (1849) problem using a zero interest rate (Samuelson, 1976).

Imputations are also undertaken, often in cavalier manner, in day-to-day life 'That drunken sailor is behaving as if there is no tomorrow [for him]' entails a criticism based on an imputed decision model of a sailor maximizing his lifetime utility in the face of a high objective probability, perceived by his critic, that the sailor *will* be alive tomorrow.

An obvious difficulty with this imputation procedure is not a poverty of candidate-maximizing models; rather, it is an embarrassing richness of candidates. Specific behaviours can be 'understood' or 'explained' by a variety of behavioural hypotheses (Machlup, 1964). Reduced-form equations can be generated by a multitude of economizing, and other, models.

Nevertheless, it seems worthwhile to attempt to explain observed behaviour in terms of solutions to problems like those posed by (2) and (3).

The observed programme (or policy) is supposed to relate the 'rate of use' to the stock of the resource. In this case, the stock is A, but what is the appropriate flow variable? This is an empirical question. One possibility is to suppose that ordinary consumption (C) is related positively to the magnitude of the asset (A). That is,

$$C = C(A); \qquad C' > 0$$

would designate an ordinary consumption function.

Another possibility would admit a broader definition of consumption to include amenity benefits. This broader view of consumption defines

$$Y = F(C, A); \qquad F_C, F_A > 0, F_{CC}F_{AA} < 0 \qquad (6)$$

where $F(\cdot)$ is a consumption aggregator. The associated programme is represented by an allocator that is in force at every point in time.

$$Y = Y(A); \qquad Y' > 0, Y'' < 0. \tag{7}$$

This latter possibility will be pursued. The analysis should be thought of as indicative of a more general class of imputation models, where flows are related to stocks in intertemporal contexts. For example, the $C = C(A)$ allocator could be explored using the same method.

The objective functional to be imputed is taken to have the additive form

$$J = \int_0^T D \cdot V(Y) dt; \qquad V' > 0, V'' < 0 \tag{8}$$

where $D \equiv \{\exp(-\delta t)\}$ is the discount factor, Y is the aggregator defined by (6) as equal to $F(\cdot)$. Utility (V) is a positive concave transform of Y. The allocator is (7) while the dynamic constraint (2) remains in force.

The aggregator (Y) is now added to the system that was explored in the previous section. The definition (6) has also been added. Consequently, if (3) can be maximized subject to (2), so can (8). Hence, if a maximized solution to (8) is to be obtained that is congruent with the allocator (7), something(s) has to 'give' in (8) to bring about the desired conformity. It is precisely this required flexibility in (8) that permits one to think about a *phantom utility functional*. In this sense, $V(\cdot)$ can be thought of as the phantom utility function, and δ as the phantom discount rate. These are to be sought.

The dynamics of the solution to (8), subject to (2) but innocent of the allocator (7), are pursued first. As in the previous section,

$$V_C = V' F_C = q \tag{4'}$$

$$\dot{q} = \delta q - \{V_A + q \cdot G'(A)\} = \delta q - \{V' \cdot F_A + \delta \cdot G'(A)\} \tag{5'}$$

$$\dot{A} = G(A) - C. \tag{2}$$

It is convenient to suppose that $F(\cdot)$ has constant returns to scale (CRTS) in C and A. Unfortunately, this imposes homotheticity in C and A on $V(\cdot)$. That is, all expansion curves (each having the same MRS_{CA}) are rays extending from the origin. This is a serious restriction. It rules out inferior goods. But as noted in the preceding section, the 'cross-partial' derivative (V_{AC}) can still be positive, negative, or zero.

Assuming that $F(\cdot)$ is CRTS, the dynamics near a singularity are characterized by

$$\begin{bmatrix} d\dot{Y} \\ d\dot{A} \end{bmatrix} = \begin{bmatrix} 0 & -V' \dfrac{F_{CC}}{V_{CC}} \cdot \dfrac{Y}{A} \left(\dfrac{G}{A} - G' \right) \\ -\dfrac{1}{F_C} & \delta \end{bmatrix} \cdot \begin{bmatrix} Y \\ A \end{bmatrix}$$

with DET [ ] < 0 if $(G/A - G') > 0$. It is sufficient for this to obtain if

$G(A)$ is 'inverted-U' shaped with $G(0) = 0$. It will be assumed here that it is the case that the average (own) rate of growth (G/A) exceeds the marginal (own) rate of growth (G') near the singularity. This is seen to be a regular saddlepoint equilibrium, as illustrated in figure 4.4.

Optimal motions of Y and A are along the stable arms leading towards (Y^*, A^*) equilibrium. Suppose these motions were to be generated by an observed $Y = Y(A)$ allocator function: how should the corresponding phantom utility functional be constructed?

Following Goldman (1968) and Lewis and Neher (1982), the first step is to note that Y and A move together along the stable arms in figure 4.4. This is consistent with a $Y = Y(A)$, $Y'(A) > 0$ allocator function.

Second, manipulate the phantom discount rate (δ) so that Y^*, A^* solves the allocator function $Y = Y(A)$. This is done with reference to the steady-state solution of $(4')$, $(5')$, and (2) with the allocator imposed and δ to be determined.

To impose the allocator, let $\bar{C}$ and $\bar{A}$ be simultaneous solutions of

$$C = G(A) \qquad \text{(from } \dot{A} = 0 \text{ in (2))}$$

$$F(C, A) = Y(A) \qquad \text{(from (6) and (7))}.$$

Then, from $(4')$ and $(5')$,

$$0 = \delta q - \frac{V_A(\bar{C}, \bar{A})}{V_C(\bar{C}, \bar{A})} \cdot q - G'(\bar{A}) \cdot q$$

or

$$\delta = \frac{F_A(\bar{C}, \bar{A})}{F_C(\bar{C}, \bar{A})} + G'(\bar{A}). \tag{9}$$

This imputation bears the following intepretation. The marginal rate of substitution of A for C (MRS_{AC}) thrown up by nature is $-dC/dA = -G'(A)$ in the steady state. The MRS_{AC} in consumption is F_A/F_C. If these two marginal rates are equal, in a steady state, then $\delta = 0$. Otherwise, as G' is found to be more positive (less negative), δ is imputed to be more positive and drives a 'wedge' between MRS_{AC} and positive $-G'(A)$. Since A/C is smaller for G' being larger, allocators that entail less A (relative to C) imply a higher imputed phantom interest rate. The higher is this δ, the less 'conservative' the programme will appear to be. This is not surprising. A society that 'reveals' itself to put a high discount on future enjoyments does so by asking its marginal asset(s) to be very productive by growing fast or by yielding large utilities. More marginal productivity in these two ways is yielded by a smaller asset.

Finally, it is required to account for the motion of the system, generated by the allocator, outside the steady state.

This is done by solving for the appropriate $V(Y)$ function in (8). Following Goldman (1968) and Lewis and Neher (1982), the problem is to impose $Y(A)$, then find V''/V'. This will define $V(Y)$ up to a positive linear transform.

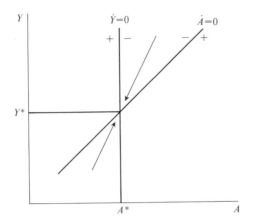

FIG. 4.4

Differentiate $(4')$ with respect to time:

$$\dot{q} = V' \cdot (F_{CC}\dot{C} + F_{CA} \cdot \dot{A}) + V'' F_C \dot{Y}.$$

Then, using the allocator (7), the aggregator (6), and rearranging,

$$\frac{V''}{V'} = \frac{1}{Y'}\left\{ \frac{1}{V'} \cdot \frac{\dot{g}}{\dot{A}} + \frac{F_{CC}}{F_C}\left(\frac{Y}{A} - Y'\right)\right\} .$$

The RHS is a function of Y: $Y = Y(A)$ entails $A = F(Y)$; $Y \equiv F(C, A)$ entails $C \equiv C(Y, A)$. So C depends upon Y as well.

To sign the RHS, note that q and A move inversely $(\dot{q}/\dot{A} = (-))$ by letting $V\{F(C, A)\}$ replace $U(C, A)$ in the previous section. However, the second term is negative only if Y/A exceeds Y'. A sufficient condition for this is that $Y = Y(A)$ be concave to the origin where $0 = Y(0)$. Moreover, the greater is Y/A relative to Y', the greater is V'' relative to V'. If Y' exceeds Y/A, then the allocator may imply that V'' is positive. Loosely put, the more 'concave' is the allocator, the greater is the 'concavity' of the phantom utility function.

Again there is no surprise here. Think of a phantom planner contemplating an accumulation of A towards an equilibrium at $\bar{A}$. He could approach $\bar{A}$ rapidly but only by lowering Y significantly, especially in the early years of the plan. These early sacrifices weigh more heavily in (8) the greater is the concavity of $V(\cdot)$. Apprehension of these utility sacrifices will deter him from imposing them. On the other hand, if $V(\cdot)$ is linear and homogeneous, then a 'most rapid approach' towards $\bar{A}$ is indicated, with maximum possible sacrifice being required along the approach to $\bar{A}$.

REVISED AND LONG-RANGE PLANNING

The second section of this paper developed a model of a resource-based economy which could be described as utilitarian in spirit, but not necessarily implementable in practice.[2] It has in its favour that it is a natural intertemporal counterpart of familiar atemporal maximizing models. But against it is a predisposition towards institutional arrangements which can discipline possibly reluctant generations of persons who do not share the ethic embodied in the programme.[3] While such plans are consistent (Blackorby *et al.*, 1973) and ethically defensible (utilitarianism), people who are required to make large consumption sacrifices towards the beginning of an accumulation phase may not concur that ultimate affluence for abstract future generations justifies poverty for their own. In short, people may not be as intertemporally altruistic as the long-range planner. All programmes in the Ramsey tradition share this difficulty.

Another, more empirical, approach was taken in the preceding section. Observing that implemented programmes prescribe positive stock-flow correlations, it was natural to ask if this rule-of-thumb procedure could be characterized as the operational solution of a long-term economizing model of the Ramsey type.

A third, but related, approach is explored in this section. Revised planning procedures are commonly employed by responsible individuals and institutions who find it practical to look ahead for a finite time and plan accordingly. The terminal date of each plan is thrust forward at the same rate that historical time passes so that the terminal date of each plan in the sequence is always the same number of years in the future.

Continuous planning revision procedures have been studied by Goldman (1968), Neher (1976), and Lewis and Neher (1982). A new plan for T years is begun at each moment as the previous plan is discarded. A sequence of initial points of T-year plans traces out an intertemporal allocation. This sequence of points can be characterized, for example, as

$$Y = Y(A).$$

Two differently motivated revised planning sequences are investigated here. The first employs ethical foundations suggested by the work of Rawls (1972). The second has legal foundations in the usufructuary traditions of English common law.

Intertemporal economic implications of Rawls's *A Theory of Justice* have been suggested, notably by Dasgupta (1974) for present purposes.[4] These purposes are best served by taking constant consumption (Y) paths to satisfy the Rawlsian maxi-min criterion: all those alive during the plan are to share equally in the benefits from the resource;

Phantom plans are constructed in figure 4.5. The upper panel shows alternate Rawlsian approaches to a predetermined A_T which is not necessarily the turnpike

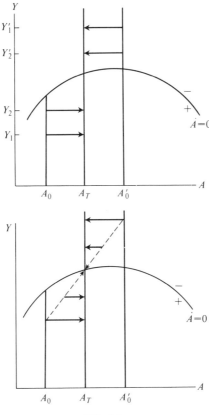

FIG. 4.5

level (Y^*, A^*) of the resource as determined by the solution of (8) and (2). Rawlsian accumulation (decumulation) can be rapid at $Y_1(Y_1')$ or slow at $Y_2(Y_2')$, reflecting the life expectancy of currently alive persons attending the constitutional convention behind the veil of ignorance. The planned positive bequest $A(T)$ satisfies their desire to provide for the welfare of the next generation. Note that relatively short accumulations (decumulations) towards $A(T)$ entail less (more) consumptions for any given $A_0(A_0')$.

Because of continual planning revision, horizontal paths like those in figure 4.5 are never completed. Given T and A_T, society is forever embarking on a new plan to reach A_T from the initial stock in time T. A revised planning path is the locus of all points with the property that $A(T) = A_T$ along the Rawlsian path emanating from the initial stock position. Given A_T and T, Y depends only on A_0 along the revised path with $Y = Y(A \mid A_T, T)$. Here, A_0 is simply written as A. These paths are shown by the broken lines on the lower panel of figure 4.5.

The simple dynamics of the biological resource serve to establish that Y is an increasing function of A along the broken lines, and that an equilibrium A

is established at A_T so that the economy ultimately achieves the desired bequest. This, however, should not be 'too large' in order not to drive Y below its maximum sustainable value.

The comparative dynamic properties of revised Rawlsian paths (broken lines) are apparent in figure 4.5 and can be stated in terms of the phantom plans which correspond to these revised Rawlsian plans. These indicate a 'steeper' approach to A_T, the shorter is the horizon of the momentary plan or the smaller is A_T. These characterize long-range phantom plans for which $-V''/V'$ is 'small'. Hence, these phantom plans can be thought of as having greater tolerance for the inequality of intertemporal income. They are less inequality-adverse. Also, the smaller is A_T, the greater $G'\{A(T)\}$, indicating a higher phantom discount rate.

While these comparative dynamic results are intuitively appealing, even self-evident, the source of A_T is somewhat obscure, and its imposition on the problem is a bit artificial. It is natural that a convention of mortal people should decide that $A_T > 0$ if they have regard at all for their successors. But it seems reasonable to suppose that their intended bequests should be related to their own contemplated consumptions in view of nature's own budget constraint (2). This suggests searching for endogenous $A(T)$ to be implemented within the revised planning framework.

One approach, taken by Dasgupta (1974, p. 409) and others, incorporates extended preferences. Another, more empirical, one is suggested by usufructuary laws and traditions which require people to 'keep the capital intact'. One version of this is 'bequeath unto others as others have bequeathed unto you'. Related to Phelps's (1966) 'Golden Rule of Accumulation', and articulated in a resource context by Solow (1974), Riley (1980), and Hartwick (1977), the injunction is against discriminating among people because of their birth dates.

Lewis and Neher (1982) and Neher (1976) have explored this approach in revised plans, which set $A(T)$ equal to A_0, and T to be the expected lifetime of the median citizen, for each momentary plan. Revised planning paths are illustrated by the broken lines in figure 4.6. Earlier results by Lewis and Neher showed that the revised plans could be represented by phantom plans incorporating independence of C and A so that the marginal utility of each is independent of the other's quantity ($U_{CA} = 0$). That result is more generally true here for any value of $U_{CA} = V' \cdot F_{CA} + V'' \cdot F_A F_C$ provided that $(G/A) > G'$ (see previous section).

Earlier qualitative results carry through to this more general case. The revised planning procedure with $A(T) = A(0)$ leads to the same steady-state equilibrium as does the original long-range plan. It is, however, less 'steep', as shown by the dotted lines in figure 4.6. The corresponding phantom plan is more inequality-adverse than is the original long-range plan, and this aversion is greater, the shorter is the planning horizon of each momentary plan.

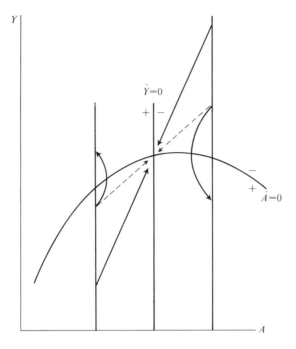

FIG. 4.6

CONCLUSIONS

Forests are not factories. Natural resources invite multiple-use management where direct benefits compete with those generated by the fruits of the harvest. Silvan scenes and toilet paper contribute jointly to the quality of life. But nature's own budget constraint imposes ultimate scarcity, so that choices must be made.

Practical cost–benefit analysis must allow for the direct enjoyment of resource stocks and for possible complementarity and substitutability between the stocks and the harvested resources. From Kurtz's early work (1968) on wealth effects in neoclassical growth models, it has been known that the analysis of this kind of problem is tedious but possible.

It is a fact that allocation decisions are actually being made all the time, in the public arena (to set aside wilderness areas, to prohibit strip mining) and in private (to fell a favourite fir tree, to build a cottage sundeck). It is clear that these decisions are often made without benefit of serious calculation or deliberate contemplation of consequence for the distribution of costs and benefits across time and among persons.

Economists have not always been able to give good advice. They are guided by training and inclination to think in terms of long-range plans, if only because short-run plans do not seem to have natural ends. Dynamic programmes are incomplete without terminal conditions.

But death is a fact of life. This consideration, coupled with the limited intertemporal altruism shared by most people, suggests that allocation plans should be made with rather shorter horizons coupled to the life expectancy of currently extant citizens.[5] These shorter plans also have the advantage of flexibility, so that they can be revised to accommodate changing circumstances: updated information, new tastes and technology, different demographic structures. It was the advantage of flexibility that motivated Goldman in his original work (1968) on revised planning processes.

Here, the prime motivation for thinking about short-term plans is the relative ease of their implementation. Practical managers seem sensitive to this virtue when they make on-the-spot decisions allowing greater harvests from more abundant stocks. But rules-of-thumb lack motivation.

The alternative of continuous planning revision, while well motivated in its day-to-day prescriptions (the equations of motion), still requires terminal conditions for each momentary plan. These were sought in the natural life-cycle of citizens and the 'keep-the-capital-intact' ethic for determining bequests.

Because long-term plans in the Ramsey tradition are so well understood, it helps to evaluate allocation sequences in terms of these plans. The phantom plan was designed for this purpose. The chief result for rule-of-thumb planning is that the average ratio of the harvest to the stock should exceed the marginal ratio as a sufficient condition for the phantom plan to incorporate diminishing marginal benefit from consumption. In short, these plans should not be too draconian. Caution may be the hallmark of reason.

In a similar way, phantom plans corresponding to sequences of revised plans are characterized by a more concave benefit function than their long-range (Ramsey) counterparts. Revised plans are more adverse to inequality of consumptions and utilities across time and generations.

ACKNOWLEDGEMENTS

An earlier version of this paper was jointly authored with Tracy Lewis and given at the World Congress of the Econometric Society (Autumn 1980). I wish to thank Tracy Lewis Partha Dasgupta, David Donaldson, Charles Blackorby, Keizo Nagatani, and Tony Scott for helpful discussions, without implicating them. The SSHRC of Canada supported the research through grants to the author and to the Programme in Natural Resource Economics at the University of British Columbia.

NOTES

1. See also Siebert (1981) for more formal analysis. D'Arge and Kogiku (1973) review much of the earlier literature.
2. Information requirements and the impossibility of forward contracting are sufficient to ensure that long-range plans will not be taken seriously. 'Agreeable plans' cope with this problem (Heal, 1973), as do continuously revised plans (Goldman, 1968, 1969; Neher, 1976; Lewis and Neher, 1982).
3. Future generations who share the same ethic have no incentive to depart from a consistent programme (Blackorby *et al.,* 1973). But tastes can change.
4. Other notable contributions to the intertemporal Rawlsian literature are Burmeister and Hammond (1977), Dixit, Hammond, and Hoel (1981), Hartwick (1977), Phelps and Riley (1978), Riley (1980), and Solow (1974).
5. An evaluation of this outcome is worth passing on. 'Society, which is expected to exist in perpetuity, should have a different standard of values as between the present and the future from that of the individual, whose appraisal of the future is governed by his own short span of life, and perhaps by a shadowy allowance for a generation or two of his descendants' (Englund, 1940).

REFERENCES

Allen, R. D. G. (1960), *Mathematical Analysis for Economists*. London: Macmillan.
Blackorby, C., Nissen, D., Premont, D., and Russell, R. (1973), 'Consistent Intertemporal Decision Making', *Review of Economic Studies* 40, 239-48.
Boulding, K. (1966), 'The Economics of Coming Spaceship Earth', in Henry Jarrett (ed.), *Environmental Quality in a Growing Economy,* Resources for the Future. Baltimore: Johns Hopkins University Press.
Brown, G. M. Jr and Hammack, J. (1973), 'Dynamic Economic Management of Migratory Waterfowl', *Review of Economics and Statistics,* 55, 73-82.
Burmeister, E. and Hammond, P. J. (1977), 'Maximum Paths of Heterogeneous Capital Accumulation and the Instability of Paradoxical Steady States', *Econometrica,* 45, 853-70.
D'Arge, R. C. and Kogiku, K. C. (1973), 'Economic Growth and the Environment', *Review of Economic Studies,* 40, 61-77.
Dasgupta, P. (1974), 'On Some Alternative Criteria for Justice Between Generations', *Journal of Public Economics,* 3, 405-23.
Dixit, A., Hammond, P., and Hoel, M. (1981), 'On Hartwick's Rule for Regular Maximum Paths of Capital Accumulation and Resource Depletion', *Review of Economic Studies,* 47, 551-6.
Donaldson, D. and Victor, P. (1976), 'On the Dynamics of Air Pollution Control', *Canadian Journal of Economics,* 1976, 492-507.
Englund, E. (1940), 'What Price Conservatism', *Land Policy Review,* 3.
Faustman, M. (first published in 1849), 'On the Determination of the Value which Forest Land and Immature Stands Passes for Forestry', in M. Gane, *Oxford Institute Papers,* no. 42.
Goldman, S. M. (1968), 'Optimal Growth and Continual Planning Revision', *Review of Economic Studies,* 35, 145-54.
Goldman, S. M. (1969), 'Sequential Planning and Continual Planning Revision', *Journal of Political Economy,* 77, 653-64.
Hartwick, J. (1977), 'Investing Returns from Depleting Renewable Resource Stocks and Intergenerational Equity', *Economic Letters,* 1, 85-8.
Heal, G. M. (1973), *The Theory of Economic Planning.* Amsterdam: North-Holland.
Hotelling, H. (1931), 'The Economics of Exhaustible Resources', *Journal of Political Economy,* 39, 137-75.

Kurtz, M. (1968), 'Optimal Economic Growth and Wealth Effects', *International Economic Review*, 9, 349–54.

Lewis, T. and Neher, P. A. (1982), 'Consistent and Revised Plans for Natural Resource Use', in L. J. Mirman and D. F. Spulber (eds), *Essays in the Economics of Renewable Resources*, Amsterdam: North-Holland.

Machlup, F. (1964), 'Professor Samuelson on the Theory of Realism', *American Economic Review*, 54, 733–5.

Neher, P. A. (1976), 'Democratic Exploitation of a Replenishable Resource', *Journal of Public Economics*, 5, 361–71.

Nordhaus, W. and Tobin, J. (1972), 'Is Growth Obsolete?' in *Economic Growth*, New York: National Bureau for Economic Research.

Phelps, E. S. (1961), 'The Golden Rule of Accumulation: A Fable for Growthmen', *American Economic Review*, 51, 638–43.

Phelps, E. S. (1966), *Golden Rules of Economic Growth*. New York: Norton.

Phelps, E. S. and Riley, J. G. (1978), 'Rawlsian Growth: Dynamic Programming of Capital and Wealth for Intergenerational "Maxi-Min" Justice', *Review of Economic Studies*, 45, 103–20.

Pontryagin, L. S. *et al.* (1964), *The Mathematical Theory of Optimal Processes*. Oxford: Pergamon.

Ramsey, F. (1928), 'A Mathematical Theory of Saving', *Economic Journal*, 38, 543–59.

Rawls, J. (1971), *A Theory of Justice* Oxford: Clarendon Press.

Riley, J. G. (1980), 'The Just Rate of Depletion of a Natural Resource', *Journal of Environmental Economics and Management*, 7, 291–307.

Samuelson, P. A. (1976), 'The Economics of Forestry in an Evolving Society', *Economic Enquiry*, 17, 446–92.

Schaeffer, M. B. (1959), 'Biological and Economic Aspects of Management of Marine Fisheries', *Transactions of the American Fisheries Society*, 88, 100–4.

Siebert, H. (1981), 'Nature as a Life Support System', Discussion Paper no. 177–81, University of Mannheim.

Solow, R. M. (1974), 'The Economics of Resources or the Resources of Economics', *American Economic Review*, 64, 1–21.

Comment   Partha Dasgupta

I am going to discuss this paper in conjunction with Professor Neher's earlier work on related issues (Neher, 1976; and Lewis and Neher, 1980). The paper under review is quite obviously part of a continuing research programme. Briefly stated, Neher is exploring the relationship between the 'democratic' exploitation of natural resource (viz. in the form of recurrent majority voting) and the 'optimal' exploitation of these resource. The analytical foundations of this question were laid by Goldman (1968), who, however, did not give his formulation quite the interpretation that Neher gives (see especially Neher, 1976). I like Professor Neher's interpretation—it is what makes the formulation interesting—and shall follow him here.

Goldman (1968) asked us to imagine that at *each* date society plans its investment policy for, say, T years; with a stipulated minimum stock level at the end of the T years. For analytical tractability he assumed that at each date society compares programmes in the light of the (discounted) sum of utilities over T years. Clearly, then, at each date society formulates a T-year plan, follows it at the first date of the plan, only to have the plan vitiated at the 'next' instant since a new plan is unfolded. And so on. Goldman (1968) analysed such a sequence of 'rolling plans' in the context of a one-good Ramsey-Solow economy. And he noted that if at each date the target capital stock T years hence is set equal to the inherited capital stock, *and* if the economy at the first instant is not (in a precise sense) capital-rich, then the sequence of such rolling plans tends in the long run to the state of affairs that a Ramsey-esque planner would aim at. Professor Neher's aim in the above paper and the two earlier ones I have referred to is to analyse this question in the context of an economy where the stock of capital not only provides future consumption benefits as a means of production but also is valuable directly as a stock. While Neher, rightly, draws attention to a number of natural resources (e.g., fisheries, clean air, etc.) with this feature, the model he works with has many additional interpretations (public capital goods; see e.g. Arrow and Kurz, 1970). (These interpretations are worth keeping in mind, because I believe Neher's analysis is pertinent to a wider class of problems than he wishes to concentrate on here. I need hardly add that usual methods of computing net national product ignore the direct value (or disbenefits) of capital assets. The social implication of this neglect is obvious: governments wedded to NNP computations gain much by veering off desirable programmes.)

For the case where the instantaneous utility function is defined on an index of income that itself is additive separable in consumption and the stock of capital (actually, a bit more is needed), Lewis and Neher (1980) have provided a fairly complete analysis of the relationship between 'democratic' resource exploitation and the 'optimal' mode. Their work significantly generalizes the results in Goldman's early work. Their central aim is to construct what they call a 'phantom' objective function, which, if invoked by a Ramsey-esque planner, would christen the democratic rule as optimal. Their most striking result is this: the 'phantom' utility function is related to the actual utility function by way of a positive concave transformation. Thus, in a precise sense the sequence of rolling plans yields a more egalitarian income flow over time than the Ramsey optimum.

There is a strong whiff of a 'revealed preference' approach to this line of enquiry, and I think it is this I find mildly unappetizing. After all, why *should* we be interested in the phantom utility function? To what end? I can see that it *is* of interest to ask what the *costs* are (in terms of welfare loss) if such a sequence of rolling plans is followed. But then, I would attempt to measure just that: the welfare loss. It seems to me that such computations would not be intolerably difficult near the steady state.

As a description of a 'democratic' exploitation rule, a sequence of rolling plans appears at first blush to be analytically appealing. But would cohorts vote so myopically as Professor Neher postulates? Since there is continual planning revision, the unfolding path is *not intertemporally consistent*. A game-theoretic resolution naturally suggests itself. The literature on this is rather large. The problem is that non-cooperative equilibria that are inter-temporally consistent aren't usually intertemporally efficient (see Phelps and Pollak, 1968, and Dasgupta, 1974)! We are faced with a dilemma.

In the above paper Neher is concerned with a broader class of instantaneous utility functions than studied in Lewis and Neher (1980), and he is faced im-mediately with a problem that was noted in Arrow and Kurz (1970), namely that there are typically multiple stationary solutions to Ramsey-esque paths, so that the long-run optimum policy depends in general on where the economy is to begin with. Characterizing optimal paths—not to mention 'democratic' policies—is a really difficult matter, and Professor Neher, not surprisingly, makes only partial progress.

REFERENCES

Arrow, K. J. and Kurz, M. (1970), *Public Investment, the Rate of Return and Optimal Fiscal Policy*. Baltimore: Johns Hopkins University Press.
Dasgupta, P. (1974), 'On Some Alternative Criteria for Justice Between Generations', *Journal of Public Economics*, 3, 405–23.
Goldman, S. (1968), 'Optimal Growth and Continual Planning Revision', *Review of Economic Studies*, 35, 145–54.
Lewis, T. and Neher, P. (1980), 'Consistent and Revised Plans for Natural Resource Use', Resources Paper no. 50, University of British Columbia Department of Economics.
Neher, P. (1976), 'Democratic Exploitation of a Replenishable Resource', *Journal of Public Economics*, 5, 361–71.
Phelps, E. and Pollak, R. (1968), 'On Second-Best National Savings and Game Equilibrium Growth', *Review of Economic Studies*, 35, 185–99.
Ryder, H. and Heal, G. (1973), 'Optimum Growth with Intertemporally Dependent Pre-ferences', *Review of Economic Studies*, 40, 1–32.

5. Modelling Fishermen and Regulator Behaviour in Schooling and Search Fisheries

James E. Wilen

If asked to point to the most important contribution that economics has made to the job of fisheries regulation, most fisheries economists would identify normative roles, as opposed to implementation roles. Economists have, especially recently, catalysed important debates which have led regulators to begin acting on efficiency, equity, and revenue generation goals in addition to the traditional goals of fishery conservation. This is evident in recent management legislation in North America, where regulators are now required by law to manage for 'optimum' yields (incorporating socioeconomic objectives) as opposed to 'maximum' yields (physical).

Beyond providing guidance at the conceptual level, very little other work has been done by economists to help regulators to *implement* management plans. This is particularly important because, like the proverbial 'slip twixt cup and lip', there are many chances for 'slips' between setting broad-scale management objectives and carrying them out at the field level. It is the implementation phase that ultimately determines success or failure, and many programmes are going or have gone awry because of the inability to forecast how the system will respond to policy changes as they are reflected in the field. Typical implementation questions that arise, for example, include the following. If limited entry permits and a buy-back system are introduced, what level will permit prices gravitate towards? If gillnet/seine catch-split targets are changed, what will happen to incomes? If trawl nets are regulated smaller, how will the industry adjust? How will increasing fuel costs affect fishing behaviour? What will the typical boat look like after limited entry is introduced?

These questions all require a shift away from the traditional normative approach in fisheries economics towards a predictive approach. Predicting behaviour requires, of course, a firm understanding of exactly how a fishery operates—what aspects of biology are important, what fishing technology looks like, how fishermen behave, how regulators react, etc. Unfortunately, very few economists have made the effort to understand these aspects of fisheries at the fishery-specific level.

This paper provides an overview of what I think are some critical aspects of regulated fisheries and then discusses their implications for developing models of regulated fishery behaviour. My focus will be on regulated fishery systems; the species biology, the fishing sectors, and the regulatory institutions and methodology will be mostly predictive rather than normative. In the next section some important characteristics of fisheries biology are discussed to provide a framework for analysis. The following section then considers regulatory behaviour from a predictive point of view—i.e., how regulators *do* regulate as opposed to how they *should* regulate. Some models are then presented of regulated fisheries in order to focus on methodological issues. There follows a discussion of fishing technology and the implications for regulation, and the final section presents a summary.

SCHOOLING VERSUS SEARCH FISHERIES

Trying to draw generalizations in a field that has as much empirical diversity as fisheries does is best attempted with caution. A look at, and particularly a comparison of, various real-world fisheries suggests, however, at least three important components that determine how a fishery evolves and responds to perturbation: the fish species biology, the fishing technology, and the regulatory structure. If we were relegated to being institutional taxonomists, we could probably find examples of fisheries that would fill many 'boxes' that might describe a variety of fishery types—categorized by biology, technology, and regulations. To take the biology characteristic, for example, there are: slow-growing species (halibut, whales) and fast-growing species (herring, anchovy); anadromous and non-anadromous; sedentary (bottom fish) and mobile (tuna) species; etc. With respect to technology, there are: troll, trawl, gillnet, seine, single, and multi-species fisheries; and so on. Examples of regulatory structures might be classified as: input- or entry-controlling; active or passive; on-line or advance forecasting; etc. Thus there are many ways in which we could classify fisheries if we were interested simply in classification.

To be more useful, I would like to suggest that, in general, the dominating characteristic of a fishery is whether it is a *schooling* fishery or a *search* fishery. These are opposite ends of a spectrum and some fisheries fall in between, but at one end are those species such as herring which become fishable only when they are densely packed. Colin Clark refers to these as Type IV fisheries,[1] and the main characteristic is that they occur at certain times in their life-cycle in concentrations that make finding and fishing for them relatively easy. At the opposite end of the spectrum are those species such as bottom fish for which fishermen must actively search to find fishable densities.[2] These, in fact, are most common, since most fish are located in 'patches' over space. Some species fall in between the poles of this spectrum, and some even have characteristics that change over the life-cycle. As an example of the latter, salmon and herring at sea are extreme versions of search fisheries (whose 'patches' are seldom found) but during spawning phases become schooling fisheries. Tuna seem to school up periodically (daily) in order to feed and then disperse rapidly. Pink shrimp during clear ocean conditions school up in dense concentrations and then disperse when, for example, the water clouds up. For both of these, one must 'search' for schools.

What is important for analysing fisheries is whether there is a phase in the species life-cycle in which they are in fishable schools that are readily found or whether they remain in more or less randomly distributed 'patches' that must be searched for. This characteristic is critical, I think, because it seems to drive both the evolution of fishing technology and the evolution of regulatory structure. For example, in schooling fisheries a net (and probably a seine net) is usually most efficient. If left unregulated, technology will probably evolve to produce a net–boat combination whose limits are defined by the physics and mechanics of setting and hauling the net around the school. This technological limit is often very large for highly concentrated schools and usually too large to ensure species preservation, so regulators generally focus on limiting capacity per net set—e.g., with mesh sizes, maximum net sizes, net design specifications, and so on. Once net limits are set, fishing technology is relatively fixed and fishermen must resort to increasing mobility (if more than one school occurs) or increasing ability to find denser schools (sonar, for example). The point, however, is that the technology is governed by the schooling nature of the fish and will be modified as regulation evolves to maintain species protection.

Another important feature of schooling fisheries that links up fishing technology and regulatory structure further is the fact that concentration remains constant and hence catch per unit effort (CPUE) is a poor measure of biomass.[3] This has important regulatory structure implications because the regulators must develop some other way of estimating biomass and monitoring catch in order to ensure adequate escapement. In British Columbia (BC) herring, for example, an alleged management advantage of forcing the fishery to use small gillnets is that 'controllability' is higher because catching rates are slower and easier to monitor.[4] In addition, because schooling fisheries may not thin out as fishing proceeds, they are very vulnerable to overharvest and hence the role of management is especially critical. Thus, the regulatory structure will generally evolve either to monitor and respond quickly, or to slow the rate of fishing, or both. Whatever happens, the important thing to note is that technology and regulatory structure are not exogenous, but in fact evolve together (or in sequence) in these fisheries. If capacity increases, management usually will take steps to preserve its biomass monitoring function and provide safety buffers by imposing inefficient gear regulations on the fleet. Fishermen, in response, will adopt methods to improve catching power within the constraints imposed by the regulations but they may be 'bound up' significantly by gear regulations. Both groups of factors will be directed by the schooling nature of the species, however, and that may give us a clue about how to predict short and long-run events. More will be said about this later.

At the other end of the spectrum are search fisheries, whose limiting factor is basically time. In these fisheries the activity of fishing is divided up between 'searching' and 'fishing'. Both activities may involve more or less separate technologies, which may be complementary or competitive. Thus, for example, a small, high-horsepower boat with lots of electronic equipment may be best for finding fish, but a larger hold-capacity design with high torque may be better for trawling once fish are found. Existing boat designs for undertaking both functions will reflect trade-offs between the two activities.

The regulation of search fisheries proceeds in several directions in practice. If the 'patches' of fish are independent biologically, then regulation will generally be aimed at ensuring that each patch that is found is not fished out. Gear restriction appear most expedient in these cases. On the other hand, if patches mix or are otherwise interdependent, regulators must ensure that aggregate catch is not too high—which can be done either by reducing the number of patches found or (and) by reducing catchability on the patches. Regulators have not generally chosen to limit searching efficiency directly but have instead, by shortening fishing seasons, reduced both search and fishing time simultaneously. Fishermen may respond, of course, by adopting methods of improving search efficiency or fishing efficiency depending upon relative costs, etc. More will be said below about these possibilities.

REGULATORY INSTITUTIONS AND REGULATOR BEHAVIOUR

One could hypothesize many things about how regulators behave, drawing on political and organizational theory and the like, but I think that in nearly all real-world cases the basic fact is that regulators are aiming towards species preservation—full stop. Thus regulators see their basic job as ensuring adequate escapement of spawning stocks and every effort will be made to ensure those targeted levels are achieved.[5] The regulatory instruments at their disposal to ensure escapement vary widely from *indirect* controls, which economists are prone to support (taxes, licences, entry permits, etc.), to direct controls, which regulators themselves have tended to adopt. Direct controls include gear restrictions, season closure, by-catch rules, etc., which directly restrict effort effectiveness or output as a binding constraint might.

A second hypothesis about regulatory institutions that is validated in real fisheries is that, by and large, *regulators will be effective* in causing no more than the targeted levels to be caught. While responses to change may vary somewhat from fishery to fishery, regulators will develop means to achieve the ends eventually. This follows from the very nature of the regulatory function i.e., that they always have the 'last move' in a sequence of regulatee-regulator interactions. Thus, if fisheries adopt a gear technology that is 10 per cent more efficient, regulators will reduce effective effort applied on the fishery by a corresponding 10 per cent in order to maintain target catch. This might be done by, for example, increasing mesh size, reducing net length, or shortening the season; but whichever method is used, the net result will be that targets will be achieved.

Beyond hypothesizing that effective effort *will* be adjusted to ensure target catches, it is difficult to go one step further and predict precisely *how* regulators will regulate effort. Evidence from real-world cases suggests that each is different and that the method that is chosen at any time may depend upon political and organization factors. This makes long-term forecasting of technology in a regulated fishery difficult, because at any point in time, the boat configuration that exists is a product of cumulative (perhaps *ad hoc*) adjustments in regulations. Thus, a fishery in which regulators successively limited troll line length, shortened seasons, increased hook spacing, and then introduced limited entry would look very much different from an otherwise identical fishery in which only the order of the regulations introductions was changed. It is even more complicated in reality because the boat-building industry also responds by developing innovations that get around direct effort controls as they become binding. Thus the end product is a result of: order of introduction, type of regulation, and order of innovative responses.

MODELLING REGULATED FISHERIES

The models in this paper represent a substantial departure from classical approaches such as those by Gordon (1954) and Scott (1955) and modern-day counterparts such as Anderson (1977) and Clark (1980a). These works all cast fisheries in an open-access equilibrium framework whereby entry of capital drives the species stock to some (generally low-level) bionomic equilibrium. Analyses of optimal regulations (e.g. taxes) are then undertaken. The important feature of these approaches is that entry and stock dynamics are assumed to determine the evolution of the fishery, which is ultimately checked at a stock level dependent on biological and economic parameters. While this general approach was perhaps relevant in the past, when many fisheries were pure open-access fisheries, most of today's fisheries simply do not fit this mould. The advent of 200-mile limits and other extensions of jurisdiction has brought most important fisheries under control of one or more regulatory authorities, and hence modern fisheries are no longer primarily pure open-access fisheries but rather, in Peter Pearse's terms, *regulated* open-access fisheries. The key difference is that fishermen do not enter and drive the stock down to some level where price equals costs. Rather, regulatory authorities *fix* a target stock level (and corresponding harvest rate) and then control the application of (generally, excess) effort applied to the fish in such a way that the target is roughly achieved. Thus, the species stock level can be regarded, at least as a first approach, as exogenously determined, and the important things to look at are how regulators control existing potential effort and how fishermen react to such controls. The models below are basically a first cut at this new (and, I believe, more appropriate) way to view modern fisheries.

Schooling fisheries

For the purpose of modelling real fisheries, the importance of the above observations is that they point to the need to look at interaction between regulators and regulatees. At the aggregate fishery level, regulators must act to prevent over-harvesting by the industry, whereas the industry might be thought of as trying to beat the regulators at their game. The industry's behaviour is not, of course, a result of carefully planned collective decisions, but is in itself the outcome of decisions made at the micro-level.

Interaction between regulators and regulatees in a schooling fishery can be formalized in a simple model as follows. First, consider an aggregate production function.

$$H = F(X, K) \qquad (1)$$

where X is a measure of the species stock, K is a measure of aggregate industry fishing capacity on the grounds, and H is aggregate harvest. We will assume for the time being that K may be produced from many inputs not necessarily efficiently combined. Not much thought has been given to the form H should take and we discuss this further in the next section. For the purposes here we simply assume that F exhibits non-increasing returns to scale and $F(0, K) = 0 = F(X, 0)$.

Define a regulated production function regulated by direct controls to be

$$H = F(\bar{X}, \theta K) \equiv f(\theta K), \qquad 0 \leqslant \theta \leqslant 1. \qquad (2)$$

For a given exogenous or pre-chosen species stock level $\bar{X}$, a particular target harvest H may be achieved by adjusting regulations to reduce potential effort K (chosen by the industry) to a level of 'effective effort' θK. The parameter θ (a scalar) captures net set restrictions, shortened seasons, area closures.

By fixing $H = \bar{H} = f(\theta K)$, the above formulation yields a *feedback regulation function* $\theta = \theta(K, \bar{H}, \bar{X})$ that establishes the severity of the controls needed to be applied to K to allow some given target catch. This formulation implies an instantaneous and perfect adjustment policy which represents an extreme in controllability, of course. Most pure schooling fisheries probably have regulatory structures that are nearly instantaneous, since close monitoring and control are essential in light of their vulnerability. In both the BC herring and river-mouth salmon fisheries, for example, openings are determined by fisheries officers *on location* after they have assessed stocks and numbers and capacity of boats present. In other fisheries, $\bar{X}$ and K are estimated and then θ is set in advance. Until recently, troll salmon fisheries (not schooling fisheries) on the Pacific coast were regulated with pre-season set openings, on-line adjustment, and pre-set (or advance-planned) adjustment, as are current Pacific troll salmon fisheries, where openings are set in advance and closures set as monitoring or cumulative catch proceeds.[6] Any of these modifications could be modelled without major changes in the qualitative results that follow.

The level of aggregate potential effort K that must be regulated is determined by the fishing industry as a whole. The industry is composed of many individual decision-making units, of course, and it is the sum of their individual decisions that produces the aggregate value of K. Let us assume that there are N members of the industry[7] and that each must decide how much potential effort to apply to the fishery. Let k_i be the amount chosen by the ith decision-maker, r the rental price of a unit of potential capacity (or generalized input price), and $P = 1$ the price per unit of fish caught. Then the ith vessel owner sees his profits to be

$$\Pi_i = \frac{k_i}{\sum\limits_{1}^{N} k_j} f\left(\theta \sum\limits_{1}^{N} k_j\right) - rk_i. \tag{3}$$

The objective function (3) reflects some of the hypotheses made earlier about behaviour in a regulated fishery. In particular, each vessel owner realizes that his profits depend upon what the regulators do (θ) and what the remaining $N - 1$ fishermen choose as their levels of k_j. A given fisherman's expected catch will be proportional to his expected share of total effort applied to the fishery. Since each fisherman would view the problem similarly, we have a non-cooperative N-person game which determines the outcome.

To examine the outcome, assume that each vessel owner makes a forecast $\hat{k}$ of his fellow fishermen's potential fishing capacity ($N - 1$) $\hat{k}$ as well as an assumption about how regulators will react in setting θ. He then optimizes by choosing a k_i that maximizes (3). He may be right or wrong in his forecasts, and an equilibrium exists only when each individual has forecast all other individuals' decision correctly and made a profit-maximizing choice, which also is the level that others expect him to choose. With respect to regulator-regulatee interaction, there are several ways to incorporate behaviour. One would be simply to include the regulator as another actor in the above described model and define the full (Nash) equilibrium as one in which all expectations, including those by fishermen about θ and those by regulators about k are fulfilled after optimal contingent choices are made. Another method would be to make the model dynamic and have expectations governed by past events, for example. The simplest way to close the model is to assume perfect and instantaneous controllability by regulators so that fishermen take $f(\theta \Sigma k_j)$ as fixed. Under this assumption, the optimal Nash equilibrium[8] for (3) satisfies

$$\frac{f}{N\bar{k}} = r\left(1 + \frac{1}{N - 1}\right). \tag{4}$$

At that point each vessel is still making a positive (but small for large N) profit equal to $rk/(N - 1)$ and the industry's total profits are $rk\{N/(N - 1)\}$. Figure 5.1 shows the regulated industry equilibrium as modelled above. Suppose that regulators desire that total harvest be $\bar{H}$ (normalized to 1, so that can be graphed on the same scale). The most efficient way to harvest would be to set $\theta = 1$ and allow only $N\bar{k}$ units of effort. But we can show that an expectation equilibrium will not be sustained at that point since $F/N\bar{k} > r\{N/(N - 1)\}$. Thus each vessel owner will apply greater effort, and θ will have to be set at lower values to keep $f(\theta N\bar{k}) = \bar{H}$. An equilibrium is reached where potential effort has expanded to $N\bar{k}$ and effective effort actually applied to $N\bar{k} = \bar{\theta} N\bar{k}$. At this point, the total costs of having excess effort to catch $\bar{H}$ are as shown above.

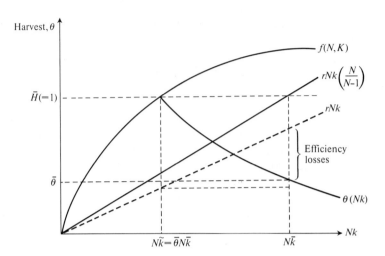

FIG. 5.1

As the model suggests, there will be a tendency towards rent dissipation, the extent of which depends upon how large N is. For large N, rent dissipation will be nearly complete with large efficiency losses where f/r is large. Given the tendency towards inefficiency and profits dissipation, and given that participants should realize this, the question arises, why does such behaviour take place? The answer is fairly simple. By fixing aggregate catch, regulators force individual units to focus on relative shares of the total rent. But since the shares sum to 1, one unit's share loss is the rest of the industry's gain and vice versa. Thus each unit must always be making a strategic decision *vis-à-vis* the rest of the industry. Unfortunately, however, disequilibrium decisions that look strategically best from the point of view of each unit have the effect, when actually enacted, of making everyone worse off. This situation is encounted in other group behaviour instances and is basically a variant of the prisoners' dilemma problem. This can be seen by supposing that we begin with all N participants selecting an effort level $k \leqslant k_0 < \bar{k}$, i.e., a disequilibrium k_0 more efficient than the equilibrium $\bar{k}$. Now, suppose that our representative fisherman contemplates increasing his potential effort to $k_0 < k^* \leqslant \bar{k}$. Table 5.1 gives his pay-off matrix; i.e., each cell shows by how much his profits would increase when the rest of the industry makes a similar adjustment or stays at k_0. Although not readily obvious by inspection, it can be shown that, whenever the industry is out of equilibrium ($k_0 < k$), the best individual strategy is to increase effort to k^* *regardless of* which strategy is anticipated by one's rivals. Thus, if one believes that the industry will maintan a level $(N - 1)k_0 < (N - 1)\bar{k}$, then column (2) yields the relevant pay-offs and the first-row entry in column (2) will be strictly positive when $k_0 < \bar{k}$. If it is believed that the industry will adjust to a larger

TABLE 5.1

i	Rest of the industry	
	Increase effort to k^* (1)	Maintain effort at k_0 (2)
Increase effort to k^*	$-rN\{\sqrt{(k_0\bar{k})} - k_0\}$	$\sqrt{(k_0\bar{k})}\left[f\left\{\left(\dfrac{N-1}{N}\right)\dfrac{1}{\sqrt{(k_0\bar{k})}} - rN\right\}\right]$
Maintain effort at k_0	$\dfrac{f}{N}\left[\dfrac{1}{1 + (N-1)\{\sqrt{(k_0\bar{k})}/k_0 - 1\}} - 1\right]$	0

$k_0 < k^* < \bar{k}$, then column (1) is relevant and losses will be minimized by also increasing k to k^*. Thus, irrespective of whether one expects rivals to follow, it always seems best to increase k above any initial level k_0 when $k_0 < \bar{k}$, even when k_0 is the rent-maximizing level k^*. The 'prisoner's dilemma' paradox is that such seemingly individually rational behaviour leads to a collective outcome where everyone is worse off.

The above model can be used to analyse the implications of various regulatory methods other than the direct method already included. For example, one can easily analyse licences on participations (i.e., on each of the N decision-makers), licences per unit of effort, taxes on effort, taxes on output, etc.[9] Extensions to allow for lagged responses, for variable participation rates, and for multiple inputs may also be incorporated. For the present purpose, however, what is important is the model's structure and how well it captures real-world fisheries' regulation environments. What I believe is crucial about this approach is the setting of individual decision-making in a gaming structure. This has not been done in other models of fisheries. It is partly a philosophical and partly an empirical issue whether we should model fishermen as parametric decision-makers *à la* standard competitive model or as actively strategic decision-makers who consider rivals' decisions in making their own. However, it is my feeling that, for tightly controlled schooling fisheries in particular, it *must* be the case that fishermen are conscious of fellow fishermen's decisions because they are sharing a *fixed* pie. This suggests that decisions will focus on share-optimizing, which in turn requires information about opponents' strategies. This is an important methodological turning point, because models that are simple extensions of atomistic perfect-competition models will yield different predictions than those incorporating gaming behaviour, particularly when expanded to the more realistic multiple-input case.[10]

Search fisheries

As discussed earlier, search fisheries combine both searching activities and fishing activities to produce total fish caught. Assume that fish are found in 'patches' and that the total number of patches found in a season depends upon the aggregate amount of time spent searching. If T is the total time available and S_i is the fraction spent searching by the ith decision-maker, then $P = g\{S_iT + (N-1)\hat{S}T\}$ represents the number of fishable patches that our representative decision-maker expects the industry to find. Assume that he also expects his share of patches found and fished to be proportional to his share of total searching time, and that his catch is proportional to the time he spends fishing (perhaps regulated by reducing gear effectiveness, etc.). Then his expected profits are

$$\Pi_i = \theta(1 - S_i)TA \left\{ \frac{S_iT}{S_iT + (N-1)\hat{S}T} \right\} g - S_iTC_s - (1 - S_i)TC_f \quad (5)$$

where C_s and C_f are costs per unit time of searching and fishing respectively and price per unit catch is assumed equal to 1. In this formulation A is a units adjustment coefficient measured in fish caught per unit time spent fishing a patch, $(1 - S_i)T$ is total fishing time, and the term in braces is the fraction of patches expected by the ith decision maker.

The above formulation is similar to the one used to model schooling fisheries, in that expected profits depend upon rivals' behaviour. In this case it is assumed that each fisherman views the principal competition as that between himself and others in the searching activity and that regulators choose directly to regulate fishing effectiveness rather than searching effectiveness. Note that we could also embed a regulatory parameter θ_s inside the searching production function to allow for the latter possibility. I can think of no fisheries where searching behaviour is stifled directly, however, so that the above formulation is probably representative.

To solve the above model, let us assume that each fisherman makes forecasts of fellow fishermen's decisions about $\hat{S}$ (the time split between searching and fishing) and about the regulators' actions on θ. An equilibrium occurs when expectations are correct and the regulators have also chosen the expected θ to ensure their target catch H. In this model θ is chosen by regulation for any given industry decision about S, such that

$$\bar{H} = \theta T(1 - S) Ag \qquad (6)$$

For simplicity, let us assume that searching time produces a proportional pay-off in patches found so that $g = kNsT$. Then $\theta(S)$ derived from (6) will be a quadratic function of S.[11] Assuming θ is taken parametrically by fishermen, the optimal searching time is found by differentiating (5) and setting equal to 0, so that

$$S_i^T = \tfrac{1}{2} - \frac{\Delta}{2\theta AKT} \qquad (7)$$

where $\Delta = C_s - C_f$. Figure 5.2 shows the result for the case where $\Delta > 0$, i.e., where searching costs per unit of time exceed fishing costs. In this example, θ is assumed to be adjusted so that $\theta = 1$ at the searching fraction (S_e^*) that yields the targeted harvest $\bar{H}$ efficiently. At the efficient level S^*, however, each industry participant will see gains associated with trying to increase his share of patches found and will increase searching time towards $\underline{S}$. As this occurs, total fishing pressure on stock will rise and regulators will have to tighten regulations on the fishing activity (e.g. by restricting gear efficiency). The end result is a regulation equilibrium S_R where too much total time is being devoted to 'over-searching' and not enough to fishing (relative to the search–fishing cost structure). In addition, regulators are forcing fishermen, when they are fishing, to be inefficient in order to maintain stock size. The opposite char-acteristics of inefficiencies would occur if fishing costs were higher than search costs per unit of time. In this case, there would be too little time devoted to searching (or too much to fishing) from an efficiency standpoint.

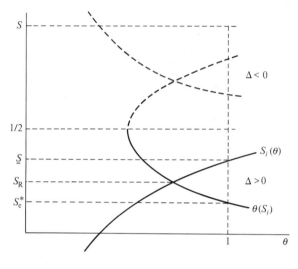

FIG. 5.2

FISHING PRODUCTION FUNCTIONS AND REGULATION

Both of the above models are simple but capture what I believe are the important features of real-world regulated fisheries; namely, the interactive nature of decision-making among regulatees and between regulators. The more interesting issues are posed once we begin disaggregating the above system, and particularly when we discuss multiple-input situations. Some of the most important conceptual issues in recent debates over the workability of direct-versus-indirect regulatory schemes have to do with input substitution possibilities. For example, the Powell River Conference brought out two points of view.[12] The first maintains that, by restricting certain key dimensions of effort, one can eventually force efficiency back into a fishery. The other view (citing failure of real-world cases) claims that the industry is likely to work around any direct controls and that, therefore, indirect measures such as individual vessel harvest quotas should be adopted. This debate basically focuses on the nature of fishing technology and has important policy implications. If direct regulations are workable, for example, questions arise such as: Which inputs should be restricted? In what sequence and to what levels should they be reduced to promote efficiency? Will rents emerge and persist with only partial controls on inputs? If direct regulations are thought to be not workable, then questions arise such as: If entry permits are allotted, how many should be given out? How will technology evolve if they are made non-transferable? If transferable quotas to harvest are used, what will the typical efficient boat look like? Will licensing programmes in several fisheries encourage specialization or multiple-fishery technology?

Both of the models discussed above aggregate inputs for simplicity of exposition. In the model of the school fishery it was assumed that potential capacity K is produced by aggregating individual production functions for k_i. By writing the regulated production function as

$$H = f(\theta k) = f\left(\theta \sum_1^N k_i\right) \tag{8}$$

we are assuming that controls are non-specific and affect each boat's fishing capacity in the same way. Once we recognize that fishing 'capacity' can be produced with multiple inputs,

$$k_i = k_i(x_i, x_2, \ldots, x_n) \tag{9}$$

it becomes important to distinguish between direct controls that restrict effort *per se*, i.e.

$$\theta k_i = \theta k_i(X_1, X_2, \ldots, X_n) \tag{10}$$

and controls that restrict particular inputs:

$$\theta \hat{K}_i = K_i(\hat{X}_1, \theta_2 X_2, \theta_3 X_3, \ldots, X_n). \tag{11}$$

In the former case it can be shown, using the schooling model, that individual boat owners will 'produce' capacity efficiently (factor proportions will be optimal) for the aggregate level being allowed, but that too much overall effort will be produced for efficiency. This is the case when regulations, for example, restrict season length or openings in order to reduce effective effort applied on the grounds. Note that we are not saying simply that there are too many boats, all of efficient design: rather, for the numbers of boats in the industry and average time allowed on the ground by regulators, boats will combine inputs in correct proportions. A completely efficient system would be likely to have a different number of boats, with different input configurations, making a different number of net sets per season.

More can be said about these issues by speculating about the likely form that a fishing production function might take. A reasonable production function for a vessel fishing more or less constant concentrations of a schooling fish is best denominated in terms something like catch per contact hour, Q. Total seasonal catch then depends upon total hours fished, T_f, which in turn is equal to total available time T minus travel time T_t, all modified by regulations on openings and closures. A complete production function might thus include:

$$C_{\text{season}} = \theta_f\{T - T_t \,(HP, \text{fuel, hull, } \ldots)\} * Q(\theta_N \text{net}, L, \ldots,$$

$$\text{hold capacity, hull, } \ldots) \tag{12}$$

This reflects the fact that total season catch depends upon catch per contact hour Q, which depends on the (regulated) net configuration, labour, other inputs, hold capacity, and hull design and size. In all schooling fisheries the terminal gear is regulated in some fashion. Q is then multiplied by total contact hours, which can be increased by building faster or more seaworthy boats and so on, but which also depends upon season closure regulations which are reflected in θ_f (the fishing time restriction parameter).

What more can be said about inefficiencies fostered by either direct fishing time restrictions (like θ_f) or by selected input restrictions like θ_N? In general, I would hypothesize that, while there is considerable substitution in the mobility production function T_t among fuel, engine size, hull design, boat size, etc., there is much less in the catch per contact-hour production function Q. Once gear restrictions on nets are set, the labour time, winches, and so on are probably related in a fixed-proportions technology. Thus, on first glance the types of controls now being employed (i.e., reducing θ_f) should influence mainly the mobility production function and leave catch per contact-hour efficiently produced. (There is always some initial inefficiency associated with $\theta_N \neq 1$, of course.) If the production functions are completely separable in inputs, changing θ_f will leave factor proportions in efficient combinations but with too much mobility being produced. In general, however, it is likely that there will be feedback between the two functions, primarily through the hull design and boat size variable. As a fishery becomes more profitable and entry occurs, regulators generally resort to shorter and shorter seasons. As they do this, fishermen will attempt (by my model) to reduce travel time by increasing mobility (there is ample evidence for this in the halibut fishery, the BC roe herring fishery, and the net salmon fisheries). However, travel speed may be increased only so much with engine changes, and thus hull configuration must be changed too—perhaps with thinner beamed boats, planing hulls, and the like. Once hull volume is reduced, it will reduce hold capacity and this may make hold capacity the limiting factor determining Q. Since the Q function is basically fixed-proportions technology, however, efficient combinations of inputs will be used to produce catch per contact-hour.

It is interesting to note that some fisheries have gone external to the fishing boat as contact-hours have been reduced by building small, fast fishing boats with small holds but by additionally hiring 'brailing' boats to handle the fish once they are netted by fishing vessels. In any case, my hypothesis is that overall effort restrictions such as short seasons (which in the BC herring case have reduced to the ridiculous level of fifteen minutes in some cases) will force fishermen to increase engine size and fuel use, alter hull design, and decrease boat size, with some feedback (possibly) into the catching functions.

Note that we can look at the problem the other way as well. If net restrictions only are used, and are successively tightened (e.g., herring gillnets lengths were cut in half in 1980), then the need for other complementary inputs, including hold capacity and hull size, will decrease (proportionately, probably), and this will spill over to the mobility production function—causing changes here too. It is possible that these changes might equip the altered boat to fish other fisheries better as well. For example, by reducing net size in salmon fleets, regulators may encourage faster boats, which might (for example) fish more for albacore.

If input-specific controls are adopted in the flexible-technology mobility production function (e.g., by fixing engine size), then extension of the model to multiple-input cases suggests that fishermen will still try and maintain too much mobility by changing factor proportions and increasing other inputs. Thus inefficiencies generated will be factor proportion inefficiences as well as overall excess effort inefficiencies. These inefficiencies will spill over into the catching function to the extent that such spill-overs are less costly than input changes in the flexible-technology production function. Generally it can be said that input-specific regulations in the flexible technology will, as they are tightened, cause factor proportions to change most towards inputs with high elasticities of substitution for the restricted input. The effect of having inputs in both production functions is to 'bind up' the elasticity of substitution for common inputs and hence to shift adjustments further away from such inputs.

With respect to search fisheries, similar hypotheses can be developed. In these fisheries we can divide up the components of seasonal catch into a catch per contact-hour per patch production function Q, which is also mainly fixed proportions in (regulated) gear, winch capacity, hold capacity, etc.; a fishing time production function $(1 - S)(\bar{T} - T_t)$, which is proportional to total time devoted to fishing and which incorporates flexibile technology in engine, fuel, hull size, hull design to produce travel time, etc.; and a fishing patch finding production function P, which is a function of search time ST_f, electronic equipment, boat design, and other less conventional factors like group behaviour and information-sharing. Thus for search fisheries, we have something like

$$C_{\text{seasonal}} = \theta_f(1 - S)\{\bar{T} - T_t(\text{HP, fuel, hull}, \ldots)\}$$
$$* Q(\theta_g\text{gear}, L, \text{hold capacity, hull}) * P(\theta_s ST_f,$$
$$(\text{hull}, HP, \text{fuel, information sharing}, \ldots) \tag{13}$$

Again, the nature of the biology will dictate the types of controls that are likely to be used by regulators. If patches are independent, regulators will want to ensure that each patch is not over-exploited and hence will probably resort mainly to gear restrictions θ_g such as hook-spacing, mesh size, troll gear restrictions, and so forth. As these are tightened they will spill over into the mobility and searching functions through hull changes and boat size changes if these are common inputs. The qualitative effect will be to encourage fishermen to increase mobility and searching capacity, which will most likely already be over-produced from an efficiency standpoint. This in turn may, in a typical sequence of regulator reactions, cause reductions in the season length as regulators try and reduce the impact of mobility, which is increasing fishing time spent on the grounds and hence exploitation rates. Note that, in the case of independent patches, regulators will be unconcerned if *more* patches are found but will be concerned if each patch is exploited more heavily. The extent to which the latter occurs will depend on relative costs in searching and fishing activities, and, as was shown earlier, reducing season length may even reduce the proportion of time devoted to fishing each patch. In that case, a tightening of gear restrictions θ_g may even allow season length restrictions θ_f to be relaxed.

If patches are interdependent, then regulators will want to reduce exploitation rates per patch and/or overall searching efficiency. In practice, this usually means that season lengths are shortened in conjunction with gear restrictions. Again, the results can be traced through, as was done in the independent patch case above.

SUMMARY AND CONCLUSIONS

In this paper I have tried to outline what I think are the most important characteristics of real-world regulated fisheries. I think that it helps first to divide up fisheries into schooling and search fisheries, because it is these characteristics that basically drive fishing technology and hence regulator behaviour. Regulator behaviour is hypothesized to focus mainly on direct regulation of specific inputs (e.g. gear) or on aggregate contact hours (e.g. season closures). These direct regulations are motivated to ensure that a given targeted catch is not exceeded. Fishermen, in turn, take the regulatory actions as more or less effective and then focus on optimizing their shares of the target catch *vis-à-vis* each other. This generally leads to too much effort being produced from an efficiency point of view but not an excessive amount being applied at the fishery from the regulators' point of view. The ramifications of regulators' action depend upon the nature of the fishery and, in particular, on the nature of the production function. My hypothesis is that the catch per contact-hour production function is basically a fixed-proportions function with the limiting factor the size and type of gear. It may have common inputs with the mobility production function in both schooling and search fisheries and with the searching production function in search fisheries. Thus regulations directed at specific inputs in the fixed-proportion catching technology (e.g. gear) may spill over into the flexible-technology mobility and search functions and cause factor proportion inefficiencies there in addition to the overall excess-capacity inefficiences. In schooling fisheries this will generally mean higher mobility, which in turn may be seen as a threat to the stock. In search fisheries gear restrictions will spill over also into the searching production function, which may be threatening if the patches are interdependent. What ultimately happens in search fisheries depends upon how fishermen choose to divide time between fishing and searching, which depends upon strategic considerations and relative costs.

If we are interested in predicting more long-run evolutionary trends in a regulated fishery, we need to hypothesize something more specific about how regulators react to perceived excess-capacity threats to stocks. As a working hypothesis I would propose that:[13] first, regulators are primarily hindsight-oriented and, second, they will generally sequentially utilize specific gear restrictions with reductions in season length. Thus we should expect to see reactions to over-capacity responded to first by gear restrictions, then by season reductions, then by further gear restrictions, etc.; in other words, generally reactions to regulations are not forecast and planned for *ex ante* but are adjusted to *ex poste*.

If more than one specific input (other than gear) is restricted, I would hypothesize that restrictions will be placed next on those inputs that seem to have changed most in response to previous actions. As discussed already, these will tend to be inputs for which elasticities of substitution with previously impacted inputs are high.

Lastly, it is worth emphasizing that what happens *in fact* in regulated fisheries is not indicative necessarily of what *should* happen. If we are interested in improving efficiency in a somewhat imperfect system, there are substantial roles for economists to play. One is to recommend wholesale changes in the nature of regulation, i.e., moving towards indirect controls which promote efficiency via price incentives. If we wish to do this there is much room to help predict just how the system will respond—for example if boats will become bigger, faster, etc. However, I am inclined to believe that we are stuck in the short run with regulatory systems that use direct controls mainly. In this (perhaps) second-best world, economists can still play a role in suggesting how to anticipate reactions and then in choosing sequences and levels of restrictions that increase rather than decrease overall efficiency. If all components of production technology were fixed proportions, for example, we could identify lowest marginal cost means of restricting effort. With some technology flexible, and some fixed and some common inputs, the issue of which path to take to minimize dead-weight efficiency losses is answerable in principle and probably in practice with a little empirical effort.

REFERENCES

Anderson, Lee G. (1976), 'The Relationship Between Firm and Industry in Common Property Fisheries', *Land Economics, 52*.

Anderson, Lee G. (1977), *The Economics of Fisheries Management*, Baltimore: Johns Hopkins University Press.

Clark, C. W. (1980a), 'Towards a Predictive Model for the Economic Regulation of Commercial Fisheries', *Canadian Journal of Fisheries and Aquatic Science, 37*.

Clark, C. W. (1980b), 'Concentration Profiles and the Production and Management of Marine Fisheries', Technical Report no. 80-8, Institute of Applied Mathematics and Statistics, University of British Columbia.

Clark, C. W. and Mangel, M. (1979), 'Aggregation and Fishiers Dynamics: A Theoretical Study of Schooling and the Purse-Seine Tuna Fisheries', *Fisheries Bulletin, 77*.

Clark, C. W. and Mangel, M. (1981), 'Optimal Allocation of Searching Effort Among Independently Fluctuating Fish Stocks', presented at the URI Workshop on Uncertainty and Fisheries Economics.

Dasgupta, P. S. and Heal, G. N. (1979), *Economic Theory and Exhaustible Resources,* Cambridge University Press.

Gordon, H. S. (1954), 'The Economic Theory of a Common Property Resource: the Fishery', *Journal of Political Economy,* 62.

Pearse, P. H. *et al.* (1979), 'Symposium on Policies for Economic Rationalization of Commercial Fisheries' (Powell River Conference), *Journal of the Fisheries Research Board of Canada,* 36.7.

Scott, A. D. (1955), 'The Fishery: The Objectives of Sole Ownership', *Journal of Political Economy,* 63.

Wilen, J. E. (1981a), 'Regulation of the BC Herring Industry', in Economic Council of Canada, *Regulation Reference Technical Report.*

Wilen, J. E. (1981b), 'Towards a Theory of the Regulated Fishery', presented at the URI Conference on Uncertainty of Fisheries Economics.

NOTES

1. Clark (1980b) discusses four types of concentration profiles (maximum concentration as a function of stock size) and analyses the implications for several fishery management alternatives.
2. For recent work in optimal searching in fisheries, see Clark and Mangel (1981).
3. Cf. Clark and Mangel (1979).
4. Wilen (1981a).
5. This and the following hypothesis may be felt by many to be oversimplifications of what is, in the real world, a complex process of trial and error, interaction by multiple parties, political logrolling, etc. While this is fully recognized, it is also the case that one must start somewhere to break this process down intellectually in order to make it tractable. It has been my observation that many real fisheries regulation processes can be assumed to be roughly if not precisely guided by these two principles.
6. Cf. Wilen (1981a) for a discussion of on-line versus advance-planned regulatory structures.
7. The assumption of a fixed N may be relaxed by assuming some sort of an entry function incorporating opportunity costs of participants, but for ease of analysis we wish to keep N exogenous. N may be looked at as the number of potential fishermen with skills sufficient to participate in a particular fishery.
8. The use of a Nash equilibrium concept may be inappropriate for some situations since time must be long enough for the equilibrium to evolve and yet short enough for those factors assumed fixed (e.g. N) to remain fixed. Without some concept of equilibrium, however, we cannot conclude much about any aspects of this interactive system.
9. Cf. Pearse *et al.* (1979).
10. Other work that develops micro-based theories of regulated fisheries are in Anderson (1977) and Clark (1980a). Both of these differ from the approach considered here in that behaviour is considered atomistic as models of perfect competition. The only other work that is similar is in Dasgupta and Heal (1979), in which a Nash equilibrium concept is utilized to discuss a common-property equilibrium. The models developed here are regulated open-access models in which regulators use direct controls in a gaming setting with regulatees.
11. We might assume diminishing or increasing returns in aggregate search time $P(NST) = (NST)^{\alpha}$; in which case S would be a non-integer polynomial like $S^{\alpha}(1-S) = \bar{H}/T^2N$. The assumption does not change results in a qualitative way.
12. Cf. Pearse *et al.* (1979).
13. These should be regarded less as fact but more as speculative thoughts based on casual observation. It would be revealing to do an anthropological organizational behaviour study of a regulatory body in order to determine whether these or other reactions tend to dominate.

Comment   **Colin W. Clark**

There are many interesting ideas in Wilen's paper above. The emphasis on implementation of economic analysis, on studying the behaviour of regulators as well as fishermen, on the differences between 'search' and 'schooling' fish species are all welcome. Yet I feel that the models that Wilen employs are far too simplistic to yield much in the way of new insights regarding these questions As pointed out in the paper by Clark, Munro, and Charles in chapter 3 above, static fishery models can, and often do, lead to unreliable and indeed theoretically incorrect predictions. For example, the whole question of over-capacity and its cure (e.g. the infamous 'buy-back' schemes), which is intimately related to non-malleability of capital, cannot even be discussed on the basis of static theories, obviously.

Unfortunately, if one wants to study strategic questions, the inappropriateness of static models places one on the horns of a dilemma. For, as everyone recognizes, dynamic game theory is so notoriously difficult as to be all but unusable in practice. But then, to paraphrase R. Pindyck, the average fisherman may be even less adept at dynamic game theory than is the average fishing economist. If so, it follows that we will probably *never* be able to predict the behaviour of fishermen (or regulators) with any degree of accuracy, no matter how much 'empirical' work is undertaken.

These arguments may appear to be leading to a vicious circle—simple models give unreliable predictions, but realistic models are too complex to be useful. But the point I am trying to make is that it is always important to be *fully aware of the limitations of one's models*. Wilen spends very little effort setting out his assumptions, or the limitations of his models—a habit that we are all perhaps too guilty of.

Two basic models are presented in the paper, one for 'schooling' fisheries and the other for 'search' fisheries. Both models are *ad hoc* and abstract, with highly aggregated variables, and both are completely static. The search model allows for two complementary inputs, searching effort and catching effort. Only catching effort is assumed to be regulated, with the unsurprising result that distortions are likely to be introduced in the allocation of effort to each activity. But, clearly, there are many aspects of searching that Wilen's analysis overlooks, including all the strategic questions of generating, sharing, protecting, and misrepresenting information. Much of fishermen's behaviour in search fisheries appears to be dominated by these considerations. How valid will predictions be that ignore these details, in terms of implementation of policy? Is it really true, as Wilen seems to be claiming at the end of his paper, that simple 'graphic' models—with a little empirical content thrown in, perhaps —will be able to encompass these important features?

The schooling fishery model is even simpler; in fact, it really has nothing to do with fisheries at all. *N* fishermen are simply competing for shares of a finite 'pie', $\bar{H}$. This game theory model is standard and the results are hardly surprising. How much of the 'rent' will be dissipated depends on parameter values (only partly described in the paper). But I do not believe that the static game model captures the way fishermen really behave. A fisherman who increases his capacity may reap only a *temporary* gain, but this may be enough to engender the capacity increase. A dynamic model ought therefore to predict *greater* degrees of over-capacity than the static model. Wilen also has to assume that the regulators' response is instantaneous (otherwise a dynamic model would emerge!). If this is unrealistic, one would expect a further incentive for over-capacity. On top of this is the incentive for over-capacity that arises during the initial development of any fishery (see Clark, Clarke, and Munro, 1979). Wilen's static model is incapable of capturing any of these effects.

Incidentally, schooling fisheries have another important characteristic that fails to show up in a static theory. There exists a *threshold* cost–price ratio, with the property that the (unregulated) bionomic equilibrium is: (1) no exploitation for c/p above the threshold, and (2) extinction for c/p below the threshold. This simple observation largely explains the notorious instability of pelagic schooling fisheries, and it is disappointing to see it disappear in an over-simplistic model.

In summary, while Wilen's paper takes up a number of interesting ideas in fishery economics, I feel that their full impact will not be realized without a great deal more work and careful dynamic modelling of the processes involved.

REFERENCES

Clark, C. W., Clark, F. H., and Munro, G. R. (1979), 'The Optimal Exploitation of Renewable Resource Stocks' Problems of Irreversible Investment', *Econometrica*, 47.

PART IV
THEORETICAL ANALYSIS OF EXHAUSTIBLE RESOURCES

Introductory Note

Tracy R. Lewis

A significant part of PRNE research has been denoted to understanding the theory of the economics of exhaustible resources. This concern is aptly reflected in the essays of this section. Since the seminal work of Hotelling in 1931, resource economists have struggled to answer two basic questions. The first is of a normative nature: given consumer preferences, and given the technology of resource extraction, how is production of the resource to be carried out efficiently? How does one optimally allocate the resource services among competing wants in different time periods? The second question is positive: how is the intertemporal production of resources in a market economy affected by the accessibility of the resource, the structure of the market for producers and consumers, and the incidence of government taxes, subsidies, and price controls applied to resource use and production?

Each of the papers and accompanying comments in this section addresses some particular aspect of these two questions. In order better to evaluate these papers and to assess their contributions to the resources literature, it is useful to review the basic model that nearly all investigators use to assess different programme of resource allocation. Following from the work of Hotelling, the most apparent feature of the model is that it is dynamic. A dynamic treatment is necessary because the production activities in different periods are naturally linked together by the availability of a scarce natural resource. As such, the model readily lends itself to analysis by capital-theoretic techniques. The model typically posits a technology describing resource extraction, and the production of services from the extracted stock. When the resource is non-renewable, decisions to extract and consume the stock are irreversible unless additional stocks may be discovered. In principle, the model can accommodate the possibility that the amount of the resource to be recovered is unknown and that the process for extracting the stock is constrained by the availability of scarce factors of production like capital.

Assuming property rights over the resource are well defined, the owner of the stock, whether a country or a firm, must choose a sequence of extraction to maximize the discounted stream of returns (or profits) given the size of the stock and the extraction technology. Several institutional factors, including the organization of producer and consumer markets, and the various kinds of government taxation and subsidization of resource production and consumption, determine the period returns from extractions. Using standard capital-theoretic analysis to solve for the optimal extraction profile, the model is intended to (a) characterize efficient resource use under different assumptions about the technology, and (b) predict the effects of imperfectly competitive markets and the imposition of resource taxation and subsidization on the time-path of extraction.

The essays in this section provide extensions to the basic Hotelling model in three important respects.

EFFICIENT EXTRACTION WITH CAPITAL

With few exceptions, theoretical analyses of resource extraction assume that only perfectly mobile factors of production, such as labour, are needed to extract the resource. Of course, in reality, non-malleable capital equipment is frequently embodied in the extraction technology. The inclusion of a capital stock into the Hotelling model complicates the analysis, since one must now consider the optimal sequencing of capital investment in order to derive efficient or profit-maximizing extraction programmes. In the Lasserre paper (chapter 6), entitled 'Exhaustible Resource Extraction with Capital', efficient–competitive extraction paths are characterized when capital is an input in the recovery process. Lasserre demonstrates how the efficient sequencing of extraction is sensitive to which specification of the capital investment function one assumes. One main result of the paper is to identify circumstances when the Hotelling prediction that (under stationary conditions) efficient extraction paths will be declining over time continues to hold when capital is required for extraction. An implication of the Lasserre analysis is that the Hotelling type of results appear to be robust to various specifications of the cost of investment function. Another primary finding is that the comparative dynamic effects of changes in the discount rate are most likely to be ambiguous when capital enters into the extraction process. Some interpretations and generalizations of the Lasserre results appear in the comments by William Schworm.

THE IMPACT OF GOVERNMENT TAXES AND SUBSIDIES ON EXTRACTION

The extractive resources sector is one of the most heavily taxed and regulated sectors in Western economies. (A discussion of the importance and pervasiveness of resource taxation and subsidation is presented by V. Kerry Smith in his comments on chapter 7.) Taxes and price controls of various kinds impact on the extractive behaviour of the firm by changing the net revenues from production in each period, which alters the relative returns from extracting in different time periods. Chapter 7, by Tracy Lewis and Margaret Slade, characterizes the effects of severance, royalty, and excess profits taxes as well as price controls and resources. The Lewis–Slade analysis departs from previous studies of resource taxation by assuming that other factor inputs must be combined with the unprocessed resource according to a Cobb–Douglas technology before it can be sold. Lewis and Slade report numerous comparative dynamic results, but their most significant finding is to demonstrate how the inclusion of a processing sector into models of resource extraction can cause the intertemporal effects of certain taxes and subsidies to be reversed. The policy implication that flows from this paper is that determining the impact of even the most simple tax instruments on extraction may be difficult when the most rudimentary elements of natural resource processing are accounted for. V. Kerry Smith comments on the limitations of the Lewis–Slade model and makes suggestions for future research.

THE IMPACT OF MARKET STRUCTURE ON EXTRACTION

Since the active participation of OPEC in world oil markets in the early 1970s resource economists have become aware of the profound impact that market structure can have on the intertemporal allocation of exhaustible resources. Recently there have been numerous theoretical anlayses which demonstrate that current resource prices tend to be higher, and the industry extraction profile tends to be tilted towards the future, in imperfectly competitive markets where the ownership of the resource is concentrated in large amounts among a few individuals. These models are partly incomplete in that they take as given the distribution of resource reserves among various users, without explaining how the division of reserves is determined. This question is taken up by Mukesh Eswaran and Tracy Lewis in chapter 8, on the 'Evolution of Market Structure in a Dominant Firm Model with Exhaustible Resources'. Specifically, Eswaran and Lewis examine the incentives for a historically dominant resource producer to maintain his strong position in the market by pre-emptively discovering new resource reserves before his rivals. The Eswaran-Lewis analysis shows that pre-emptory exploration by the dominant firm is less profitable when the new reserves are located in small amounts in numerous distinct locations. The paper suggests that the degree of concentration in reserve ownership is apt to be highest for those natural resources that are found in large quantities in a few locations. Hence the structure and performance of some resource markets may be affected by the geological characteristics of the resource.

6. Exhaustible Resource Extraction with Capital

Pierre Lasserre

INTRODUCTION

Little attention has been devoted in the exhaustible resource literature to the importance of factors of production, capital in particular, in the extraction process. Given that the approach used to deal with extraction problems has been basically capital-theoretic, one may wonder to what extent the presence of one or several other assets or stocks in those problems might affect the traditional results.

In this paper, we investigate the effects of introducing capital on two well-known results of the exhaustible resource literature: the result that the extraction rate diminishes over time, and the result that a rise in the interest rate implies a faster extraction programme. Both issues have already received some attention, but we hope to throw some more light on the effects of introducing capital, by casting the analysis into a more general framework, by focusing alternatively on the major approaches to investment that have been applied to the conventional firm, and by adapting to the extractive firm some of the analytical methods that are routinely used in standard microeconomics. The analysis does not involve uncertainty and ignores the issues associated with exploration.

In the next section, we propose various ways of introducing capital in extractive models and examine their effects on extraction profiles. We then use a model with many factors of production but with perfectly malleable capital in order to investigate, following Neher (1981), under what circumstances a rise in the interest rate accelerates extraction. The final section provides a brief summary and conclusion.

THE EXTRACTION PROFILE

A great deal of effort has been devoted to characterizing the extraction profile of exhaustible resources. Gray (1914) initiated this long tradition, which found other major benchmarks with the work of Hotelling (1931), Paish (1938), and Scott (1955); took momentum in the recent period with such research as that by Schulze (1974), Levhari and Liviatan (1977), and most of the contributors to the book edited by Mason Gaffney (1967), in particular Scott and Herfindahl; and has now reached maturity, that is to say the status of a full chapter (chapter 6), in the book by Dasgupta and Heal (1979). The major result applies to the individual mine as well as to industry as a whole in the absence of technical change or demand shifts. It calls for a progressive reduction in the extraction rate as time goes by. Being somewhat unrealistic, that result has also generated a search for exceptions, the most meaningful of which arise when the resource is not homogeneous and/or when capital and investment come into the picture. Two papers, one by Puu (1977) and one by Campbell (1980), fall into the last category and make the connection with an older and less well-known line of research on capital and extraction which is represented by Massé (1962, 348-53), Billiet (1959), and Ventura (1964) and has provided an early mathematical treatment to the issue of the capacity choice discussed by Scott (1967) or dealt with by Helliwell (1978) and Bradley *et al.* (1981). Other authors have attempted to provide general treatments for the problem of resource use with capital. Smith (1968) considers extraction with perfectly malleable capital. His paradoxical result—that industry output increases over time despite resource homogeneity—relies on his very special behavioural assumption that the increase in industry capital is proportional to the gap between price and unit cost. Burt and Cummings (1970) propose a discrete-time model of resource extraction with many capital stocks; however, the paper does not emphasize the qualitative description of the extraction and investment trajectories implied.

Before going over the distinctive features of those models with capital, a word on maintained assumptions is warranted. The diminishing extraction rate is the counterpart of the increasing implicit price of the resource, which itself arises from a standard asset management argument: the own interest rate on an otherwise unproductive asset must equal the general rate of interest. It follows that exceptions to the diminishing extraction rate rule may result from two kinds of causes: first, when something breaks or complicates the link between the implicit extraction cost and the extraction rate, as may happen in the presence of capital; second, when the cause itself disappears, as may be the case when the resource is heterogeneous. Indeed, when the resource is heterogeneous, its implicit price may decrease and increasing extraction rates may follow (Levhari and Liviatan, 1977). In this section of the paper, since we investigate how the introduction of capital may affect the result that the extraction rate diminishes, we assume that all other conditions for this result are satisfied; in particular, we assume that the resource is homogeneous, that there is no technical change, and that the demand, whether elastic or not, does not shift over time (Stiglitz, 1976).[1]

Capital raises the issues associated with its durability and its lack of malleability. Those have been addressed in various ways which carry specific assumptions with them: irreversibility, adjustment costs, and the putty-clay hypotheses, for example. We shall deal with the issue of capital in a somewhat systematic way, by proposing models of the extractive firm which can be classified according to those key assumptions.

We start with a model of the firm characterized by a concave production function of several factors, some having the dimension of stocks and the others called variable factors, having the dimension of flows. There are no adjustment costs to any factors, nor any irreversibility. The sole constraint on factors of production is that they should be non-negative. It is also assumed that the industry is competitive or managed by a social planner, so that there are no attempts to extract any monopoly rent. The output price may not be constant over time, but is given by a time-autonomous function of output which is such that demand 'chokes off' at some finite price. The price trajectory is somehow known to the firm. Factor prices are assumed to be constant. Finally, and this is the difference between this model and any early neoclassical model of investment (Jorgenson, 1963), the firm extracts ore from a finite homogeneous reserve stock, R. The problem is (time subscripts will be omitted later on when no ambiguity arises):

$$\max_{\{I_t, L_t\}T2} \int_{T1}^{T2} \gamma_t \cdot \{p_t \cdot f(x_t, L_t) - w' \cdot L_t - \phi' \cdot I_t\} \cdot dt + \gamma_{T2} \cdot \phi' \cdot x_{T2} \qquad (1)$$

subject to

$$\text{(a) } \dot{x}_t = I_t; \qquad \text{(b) } x_{T1} = x_1; \qquad \text{(c) } x_t \geqslant 0, t\epsilon(T1, T2) \qquad (2)$$

$$L_t \geqslant 0 \qquad (3)$$

$$\text{(a) } \dot{R}_t = -q_t = -f(x_t, L_t); \qquad \text{(b) } R_{T1} = R_1; \qquad \text{(c) } R_t \geqslant 0, t\epsilon(T1, T2) \qquad (4)$$

where p_t, w, and ϕ are, respectively, the price of the output flow, the rental prices of the variable factors, and the asset prices of the stock factors at time t; x_t, I_t, and L_t are, respectively, a vector of factor stocks, the vector of adjustments to those stocks, and a vector of variable factors; $\gamma_t = \exp\{-r \cdot (t - T1)\}$; $T1$ and $T2$ are, respectively, the initial and final extraction dates. The production function, $f(x_t, L_t)$ is assumed to be concave and twice differentiable and satisfies the Inada conditions. This guarantees that extraction does occur. Since the resource is homogeneous and the price is bounded, the extraction period is finite (Salant *et al.*, 1981).

   Although all conditions for the application of the maximum principle are not met, it does yield the solution in this problem. The current-value Hamiltonian, simply called Hamiltonian in the rest of the paper, is:

$$M = (p - \mu) \cdot f(x, L) - w' \cdot L - (\phi' - \lambda') \cdot I \qquad (5)$$

where μ and λ are, respectively, the costate variable (or shadow price) associated with R and the vector of costate variables (or shadow prices) associated with x. One notes that M is linear in I, so that the optimum decision depends on the sign of each element in the vector of switching functions, $\sigma(t) = (\lambda_t - \phi)$. Consider the case where each switching function is null. Then

$$\lambda_t = \phi, \qquad (6)$$

and

$$\dot{\lambda}_t = \dot{\phi} = 0. \qquad (7)$$

The first-order conditions governing the costate variables are:

$$(\dot\lambda - r\lambda) \cdot \gamma(t) = -\frac{\partial}{\partial x}\{\gamma(t) \cdot M\} \quad \text{and} \quad (\dot\mu - r\mu) \cdot \gamma(t) = -\frac{\partial}{\partial R}\{\gamma(t) \cdot M\}$$

or

$$\dot\lambda = r\lambda - (p - \mu) \cdot f_x \qquad (8)$$

and

$$\dot\mu = r \cdot \mu. \qquad (9)$$

Substituting (6) and (7) into (8), we have a conventional user cost relation, except that the output price has been corrected to reflect the implicit value of the resource:

$$(p - \mu) \cdot f_x = r \cdot \phi. \qquad (10)$$

Equation (10) defines a singular path for x. That such a path is preferable to any other one results from the fact that the indeterminary of I in the maximization of the Hamiltonian, when $\sigma = 0$, means that no marginal change in x could affect the objective functional. Furthermore, by the concavity of f, each vector x_t^* so characterized is a unique maximum. Hence the singular path cannot be improved upon. Now, if $x_t \neq x_t^*$, the optimal policy is to bring x instantaneously to x^*. That the move is instantaneous results from the bang-bang nature of the problem, and the absence of bounds on I. That the optimal move is towards x^*, not away from it, again results from the concavity of the production function.

Now the Hamiltonian must also be maximized with respect to L. Hence,

$$(p - \mu) \cdot f_L = w. \qquad (11)$$

Expressions (10) and (11) implicitly define the solutions x^* and L^* as functions of $p - \mu$, w, $r \cdot \phi$. They can be interpreted as first-order conditions for the maximization of the modified Hamiltonian, defined at its maximum as:

$$H^* (y, v, w) = y \cdot f(x^*, L^*) - w' \cdot L^* - v' \cdot x^* \qquad (12)$$

where $v = r \cdot \phi$ and $y = p - \mu$. Since f is concave, H^* can be interpreted as an implicit profit function with the usual properties (Diewert, 1974):

H^* is decreasing in w and v, and increasing in y; H is convex; $\partial H^*/\partial w = -L^*$; $\partial H^*/\partial v = -x^*$; $\partial H^*/\partial y = f(x^*, L^*) = q^*$.
This last expression, Hotelling's theorem, can be differentiated totally in order to study the behaviour of q^* over time (asterisks will be omitted in the rest of the argument). One gets

$$\dot q = H_{yy} \cdot \dot y. \qquad (13)$$

Since the market price is a time-autonomous function of output, $p = p(q)$, we have

$$\dot{y} = p_q \cdot \dot{q} - \dot{\mu}$$

so that, substituting into (13),

$$\dot{q} \cdot (1 - H_{yy} \cdot p_q) = -H_{yy} \cdot \dot{\mu}. \tag{14}$$

Since H_{yy} is non negative, p_q non-positive, and $\dot{\mu}$ positive, we get the usual result that the extraction rate diminishes over time.[2]

As could be expected from a model that reflects only the durability of capital, and not its lack of malleability, the pattern of diminishing extraction rates is not affected.

We now show that the sign of the change in the extraction rate is not affected either by a fairly common way to model the lack of malleability of capital, the assumption that investment is non-negative. Consider the same problem as previously, but with the following two supplementary assumptions:

$$\text{(d)} \ I \geqslant 0, \ t\epsilon(T1, T2) \tag{2}$$

and the scrap value of the firm is null, since assumption (2d) means that the equipment has no alternative use outside the firm.

The Hamiltonian of the problem is still given by (5), but one must take account of (2d) in its maximization. As before, since M is linear in I, three phases must be distinguished for each stock x_j: phase a, where $\phi_j - \lambda_j < 0$, I_j is infinite, and x_j registers a discrete increase; phase b, where $\phi_j = \lambda_j$, and I_j is not determined by the maximization of the Hamiltonian; phase c, where $\phi_j - \lambda_j > 0$, I_j would be infinite and negative if it were not for the non-negativity constraint, but the latter is binding and $I_j = 0$. The following remarks are in order. First, since $x_j(t)$ is continuous during phases b and c, its costate variable is continuous during those phases. Consequently, a transition from phase c, when $\phi_j - \lambda_j > 0$, to phase a, when $\phi_j - \lambda_j < 0$, must involve a passage in phase b, when $\phi_j = \lambda_j$; second, since it involves a discrete change in x, any occurrence of phase a must be instantaneous.

In the rest of this section, we shall use the superscripts a, b, c, to denote those stock factors, stock adjustments, stock asset prices, or implicit prices that are (or pertain to stock factors that are) in phases a, b, or c, respectively. Consider now a situation where all stock factors are either in phase b or phase c, when I is finite. Since $\lambda^b = \phi^b$, it follows from (8) that

$$r \cdot \phi^b = y \cdot fx^b(x^b, x^c, L). \tag{15}$$

Expression (11) is unaffected by the new constraint; combined with (15), it implies that the restricted modified Hamiltonian, defined below at its maximum, is being maximized:

$$\tilde{H}(y, v^b, w, x^c) = y \cdot f(x^{b*}, x^c, L^*) - w' \cdot L^* - v^{b'} \cdot x^{b}*. \tag{16}$$

$\tilde{H}$ differs from H^* in that it has only a subset of stock factor user-costs as arguments, these that pertain to stocks currently being adjusted, and it has some stocks, those which are currently fixed, as arguments. Clearly, $\tilde{H}$ can be interpreted as a restricted profit function, with the following properties (Lau, 1976): $\tilde{H}$ is convex in y, y^b, and w; $\partial \tilde{H}/\partial w = -L$; $\partial \tilde{H}/\partial v^b = -x^b$; $\partial \tilde{H}/\partial x^c = -v^c$; $\partial \tilde{H}/\partial y = q$. Differentiating this last expression with respect to time, one has, following the same argument as in the previous case,

$$\dot{q} \cdot (1 - \tilde{H}_{yy} \cdot p_q) = -\tilde{H}_{yy} \cdot \mu \tag{17}$$

since $\dot{x}^c = 0$. This expression, which implies that q does not increase over time, is valid whenever all stocks are in phases b or c, although $\tilde{H}$ must be redefined whenever a stock switches from one phase to the other. Given the possibility of a third phase, one may wonder about the generality of this result. However, it is sub-optimal to move from phase b to phase a when, as assumed, prices do not have discontinuities. The reason is intuitively obvious: in phase b, when $\lambda^b = \phi^b$, the maximum principle leaves the stock adjustment, I^b, indeterminate precisely because no marginal change in the levels of the corresponding factor stocks can increase the Hamiltonian or, consequently, the objective functional. So, whenever possible, it is optimum for a stock to be in phase b. Since upward stock adjustments are feasible in phase b, λ^b will not be allowed to increase in such a way as to become higher than ϕ^b. It follows that phase a can occur only as an initial instantaneous build-up of capital,[3] so that (17) holds all the time except, possibly, at $T1$. So even in the presence of non-negativity constraints, the rate of output is non-increasing.

Are there any interesting special cases? Campbell (1980) presents an elegant treatment of a problem whose optimum involves a constant extraction rate over an initial period. In his model the short-run marginal extraction cost increases with output and the firm faces a capacity constraint, $q \leqslant \bar{q}$, with $\bar{q}$ directly proportional to the level of capital, the unique stock factor that may be acquired in any positive amount but has no alternative use. This is clearly a special case of the model just described, and we can make use of (17) to infer conditions on the technology that produced Campbell's result. With only one stock factor, K, $\tilde{H}$ reduces to

$$\tilde{H}(y, w, K) = y \cdot f(K, L^*) - w' \cdot L^* \tag{16a}$$

when K is currently fixed, or

$$H^*(y, w, v) = y \cdot f(K^*, L^*) - w \cdot L^* - v \cdot K^* \tag{16b}$$

when K is being adjusted. In both cases, (17) holds provided the appropriate function is used. Although this is not crucial to our interpretation, we can also make use of Campbell's result that K is adjusted only at the initial time, which implies that $\tilde{H}(y, w, K)$ is the appropriate function to use. Following Campbell, we also assume that the output price is constant, which implies that

$$p_q = 0.$$

Accordingly, (17) reduces to

$$\dot{q} = -\tilde{H}_{yy}(y, w, K) \cdot \dot{\mu}.$$

A constant extraction rate, $\dot{q} = 0$, implies $\tilde{H}_{yy} = 0$, which requires $\tilde{H}$ to be linear in y. Considering (16a), this means that L^* is insensitive to y. In other words, the marginal cost curve is vertical at the output rate considered. Following the same argument, a diminishing extraction rate requires the marginal cost curve to be upward-sloping at the levels of output that prevail towards the end of the extraction period, when y is low. Since K is constant, we have just characterized two parts of the same marginal curve: an upward-sloping part at low levels of y, a vertical part at higher levels of y, as shown in figure 6.1.

Figure 6.1 clearly shows how the reduction in y, which results from the increase in μ over time, may have no effect on extraction as long as the marginal cost curve, *MC,* is vertical, but will cause output to diminish when y becomes low enough to correspond to the upward-sloping part of the curve. It will also be noted that Campbell's assumption that the upward-sloping part of the marginal cost curve is independent of K is not crucial to his result.

So far, we have seen that perfectly malleable capital, even with no alternative use outside the firm, does not affect the standard Hotelling result that the output of a mine or extractive industry does not increase over time. The lack of malleability of capital may also result from internal technological constraints. A primitive way to introduce such constraints is to impose an upper bound on

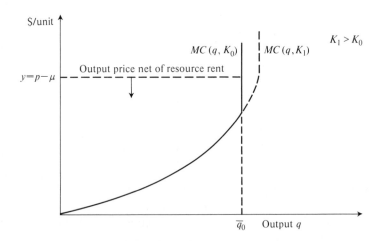

FIG. 6.1 The technology in Campbell's (1980) model

investment. Puu (1977) studies such a model; its solution consists in a phase of increasing output followed by a phase of decreasing output. However, he uses a model with variable grade, for which it is known that the standard result does not necessarily hold. Does his result depend on that particular assumption, or does it follow from the upper bound that is imposed on investment? Let us use the same model as before, with an additional constraint:

$$(2d)\, I_t \leqslant \bar{I}. \tag{2}$$

As before, we have a bang-bang problem, which involves three possible alternative policies for each stock x_j, according to whether $\lambda_j > \phi_j$ (phase a), $\lambda_j = \phi_j$ (phase b), or $\lambda_j < \phi_j$ (phase c). In the absence of an upper bound on I, phase a was shown to involve an instantaneous upward jump in the stock considered. This could be observed only at $T1$, so that, during the extraction period $(T1, T2)$, all stocks were in either phases b or c, $\dot{q}$ was given by (17) and was consequently non-positive. This is no longer true in presence of an upper bound on I, and it could be shown that the optimal policy, during phase a, consists in increasing the stock as fast as possible, at a rate $I^a = \bar{I}^a$. The optimal extraction policy, derived from (8) and $\lambda^b = \phi^b$, must now satisfy:

$$\dot{q} \cdot (1 - \bar{H}_{yy} \cdot p_q) = -\bar{H}_{yy} \cdot \dot{\mu} + \bar{H}_{yx}{}_a \cdot \bar{I}^a. \tag{17a}$$

In the absence of any *a priori* restriction on the vector $\bar{H}_{yx}{}_a$, the sign of $\dot{q}$ cannot be inferred. This result is not surprising, as intuition and Puu's result lead one to conjecture that, if initial factor stocks are low, the firm goes through an initial period during which it builds up its capacity (phase a) and finishes its extractive life with a period in which it wished it owned less factor stocks, as the equipment has no alternative use, but cannot get rid of them (phase c). Indeed, since we know that the implicit factor stock prices are continuous functions of time in this problem, and since, in the absence of alternative uses for the stocks, they must tend towards zero as t approaches $T2$, it is easily proven that all stocks must be in phase c towards the end of the extraction period. What happens before that is not as clear. One would like to conjecture that the (bliss) phase b, when the firm is perfectly happy with the amount of equipment it owns, is short-lived to the point of being instantaneous. But if one imposes $\lambda^b = 0$ and differentiates (8) with respect to time, one finds that this is not necessarily the case, unless there is only one factor of production, as in the model of Puu.

So it appears that the lack of malleability of capital, even when it is introduced in a primitive fashion, by imposing upper and lower bounds on investment, affects Hotelling's result about the direction of the change in the extraction rate. One would expect this to be also the case when the lack of malleability takes the more sophisticated form of adjustment costs. In Lasserre (1981, chapter 2) we studied a model of factor demands and output supply for an extractive firm that faced costs when adjusting its factor stock levels. Unfortunately, we were able to provide only an implicit characterization of the solution, in the form of a system of differential equations. Here, we characterize the optimum programme explicitly, for a one-factor model with separable adjustment costs. The problem is to choose $I(t)$ so as to maximize

$$\int_{T1}^{T2} \gamma_t \cdot \{p \cdot f(x) - C(I) - \phi \cdot I\} \cdot dt + \gamma_{T2} \cdot \phi \cdot x_{T2} \qquad (18)$$

subject to

$$\text{(a) } \dot{x} = I; \qquad \text{(b) } x_{T1} = x_1, \text{ given}; \qquad \text{(c) } x \geqslant 0. \qquad (2)$$

$$\text{(a) } \dot{R} = -f(x); \qquad \text{(b) } R_{T1} = R_1; \qquad \text{(c) } R \geqslant 0. \qquad (4)$$

where $C(I)$ is a convex adjustment cost function which reaches a minimum of $C(0) = 0$ and tends to positive infinity when $|I|$ tends to infinity. The term $\phi \cdot I$ under the integral may be positive or negative, which implies that the equipment can be resold at no loss, and that the adjustment costs, $C(I)$, are internal to the firm. Consistent with the assumption that the equipment has an alternative use, there is a scrap value to the firm; as formulated, it can be realized at no cost, under the assumption that the adjustment costs affect only the operating firm and disappear at $T2$.[4] If we ignore those problems that might be associated with using the maximum principle in presence of non-negativity constraints on the state variables, conditions for using it are met. The Hamiltonian is

$$H = y \cdot f(x) - C(I) - (\phi - \lambda) \cdot I. \qquad (19)$$

It is maximized when

$$C'(I) = -(\phi - \lambda). \qquad (20)$$

Other first-order conditions are:

$$\dot{\lambda} = \lambda r - y \cdot f_x \qquad (21)$$

$$\dot{\mu} = r \cdot \mu. \qquad (22)$$

The transversality conditions are: $H = 0$, or, since $I(T2) = 0$ in the absence of adjustment costs after $T2$,

$$\mu(T2) = p\{f(x_2)\} \qquad (23)$$

and

$$\lambda(T2) = \phi. \qquad (24)$$

The Legendre second-order conditions are satisfied, since $f(x)$ is concave as well as $-\{C(I) + \phi \cdot I\}$.

Proposition 1. If $\lambda > \phi$, $\dot{\lambda} < 0$.
   Proof. If $\lambda > \phi$, we have $I > 0$, $\dot{q} > 0$, $\dot{p} < 0$, $\dot{y} < 0$.

Differentiating (21), we get

$$\ddot{\lambda} = \dot{\lambda} r - \dot{y} \cdot f_x - y \cdot f_{xx} \cdot I. \tag{25}$$

Suppose that $\dot{\lambda} \geqslant 0$; then by (25), $\ddot{\lambda} > 0$. It follows that λ will keep increasing so that the transversability condition (24) will not be met. Hence $\dot{\lambda}$ must be negative.   Q.E.D.

Proposition 2. If $\lambda = \phi$, $\dot{\lambda} < 0$ unless $t = T2$.

Proof. Using a similar argument as in proposition 1, one can show that $\dot{\lambda}$ must not be positive unless $t = T2$. Hence $\dot{\lambda} \leqslant 0$. Suppose that $\dot{\lambda} = 0$. Since $\lambda = \phi \Rightarrow \dot{y} < 0$ and $I = 0$, it follows from (25) that $\ddot{\lambda}$ is positive. But if so, $\dot{\lambda}$ will become positive, which was just shown not to be feasible unless $t = T2$. Hence $\dot{\lambda} < 0$ unless $t = T2$.   Q.E.D.

Proposition 3. $\dot{\lambda}(T2) = r \cdot \phi$ unless $x(T2) = 0$.

Proof.

$$\lim_{t \to T2} \dot{\lambda} = \lim_{t \to T2} \lambda \cdot r - \lim_{t \to T2} y \cdot f_x, \qquad \text{by (21)}$$

$$= r \cdot \phi - 0 \cdot \lim_{t \to T2} f_x, \qquad \text{using (23) and (24)}$$

$$= r \cdot \phi$$

unless x tends towards zero.   Q.E.D.

From propositions 1–3 we deduce the following:

1. If $\lambda > \phi$ at some date during the extraction period, then $\lambda(T1) > \phi$ (from proposition 1).
2. The trajectory of λ can cross the $\lambda = \phi$ line at most once and from above (from proposition 2).
3. If $\lambda > \phi$ at some date during the extraction period, the trajectory of λ must cross the $\lambda = \phi$ line (from proposition 3, since x cannot tend towards zero if λ tends towards ϕ from above, as this implies that x is increasing, and since λ must tend towards ϕ from below, if $x(T2) > 0$). As a result, referring to figure 6.2(a), the optimum programme must either follow pattern 1, which we label 'scarce capital', or pattern 2, which we label 'abundant capital'. Pattern 3 is an important limiting case, to which we shall refer later.

As when investment was bounded, a programme such as pattern 1, which involves an increasing rate of extraction during an initial period, followed by a period of decreasing output towards the end of the extractive life, may be optimum if the initial capital stock is low. On the contrary, if the initial capital stock is high enough, the standard pattern of decreasing output

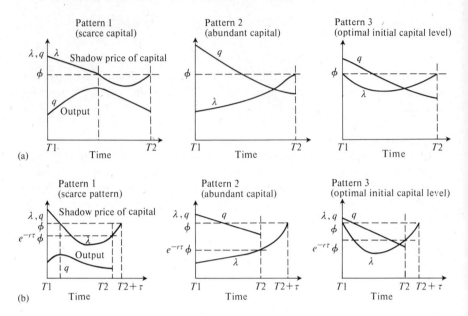

FIG. 6.2   (a) Optimum programmes with costs of adjustment; (b) optimum programmes
with costs of adjustment that persist after exhaustion

will obtain. We believe but have not been able to prove that this is also the
case for a model with many factors of production.[5]

One weakness of cost of adjustment models of investment is their inability
to explain the inherited capital level, x_1, in a satisfactory manner. One has to
believe that the same adjustment cost regime applies during the construction of
a firm as during its active existence. A better view of the world, represented
by the putty-clay hypothesis and refined by the putty-semi-putty hypothesis
(Fuss, 1977), holds that something irreversible happens at the creation time
which narrows the *ex post* choice set of the firm. In Lasserre (1981), this idea
is adapted to mean that adjustment costs are negligible *ex ante*, so that a firm
can select any scale of operation and factor proportions to start with, but that
adjustment costs become present *ex post* if the firm wants to modify its initial
choice. For problem (18) this amounts to making the initial equipment level
a choice variable. The investment programme $I(t)$ is then selected accordingly.
If we call $V(x_1, R_1, \phi, r)$ the maximized value function obtained by solving
problem (18) for a given initial level of x, x_1, the *ex ante* choice consists in
choosing x_1 so as to maximize

$$V(x_1, R_1, \phi, r) - \phi \cdot x_1. \qquad (26)$$

Since $f(x)$ satisfies the Inada conditions, it can be shown that V is concave and differentiable in x_1 and that an interior solution to (26) exists. That solution must satisfy

$$V_{x_1} = \phi$$

or

$$\lambda(T1) = \phi. \tag{27}$$

Consequently, when the initial level of capital is a decision variable, the optimum extraction pattern is pattern 3 (figure 6.2(c)), and it follows that the standard Hotelling's result applies again!

Besides the very sensible extraction pattern implied, this model describes the investment pattern qualitatively. A surprising result implied by proposition 3, which states that λ is increasing when time approaches $T2$, is that investment is becoming less negative when t approaches $T2$, a feature that gets an intuitive explanation from the fact that, in (21), the change in the opportunity cost of capital can be attributed to two sources. The first one, λr, reflects the fact that capital is a financial asset which must produce capital gains unless it generates other benefits. Those are productive services, the second source of changes in λ and the second term in (21); they tend to be dominated by the first term towards the end of the extraction phase because y, the value of one extracted ore unit net of its resource opportunity cost, becomes very small when the horizon is near.

A word on the putty–clay hypothesis will complete this review of alternative ways to introduce capital in exhaustible-resource models. Two versions must be considered. In the first one, only stock factors are fixed *ex post*, while the proportion of variable factors to fixed factors may vary. This is the standard extraction case with increasing marginal costs, which is known to involve a diminishing extraction rate. In the second version, both stock factor levels and factor proportions are fixed *ex post*. In that case, output is constant. Again, Hotelling's result holds as a limiting case.

THE EFFECT OF THE INTEREST RATE

Even a partial survey of the effects of capital and investment on resource extraction could not leave out a discussion on the role of the interest rate. Since Neher (1981) covers the key aspects of this question in an attractive and elegant fashion, we shall only discuss his points briefly, derive them in the more general framework of the model used in the previous section, and provide a few additional results. We shall consider two alternative interest rates, with $r_0 < r_1$. Subscripts 0 and 1, associated with any relevant variable, will refer to the optimum value of that particular variable when $r = r_0$ or $r = r_1$ respectively. Without loss of generality, the initial extraction date will be $t = 0$ and the terminal time will be noted $T_i, i = 0, 1$, unless the extraction period is infinite.

The traditional view is that extraction is faster, the higher the interest rate, as the opportunity cost of postponing a revenue rises with the interest rate. The notion of a faster extraction is not without ambiguity. When T is finite one could say that extraction is faster when $r = r_1$ than when $r = r_0$ if $T_1 < T_0$. Indeed, Levhari and Liviatan (1977) show that $\partial T/\partial r < 0$. Unfortunately, for many exhaustible-resource models the extraction period is infinite. Such would be the case for our model of the last section had we not postulated that demand choked above a certain price. An alternative concept of speed of extraction compares extraction rates: extraction is said to be faster at r_1 than r_0 if the extraction rate is higher at r_1, other thing equal. A privileged date for other things to be equal is $t = 0$, as this is when the resource stocks are identical under the two alternative programmes. Indeed, whether T is finite or not, $\partial q(0)/\partial r \geqslant 0$ in all 'traditional' extraction models.[6] This last concept may be deceptive, however, for one can conceive of a resource for which $\partial q/\partial r \geqslant 0$ at some reserve level and $\partial q/\partial r < 0$ at some other level. In fact, this is the essence of Neher's (1981) 'Double Cross', an example of an extraction model with capital for which the industry price paths at two alternative interest rates cross twice. Given this possibility, one would like to suggest two alternative definitions of 'faster extraction'. Under the strong definition, extraction is said to be faster at r_1 than r_0 if $\partial q/\partial r \geqslant 0$ at any reserve level; under the weak definition, extraction is said to be ultimately faster at r_1 than r_0 if there exists a level of reserves below which $\partial q/\partial r \geqslant 0$. Such a distinction between a strong and a weak definition of 'faster extraction' may also usefully be extended to cases where T is finite, for it is easily seen that $\partial q/\partial r \geqslant 0$ at any reserve level implies $\partial T/\partial r \leqslant 0$ whatever the initial reserve level (a 'strong' concept of faster extraction) and that, if $\partial q/\partial r \geqslant 0$ when reserves are below a certain level, $\bar{R}$, then $\partial T/\partial r \leqslant 0$ if the initial reserve level is not greater than $\bar{R}$ (a 'weak' concept of faster extraction).

Before providing a few results on the effect of the interest rate on the extraction speed, we show briefly how the presence of capital may affect the traditional result, as an increase in r increases the user cost of capital and provides an incentive for slow extraction that might offset the increased extractive impatience that underlies the traditional result.[7] Consider the model of extraction with perfectly malleable capital that was studied in the previous section. It is recalled that $q = H_{\hat{y}}^*(y, v, w)$. The interest rate affects q through y, the net-of-resource-rent output price, and through v, the user-cost of capital, as

$$y = y(R, r, \phi, w), \qquad \text{at the optimum, and } v = r \cdot \phi.$$

It follows that

$$\frac{\partial q}{\partial r} = H_{yy}^* \cdot \frac{\partial y}{\partial r} + H_{yv}^* \cdot \frac{\partial v}{\partial r} \cdot$$

$$= H_{yy}^* \cdot \left(p_q \cdot \frac{\partial q}{\partial r} - \frac{\partial \mu}{\partial r} \right) + H_{yv}^* \cdot \frac{\partial v}{\partial r}$$

and

$$\frac{\partial q}{\partial r} \cdot (1 - p_q \cdot H^*_{yy}) = -H^*_{yy} \cdot \frac{\partial \mu}{\partial r} + H^*_{yv} \cdot \phi. \tag{28}$$

Since p_q is non-positive and H^* is convex in y, $\partial q/\partial r$ has the sign of the right-hand side of (28). For a homogeneous resource, when capital is perfectly malleable, $\partial \mu/\partial r \leqslant 0$, so that the first term on the RHS of (28) is non-negative. It follows that, in the absence of capital, when $H^*_{yv} = 0$, $\partial q/\partial r$ is non-negative, which is the traditional result. Focusing now on the second term on the RHS of (28), each term in the vector H^*_{yv} represents the effect on output of an increase in one particular stock-factor price, ignoring the impact of that price increase on output price y. In general, this effect may be positive or negative, so that the combined effect $H_{yv} \cdot \phi$ is unsigned. When there are only stock factors, as in Neher's one-factor model, this combined effect can be signed because the increase in factor prices is equivalent to a reduction in the output price, which is known to have a negative impact.[8] When the resource is plentiful and $\partial \mu/\partial r = 0$, (28) shows that the effect on the extraction rate of an increase in the interest rate reduces to its effect through factor prices, which is negative when there are only stock factors. In general, it appears that a rise in the interest rate may affect the rate of output positively or negatively, but that the effect is more likely to be positive, the scarcer is the resource relative to capital. This is the essence of Neher's (1981) paper.[9]

This finding satisfies one's intuition and leads to more specific questions. It is clear that, when capital is not under the control of the firm, a rise in the interest rate implies a faster extraction programme whatever the level of reserves. When capital is variable, however, since the resource becomes relatively scarcer as extraction proceeds, one may wonder whether there is a reserve level below which a rise in the interest rate will imply a faster extraction (the weak definition). It turns out that this is not necessarily the case, but propositions 3 and 5 provide two situations where this is true:

Propsoition 1. If the demand does not choke, then there is a reserve level below which a rise in the interest rate implies a faster extraction.

Proposition 2. If the production function satisfies the Inada conditions, then there is a reserve level below which a rise in the interest rate implies a faster extraction.

Proofs. Both proofs rely on a comparison between $\dot{q}_0$ and $\dot{q}_1$, when t tends towards infinity in the case of propositon 3, and when t tends toward T_0 or T_1 in the case of proposition 4. When the demand does not choke, p tends towards infinity and q tends towards zero as t tends towards infinity. Since $p = \mu + c$, where c represents the marginal extraction cost, and since, with a concave production function, c does not increase as q diminishes, the trajectory of μ tends towards the trajectory of p as q approaches zero. It follows that

$$\lim_{t \to \infty} \dot{p}/p = \lim_{t \to \infty} \dot{\mu}/\mu.$$

But $\dot{\mu}_0/\mu_0 = r < \dot{\mu}_1/\mu_1 = r_1$. Consequently, when t tends towards infinity, $\dot{p}_0/p_0 < \dot{p}_1/p_1$, which implies that $\dot{q}_0/q_0 > \dot{q}_1/q_1$. In order that both q_0 and q_1 tend towards zero while q_1 diminishes at a faster rate when t tends towards infinity, it is necessary that

$$q_1(t) > q_0(t) \text{ when } t \to \infty$$

This establishes proposition 3.

When the demand does not choke, proposition 4 follows from proposition 3. We now assume that there is an upper limit, $\bar{p}$, to the output price, which implies that extraction takes place over a finite period. If the production function satisfies the Inada conditions, it can be shown that $\mu(T) = \bar{p}$, which reflects the fact that $q(t)$ tends towards zero as t approaches T, so that marginal factor products tend towards infinity and the marginal cost tends towards zero. This has two interesting implications. First, since $\mu_0(T) = \mu_1(T)$, $\dot{\mu}_0(t) < \dot{\mu}_1(t)$ when t approaches T. Second, since $p = \mu + c$ and c tends towards zero, $\dot{p} = \dot{\mu}$ when t tends toward T. It follows that $\dot{p}_0(t) < \dot{p}_1(t)$ when t tends towards T_0 (in the case of $\dot{p}_0(t)$) or T_1 (in the case of $\dot{p}_1(t)$). This is illustrated in figure 6.3. The slopes of p_1 and p_0 at T_1 and T_0 respectively are uniquely defined by $\bar{p}$ and the appropriate level of r. But the relative position of T_1 and T_0 depends on the initial level of μ_0 and μ_1, itself a function of the initial reserve level. It is clear however that the last reserve unit is extracted faster when $r = r_1$ than when $r = r_0$, which implies that there is a level of reserves below which extraction is faster the higher is the interest rate. This establishes proposition 4.

Propositions 3 and 4 confirm one's intuition that, although the presence of capital may affect the traditional view on the effect of the interest rate, that

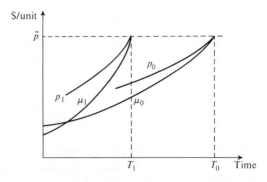

FIG. 6.3 Terminal conditions when the production function satisfies the Inada conditions and demand chokes at $\bar{p}$

view remains valid for a resource that approaches exhaustion. Such intuition must be taken cautiously, however, as can be seen from the following counter-example. Suppose that the technology is such that the minimum marginal cost is $c(r)$, with $c(r_0) < c(r_1)$, as would be the case, for example, if the production function were linear in a unique stock factor. We know that $\mu_0(T_0) = \bar{p} - c(r_0)$ and $\mu_1(T_1) = \bar{p} - c(r_1)$. It follows that $\mu_1(T_1)$ may be sufficiently lower than $\mu_0(T_0)$ for $\dot{\mu}_1(T_1)$ to be lower than $\dot{\mu}_0(T_0)$, despite the fact that μ_1 grows at a higher rate than μ_0. If, as drawn in figure 6.4, the marginal costs are respectively constant over time this is sufficient for

$$\dot{q}_0(T_0) > \dot{q}_1(T_1).$$

In this case, a rise in the interest rate implies a slower extraction at any reserve level. Capital remains scarce relative to the exhaustible resource over the whole extraction programme.

SUMMARY AND CONCLUSION

We have explored some ways and effects of introducing capital in extractive models. The emphasis was put on two well-known results: the proposition that the output of an extractive firm or industry should not increase over time, and the proposition that a rise in the interest rate speeds up extraction. When capital is introduced in a somewhat primitive fashion, where only its durability is taken into account, the standard result on the extraction profile remains valid. It is the second key characteristic of capital, its imperfect malleability, that may affect the result, as a firm may find itself in a position where it is optimum progressively to build up its capacity before adopting the standard attitude of reducing output in response to a rising resource opportunity cost and, possibly, to the reduction in the remaining operative life of equipment.

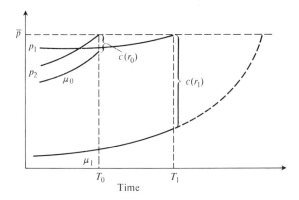

FIG. 6.4 Counter-example

The standard result appears to be fairly robust, however, and it is valid again in the case of a more sophisticated one-factor adjustment cost model where the initial factor stock is not left unexplained but results from a rational *ex ante* decision of the firm.

A rise in the interest rate may slow down extraction in the presence of capital, but, unlike the previous case, the key characteristic at play is the durability of capital. Neher's (1981) conclusion that this result obtains only if capital is scarce relative to the exhaustible resource was re-established and explored further. If the demand does not vanish at high prices, or if the production function satisfies the Inada conditions, there exists a reserve level below which the exhaustible resource is scarce enough relative to capital for the conventional effect of a rise in the interest rate to obtain. Under other characteristics of the market and the technology, however, the scarcity of the resource will indeed increase over time but may never outweigh that of capital. In such cases, a rise in the interest rate may slow down extraction even if the resource approaches exhaustion.

Throughout the paper, the methods and results of static duality theory were applied to maximized Hamiltonians, allowing the derivation of fairly general results in a simple fashion.

NOTES

1. Aggregation problems may be perverse in the presence of exhaustible resources (Blackorby and Schworm, 1980). In fact, Lasserre (1982) shows that, even when the conditions outlined below are met, the extraction rates of all individual firms may not decrease over time although industry output conforms to the Hotelling pattern.
2. If the aggregation problem is addressed adequately, this result does not follow for all firms (see n. 1).
3. In the foregoing argument, since we are considering upward jumps only, the non-negativity constraint on I can be ignored, so that the argument of Arrow and Kurz (1970, p. 57) can be used as a formal proof.
4. If adjustment costs persists at $T2$, the firm faces a standard extraction problem without capital, that of extracting a stock, x_2, at a rate $I = \dot{x}$ using a technology characterized by the cost function $C(I)$, given that the output price will stay at ϕ. For this well-known problem, the imputed price of the resource (capital), λ, grows at the discount rate to reach the output price, ϕ, at the end of the extraction (dismantling) period, with output (negative investment) reaching zero at that time (Lasserre, 1981, chapter 2; and also Schulze, 1974). If τ is the length of the dismantling period that starts at $T2$, the imputed value of capital at $T2$ is $\lambda(T2) = e^{-r\tau} \cdot \phi$. The whole foregoing treatment of the cost of adjustment model can be adapted by substituting this terminal value to that given by (24). For more comments see n. 5.
5. If adjustment costs persist after $T2$, it is easily checked that proposition 1 holds, proposition 2 holds even at $t = T2$ and proposition 3 now reads: $\lambda(T2) = r \cdot e^{-r\tau} \cdot \phi + [C(I) + (\phi - \lambda(T2)) \cdot I] \cdot f_x(x)/f(x)$, with $I = I(T2) < 0$ and $x = x(T2) > 0$. The same qualitative results obtain, with figure 6.2(a) being replaced by figure 6.2(b). There are now two distinct phases in the life of the mine: during the first one, the firm extracts ore while adjusting its capital stock upward or downward: during the second phase, the mine does not produce any longer but progressively dismantles its capital stock. The first phase ends at $T2$ when the shadow price of capital reaches

its market opportunity cost, $e^{-r\tau} \cdot \phi$. The second phase ends at $T2 + \tau$ and last longer, the higher is the initial capital, because the stock of capital still in place at $T2$, x_2, is higher, the higher is x_1. This can be shown by contradiction. Let the indices a and s refer to the cases of abundant and scarce initial capital respectively. If $x^a(T2^a) < x^s(T2^s)$, by (21), $\dot{\lambda}^a(T2^a - \epsilon) < \dot{\lambda}^s(T2 - \epsilon)$, since f is concave. But this implies that the trajectory of λ^a tends to the trajectory of λ^s from above if those are represented on such a time scale that $T2^a$ and $T2^s$ are represented by the same point (figure 6.5). This in turn implies that $I^a > I^s$ towards $T2$. So if $x^a(T2^a) < x^s(T2^s)$, I^a must have been inferior to I^s, requiring $\lambda^a < \lambda^s$, at some earlier time. The trajectories of λ^a and λ^s must have crossed as indicated in figure 6.5 at, say, $T2 - \hat{t}$. At $T2 - \hat{t}$, $\lambda^a = \lambda^s$, $x^a < x^s$, and $y^a = y^s$. Hence by (21) $\dot{\lambda}^a < \dot{\lambda}^s$, which contradicts figure 6.5. Hence the initial proposition, $x^a(T2^a) < x^s(T2^s)$, cannot hold, hence $x^a(T2^a) \geqslant x^s(T2^s)$.

6. By 'traditional' models, we mean positive discount rate models of present-value or additive-utility maximization without capital, such as Hotelling (1931), Levhari and Liviatan (1977), or Schulze (1974).

7. In the Lewis–Slade paper (chapter 7 below), this double effect of the interest rate r could be investigated if some of the factor prices in q were treated as user costs, that is to say were made functions of r.

8. If $\partial v / \partial r = \phi$, $(\partial v / \partial r) / v = 1/r$, which means that all factor prices have been increased by the same percentage $1/r$.

9. As Neher's illustration relies on several explicit integrations, it was confined to a one-factor model with linear technology under the assumption that demand does not choke. (28) is valid for any concave production function of m variable factors and n perfectly malleable stock factors for which a solution to the mine problem exists; we assume $p_q \leqslant 0$, but there may be an upper limit to the prices that command a positive demand.

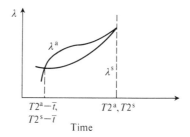

FIG. 6.5 Shadow price trajectories if $x^a(T2^a) < x^s(T2^s)$

REFERENCES

Arrow, K. J. and Kurz, M. (1970), *Public Investment, the Rate of Return, and Optimal Fiscal Policy*, Baltimore: Johns Hopkins University Press (for Resources for the Future).

Billiet, A. (1959), 'Sur la recherche de l'optimum d'exploitation d'un gisement minier de capacité incertaine', *Revue française de Recherche opérationnelle*, 10, 21–4.

Blackorby, C. and Schworm, W. (1980), 'Rationalizing the Use of Aggregates in Natural Resource Economics', Discussion Paper no. 80-19, Department of Economics, University of British Columbia.

Bradley, P. G., Helliwell, J. F., and Livernois, J. R. (1981), 'Efficient Taxation of Resource Income: The Case of Copper Mining in British Columbia', *Resources Policy*, 7, 3, 161–70.

Burt, O. R. and Cummings, R. G. (1970), 'Production and Investment in Natural-resource Industries', *American Economic Review*, 60, 576–90.

Campbell, H. F. (1980), 'The Effect of Capital Intensity on the Optimal Rate of Extraction of a Mineral Deposit', *Canadian Journal of Economy*, 13, 349–56.

Dasgupta, P. S. and Heal, G. M. (1979), *Economic Theory and Exhaustible Resources*, Cambridge University Press.

Diewert, W. E. (1974), 'Applications of Duality Theory', in M. D. Intrilligator and D. A. Kendrick (eds), *Frontiers of Quatitative Economics*, vol. II. Amsterdam: North-Holland.

Fuss, M. A. (1977), 'The Structure of Technology Over Time: A Model for Testing the "Putty-clay" Hypothesis', *Econometrica*, 45, 1797–1821.

Gaffney, M. (ed.) (1967), *Extractive Resources and Taxation*, Madison: University of Wisconsin Press.

Gray, L. C. (1914), 'Rent Under the Assumption of Exhaustibility', *Quarterly Journal of Economics*, 28, 466–89; reprinted in Mason Gaffney (ed.), *Extractive Resources and Taxation*, Madison: University of Wisconsin Press.

Helliwell, J. F. (1978), 'The Effects of Taxes and Royalties on Copper Mining Investment in British Columbia', *Resources Policy*, 4, 1, 35–44.

Herfindahl, O. C. (1967), 'Depletion and Economic Theory', in M. Gaffney (ed.), *Extractive Resources and Taxation*, Madison: University of Wisconsin Press.

Hotelling, H. (1931), 'The Economics of Exhaustible Resources', *Journal of Political Economy*, 39, 137–75.

Jorgenson, D. W. (1963), 'Capital Theory and Investment Behaviour', *American Economic Review*, Papers and Proceedings, 53, 247–59.

Lasserre, P. (1981), 'Generalized Irreversibility and *Ex Ante* Factor Demands with an Application to Mining', *Cahier de recherche* no. 8116, Department of Economic Science and the Centre for Economic Research and Development, University of Montreal.

Lasserre, P. (1982), 'Market Price and Individual Extraction Profiles for a Competitive Extractive Industry', unpublished mimeograph, Department of Economic Science, University of Montreal.

Lau, L. J. (1976), 'A Characterization of the Normalized Restricted Profit Function', *Journal of Economic Theory*, 12, 131–63.

Levhari, D. and Liviatan, N. (1977), 'Notes on Hotelling's Economics of Exhaustible Resources', *Canadian Journal of Economics*, 10, 177–92.

Masse, P. (1962), *Optimum Investment Decisions*, Englewood Cliffs, NJ: Prentice-Hall.

Neher, P. A. (1981), 'Rent-A-Rig II', Resources Paper no. 68, Department of Economics, University of British Columbia.

Paish, F. W. (1938), 'Causes of Changes in Gold Supply', *Economica*, 5, 379–409.

Puu, T. (1977), 'On the Profitability of Exhausting Natural Resources', *Journal of Economic and Environmental Management*, 4, 185–99.

Salant, S., Eswaran, M., and Lewis, T. (1981), 'The Length of Optimal Extraction Programs when Depletion Affects Extraction Costs', Resources Paper no. 61, Department of Economics, University of British Columbia.

Schulze, W. D. (1974), 'The Optimal Use of Non-renewable Resources: the Theory of Extraction', *Journal of Economic and Environmental Management*, 1, 53–73.

Scott, A. (1955), *Natural Resources: The Economics of Conservation*, University of Toronto Press.

Scott, A. (1967), 'The Theory of the Mine Under Conditions of Certainty', in Gaffney M. (ed.), *Extractive Resources and Taxation,* Madison: University of Wisconsin Press.

Smith, V. L. (1968), 'Economics of Production from Natural Resources', *American Economic Review,* 68, 409–31.

Stiglitz, J. E. (1976), 'Monopoly and the Rate of Extraction of Exhaustible Resources', *American Economic Review,* 66, 655–61.

Ventura, E. M. (1964), 'Operations Research in the Mining Industry', in D. B. Hertz and R. T. Edison (eds), *Progress in Operations Research,* vol. 2, section 4.4, New York, Wiley, 315–16.

Comment   William Schworm

INTRODUCTION

Since publication in 1931, Hotelling's model of non-renewable resource extraction has provided the paradigm for analysing the production aspects of the extraction process. There are several well-known results that are implied by Hotelling's model and some of its generalizations. One is that, for competitive equilibrium price paths, the optimal rate of resource extraction is decreasing over time. A second implication is that a permanent increase in the interest rate causes a more rapid depletion of the resource. Both of these propositions have been examined extensively in generalizations of Hotelling's model, and there is substantial knowledge of conditions under which these implications are not valid. Little is known about the validity of these two propositions, however, if capital equipment is used in the extraction process.

Professor Lasserre investigates the validity of these two propositions when capital is an input in the extraction process. Several different specifications of capital in the extraction process are investigated. Conditions are found under which the optimal extraction rate is declining over the life of a resource, but conditions are also found under which the optimal extraction rate increases over an initial time period. The effect of an interest rate change on the extraction path is shown to be ambiguous once capital is included in the model even if capital is treated in the simplest possible manner.

There has been a relatively small literature on the use of capital in the extraction process. In Smith (1968), Burt and Cummings (1970), and Diewert and Lewis (1981), quite general models of extraction and investment decisions are constructed which apply to both renewable and non-renewable resources. In the first two papers, however, little attention is paid to the qualitative properties of the extraction path, and in the Diewert–Lewis paper few results are obtained in the two-stock case owing to the generality of the model. Clark, Clarke, and Munro (1979) investigate a specific model of a renewable resource with irreversible investment. However, the structure of the solution depends on the resource being renewable, and no attention is devoted to the solution in the non-renewable case.

There are several papers that are more directly concerned with the interaction of the optimal capital path and the optimal extraction path. Massé (1962), Billiet (1959), and Ventura (1964) investigate the extraction and investment decisions in very specific models of the extraction process. In more recent work, Crémer (1979) and Hanson and Lee (1979) investigate the effect of capital on the qualitative properties of the extraction path. Although Crémer assumes capital has a fixed input–output coefficient, Hanson and Lee assume a general technology with irreversible investment and variable utilization. Campbell (1980) and Crabbé (1982) have specified conditions under which the optimal extraction path is a constant over at least part of the life of a non-renewable resource when capital constrains the extraction rate. In several special models of resource extraction with capital, Neher (1978, 1981) has shown that changes in the interest rate do not have a determinate effect on the optimal extraction path if capital is used in the extraction process.

The results of multi-stock growth models (see for example, Hadley and Kemp, 1971, or Burmeister, 1980, or the results of the Diewert–Lewis, 1981 model) make one sceptical of obtaining strong results in an intertemporal optimization problem with both a resource stock and a capital stock. There are several characteristics of the non-renewable resource model, however, that make interesting qualitative results more likely. First, there is the simple equation of motion for non-renewable resources. The rate of decline of the resource stock is equal to the extraction rate. Second, under reasonably general conditions the steady state for the model occurs when there is no resource remaining. Therefore, there is a simple characterization of the steady state and the steady state is invariant to the parameters. Third, there is a strong restriction imposed on price paths by competitive equilibrium conditions. Finally, the special contribution of this paper is to use optimization conditions to restrict the admissible values of the initial capital stock.

I begin by describing and discussing the models analysed by Professor Lasserre, and go on to summarize and explain the results obtained by him on the shape of the extraction path. I then discuss the results obtained on the impact of interest rate changes on the extraction path, and offer suggestions for further research in the concluding section.

THE MODEL

In Professor Lasserre's model, the resource extraction industry is represented as a single, aggregative firm. This industry treats the output price path as exogenous and known. The equilibrium price path is determined by the industry output path and the autonomous inverted demand function, $p_t = P(q_t)$, which is assumed to have a finite choke price, $P(0)$. The firm faces exogenous factor prices: w for variable inputs, L, and ϕ for the capital input χ. These factor prices are assumed to be known and constant over time. Although Professor Lasserre treats χ as a vector in part of his paper, I will treat it as a scalar primarily for expositional reasons.

The extraction of the resource is modelled as the output of a productive process. The technology of this process is modelled by a production function f such that

$$q_t = f(\chi_t, L_t) \tag{1}$$

where q_t is the resource extraction rate. The production function is assumed to be concave and twice-differentiable and to satisfy the conditions.

The firm begins with a given amount of the resource, R_0, and the extraction path is related to the resource path by

$$\dot{R}_t = -q_t \tag{2}$$

where $R_t \geqslant 0$ and $q_t \geqslant 0$. Also, the firm has an initial capital stock vector, χ_0, and the capital path is related to the investment path by

$$\dot{\chi}_t = I_t \tag{3}$$

where $\chi_t \geqslant 0$.

Professor Lasserre models the cost of investment goods in several different ways. For the moment, investment costs are denoted by $C(I)$ and several different specifications of this cost are given below.

The value of the extractive industry is the present value of its cash flow plus the value of its terminal capital stock:

$$\int_0^T \gamma_t \{p_t q_t - w \cdot L_t - C(I_t)\} dt + \gamma_T \phi \chi_T \tag{4}$$

where γ_t is the discount rate and $r = -\dot{\gamma}_t/\gamma_t$ is the constant, instantaneous interest rate. The terminal extraction date, T, is endogenous and is known to be finite because of the assumptions on the production function and the demand function.

The industry's optimization problem is to choose (q_t, L_t, I_t) for all t to maximize (4) subject to (1), (2), and (3). The competitive equilibrium price path, which is treated as exogenous by the industry, is given by the output price path and the demand function.

Four distinct specifications of the cost of investment are used in the paper. The first specification follows from the assumption that capital is perfectly malleable:

$$C(I) = \phi I, \qquad \text{with } -\infty \leqslant I \leqslant +\infty. \tag{5}$$

The cost of investment is the acquisition cost in the market, and investment can take on arbitrary positive or negative values. For this specification to be correct there must be perfect used capital markets in which the industry can sell used capital at parametric prices.

The second specification is the case of irreversible investment:

$$C(I) = \phi I, \qquad \text{with } 0 \leqslant I \leqslant +\infty. \tag{6}$$

Although the industry can buy new capital at a parametric price, capital cannot be sold once it has been acquired.

The third specification is the adjustment cost model of investment:

$$C(I) = \phi I + c(I), \qquad \text{with} -\infty \leqslant I \leqslant +\infty \tag{7}$$

with c strictly convex. To acquire capital, the industry must pay not only the market price of investment goods but also the adjustment costs associated with altering the capital stock in the industry.

The final specification is a combination of the first and third specification which has been developed in Professor Lasserre's thesis (1981). It is assumed that at the initial date the firm can choose the initial capital stock without bearing adjustment costs. Therefore, the cost of initial capital construction is ϕK. After the initial capital stock is in place, however, any later changes in the capital stock will incur adjustment costs. Therefore, in this specification capital is malleable at $t = 0$ but the adjustment cost model is applicable for $t > 0$.

THE SHAPE OF THE OPTIMAL EXTRACTION PATH

In this section, I explain and provide a minor generalization of Professor Lasserre's results on the influence of capital on the shape of the optimal extraction path.

The industry's optimization problem is characterized by the following Hamiltonian:

$$H(p - \mu, w, \chi) + G(\lambda) = \max_{(q,L,I)} \{p \cdot q - w \cdot L - \mu q - C(I) + \lambda I | q \leqslant F(L, \chi)\}. \tag{8}$$

The additive structure of the Hamiltonian is a consequence of the additive separability of I from (q, L) in the objective function in (8).

Assuming that factor prices are constant over time, and using the relationship

$$\frac{\partial H(p - \mu, w, \chi)}{\partial p} = \dot{q},$$

one can derive the following useful identity, which must be satisfied along optimal extraction paths:

$$\dot{q} = \frac{\partial^2 H(p - \mu, w, \chi)}{\partial p^2} (\dot{p} - \dot{\mu}) + \frac{\partial^2 H(p - \mu, w, \chi)}{\partial p \partial \chi} I. \tag{9}$$

Using the demand relation, $p = P(q)$, one obtains

$$\dot{q} = \left(-\frac{\partial q}{\partial p} r\mu + \frac{\partial q}{\partial \chi} I \right) \bigg/ \left(1 - \frac{\partial q}{\partial p} P'(q) \right) \tag{10}$$

where

$$1 - \frac{\partial q}{\partial p} P'(q) > 0$$

and $\partial q / \partial p > 0$.

I make the following assumption about the technology which is not assumed by Professor Lasserre.

Assumption. $\partial q / \partial \chi > 0$.

The following proposition follows immediately from this assumption and (10).

Proposition 1. If $I(t) \leqslant 0$, then $q(t) < 0$ and $\dot{p}(t) > 0$.

This proposition holds for any of the four specifications of the cost of capital since the properties of G and, hence, the properties of c were not used in the derivation of the proposition. Therefore, the standard Hotelling result on the monotonicity of the output and price path are valid in the presence of capital if capital is not increasing over the extraction period. Therefore, to find circumstances in which the Hotelling result is valid, one needs to find conditions that imply that optimal investment is non-positive over the life of a resource. It seems likely that there are interesting circumstances in which this is true, since the optimal capital stock is decreasing over the life of the resource if capital is malleable. Also, if the capital stock is fixed over the life of the resource, then the extraction rate declines over time.

In the case of irreversible investment, it has been shown by several people, including Professor Lasserre, that all investment occurs at $t = 0$. The reason is that the optimal capital stock path with malleable capital is non-increasing. As a consequence, the optimal capital path with the constraint that capital cannot be strictly decreasing will also be non-increasing. Therefore, the capital stock after the initial instant will be a constant over the life of the resource. The proposition implies then that the extraction rate is non-increasing over the life of the resource.

In the case with adjustment costs, and a given initial capital stock, the shape of the extraction path depends on the initial capital stock. Following Professor Lasserre, define capital as scarce if the initial capital stock is such that the shadow value of capital exceeds the market price of capital, $\lambda > \phi$. Define capital as abundant if $\lambda < \phi$ and define the initial capital stock as optimal if $\lambda = \phi$. It is easy to see that $I(0) \gtrless 0$ as $\lambda \gtrless \phi$ under the usual assumptions on $c(I)$. To determine the shape of the output path, however, one must know the global properties of the investment path.

Professor Lasserre has shown that, if capital is the only factor of production, then initial capital optimality or abundance implies that investment is non-positive for all t. This fact plus proposition 1 implies that the extraction rate is decreasing over the life of the resource. The result depends on the following lemma.

Lemma. If $\lambda_t \leqslant \phi$, then $\lambda_s \leqslant \phi$ for all $s \geqslant t$.

This lemma insures that, if capital is not scarce at any time, then it will never be scarce at a later date. Therefore, if the initial capital stock is abundant or optimal, then capital will be non-scarce over the entire life of the resource. As a consequence, under these conditions investment is never positive.

Although Professor Lasserre has proved this lemma only when there is a single factor of production, a straightforward modification of his procedure proves the lemma when there are many variable inputs if one maintains the assumption that $\partial q/\partial \chi > 0$. Therefore, the following proposition can be proved for the general model with adjustment costs presented in the preceding section.

Proposition 2. If the initial capital stock is abundant or optimal so that $\lambda_0 \leqslant \phi$. then $I_t \leqslant 0$, $\dot{q}_t \leqslant 0$, and $\dot{p}_t \geqslant 0$ for all t.

If capital is scarce initially, then investment is positive over some initial extraction period. As a consequence of the increasing capital stock, the extraction rate can be increasing over this initial period. Therefore, if there are adjustment costs of investment and an arbitrary initial capital stock, the proposition that the extraction rate is monotonically decreasing is not generally valid.

In the fourth model considered, Professor Lasserre has suggested that the initial capital stock should not be treated as arbitrary. Instead, the initial capital stock is a consequence of an optimization decision about the amount of capital with which to begin the extraction process, given that the industry will face adjustment costs for any later alterations in the capital stock. This is the most important point in the paper. The use of optimization conditions for the initial capital stock not only adds realism to the model but also strengthens the implications of the model. In particular, if firms choose the capital stock optimally at $t = 0$, then $\lambda_0 = \phi$ and the hypothesis of proposition 2 is alsways satisfied as an optimality condition. Hence, the following is a corollary of proposition 2.

Corollary. If χ_0 is chosen optimally, then $I_t \leqslant 0$, $\dot{q}_t \leqslant 0$, and $\dot{p}_t \geqslant 0$ for all t.

To summarize, the most important contribution of this paper is to show that capital can be introduced into the extractive process in a reasonably complex manner without invalidating the general result that extraction decreases over time. This result is obtained by exploiting optimality conditions to restrict the initial capital stock chosen prior to the beginning of the extraction process. This general idea should prove to be useful in other contexts where there is a natural point in time at which production begins.

THE EFFECT OF THE INTEREST RATE ON THE EXTRACTION PATH

In the Hotelling model, with no capital an increase in the interest rate causes a more rapid depletion of the resource. Professor Lasserre examines the case in which capital is malleable and shows that the result does not hold in general if capital is used in the extraction process. The extractive firm is assumed to have a general, convex technology. Therefore, Professor Lasserre's result generalizes the similar result obtained by Neher (1981).

The reason that capital changes the standard result is that the interest rate is a component of the rental cost of capital. A change in the interest rate not only causes a change in the present value of funds but also increases the cost of capital and, hence, the extraction costs. Although the decrease in the present value of future funds induces more rapid depletion, the increase in extraction costs induces slower depletion. The net effect is ambiguous. Professor Lasserre does show that, under certain reasonable conditions, a rise in the interest rate implies faster extraction if the initial reserves are low enough.

Although Professor Lasserre does not examine cases with non-malleable capital, it appears that his results would generalize. As an example, consider the case with adjustment costs and a fixed initial capital stock. The effect of the interest rate on extraction is given by

$$\frac{\partial q}{\partial r} = - \left(\frac{\partial q}{\partial p} \frac{\partial \mu}{\partial r} - \frac{\partial q}{\partial \chi} \frac{\partial \chi}{\partial r} \right) \bigg/ \left(1 - \frac{\partial q}{\partial p} P'(q) \right). \tag{11}$$

If μ is independent of χ, and if $\partial\chi/\partial r = 0$, then an increase in the interest rate for a given level of reserves increases extraction. But an increase in the interest rate can induce a lower capital stock and, hence, a lower rate of extraction for a given level of reserves. In general, the net effect is ambiguous.

CONCLUSIONS

The introduction of capital into the resource extraction process greatly complicates the characteristics of the optimal resource path. Professor Lasserre has shown, however, that some interesting results can be obtained in resource models with capital equipment.

There are several areas in which I think further research in this area could be fruitfully pursued. One is to examine the investment–extraction behaviour when there are cyclical shifts in the demand function or variations in factor prices over time. A second area is to examine the effects of relaxing the stringent assumptions about the existence of perfect capital markets or futures markets. This would require a more serious examination of the interaction between financial policy and intertemporal resource extraction. A third aspect of the standard models that should be investigated is the assumption of an aggregate technology to characterize feasible industry extraction paths. It is possible that some results are dependent on the assumption of an aggregate technology.

Perhaps the greatest complexity that arises from a consideration of capital in the resource extraction process is in the specification of theoretically consistent extraction and investment equations that can be estimated with available data. This is an extremely important area for future research. Too much current empirical research ignores the dynamic properties of the extraction process. In addition, most empirical research ignores the existence of capital as a factor of production in the extraction process. An exception is Professor Lasserre's thesis, in which he models the extraction and investment equations derived from a dynamic optimization problem. Much more research of this sort is needed.

REFERENCES

Billiet, A. (1959), 'Sur la recherche de l'optimum d'exploitation d'un gisement minier de capacite incertaine', *Revue française de recherche opérationnelle,* 10, 21-4.

Burmeister, E. (1980), *Capital Theory and Dynamics,* Cambridge University Press.

Campbell, H. F. (1980), 'The Effect of Capital Intensity on the Optimal Rate of Extraction of a Mineral Deposit', *Canadian Journal of Economy,* 13, 349-56.

Crémer, J. (1979), 'On Hotelling's Formula and the Use of Permanent Equipment in the Extraction of Natural Resources', *International Economic Review,* 20, 317-24.

Bart, O., and Cummings, R. (1970), 'Production and Investment in Natural Resource Industries', *American Economic Review,* 60, 576-90.

Clark, W., Clarke, F., and Munro, G. (1979), 'The Optimal Exploitation of Renewable Resource Stocks: Problems of Irreversible Investment', *Econometrica,* 47, 25-47.

Crabbé, P. (1982), 'The Effect of Capital Intensity of the Optimal Rate of Extraction of a Mineral Deposit', *Canadian Journal of Economics,* 15, 534-41.

Diewert, E. and Lewis, T. (1981), 'The Comparative Dynamics of Efficient Programs of Capital Accumulation and Resource Depletion', Resource Paper no. 59, Department of Economics, University of British Columbia.

Hadley, G. and Kemp, M. (1971), *Variational Methods in Economics,* Amsterdam: North-Holland.

Hanson, D. and Lee, S. (1979), 'Oil Supply and the Producer Price Path', Working Paper no. 125, Department of Economics, Southern Methodist University, Dallas.

Hotelling. H. (1931), 'The Economics of Exhaustible Resources', *Journal of Political Economy,* 39, 137-75.

Lasserre, P. (1981), 'Factor Demands and Output Supply by the Extractive Firm: Theory and Estimation', unpublished PhD thesis, University of British Columbia.

Massé, P. (1962), *Optimum Investment Decisions,* Englewood Cliffs, NJ: Prentice-Hall.

Neher, P. A. (1978), 'Rent-A-Rig', Resources Paper no. 29, Department of Economics, University of British Columbia.

Neher, P. A. (1981), 'Rent-A-Rig II', Resources Paper no. 68, Department of Economics, University of British Columbia.

Smith, V. (1968), 'Economics of Production from Natural Resources', *American Economic Review,* 58, 409-31.

Ventura, E. M. (1964), 'Operations Research in the Mining Industry', in D. B Hertz and R. T. Edison (eds), *Progress in Operations Research,* Wilby, vol. 2, New York, Wiley, section 4.4, 315-16.

7. The Effects of Price Controls, Taxes, and Subsidies on Exhaustible Resource Production

Tracy R. Lewis and Margaret Slade

INTRODUCTION

Current policies for utilizing scarce natural resources often call for taxes, subsidies, and price controls.[1] There are two reasons why equity and efficiency might require the government to intervene in private exhaustible-resource markets. First, it is generally believed that natural resources belong in the public domain. Hence, the rents obtained from extracting these resources should not accrue to private concerns. Many devices for collecting and redistributing resource rents have been proposed and tried. These include profit taxes, royalty payments, excise or severance taxes, and price controls on intermediate or final products.

Second, it is argued that taxes or subsidies may correct inefficiencies that exist in resource markets and elsewhere in the economy. Depletion allowances and other favourable tax provisions have been instituted to encourage more rapid and complete development of energy resources. On the other hand, surcharges on resource consumption have been proposed to prevent myopic producers from depleting stores of strategic nonrenewable resources too rapidly.

Although resource taxes and price controls are widely advocated and used, little has been done to assess the effects that these instruments have on the intertemporal supply of exhaustible resources. This is a difficult subject because it requires knowledge of how the firm's production decision in each time period is affected by past and future taxes and subsidies. However, progress has been made on solving this problem in the interesting work of Burness (1976), Sweeney (1977), Microeconomic Associates (1977), Dasgupta, Heal, and Stiglitz (1980), and Conrad and Hool (1981).[2] These papers examine the effect that taxes, subsidies, and price controls have on extraction profiles under competitive conditions. To simplify matters, these authors assume that the extracted resource is sold without prior processing. Hence all taxes, subsidies, and royalties apply to the unprocessed resource.[3] This assumption, which turns out to be important in deriving results, will be discussed further below. While these studies ignore certain real-world complexities of resource extraction, they provide a first step towards understanding the comparative dynamics of extractive industries. The principal conclusions that emerge from this literature are as follows:

1. The imposition of a constant tax per unit of ore extracted (sometimes called a severance tax) will cause the resource to be extracted less rapidly and, when costs vary across deposits, may cause cumulative extraction to fall. Likewise, a subsidy that reduces unit extraction cost by some constant

amount will increase the rate of extraction and may increase cumulative extraction.

2. The imposition of a royalty, which is a constant proportion of final-product price, will cause extraction to proceed more rapidly/at the same rate/more slowly depending on whether the discounted market price of the extracted resource increases/remains unchanged/decreases over time. When ore varies in production cost, cumulative extraction may fall as a result of the royalty.

3. A price control placed on the resource will cause extraction to proceed more rapidly/at the same pace/more slowly depending on whether the discounted difference between the market price and the controlled price increases/remains unchanged/decreases over time. It may also cause the cumulative amount of production to fall.

Conclusions 2 and 3 are particularly interesting because they indicate when royalties and price controls are non-distortionary.

This paper examines the effects of various tax instruments on resource extraction under more general and realistic circumstances than have previously been considered. We assume that the extracted resource is used with other inputs as an intermediate product in the production a final good.[4] The motivation for this assumption comes from observing that extracted resources are almost always subjected to some degree of processing prior to marketing. For example, crude petroleum is refined and combined with chemical additives before it is sold as gasoline; bauxite is mixed with reagents to form alumina (Al_2O_3), which in turn is electrolytically separated into aluminium and oxygen; and iron ore is smelted to form pig iron, refined to separate out impurities, and combined with carbon and ferroalloys before it is sold as steel. Taxation can occur at many different stages of processing. With copper, for example, ore, concentrate, blister, or refined metal can be taxed.

The amount of processing prior to marketing is important in assessing the impact of resource taxation. Generally, the effect of a tax on extraction will depend on whether it applies directly to the extracted resource or to a final good that uses the resource as an input. With the exception of a severance tax, which falls directly on the extracted resource, most taxes and royalties are collected further 'downstream' once the resource has been combined with other inputs to produce a refined product. Because the value of the unprocessed resource is difficult to establish (since it is a firm-specific stock, which is usually not traded in a market), it is easier to tax a processed product, which has a market price.

This suggests that the change in extraction resulting from a particular tax or subsidy will depend on where it falls, on how it affects input and output prices, and on the possibilities for substituting between the resource and other inputs in producing a final product. A general model for studying these effects is developed in Diewert and Lewis (1981). In particular, they examine the effect that a tax on an end-of-period stock has on extraction profiles. They show that, if the technology set is restricted to satisfy certain sufficient conditions, it is possible to evaluate the effects that many different tax policy instruments have on extraction profiles by transforming each tax or subsidy into an equivalent stock tax. A constant-returns-to-scale, Cobb–Douglas production technology satisfies these conditions.

In this paper, we exploit this property of the Cobb–Douglas technology to obtain comparative-dynamic results for changes in royalties, cost subsidies, favourable tax treatment, and price controls. This analysis allows us to identify conditions on (1) the relative shares of output attributed to the resource and other inputs, (2) the time-paths of input and output prices, and (3) the rate of discount, that determine how the extraction profile responds to a particular tax or subsidy. Our formulation has the advantage that in most instances conditions (1)–(3) can be determined empirically.

The outline of the paper is as follows. In the next section we introduce the model and state a result about the comparative-dynamic effects of a tax (or subsidy) that is based on the firm's current stock of resources. This result has an intuitive interpretation, which is an aid in understanding how tax policy affects extraction. It is also seen that the conclusions from the investigations mentioned above can be derived as a special case of our model and the stock tax result. We then provide some general comparative-dynamic results on the effects of changes in relative market prices on profit-maximizing extraction, output, and input-use paths of a firm. These general results are then used to analyse the impact of some specific resource tax and subsidy policies. The final section summarizes our results and puts forth some suggestions for further work in this area.

THE MODEL AND SOME PRELIMINARY RESULTS

Description of the competitive extractive firm

The following model is a special case taken from Diewert and Lewis (1981). We focus on an extractive industry where firms take input and output prices as given. (Possible modifications to this price-taking assumption will be discussed in the concluding section.[5] A typical firm in this industry has production possibilities that are described by a single period technology set, $S(y, \vec{x}, s_0, s_1)$, where y is current-period output of some good, $\vec{x} = (x^1, x^2, \ldots, x^m)$ is an m-dimensional vector of current period inputs, s_0 represents the size of the resource stock at the beginning of the production period, and s_1 is the stock remaining at the end of the period. Hence, s_1 becomes the stock available to the firm at the start of the next period. The technology set S indicates the trade-offs between producing more current output, y (or using fewer current inputs, $\vec{x}$), and running down the end-of-period stock, s_1. If the resource were renewable like a forest or fishery, S would also depend on the natural rate of growth of the stock.

An equivalent but more convenient representation of the technology set is the variable profit function. Assuming the producer maximizes profits for a given s_0 and s_1, we define the one-period variable profit function π as

$$\pi(p, \vec{q}, s_0, s_1) = \begin{cases} \sup\limits_{y, x} \{py - qx : (y, \vec{x}, s_0, s_1) \in S\} \text{ if there exists a} \\ \qquad\qquad\qquad\qquad\qquad (y, \vec{x}) \text{ such that} \\ \qquad\qquad\qquad\qquad\qquad (y, x, s_0, s_1) \in S \\ -\infty \qquad\qquad\qquad\qquad \text{otherwise} \end{cases} \quad (1)$$

where p is the output price and $\vec{q} \gg 0_m$ is the vector of market prices corresponding to the vector $\vec{x}$. Notice that there are no market prices corresponding to s_0 and s_1. Irrespective of the properties of S, it can be shown that $\pi(p, \vec{q}, s_0, s_1)$ is a convex and positively linearly homogeneous function in p and $\vec{q}$.[6] Furthermore, assuming π is differentiable at $(p, \vec{q}, s_0, s_1)$ with respect to p and the components of $\vec{q}$, we know from Hotelling's Lemma that

$$y(p, \vec{q}, s_0, s_1) = \partial\pi/\partial p \qquad\qquad (2a)$$

$$x(p, \vec{q}, s_0, s_1) = -\nabla_{\vec{q}}\pi \qquad\qquad (2b)$$

where $y(p, \vec{q}, s_0, s_1)$ and $x(p, \vec{q}, s_0, s_1)$ is the solution to the maximization problem defined in (1) and $\nabla_q \pi = (\partial\pi/\partial q^1, \ldots, \partial\pi/\partial q^m)$. The connection between the technology set S and the one-period variable profit function, π, is illustrated below when we consider some specific technologies.

We can now consider the firm's profit-maximizing production and extraction choices over time. Assume that the firm has a $(T + 1)$-period horizon, where T is an arbitrary positive but finite number. Then the firm's maximization problem can be written in terms of the variable profit function as follows:[7]

$$\max_{s_1 \geqslant 0, s_2 \geqslant 0 \ldots s_T \geqslant 0} \left\{ \sum_{t=1}^{T} \delta^{t-1}(\pi_t - \tau_t s_t) \right\} \equiv V \qquad\qquad (3)$$

where $\pi_t = \pi(p_t, \vec{q}_t, s_{t-1}, s_t)$ is the one-period profit function defined by (1)

$p_t > 0$ is the output price in period t, $t = 1, 2, \ldots, T$

$\vec{q}_t \gg 0_m$ is the vector of variable input prices in period t

$s_{t-1} > 0$ is the initial stock of the resource

$s_t \geqslant 0$ is the stock available to the firm at the beginning of period $t + 1$ (note that $s = (s_1, s_2, \ldots, s_T)$ is the vector of decision variables in the maximization problem (3))

$\delta = 1/(1 + r) > 0$ is the constant discount factor; i.e., r is the constant rate of discount

τ_t is the stock tax (or subsidy) rate that the firm must pay on its holdings of the resource at the end of period t

V is the firm's value function, which is defined to be the maximum discounted stream of profits that the firm can earn over the T-period horizon.

The tax variables, τ_t, have been introduced for two reasons: (1) in some instances governments may be interested in imposing such taxes (or subsidies) in order to encourage depletion or conservation of the resource stock; (2) more importantly, developing the comparative-dynamic properties of our model with respect to these variables helps us derive comparative-dynamic results for other tax instruments.

One significant restriction of our formulation is that the extraction horizon is presumed to be given exogenously. In particular, we ignore the possibility that T may be influenced by government tax policy. There are, however, two scenarios where it seems reasonable to regard the life of a mine to be insensitive to changes in tax policy. First, the useful lifetime of a mine might be determined by initial investment. If investment in capacity tends to be lumpy and expensive, it may be economical to mine the resource only until the initial stock of capital wears out. Admittedly, this is a makeshift justification for regarding T as being fixed. If initial investment is important in determining the extraction horizon, it should be modelled explicitly in our analysis. This extension to the model will be discussed in the final section. Second, it is possible to regard T as the optimal lifetime of the mine for a given programme of government taxes and subsidies. In general, T will be insensitive to small changes in one of the taxes or subsidies. Hence, our comparative-dynamic results will at least hold locally (i.e. for small variations in tax rates) when T is chosen by the firm owner.

The comparative-dynamic effects of variations in stock taxes

The general method for obtaining comparative-dynamic results on the effect of variations in prices and tax rates on optimal stock choices is as follows. We assume that the solution $s^* = (s_1^*, s_2^*, \ldots, s_T^*)$ to (3) is unique and that $s_t^* > 0$ for all t, so that we have an interior solution. Further, we suppose that s^* satisfies the first-order conditions for the maximization of (3) and that π_t^* is twice continuously differentiable around $(p_t, \vec{q}_t, s_{t-1}^*, s_t^*)$. Then assuming that the second-order sufficient conditions for an unconstrained interior maximum hold, we can totally differentiate the first-order conditions for the maximization of (3) with respect to the various price and stock tax components to obtain our desired comparative-dynamic results.

This procedure, which is outlined in Diewert and Lewis (1981), is used to derive comparative-dynamic effects of changes in the stock taxes, τ_t. Following the terminology of Diewert (1974, pp. 144-5), we say that the stocks s_t and s_{t-1} are substitutes (strong substitutes) if $\partial^2 \pi / \partial s_t \partial s_{t-1} \geq 0$ (>0). Otherwise the stocks are referred to as complements. Typically, the stocks will be substitutes (see Diewert and Lewis, 1981, p. 43). We can now state a useful result (proved in Diewert and Lewis, 1981) about the effects of stock taxes on optimal extraction.

Proposition 0. If beginning and end-of-period stocks are substitutes (i.e., $\partial \pi^2 / \partial s_t \partial s_{t-1} \geq 0$), then $\partial s_t / \partial \tau_{t'} \leq 0$ (<0 when $\partial^2 \pi / \partial s_t \partial s_{t-1} > 0$) for $t, t' = 1, \ldots, T$.

Thus if any stock tax increases, each optimal stock will decrease so that cumulative extraction as of time t will increase. It is interesting to note that a change in one tax produces a sort of rippling effect on the stock levels throughout the entire time period. In addition, proposition 0 holds for arbitrary sequences of input and output prices, provided that there is an interior solution to the firm's maximization problem in (3).

Under certain conditions, the imposition of a royalty or a price control is equivalent to increasing or decreasing one or more of the stock taxes. In order to illustrate this we turn to the special case previously considered in the literature, where the unprocessed resource is sold directly as a final product. In this instance, the one-period variable profit function can be written as

$$\pi_t = p_t R_t - \phi(R_t, s_{t-1})$$

where $R_t = s_{t-1} - s_t$ is the amount extracted in period t, p_t is the price of the extracted resource, and $\phi(R_t, s_{t-1})$ is the total cost of extracting R_t when the current stock of the resource is s_{t-1}. (Note that the dependence of extraction costs on input price q is suppressed.) It is frequently assumed that marginal extraction costs increase with the amount extracted per time period and increase as the current stock decreases. The second assumption captures the fact that extraction becomes more difficult as the more readily available and higher-grade ores become depleted. These two assumptions imply that

$$\phi_{R_t R_t} > 0 \text{ and } \phi_{R_t s_{t-1}} \leqslant 0.$$

If in addition we assume that the marginal cost of depleting the stock to a fixed end-of-the-period level, $\bar{s}_t$, is increasing in R_t, or, equivalently, if it is increasing in s_{t-1}, since $R_t = s_{t-1} - \bar{s}_t$, we have

$$\frac{d}{ds_{t-1}} \phi_{R_t}(R_t, s_{t-1}) = \frac{d}{ds_{t-1}} \phi_{R_t}(s_{t-1} - s_t, s_{t-1}) = \phi_{R_t R_t} + \phi_{R_t s_{t-1}} > 0.$$

Given this assumption, we note that

$$\pi_{s_t s_{t-1}} = \phi_{R_t R_t} + \phi_{R_t s_{t-1}} > 0$$

so that s_t and s_{t-1} are substitutes.

We shall further simplify matters by assuming that the price of the exhaustible resource appreciates at some constant rate $\bar{a}$ over time, so that $p_t = (1 + \bar{a})^t p_0$ for all t.

Now let us examine the effect on extraction of a royalty that is a percentage of output price. Suppose that some fraction, B, $(0 < B < 1)$ of sales revenues is collected. The imposition of the royalty is equivalent to decreasing the output price that firms receive to $(1 - B)p_t$. In this case, the variable profit function becomes

$$\pi\{p_t(1 - B), s_{t-1}, s_t\} = p_0(1 - B)(1 + \bar{a})^t R_t - \phi(R_t, s_{t-1})$$

$$= p_0(1 - B)(1 + \bar{a})^t(s_{t-1} - s_t) - \phi(R_t, s_{t-1}). \quad (4)$$

Substituting this expression for net profits into (3) and collecting terms involving s_t and s_{t-1}, we find that the firms' maximization problem with royalty payments can be written as

$$\max_{s_1 \geqslant 0, \ldots, s_T \geqslant 0} \left[\sum_{t=1}^{T} \delta^{t-1} \{\pi(p_t, s_{t-1}, s_t) - \tau_t s_t\} \right] \tag{5}$$

where

$$\tau_t = p_0 (1 + \bar{a})^{t-1} B\{(1 + \bar{a})/(1 + r) - 1\}. \tag{6}$$

Notice that (6) is in a form so that we can use our result on stock taxes in order to analyse the impact of royalties on resource production.[8] It follows from (6) that

$$\frac{d\tau_t}{dB} \begin{array}{c} > \\ = \\ < \end{array} 0 \quad \text{as } (1 + \bar{a}) \begin{array}{c} > \\ = \\ < \end{array} (1 + r). \tag{7}$$

According to (7) and our proposition 0, the imposition of a royalty causes extraction to proceed more rapidly/at the same pace/more slowly depending on whether the rate of discount is less/equal/greater than the rate of price appreciation (see result 2 in the introductory section).

Other results on severance taxes and price controls that are reported in the resource taxation literature may be derived from our model using the same method. This method represents the effect of a change in price induced by a tax or subsidy as a change in stock taxes, τ_t. The fact that prices are multiplied by terms that are linear in the stocks, s_t (see (4)), allows us to add up all the price terms involving s_t in order to obtain the stock taxes τ_t. In what follows, we will exploit this property of the model to examine the effects of resource taxation under more general circumstances.

Accordingly, we now turn to the case where the extracted resource, R, is refined and combined with other inputs like capital, labour, and other raw materials before it is sold. Let Q, the marketed product, be equal to $f(R, \vec{x})$ where f is a production function that depends on R and other inputs x_i, for $i = 1, 2, \ldots, m$. Let p_t and $\vec{q}_t$ be the tth-period prices of the output, Q, and the inputs, $\vec{x}$, respectively. If we assume that f is linearly homogeneous, we have

$$\pi(p_t, \vec{q}_t, s_{t-1}, s_t) = \sup_{\vec{x}_t} \left\{ p_t f(R_t, \vec{x}) - \vec{q}_t \cdot \vec{x} - \phi(R_r, s_{t-1}) \right\}$$

$$= R_t \sup_{\vec{x}_t/R_t} \left\{ p_t f\left(1, \frac{\vec{x}_t}{R_t}\right) - \vec{q}_t\left(\frac{\vec{x}_t}{R_t}\right) \right\} - \phi(R_t, s_{t-1})$$

$$= R_t \cdot g(p_t, \vec{q}_t) - \phi(R_t, s_{t-1}) \tag{8}$$

where the second line follows from the linear homogeneity of $p_t f(R_t, \vec{x}_t) - \vec{q}_t \cdot \vec{x}_t t$ and the third line results once the maximization with respect to $\vec{x}_t/R_t$

in the second line has been carried out. We have thus established the following lemma.

Lemma. Suppose that $f(\ )$ is linearly homogeneous; then the variable profit function can be written as

$$\pi(p_t, \vec{q}_t, s_{t-1}, s_t) = R_r \cdot g(p_t, \vec{q}_t) - \phi(R_t, s_{t-1})$$

where $g(\ )$ is some function of output and input prices.

Another implication of our constant-returns-to-scale assumption is that the price and availability of resource substitutes will not affect the rate at which the resource is extracted. Suppose there exists a substitute for the resource denoted by v which can be substituted for R in production at a rate $h(v)$, where h is increasing. Total output is then given by $f\{R + h(v), x\}$. Let $p_{v,t}$ be the price of v. It then follows that the variable profit function, in this case denoted by $\pi(p_t, p_{v,t}, \vec{q}_t, s_{t-1}, s_t)$, is given by

$$\pi(p_t, p_{v,t}, \vec{q}_t, s_{t-1}, s_t)$$

$$= \sup_{v_t, \vec{x}_t} \left\{ [p_t f\{R_t + h(v_t), \vec{x}_t\} - p_{v,t} v_t - \vec{q}_t \cdot \vec{x}_t - \phi(R_t \cdot s_{t-1})] \right\}$$

$$= \sup_{v_t} \left\{ \{R_t + h(v_t)\} \underbrace{\sup_{x_t} \left[p_t \frac{f(1, \vec{x}_t)}{R_t + h(v_t)} - \vec{q}_t \cdot \left\{ \frac{\vec{x}_t}{R_t + h(v_t)} \right\} \right]}_{R(t)+h(v_t)} \right.$$

$$\left. - p_{v,t} v_t - \phi(R_t, s_{t-1}) \right\}$$

$$= \sup_{v_t} \ \{R_t + h(v_t)\} g(p_t, \vec{q}_t) - p_{v,t} v_t - \phi(R_t, s_{t-1})$$

$$= R_t g(p_t, \vec{q}_t) - \phi(R_t, s_{t-1}) + \sup_{v_t} \{h(v_t) g(p_t, \vec{q}_t) - p_{v,t} v_t\}$$

$$= \pi(p_t, \vec{q}_t, s_{t-1}, s_t) + \sup_{v_t} \{h(v_t) g(p_t, \vec{q}_t) - p_{v,t}, v_t\}. \tag{9}$$

Hence the profitability of resource extraction is independent of the use of substitute inputs.[9]

According to the lemma, if there are constant returns to scale in the production of Q, the variable profit function has price terms that are multiplied by linear stock terms. In the sections that follow we use this property in conjunction with our stock tax results to examine the effects of different taxes and subsidies on optimal extraction. In particular we assume that $f(R, x)$ is a Cobb-Douglas production function with constant returns to scale. Further, we suppose that there is just one input besides the resource, which we call x.

However, the results we obtain generalize to the case of N inputs. In the two-input Cobb–Douglas case we have

$$Q_t = A_t R_t^\alpha x_t^{1-\alpha}, \qquad A_t > 0, 0 < \alpha < 1 \tag{10}$$

where α and $1 - \alpha$ are the output shares attributed to R_t and x_t respectively. Without loss of generality we assume that $A_t = 1$ for all t. The variable profit function corresponding to (10) can then be written as

$$\pi(p_t, q_t, s_{t-1}, s_t) = R_t(p_t)^{1/\alpha}(q_t)^{(\alpha-1)/\alpha} K - \phi(R_t, s_{t-1});$$
$$K = (1-\alpha)^{(1-\alpha)/\alpha} - (1-\alpha)^{1/\alpha} \tag{11}$$

and the input-demand function $x(R, p, q)$ is given by

$$x = \frac{-\partial \pi(p_t, q_t s_{t-1}, s_t)}{\partial q_t} = R_t \left(\frac{p_t}{q_t}\right)^{1/\alpha} (1-\alpha)^{1/\alpha} \tag{12}$$

Our interest here is to derive some qualitative comparative-dynamic results for the effects of various taxes and subsidies on resource extraction. In this regard, the Cobb–Douglas specification is convenient because we can interpret the stock effects of taxes and subsidies in terms of the resource production share parameter α. We recognize, however, that the Cobb–Douglas form is restrictive and not necessarily representative of conditions in many extractive industries. Hence we regard our results as merely being suggestive of the results that might emerge from different production conditions.[10] In subsequent work we plan to estimate technologies for specific industries in order to study the quantitative impact of resource taxation.[11]

GENERAL COMPARATIVE-DYNAMIC EFFECTS OF A PRICE CHANGE

In this section we derive some general comparative-dynamic results. We allow for either a change in final product price or input prices to occur and then trace the impact of these changes on extraction, final-goods production, and input use. With these general results we will then analyse specific resource taxes in the next section. There we show how a particular tax or subsidy is equivalent to changing either the final product price, p_t, or the input price q_t. Using this knowledge we appeal to the pertinent results in this section to study comparative dynamics.[12]

In the following, we assume (1) that input prices are constant, so that $q_t = q$ for all t, and that (2) final-product price appreciates at a constant rate $\bar{a} \geqslant 0$, so that $p_t = (1 + \bar{a})^t p_0$. The first assumption seems innocuous. The second assumption could be weakened to allow for small temporal variations in the rate of appreciation. There is little to be gained from this, however. The role of assumption (2) will be explained below.

Consider a change in the final-product price from p_t to p_t' where

$$p'_t = p_t - \Delta_t$$
$$= p_0(1 + \bar{a})^t - d_0(1 + g)^t \qquad \text{for } t = 1, 2, \ldots, T. \qquad (13)$$

In (13) we restrict the variation Δ_t to be growing or declining at some rate g. The constant d_0, which may be positive or negative, is a scale parameter. Notice, when $(1 + \bar{a}) = (1 + g)$, Δ_t is just a proportion of the original price p_t. Using (11) and (13), we can write the variable profit function corresponding to new prices, denoted by $\pi(p'_t, q, s_{t-1}, s_t)$, as

$$\pi(p'_t, q, s_{t-1}, s_t) = \pi(p_t, q, s_{t-1}, s_t)$$
$$+ R_t[\{p_0(1+\bar{a})^t - d_0(1+g)^t\}^{1/\alpha} - \{p_0(1+\bar{a})^t\}^{1/\alpha}]q^{(\alpha-1)/\alpha}K.$$

Using this expression for variable profits in (3) and collecting terms in s_t, we can write the maximization problem for the firm as

$$\max_{s_1 \geqslant 0,\ldots,s_T \geqslant 0} \sum_{t=1}^{T} \left(\frac{1}{1+r}\right)^{t-1} \pi(p_t, q, s_{t-1}, s_t) - \sum_{t=1}^{T} \left(\frac{1}{1+r}\right)^{t-1} s_t \tau_t \qquad (15)$$

where

$$\tau_t = [\{p_0(1+\bar{a})^t - d_0(1+g)^t\}^{1/\alpha} - \{p_0(1+\bar{a})^t\}^{1/\alpha}]q^{(\alpha-1)/\alpha}K$$

$$- \frac{[\{p_0(1+\bar{a})^{t+1} - d_0(1+g)^{t+1}\}^{1/\alpha} - \{p_0(1+\bar{a})^{t+1}\}^{1/\alpha}]q^{(\alpha-1)/\alpha}K}{(1+r)}.$$

Differentiating τ_t with respect to d_0 we see that the derivative of (16) is equal in sign to

$$\frac{d\tau_t}{dd_0} \overset{s}{=} \left(\frac{1+g}{1+r} - \left[\frac{\{p_0(1+a)^t - d_0(1+g)^t\}}{\{p_0(1+a)^{t+1} - d_0(1+g)^{t+1}\}}\right]^{(1-\alpha)/\alpha}\right) \qquad (16)$$

where 's' means equal in sign. For most applications we shall be able to sign $d\tau_t/dd_0$, and $d\tau_t/dd_0$ will have the same sign in each period. This needn't occur in general if prices increase or decrease at varying rates.

Combining expression (16) with proposition 0, we establish proposition 1.

Proposition 1. If $d\tau_t/dd_0$ has the same sign for $t = 1, 2, \ldots, T$, then

$$\frac{ds_t}{dd_0} \overset{>}{\underset{<}{=}} 0 \text{ as } \frac{(1+g)}{(1+r)} \overset{<}{\underset{>}{=}} \left[\frac{\{p_0(1+\bar{a})^t - d_0(1+g)^t\}}{\{p_0(1+\bar{a})^{t+1} - d_0(1+g)^{t+1}\}}\right]^{(1-\alpha)/\alpha}. \qquad (17)$$

It turns out that condition (17) stated in proposition 1 is also sufficient to determine the comparative-dynamic impact of certain cost subsidies that we consider later. These subsidies have the effect of changing input prices.

Proposition 1 only indicates how *cumulative* extraction up to any time t is affected by tax policy. One would also like to know how extraction in each period is affected. Additional results on the comparative effects of tax policy on extraction, output, and input profiles can be obtained for the case where extraction costs are independent of the amount previously extracted, i.e. when $\phi(R_t, s_{t-1}) = \phi(R_t)$. The extent to which this cost structure approximates actual production conditions varies by industry.[13] When extraction costs depend on current extraction only, it is straightforward to show that the solution to (3) is characterized by the condition[14]

$$\left(\frac{1}{1+r}\right)^t \frac{d\pi_t}{dR_t} = \lambda = \left(\frac{1}{1+r}\right)^{t+1} \frac{d\pi_{t+1}}{dR_{t+1}}. \tag{18}$$

This condition is a variant of the famous Hotelling rule: in equilibrium the net marginal return from extraction rises at the market rate of interest.

Substituting for the marginal profit terms in (18), we obtain

$$(p_t)^{1/\alpha} q^{(\alpha-1)/\alpha} K - \phi'(R_t) = \frac{p_{t+1}^{1/\alpha} q^{(\alpha-1)/\alpha} K - \phi'(R_{t+1})}{(1+r)} \tag{19}$$

or

$$\frac{(p_t^{1/\alpha}) q^{(\alpha-1)/\alpha} K - \phi'(R_t)}{(p_{t+1}^{1/\alpha}) q^{(\alpha-1)/\alpha} K - \phi'(R_{t+1})} = \frac{1}{1+r}.$$

Looking at equation (19), it is possible to characterize the optimal extraction horizon for some cases of interest. Suppose $p_t = p_{t+1}$ for all t, so that nominal (undiscounted) output price is constant. Then (19) implies $\phi'(R_{t+1}) < \phi'(R_t)$ or $R_t > R_{t+1}$, since ϕ' is increasing. We thus obtain a strictly decreasing extraction profile, which is represented in figure 7.1(a).

An increasing extraction path, as depicted in figure 7.1(b), results if real (discounted) output price is non-decreasing, i.e., if $p_{t+1} \geqslant p_t(t^1 + r)$ or $\bar{a} \geqslant r$. For this case, by rewriting (19), we obtain

$$\frac{\phi'(R_{t+1})}{1+r} - \phi'(R_t) = (p_0)^{1/\alpha} q^{(\alpha-1)/\alpha} K \left\{\left(\frac{1+\bar{a}}{1+r}\right)^{1/\alpha} - 1\right\} (1+\bar{a})^{t/\alpha} > 0. \tag{20}$$

Equation (20) implies that $\phi'(R_{t+1}) > \phi'(R_t)(1+r) > \phi'(R_t)$ so that R_t is increasing. This case is interesting because the literature on exhaustible resources usually concludes that mine output falls over time.

In what follows, we maintain the assumption that cost depends only on current extraction, and additionally assume that the firm eventually extracts its entire available stock s_0. (When extraction cost depends on the current stock, exhausting the available stock may not be optimal.) With this assumption, we determine how the extraction profile tilts if we change relative prices. Let R_t and R'_t denote the profit-maximizing extraction paths for the original and new set of prices. Then R'_t is characterized by

$$\frac{\phi'(R'_{t+1})}{1+r} - \phi(R'_t) = \left[\left|\frac{p_0(1+a)^{t+1} - d_0(1+g)^{t+1}}{1+r}\right|\right]^{1/\alpha}$$

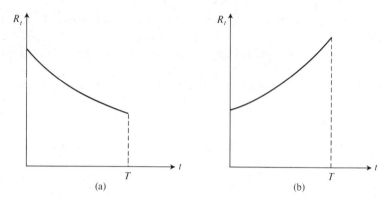

FIG. 7.1 (a) Extraction profile, $a = 0$; (b) extraction profile, $\bar{a} > r$

$$- \{p_0(1 + \bar{a})^t - d_0(1 + g)^t\}^{1/\alpha} \Bigg] q^{(\alpha - 1)/\alpha} K. \tag{21}$$

Subtracting (21) from (20), and using (15), we obtain

$$\left| \frac{\phi'(R_{t+1})}{1 + r} - \phi'(R_t) \right| - \left| \frac{\phi'(R'_{t+1})}{1 + r} - \phi'(R'_t) \right| = \tau_t. \tag{22}$$

Suppose $d\tau_t/dd_0 < 0$ so that the LHS of (22) is negative. Then rewriting (22), we obtain

$$\frac{\phi'(R_{t+1}) - \phi'(R'_{t+1})}{(1 + r)} < \phi'(R_t) - \phi'(R'_t). \tag{23}$$

Now there must exist some time $\hat{t} \leqslant T$ when $T'_t \geqslant R_t$. Otherwise, R'_t would be less than R_t for all t and the total amount extracted under prices p'_t would be less than s_0, which is ruled out by assumption. If $\hat{t} < T$, equation (23) implies

$$\frac{\phi'(R_{\hat{t}+1}) - \phi'(R'_{\hat{t}+1})}{(1 + r)} < 0 \text{ or } R'_{\hat{t}+1} > R_{\hat{t}+1} \tag{24}$$

since ϕ' is strictly increasing. But if $\hat{t} + 1 < T$, a similar argument implies that $R_{\hat{t}+2} > R_{\hat{t}+2}$. Generally, we can show that $R'_t > R_t$ for t satisfying $\hat{t} < t \leqslant T$. This implies $\hat{t} > 1$, otherwise $R_t \geqslant R'_t$ for all t (with strict inequality for some t), which is impossible. We have thus established proposition 22.

Proposition 2a. If (1) $\phi(R_t, s_{t-1}) = \phi(R_t)$; (2) it is optimal to extract the entire stock, and (3) $d\tau_t/dd_0 < 0$ for $t = 1, \ldots T$, then there exists a $\hat{t}$ satisfying $1 < \hat{t} \leqslant T$ such that:

$$\frac{dR_t}{dd_0} \left| \begin{matrix} \leqslant \\ = \\ > \end{matrix} \right| 0 \text{ for } t \left\{ \begin{matrix} \leqslant \\ = \\ > \end{matrix} \right\} \hat{t} ; t = 1, \ldots, T.$$

Using a similar argument, we can establish the counterpart to proposition 2a.

Proposition 2b. If conditions (1) and (2) of proposition 2a are satisfied, and if (3), $d\tau_t/dd_0 > 0$ for $t = 1, \ldots, T$, then there exists a $\hat{t}$ satisfying $1 < \hat{t} \leqslant T$ such that

$$\frac{dR_t}{dd_0} \begin{Bmatrix} > \\ = \\ < \end{Bmatrix} 0 \text{ for } t \begin{Bmatrix} < \\ = \\ > \end{Bmatrix} \hat{t} \, ; t = 1, \ldots T.$$

These results are depicted in figure 7.2 for the case where extraction is decreasing.

We can derive some comparative-dynamic effects of changes in the interest rate, r, using the same technique. It is well known that, *ceteris paribus*, extraction proceeds more rapidly with higher discount rates. This is because the resource becomes more valuable in current consumption. It is worthwhile noting that this effect can be overturned if market prices are indexed to the interest rate. Suppose that the rate of appreciation of output price is tied to the interest rate such that

$$1 + \bar{a} = (1 + r)m; \; m > 0. \tag{25}$$

When $m = 1, (m < 1$ or $m > 1)$, the real (discounted) price is either constant, is decreasing, or is increasing at a constant rate. Now let R_t^1 and R_t^2 be the profit-maximizing extraction paths corresponding to different discount rates r_1 and r_2 respectively. For m sufficiently large, an increase in r, say, from r_1 to r_2, tilts the extraction profile towards the future. To see this substitute the expression for $1 + \bar{a}$ in (25) into equation (2) to obtain

$$\frac{\phi'(R_{t+1}^i)}{1 + r^i} - \phi'(R_t^i) = p_0^{1/\alpha}(Kq^{(\alpha-1)/\alpha}) \{m^{1/\alpha}(1 + r^i)^{(1-\alpha)/\alpha} - 1\}m^{t/\alpha}(1 + r^i)^{t/\alpha}$$

for $i = 1, 2,$ (26)

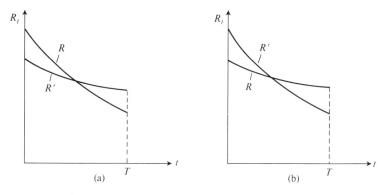

FIG. 7.2 (a) Tilting effect when $d\tau_t/dd_0 < 0$; (b) tilting effect when $d\tau_t/dd_0 > 0$

If $m > (1 + r^i)^{\alpha-1}$ the RHS of (26) is positive and increasing in r, which implies

$$\frac{\phi'(R_{t+1}^2)}{1 + r^2} - \phi'(R_t^2) > \frac{\phi'(R_{t+1}^1)}{1 + r^1} - \phi'(R_t^1) \tag{27}$$

since $r_2 > r_1$. Arguing as we did above, there exists some time $\hat{t} \leqslant T$ such that $R_{\hat{t}}^2 \geqslant R_{\hat{t}}^1$. It follows from (27) that $R_{\hat{t}+1}^2 > R_{\hat{t}+1}^1$ if $\hat{t} < T$, since $r^2 > r^1$. We can deduce that $R_t^2 > R_{t-1}^1$ for t satisfying $\hat{t} < t \leqslant T$ by repeating this same argument. But since $R_t^1 > R_t^2$ for $t = 1, \ldots \hat{t} - 1$, it follows that $\hat{t}$ satisfies $1 < \hat{t} \leqslant T$. Therefore, we find that

$$R^2(t) \begin{Bmatrix} < \\ = \\ > \end{Bmatrix} R^1(t) \text{ for } t \begin{Bmatrix} < \\ = \\ > \end{Bmatrix} \hat{t},$$

as was to be demonstrated, i.e. extraction may be less rapid under higher discount rates when output price is indexed to the interest rate.

It is also possible to derive results on the effect of changes in relative prices on the time-paths of output Q_t and input x_t. The expressions for Q_t and x_t are

$$Q_t = R_t \left| \frac{(1 + \bar{a})^t p_0 - d_0(1 + g)^t}{q_t} \right|^{(1-\alpha)/\alpha} (1 - \alpha)^{(1-\alpha)/\alpha} \tag{28a}$$

$$x_t = R_t \left| \frac{(1 + \bar{a})^t p_0 - d_0(1 + g)^t}{q_t} \right|^{1/\alpha} (1 - \alpha)^{(1-\alpha)/\alpha} \tag{28b}$$

for the case where output prices are perturbed. Differentiating these equations with respect to d_0 we obtain (recognizing that R_t is implicitly a function of d_0)

$$\frac{dQ_t}{dd_0} = \left\{ \frac{dR_t}{dd_0} - R_t \frac{1 - \alpha}{\alpha} \frac{(1 + g)^t}{q_t} L_t^{-1} \right\} L_t^{(1-\alpha)/\alpha} (1 - \alpha)^{(1-\alpha)/\alpha} \tag{29a}$$

$$\frac{dx_t}{dd_0} = \left\{ \frac{dR_t}{dd_0} - \frac{R_t}{\alpha} \frac{(1 + g)^t}{q_t} L_t^{-1} \right\} L_t^{1/\alpha} (1 - \alpha)^{(1-\alpha)/\alpha} \tag{29b}$$

where

$$L_t = \frac{(1 + \bar{a})^t p_0 - d_0(1 + g)^t}{q_t}.$$

Hence dQ_t/dd_0 and dx_t/dd_0 are negative whenever dR_t/dd_0 is negative; otherwise they are of indeterminate sign.

The effect of a price change on total production over the T-period horizon is given by

$$\frac{d\Sigma Q_t}{dd_0} \underset{S}{\equiv} \sum_{t=1}^{T} \frac{dR_t}{dd_0} L_t^{(1-\alpha)/\alpha} - \frac{1 - \alpha}{\alpha} \sum_{t=1}^{T} R_t \frac{(1 + g)^t}{q_t} L_t^{(1-2\alpha)/\alpha} \tag{30}$$

If $d\tau_t/dd_0 > 0$, proposition 2b implies that

$$\frac{dR_t}{dd_0} \begin{Bmatrix} \geq \\ = \\ \leq \end{Bmatrix} 0 \text{ for } t \begin{Bmatrix} \leq \\ = \\ > \end{Bmatrix} \hat{t}.$$

When L_t is increasing over time (this will occur in most of our examples) there exists an upper bound on the first term on the RHS of (30).

$$\sum_{t=1}^{T} \frac{dR_t}{dd_0} L_{t-1}^{(1-\alpha)/\alpha} \leq \sum_{t=1}^{\hat{t}-1} \frac{dR_t}{dd_0} L_{t-1}^{(1-\alpha)/\alpha} + \sum_{t=\hat{t}}^{T} \frac{dR}{dd_0} L_{t-1}^{(1-\alpha)/\alpha}$$

$$= L_{t-1}^{(1-\alpha)/\alpha} \sum_{t=1}^{T} \frac{dR_t}{dd_0} = 0. \tag{31}$$

The last equality in (31) follows from our assumption that $\Sigma_{t=1}^{T} R_t = s_0$. Combining (30) and (31) we have $d(\Sigma_{t=1}^{T} Q_t)/dd_0 < 0$ whenever $dT/dd_0 > 0$ for all t and L_t is increasing. When $d\tau_t/dd_0 = 0$ for all t it follows that $dR_t/dd_0 = 0$ for all t and (30) indicates that $d(\Sigma_{t=1}^{T} Q_t)/dd_0 < 0$. The sign of $d(\Sigma_{t=1}^{T} Q_t)/dd_0$ appears to be indeterminate when $d\tau_t/dd_0 < 0$.

THE EFFECTS OF TAXES AND SUBSIDIES ON EXTRACTION AND PRODUCTION

Royalties

Royalties are frequently used by governments to appropriate some of the rents from resources extraction. They are attractive because they are easier to administer than property taxes. Unlike severance taxes, which are a per-unit charge on the unprocessed resource, royalties are usually collected as a constant proportion of the processed resource price, P_t. As mentioned above, when the resource is sold directly as a final good, royalties cause cumulative extraction up to any time t to decrease if the real final-product price is not rising over time. Below we show how this conclusion may be changed when additional inputs are used in producing a final good.

A royalty is typically a fixed proportion, B, of the final-product price, p_t, with $0 < B < 1$. The royalty thus changes the producer price from p_t to $(1 - B)p_t$, implying that $g = \bar{a}$ and $d_0 = B$ in terms of (13). The stock tax resulting from the royalty is, from (15),

$$\tau_t = [\{p_0(1 + \bar{a})^t (1 - B)\}^{1/\alpha} - \{p_0(1 + \bar{a})^{t-1}\}^{1/\alpha}] K q^{(\alpha-1)/\alpha}$$

$$- [\{p_0(1 + \bar{a})^{t+1} (1 - B)\}^{1/\alpha} - \{p_0(1 + \bar{a})^{t+1}\}^{1/\alpha}] K q^{(\alpha-1)/\alpha}/(1 + r). \tag{32}$$

Substituting for g and d_0 in (16) and rearranging, we obtain

$$\frac{d\tau_t}{dB} \underset{=}{\overset{S}{\gtrless}} \left| \frac{(1 + \bar{a})^{1/\alpha}}{(1 + r)} - 1 \right|. \tag{33}$$

Combining (33) with proposition 1 yields

$$\frac{ds_t}{dB} \gtrless 0 \text{ as } (1+r) \gtrless (1+\bar{a})^{1/\alpha} \qquad \text{for } t = 1, \ldots, T. \qquad (34)$$

Notice from (33) that, if r and $\bar{a}$ are constants, an increase in the royalty rate, B, affects taxes in the same way in all periods, allowing us to sign ds_t/dB using proposition 0. Unfortunately, if the rate of price appreciation is alternately greater than and less than r in different periods, we generally cannot sign ds_t/dB.

The information in (34) is summarized in figure 7.3. The relative values of $\bar{a}$, r, and α for which the imposition of a royalty causes cumulative extraction (the total amount extracted to date) to decrease or increase are indicated by areas A and B, respectively. Points in $\bar{a}$-r space lying above/below the 45° line depict situations where the real final product price is rising/falling over time. The polar case, where $\alpha = 1$ (the extracted resource is the final product), is depicted in figure 7.3(a). It is obvious from figure 7.3(b) that the smaller the resource share, the more likely it is that royalties will have counter-intuition effects. This is an interesting conclusion because, typically, resource shares of refined products are small (as little as 5 per cent for refined aluminium, for example).

When extraction costs are independent of the current stock and it is optimal to extract the entire stock, we can utilize proposition 2 and equations (28)–(31) to establish the results summarized in table 7.1.

Casual empiricism suggests that, on average, the real price of many resource-derived goods has been falling. If this is true, and if the resource share in production is high, then the effects of a royalty are to decrease extraction and production in the short run. This is case A, represented by area A in figure 7.3. In this instance, the stock that is conserved in early periods eventually provides for greater extraction later on. This tilting of the extraction path towards greater conservation may be beneficial if there is a tendency for producers to extract resources 'too fast' from a social viewpoint.

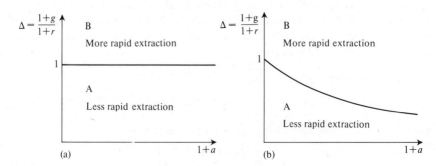

FIG. 7.3 Effects of a royalty: (a) $\alpha = 1$; (b) $\alpha < 1$

TABLE 7.1

Effects of a royalty increase: stock-independent extraction costs

Case A: Real output prices falling and a high resource share ($d\tau_t/dB < 0$)

	Variable			
Time	R_t	Q_t	x_t	$\sum_{t=1}^{T} Q_t$
Before $\hat{t}$	−	−	−	
After $\hat{t}$	+	?	?	?

Case B: Real output prices non-decreasing or a low resource share ($d\tau_t/dB > 0$)

	Variable			
Time	R_t	Q_t	x_t	$\sum_{t=1}^{T} Q_t$
Before $\hat{t}$	+	?	?	
After $\hat{t}$	−	−	−	−

One argument against using royalties for collecting revenue is that they reduce the profitability of resource extraction and exploration. This problem is
discussed below. In addition, many energy experts feel that we should use up
our conventional sources of energy at normal rates now, since substitute supplies
will be available later on. There is concern that royalties may impede resource
flows required for present consumption.

We find that under plausible conditions, as stated in Case B, the rate of
resource use may increase in the near term as a result of a royalty. This will
be at the expense of decreased extraction and final-goods production in later
periods. Case B occurs when α, the resource share in the production of the
final good, is low and when $\bar{a}$, the rate of price appreciation, is high (compare
figures 7.3(a) and (b)). Thus, a royalty is likely to speed up extraction if the
resource is highly refined and extensively treated before it is sold as a final
product and if final product prices are rapidly appreciating. Whether or not
these conditions are met in practice is an empirical matter. Looking at engineering data for copper and aluminium ingots, we found that the resource share, α, is
appropriately 0.33 for copper and 0.05 for aluminium. The rate of appreciation
of deflated metal price (refined metal price deflated by an index of input prices)
was found to be 0.014 for copper and 0.003 for aluminium.[15] Therefore
$(1 + \bar{a})^{1/\alpha}$ is 1.042 for copper and 1.055 for aluminium. If the real discount
rate is 4 per cent or less, we would find that the imposition of a royalty on the

sale of these metals would speed up ore extraction. While these numbers are only crude estimates, they do suggest the possibility that the imposition of a royalty may speed up rather than slow down the rate of use of some resources.

According to (33) and (34), there is a knife-edge case, $(1 + \bar{a})^{1/\alpha} = (1 + r)$, where $ds_t/dB = dR_t/dB = 0$. Here the royalty is non-distortionary in that it has no effect on the profit-maximizing extraction path. Overall, the royalty is distortionary, though, because it reduces the marginal profitability of extraction. In the stock-independent cost case, marginal profitability is measured by the shadow price λ defined by

$$\lambda = \left(\frac{1}{1+r}\right)^{t-1} \frac{d\pi_t}{dR_t} = \left(\frac{1}{1+r}\right)^{t-1} [\{(1-B)p_0(1+\bar{a})^{t-1}\}^{1/\alpha}q^{(\alpha-1)/\alpha}K - \phi'(R_t)]$$
(35)

which is decreasing in B. The shadow price is the value of an additional unit of the stock. Thus, in an expanded analysis that allowed for exploration, the imposition of a royalty would decrease the incentive to find new reserves.

Cost subsidies and favourable tax treatment

It is occasionally argued that preferential treatment for resource firms, such as subsidization and favourable taxation, is required to encourage adequate development of key resources because of the risk borne by the firms in finding and recovering ore deposits. In addition, resource prices fluctuate owing to political and economic uncertainty, thus increasing the risk of extraction and production.

This section investigates two forms of preferential treatment. The first type is a subsidy that reduces the price, q, of complementary inputs like capital that are combined with the resource to produce a refined product. The second type involves reducing the effective cost of extraction. This is accomplished by allowing firms to deduct an inflated proportion of actual extraction costs from their taxable income.

In the first case, we assume that a fraction, w, of the input price is paid by the government so that the price to the firm becomes $(1-w)q$. Under these conditions the variable profit function, $\pi\{p_t, (1-w)q, s_{t-1}s_t\}$, is

$$\pi\{p_t, (1-w)q, s_{t-1}s_t\} = R_t[\{p_0(1+\bar{a})^t\}^{1/\alpha}\{(1-w)q\}^{(\alpha-1)/\alpha}K] - \phi(R_t, s_{t-1}).$$
(36)

Rewriting (36) slightly yields

$$\pi\{p_t, (1-w)q, s_{t-1}, s_t\} = R_t[\{(1-w)^{\alpha-1}p_0(1+\bar{a})^t\}^{1/\alpha}q^{(\alpha-1)/\alpha}K] - \phi(R_t, s_{t-1}).$$
(37)

We see that the cost subsidy is operationally equivalent to inflating the output price by the factor $(1-w)^{\alpha-1} > 1$.

In the second case we introduce a constant profit tax, v, with $0 < v < 1$ which is applied to taxable profits, $\tilde{\pi}_t$, given by

$$\tilde{\pi}_t = R_t[\{p_0(1+\bar{a})^t\}^{1/\alpha}q^{(\alpha-1)/\alpha}K] - (1+z)\,\phi(R_t, s_{t-1}) \qquad (38)$$

where $z > 0$ is the inflated proportion of extraction costs that can be applied against taxable income. After-tax variable profits, denoted by $\pi_t(P_t, q, s_{t-1}, s_t/z)$, is

$$\pi_t(p_t, q, s_{t-1}, s_t|z)$$

$$= \pi_t(p_t, q, s_{t-1}, s_t) - v\tilde{\pi}_t$$

$$= \{1 - v(1+z)\}\,[R_t\{p_0(1+\bar{a})^t\}^{1/\alpha}q^{(\alpha-1)/\alpha}K - \phi(R_t, s_{t-1})]$$

$$+ zv[R_t\{p_0(1+\bar{a})^t\}^{1/\alpha}q^{(\alpha-1)/\alpha}K]$$

$$= \{1 - v(1+z)\}\left(\pi(p_t, q, s_t, s_{t+1}) + \frac{zv}{1-v(1+z)}\,[R_t\{p_0(1+\bar{a})^t\}^{1/\alpha}q^{(\alpha-1)/\alpha}]\right).$$

$$(39)$$

Subsidizing the purchase of inputs and reducing extraction cost through favourable taxation turn out to have the same qualitative effects on extraction and production. By substituting the expression for variable profits in (37) into the firm's maximization problem in (15), we see that the effective stock tax becomes

$$\tau_t = [\{p_0(1-w)^{\alpha-1}(1+\bar{a})^t\}^{1/\alpha} - \{p_0(1+\bar{a})^t\}^{1/\alpha}]\,q^{(\alpha-1)/\alpha}K$$

$$- \frac{[\{p_0(1-w)^{\alpha-1}(1+\bar{a})^{t+1}\}^{1/\alpha} - \{p_0(1+\bar{a})^{t+1}\}^{1/\alpha}]\,q^{(\alpha-1)/\alpha}K}{(1+r)}. \qquad (40)$$

Differentiating (40) with respect to w yields

$$\frac{d\tau_t}{dw} \underset{=}{S} \left\{1 - \frac{(1+\bar{a})^{1/\alpha}}{(1+r)}\right\}. \qquad (41)$$

In equation (39), the constant $\{1 - v(1+z)\}$ multiplying the terms in large round brackets is an effective profit tax. It is well known that a constant profit tax does not affect a firm's profit-maximizing decision.[16] Hence we can substitute our expression (36) for variable profits (ignoring the multiplicative term $1 - v(1+z)$) into the firm's maximization problem in (16) to derive the effective stock tax:

$$\tau_t = \frac{z \cdot v}{1 - v(1+z)}\,Kq^{(\alpha-1)/\alpha}p_0^{1/\alpha}(1+\bar{a})^{t/\alpha}\left\{1 - \frac{(1+\bar{a})^{1/\alpha}}{(1+r)}\right\}. \qquad (42)$$

Differentiating (42) with respect to z, we obtain

$$\frac{d\tau_t}{dz} \underset{=}{S} \left\{1 - \frac{(1+\bar{a})^{1/\alpha}}{(1+r)}\right\}. \qquad (43)$$

Combining equations (41) and (43) with proposition 1, we have

$$\frac{ds_t}{dw} \left\lvert \begin{matrix} < \\ = \\ > \end{matrix} \right. 0 \text{ as } (1+r) \left\lvert \begin{matrix} > \\ = \\ < \end{matrix} \right. (1+\bar{a})^{1/\alpha} \qquad \text{for } t = 1, \ldots, T. \qquad (44a)$$

$$\frac{ds_t}{dz} \left\lvert \begin{matrix} < \\ = \\ > \end{matrix} \right. 0 \text{ as } (1+r) \left\lvert \begin{matrix} > \\ = \\ < \end{matrix} \right. (1+\bar{a})^{1/\alpha} \qquad \text{for } t = 1, \ldots, T. \qquad (44b)$$

This information is schematically presented in figure 7.4. Further comparative-dynamic effects for the stock-independent cost case are summarized in table 7.2.

We see from (44) and table 7.2 that the effects on extraction and production of either an input-cost subsidy or an increase in extraction-cost tax deductions are similar. It is also clear from (34) and (44) that royalties and cost subsidies affect extraction and production in opposite ways.

A standard argument for subsidizing either output expenses or extraction costs is to encourage more rapid and more complete recovery of resources in extractive industries. However, we note that in case B (non-decreasing real output prices or a low resource share) cost subsidization will cause firms to extract and produce less rapidly.

Price controls

Petroleum and natural gas are examples of exhaustible resources that have been subject to price controls. Presumably, the reason for forcing prices below their market-clearing level was to protect consumers from the vagaries of the market an to prevent oil companies from earning 'super-normal' windfall profits from OPEC price increases. Price controls have also forced prices above market-clearing values, as when producer-countries have attempted to charge monopoly prices but have been unsuccessful at restricting output.

Formally, controlling prices is the same as levying a tax on producers equal to the difference between the market price p_t and the controlled price $p_{c,t}$.

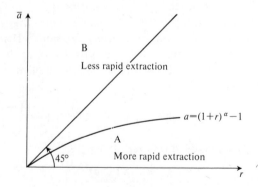

FIG. 7.4 Effects of a cost subsidy or tax break, $\alpha < 1$

TABLE 7.2

Effects of subsidizing input or extraction costs:
stock-independent extraction costs

Case A: Real output prices falling and a high resource share* $(d\tau_t/dw, d\tau_t/dz > 0)$

Time	R_t	Q_t	x_t	Q_t $t=1$
Before $\hat{t}$	+	+	+	?
After $\hat{t}$	−	? (−)	? (−)	(−)

Case B: Real output prices non-decreasing, or a low resource share* $(d\tau_t/dw, d\tau_t/dz < 0)$

Time	R_t	Variable Q_t	x_t	ΣQ_t
Before $\hat{t}$	−	? (−)	? (−)	+
After $\hat{t}$	+	+	+	

*The signs in parenthesis pertain to the tax break case.

In terms of equation (13), the size of the tax can be represented by the term $d_0(1 + g)^t$. Equations (15) and (16) respectively represent the effective stock tax τ_t and the derivative of τ_t with respect to d_0 for the price control case. Generally, the sign of $d\tau_t/dd_0$ is indeterminate, so we shall consider some special cases.

Examining the case where $d_0 \cong 0$ yields some insights about the effects of instituting small price controls. Let $\bar{\Delta} = (1 + g)/(1 + r)$. When $\bar{\Delta} > 1 (<1)$ the real value of the price gap is increasing (decreasing); one may envision this as a gradual imposition (lifting) of price controls. For $d_0 \cong 0$ we can rewrite (17) as

$$\frac{ds_t}{dd_0} \underset{<}{\overset{>}{=}} 0 \text{ as } \bar{\Delta} \underset{>}{\overset{<}{=}} (1 + \bar{a})^{(\alpha-1)/\alpha}. \qquad (45)$$

These conditions are summarized in figure 7.5. The comparative-dynamic effects on production and extraction in the stock-independent cost case appear in table 7.3.

When $\alpha = 1$, we obtain the known result that price controls cause extraction to increase/remain unchanged/decrease if the real gap between the controlled and uncontrolled price is increasing/constant/decreasing over time. When $\alpha < 1$, as in figure 7.5(b), price controls cause extraction to increase unless Δ is small, which means that the control is rapidly phased out.

TABLE 7.3

Effects of marginal price controls

Case A: $(1 + g)/(1 + r) < (1 + \bar{a})^{(\alpha-1)/\alpha}$

Time	Variable			
	R_t	Q_t	x_t	ΣQ_t
Before $\hat{t}$	−	−	−	?
After $\hat{t}$	+	?	?	

Case B: $(1 + g)/(1 + r) > (1 + \bar{a})^{(\alpha-1)/\alpha}$

Time	Variable			
	R_t	Q_t	x_t	ΣQ_t
Before $\hat{t}$	+	?	?	−
After $\hat{t}$	−	−	−	

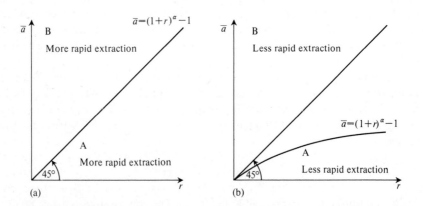

FIG. 7.5 Effects of price controls: (a) $\alpha = 1, d_0 \cong 0$; (b) $\alpha < 1, d_0 \cong 0$

CONCLUSIONS

This paper analyses the qualitative effects of resource tax and subsidy policies. We have focused on policies that change relative input and output prices faced by competitive extractive firms, assuming a Cobb–Douglas technology for final-goods production. We develop a general method for evaluating tax effects, which involves transforming many different tax policy instruments into equivalent taxes on end-of-period stocks. The main policy implications that emerge from our study are as follows.

1. The impact of a tax or subsidy depends on where it is placed. It may fall directly on the extracted resource, as in the case of a severance tax, or it may apply to a processed product which uses the resource as an input. In the latter case, the rate of appreciation of the processed product price relative to the discount rate and the share of production attributed to the resource input determine the temporal effects of the tax.
2. The effect of a tax or subsidy on extraction and production can be reversed depending on whether the resource share in production is high or low. For example, a royalty can cause extraction to increase and a cost subsidy can cause extraction to fall when the resource share is low. These results run counter to what is normally reported in the literature (based on the assumption that the resource share is one).[17]
3. The taxes and subsidies we have investigated are all distortionary in one way or another. Even in cases where the rate of extraction is unaffected, taxes affect the time-paths of production and input use and the incentives to explore for new deposits.

There are several directions in which our analysis might be extended. First, the conditions characterizing the effects of different tax policies are all in terms of parameters that can be estimated. An empirical investigation of particular extractive industries, allowing for more general technologies than the Cobb–Douglas, would be a way to utilize and test our model. In fact, such an investigation is already under way.

Second, our analysis of tax policy could be extended to situations where a firm extracts more than one metal from the same ore. Such conditions are common in the mineral industries. For example, silver, gold, and molybdenum are often by-products of copper production. In such instances, a tax levied on one metal will also affect the extraction and production of the others. A partial characterization of this general case is contained in Diewert and Lewis (1981). However, the prospects for obtaining further analytical results are limited by the complexity of the problem.

Third, our current model is not well suited to studying the effects of market structure and tax policy on resource use. In particular, we assume that firms regard prices as parametric. It might be possible to adapt the model for studying monopolistic behaviour under taxation by parameterizing the demand curve that faces the monopolist. One could then analyse shifts in demand caused by government tax policy.

Finally, although the results presented here are qualitative, the model we have employed is particularly well suited for obtaining quantitative measures of distortions in output and productive efficiency caused by government taxation.

NOTES

1. For discussions of such policies see for example Brannon (1975), Gaffney (1967), and Gillis *et al.* (1977).
2. The papers mentioned above have been singled out because they are closest in spirit to this one. However, there is a large literature on resource taxation, both theoretical and empirical. Several PNRE members have written on the subject; for example, Bradley, Helliwell, and Livernois (1981), and Scott (1955, 1967). For a recent survey of the taxation literature, see Helliwell and Heaps (1983).
3. Conrad and Hool (1981) compare taxes on final products versus taxes on ore, but there are no other (non-resource) inputs that enter into the production phase.
4. The words 'final goods' are used here to denote any degree of processing. Thus, a final good could be a concentrate or a refined metal.
5. We assume that prices are determined in world or perhaps in national markets. Therefore, we assume that the firms in question are price-taking producers. Our analysis thus applies to situations in which taxes are applied to a group of firms, perhaps within a region or a country, that together comprise a small portion of the total market. For example, the taxation of domestic petroleum suppliers within the United States and Canada would seem to be an appropriate case for our analysis.
6. These properties as well as additional characteristics of the model are formally derived in Diewert and Lewis (1981).
7. Diewert and Lewis (1981) allow for any of the resource left over after time T to be salvaged and sold as scrap. Here for simplicity we assume the scrap value is zero.
8. The maximization (5) also involves a term $-Bp_0 (1 + \bar{a})S_0$. However, because S_0 is fixed, adding this term will not affect the result. Equation (6) is not exact for τ_T unless $s_T = 0$.
9. This is a partial-equilibrium result. If the price of the substitute changes, causing a significant variation in output, Q, this will eventually affect resource use by altering the final product price P_t.
10. The implications of alternative production conditions are explored in Slade (1982a).
11. One such investigation is reported in Slade (1982b).
12. The effects of changes in p and q were previously examined by Scott (1967).
13. For example, the cost of extraction can be virtually independent of the stock remaining in the case of strip mining.
14. In this case the firm's variable profit function may be written as $\pi(p_t, q_t, R_t)$, and its maximization problem becomes

$$\max_{R^1 \geqslant 0, \ldots, R_T > 0} \sum_{t=1}^{T} \delta^{t-1} \{\pi(p_t, q_t, R_t)\}$$

$$\text{subject to} \quad \sum_{t=1}^{T} R_t \leqslant s_0.$$

Assuming an interior solution to this problem exists, it can be characterized in terms of (18).
15. Equations of the form $p_t = p_0 e^{\bar{a}t}$ at were estimated for both metals using annual time-series data for the period 1947–79.
16. In the formulation of (39) we are assuming that interest income is not taxed. If it were, then the effective discount rate would vary with the tax.
17. These results are similar to ones derived in Paish (1938) and Scott (1967).

REFERENCES

Bradley, P. G., Helliwell, J. F., and Livernois, J. R. (1981), 'Efficient Taxation of Resource Income: The Case of Copper Mining in British Columbia', *Resources Policy,* 7.

Brannon, G. M. (ed.) (1975), *Studies in Energy Policy,* Cambridge: Ballinger.

Burness, H. Stuart (1976), 'On the Taxation of Nonreplenishable Natural Resources', *Journal of Environmental Economics and Management,* 3(4).

Conrad, R. F. and Hool, B. (1981), 'Resource Taxation with Heterogenous Quality and Endogenous Reserves', *Journal of Public Economics* 16(1).

Dasgupta, P., Heal, E., and Stiglitz, J. (1980), 'The Taxation of Exhaustible Resources', Working Paper no. 436, National Bureau of Economic Research, Cambridge, Massachusetts, January.

Diewert, W. E. (1974), 'Applications of Duality Theory', in M. Intriligator and D. Kendrick (eds), *Frontiers of Quantitiative Economics,* vol II, Amsterdam: North-Holland.

Diewert, W. E. and Lewis, T. R. (1981), 'The Comparative Dynamics of Efficient Programs of Capital Accumulation and Resource Depletion', PNRE Discussion Paper no. 59, Department of Economics, University of British Columbia.

Gaffney, Mason (ed.) (1967), *Extractive Resources and Taxation,* Madison: University of Wisconsin Press.

Gillis, S. M. *et al.* (1977), *Taxation and Mining,* Lexington: Ballinger.

Helliwell, J. F. and Heaps, T. (1983), 'The Taxation of Natural Resources', in M. Feldstein and A. Auerback (eds), *Handbook of Public Economics,* Amsterdam: North-Holland.

Microeconomic Associates (1977), 'An Economic Analysis of the Conservation of Depletable Natural Resources', Berkeley, California.

Paish, F. W. (1938), 'Causes of Changes in Gold Supply', *Economica,* 5.

Scott, A. D. (1955). *Natural Resources: The Economics of Conservation,* University of Toronto Press.

Scott, A. D. (1967), 'The Theory of the Mine Under Conditions of Certainty', in *M. Gaffney* (ed.), *Extractive Resources and Taxation,* Madison: University of Wisconsin Press.

Slade, M. E. (1982a), 'Taxation of Nonrenewable Resources: A Production-Function Approach', PNRE Working Paper no. 81, Department of Economics, University of British Columbia.

Slade, M. E. (1982b), 'Taxation and the Supply of Exhaustible Resources: Theory and Practice', PNRE Working Paper no. 83, Department of Economics, University of British Columbia.

Sweeney, James L. (1977), 'Economics of Depletable Resources: Market Forces and Intertemporal Biases', *Review of Economic Studies,* 44.

Comment   V. Kerry Smith

INTRODUCTION

The extractive sector of most nations (developed and developing alike) is generally subject to a wide array of taxes. Severance, royalty, excess profits, and other taxes have all been imposed on extractive firms. Moreover, in many countries (the United States is one notable example) these taxes have had a long and involved history. Yet despite their long-term presence and continued use as policy instruments, we know very little of their impacts on the extraction profile of a non-renewable resource. The purpose of the Lewis–Slade paper above is to consider the implications of these types of policy instruments for the intertemporal allocation of exhaustible natural resources. In contrast to nearly all past work, however, these authors consider taxes, subsidies, and price controls in a framework that recognizes the processing required before the resources can be sold. For the most part the existing literature has assumed that the firms involved in extracting specific resources can market each output directly.[1]   Indeed, these past efforts have represented the extraction technology itself in such simple terms that they do not adequately describe the complexities of most mining activities (see Harris and Skinner, 1982, and Mikesell, 1979, chapter 2, for discussion of some specific examples). Since these taxes generally apply to the resource (i.e., before extensive processing), it is important to incorporate a plausible description of the extraction and processing technologies in any evaluation of the implications of taxes on the availability of natural resource ouputs. Lewis and Slade take some important first steps toward meeting these objectives in their analysis.

Before turning to the details of their analysis, it may be desirable to provide some indirect empirical motivation for their study. While taxes on the extractive sector have been present 'on the books' for a long time, changes in the codes, 'loopholes', and the collection of 'all other factors' that can be enumerated as potential influences on extraction profiles might well lead one to suggest that their empirical relevance is probably marginal at best.

There are at least two sources of information to evaluate this conjecture. The first involves hypothetical calculations of the implications of specific tax provisions, such as the percentage depletion allowance, for specific natural resources. These studies translate a given tax code into its prospective impacts on a hypothetical firm's costs and compare them on a per-unit-of-output basis with prices at various stages of operations. Brannon (1975) performed one such calculation for the United States considering energy related natural resources. Table C7.1 reproduces his estimates. The tax benefits as a percentage of price range from approximately 4 to nearly 20 per cent of the prices at the point of extraction and from 3 to 13 per cent as a proportion of the delivered prices of these resources. Thus, based on these calculations for these minerals in the United States, taxes would be judged to be quantitatively important components of resource prices. Moreover, the degree of processing of resource inputs also affects the magnitude of their impact.

A second, more direct, source of information can be found in the actual price movements of natural resources. Over the past few years a series of authors, initiated by the work of Heal and Barrow (1980), have attempted to investigate the empirical consequences of Hotelling-based models of natural resources. That is, they have examined the prospects for arbitrage relationships between the rate of change in specific resources' prices and the rate of return to other assets. The models have performed reasonably well in explaining short-term price movements using monthly data over fairly limited time horizons (see Heal and Barrow, 1980, and Kroch, 1983). However, the record with long-term annual price data has been substantially more limited.[2] In an attempt to explain these disparate performance patterns, Heal and Smith (1981) have investigated

TABLE C7.1

Brannon's analysis of net value of tax benefits for selected energy resources as a percentage of the delivered price to electric utilities in the United States*

Level of processing	Resource			
	Oil	Natural gas	Coal	Uranium
	%	%	%	%
Tax benefit as percentage of price at mine/well mouth	18.4	18.4	4.1	8.6
Tax benefit† as percentage of delivered price	12.9	11.7	3.4	2.8

* This table is based on table 1.5 in Brannon (1975, p. 18).

† The distinction between these two percentages (i.e. mine/well mouth versus delivered) is calculated based on price at delivery relative to that at the point of extraction.

the role of tax changes, stockpile policies, import duties, and discoveries as potential determinants of the stability of arbitrage models for eight minerals prices over the period 1926-70. These results clearly indicate that changes in tax policy are associated with shifts in the estimated parameters of these models for six of the eight minerals. (The Appendix to this paper provides an indication of the evaluation method and the Heal–Smith findings.)

Thus, with the benefit of both types of empirical information, it seems reasonable to conclude that the Lewis–Slade analysis considers a problem that is theoretically interesting and quantitatively important for the prospective availability of natural resources. In what follows, we will briefly summarize their approach for analysing these policy instruments, consider the implications of their model's structure for the results derived, and attempt to judge the plausibility of the model in comparison with what we know of extractive industries. Finally, some attention will be given to the research directions their paper has identified.

THE LEWIS–SLADE MODEL: FINDINGS AND EVALUATION

The Lewis–Slade model assumes that: (1) output prices are given; (2) the firm seeks to maximize discounted profits over a finite time horizon that is defined exogenously; (3) the stock of available resources is known; (4) the production technology for the natural resource output can be described with a constant returns to scale (CRTS), two-factor-input (i.e., natural resources and something else), Cobb–Douglas technology; and (5) extraction costs are generally a function of the level of the extracted resource only. Within this setting the authors consider the effects of changes in output prices and tax rates on the optimal stock-holding decisions of the firm. Thus, their results evaluate the implications of these factors for interior solutions to the firm's maximization problem. Comparative analysis of the properties of these solutions permits Lewis and Slade to describe the extraction profile under each of four classes of exogenous influences on firm behaviour. Table C7.2 summarizes their results for the extraction profile, R_t, produced natural resource output, Q_t, the use of the additional productive input, X_t, and the cumulative production of resource outputs over the time horizon, ΣQ_t, for each of the four policy instruments.

Their model separates the extraction from the ore concentration, refining, and processing technologies. While the general principles used to derive their solutions do not require this assumption, their specific results for each policy instrument do. The overall approach used to evaluate these changes in exogenous conditions facing the firm relies on translating each proposed change to an equivalent tax on the stock of the resource. That is, the authors use an important theorem derived by Diewert and Lewis (1981) on the effects of stock taxes on optimal extraction to establish the sign of the effects of each of the four policy instruments. This theorem established an inverse relationship between stock taxes in period t and the stocks held in the periods after t when the beginning and end-of-period resource stocks are substitutes in their effects on the firm's profits (see proposition 0 in the above paper).

With the Cobb–Douglas technology, the firm's profit function is given as

$$\pi(p_t, q_t, s_{t-1}, s_t) = R_t(p_t)^{1/\alpha}(q_t)^{(\alpha-1)/\alpha} K - \phi(R_t, s_{t-1}) \qquad (1)$$

where: p_t = price of natural resource product
$\quad\quad\quad s_t$ = stock of natural resource in t
$\quad\quad\quad R_t$ = $s_{t-1} - s_t$
$\quad\quad\quad q_t$ = price of factor input X_t
$\quad\quad\quad \alpha$ = elasticity of productivity for resource input R_t
$\quad\quad\quad \phi(\cdot)$ = extraction cost function
$\quad\quad\quad K$ = constant $(= (1-\alpha)^{(1-\alpha)/\alpha})$
$\quad\quad\quad \pi(\cdot)$ = per-period variable profit function

All of the Lewis–Slade results in table C7.2 assume $\phi(R_t, s_{t-1}) = \phi(R_t)$. Therefore, the assumption that marginal extraction costs increase with the amount extracted per time period will assure that s_t and s_{t-1} are substitutes.

The results in table C7.2 highlight the importance of the production technology for refining and processing the resource for the extraction profile. There are reversals in the shifting of extraction from present to future depending upon the resource's output share (i.e., whether α is small or large). This finding is quite clearly a more general statement of the impacts of taxes on extraction.

TABLE C7.2

Summary of Lewis–Slade comparative dynamic results for stock-independent extraction costs

Type of change	Assumption*	R_t		Q_t		X_t		ΣQ_t	
		Before $\hat{t}$	After $\hat{t}$	Before $\hat{t}$	After $\hat{t}$	Before $\hat{t}$	After $\hat{t}$	Before $\hat{t}$	After $\hat{t}$
Price change	$d\tau/dd_0 < 0$	−	+	−	?	−	?	?	?
	$d\tau/dd_0 > 0$	+	−	?	−	?	−	−	−
Royalties	Real output prices falling and high resource share	−	+	−	?	−	?	?	?
Subsidizing extraction cost	Real output prices falling and high resource share	+	−	+	?	+	?	?	?
	Real output prices non-decreasing or low resource share	−	+	?	+	?	+	+	+
Marginal price controls	$\dfrac{1+g}{1+r} < (1+\bar{a})^{\frac{\alpha-1}{\alpha}}$	−	+	−	?	−	?	?	?
	$\dfrac{1+g}{1+r} > (1+\bar{a})^{\frac{\alpha-1}{\alpha}}$	+	−	?	−	?	−	−	−

* ? designates the equivalent tax on the stocks of the resource to the price change. d_0 is a constant base change in the resource price; g is the rate of change in the price control; r is the real rate of interest; $\bar{a}$ is the exogenously specified rate of change in the resource output's price; α is the output elasticity for the resource input (R_t); t designates t with $0 < t < T$ where T is end-point for the firm's planning horizon.

For example, the earlier literature does not indicate that we can expect different effects from a royalty depending on the firm's technology (see Conrad and Hool, 1981, or Dasgupta and Heal, 1979, chapter 12). However, these results are not derived without cost (i.e., in terms of the need to adopt restrictive assumptions).

In order to explore these costs as potential qualifications to the applicability of the model's results, we have organized some comments and questions on the model into three general areas: the role of substitution in the production technology; the modelling of extraction—usage of inputs and geological constaints; and the endogeneity of the firm's time horizon.

The role of substitution in the production technology

There are two input substitution issues that must be considered in evaluating the Lewis–Slade model. The first concerns the prospects for substitution among different types of resources. Here the authors demonstrate that, if the technology can be considered weakly separable in a resource aggregate, $\bar{R}_t$, and that aggregate is related to R_t and a substitute resource, V_t, as in equation (2) below, then the profitability of resource extraction is independent of the use of substitute inputs.

$$\bar{R}_t = R_t + h(V_t). \tag{2}$$

This is an important finding, which is not developed fully by the authors. Indeed, it does tend to lessen the restrictive character of their production specification. As the authors acknowledge at the outset of their paper, most extractive production activities involve several natural resources. The processing activities to transform iron ore to steel require a sequence of processing steps, materials to remove impurities, as well as a variety of alloying elements depending on the character of the final outputs produced. Similar types of transformations are required for most metals. Equally important, the degree of substitution between these resource inputs may well be quite limited. Physical laws often limit the range that can be tolerated in the composition of the materials charge that is to be refined (see Kopp and Smith, 1980, for further discussion). Fortunately, the Lewis–Slade hierarchical production structure is quite flexible in its ability to accommodate diverse input relationships. While the elasticity of substitution between the resource aggregate (designated here as $\bar{R}_t$) and X_t is unity, the elasticity between R_t and V_t is *not*. It is given as

$$\sigma_{RV}^{Q} = \frac{\sigma_{RV}^{\bar{R}} - (1 - \alpha)}{\alpha}$$

where σ_{RV}^{Q} = Allen elasticity of substitution between R and V holding Q constant

$\sigma_{RV}^{\bar{R}}$ = Allen elasticity of substitution between R and V holding $\bar{R}$ (the resource aggregate) constant

For small values of the output elasticity, α, and for $\sigma_{RV}^{\bar{R}}$, the specification can accommodate two resource inputs that are complements in the production Q_t:

$$\sigma_{RV}^{\bar{R}} = -\left(\frac{h'(V)}{Vh''(V)} + \frac{\{h'(V)\}^2}{Rh''(V)} \right) \qquad (4)$$

With $h'(V) > 0$ and $h''(V) < 0$, we can expect that $\sigma_{RV}^{\bar{R}} > 0$.

This flexibility is potentially important, since recent estimates of the elasticity of substitution between materials and between energy inputs to the primary metals sector indicate fairly diverse relationships between resource inputs. More specifically, Hazilla and Kopp (1982) have recently used the updated Faucett data over 1958-74 to estimate hierarchical translog cost functions for this sector (along with a majority of the thirty-six other sectors in these data). In contrast to the models reported by Jorgenson and Fraumeni (1981) with these same data, these authors explicitly estimate sub-functions for each of three types of resource inputs: minerals I, minerals II, and energy. Table C7.3 reports the estimated Allen elasticities of substitution holding the respective sub-function aggregate constant (the equivalent to our $\sigma_{RV}^{\bar{R}}$). These estimates are calculated at the mean predicted cost shares for the respective inputs, and indicate the wide range of potential associations—from high degree of substitution, as with copper and aluminium in minerals aggregate I, to strong complementarities exhibited in the minerals aggregate II.

While the Lewis-Slade specifications impose restrictions on the feasible sets of relationships between resource inputs (their equations (3) and (4) can be combined to describe the exact nature of the restrictions in relation to $h(V)$), it is not as restrictive as one might have suspected from the aggregate Cobb-Douglas specification.

Unfortunately, the second aspect of input substitution—between the resource aggregate and X—is quite restrictive. The Cobb-Douglas specification implies an unitary substitution elasticity. It is difficult to judge how inappropriate this assumption is. The existing results for industry-level substitution elasticities including natural resource inputs are quite limited. While it is possible to use two recent studies to gauge the plausibility of a unitary-substitution elasticity, it should be acknowledged that the available information is too limited to claim that these are consensus estimates. Table C7.4 reports the Hazilla-Kopp unpublished estimates for the metal mining and primary metals sectors using a CRTS translog aggregate cost function with capital, labour, energy, and materials inputs. The table also summarizes the Moroney-Trapani (1981) findings for copper rolling and drawing, blast furnaces and basic steel, and primary aluminium using a capital, labour, and materials specification.

For the most part these estimates suggest a unitary elasticity of substitution is implausible. If we treat either capital or labour as the alternative factor, the estimated elasticities with materials are generally quite different from unity. The only exception to this conclusion arises with Moroney and Trapani's estimates for the blast furnace and basic steel industry. Of course, it should

TABLE C7.3

*Hazilla–Kopp elasticities of substitution for materials and energy
sub-function—primary metals sectors*

	A Minerals aggregate I			
	Aluminium	Iron and Steel	Chrome	Copper
Aluminium	−7.574			
Iron and Steel	0.119	−0.727		
Chrome	0.165	1.459	−0.383	
Copper	2.205	0.219	−0.920	−0.680

	B Minerals aggregate II				
	Cadmium	Cobalt	Columbium	Titanium	Vanadium
Cadmium	−78.261				
Cobalt	−10.493	−4.112			
Columbium	−9.495	4.981	−4.899		
Titanium	5.390	1.214	−0.463	−0.369	
Vanadium	2.885	−2.325	2.008	0.163	−0.673

	C Energy		
	Fuel	Electricity	Natural gas
Fuel	−0.527		
Electricity	−0.362	−1.469	
Natural gas	0.732	2.204	−3.387

be acknowledged that these comparison are judgemental evaluations and not statistical tests. None the less, they do provide motivation for consideration of the sensitivity of the Lewis–Slade results to the specification of the production technology for resource processing.

Modelling extraction activities

The Lewis–Slade specification for the production activities of an extractive firm separates mining and processing technologies in the definition of the profit function. This formulation of the problem seems quite appropriate. The production of most geochemically scarce metals involves two distinct stages: mining of the ore deposit, and separating the ore mineral to form a concentrate (see Harris and Skinner, 1982, p. 261, for some specific examples). None the less, their formulation does have some limitations.

The first of these stems from the assumption that factor input prices can be ignored in the specification of the extraction cost function, $\phi(\cdot)$. If common inputs are used in mining operations as in the processing stages, then a recognition of their role in $\phi(\cdot)$ will increase the ambiguity in signing the effects of

TABLE C7.4

Estimates of Allen elasticities of substitution by sector and author

I Hazilla–Kopp—KLEM framework, CRTS translog, 1958–74*

B Primary metals

	K	L	E	M
K	−0.948			
L	1.201	−0.803		
E	−1.008	−1.661	−23.629	
M	−0.262	0.180	2.007	−0.120

A Copper rolling and drawing†

	K	L	E	I	M
K	−4.152				
L	−0.296	−2.477			
E	−0.775	1.917	−12.919		
I	−0.437	1.950	−1.870	−1.676	
M	1.599	0.037	1.639	0.282	−0.794

II Moroney–Trapani—KLM framework, CRTS translog, neutral technical change, 1954–74

A Copper rolling and drawing†

	K	L	N	S
K	0.09			
L	2.46	−1.39		
N	0.18	0.43	−0.27	
S	−3.51	−2.55	0.54	3.53

B Primary aluminium

	K	L	N
K	−0.12		
L	−0.13	−0.79	
N	0.47	1.33	−2.90

C Blast furnaces and basic steel

	K	L	N	S
K	−1.24			
L	0.95	−1.15		
N	1.08	1.14	−6.41	
S	−0.90	0.20	0.39	0.72

* The Hazilla–Kopp estimates for primary metals are based on a hierarchical cost function with minerals I and minerals II aggregated to form non-fuel minerals in IB. I refers to intermediate inputs, which is separated for their primary metals model.

† The Moroney–Trapani work distinguishes primary sources (*N*) from scrap (*S*) in copper rolling and drawing and blast furnaces and basic steel. With the former the sample is 1958–74.

policy instruments on the non-resources input. For example, in the case of variations in the product price, the demand for X_t would be written as

$$x_t = \frac{R_t}{\alpha} \left| \frac{(1 + \bar{a})^t p_0 - d_0(1 + g)^t}{q_t} \right|^{1/\alpha} (1 - \alpha)^{1/\alpha} + \phi_{q_t}(R_t, q_t). \qquad (5)$$

Since R_t is implicitly a function of the parameter, d_0, we must sign $\phi_{q_t} R_t$ to describe unambiguously the impacts of price changes on input usage. While one might argue that $\phi_{q_t} R_t > 0$ for most cases, this would conflict with sign for the first term in most of the Lewis–Slade analyses of X_t (see their equation (29b) as one example)). Similar arguments can be developed for the remaining policy instruments. Thus, a more complete description of the role of inputs in extraction activities would reduce the ability of their model to explain the effects of policy instruments on input usage.

There are two further reasons for questioning their description of extractive activities. However, these issues can be as easily raised with most models for an extractive firm's behaviour. They arise from the constraints imposed on extraction by the geological conditions for mineral deposits. In describing the extraction cost function and its relationship to R_t and s_{t-1}, it is important to identify whether these cost changes are assumed to arise from activities within a single deposit or across many deposits. Their argument appears most relevant to the analysis of extraction costs across different deposits that vary in grade rather than within a single deposit. This would suggest that the marginal profitability condition (i.e., the value of an additional unit of stock as given in their equation (35)) used to relate their results to incentives for exploration is misleading. It should not be derived under an assumption of stock-independent extraction costs. The introduction of exploration into the model acknowledges the possibility of multiple deposits and identifies the activities necessary to find new ones. Thus the relevant extraction cost function would include both the flow and stock effects.

A final consideration in the modelling of extraction costs concerns the smooth, continuous increase in costs with depletion of the stock. Harris and Skinner (1982) argue that for the geochemically scarce minerals this may not be a good approximation to the actual costs associated with extracting from different types of deposits. Using the example of switching from sulfide ores as a source of copper to processing copper present in biotite, there will be a dramatic shift in costs, even under optimistic assumptions with respect to the amount of overburden and the efficiencies of the concentration and smelting activities (see Harris and Skinner, 1982, pp. 261-4). Moreover, these same features are likely to be present for most geochemically scarce minerals. Consequently, there may be a need to consider the sensitivity of the results to discontinuities in the extraction costs.

The firm's time horizon for extractive activities

The Lewis–Slade method for analysing the impacts of exogenous policy changes on the competitive firm's extraction profile requires that the firm's time horizon, T, be given. They acknowledge that this is a restrictive assumption and that a framework in which T was endogenous would be preferable. None the less, their analysis does not seem to identify an important aspect of their findings, which stems from the fixed time horizon assumption. A fixed time horizon, together with the assumption of full depletion of the resource, assures that extraction profiles will be tilted as a result of any policy action. Whether there is decreasing or increasing extraction in response to the policy, neither can be sustained over the full time horizon and have the solution consistent with the firm's constraints. Thus, while the initial magnitude of the impact of the policy instruments considered by Lewis and Slade may be small, the shape of the profile itself is most clearly affected by this fixed time horizon assumption.

SUMMARY

The Lewis–Slade paper has provided a substantial advance over our existing knowledge of the effects of taxes on the behaviour of extractive firms. In the process it has served to identify an array of research issues that require further attention. The authors highlight three possibilities:

1. more general specifications for the firm's processing technology;
2. accounting for the impacts on firms that extract more than one metal from the same ore;
3. considering the implications of tax policy under different market structures.

This analysis of their paper endorses these suggestions. Our findings indicate that the Lewis–Slade framework is not as limiting as the authors imply for inter-resource substitution. It can accommodate a range of possible substitution relationships between these minerals. However, the Cobb–Douglas specification does restrict the types of resource/non-resource input relationships. Based on the available empirical estimates, the Cobb–Douglas assumptions would seem implausible. Thus this is clearly an important area for further research.

In addition to these issues we have also considered the authors' characterization of the extraction cost function and the assumption of an exogenous time horizon. Both were found to play important roles in the Lewis–Slade findings and therefore warrant more detailed research evaluating the sensitivity of this model's conclusions to modifications in these assumptions.

ACKNOWLEDGEMENT

Thanks are due Ray Kopp for making the results of the Hazilla–Kopp (1982) analysis available to me.

Appendix

TABLE CA7.1
Definition of variables

Variable	Definition	Source
RX_iL1, RX_iL2	Percentage change in X_i resource price ($\Delta p_t/p_t$, lagged (L) one or two periods	Manthy (1978)
$DFR1$, $DFR1L1$,	Change in prime commerical rate (4 to 6 months) $= r_t - r_{t-1}$ and lagged values of this change	*Historial Statistics of the US, 1900–1970*
PZX, $PZXL1$, $PZXL2$	The change in cumulative amount extracted to time t (Z_t) relative to the lagged price of resource X and lagged values of this ratio	Manthy (1978)
PqX $PqXL1$	The change in the current period's output of resource X relative to the lagged price of X and lagged values of this ratio	Manthy (1978)
ΔWX	The change in the hourly wage rate for bituminous coal mining (as a proxy for wage rate for all extractive labour) relative to the lagged price of the X resource	*Historical Statistics of the US, 1900–1970*
$\Delta R1X$	Change in the prime commercial rate (4 to 6 months) relative to the lagged price of the X resource.	*Historical Statistics of the US, 1900–1970*

Source: Heal and Smith (1981).

TABLE CA7.2

An evaluation of non-market influences on arbitrage models for copper, zinc, anthracite coal, and bituminous coal*

Coefficient	Manganese					Lead				Anthracite coal	Bituminous coal
	TAX	ADUTY	DUTY	DIS	STP	TAX	DUTY	DIS	STP	TAX	TAX
TXL1	+	+		+		+					
RXL2	+	+				+	—				
DFR1											
DFR1L1											
DRF1L2											
PZX	—										
PZXL1	—										
PZXL2	—										
PqX	—			+		+					
PqXL1				—							
PqXL2											
ΔWX											
ΔR1X	+				+						

* The cells of the table with (+) or (−) signs indicate statistically significant associations between the *DFBETA* for the relevant coefficient and the effect identified. The sign indicates the sign of the associated regression coefficient. *TAX* refers to a dummy variable indicating the year preceding each change in the depletion allowance as it affected each mineral. Since all the minerals were not changed simultaneously, this variable is potentially different for each mineral. *DUTY* refers to a dummy variable for the year after import policies changed for each mineral. *ADUTY* measures the revised average duty when this was the change in import policy relevant only for manganese). *DIS* measures discoveries as a percentage of the average discovery of the relevant mineral in the sample period. *STP* refers to a qualitative variable for the year following a change in US stockpile policies.

TABLE CA7.3

*An evaluation of non-market influences on arbitrage models for
copper, zinc, iron ore, and tin**

Coefficient	Copper TAX	Copper STP	Zinc TAX	Zinc DUTY	Zinc DIS	Zinc STP	Iron ore TAX	Iron ore STP	Tin TAX	Tin STP
$RXL1$						+				
$RXL2$						+				
$DFR1$										
$DFR1L1$										
$DRF1L2$										
PZX	−		−				−			
$PZXL1$	−	−	−		−		−			
$PZXL2$	−		−		−		−			
PqX	−				+		−			
$PqXL1$	+						−			
$PqXL2$	+		+				+		+	
ΔWX		+			+		−			
$\Delta R1X$	+						−		+	

* The cells of the table with (+) or (−) signs indicate statistically significant associations between the *DFBETA* for the relevant coefficient and the effect identified. The sign indicates the sign of the associated regression coefficient. *TAX* refers to a dummy variable indicating the year preceding each change in the depletion allowance as it affected each mineral. Since all the minerals were not changed simultaneously, this variable is potentially different for each mineral. *DUTY* refers to a dummy variable for the year after import policies changed for each mineral. *ADUTY* measures the revised average duty when this was the change in import policy (only relevant for manganese). *DIS* measures discoveries as a percentage of the average discovery of the relevant mineral in the sample period. *STP* refers to a qualitative variable for the year following a change in US stockpile policies.

NOTES

1. Conrad and Hool (1981) is the one exception in the literature. However, their analysis relates to a very simple, fixed-coefficient model in which marketed output is a fixed fraction of the extracted ore.
2. See Heal and Barrow (1981) and Smith (1981) as examples.

REFERENCES

Brannon, Gerald M. (1975), 'Existing Tax Differentials and Subsidies Relating to the Energy Industries', in G. M. Brennon (ed.), *Studies in Energy Policy,* Cambridge, Mass.: Ballinger.

Conrad, Robert F. and Hool, Bryce (1981), 'Resource Taxation with Heterogeneous Quality and Endogenous Reserves', *Journal of Public Economics,* 16, 17–34.

Dasgupta, Partha S. and Heal, Geoffrey M. (1979), *Economic Theory and Exhaustible Resources,* Cambridge University Press.

Diewert, W. Erwin and Lewis, Tracy R. (1981), 'The Comparative Dynamics of Efficient Programs of Capital Accumulation and Resource Depletion', University of British Columbia, Program in Natural Resource Economics, Discussion Paper no. 59.

Harris, DeVerle P. and Skinner, Brian J. (1982), 'The Assessment of Long-Term Supplies of Minerals', in V. Kerry Smith and John V. Krutilla (eds), *Explorations in Natural Resource Economics,* Baltimore: Johns Hopkins University Press.

Hazilla, Michael and Kopp, Raymond J. (1982), 'Assessing US Vulnerability to Material Supply Disruptions: The Case of Non-Fuel Minerals', *Resources for the Future,* February.

Heal, Geoffrey and Barrow Michael (1980), 'The Relationship Between Interest Rates and Metal Price Movements', *Review of Economic Studies,* 47, 161–82.

Heal, Geoffrey and Barrow, Michael (1981), 'Empirical Investigations of the Long-term Movement of Resource Prices: A Preliminary Report', *Economic Letters,* 7, 95–103.

Heal, Geoffrey M. and Smith, V. Kerry (1981), 'An Econometric Evaluation of Long-run Movements of Mineral Prices', paper presented at 1981 Annual Meetings of Association of Environmental and Resource Economists, Washington, DC.

Hotelling, Harold (1931), 'The Economics of Exhaustible Resources', *Journal of Political Economy,* 39, 137–75.

Jorgenson, Dale W. and Fraumeni, Barbara M. (1981), 'Relative Prices and Technical Change', in Ernst R. Berndt and Barry C. Field (eds), *Modeling and Measuring Natural Resource Substitution,* Cambridge, Mass.: MIT Press.

Kopp, Raymond J. and Smith, V. Kerry (1980), 'Measuring Factor Substitution With Neoclassical Models: An Experimental Evaluation', *Bell Journal of Economics,* 11, 631–55.

Kroch, Eugene (Forthcoming) 'Identifying Hotelling Rents in Metal Markets', *Review of Economics and Statistics.*

Manthy, Robert S. (1978), *Natural Resource Commodities: A Century of Statistics,* Baltimore: Johns Hopkins University Press.

Mikesell, Raymond F. (1979), *The World Copper Industry: Structure and Economic Analysis,* Baltimore: Johns Hopkins University Press.

Moroney, John R. and Trapani, John M. (1981), 'Alternative Models of Substitution and Technical Change in Natural Resource Intensive Industries', in Ernst R. Berndt and Barry C. Field (eds), *Modeling and Measuring Natural Resource Substitution,* Cambridge, Mass.: MIT Press.

Smith, V. Kerry (1981), 'The Empirical Relevance of Hotelling's Model for Exhaustible Natural Resources', *Resources and Energy,* 3, 105–17.

8. Evolution of Market Structure in a Dominant Firm Model with Exhaustible Resources

Mukesh Eswaran and Tracy R. Lewis

INTRODUCTION

The recent emergence of natural resource cartels like OPEC have prompted economists to study the effects of market structure on exhaustible resource use. The extensive literature on this subject is nicely summarized in Dasgupta and Heal (1979), especially chapter 11. Most of this literature ignores the questions of how the supply side of the market evolves over time, and what factors determine the initial distribution of reserves among competing suppliers.[1] For example, it would be interesting to know why some resource markets are more concentrated (in terms of reserve ownership) than others.[2]

Certainly, the geographical distribution of reserves partially determines concentration. Also, suppliers can augment their stocks by exploring for new sources or by acquiring reserves from other firms. Reserve acquisition of this type has occurred occasionally in markets for copper, bauxite, and molybdenum.[3] The structure of some of these markets has evolved in this way. Initially, large reserves are discovered by one or a few suppliers who become leading firm(s) in the industry. These firms maintain a dominant position by supplementing their stock through exploration and acquisition of reserves from smaller suppliers. In the long run a dominant firm (cartel)—competitive fringe industry structure results from this process.

This description of how some resource markets evolve over time suggests several questions to us. Are there 'first-in' advantages in exhaustible resource industries? Is there an incentive for a dominant firm to maintain and enhance its position in the market? Is there a natural or stable size for a dominant firm? To what extent can a cartel prevent competition from fringe producers by pre-emptive exploration and acquisition?[4]

In this paper we try to answer these questions by looking at a sample dominant firm–competitive fringe model of a resource industry where the ownership of reserves is endogenously determined. We assume that the dominant firm or cartel initially controls a significant portion of known reserves. The industry also consists of a group of competitive fringe suppliers who each own a small fraction of the available stock. We assume that there is some additional stock contained in separate 'pools' (locations) that have not yet been discovered and claimed. The reserves in a given pool are obtained by discovering the pool first. Resource exploration is assumed to be a deterministic process, so that a pool is claimed by the firm spending the most on exploration. An alternative assumption is that all of the resource has been discovered, but that some of it is owned by the government. Firms can augment their supplies by bidding the most for new reserves as they are auctioned off by the government.

Formally, we model resource supply as two sequential discrete processes. First, firms acquire resource stocks through competitive exploration and development. Second, firms extract and sell resources from their reserves once the ownership of the stock is determined. Logically, we must assume that firms can predict the outcome of the second post-acquisition phase of supply in order to form expectations about the profitability of acquiring resource stocks during the initial supply phase.[5] In particular, we assume that during the extraction phase the dominant firm acts as an intertemporal Stackelberg price-leader. It announces a time-path of prices, assuming that fringe producers react by choosing a profit-maximizing extraction programme. This process, which is characterized in Salant (1976, 1981), Lewis and Schmalensee (1980a, b, 1983), and Ulph and Folie (1980), results in a well defined extraction equilibrium. We assume that firms can calculate the resulting equilibrium level of profits, for all allocations of initial reserves between the dominant firm and the competitive fringe. This information is then used by firms to determine the optimal expenditure for acquiring reserves during the exploration phase of supply. We note that this formulation ignores the possibility that exploration may be uncertain, and that firms may explore and extract simultaneously. This is done to maintain tractibility, but we are not convinced that the predictive content of our model would change significantly if these complications were introduced.

Our analysis begins in the next section where we characterize extraction equilibria for the dominant firm–competitive fringe model in terms of the initial reserves controlled by the dominant firm. This information is then used to analyse the reserve acquisition process. We assume that the resource is distributed in discrete amounts among N distinct pools. Firms acquire the reserves contained in a particular pool by outspending their rivals in exploration. Alternatively, reserves—already known to exist—are acquired through the process of competitive bidding. We are interested in determining the dominant firm's ability to limit competition from the fringe by pre-emptive discovery of new reserves. We find that in some instances fringe suppliers who manage to acquire some of the stock benefit from higher prices brought about by the presence of the dominant firm.[6] This free-rider effect reduces the dominant firm's incentives to outspend its fringe rivals in exploration. We demonstrate that the prospects for pre-emption are best when the resource is concentrated in large amounts in a small number of pools. This is because the cost to the dominant firm of acquiring reserves increases when the available resource is distributed in many separate pools.

There are other instances, described by Ulph and Folie (1980), when fringe supplier profits fall as the dominant firm acquires additional reserves. In this case we demonstrate the profitability of complete pre-emptive discovery/ acquisition of all available reserves by the dominant firm.

We go on to examine pre-exploration behaviour of the dominant firm which reduces the eventual costs of reserve acquisition. The dominant firm can influence the value of undiscovered resources by signing long-term contracts with consumers prior to exploration or acquisition of reserves. For example, the value of reserves to the fringe may decline if the cartel commits itself to selling additional resources at lower prices during initial periods of the extraction horizon. We show that this policy is effective because it decreases the costs of resource acquisition more than it reduces the value of new reserves to the dominant firm. By depressing resource prices, the dominant firm reduces the free-rider benefits accruing to fringe producers, and it makes pre-emptive reserve acquisiton more attractive. This is illustrated with an example in which we show that complete pre-emption of available reserves is made profitable by deflating resource prices. Also, we note that there is empirical support for this behaviour as it has been suggested that AMAX, the leading molybdenum producer, has depressed current selling prices to decrease the future costs of acquiring reserves.[7]

The analysis is concluded with a summary of results and suggestions for further work.

THE PRICE LEADERSHIP EXTRACTION MODEL

Assumptions

Following Salant (1976), we consider an exhaustible resource market where consumers purchase supplies at the same price from independent firms. For the time being we assume that the initial resource stock is distributed between a dominant firm, or cartel, and a group of fringe suppliers. The question of how this distribution is determined is the subject of the next two sections. The cartel sets current and future prices in the market by signing binding long-term service contracts with consumers to supply quantities of the resource at specified prices.[8] Fringe producers choose a sales path to maximize discounted profits taking prices as given in each period. Hence, the cartel chooses a price path, supported by its sales, to maximize discounted profits, subject to the supply response of the fringe.

Note that this is a Stackelberg price leader-follower formulation, whereas the Salant (1976) model assumes Cournot–Nash behaviour for all firms. Under conditions to be specified below, the two approaches are equivalent, yielding the same price and quantity paths in equilibrium (see Lewis and Schmalensee, 1983).

Let $q(t)$ be total market sales and $q^c(t)$ and $q^f(t)$ be the sales of the cartel and competitive fringe, respectively. Following Salant (1976), we assume that there is a stationary inverse demand function $p(q)$, with $p'(q) < 0$ and a finite choke price F, and that the coefficient of price elasticity $e(q) = (-dq/dp)/(p/q)$ is strictly decreasing in q.

In much of our analysis, zero marginal extraction costs are assumed. (The introduction of constant positive marginal extraction costs does not change our results.) However, the assumption that all producers face the same constant extraction costs is not innocuous, as is demonstrated by Ulph and Folie

(1980). The implications of marginal extraction costs varying across different resource deposits is examined in the next section.

Finally, an important assumption of our model is that the cartel can credibly commit itself to support the price it announces for each time period. This is equivalent to requiring the existence of a futures market for the resource, where extractors can contract with consumers for current and future deliveries of the resource. In the absence of complete futures markets, the ability of the cartel to commit itself to a stream of future prices is diminished. In fact, in this case the cartel may profitably deceive fringe suppliers by announcing price paths that it knows it will want to change later on (see Lewis and Schmalensee, 1983 and Newbery, 1981).[9] The problem of characterizing equilibria in the absence of futures markets is not our main concern in this paper, so we will not deal with it here except for a brief discussion in the concluding section.

Properties of equilibria

In equilibrium, the cartel announces a time-path for prices that maximizes its discounted profit subject to the profit-maximizing response of the price-taking fringe. Taking the response of the fringe suppliers as given, straightforward maximization of cartel profits yields the necessary conditions (1)-(4) for a Stackleberg equilibrium:[10]

$$e^{-rt}MR^c(q^c, q^f) \equiv e^{-rt}\{p(q^c + q^f) + \frac{dp}{dq} q^c\} = MR_0^c \tag{1}$$

$$\int_0^T q^c(t)dt = I^c \tag{2}$$

$$e^{-rt}p(q^c + q^f) = p_0 \text{ whenever } q^f > 0 \tag{3}$$

$$\int_0^S q^f(t)dt = I^f. \tag{4}$$

Equation (3) is an equilibrium arbitrage condition that holds whenever price-taking fringe suppliers produce. Given this condition, the cartel maximizes profits by equating discounted marginal revenue (calculated along its excess demand curve) across all time periods as indicated in equation (1). The resource constraints are given by (2) and (4), where T and S denote the extraction horizons, and I^c and I^f represent the initial reserves of the cartel and competitive fringe, respectively.

Salant (1976) shows that the intertemporal equilibria described by the equations above consists of two phases. Initially, both the competitive fringe and the cartel operate during a phase in which price rises at the rate of interest. Eventually, at time $S < T$, fringe supplies are exhausted and the entire market is left to the cartel, which then operates as a monopoly with $\dot{p}/p < r$.[11]

Lewis and Schmalensee (1980b) analyse the effects on equilibria of changes in fringe and cartel initial resource endowments. These results are summarized here, for use in the following two sections. Let $p_0(I^c, I^f)$ and $MR_0^c(I^c, I^f)$ (defined by equations (3) and (1), respectively) denote the constant discounted price and marginal revenue accruing to fringe suppliers and the cartel, respectively, in market equilibrium; and let $W^c(I^c, I^f)$ and $W^f(I^c, I^f)$ represent total discounted profits earned by the cartel and competitive fringe sector. Some of the comparative static effects of variations in the initial reserve levels are given below (see Lewis and Schmalensee, 1980b, pp. 140-2, 151-3 for details).

$$dW^c/dI^c = MR_0^c, \, dW^f/dI^f = p^0 \tag{5}$$

$$dMR_0^c/dI^i, \, dp_0/dI^i < 0 \qquad \text{for } i = c, f \tag{6}$$

$$dW^c/dI^c - dW^c/dI^f = p_0, \, dp_0/dI^c - dp_0/dI^f > 0 \tag{7}$$

$$d(W^c + W^f)/dI^c - d(W^c + W^f)/dI^f > 0. \tag{8}$$

According to (5) and (6), the marginal value of reserves to the cartel and competitive fringe represented by MR_0^c and p_0, respectively, decline with greater initial reserves. Total and average cartel profits increase, as reserves shift from the competitive fringe to the cartel, as indicated by the first part of equation (7). This occurs because the cartel simultaneously obtains more of the resource, and reduces the reserves of rival suppliers. The second part of equation (7) implies that fringe suppliers who continue to hold resources also benefit by a shift in reserves from the fringe sector to the cartel. This is the 'free-rider' effect we mentioned above. Equation (8) shows that total industry profits increase with the relative size of the cartel.

DOMINANT FIRM PRE-EMPTION

A case where fringe producers benefit from the presence of the cartel

We now consider the struggle between the cartel and the competitive fringe to acquire initial reserves. For simplicity, suppose that the available resource stock is a fixed known amount, I. Initially, the cartel controls $I^c > 0$ of the stock, the fringe collectively owns $I^f \geqslant 0$, and there is a residual, $D = I - I^c - I^f > 0$ left to be claimed and discovered.[12] D is equally divided among N distinct sources or 'pools', each containing D/N of the stock. (Alternatively, we can imagine that D is initially controlled by N equal-sized fringe suppliers, and that the dominant firm may increase its stock by buying out some of these producers.)

The stock contained in a particular pool is captured by the firm that spends the most in finding that source. There is simultaneous and unrestricted competition for each of the N pools. This means that the eventual winner of each pool must spend at least the maximum amount that the pool would be worth to some other producer.

Let us calculate the net return to the cartel of acquiring some amount $E < D$ of the residual reserves. Assume that the stock in each pool is $\Delta = D/N$. Assuming

E is divisible by Δ, the cartel must acquire $N_E = E/\Delta$ pools. Consider a fringe supplier who competes for one of the N_E pools. If he should capture that pool, and the cartel acquires the other $N_E - 1$ pools, the fringe producer earns extraction profits equal to

$$\Delta p_0\{I^c + (N_E - 1)\Delta\} \tag{9}$$

where p_0 is expressed as a function of the reserves owned by the cartel. Equation (9) represents the value of *each* pool to a potential fringe supplier. In order for the cartel to capture all N_E pools, it must spend at least

$$N_E\Delta p_0\{I^c + (N_E - 1)\Delta\} = Ep_0(I^c + E - \Delta) \tag{10}$$

where we have used $N_E\Delta = E$ in deriving (10). The cartel's net return of acquiring E reserves, assuming the stock per pool is Δ, denoted by $R_\Delta(E)$, is equal to

$$R_\Delta(E) = W^c(I^c + E) - W^c(I^c) - p_0(I^c + E - \Delta)E \tag{11}$$

where W^c is written as a function of the cartel reserves. A necessary condition for the acquisition to be profitable is that $R_\Delta(E) > 0$. We can rewrite $W^c(I^c + E)$ as

$$W^c(I^c + E) = \int_{I}^{I^c+E} W^{c'}(z)\mathrm{d}z + W^c(I^c). \tag{12}$$

Substituting the expression (7) for $W^{c'}$ into (12), we obtain

$$W^c(I^c + E) - W^c(I^c) = \int_{I^c}^{I^c+E} p_0(I^c + z)\mathrm{d}z. \tag{13}$$

According to (7), p_0 is strictly increasing. Hence there exists a $\hat{z} \in (0, E)$ such that

$$W^c(I^c + E) - W^c(I^c) = p_0(I^c + \hat{z})E. \tag{14}$$

Substituting this expression into (11) we obtain

$$R_\Delta(E) = \{p_0(I^c + \hat{z}) - p^0(I^c + E - \Delta)\}E \tag{15}$$

Equation (15) implies that the sign of $R_\Delta(E)$ depends on the size of Δ. If Δ is large, so that the residual stock is concentrated in a few pools, then acquisition by the cartel is profitable. Also, some amount of acquisition, for example $E = \Delta$, is profitable for any Δ. But for a given E, if Δ is sufficiently small, then $R_\Delta(E)$ is negative, and the acquisiton of E reserves is not feasible. The reason for this is that each additional pool that is captured by a fringe producer reduces the value of reserves to that producer as well as to the rest of the fringe. But if the amount contained in each pool is small, then the decrease in the value of reserves arising from a transfer of one pool from the cartel to the fringe is small. This enhances the incentive for fringe suppliers to acquire new reserves, which is reflected in a higher average acquisition price $p_0(L^c + E - \Delta)$ to the cartel.[13]

In general, it does not seem possible to say much about the size of the optimal acquisition and how it depends on Δ. While we do know that the profitability of any acquisition varies directly with average pool size, it does not seem possible to analytically show, for example, that the optimal amount to acquire increases with Δ. Part of the ambiguity arises because of integer problems associated with the discrete nature of our problem. The optimal acquisition E^*, satisfies the condition

$$R_\Delta(E^* + \Delta) - R_\Delta(E^*) = \int_{E^*}^{E^*+\Delta} R'_\Delta(x)dx \leqslant 0 \qquad (16)$$

assuming $E^* < D$. Differentiating (11) with respect to E and using (7), we obtain

$$R'_\Delta(E) = W^{c'}(I^c + E) - p'_0(I^c + E - \Delta)E - p_0(I^c + E - \Delta)$$
$$= p_0(I^c + E) - p_0(I^c + E - \Delta) - p'_0(I^c + E - \Delta)E \qquad (17)$$

Equation (17) implies that $R'_\Delta(E) < 0$ for $E > \Delta$ when p_0 is a concave (or linear) function of cartel reserves. This together with (16) implies that $E^* = \Delta$ when $p''_0 \leqslant 0$. In this case the degree of pre-emptive acquisition by the cartel is quite limited. When p_0 is convex the optimal acquisition is potentially greater than Δ.

An example. Typically, the sign of p''_0 can be determined only by computing the equilibrium for the post-acquisition game. We have done this for a linear demand example where

$$P(Q) = 10 - Q$$

and the total available resource stock is 30 units.[14] Extraction costs are zero, and the discount rate $r = 0.10$. In figure 8.1 we have graphed p_0, the present value price of the resource in the first phase of the equilibrium as a function of amount of reserves held by the cartel at time zero. As the graph indicates, p_0 is increasing and strictly convex in the amount of resource held by the cartel.

In table 8.1 we tabulate the present value profits to the cartel and fringe for a range of possible configurations of the final reserve holdings. Also listed are the present value prices in the first phase of the Stackelberg equilibrium. Using this information and equation (11), it is possible to compute the returns to the cartel of pre-empting an amount E of the resource, given Δ and some initial configuration of reserve holdings. For purposes of illustration we assume that the fringe and cartel initially hold 10 and 16 units of the resource and that an additional amount of 4 units remains to be recovered (i.e., $I^f = 10, I^c = 16$, and $D = 4$). In table 8.2 we present the returns to the cartel of pre-empting amounts, E, of the additional resource for various assumed values of Δ. (The amount E must, of course, be a multiple of Δ.)

Table 8.2 reveals that, while the returns to the cartel of pre-empting an

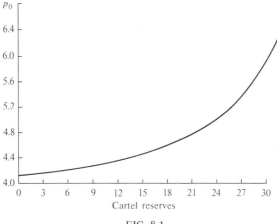

FIG. 8.1

amount equal to 2Δ are positive, the present value profits of the cartel, net of acquisition costs, are maximized for $E = \Delta$. This appears to be true irrespective of the distribution of the initial reserves between the fringe and cartel and of the size of D. Hence, at least for this example, the profitability and extent of pre-emptive acquisition is quite limited. In the next section we see how these results are modified when the cartel can deflate resources prices to decrease acquisition costs.

Acquisitions by the fringe

It is interesting to enquire if a fringe producer can profitably buy reserves from the cartel. Suppose a fringe supplier contemplates purchasing F reserves from the cartel which initially owns stock I^c. The acquisition by the fringe firm will be profitable only if

$$p_0(I^c - F)F \geqslant W^c(I^c) - W^c(I^c - F). \tag{18}$$

Following the analysis of equations (12) and (13), we can rewrite (18) as

$$p_0(I^c - F)F \geqslant p_0(z)F; \quad z \in (I^c - F, I^c) \tag{19}$$

Since p_0 is strictly increasing, the condition in (19) is always violated. Hence, at least for this case, the cartel will never divest itself of resource holdings. In the next section we examine a case in which this conclusion is reversed.

A case where fringe suppliers are harmed by the presence of the cartel

Ulph and Folie (1980) have constructed a case where the competitive fringe owners of reserves are harmed by the presence of the cartel. They assume that the dominant firm initially owns I^c reserves that can be extracted cost-lessly. Collectively, the fringe controls a smaller amount of reserves I^f, which can be extracted at a unit cost c. They show that, when I^f is sufficiently small and c is sufficiently large, the equilibrium consists of an initial phase during

TABLE 8.1

Reserves		Present value profits		Present value
Fringe	Cartel	Fringe	Cartel	price, p_0
10.0	20.0	45.93	85.20	4.59
10.2	19.8	46.73	84.28	4.58
10.4	19.6	47.52	83.36	4.57
10.6	19.4	48.32	82.45	4.56
10.8	19.2	49.11	81.54	4.55
11.0	19.0	49.90	80.63	4.54
11.2	18.8	50.69	79.72	4.53
11.4	18.6	51.48	78.82	4.52
11.6	18.4	52.26	77.92	4.51
11.8	18.2	53.05	77.02	4.50
12.0	18.0	53.83	76.12	4.49
12.2	17.8	54.61	75.22	4.48
12.4	17.6	55.39	74.33	4.47
12.6	17.4	56.16	73.44	4.46
12.8	17.2	56.94	72.55	4.45
13.0	17.0	57.71	71.66	4.44
13.2	16.8	58.49	70.78	4.43
13.4	16.6	59.26	69.89	4.42
13.6	16.4	60.03	69.00	4.41
13.8	16.2	60.80	68.12	4.41
14.0	16.0	61.57	67.24	4.40
14.2	15.8	62.33	66.36	4.39
14.4	15.6	63.10	65.48	4.38
14.6	15.4	63.86	64.61	4.37
14.8	15.2	64.63	63.73	4.37
15.0	15.0	65.40	62.86	4.36
15.2	14.8	66.15	61.99	4.35
15.4	14.6	66.91	61.12	4.34
15.6	14.4	67.67	60.25	4.34
15.8	14.2	68.43	59.39	4.33
16.0	14.0	69.19	58.52	4.32
16.2	13.8	69.95	57.66	4.32
16.4	13.6	70.71	56.79	4.31
16.6	13.4	71.47	55.93	4.31
16.8	13.2	72.22	55.07	4.30
17.0	13.0	72.98	54.21	4.29

which the cartel and fringe both produce. In addition, the discounted net price received by fringe producers, p_0, decreases as the cartel increases its reserve holdings; i.e., $p_0'(I^c) < 0$.[15]

Under these conditions pre-emptive reserve acquisition is always profitable for the cartel. To see this, suppose that the cartel begins with I^c reserves and assume that there is an additional stock of D still available. It is easy to show that total industry profits increase as total reserves controlled by the cartel increase. Hence, for $E < D$,

$$W^c(I^c + E) + p_0(I^c + E)(\bar{I} - I^c - E) > W^c(I^c + E - \Delta)$$
$$+ p_0(I^c + E - \Delta)(\bar{I} - I^c - E + \Delta) \qquad (20)$$

TABLE 8.2

Δ	E	$R_\Delta(E)$
0.4	0.4	0.00324
	0.8	0.00008
	1.2	−0.00999
	1.6	−0.02750
	2.0	−0.05300
	2.4	−0.08710
	2.8	−0.13042
	3.2	−0.18364
	3.6	−0.24753
	4.0	−0.32278
0.8	0.8	0.01314
	1.6	0.00069
	2.4	−0.04148
	3.2	−0.11798
	4.0	−0.23406
1.0	1.0	0.02068
	2.0	0.00138
	3.0	−0.06602
	4.0	−0.19094
2.0	2.0	0.08544
	4.0	0.01238
4.0	4.0	0.36530

where $\bar{I}$ is the total resource stock, and $\bar{I} - I^c - E$ is the stock held by the fringe, assuming the cartel controls $I^c + E$ of the resource. Since by assumption p_0 is a decreasing function, equation (20) implies

$$W^c(I^c + E) > W^c(I^c + E - \Delta) + p_0(I^c + E - \Delta)\Delta. \qquad (21)$$

Suppose the cartel has acquired $E - \Delta$ reserves. Then (11) implies that the net increase in profits obtained by capturing an additional pool is given by

$$R_\Delta(E) - R_\Delta(E - \Delta) = W^c(I^c + E) - W^c(I^c + E - \Delta) - \{p_0(I^c + E - \Delta)(E) $$
$$- p_0(I^c + E - 2\Delta)(E - \Delta)\} \qquad (22)$$

where the expression in braces represents the increase in acquisition costs. Since p_0 is a decreasing function, we can use (22) to show

$$R_\Delta(E) - R_\Delta(E - \Delta) \geqslant W^c(I^c + E) - W^c(I^c + E - \Delta) - p_0(I^c + E)\Delta. \quad (23)$$

It follows from equations (23) and (21) that $R_\Delta(E + \Delta) - R_\Delta(E) > 0$, so that the incremental return to acquiring additional reserves is positive. Hence, any situation in which the fringe holds reserves is unstable because there is an incentive for the fringe members to sell out to the dominant firm. In fact, fringe suppliers who hold on to their stock are made worse off in the long run.[16]

LOWERING PRICES AND PRE-ACQUISITION BEHAVIOUR

Let us return to our original model, where there are zero marginal extraction costs associated with all reserves. Suppose that the cartel decides to acquire $E \leqslant D$ reserves. We know that the reserve acquisition price, p_0, is strictly increasing in the amount of the stock held by the cartel. So one way for the cartel to reduce this price would be for it to divest itself of some fraction of its resource stock. For example, the cartel could enter into future contracts with fringe suppliers, agreeing to sell them some amount Q of its extracted resource over time at competitive market prices. This would mean that an additional Q reserves would not be controlled by fringe suppliers so that the competitive price for reserves would become $p_0(I^c + E - Q)$. Alternatively, the cartel could sign futures contracts to sell an extra Q units to consumers at competitive prices, $p_0(I^c + E - Q)$. In either case, this commitment to sell resources at deflated prices would decrease the value of acquiring additional reserves to the fringe. Of course, in the process of deflating prices, the cartel would also be depreciating the value of its own reserves. However, it is possible to show that, on balance, the decrease in acquisition costs would outweigh the decrease in cartel reserve value for small Q. Let

$$V(E, Q) = W^c(I^c + E - Q) + Qp_0(I^c + E - Q) - Ep_0(I^c + E - \Delta - Q) - W^c(I^c) \tag{24}$$

be the return to the cartel of acquiring E reserves through exploration or bidding, given that Q units of the resource are to be sold at the cometitive present value price, $p_0(I^c + E - Q)$. The partial derivative of $V(E, Q)$ with respect to Q is given by

$$\frac{\mathrm{d}V}{\mathrm{d}Q}(E, Q) = -Qp_0'(I^c + E - Q) + Ep_0'(I^c + E - \Delta - Q) \tag{25}$$

where we have used (7) to obtain the right-hand side of (25). Evaluating (25) at $Q = 0$, it follows that

$$\frac{\mathrm{d}V}{\mathrm{d}Q}(E, 0) > 0. \tag{26}$$

Thus, given E, it is profitable for the cartel to commit at least some amount of the resource to be sold at deflated prices. This is warranted because of a reduction in the acquisition price faced by the dominant firm. On the other hand, evaluating (25) at any $Q \geqslant E$, we obtain

$$\frac{\mathrm{d}V}{\mathrm{d}Q}(E, Q \geqslant E) < 0 \tag{27}$$

if the initial price p_0 is convex in its argument—which it is when the demand function is linear, for example. In such cases, it is never optimal for the cartel to commit all of or more than the amount pre-empted to be sold at deflated prices; the benefits of lower acquisition costs are more than offset by the lower price received for the resource when ownership is transferred to the fringe.

The profitability of depressing the acquisition price by selling part of the resource at competitive prices will, in general, affect the optimal amount E^* of the resource that the cartel pre-empts. Given E, let $Q(E)$ denote the optimal quantity of the resource to sell at competitive prices; i.e., $Q(E)$ solves

$$\max_{Q} \; V(E, Q). \tag{28}$$

Substituting for $Q(E)$ into (24) and totally differentiating with respect to E yields, upon using the envelope theorem,

$$\frac{dV}{dE}\{E, Q(E)\} = W'^c(I^c + E - Q) + Qp_0'(I^c + E - Q) - p_0(I^c + E - \Delta - Q)$$

$$- Ep_0'(I^c + E - \Delta - Q).$$

Upon invoking (7) and using the first-order condition for (28), the above expression reduces to

$$\frac{dV}{dE}\{E, Q(E)\} = p_0(I^c + E - Q) - p_0(I^c + E - \Delta - Q) > 0 \tag{29}$$

since p_0 is increasing in its argument. It follows from (29) that, for $E < D$,

$$V\{E + \Delta, Q(E + \Delta)\} - V\{E, Q(E)\} = \int_{E}^{E+\Delta} \frac{dV}{dz}\{z, Q(z)\}dz > 0$$

so that complete pre-emptive acquisition of all D available reserves is profitable.

The above result is verified in the numerical example for the linear demand case introduced in the previous section. The return function $V(E, Q)$ is graphed in figure 8.2 for various values of E, assuming $I^c = 16, I^f = 10 \, p = 4$ and $\Delta = 1$. (All the information required to construct figure 8.2 contained in table 8.1.)

According to the figure, $V(E, Q)$ is maximized at $E = D = 4$; i.e., cartel profits are maximized by complete pre-emption. In the previous section we saw that, when $Q = 0$, the cartel optimally pre-empts $E = \Delta = 1$. Thus, the cartel's strategy of divesting part of its reserves at competitive prices not only enhances the profitability of pre-emption but also dramatically increases the amount acquired.

Consumers also benefit by the cartel's strategy of deflating prices. From figure 8.2 we see that when $E = 4$, $Q(E) = 3.6$. In this case it is as if $I^f + Q = 13.6$ units of the resource are being sold by competitive fringe producers. On the other hand, when $Q = 0$, and $E = 1$, as in the example of the previous section, then $I^f + 3 = 13$ units of the resource are competitively controlled. Hence, present value competitive price p_0 is lower, and consumers are better off, when the cartel is able to depress prices.[17]

In fact, when p_0 is a linear function of cartel reserves, equation 29 implies

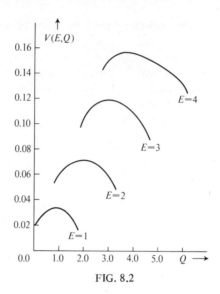

FIG. 8.2

that $Q(E) = E$. It is still profitable for the cartel to pre-empt all available reserves (i.e., $E^* = D$), but it is as if $I^f + D$ units of the resource are being sold by competitive producers. In this case the equilibrium price path for the resource is not affected by the pre-emptive behaviour of the cartel.

SUMMARY

In this paper we attempted to endogenize the reserve-acquiring process. Our motivation for doing this is to rationalize the various patterns of resource ownership that one observes in different industries. It seems peculiar to us that some resource markets are relatively concentrated while others, like the coal market, are not. We try to explain these differences by looking at the incentives for dominant firms to pre-empt rival competition by capturing additional stocks. We find that the ability of a cartel to monopolize the market depends on the extent to which fringe producers benefit by the presence of the cartel,[18] the degree of concentration of new reserves in separate locations and the ability of the cartel to control long-run prices.

Two primary conclusions emerge from our analysis. First, even though total industry profits increase with concentration, it is not always possible for large firms to completely monopolize the market by bidding away all the resources from smaller fringe suppliers. Second, the dominant firm may voluntarily commit itself and the rest of the industry to charging lower prices for the resource in order to depress the value of new reserves to the fringe. This strategy makes it feasible and optimal—at least in some cases—for the cartel to pre-empt all of any new reserves that might become available through discovery or bidding.

There are several possible extensions of our analysis. It is conceivable that one could study the intertemporal stability of cartels in resource markets with our model. There has been a lot of informal discussion of cartel stability, particularly with regard to the world oil market, and the long-run viability of OPEC. One could perhaps apply some of the recent results of d'Aspremont *et al.* (1981) and Domsimoni *et al.* (1981) on cartel stability in static markets to our model in order to study dynamic stability questions.

A second extension of our model would be to allow exploration and extraction to occur simultaneously, as in the interesting analysis of Pindyck (1978). In this case, exploration would become a real time process. Firms would need to discover new stocks in time to replenish their reserves as they were depleted by extraction. Inefficiencies in exploration might occur because there would be incentives for suppliers to explore more rapidly in order to be the first to discover a given resource deposit.

A third extension of the model would be to examine other intertemporal equilibria, and equilibria for other market structures. For example, we might analyse reserve acquisition, when complete futures markets for the resource did not exist. In this case, it would not be possible for firms to commit themselves to an entire time-path of supply. This would involve investigating the so-called closed-loop equilibria, which have been studied recently by Newbery (1980), Eswaran and Lewis (1982), and Reinganum and Stokey (1981). We might also study other structures besides the dominant firm–competitive fringe one.

NOTES

1. One notable exception is the interesting analysis by Salant *et al.* (1980).
2. The issue of how one measures concentration in resource markets is itself an interesting problem. Should one use figures on current *stocks* or on current *extraction* to compute concentration measures? This and related questions are discussed in Slade (1981) and Lewis and Schmalensee (1980a).
3. For example, see 'Molybdenum: Outlook Remains Good as New Mine Properties are Sought', *Engineering and Mining Journal,* March 1980, pp. 99–103.
4. The term 'pre-emptive' is borrowed from the thought-provoking papers by Eaton and Lipsey (1977) and Gilbert and Newbery (1982).
5. The logical necessity of this has been emphasized by Dixit (1980) in a different context.
6. Similarly, free-rider effects have been noted in discussions of cartel stability (see Stigler, 1964, and firm takeovers see Grossman and Hart, 1980).
7. For example, see *Molybdenum,* May 1979 (US Department of the Interior).
8. Long-term service contracts are common in domestic resource industries where they can be enforced at low cost. In international markets, like the world oil market, long-term agreements are less common because of the difficulty of enforcing contracts between different nationals.
9. Also see Kydland and Prescott (1977) for a discussion of dynamic inconsistency in leader–follower situations.
10. These are equivalent to equations (1)–(4) in Salant (1976). Henceforth, time arguments are deleted where no confusion exists.

11. Under different conditions, the order of production may be reversed. Lewis and Schmalensee (1980b) show that there is an initial phase when only the cartel produces if $dE(Q)/dQ > 0$ along the market demand curve. Ulph and Folie (1980) examine the effect of introducing different, but constant, marginal extraction costs on the order of production between the fringe and cartel.
12. The process by which $\bar{I}^c$ and $\bar{I}^f$ are determined will not concern us here.
13. It is interesting to note that a similar result has been noted by Grossman and Hart (1980) in their analysis of firm takeovers. They show that takeover bids may not succeed with numerous small stockholders because of free-rider effects.
14. Details of the calculaton are availabe from the authors.
15. The Ulph and Folie model assumes Cournot–Nash behaviour. However, as in the Salant model, it can be demonstrated that the Stackelberg and Cournot–Nash equilibria coincide.
16. This phenomenon is similar to the 'turning' effect described by Schelling (1960). There, racially mixed neighbourhoods are inherently unstable because neighbours of different race are not compatible with each other. Thus, one group is likely to buy out the other, until the neighbourhood becomes homogeneous.
17. Lewis and Schmalensee (1980b, pp. 151–3) show that consumer surplus increases with the amount of reserves controlled by the fringe.
18. If the demand function were of constant elasticity, for example, and extraction costs zero for both the cartel and the fringe, the latter would not benefit from the formation of a cartel. As is well known, the Stackelberg equilibrium coincides with the competitive equilibrium in this case and is independent of the reserve distribution. In this case, the final distribution of reserves is indeterminate since the returns to both the cartel and the fringe of acquiring additional reserves are the same. However, the final distribution of reserves has little relevance in this situation since all possible reserve distributions lead to socially optimal outcomes.

REFERENCES

d'Aspremont, C. *et al.* (1981), 'On the Stability of Collusive Price Leadership', Working Paper no. 8101, Catholic University of Louvain.

Dasgupta, P., and Heal, G. (1979), *Economic Theory and Exhaustible Resources,* Cambridge University Press.

Dixit, A. (1980), 'The Role of Investment in Energy-Deterrence', *Economic Journal.*

Domsimoni, M. P. *et al.* (1981), 'Stable Cartels', Working Paper no. 8112, National Institute of Statistical and Economic Studies.

Eaton, C., and Lipsey, R. (1977), 'The Theory of Market Pre-emption: The Persistence of Excess Capacity and Monopoly in Growing Spatial Markets', *Economica.*

Eswaran, M., and Lewis, T. (1982), 'Alternative Concepts of Intertemporal Equilibria in Natural Resource Models', mimeo.

Gilbert, R. and Newbery D. (1982), 'Pre-emptive Patenting and the Persistence of Monopoly', *American Economic Review.*

Grossman, S. and Hart, O. (1980), 'Takeover Bids, the Free Rider Problem, and the Theory of the Firm', *Bell Journal of Economics.*

Kydland, R., and Prescott, E. (1977), 'Rules Rather than Discretion', *Journal of Political Economy.*

Lewis, T. and Schmalensee, R. (1980a), 'On Oligopolistic Markets for Non-renewable Resources', *Quarterly Journal of Economics.*

Lewis, T. and Schmalensee, R. (1980b), 'Cartel and Oligopoly Pricing of Non-replenishable Natural Resources', in P. T. Lui (ed.), *Dynamic Optimization and Mathematical Economics,* New York: Plenum Press.

Lewis, T. and Schmalensee, R. (1983), 'Cartel Deception on Non-renewable Resource Markets', *Bell Journal of Economics.*

Newbery, D. (1980), 'Oil Prices, Cartels, and the Problem of Dynamic Inconsistency', *Economic Journal.*

Pindyck, R. S. (1978), 'The Optimal Exploration and Production of Non-renewable Resources', *Journal of Political Economy,* pp. 00–00.

Reinganum, J. and Stokey, N. (1981), 'Oligopoly Extraction of a Non-renewable, Common Property Resource: the Importance of the Period of Commitment in Dynamic Games', Working Paper no. 508, Chicago: Northwestern University.

Salant, S. W. (1976), 'Exhaustible Resources and Industrial Structure: A Nash–Cournot Approach to the World Oil Market', *Journal of Political Economy.*

Salant, S. W. (1982), *Imperfect Competition in the World Oil Market: A Computerized Nash-Cournot Model,* Lexington, Mass.: Lexington Books.

Salant, S., Switzer, S., and Reynolds, R. (1980), 'Losses from Merger: A Comparative Static Analysis of Cournot Equilibria', Federal Trade Commision Working Paper.

Schelling, T. (1960), *Strategy of Conflict*, Cambridge, Mass.: Harvard University Press.

Slade, M. (1981), 'Measures of Market Power in Extractive Industries: The Legacy of U.S. vs. General Dynamics', Working Paper, University of British Columbia.

Stigler, G. J. (1964), 'A Theory of Oligopoly', *Journal of Political Economy*, p. 00–00.

Ulph, A. and Folie, M. (1980), 'Exhaustible Resources: An Intertemporal Cournot–Nash Model', *Canadian Journal of Economics.*

Comment   Partha Dasgupta

This is an exceptionally fine paper and will be widely read. Eswaran and Lewis are concerned with the incentives for discovering new deposits of an exhaustible resource when the existing market consists of a resource cartel and a competitive fringe. In order to concentrate on strategic aspects of the matter, they eschew uncertainty in the discovery process and suppose there to be a known number of identical additional deposits for which agents can bid. In this way the authors simplify the problem to one of bidding for a given number of prizes among asymmetrically placed agents. This is a beautiful simplification, and Eswaran and Lewis make full use of its potency in their paper.

Now, the relative incentives among resource-owners to acquire additional deposits depend, among other things, on the existing distribution of *owned* reserves. In order to calculate these incentives one needs first to describe the intertemporal oligopoly equilibrium outcome for a given distribution of owned reserves. In fact, quite a bit is known about such equilibrium paths and the profits (or rents) enjoyed by resource-owners along them. The authors exploit this information (equations (5)-(8)) very effectively to say several precise things about the relative incentives.

For the most part Eswaran and Lewis study what theorists might call the 'standard case', where extraction costs are nil and demand elasticity is a decreasing function of output. (In fact, these are sufficient conditions for establishing the comparative dynamics in equations (5)-(8).) They wish to study the extent to which the cartel is able to outbid fringe suppliers and, in particular to identify conditions under which it can pre-empt *all* new discoveries. They note that in the 'standard case' fringe owners who acquire additional reserves benefit from the higher prices brought about by the presence of the cartel. It is this free-rider feature that dilutes the cartel's incentives for acquiring additional reserves. The authors show that, nevertheless, in the standard case there can be complete pre-emption on the part of the cartel if additional reserves are concentrated in a few deposits, but that the cartel will acquire only a fraction of new deposits if their number is large.

Given the occasion, Eswaran and Lewis, rightly, concentrate their attention on resource markets. Their arguments therefore depend heavily on the characteristics of intertemporal oligopolistic equilibria in markets for exhaustible resources. This is the strength of the paper, because it allows the authors to trace the reasons why the payoffs to the various resource-owners have the properties they are assumed to have. But for the reader who is not as much of an expert in resource economics as the authors, this may be the paper's weakness, because it seems to me that the basic insights the authors obtain from their analysis are of wider interest. In what follows I shall therefore discuss a bidding game and *assume* certain properties of the payoff functions so as to draw out conditions under which complete pre-emption is the equilibrium outcome.

For simplicity, suppose there to be two agents: a cartel and its rival. There are $N(\geq 1)$ patents to be won. They are identical in their economic effects. The payoff to the cartel in winning $K(0 \leq K \leq N)$ patents is $V_C(K)$ and for the rival $V_r(K)$. I assume

$$V_c(K + 1) > V_c(K) > 0 \qquad \text{for } 0 \leq K \leq N - 1$$
$$V_r(K + 1) > V_r(K) \qquad \text{for } 0 \leq K \leq N - 1$$
$$V_c(K) > V_r(K) \qquad \text{for } 0 \leq K \leq N$$

and

$$V_r(0) = 0.$$

For simplicity I want to consider the case where the rival's payoff is *super-additive*:

$$V_r(K)/K \geq V_r(J)/J \qquad \text{for } J < K.$$

Suppose the cartel bids first. If it wants to win precisely $K(0 \leq K \leq N)$ patents in such a situation, then it should bid nothing for $(N - K)$ of them and $H(K)$ for *each* of the rest, where

$$H(K) = \{V_r(N) - V_r(N - K)\}/K.$$

Were it to do this, the *net* payoff to it (in obtaining K patents) is

$$M(K) = V_c(K) - KH(K) = V_c(K) - V_r(N) + V_r(N - K).$$

The cartel's problem is to choose K so as to maximize $M(K)$. A *sufficient condition* for *complete pre-emption* is therefore

$$M(K + 1) \geqslant M(K) \qquad \text{for all } K$$

or

$$V_c(K + 1) + V_r\{N - (K + 1)\} \geqslant V_c(K) + V_r(N - K) \qquad \text{for all } K.$$

In other words, *total* industry profits are rising with the number of patents captured by the cartel.

Although the model presented here is not identical to the one Eswaran and Lewis discuss in their paper, I think it does explain why in the standard case the resource cartel will completely pre-empt if the number of additional deposits to be bid for is small.

PART V
EMPIRICAL ANALYSIS OF EXHAUSTIBLE RESOURCES

Introductory Note

John F. Helliwell

This section contains three papers concerned with empirical modelling of the discovery and production of extractive resources. Russell Uhler deals with natural gas discoveries; Harry Campbell and Doug Wrean model the development costs of established uranium deposits, and Paul Bradley uses earlier empirical mining models by himself and others to emphasize the importance of irreversible investments in reproducible capital.

The paper by Uhler deals with aggregate natural gas discoveries in Alberta, treating new discoveries separately from increases in reserves (called appreciation) attributable to earlier discoveries. Wellhead prices, which are calculated with allowance for taxes, royalties, and the likely delay between discovery and production, are found to influence both the pace of new discoveries and the ultimate amount of reserves appreciation.

Uhler's work has ranged from disaggregated stochastic modelling of exploration, with no explicit role for economic variables like costs and prices, to the current aggregate equations for additions to natural gas reserves determined chiefly by natural gas wellhead prices and cumulative discoveries. The discussants both note that this paper adds a new dimension to Uhler's previous work, but note the absence of features that characterized some of his earlier work: separate stochastic treatment of occurrence and size of discoveries, the disaggregation of data into plays, and the use of functional forms that permit specific cost functions to be identified. Uhler's work has shown that it is frequently necessary to aggregate data, or to compress certain features of a more general model, to obtain equations suitable for estimation. His results so far indicate that it is difficult to obtain robust parameter estimates of the economic structure of petroleum exploration decisions, and hence that progress towards the estimation of a more comprehensive model may be slow.

The paper by Campbell and Wrean develops estimates of the supply price of uranium from five actual or proposed open-pit uranium mines in Saskatchewan. The authors start with separate cost functions for capital and operating costs, and then calculate the mine life that maximizes the net present value of each deposit for each combination of uranium price and mill operating rate. These present value grids are constructed from pre-tax and post-tax points of view. Divergences between the points of maximum present value are then used to indicate the effects of taxation on the firm's choice of scale and mine life. The difference between the highest social value of the mine and the social value of the mine chosen by the firm can thus be used to provide a measure of the economic costs, imposed by the system of taxes and royalties.

In her comments, Nancy Olewiler notes that the authors assume, without testing against alternative production profiles, that the mill refines ore at a constant rate over its lifetime while the mine extracts material at a constant rate. The assumed cylindrical ore body and constant slope of the walls of the open pit imply a rising proportion of waste to ore. Therefore, there must be a stockpile of ore built up by the mining operation before the mill commences, because the waste material is separated from the ore before the ore goes to the mill. There is thus, she suggests, likely to be room for further optimization by the firm as well as scope for extending the analysis to include other stages of decision-making, especially acquisition of mineral or exploration rights, exploration activity, and the response of the mine to conditions that change after the initial planning decision has been made.

The most notable feature of the Campbell and Wrean empirical results is that the social present value surface is rather flat over a fairly wide range of mine lives and sizes. This means that taxes and royalties that substantially alter mine development decisions may not have a substantial effect on the total value of the project.

Another feature of the results is that the model predicts optimal rates of extraction and milling higher than those actually planned for the mines in question. The authors attribute this to the likely effects of uncertainty, since their analysis does not contemplate the possibility of unfavourable changes in costs and prices after the mine development decision has been made. Given the basic result that mine size can often be varied substantially (*ex ante*) without causing large changes in present value, and that capital expenditures are irreversible, reductions in scale to reduce risk are likely to provide fairly low-cost insurance. The discussant notes that the model could usefully be extended to capture this possibility explicitly.

The discrepancy between actual and theoretically optimal mine scale is also emphasized in the paper by Paul Bradley. Based on a number of earlier applied mining models by himself and others, Bradley's emphasis is on the importance of irreversible investment in reproducible capital. These studies, like that by Campbell and Wrean, show that 'present value is not highly sensitive to the extraction rate over a broad range surrounding the optimal point'. Bradley argues that smaller scale, by increasing the expected net present value per dollar invested, provides an attractive option if mine developers are risk-averse, if mine development expenditures are largely irreversible, or if they face a rising price of capital.

The link between irreversible capital expenditures and the relative constancy of mine output, which is so important in the applied papers of Campbell and Wrean, and by Bradley, is also addressed in the theoretical paper in Part IV by Pierre Lassere (chapter 6 above) although Lassere does not treat explicitly the important link between uncertainty and irreversibility.

9. The Supply of Natural Gas Reserves in Alberta

Russell S. Uhler

INTRODUCTION

In trying to explain crude oil and natural gas discoveries, a question that naturally arises is, how best to measure the amounts discovered? This question arises because (1) when a reservoir is first discovered the amount of reserves it contains is only imprecisely measurable, and (2) the amounts that are reported initially and that get reported ultimately depend upon economic conditions both at the time of discovery and subsequent to it.

Most studies that have tried to explain the time pattern of oil and gas discoveries have used data on the amounts discovered in each period as they are reported from the perspective of the most recent period in the data set. Although this approach takes into account the natural appreciation behaviour of reserves estimates as reservoirs are developed, and accounts to some extent for the impact of changing economic conditions on reserve appreciation, it has the weakness that observations on the amounts discovered depend upon the particular reference point taken. If taken from the perspective of time period t, for example, reserves discoveries in this period will be different than if taken from the perspective of period $(t + 1)$, because changes in economic conditions between the two periods cause estimated discoveries in period t to change.

This weakness can be overcome by separating initial reported discoveries and additions arising from appreciation. The purpose of this paper is to construct a model that creates such a separation. Effectively, there will be two models: one to explain initial discoveries of non-associated natural gas, and the other to explain appreciation of these discoveries. They are linked by the common factors that are important in explaining discoveries and their appreciation. Discoveries will be measured at their initial reported amounts and a model will be constructed that shows the impact of economic and other factors on these discoveries. The initial discovered amounts are then appreciated in accordance with a well-known appreciation formula which has been modified to allow for the effect of price changes on both the rate of appreciation and the level of ultimate appreciation. Thus, price changes have two primary effects: they serve to explain the level of discoveries through their effect on current exploratory activity, and they serve to explain the appreciation of reserves that have been discovered in all previous periods.

In the next section the discovery and appreciation models and the link between them are outlined, and in the following section the prices that should appear in each of the models are considered. In the final section the estimates of the parameters of the models are presented and the results are evaluated.

NATURAL GAS DISCOVERIES AND APPRECIATION

Before attempting to specify a model to explain the time pattern of non-associated natural gas discoveries,[1] it is useful to consider conditions that make oil and gas discovery processes somewhat different from the usual production processes and that therefore affect the applicability of the methodology that is usually used to explain these processes. It should be made clear at the outset that we are considering a discovery process that involves two products: crude oil, including solution and associated (natural) gas, and non-associated natural gas. Of course, there are a number of conditions that make oil and gas discovery processes different from ordinary production processes. Foremost among them is the uncertainty of success. But what is most important from the standpoint of determining the impact of relative prices is not the total discoveries of oil and gas but their relative proportions. Although relative prices may dictate a particular desired mix of oil and gas discoveries, this outcome may not be realized because of the inability of firms to distinguish accurately between gas prospects and oil prospects. This is particularly true in the early part of the exploration of a sedimentary basin before a significant amount of geological, geophysical, and drilling evidence has been accumulated. In short, the desire to be at a particular point on the transformation function does not necessarily get you there. Because of this fact, any model that relies on relative prices to explain the mix of oil and gas discoveries will almost certainly be limited in its explanation of these data.

With this problem in mind, two approaches to determining a natural gas supply relationship might be considered. The first is to assume that firms in the industry make choices in an attempt to maximize their profits. Under this assumption it is possible to specify a maximized profit function from which output supply and input demand relationships can be derived. Since we are interested in the non-associated gas supply relationship here, this approach seems to be applicable. Moreover, it has the advantage of easily handling the multiple-output case. However, it is suggested with the warning that, in view of the problem mentioned above, relative prices cannot be expected to provide a very good explanation of discoveries. Nevertheless, one can hope that the actual mix of discoveries will be close enough to the desired mix to allow prices to provide a useful level of explanatory power.

The other approach is one that I have used previously, which is to divide exploratory inputs into oil-intent and gas-intent categories and to estimate the oil and gas discovery functions separately. At first glance this approach may seem to avoid the problem just considered in that it does not rely on relative prices to allocate exploratory inputs in the search for oil and gas. But when it is recognized that intent does not necessarily get the desired result, it is clear that this approach offers little improvement. Moreover, there is reason to believe that the data available for classifying drilling effort and other exploratory inputs by intent are deficient. Thus we see that both of these approaches have limitations that are related to the inability to model production processes that achieve other than the desired outcome. Unfortunately, there does not seem to be an alternative approach that does not have this limitation.

In this paper I will use the first approach and specify an output supply relationship that is derived from a maximized profit function given by

$$\Pi^*(P, Z) = \max_{Y} \ \{PY : T(Y, Z)\} \qquad (1)$$

where P is a vector of output and input prices, Y is a vector of outputs (oil and non-associated gas) and exploratory inputs, and $T(Y, Z)$ is a transformation function relating inputs and outputs. The vector Z contains the variables cumulative unappreciated discoveries of gas and cumulative unappreciated discoveries of oil. These variables shift the transformation function and reflect the effects of knowledge and the exhaustion of remaining undiscovered reserves. The rationale for the specification of these variables is considered in detail in Uhler (1979).[2]

Output supply and input demand functions can be derived from equation (1) using Hotelling's rule. In particular, the supply function for gas is given by

$$\partial \Pi^* / \partial p_g = y_g = G(P, Z) \qquad (2)$$

where p_g is the price of gas and y_g is the quantity of gas discovered. Thus, gas discoveries depend upon the prices of gas and oil, the prices exploratory inputs, and the cumulative discoveries of gas and oil.

The next step is to specify a functional form for either the profit function or the supply function. Recently, it has become fashionable to specify a functional form for the profit function that provides a second-order approximation in input and output prices to an arbitrary profit function and that has other desirable properties as well. In the final section of the paper I consider specifications for the supply and profit functions and estimate the parameters and compare their parameter estimates.

Appreciation of reserves

It is well known that one of the characteristics of oil and gas reservoirs is that the estimated amount of recoverable reserves usually increases following initial discovery. This process of 'appreciation' is due largely to the time required to delineate and develop a reservoir. But there is also good reason to suspect that the level of ultimate appreciation of a discovery is influenced by the price of the resource in that higher prices will make it worthwhile to recover a higher proportion of the contents of the reservoir and thus will affect its ultimate appreciation. The effect of higher prices on reservoir appreciation also applies to that class of reservoirs discovered in the past but evaluated as non-commercial under the prevailing set of economic conditions. Higher prices can change the evaluation of some of these discoveries dramatically, so that in terms of the usual view of reservoir appreciation they can be considered as reservoirs whose appreciation is due entirely to changes in prices. This is not to say that further development of these structures will not result in still more appreciation; once they become economic, appreciation may be expected to continue in the normal way.

Thus we can see that natural gas reserve additions can be expected to come from three sources: (1) discoveries of new reservoirs, (2) appreciation of recoverable reserves from known producing reservoirs, and (3) appreciation of reserves in reservoirs that, under the economic conditions that existed at the time of discovery, were classified as uneconomical. Although it is probably true that gas reserves in the third category have accounted for most of the appreciation that is due strictly to changes in economic conditions, because of data limitations it is not possible to identify appreciation of reserves from each of these sources separately. Thus, appreciation from these two sources will be combined and it will be explained by both economic and time variables.

It is now useful to state the problem more formally so that a model structure for analysing the appreciation data can be created. Let $y_{t\tau}$ be the gas reserves that in time period τ are associated with the reserves that were discovered in period t. Also, let y_t be the reserves that are reported as being discovered in period t and let $A(\tau - t, p_\tau)$ be an appreciation function. Under these conditions we can write

$$y_{t\tau} = y_t A(\tau - t, p_\tau). \tag{3}$$

Cumulative appreciated discoveries viewed from the perspective of time τ are given by

$$R_\tau = \sum_{t=1}^{\tau} y_{t\tau}. \tag{4}$$

In terms of the earlier discussion y_t is unappreciated discoveries in period t and $A(\tau - t, p_\tau)$ is the function that appreciates them over time and that depends upon the prevailing price in period τ, p_τ. Equation (4) simply states that cumulative discoveries is the sum of the appreciated discoveries of each vintage.

Figure 9.1 illustrates this process graphically. In each time period the magnitude of discoveries is indicated by the height of the vertical line at that point in time. Reserves discovered in each period then appreciate over time in accordance with the illustrated curves. The asymptotic value that each of these curves approaches depends on the price at time τ. Total discoveries at time τ is just the vertical summation of all of the curves at that time. Note, however, that the vertical summation of the curves at each point in time is not the total reserves discovered up to that time because each curve in the diagram is contructed on the basis of the price prevailing at time τ. The higher is the price, the higher is the asymptotic value approached by each of these curves.

The effect of an increase in the price of gas at time τ on cumulative discoveries

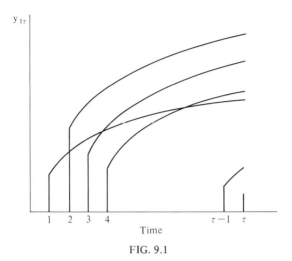

FIG. 9.1

is given by

$$\partial R_\tau / \partial p_\tau = \sum_{t=1}^{\tau} y_t \partial A / \partial p_\tau + A \partial y_\tau / \partial p_\tau. \qquad (5)$$

The first τ term on the right measures the rise in reserves of each vintage owing to the rise in appreciation caused by the price increase and the last term measures the effect of the price increase on discoveries at time τ.

CHOOSING THE PRICES

It is clear from the previous section that prices are believed to play an important role in both the discovery of reserves and their subsequent appreciation. But, which prices create the economic incentive for reserve additions from each of these sources? The answer to this question depends upon one's view of the process of reserve additions. If the view taken in this paper is followed, then reserves are discovered by expenditure on exploratory activity and subsequently appreciate by expenditure on reservoir development. The price that provides an incentive for new reservoir discoveries is the price of reserves in the ground, which is the per-unit asset value of reserves. On the other hand, the decision to develop a reservoir and thus set the process of reserves appreciation in motion depends upon the wellhead price, or, more accurately, on the netback price. It is this price that must at least equal the unit economic cost of carrying out investment in reservoir development for appreciation to occur. Thus, the separation of the process of reserves additions into the initial discovery and appreciation stages requires two different but related set of prices to be used to help explain the levels of these activities.[3] In view of these facts, before presenting the results of estimating the discovery and appreciation models described above, it is useful to consider some of the important aspects of calculating the price of natural gas reserves in the ground.

The exploration of the Western Canadian Sedimentary Basin has yielded substantial discoveries of non-associated natural gas. However during much of the period between 1947 and the present the markets for natural gas were such that most new discoveries in this region faced long periods of delay before they could be marketed. This was especially true if discoveries were in relatively remote locations which were far from cities and regional pipeline transport facilities. After the construction of major inter-provincial pipelines and other pipelines connecting with those in the United States, markets for natural gas improved and delay times were reduced.

The period of delay between discovery and extraction is of interest here because it has an important bearing on the determination of the price of gas reserves in the ground, these prices being the ones that provide an important part of the economic incentive for natural gas exploration. The methodology used in calculating gas reserves prices is very similar to that used in calculating oil reserves prices. It is outlined in Uhler (1981) and will not be repeated here. But for oil discoveries in the Western Canadian Sedimentary Basin the period of delay between discovery of conventional reserves and their extraction has been small, limited mainly to the time it takes to delineate newly discovered reservoirs and to bring them into full production, so that delay times were not important in the calculation of oil reserves prices. On the other hand, delay times for natural gas discoveries over most of the period in question have been significant and have had a major impact on exploration incentives for natural gas. Since delay times have such an important bearing on determining the price of gas reserves, as well as being of interest in their own right, I will consider their calculation in some detail.

To proceed in an orderly manner I must make some assumptions. The first is that there is roughly a constant relationship between the extraction rate and the volume of reserves required to support the extraction rate. This assumption may seem unrealistic in view of the fact that reservoirs vary considerably in their productive capability and that the least-cost reservoirs will tend to be exploited first. But remember that we are aggregating over a large number of reservoirs and that the most productive and the least-cost resevoirs are not necessarily found first, so that in the aggregate the assumption is quite plausible.

The second assumption that I make is that, if the available stock of discovered reserves will support an extraction rate that is higher than the market demand, then this extraction is allocated in such a way that only a portion of the reserve stock is producing at full capacity rather than the entire stock producing at less than full capacity. The economics of reservoir development supports this assumption and, moreover, it is supported by the empirical evidence.

The third assumption is that reservoirs get produced on a 'first-discovered-first-produced' basis so long as the discoveries are judged to be commercially viable. Although there are obvious cases where this assumption is violated, non-associated gas reservoirs in this region are homogeneous enough to make the assumption innocuous.

The model used to estimate delay times is a simple one. Current production is viewed as coming from reserve stocks of various vintages. Some of these reserve stocks are in reservoirs in their initial year of production while others are in reservoirs that are near the end of their production lives. To determine delay time we need to know what the extraction rate is in the first-year class, given that the aggregate extraction rate over all year classes is an amount, say, Q, under some assumption about how the extraction rates of various vintages change over time. If extraction rates are constant over time then the calculation is trivial. It is just the aggregate extraction rate divided by the period of production, say, T. Constant extraction rates are unrealistic, however. Most reservoirs exhibit production decline over time. We will assume that exponential decline at rate θ is a reasonable approximation. Then if q_1 is the production rate from reserves in the first-year class, it can be determined from the following equation:

$$\int_0^T q_1 e^{-\theta t} dt = Q. \tag{6}$$

The delay time for newly discovered reserves is then the excess productive capacity of the reserve base divided by q_1. This, of course, presumes that the aggregate extraction rate is expected to remain constant at Q. If the extraction rate is growing over time, then all of the growth in any period gets allocated to those reserves that are waiting for an opportunity to begin production. Since the aggregate extraction rate is now higher, greater production capacity is required to enter the first-year class in order to maintain the higher aggregate rate. Such growth can reduce delay times dramatically. To see this consider the following simple example. Current production is 2 tcf(10^{12} ft^3) per year allocated over a twenty-year production period so that there are twenty vintages of producing reserves. Suppose there is 1 tcf per year of excess productive capacity and that $\theta = 0.05$. In this case $q_1 = 0.16$ tcf, so that this amount of production enters each year in order to maintain total production at 2 tcf. This gives a delay time of 6.25 years for newly discovered reserves. However, if production grows by 0.20 tcf per year, then the delay time is reduced to 2.75 years, since all of this growth in production is allocated to the first-year class. Actually, the delay time would be even smaller, because this example does not take into account that the aggregate production rate is now greater, which leads to greater total decline, which in turn allows more production to enter the first-year class. It should be noted that these calculations are quite sensitive to the parameter, θ, so that the delay times that are presented below should be evaluated with this in mind.

The next requirement is to calculate excess production capacity. If an average production period of twenty years is assumed, then excess production capacity can be determined from data on actual recoverable reserves and production rates.

However, this calculation is complicated by two factors: (1) if based on re-coverable reserves, excess production capacity will undoubtedly be understated because of the conservatism of recoverable reserves estimates, and (2) the '30-year rule' of the Alberta government, which requires that excess production capacity is only that amount of reserves that is in excess of thirty years' supply at current production rates.

Even though it provides a conservative estimate, for the purposes of this paper excess capacity will be based on estimates of recoverable reserves and will be calculated as the productive capacity of the reserve base, which is in excess of the producing reserve base. The producing reserve base is estimated as twenty times the current rate of production. As for the potential constraint imposed by the thirty-year rule, the evidence is that it has not been binding. During the 1970s the gas life index averaged well under thirty years when calculated on the basis of recoverable reserves. In other words, the Energy Resources Conservation Board (ERCB) has been recognizing reserves that are somewhat larger than those that are defined as recoverable in applying the thirty-year rule.

The next step is to actually calculate the expected time of delay between the discovery of new gas reserves and the beginning of their production for the period 1947 to the present. Table 9.1 presents some estimated delay times for this period based on the model that was just described. The growth in the production rate was estimated as the difference between this period's and last period's production. A twenty-year production period is assumed and a decline rate of 0.05 is specified. This table shows that, for the early period of explora-tion in Alberta, the expected delay time between discovery and marketing of natural gas reserves was, on average, about twenty-five years. Such long delay times reduced the value of natural gas reserves in the ground to such a low level that, except in special circumstances, the incentive to search for them was nil.

It is also apparent from table 9.1 that delay times decreased dramatically during the 1960s and 1970s. Most of this can be attributed to the significant growth in markets that occurred during this period. However, by the end of the decade delay times had risen again, reflecting the surge in additions to natural gas reserves, both through new discoveries and through the appreciation of known reserves, and the failure of markets to keep up with this growth.

As noted earlier, the calculation of natural gas reserves prices presented here follows the methodology used in calculating oil reserves prices as given in Uhler (1981). The prices are essentially the unit present value of natural gas reserves and are derived from knowledge of wellhead prices, extraction costs, optimal production behaviour, etc. They also take into account the impact of the tax rules that prevailed at the time and the effect of delay time as described above. Table 9.1 presents these results. The first thing to notice about the price series given in this table is that the composite price of gas is much higher than the well-head price of raw gas. This is because the composite price includes the value of the gas co-products propane, butane, pentanes, and sulphur, which add substantially to its value. In the future the wellhead price of gas will refer to its composite price.

TABLE 9.1

Natural gas prices and delay times in Alberta

Year	Wellhead price: gas ($/mcf)	Composite wellhead price ($/mcf)	Delay time (years)	Reserves price ($/mcf)
1947	0.0680	0.0680	–	–
1948	0.0640	0.1055	16.53	0.0113
1949	0.0620	0.1028	24.70	−0.0076
1950	0.0580	0.0947	12.46	−0.0232
1951	0.0610	0.0972	25.03	−0.0116
1952	0.0930	0.1323	36.35	−0.0015
1953	0.0920	0.1324	36.24	−0.0016
1954	0.0910	0.1310	28.84	−0.0007
1955	0.0930	0.1374	25.30	0.0038
1956	0.0950	0.1417	48.76	0.0002
1957	0.1010	0.1556	28.91	0.0010
1958	0.1080	0.1481	15.39	0.0023
1959	0.0950	0.1411	12.97	0.0047
1960	0.0970	0.1455	12.78	0.0103
1961	0.1200	0.1773	8.52	0.0139
1962	0.1270	0.1966	3.96	0.0414
1963	0.1390	0.2440	7.43	0.0447
1964	0.1470	0.2597	6.65	0.0522
1965	0.1450	0.2699	7.06	0.0540
1966	0.1520	0.2992	8.26	0.0488
1967	0.1570	0.3324	6.82	0.0508
1968	0.1570	0.3586	5.27	0.0582
1969	0.1580	0.3227	2.90	0.0586
1970	0.1650	0.2902	2.23	0.0441
1971	0.1640	0.2934	1.95	0.0506
1972	0.1700	0.3223	1.28	0.0659
1973	0.1900	0.3780	1.87	0.0728
1974	0.3000	0.6520	3.29	0.1078
1975	0.6400	1.0785	2.45	0.1768
1976	1.0200	1.4401	2.62	0.2870
1977	1.3100	1.7880	2.59	0.3847
1978	1.5500	2.0538	6.90	0.2228
1979	1.8000	2.4125	4.11	0.3102

It is also clear from this table that, during the early period of exploration in Alberta, the price of gas reserves was very low. The negative price indicates that, on average, losses would have been incurred to market the gas reserves at prevailing prices. These data thus indicate that during this period there was no economic incentive to search for gas, which re-enforces the view that the major portion of all gas discovered during this time was discovered during the search for oil. However, there are accurate data that indicate that some gas-intent exploratory and development drilling did occur during this period. But remember that these calculations only reflect the average conditions that existed. Certainly, there were special situations in which it was attractive to find and develop gas reserves. Gas in certain locations could have been marketed quickly and inexpensively.

It is also evident from table 9.1 that the price of gas reserves rose markedly during the early 1960s and again in the mid-1970s, thus creating a strong incentive to explore for additional gas reserves. But starting in 1978 delay times again rose as markets for increased reserves failed to develop and the price of reserves in the ground took a sharp drop. Although it is not indicated in table 9.1, the situation has not improved in 1980 and 1981.

DATA ANALYSIS

In this section the results of estimating gas discovery and appreciation functions are presented. The results of estimating equation (2), the gas discovery equation, are considered first. It will be recalled that the amount of gas discoveries depends upon output and input prices and on cumulative reserves discoveries of both gas and oil. The specification of the output prices was discussed in detail in the previous section, and the rationale for the specification of cumulative discoveries has been outlined and will be considered further in the material that follows. What hasn't been considered up to this point is the choice of the exploratory inputs, and hence the input prices, which will be specified in the equation.

In a previous study I argued for the use of three exploratory inputs: exploratory drilling, geophysical effort, and land under exploration. In this study I am dropping land as an input. One can argue that in each year drilling and geophysics are supplied at a reasonably constant price to the industry operating in Alberta. However, this is obviously not true of land. Its price is determined by industry demand.

Thus, this study will use two input prices: the price of drilling effort as measured by the price of exploratory wells, and the price of geophysical effort as measured by the price of a geophysical crew-week. There is one aspect of calculating the prices of these inputs that should be noted. The Alberta government has offered exploratory drilling incentive and geophysical incentive grants to the oil and gas industry operating in Alberta. These grants have served to reduce the actual prices paid by the industry and are accounted for in the prices used in this study.

Now consider the estimation of equation (2). The first step is to specify a functional form for this equation which not only includes the variables that have already been suggested but also has other desirable properties. One desirable property suggested by economic theory is that this equation be homogeneous of degree zero in prices. In view of the earlier discussion, another desirable property is that it be derived from a profit function that is linearly homogeneous and provides at least a second-order approximation in prices to an arbitrary profit function. The following specification of the discovery and profit functions satisfies these criteria. The discovery function is given by

$$y_g = \alpha_1 + \sum_i \beta_{1j} p_j' + \sum_k \gamma_{1k} z_k \tag{8}$$

where p'_j are the price ratios with the price of drilling chosen as the numeraire. Ths is derived from the normalized quadratic profit function of the form

$$\Pi^*(P', Z) = \alpha_0 + \sum_i \alpha_i p'_i + 1/2\sum_i \sum_j \beta_{ij} p'_i p'_j + \sum_i \sum_k p'_i z_k. \tag{8}$$

Equation (7) relates current gas discoveries to current normalized input and output prices and to cumulative discoveries of gas and oil. There is reason to believe, however, that adjustments to price signals in this industry take longer than one year, so that in the empirical work prices lagged by one period are used in place of current prices.[4] It will also be noted that equation (7) calls for the specification of both the cumulative discoveries of gas and the cumulative discoveries of oil. Since these variables are highly correlated, the empirical work was carried out using only the cumulative discoveries of gas in the specification. With these changes equation (7) was estimated using ordinary least squares. The estimated equation is given by

$$y_{g,t} = 0.08 + 0.52p'_{g,t-1} + 0.005p'_{0,t-1} + 0.08p'_{h,t-1}$$
$$\phantom{y_{g,t} = } (0.72)\ (0.20) (0.02) (0.22)$$
$$\phantom{y_{g,t} = }+ 0.16z_{g,t} - 0.02\ z^2_{g,t} R^2 = 0.26$$
$$\phantom{y_{g,t} = }(0.20) (0.016)$$
$$\tag{9}$$

where $y_{g,t}$ is the current unappreciated level of non-associated gas discovered. The standard errors are in parentheses below the coefficients. The data for this and subsequent discovery equations cover the period 1950-78. The variables $p'_{g,t-1}$, $p'_{0,t-1}$, and $p'_{h,t-1}$ are the price of gas reserves, the price of oil reserves, and the price of geophysical effort all relative to the price of drilling, $p_{d,t-1}$. The variable $z_{g,t}$ is cumulative gas discoveries up to the beginning of the current period. The equation shows that gas discoveries are positively related to the price of gas and the elasticity at the means is 0.71. Neither the price of oil nor the price of geophysics contributes very much to explaining the variation of y_g. Surprisingly, using this specification, not even cumulative discoveries is significant even though the coefficients on this variable and its squared value do have the expected signs. The coefficient of determination for this equation is 0.26, suggesting that the variables as a group have a very low level of overall explanatory power. The price of gas is the only variable that provides a significant amount of explanatory power.

In view of these relatively poor results it was decided to consider a specification of the discovery function using the prices instead of the price ratios. This equation is no longer homogeneous of degree zero in prices, nor can it be derived from a linear homogeneous profit function. Nevertheless, one may be willing to scarifice these properties in the interest of better explanatory capability. This estimated equation is given by

$$y_{g,t} = -0.43 + 6.34p_{g,t-1} + 0.07p_{0,t-1} + 7.04p_{h,t-1} \tag{10}$$
$$\phantom{y_{g,t} = }(0.61)\ (2.43) (0.30) (3.14)$$

$$-0.92p_{d,t-1} + 0.43z_{g,t} - 0.047z_{g,t}^2 \qquad R^2 = 0.45. \qquad (10)$$
$$(3.65) \qquad\quad (0.19) \qquad (0.016)$$

Although still not particularly good, it provides a significant improvement over the previous equation. The price of gas still provides a significant contribution towards explaining discoveries, as now does cumulative discoveries. The gas price elasticity at the means is measured as 0.87, a value similar to that obtained in the previous equation. Neither the price of oil reserves nor the price of drilling effort contribute very much to explaining gas discoveries, even though the coefficient on drilling does have the expected sign. The coefficients indicate that, as cumulative discoveries increase, the discovery rate of gas rises until $z_g = 4.57$ tcf, after which further increases cause discoveries to decline. According to this, the exhaustion effect has predominated since about 1958. Thus, the recent surge in the discoveries of new gas reservoirs is explained primarily by price increases. In other words, price increases have shifted the whole $Y_{g,t} = f(Z_{g,t})$ curve upwards.

The price of geophysical effort provides significant explanatory power in this equation yet has the wrong sign. This might be explained by the difficulties involved in measuring the price of geophysics. As measured, the price of geophysics has increased in recent years but a crew-week today clearly provides more units of geophysical effort than previously. If effort could be measured in more appropriate units, one might well have observed a decline in the price of geophysics in recent years instead of an increase, which might have led to the expected inverse relationship between geophysics prices and discoveries.

It is also of interest to present the regression results in which prices are not lagged. This is given by

$$y_{g,t} = -1.20 + 1.39p_{g,t} + 0.46p_{0,t} + 6.91p_{h,t}$$
$$(0.44) \ (1.37) \qquad (0.21) \qquad (3.04)$$

$$+ 0.74p_{d,t} + 0.56z_{g,t} - 0.054z_{g,t}^2 \qquad R^2 = 0.52 \qquad (11)$$
$$(2.90) \qquad (0.17) \qquad (0.015)$$

This equation is similar to equation (10) but differs in two main respects. The coefficient on p_g is much smaller and less stable, which suggests that current price increases have a smaller impact on discoveries than do lagged price increases. This is consistent with the argument that adjustment of discoveries to price changes takes more than one year in this industry. The other main difference is that the coefficient on oil price is higher and more stable than before. This is a result that I would have expected in the first place, since much of the effort of searching for oil has resulted in gas discoveries. The significance of the price of geophysics can be explained as before. Cumulative discoveries continue to provide a significant amount of explanatory power in this question.

Let us now turn to the estimation of the non-associated gas reserves appreciation function. However, before we can proceed with estimation it is first necessary to specify a functional form for this function. It has been indicated that appreciation should depend upon the time since discovery to account for 'normal' reservoir appreciation behaviour and on wellhead price to account for the effect of price changes on recovery fractions of reservoirs, especially including the reservoirs that at the time of discovery were judged to have essentially zero recovery fractions owing to economic conditions. The appreciation function that is used here is given by:[5]

$$A(\tau - t, q_\tau) = 1 + \eta[1 - \exp\{\phi(\tau - t)\}] q_\tau^\lambda \tag{12}$$

where q_τ is the wellhead price of gas. As is apparent from equation (3), the appreciation function is the ratio of reserves $\tau - t$ years after the discovery year to the reserves in the discovery year, t. The asymptote of appreciation function given by this equation is $1 + \eta q_\tau^\lambda$ and thus depends upon wellhead price and the parameters η and λ. Figure 9.2 illustrates the effect of wellhead price on the appreciation curve.

In order to estimate the parameters of equation (12), one requires data on reserves for each year subsequent to the initial discovery year for each vintage of discovery. From these data the ratio of reserves in each subsequent year to the initial year are formed, which, along with the wellhead price, completes the data set. To clarify the construction of the data set, consider an example involving only two vintages of discoveries, say, 1950 and 1958 vintage discoveries. For k years after the discovery, the data formed from these two vintages consist of the ratio of reserves k years after the discovery to the initial amount. Obviously, there are more observations the earlier the vintage of the discovery. The observation on wellhead price of the 1950 vintage discoveries, say, one year after discovery would be the 1951 wellhead price, whereas for the 1958 vintage it would be the 1959 price; etc. Using the data constructed in this way equation (12) was estimated using nonlinear least squares and is given by

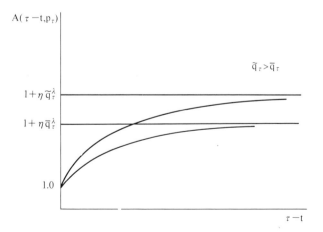

FIG. 9.2

$$A(t, q) = 1 + 4.95g_\tau^{0.21} \quad \{1 - \exp(-0.28t)\} \tag{13}$$
$$(0.30)\,(0.08) \qquad\qquad (0.07)$$

where q_τ is the wellhead price and t is the time since initial discovery. The estimated standard errors of the estimated parameters are given in parentheses below the estimates and indicate that these estimates are very stable. The estimated asymptote of the appreciation function is given by

$$A(\infty, q_\tau) = 1 + 4.95\, q_\tau^{0.21} \tag{14}$$

indicating that the higher wellhead prices lead to higher ultimate appreciation.

It is interesting to use these results both to forecast reserve additions in some time period and to forecast ultimate gas discoveries. Two sets of calculations will be made. The first set, which are presented in table 9.2, show forecasted reserve additions in the period 1979–82 as well as ultimate discoveries under the assumption that prices remain constant at their 1978 levels. The value of cumulative discoveries for 1978 in table 9.2 is obtained by appreciating all past discoveries to 1978 in accordance with our estimated appreciation equation. The value of cumulative discoveries for 1982 involves the further appreciation of discoveries made prior to 1979 as well as the post-1978 forecasts of the discovery equation (10), with prices held constant at their 1978 levels. These forecasted discoveries in the interval 1979–82 are, of course, appreciated up to 1982. Thus, the reserve additions between 1978 and 1982 consist of the appreciation of all discoveries including those that are forecasted plus new initial reserves discoveries. Table 9.2 shows clearly that the bulk of reserve additions occur as a result of the appreciation of past discoveries. Very few new discoveries are forecasted by the model under the scenario of constant economic conditions.

This table also presents estimates of ultimate cumulative discoveries under these same fixed economic conditions. It is clear that forecasted ultimate

TABLE 9.2

Forecasts of non-associated natural gas reserve additions and ultimate discoveries (constant 1978 price)

Year	Cumulative discoveries* (tcf)
1982	87.00
1978	77.30
Reserves additions, 1978–82	9.70
Due to appreciation	9.58
Due to new discoveries	0.12
	9.70
Ultimate discoveries	91.00

* Discovery rate based on equation (10).

discoveries are only slightly larger than those forecasted to 1982. This is because the model does not predict significant levels of new discoveries and the further appreciation of previous discoveries will not be large under static 1978 economic conditions.

The second set of calculations will show the effect of rising gas prices, other prices constant, on the level of ultimate discoveries. But before considering the effect of these increasing prices using both equations (10) and (11) as forecasting equations, it is instructive to reconsider equation (5) in the light of the recognition that both wellhead and reserves prices enter the model, and to use the modified equation to determine the wellhead price elasticity of cumulative appreciated discoveries. This modified equation is given by

$$\partial R_\tau/\partial q_\tau = \sum_{t=1}^{\tau} y_t\, \partial A/\partial q_\tau + A(\partial y_\tau/\partial p_\tau)(\partial p_\tau/\partial q_\tau). \tag{5a}$$

The first τ terms on the right recognize the impact of an increase in the wellhead price on cumulative discoveries through its effect on the appreciation of these discoveries, and the last term recognizes the impact of increases in the wellhead price on current discoveries through its effect on the price of reserves. Evaluating this equation for values of the variables in 1978 and allowing for a wellhead price increase of $0.10 per mcf ($10^3$ ft^3) yields an increase in reserves of 1.1 tcf, of which 0.71 tcf comes from the appreciation of previous discoveries and 0.39 tcf comes from appreciated current discoveries. Evaluated at 1978 values of R and q, this gives an elasticity of 0.27. However, this level of increase in discoveries will not remain constant for further increases in price because of the dynamic nature of the discovery equation. We cannot allow very large increases in cumulative initial discoveries while attempting to hold them constant in the evaluation of this equation because increases in this variable causes the discovery rate to fall.

It is more useful to use the estimated equations to forecast discoveries and their appreciation for various levels of wellhead prices, taking into account the fact that increments to cumulative initial discoveries cause the discovery rate to fall. Thus we have a situation in which price increases cause the discovery rate and the appreciation of those discoveries to rise but where this is offset by the reduction in the discovery rate caused by the depletion effect of rising levels of the variable z_t. Table 9.3 presents these results using two of the estimated discovery equations. Comparing the estimates of cumulative discovery potential shown in table 9.3 with that in table 9.2 clearly indicates that increasing wellhead and reserves prices can be expected to add substantially to the total discoveries of non-associated natural gas in Alberta. The price increase indicated in this table more than offset the depletion effects of cumulative discoveries, so that instead of quickly rising to a stable maximum, as they would under static economic conditions, discoveries continue to grow as prices rise.

It is also apparent that the two discovery equations provide substantially

TABLE 9.3

*Forecasts of cumulative appreciated non-associated natural gas discoveries:
increasing wellhead price*

Wellhead price ($/mcf)	Cumulative discoveries (tcf)	
2.15	91.70*	92.20†
2.65	105.40	98.10
3.15	118.10	103.50
3.65	130.00	108.30

* Discovery rate based on equation (10).
† Discovery rate based on equation (11).

different forecasts. Although they start out at about the same level, under the estimates of equation (10) discoveries rise much more quickly as wellhead price increases than they do when the estimates from equation (11) are used. This is not surprising in view of the relative magnitudes of the natural gas price coefficients in each equation, but it still does not tell us which forecast is best. It will be recalled that equation (11) had the best overall fit but that the gas price coefficient had a relatively large variance, whereas equation (10) had a poorer overall fit but the gas price coefficient was relatively stable. Rather than chose between these two forecasts, it is probably best to interpret both of them with extreme caution.

Finally, it is of interest to compare the forecasts in table 9.3 with some recently made by the ERCB (1978) for Alberta. They estimate 110 tcf and possibly 130 tcf of proven initial recoverable reserves by the 1990s. Although their estimates are not based on an explicit model, they are 'based on an analysis of historical growth rate and a projection of the growth trend assuming that favourable economic incentives and full marketing opportunity for gas will exist in the future'. The forecasts in table 9.3 are very similar to the ERCB estimates, but this should not be surprising given that these results are also based on an analysis of historical growth rates and a projection of the growth trend assuming favourable economic incentives with, just possibly, a little extra thrown in.

ACKNOWLEDGEMENTS

I would like to thank Stephen Tierney for research assistance and Olga Betts for text processing. The research reported in this paper was supported by EMR Research Agreement 277/8/79 and by UBC's Programme in Natural Resources Economics financed by the SSHRCC.

NOTES

1. Currently, non-associated gas comprises about 85 per cent of Alberta reserves.
2. Cumulative appreciated reserves of oil and gas could also serve as proxy variables, but they would not provide a stable series over time and are thus, in my judgement, less suitable than those suggested.
3. If one considers a reserves additions model, in which categories of drilling are not distinguished and this drilling has the purpose of both adding to reserves and establishing productive capacity, the relevant price in such a model is the netback price alone. The incentive to drill any well then depends upon the present value of net revenue, which in turn depends upon present and future netback prices. The price of reserves in the ground does not play a role in such a model.
4. For a more flexible adjustment process which can be used in connection with models of this variety, see Woodland (1977).
5. This equation is a modified version of a formula used in the engineering literature to approximate the appreciation behaviour of oil and gas reservoirs. The modification incorporated here is to recognize explicitly the impact of price on reservoir appreciation.

REFERENCES

Energy Resources Conservation Board (1978), *The Supply and Demand for Alberta Gas,* ERCB Report 78-E, Calgary, Alberta, May 1978.

Energy Resources Conservation Board (1979), *Alberta's Reserve of Crude Oil, Gas, Natural Gas Liquids, and Sulphur.* ERCB Report 79-18, Calgary, Alberta, August 1979.

Uhler, Russell S. (1979). *Oil and Gas Finding Costs,* Canadian Energy Research Institute, Study no. 7, Calgary, Alberta, September 1979.

Uhler, Russell S. (1981), 'Oil Reserves Prices', Resources Paper no. 68, University of British Columbia, June 1981.

Woodland, Alan (1977), 'Estimation of Variable Profit and Planning Price Functions for Canadian Manufacturing, 1947-1970', *Canadian Journal of Economics*, 10, 355-77.

Comment   Robert S. Pindyck

I found Russell Uhler's paper both interesting and innovative. The problem of estimating supply functions for natural gas (and other hydrocarbon resources) is an important and difficult one. Better estimates of supplies and supply functions are needed as an input to the formulation of energy policy, and a better understanding of the supply process is needed as a management tool for energy-producing companies. I found this paper interesting in and of itself, but it is also nice to see that Russell Uhler is continuing to pursue research in this important area.

I think that this paper will also serve to stimulate further work in this area; as I read it a number of issues and concerns came to mind. The comments that I offer below should be viewed not as criticisms of this paper, but rather as thoughts that might be suggestive of the directions that further work might take. In particular, I would like to discuss the issue of 'jointness' in the oil and gas discovery process, and the issue of risk stemming both from price and cost uncertainty, and from the stochastic nature of the discovery process. I will conclude with some minor comments relating to the model and the statistical results.

OIL AND GAS AS JOINT PRODUCTS

The estimation of natural gas supply functions is of course complicated by the fact that natural gas and oil are often discovered jointly (and sometimes produced jointly) and that jointness is stochastic in nature. This is a problem that Uhler recognizes and deals with at the outset. As he points out (p. 264).

although relative prices may dictate a particular desired mix of oil and gas discoveries, this outcome may not be realized because of the inability of firms to distinguish accurately between gas prospects and oil prospects. . . . Because of this fact, any model that relies on relative prices to explain the mix of oil and gas discoveries will almost certainly be limited in its explanation of these data.

The approach Uhler uses is to assume that the actual mix of discoveries will be close to the desired mix. If this is indeed the case, then equations can be estimated from a restricted profit function based on the assumption that 'firms in the industry make choices in an attempt to maximize their profits'. (Note, by the way, that this also assumes risk neutrality on the part of firms.)

I think this is probably a reasonable approach, although there are others (in addition to dividing exploratory inputs into oil-intent and gas-intent categories and estimating the oil and gas discovery functions separately), and it might be interesting to pursue them, perhaps as part of an extension of this current work. One alternative approach is that used by Paul MacAvoy and me in our work some years ago on US natural gas and oil markets.[1]

MacAvoy and I viewed exploratory behaviour as a kind of portfolio selection problem. In particular, we saw decisions to undertake drilling ventures as analogous to decisions to purchase stocks, except that drilling ventures could be characterized along two dimensions. One dimension is the trade-off between risk and return (i.e., some ventures are higher risk but with a higher expected return). The second dimension relates to the relative *a priori* probabilities of finding gas or oil. Given this approach, we specified equations for exploratory drilling, oil, and gas success ratios, and average sizes of find based on approximations to a single-period capital asset pricing model for the valuation of the venture.

Looking back, I cannot say that our approach was particularly successful. Part of the problem was our use of pre-1973 data (so there was limited price variability), and the fact that we in large part ignored the dynamic aspects of the problem. Uhler's results in this paper seem tighter statistically, and more realistic. None the less, I think that further work in this area does need to deal with the stochastic aspect of the jointness of the oil and gas discovery process, as well as the problem of risk and returns in exploration ventures.

IMPLICATIONS OF UNCERTAINTY

Uncertainty is an inherent aspect of the gas and oil discovery process, and, as I mentioned above, needs to be dealt with seriously. I have already discussed the fact that at the micro-level the discovery 'response function' is inherently stochastic; i.e., a given amount of exploratory effort will result in a partly unpredictable quantity of new reserves. However, there is another form of uncertainty that in my view also needs to be dealt with.

That second form of uncertainty has to deal with *future prices*, and has serious implications for the valuation of in-place reserves. As can be seen in his table 9.1, Uhler calculates values (prices) for reserves that are quite low throughout the period of interest. It seems to me that his method may have understated the values, particularly in the 1970s—a decade in which there was considerable uncertainty over *future* gas (and oil) prices.

As I have noted elsehwere,[2] one can view in-place reserves as options on future production. In other words, if the future price of the gas or oil turns out to be higher than the cost of extraction, it may well be desirable to 'exercise' the option and produce the resource, but if instead price falls (or does not rise sufficiently), so that production would be unprofitable, the option need not be exercised, and the only loss is the cost of discovering or purchasing the reserve. But as with financial options, this means that future price uncertainty makes the current value of a unit of reserves *larger* than the current price net of extraction cost. (Putting it another way, the value of an in-place reserve is a convex function of the price of the resource, so, by Jensen's inequality, price uncertainty raises the value.)

Testing this notion requires some estimate of the variance of expected future price. For the 1970s such an estimate might be obtained from a sample of forecasts taken at different points in time. It would be interesting to see whether an estimated price variance variable turns out to be statistically significant if inserted on the right-hand side of Uhler's equation (9).

MINOR COMMENTS

I will close with a few particular comments. First, it should be noted on p. 265 that variables relating to cumulative unappreciated discoveries of gas or oil make sense only if the data are regional, or if the distribution of reserves is more or less homogeneous. Second, estimates of the 'delay time' (p. 269) are made with error, and it would be interesting to know what implications errors in this estimated variable would have for the estimation of the supply relationship. Third, note that the insignificant oil price variable in equations (9) and (10) is disturbing since (as discussed earlier) theory tells us that this variable should indeed be significant. Finally, note that the estimated standard errors of the estimated parameters in equation (13) have limited meaning. I don't know what kind of nonlinear estimation algorithm was used in the estimation of (13), but presumably the estimated standard errors refer only to a linearization at the last iteration.

NOTES

1. That work is described in P. W. MacAvoy and R. S. Pindyck, *The Economics of the Natural Gas Shortage (1960–1980),* Amsterdam: North-Holland, 1976, and in R. S. Pindyck, 'Higher Energy Prices and the Supply of Natural Gas', *Energy Systems and Policy,* Fall. 1977.
2. See R. S. Pindyck, 'The Optimal Production of an Exhaustible Resource when Price is Exogenous and Stochastic', *Scandinavian Journal of Economics,* June 1981.

Comment   G. C. Watkins

INTRODUCTION

The Uhler paper relates to a very important issue—how to project the future supply of natural gas in Alberta. Alberta has been and still is the predominant source of gas in Canada, accounting for 71 per cent of established Canadian reserves and 86 per cent of Canadian production of natural gas in 1980.

The reason why the prospects for Alberta natural gas are so important is two-fold. First, information on future Alberta gas supply is mandatory for any general assessment of the Canadian energy outlook and in particular in evaluating the role of frontier gas. Second, and more specifically, projections of Alberta gas supply are incorporated directly in the current formulae used by the Alberta Energy Resources Conservation Board (ERCB) and the National Energy Board (NEB) to determine any 'surplus' gas that may be available for export.

So the topic covered by Russell Uhler is especially timely in that it confronts some pressing policy issues. It is also a topic where work with Canadian data has not been extensive; much of what has been done is by Uhler himself (see Uhler and Bradley, 1970; Uhler, 1976, 1977, 1979).

In this discussion of Uhler's current paper I start by making some general points, seeking to place Uhler's work in a broader context, and then make several more detailed comments.

GENERAL COMMENTS

The key feature of Uhler's current model is the distinction he makes between new discoveries and their subsequent appreciation, often called 'extensions and revisions'. Ignoring this distinction can lead to erroneous analysis of discovery trends. Let me give an example, in this case for crude oil rather than gas. The mid-1960s saw a sharp increase in Alberta oil reserve additions, which induced strong pressure to move more Canadian oil to the United States, and the outlook for oil supply became quite euphoric. Not long thereafter, reserve additions declined and a much more conservative attitude prevailed. The mid-1960s oil reserve increases were partly attributable to the Rainbow–Zama play in north-west Alberta, but they also included substantial amounts of appreciation to existing reserves, mainly a result of the stimulus given to enhanced recovery by changes to the Alberta pro-rationing system in 1964. Such appreciation was more in the nature of a once-for-all stock adjustment, not a long-term trend.

Uhler's empirical application of his model is highly aggregative. The gas discovery data are not segregated by geological play, and yet it is the play—the discovery of significant petroleum deposits in a particular geological formation—that is the key determinant of the characteristics of discovered reserves. Combining data across plays thus can lead to classical aggregation problems if the nature of the plays were disparate. Uhler is well aware of this problem. As he says in one of his earlier papers,

Recall that I have emphasized the importance of using the petroleum play as the most natural unit of aggregation. The reason is that we know a good deal about how the rate of reservoir discovery in a petroleum play behaves with respect to the current and cumulative levels of exploratory effort. We also know that the largest reservoirs in a play tend to be found early and that their average size declines over the course of the play. . . . The econometric studies, however, have constructed models of the supply process which are designed to use data which is aggregated over many plays. Thus the discovery rate of reserves in the aggregate data consists of the summation of the discovery rates in all the plays which are currently active. . . .
Thus we see that, though these aggregate models seem to be one way to incorporate the effect of new play discoveries on the reserves discovery rate, in my view it is quite likely that they will lead to erroneous forecasts. [Uhler, 1977, pp. 34–5]

Perhaps the justification for the aggregation procedure followed in Uhler's current paper is in Uhler (1979), where he points out that in comparison with oil the gas play features are much less pronounced:

the structure of gas plays in Alberta is even more complex than oil plays. In fact it was suggested earlier that in Alberta gas plays have never existed in the true sense because plays are as much an economic phenomenon as they are a physical one. In other words, the right economic circumstances must exist to generate high levels of exploratory activity which result in rapid increases followed by sharp declines in the discovery rate. Such conditions have not typically existed for gas so the discoveries in particular formations tend to be spread out over long periods of time, sometimes with several peaks in the discovery rate. Thus gas discoveries do not lend themselves to play analysis. [Uhler, 1979, p. 41]

However, my guess is that the aggregation across plays problems may become more severe in relation to current developments, because some of the more prolific new Alberta gas plays—such as the deep basin play—have quite different geological characteristics, especially areal and recovery factor elements, than previous plays.

Another feature of Uhler's current model is its 'reduced form'. Gas discoveries arise from the results of geophysical and drilling activity. The pattern of success, or otherwise, of exploration activity can show a trend as a function of economic and underlying physical parameters. The same comment applies to the size of discoveries. While earlier work by Erickson and Spann (1971) is fraught with conceptual and econometric problems, it is still useful to recall their basic identity:

$$ND_g \cong W \times SR \times AD_g \tag{1}$$

where:

$$
\begin{aligned}
ND_g &= \text{natural gas discoveries} \\
W &= \text{wildcat wells drilled} \\
SR &= \text{success ratio} \\
AD_g &= \text{average gas discovery size.}
\end{aligned}
$$

In his 1976 paper Uhler (pp. 75-6) separated out the elements that lead to gas discovery much along the lines of equation (1), characterizing the first stage as the use of search-related resources to locate promising wildcat drilling sites; the number of site locations in a given time interval was treated as a Poisson variate with its mean rate (intensity) depending on the amount of resources allocated to the searching effort. A second stage involved drilling prospective sites, also treated as a Poisson process. The third stage was the reserve discovery process. Given that a site is drilled, and given the probability of finding petroleum, the number of reservoirs discovered (N_t) was treated as a function of λ_t, where

$$\lambda_t = \theta_t p_t q_t$$

and:

$$
\begin{aligned}
\lambda_t &= \text{intensity of effort} \\
p_t &= \text{probability of drilling a given site} \\
q_t &= \text{probability of discovery.}
\end{aligned}
$$

Uhler then makes a distinction between prospective oil and gas locations, and an associated division of exploratory effort. Discovered reservoirs are then translated into reserves by applying a lognormal size distribution of discoveries. Uhler incorporates the contrary effects on the discovery rate of sampling without replacement and the acquisition of geological knowledge by including cumulative exploratory footage per unit area in a way that allows growing knowledge to push up the mean number of discoveries while simultaneously exhausting the number of reservoirs; eventually, the exhaustion effect dominates.

It is not my intention to go into the Uhler (1976) model in detail; in passing let me mention that the model omits explicit inclusion of economic variables on the stages outlined, in particular on the characteristics of prospects accepted for drilling. My intention is simply to show the way the various components of the new discovery process can be broken down, thereby indicating the extent to which the current Uhler model compresses this whole procedure.

Uhler's current discovery model is a linear function:

$$y_g = f(p_g, p_0, p_h, p_d, Z_g, Z_g^2)$$

where:

y_g	=	new gas discoveries (unappreciated)
p_g	=	price of gas reserves in the ground
p_0	=	price of oil reserves in the ground
p_h	=	price of geophysics
p_d	=	price of drilling
Z_g	=	cumulative new gas discoveries.

The three petroleum price variables are the economic parameters introduced to account for shifting exploration margins; the price of drilling enters as part of the production/cost function element—a feature of Uhler's (1979) paper. The quadratic function in Z_g, cumulative discoveries, is intended to accommodate the combination of the knowledge and depletion effects, with the second-degree term (expected to be negative) reflecting the exhaustion effect and the first-degree term reflecting the acquisition of knowledge effect.

This model can be interpreted as a reduced form of the underlying new discovery process discussed above, which identified the separate elements combining to generate new discoveries, typified by geophysical activity, the selection of prospects, drilling, and the evaluation of discoveries. Such an aggregated reduced-form model may well be able to generate a useful description of new discoveries over time, but combining all these elements does mean the different structural characteristics shown in other modelling efforts and in some of Uhler's work are not identified. Thus, the model does not rely in any explicit way on statistical regularities relating to occurrences of petroleum which have emerged from earlier work—the lognormal size distribution of reserves and the Poisson or negative binominal distribution of areal reservoir density. These distributional characteristics could represent some fundamental physical process, and in my opinion preferably should be incorporated in gas supply modelling efforts.

Gas costs cannot be estimated from the model, in part a consequence of the aggregated 'reduced-form' specification. Cost information is important in the Canadian context, where the question of the economic ranking of alternative sources of gas supply is critical. Put another way, the Uhler model does not provide specific information on the nature and shape of the gas supply curve, although some information can be derived indirectly by varying prices and assuming price marginal cost equivalence.

Let me now turn to the question of reserve appreciation. One interesting aspect of oil and gas reserve appreciation is the difference between their respective extents. For example, the Alberta Energy Resources Conservation Board (1969) estimated 'normal' appreciation of gas reserves as approximately four times the discovery year estimate; for oil the corresponding multiple was nine (figures V-4 and V-9). The reason for such a difference seems to lie in the distinction between appreciation of 'in-place' reserves and the appreciation in the recovery factor.[1] In the case of gas, appreciation relates primarily to the in-place estimates; the recovery factor shows little variation over time and what variation is displayed seems to be of a declining trend;[2] gas recovery factors are usually at high levels of around 70 per cent or more. The case of oil is quite different, where about two-thirds of appreciation relates to oil in-place and one-third to recovery factor increases. The oil recovery factor is normally much lower than for gas—a representative figure would be 33 per cent—and the scope for it to increase through introduction of enhanced recovery schemes is correspondingly greater.

These differences between the nature of oil and gas appreciation suggest a reason why aggregation across plays in the case of gas may be more tolerable than in the case of oil. I hypothesize that one of the main distinctions between plays in the case of oil is the difference between recovery factors. Such a variation in the case of gas is more muted, and to this extent gas plays are more homogeneous than oil plays, and hence more plausibly aggregated.

One feature of reserve appreciation data is that the considerable degree of variation in appreciation by reservoir reflects not only the nature of the pools themselves, but also vagaries in the timing of their discovery, and in particular whether they were discovered near the beginning or the end of a year: pools discovered near the end of a year would undergo much greater relative appreciation in future years. Again, this aspect supports aggregation of the data, in the hope that things will average out. But it is also a feature that blurs the distinction between initial discoveries and appreciation.

The original work on 'normal' reserve appreciation by the Alberta Board utilized a 'response' function[3] of the form

$$A = 1 + K(1 - e^{-t/L}) \tag{2}$$

where:

A	=	appreciation in relation to initial year reserve
K	=	a scale constant
t	=	time
L	=	a fitting constant.

Note that as $t \rightarrow 0$, $A \rightarrow 1$; as $t \rightarrow \infty$, $A \rightarrow K + 1$. The equation made no provision for the influence of economic parameters. And at the time it was first estimated (1969) the exclusion of economic parameters was not a serious omission. Natural gas prices, especially in real terms, had shown little variation over quite an extensive period, so in terms of analysing historical trends it is unlikely that economic parameters would have emerged as significant variables.

Uhler's appreciation equation modifies equation (2) in a straightforward way by including the wellhead price of gas (q_t) as an adjustment to the upper asymptote, which becomes $1 + Kg_t^{\lambda}$ where λ is the estimated parameter.

Other work on reserve appreciation by economists is quite sparse. MacAvoy and Pindyck (1973) distinguished between extensions and revisions, treating extensions of non-associated gas as

$$XN = f(WXT_{-1}, DN_{-1}) \tag{3}$$

where:

XN = reserve extensions, non-associated gas
WXT = total exploratory wells
DN = total new discoveries of non-associated gas

while the corresponding equation for revisions was:

$$RN = f(\Delta YT_{-1}) \tag{4}$$

where:

RN = reserve revisions, non-associated gas
YT = year end total gas reserves (associated and non-associated)

MacAvoy and Pindyck suggest extensions and revisions depend on price incentives, past discoveries of gas, existing reserves levels and the cumulative effect of past drilling. Ostensibly, function (3) does not include economic parameters, but they enter through the response of exploratory drilling and new discoveries to economic incentives.[7]

The Uhler appreciation equation introduces economic incentives, but by treating appreciation essentially as a function of time, does not attempt to allow for fluctuations in the pattern of appreciation induced by changing economic or underlying physical conditions. For instance, the Uhler equation does not accommodate the manner by which higher prices may encourage a lot of flank reservoir drilling, lead to substantial appreciation over a short period rather than a smooth process over time. One way such impacts might be comprehended by the model is to include a drilling variable relating to development wells, or one of the finer distinctions of the exploratory drilling category, such as outpost wells.

SPECIFIC COMMENTS

On grounds of data limitations, Uhler combines what he calls category 2, namely appreciation of recoverable reserves from known producing reservoirs, and category 3, appreciation of reserves and reservoirs which at the time of discovery were classified as uneconomic. An additional reason for combining 2 and 3 is that the distinction between them is not clear. Some of the appreciation from existing reservoirs, for example the drilling of fringe wells into thin pay zones, may require as much of a change in economic conditions as does the requirement to bring on stream reservoirs previously considered uneconomic.

The relationship between the extraction rate and the volume of reserves can be affected by contractual arrangements and normal contractual rates of take. It is these that typically govern the installation of reservoir capacity. While Uhler rightfully says that most reservoirs exhibit production decline over time, the typical contractual arrangements are such that for a quite considerable period there would be no productivity decline, since the contractual rate of take would be less than the maximum rate of production, so that it may be several years before the productivity decline aspects hit.

Reference is made by Uhler (see Table 9.1 above) to the expected delay between discovering and marketing of natural gas averaging twenty-five years in the early period of exploration in Alberta. I think this gives a rather distorted view, because the expected delay time would also relate to the expected, not current, rate of production; undoubtedly the expectation was that the rate of production would rise very significantly once projects for export of natural gas from Alberta got under way.

The gas price elasticities estimated by Uhler of 0.7 to 0.8 are substantial, since presumably these are short-run elasticities. Because his equations (9) and (10) are dynamic through the Z_g variable (cumulative new discoveries), intermediate and long-run elasticities could be derived. The point of inflexion (1958) calculated for the Z_g variable after which 'exhaustion' effects predominate is curious, as 1958 seems far too early; at this time the drilling density for Alberta was relatively low. For example, in 1958 the exploratory drilling density was about 1 well per 50 square miles of sedimentary area, while the Alberta Energy Resources Conservation Board (1969) estimated the ultimate drilling density would be 1 well per 8 square miles. (See pp V-4 and V-18). One could argue, as does Uhler, that the recent surge in discoveries is explained primarily by price increases, but also there were substantial new discoveries in the 1960s in new plays (see Uhler, 1979, p. 10). Moreover, recent discoveries also represent the evaluation of new plays. In other words, even now we may not have reached the 'exhaustion' decline stage.

One final comment: there is no provision for technical change in the model. Given changes in drilling efficiency and other activities associated with the discovery and development of new reserves over the estimation period, I suggest technical change may well be a significant variable.

Overall, Uhler's paper makes an important contribution to analysis of gas supply. It is to my knowledge the first econometric model using Canadian data that pursues separate treatment of new discoveries and their subsequent appreciation. The model can be used to elucidate some of the implicit price parameters that may underlay projections of ultimate Alberta reserve potential. The way the model sheds light on these important unknowns will be helpful in policy assessment; the model specification is also applicable to other regions.

NOTES

1. Broadly speaking, recoverable reserves is the product of reserves in place and the recovery factor.
2. Apparently attributable to adverse reservoir performance not being recognized until some producing history has been obtained (see ERCB, 1969, p. V-15).
3. See Oil and Gas Conservation Board (OGCB) (1968, p. 128). The equation related to Newton's law of cooling; see Eckman (1948), p. 30.
4. Khazzoom (1971) has also estimated models for extension and revisions as a function of the price of gas, oil and NGLs, new discoveries (lagged) and lagged revisions and extensions.

REFERENCES

Eckman, D. P. (1948), *Principles of Industrial Process Control,* New York: John Wiley.

Energy Resources Conservation Board (1968), *Reserves of Crude Oil, Gas, Gas Liquids and Sulphur, Province of Alberta,* OGCB Report 69-18.

Energy Resources Conservation Board (1969) *Reserves of Crude Oil, Gas, Gas Liquids and Sulphur.* 70-18.

Erickson, E. and Spann, R. (1971) 'Supply and Response in a Regulated Industry: The Case of Natural Gas', *Bell Journal of Economics and Managment Science,* 2, 94-121.

Hotelling, H. (1931), 'The Economics of Exhaustible Resources', *Journal of Political Economy,* 39, 137-75.

Hotelling, H. (1932), 'Edgeworth's Taxation Paradox and the Nature of Demand and Supply Functions', *Journal of Political Economy,* 40, 577-616.

Khazzoom, J. Daniel (1971), 'The FPC Staff's Econometric Model of Natural Gas Supply in the United States', *Bell Journal of Economics and Management Science,* 2, 51-93.

MacAvoy, P. W. and Pindyck, R. S. (1973), 'Alternative Regulatory Policies for Dealing with Natural Gas Shortages', *Bell Journal of Economics and Management Science,* 4, 454-98.

National Energy Board (1979), *Canadian Natural Gas, Supply and Requirements.*

Uhler, Russell S. (1976), 'Costs and Supply in Petroleum Exploration: The Case of Alberta', *Canadian Journal of Economics,* 9, 72-90.

Uhler, Russell S. (1977), 'Economic Concepts of Petroleum Energy Supply', in G. C. Watkins and M. Walker (eds), *Oil in the Seventies,* the Fraser Institute, pp. 5-42.

Uhler, Russell S. (1979), *Oil and Gas Finding Costs,* Canadian Energy Research Institute, Study no. 7.

Uhler, Russell S (1982), 'The Supply of Natural Gas Resources in Alberta', Department of Economics, University of British Columbia, Resources Paper no. 74.

Uhler, Russell S. and Bradley, Paul G. (1970), 'A Stochastic Model for Determining the Economic Prospects of Petroleum Exploration over Large Regions,' *Journal of the American Statistical Association,* 65, 623-30.

10. Deriving the Long-run Supply Curve for a Competitive Mining Industry: The Case of Saskatchewan Uranium

Harry F. Campbell and Douglas L. Wrean

INTRODUCTION

In this paper we describe a general methodology for modelling open-pit mines and deriving long-run marginal cost curves on a mine-by-mine basis for the mineral in question. The next section outlines the approach in very general terms and shows how it is related to the standard economic models of mining. In the following section the more detailed structure of the applied model is described. The final section describes an application of the model to a group of five uranium mines in northern Saskatchewan. A long-run supply curve is obtained for each mine and some predictions of uranium supply are discussed. In our view, the techniques outlined in this paper will be of value in predicting and assessing for public policy purposes all aspects of the impact of a proposed open-pit mine or series of mines.

A MODEL OF A MINING FIRM

Our model of mineral extraction differs from the conventional model (see for example Levhari and Liviatan, 1977, and additional references cited there) in that we distinguish between capital and operating costs. Capital costs are incurred prior to the mining and milling of the ore and are determined by the chosen capacity of the mining and milling plant: $K = K(x)$, $K'(x) > 0$, where K is capital cost incurred in year 0 and x is the annual throughput of ore. Capital expenditures are assumed to be irreversible. Our operating cost function is a particular form of a general function which is popular in the literature. The general form is

$$C_t = C(x_t, X_t), \qquad C_{x_t} > 0, C_{X_t} > 0$$

where C_t is total operating cost at time t, x_t is the rate of throughput, and X_t is cumulative extraction. We use a separable form of this operating cost function:

$$C_t = C(x_t)\, g(X_t), \qquad C_{x_t} > 0, C_{x_t x_t} \overset{>}{\underset{<}{=}} 0, g_{X_t} > 0.$$

Our cost function allows the possibility of continually decreasing average variable costs over the range of possible extraction rates, and it recognizes that operating costs will rise with cumulative extraction as ore of a given grade becomes less and less accessible.

We assume that our mining firm is a price-taker in both input and output markets. For the moment we will assume that the firm is risk-neutral and that it maximizes the expected net present value of the mine. Its expectation is assumed to be that input and output prices will remain constant over the life of the mine. The maximization of expected net present value results in a mining firm with a finite life selling at a constant expected price. This is perhaps a common enough phenomenon in the world of mining, but an unusual one in the mining economics literature. Schulze (1974) presents the most rigorous analysis we have seen of individual firm behaviour within a competitive mining industry. In that analysis, each firm faces a constant mineral price but controls only a unit deposit so that extraction is instantaneous.

In our model we assume that the mine-owner chooses to exploit the mineral deposit at a constant rate. The reasoning underlying this assumption has already been developed in Campbell (1980). A mining firm that faces a substantial initial investment in plant capacity will not find it optimal to maintain idle capacity for most of the mine's life. Consequently, instead of choosing a declining output path as in the conventional model, the mine-owner will operate at a constant rate for much of the mine's life. If the marginal cost of capacity is relatively high, the proportion of the mine's life characterized by capacity output will be correspondingly high. For mathematical convenience we assume that the mine operates at capacity over its whole life.

Assuming that a constant rate of extraction is chosen to maximize the expected net present value (NPV) of the mineral deposit, the firm's maximization problem becomes

$$\max_{NPV} = \int_0^T e^{-rt} \{px - C(x)g(X_t)\} \, dt - K(x) \tag{1}$$

$$\text{s.t. } x \cdot T \leqslant \bar{X}$$

where p is expected mineral price; $C(x)$ is the expected total operating cost at the extraction rate x; $g(X_t)$ is a scalar which augments total operating cost as extraction proceeds to reflect the increasing inaccessibility of ore of a given grade; $K(x)$ is the capital cost of plant capable of operating at rate x; r is the discount rate; $X_t = x \cdot t$ is cumulative extraction; and $\bar{X}$ is the initial size of the mineral deposit. The solution to this problem is obtained by a simple application of nonlinear programming techniques. The Lagrangean function is

$$L = F(x, T; r, p) + \lambda(\bar{X} - xT) \tag{2}$$

where $F(x, T; r, p)$ is the general form of the *NPV* function. The Kuhn Tucker conditions are:

$$F_x - \lambda T \leqslant 0 \tag{3}$$

$$F_T - \lambda x \leqslant 0 \tag{4}$$

$$(F_x - \lambda T)x = 0 \tag{5}$$

$$(F_T - \lambda x)T = 0 \tag{6}$$

$$\bar{X} - xT \geqslant 0 \tag{7}$$

$$(\bar{X} - xT)\lambda = 0 \tag{8}$$

$$x \geqslant 0, T \geqslant 0 \tag{9}$$

$$\lambda \geqslant 0 \tag{10}$$

It will be instructive to consider one method of solving conditions (3)–(10) for the optimal values of x and T since it is the basis of the algorithm used to solve our applied model. Assume that in condition (9) the inequalities hold. This means that it is in fact optimal to exploit the deposit as opposed to leaving it in the ground. It may be optimal to extract only part of the deposit, in which case the shadow-price, λ, equals zero; or it may be optimal to extract the whole deposit, in which case $\lambda \geqslant 0$. If $\lambda = 0$, we get

$$F_T = 0 \tag{11}$$

from (6); and if $\lambda > 0$ we get

$$xT = \bar{X} \tag{12}$$

from (8). Given values of p and r, equation (11) can be solved for the terminal time, T, corresponding to each of a range of possible extraction rates. The (x, T) pairs for which $xT \leqslant \bar{X}$ correspond to situations in which $\lambda = 0$. When $xT > \bar{X}$, then $\lambda > 0$ and the T value is re-set to $\bar{X}/x$ as indicated by equation (12). The modified set of (x, T) combinations is then used to evaluate the *NPV* function and the (x, T) pair corresponding to maximum net present value is determined by inspection. If this maximum *NPV* turns out to be negative, then we conclude that the equalities in condition (9) hold and the deposit will not be exploited.

If the process just described is repeated for a range of possible mineral prices, a grid consisting of net present values resulting from a set of (p, x) combinations can be obtained. In each row of this grid there will be a maximum value of *NPV* corresponding to the optimal extraction rate for a given price, while in each column *NPV* rises as p rises with the extraction rate held constant. The information reported in this grid can be used to derive average and marginal long-run cost curves of the kind proposed by Bradley (1979) for the mining firm.

Bradley has proposed definitions of long-run average and marginal costs of output from an exhaustible resource stock which have the same basic properties as the concepts of long-run average and marginal cost in the conventional theory of the firm. These properties are that long-run average cost (*LRAC*) defines the break-even price of output, and equating long-run marginal cost (*LRMC*) with price defines the profit-maximizing rate of output in the long run. A break-even price for the resource at a rate of extraction x is that sum of money, P_{AC}, which, when received for each unit of the resource at the time of production, ensures that the net present value of the mine is zero. Thus, the break-even price for a given extraction rate, x, is the solution to

$$NPV = P_{AC} \int_0^T e^{-rt} x \, dt - PVTC(x) = 0 \qquad (13)$$

where $PVTC(x)$ is the present value of total cost when extraction is conducted at rate x:

$$PVTC(x) = \int_0^T e^{-rt} C(x)g(x, t) \, dt + K(x). \qquad (14)$$

Hence long-run average cost is given by

$$P_{AC} = LRAC(x) = PVTC(x) \bigg/ \int_0^T e^{-rt} x \, dt. \qquad (15)$$

The $LRAC$ for each x can be read off the appropriate column of the NPV grid as that p value which corresponds to $NPV = 0$.

The long-run profit-maximizing rate of extraction at a given price of output, P_{mc}, is the rate for which marginal net present value of revenues equals marginal net present value of costs:

$$\frac{d}{dx} \left(P_{mc} \int_0^T e^{-rt} x \, dt \right) = \frac{d}{dx} PVTC(x) \qquad (16)$$

$$P_{mc} = LRMC(x) = \frac{d}{dx} \{PVTC(x)\} \bigg/ \frac{d}{dx} \left(\int_0^T e^{-rt} x \, dt \right). \qquad (17)$$

The points (P_{mc}, x) on the $LRMC$ curve can be obtained from the rows of the (p, x) grid: in the row corresponding to each price p, there is maximum net present value at some level of extraction x, and this (p, x) combination is a point on the $LRMC$ curve.

The portion of the $LRMC$ curve lying above the $LRAC$ curve has the usual interpretation as the firm's long-run supply curve. The horizontal sum of the various mines' long-run supply curves is the industry long-run supply curve, where the 'long run' is short enough to exclude the exit from the industry of exhausted mines and the entrance to the industry of new deposits which have been located by exploration.

AN APPLICATION OF THE MODEL

The model that we use to derive supply curves for a series of Saskatchewan uranium mines differs from the model described in the preceding section of the paper in three ways. First, the theoretical model is constructed as if mineral extraction were a single activity with an operating and capital cost function. In our applied model we identify a number of distinct activities including mining, hauling, milling, and operating a townsite, and we have an operating and capital cost function for each activity. Second, equations (4) and (6), which ensure that the mining of the deposit is not carried on after it has ceased to be profitable, are given a specific form derived from a series of assumptions about the geometry of the ore deposit. Third, we introduce into the applied model the rather complex mix of federal and provincial taxes to which the Saskatchewan uranium mines are subject.

We find it convenient to distinguish between the mining and milling divisions of the firm. The milling division mills ore at the constant rate, x. It incurs an initial capital cost associated with setting up the milling plant and providing accommodation for its employees, and it incurs costs in the operation of these facilities. It purchases ore from the mining division at a minehead price which is an internal accounting price set at the value of the milled product obtained from each ton of ore less the unit operating cost of the milling facilities. The minehead price[1] for each milling rate, x, is thus set at the highest value consistent with continued operation of the milling division at that rate. All resource rent that accrues to the mining firm plus the quasi-rent on the milling division's fixed capital is treated as if it were appropriated by the mining division.

The mining division mines and hauls material from the open pit at some constant rate q. Since the material removed from the pit consists of both waste rock and ore, $q > x$. The initial capital costs associated with setting up the mining division consist of the costs of uncovering the ore deposit, the cost of mining and hauling equipment, and the cost of providing accommodation for miners. The distinction between the milling and mining sections of the townsite is purely expositional and it disappears when the equations of the model are assembled. The mining division incurs the costs of operating the mining and hauling plant and its portion of the townsite.

The cost functions we use are derived from a set reported in an earlier paper by Campbell and Scott (1980). In that paper a set of operating and capital cost functions for the mining and milling processes of the form $K = CZ^{\alpha}$ is used, where K is total capital or unit operating cost, C and α are constants, and Z is the mining or milling rate expressed in tons per day. The cost functions for the townsite are of a different form: the capital cost function is of the form $K = C + \alpha N$, where K is total capital cost and N is town population; and the function describing monthly town operating costs is of the form $K = CN$. Town population is assumed to be a multiple, *POPD*, of the combined mining and milling labour force. Mining and milling labour forces are each described by a function of the form CZ^{α} and the parameters of these functions are reported in the Appendix. Obviously, the values of the parameters C and α are different for different cost functions. With one exception we have adopted the following procedure in converting the cost functions reported in the Campbell and Scott paper, which were for uranium mines operating in northern Australia in 1976, to functions that could be used for evaluating the Saskatchewan deposits: the values of the scale parameters, α, were retained and the values of the constants, C, were converted to 1976 Canadian dollars and then inflated to 1979 Canadian dollars. The one exception is the Cluff Lake deposit, which is much richer than any of the Australian deposits for which cost data were available. For this deposit the Australian values of the scale parameters were retained, but a separate set of estimates of the constants C in the mining, milling, and hauling cost functions were obtained from interviews with industry and government sources. The cost parameters, together with a brief note on sources, are reported in the Appendix.

We have referred to the requirement that the mining firm operating in a remote region provides accommodation for its employees. There are two basic methods of meeting this requirement. One is to construct a full-scale town for the employees and their families. The other is to construct accommodation for the employees alone and to transport the employees from their homes to the mine for short periods of employment. Both methods have been considered in northern Saskatchewan. In our model we make the rather unrealistic assumption that the two types of accommodation share the same operating and capital cost functions. The costs of accommodation will not be the same, however, because the population of the full-scale town will be a multiple of that of the mining camp. The savings in capital and operating costs involved in opting for the latter alternative may be partially or wholly offset by transport costs, and we incorporate estimates of these costs in our model. We pay no attention, however, to the possibility of mine and mill operating costs varying with the type of accommodation provided through the equalization of net advantage to employees across mines. The issue is examined by Cummings and Mehr (1977) and Cummings and Schulze (1980).

It will be recalled that our technique for solving for the mining firm's optimal rate of extraction involves calculating the net present value of the mine for a range of possible extraction rates. Once an extraction rate, x, is selected, the operating costs of the mill are known and the minehead price of ore can be identified. Since all rents are regarded as being appropriated by the mining division, the problem reduces to solving for an optimal management programme for the mine, given the minehead price. It should be noted, however, that, since the minehead price of ore is set at a level that yields a negative quasi-rent on the milling division's fixed capital, the mining division must include the capital costs of the mill along with those of the mine in deciding upon the net present-value-maximizing extraction programme for the firm.

In order to apply the model of the previous section of the paper we need to have, in addition to the set of cost functions described above, a specific form of the function $g(X_t)$ which indicates how mining costs increase with the cumulative output of ore. This specific form is obtained from a set of assumptions about the physical structure of the deposit and the open-pit mine. These assumptions are described and explored in Campbell and Scott (1980), and we deal with them only briefly here. The ore deposit is assumed to be a vertical cylinder, with a given height and radius, the top of which is a given distance below the ground. At time T, when the economic portion of the orebody has been recovered, the open pit is an inverted truncated right cone with a slope that is assumed to be exogenously determined by considerations of slope stability. The base of the cone is a circle on the earth's surface while its top is the cross-section of the ore deposit at terminal depth. This structure is illustrated in figure 10.1. The exploitation of the orebody is assumed to proceed first by the removal of the overburden, a process that is regarded as a capital investment, and then by reaming the inside surface of the cone to expose successive cross-sections of the ore deposit at the top of the cone. These cross-sections are assumed to be of constant average grade.

It is clear from the diagram that as mining proceeds the amount of waste that has to be reamed out to expose an orebody cross-section of given thickness increases. The ratio of waste to ore mined at a given time t is defined as the marginal stripping ratio, $\bar{S}_t$. The ratio of waste to ore mined over the entire life of the mine is defined as the average stripping ratio. It can be shown that, for a given physical structure of the deposit and the open pit, the marginal and average stripping ratios are functions of the cumulative output of ore:[2]

$$S_t = S(x \cdot t) \qquad\qquad (18)$$

$$\bar{S} = \bar{S}(x \cdot T). \qquad\qquad (19)$$

The unit cost of mining a ton of ore is given by the unit cost of mining a ton of material (waste and ore) multiplied by $(1 + S_t)$. Since the marginal stripping ratio S_t rises with cumulative output, the unit cost of mining a ton of ore rises as extraction proceeds, even though the unit cost of mining material remains constant.

Bearing in mind that we have identified three activities associated with 'mining' and two with 'milling', let us assume for ease of exposition that mining and milling costs are each represented by one operating and one capital cost function. The total operating cost functions can be represented as $CM(q)$ for

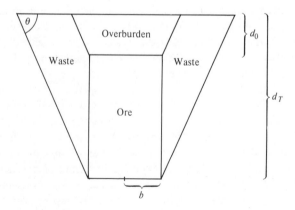

FIG. 10.1 A cross-section of the open-pit mine

mining, and $CL(x)$ and for milling. The unit operating cost of mining material from the open pit is $CM(q)/q$, and hence, from (18), the unit operating cost of mining ore is

$$CM(q)/x = \{CM(q)/q\}\{1 + S(x \cdot t)\}. \tag{20}$$

since $x = q/(1 + S_t)$. Assuming that the mine and the mill have the same life,[3] and that the mining and milling rates are constant, the mining rate necessary to supply the mill with ore at an average rate x is

$$q = x\{1 + \bar{S}(x \cdot T)\}. \tag{21}$$

Since the marginal stripping ratio rises over time and the rate of mining material is constant, the rate of mining ore must be declining. The discrepancy between the declining rate of mining ore and the constant mill feed is resolved by means of a stockpile of mined ore.[4]

Given that all rent accruing to the firm is appropriated by the mining division (including the negative rent earned by invested capital in the milling division), the maximization problem reduces to one of maximizing the net present value of the mining division of the firm. It will be recalled from our earlier discussion of the technique for solving this maximization problem that the critical step was the solution to equation (11), which ensures that extraction is terminated at the optimal time (assuming that it is profitable at some initial time). In terms of the maximization of the net present value of the mining division of the firm, the mine should be closed when unit mine operating costs have risen to the level of the minehead price of ore. Corresponding to equation (11), we have

$$P - CL(x)/x = \{CM(q)/q\}\{1 + S(x \cdot T)\} \tag{22}$$

where the left-hand side is the minehead price of ore, as defined earlier, and the right-hand side is the unit cost of mining ore at terminal depth T. Since we have introduced the distinction between mining and milling rates into the problem we need to add equation (21) to the optimizing routine. Equations (21) and (22) are two equations in the three unknowns x, q, and T. For any given value of x, values of q and T can be obtained as solutions to these equations. The solution values (x, T) for a range of x values can then be used in the maximization process in the same way as the solution values of equation (9) were used in the preceding section. The net present value grid can be constructed as before, and long-run average and marginal costs can be derived.

Before turning to a discussion of the cost curves obtained in this way for the Saskatchewan mines, we introduce into the model the federal and provincial tax systems within which these mines will operate. Because of the complexity of these systems, a detailed analysis of their effects would be very lengthy, and consequently we confine ourselves in the final section to a comparison of the 'tax' and 'no-tax' cases.

The uranium mines modelled in this paper are subject to federal and provincial corporate income taxes and Saskatchewan uranium royalties. The tax base for corporate income taxes is described in Mackenzie and Bilodeau (1979). In our calculations we have assumed that each mine is operated by a one-mine company so that the various allowances and deductions that can be applied against company income are applied against income from the mine being modelled, and that the financing for each mine is done on an equity basis so that there are no interest deductions in the computation of the tax base.

THE SUPPLY OF SASKATCHEWAN URANIUM

Uranium has been mined in Saskatchewan since the opening in 1953 of an underground mine operated by the federal government at Uranium City. More recently a large open-pit mine at Rabbit Lake has been developed, and in its first five years of operation has produced more than 15 million pounds of uranium oxide. Since the opening of the Rabbit Lake mine Saskatchewan has been the focus of steadily increasing exploration effort. By 1979 over a hundred companies were participating in this search, three times the number involved in 1976. Companies presently exploring for uranium in Saskatchewan, usually on a joint venture basis, include federal and provincial crown corporations and private concerns from Canada, the United States, West Germany, and France. The outcome of this exploratory effort has been the discovery of 'about a half-dozen new orebodies with commerical potential'.[5] Of these discoveries three can be considered major finds that will undoubtedly join Rabbit Lake as producing open-pit mines. These are the deposits at Cluff Lake (the 'D', 'N', and 'Claude' orebodies), Midwest Lake, and Key Lake (the Gaertner and Deilmann orebodies). None of the other deposits is assured of being exploited, although in some cases such as the Collins Bay deposit the likelihood is quite high.

For the purposes of the present study our attention will be directed at the existing open-pit mine at Rabbit Lake and the three discoveries that seem assured of being developed as open-pit mines. These mines will contribute the bulk of the supply of uranium from the province in the 1980s and the characteristics of the deposits have been established with reasonable precision. The Rabbit Lake deposit, which started to be exploited in 1974, contains about 40 million pounds of uranium with a grade of 0.4 per cent. Although this ore is not as rich as at the other deposits examined in this study, the Rabbit Lake deposit is overlaid by a relatively small amount of overburden and is commercially attractive. Five uranium deposits have been located at Cluff Lake. The most spectacular of these is the 'D' orebody, a small shallow deposit with an unprecedented average grade of 7 per cent. The richness of this deposit and its relative ease of access make it a particularly attractive prospect. The Cluff Lake Board of Inquiry has submitted a lengthy assessment of a proposal to mine this deposit (referred to as Phase I) and the province has indicated its approval. Phase II of the Cluff Lake development will involve sequential mining of the 'N' and 'Claude' deposits. The 'Claude' deposit consists of 13 million pounds of uranium oxide with an average grade of 0.5 per cent, while the 'N' deposit contains 18 million pounds with an average grade of 0.4 per cent. Twin deposits each containing about 75 million pounds of uranium oxide at a grade of over 2 per cent will be exploited sequentially at Key Lake. The Gaertner orebody will be exploited first, as it is slightly larger, richer, and more accessible. Despite the large amount of overburden and water overlying these deposits, their size and grade make them the most valuable of the mines modelled here. The owners of these deposits have applied for permission to proceed with mining and a board of inquiry is examining their proposal. The Midwest Lake orebody contains about 55 million pounds of uranium oxide. The ore grade is 1.25 per cent, but the orebody is quite inaccessible, lying 200 metres below an arm of Midwest Lake. Application for permission to develop this deposit has not yet been made. Appendix table A10.1 gives details of the characteristics of these deposits and the open pit that will be formed to extract them.

Each of the deposits has special features from a modelling point of view. The Rabbit Lake mine is already in operation, and comparison of its observed mining rate with the rate predicted by our model will serve as a check on the model's accuracy. This comparison cannot be too precise since our model is based on the tax structure, uranium price, and mining costs of 1979, whereas the planning period for Rabbit Lake was in the early 1970s. The Cluff Lake 'D' orebody is of such high grade that special precautions will have to be taken in mining and milling it in order to protect personnel from radiation hazards. In discussion with industry sources it was made clear to us that a special set of cost curves would need to be constructed for this mine and mill (see the Appendix).

Phase II of the Cluff Lake development, which involves sequential mining of the 'Claude' and 'N' deposits, is scheduled to begin after Phase I is completed. The Key Lake property also consists of twin deposits to be exploited sequentially. Our mode of this sequential development assumes that the capacity of the mill remains constant over the life of both deposits. The Midwest Lake deposit is the simplest from a modelling viewpoint. It is a single orebody of average grade, and although it is still in the planning stage fairly detailed information about the deposit is available. For this reason we use it for illustrative purposes and present complete results for this mine, including both the (p, x) grid and the supply curves it generates. For the other four mines we present only the supply curves obtained from the model.

For each mine a (p, x) grid is calculated on both a before- and after-tax basis. The before-tax grid for the Midwest Lake mine is reported in table 10.1. The entries in bold type indicate points on the before-tax marginal cost curve, which is labelled *MC* in figure 10.2. We are interested in the before-tax situation because the marginal cost curve indicates the optimal extraction rate at each price from a social point of view if there are assumed to be no externalities and society is risk-neutral (or if through pooling the project does not affect

TABLE 10.1

The before-tax (p, x) grid for the Midwest Lake Mine

	Milling Rate (tons of ore per day)																		
	100	300	500	700	900	1100	1300	1500	1700	1900	2100	2300	2500	2700	2900	3100	3300	3500	3700
61	881	1692	1974	2106	2179	2223	2249	2265	2276	2284	2284	2284	2285	**2286**	2281	2274	2267	2260	2254
58	834	1603	1869	1993	2062	2103	2127	2142	2151	**2158**	2157	2157	2157	2157	2152	2145	2138	2131	2124
55	788	1514	1765	1881	1945	1983	2005	2018	2027	**2032**	2031	2030	2029	2029	2023	2016	2008	2001	1994
52	741	1425	1660	1769	1828	1864	1883	1895	1902	**1906**	1904	1902	1901	1900	1894	1886	1879	1872	1864
49	694	1336	1556	1657	1711	1744	1761	1771	1777	**1780**	1778	1775	1773	1772	1765	1757	1749	1742	1735
46	647	1246	1451	1545	1595	1624	1639	1647	1652	**1654**	1651	1648	1645	1643	1636	1628	1620	1612	1605
43	600	1157	1347	1433	1478	1504	1517	1524	1527	**1529**	1524	1521	1517	1514	1507	1499	1491	1483	1475
40	554	1068	1242	1320	1361	1384	1395	1400	1402	**1403**	1398	1393	1389	1386	1378	1370	1361	1353	1345
37	507	979	1138	1208	1244	1264	1273	1277	**1277**	1277	1271	1266	1261	1257	1249	1241	1232	1223	1215
34	460	890	1033	1096	1128	1144	1151	**1153**	1153	1151	1145	1139	1134	1128	1120	1111	1102	1094	1085
31	413	800	929	984	1011	1024	1029	**1030**	1028	1025	1018	1012	1006	1000	992	982	973	964	955
28	367	711	824	872	894	904	**907**	906	903	899	891	884	878	871	863	853	844	834	826
25	320	622	720	760	777	785	**785**	782	778	773	765	757	750	743	734	724	714	705	696
22	273	533	615	647	660	**665**	663	659	653	647	638	630	622	614	605	595	585	575	566
19	226	444	511	535	544	**545**	541	535	528	521	512	503	494	486	476	465	455	446	436
16	179	355	406	423	**427**	425	419	412	403	395	385	375	366	356	346	336	326	316	306
13	133	265	302	**311**	310	305	297	288	279	269	258	248	238	228	218	207	197	186	176
10	86	176	197	**199**	193	185	175	165	154	143	132	121	110	100	89	78	67	57	46
7	39	87	**93**	87	77	65	53	41	29	17	5	-6	-17	-28	-39	-50	-61	-72	-82
4	-7	-1	-11	-25	-39	-54	-68	-82	-95	-108	-120	-133	-145	-156	-168	-179	-191	-202	-212

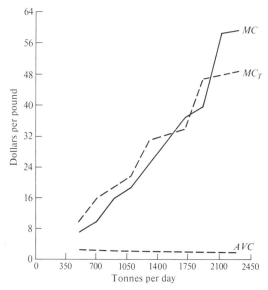

FIG. 10.2 Midwest Lake cost curves

the variability of the overall return from the social portfolio). This optimal extraction rate can be used as a yardstick in assessing the effects of the tax regime within which the mines operate.

The after-tax marginal cost curve is derived in the same way, but from a table of private net present values. This table shows that, while there is a maximum net present value in each row, the functions describing net present value as the milling rate increases and uranium price is held constant have fairly flat ranges around their maximum points.[6] Since we have assumed risk neutrality we can argue that the firm will choose the milling rate corresponding to maximum present value and consequently that the after-tax marginal cost curve, MC_T, will be the set of points (p, x_{max}) when x_{max} is the milling rate that maximizes net present vaue for mineral price p. If we wished to introduce risk aversion, we could argue that the firm evaluates increments in capacity against the standard of a marginal benefit–cost ratio in excess of unity. The marginal cost curve would then be the set of points $(p, x_{1.1})$, for example, where p is mineral price and $x_{1.1}$ is the milling rate at which the marginal benefit–cost ratio is 1.1 or whatever was the appropriate allowance for risk. The marginal cost curve calculated on this basis would include the cost of risk and would be to the left of the MC curve. Since we have no model that enables us to determine the appropriate degree of risk aversion, we have used a cut-off marginal benefit–cost ratio of unity to calculate the MC_T curve that is drawn in figure 10.2.

A striking feature of our model of the Midwest Lake mine is that, over a large range of output, the effect of the tax system is to speed up extraction. For example, at a price of $40 the privately optimal rate of production is 1900 tonnes per day whereas the socially optimal rate is 1700 tonnes. A glance

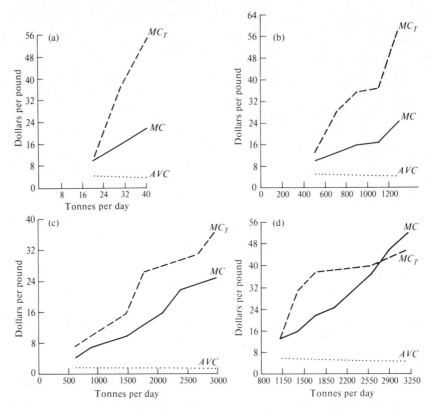

FIG. 10.3 Cost curves for four mining projects: (a) Cluff Phase I; (b) Cluff Phase II; (c) Key Lake; (d) Rabbit Lake

at figure 10.3, which shows the marginal cost curves for the other four projects in our study, shows that this feature is shared with the Rabbit Lake mine but not with the other three mines. In fact, in the case of the Cluff Lake Phase I project, the privately optimal rate of production is only slightly over half of the socially optimal rate. The tax regime within which these mines operate is quite complex, and we have not been able to uncover any simple reason why one set of tendencies dominates in the case of two of the mines and another set in the case of the other three.

While our results for the Midwest Lake mine suggest that the tax system creates a divergence between the privately and socially optimal extraction rates, the costs of this distortion are relatively small. For a uranium price of $25 per pound the present value of the mine gross of tax reaches a maximum of $785.48 million at a milling rate of 1300 tons per day. At the privately optimal milling rate of 100 tons per day, the gross of tax present value is $785.05 million. Thus the cost of the tax distortion is less than $0.5 million. The effectiveness of the tax system can be gauged from table 10.2, which shows the breakdown of the present value of the mine at the privately optimal milling

TABLE 10.2
Present values of the Midwest Lake Mine at a price of $25

	Present value ($ million)
Federal corporation tax	161.73
Provincial corporation tax	53.91
Provincial basic royalty	29.97
Provincial graduated royalty	304.64
Private share	234.79
Total	785.04

rate for the $25 price. The combined effect of the various taxes is to capture around 70 per cent of net present value.

In figures 10.2 and 10.3 we have reported the average variable cost curves for each mine. Since our model is a planning model it tells us little about the reaction of an established mine to changes in uranium price. If price net of the basic royalty dropped below the average variable cost, we would predict that the mine and mill would shut down at least temporarily unless there were significant shut-down costs. Since average variable costs are low relative to current uranium price (about Can $25 per pound) this prediction is not of much practical significance.

We have now established long-run marginal cost curves for each of five uranium mines. The Rabbit Lake mine is already in operation, milling at a rate of 2000 tons per day and producing around 5 million pounds of U_3O_8 per year though historically it has produced less. It is expected to be exhausted around 1985. From the viewpoint of 1979, when our study commenced, the other four mines were still in the planning stage and the price of U_3O_8 was around US $40 per pound. If we supposed that Can $25 was a reasonable estimate of the long-run price of U_3O_8 (the current price is around US $20), our supply curves would predict that Cluff Lake Phase I would mill at 20 tons per day, producing 1.08 million pounds of U_3O_8 per year; Cluff Lake Phase II would mill at 1500 tons per day producing 1.67 million pounds per year. Key Lake would mill at 1500 tons daily, producing 30.19 million pounds annually, and Midwest Lake would mill at 1100 tons per day producing 10.62 million pounds per year. It should be noted that these predictions are at variance with the reportedly planned milling rates of 90, 700, 750, and 600 tons per day and uranium outputs of 4, 4, 12, and 4.5 million pounds of uranium oxide. The planned rate of 90 tons per day for Cluff Lake Phase I is a provincially regulated rate which is higher than the present-value-gross-of-tax-maximizing rate of 50 tons per day, which in turn is higher than the private optimum of 20 tons per day.

It can be seen that, with the exception of Cluff Lake Phase I, our estimates of milling rates and uranium output exceed the planned rates. A clue to one reason for this finding lies in the fact that our estimates of uranium output do not err by the same factor as do our estimates of milling rates. This implies a different relationship between milling rate and uranium output in our model than exists for these mines. A readily identifiable source of this divergence is the difference between published ore grades for a deposit and the grade of ore that will actually enter the mill. The latter is often lower than the former, because of the inclusion in the mill feed of rock or ore of very low grade. While it may not be economic to mill this material on its own, it may also not be economic to separate this material from the ore. Much of the divergence between our estimates and the planned levels of uranium output for the Key and Midwest Lake mines is probably attributable to this source of error. *Ad hoc* adjustments to our model, reducing ore grades and increasing amounts of ore correspondingly, lead to lower predicted levels of uranium output. Such adjustments also lead to estimates of mine lives much closer to those that have been planned. Other factors that may have biased our output predictions upwards are our assumption of risk neutrality, and the possibility that our cost functions are not taking adequate account of the higher grades of ore found in Saskatchewan.

If we accept the planned starting dates for the four mines and use our predictions as to milling rates and mine lives, we obtain the supply profile reported in table 10.3. As information becomes available about the physical characteristics of deposits located by exploration, these can be modelled and added to the supply profile. While we do model the construction period for each mine, as

TABLE 10.3
Output of Saskatchewan uranium mines (millions of pounts U_3O_8)

Year	Rabbit Lake	Cluff Phase I	Cluff Phase II	Key Lake	Midwest Lake	Total
1980	5.00	–	–	–	–	5.00
1981	5.00	1.08	–	–	–	6.08
1982	5.00	1.08	–	–	–	6.08
1983	5.00	1.08	–	30.19	–	36.27
1984	5.00	1.08	1.67	30.19	–	37.94
1985		1.08	1.67	30.19	–	32.94
1986		1.08	1.67	30.19	10.62	43.56
1987		1.08	1.67	29.28	10.62	42.65
1988		1.08	1.67		10.62	13.37
1989		1.08	1.67		10.62	13.37
1990		1.08	1.67		10.62	13.37
1991		0.23	1.67		1.91	3.81
			(cont'd)			(cont'd)

Notes: The Rabbit Lake output is approximately equal to the actual output of this mine. The outputs for the other mines are our predicted rates of output at an expected price of Can \$25 per pound of U_3O_8. The Cluff Lake Phase II mine continues producing at the rate reported until the year 2002.

well as the length of the mine life, we have not used our model to predict starting times for mining because of the uncertainty about the amount of time necessary to conduct the required impact assessment. Instead, we have relied on the educated guesses of industry and government officials. At the time of writing it seems as if the Collins Bay deposit might be the next to go into production after Midwest Lake but we do not care to speculate on the starting date. Table 10.3 contains our prediction of Saskatchewan uranium supply in the current decade, based upon our information and assumptions.

APPENDIX

THE COST FUNCTIONS

The following tables report the parameters of the cost functions used in modelling the Saskatchewan uranium mines with the exception of the Cluff 'D' deposit which is treated separately below.

The capital cost functions

	Parameters		Price index
	C	α	
Mining equipment	26,060	0.83	D 603800
Milling plant	527,520	0.70	D 603800
Town	18,920,000	47,300	D 481602

Source: the C parameters of the capital cost functions reported in Campbell and Scott (1980), Appendix 2, were converted to 1976 Canadian dollars using an early 1976 exchange rate of Can $1.295. Thes estimates were then updated to 1979 Canadian dollars using Cansim price indices. The parameter for the town capital cost function was derived in the same way, while the parameters for the mining and milling capital cost functions are same as those reported in the Campbell and Scott paper. Since most of the mine data available to use are expressed in metric tons, the C parameters of the mining and milling cost functions were adjusted accordingly.

The operating cost functions

	Parameters		Price index
	C	α	
Unit mining cost	8.93	-0.14	D 5278
Unit haulage cost	1.69	-0.05	D 5278
Unit milling cost	77.12	-0.16	D 5278
Mining and haulage labour force	14.7	0.30	
Milling labour force	8.5	0.30	
Town operating cost	25.98	–	D 5278
Fly-in service	216.80		

Source: the C values were obtained from the values reported in Appendix 2 of the Campbell and Scott paper in the same manner as for the parameters of the capital cost

TABLE A10.1

Description of proposed uranium mines in Saskatchewan

Name of mine	Orebody	Ore (millions of tons)	Grade (% U_3O_8)	Pit slope (degrees)	Depth of overburden (metres)	Max. depth of deposit (metres)	Planned output rate (millions of lbs U_3O_8 per year)
Cluff Lake Phase I	D	0.073[1]	7.0[2]	37[3]	6[4]	30[5]	4[6]
Cluff Lake Phase II	Claude	1.2[7]	0.5[8]	37[9]	10[10]	100[11]	4[12]
	N	2.0[13]	0.4[14]	37[15]	10[16]	80[17]	4[18]
Key Lake	Gaertner	1.23[19]	2.84[20]	37[21]	50[22]	80[23]	12[24]
	Deilmann	1.57[25]	2.11[26]	37[27]	90[28]	170[29]	12[30]
Rabbit Lake		4.5[31]	0.4[32]	20[33]	10[34]	140[35]	5.5[36]
Midwest Lake		2.0[37]	1.25[38]	37[39]	170[40]	205[41]	4.4[42]

Footnotes:

[1]*CLBI*, p. 19   [2]*CLBI*, p. 18   [3]Assumed to be the same as Key/Midwest Lake   [4]*Northern Miner*, 19 July, 1979, p. B23   [5]*CLBI*, p. 18
[6]SMDC, p. 28   [7]Munday, p. 103   [8]Munday, p. 103   [9]See n. 3   [10]Tapaninen, p. 59   [11]Tapaninen, p. 59   [12]SMDC, p. 28
[13]Munday, p. 103   [14]Munday, p. 103   [15]See n. 3   [16]Tapaninen, p. 61   [17]Tapaninen, p. 61   [18]SMDC, p. 28   [19]Munday, p. 103,
and *KLBI*, 'Economic Impact', p. 1   [20]Munday, p. 103   [21]*KLBI*, p. 4.3.2   [22]*KLBI*, p. 4.7.2   [23]*KLBI*, p. 4.7.2   [24]SMDC, p. 26
[25]Munday, p. 103, and *KLBI*, 'Economic Impact', p. 1   [26]Munday, p. 103   [27]*KLBI*, p. 4.3.3.   [28]*KLBI*, p. 4.3.3.   [29]*KLBI*, p. 4.3.3
[30]SMDC, p. 26   [31]Munday, p. 103   [32]Munday, p. 103   [33]Inferred from Hoeve, p. 115   [34]Inferred from Hoeve, p. 117   [35]*Northern Miner*, 19 July 1979, p. B7   [36]*Northern Miner*, 21 August 1980, p. B6   [37]*MLS*, 'Introduction'   [38]*MLS* 'Introduction'   [39]*MLS* 'Project Development'   [40]*MLS* 'Project Development'   [41]*MLS* 'Project Development'   [42]*MLS* 'Project Development'

Sources:

Esso Minerals Canada, *Midwest Lake Uranium Deposit Project Summary (MLS)*
Hoeve, J. (1977), 'Uranium Metallogenic Studies, II: Rabbit Lake, Mineralogy and Geochemistry', in *Summary of Investigations, 1977, MacDonald, Saskatchewan Geological Survey*, ed. Christopher and Macdonald, Saskatchewan Department of Mineral Resources, pp. 331–54 (Hoeve)
Key Lake Mining Corporation (1980), *Submission to the Key Lake Board of Inquiry (KLBI)*
Munday, R. J. (1978), 'Uranium Mineralization in Northern Saskatchewan', *Canadian Mining and Mettalurgical Bulletin*, 71 (Munday)
Saskatchewan Department of the Environment (1978), *The Cluff Lake Board of Inquiry, Final Report (CLBI)*
Saskatchewan Mining Development Corporation(1979) *1979 Annual Report* (SMDC)
Tapaninen, K. (1976), 'Cluff Lake Area', GAC–MAC Meeting, Edmonton, Field Trip no. A-1 (Tapaninen)

functions. The value of *POPD* is set at 2.8 as in the Campbell and Scott paper except where a programme of flying workers into the mine site is adopted. Such a programme is modelled by setting *POPD* = 1.0, assuming a one-week rotation, and adding fly-in costs to the monthly operating costs of the mine and mill. These costs are described by the function $K = CN$, where K is monthly fly-in cost, C is the parameter reported in the table, and N is town population or, in this case, total labour force. The value of the parameter C is based on a commercial air fare for a trip out of Saskatoon of the distance to the uranium mining sites.

The Cluff Lake 'D' deposit

The Cluff Lake 'D' deposit has two characteristics that make the use of the mining and milling costs functions described above inappropriate: it is of a much smaller size in terms of ore tonnage, and the ore is much richer than in the other mines. The values of the parameters that describe scale effects are retained, but alternative values for some of the C parameters were calculated from cost estimates obtained from conversations with industry and government officials. The alternative parameter values are:

Capital costs

	C
Mining equipment	105310
Milling plant	2094348

Operating costs

Unit mining cost	65.08
Unit milling cost	745.36

Transportation cost

We have used $0.50 per pound as an estimate of the cost of shipping yellow cake to market.

Interest rate

We have used a real rate of interest of 5 per cent per annum in all net present value calculations reported in this paper.

THE MINE DATA

The physical characteristics of the orebodies are described in the table A10.1 and the sources of the data are given as footnotes. These figures relate to figure 10.1 in the following ways: the grade is the constant average grade of a cross-section of the orebody; the slope is the angle θ; the depth of overburden is d_0; and the maximum depth of the deposit is the maximum possible value for d_T; of course, as explained in the text, it may not be economical to continue mining to this depth, although in the case of all the mines modelled in this paper the optimal terminal depth d_T coincides with the maximum depth.

NOTES

1. The product of a uranium mine–mill complex is yellowcake, which is 80–85 per cent uranium oxide (U_3O_8). Yellowcake is sold on a U_3O_8 content basis and the quoted price of uranium is actually the price per pound of U_3O_8. When ore grades are reported they usually indicate the percentage by weight of U_3O_8 that could be obtained from the ore with 100 per cent recovery.
2. For a derivation of these formulae see Campbell and Scott (1980, Appendix 1), where the marginal and average stripping ratios are expressed as functions of current and terminal depths, respectively. Since depth depends on cumulative extraction, these functions can be rewritten in the general form described here. The particular form of the expression $\{1 + S(x \cdot t)\}$ is $\{(xt + 2\Pi\alpha bd_0)/(2\Pi ab^2 \tan\theta) + 1\}^2$ where d_0, b, and θ are parameters of the open-pit deposit as illustrated in figure 10.1, and α is the density of the deposit.
3. This assumption is for convenience. It is easy to amend equation (21) to include a variable representing the ratio of the economic life of the milling plant to that of the mining plant. This ratio then becomes an optimizing variable. See Campbell and Scott (1980, p. 44) for details.
4. See Campbell and Scott (1980, pp. 41-2) for a discussion of the assumption of a constant mining rate and the role of a stockpile of mined ore.
5. See various issues of *The Orange Disc* published in Pittsburgh by Gulf, and especially the Spring 1979 issue, vol. 23, n. 9.
6. When the (p, x) grid is calculated with a finer x dimension it can be seen that some of its rows have local maxima in the region of the global maximum. These perturbations are very slight and are caused by the discreteness of some of the tax calculations, especially the earned depletion allowance against corporation income tax.

REFERENCES

Bradley, P. G. (1979), 'Production of Depleting Resources: A Cost-curve Approach', UBC Department of Economics Resources Paper no. 41, p. 35.

Campbell, H. F. (1980), 'The Effects of Capital Intensity on the Optimal Rate of Extraction of a Mineral Deposit', *Canadian Journal of Economics,* 13, 349-56.

Campbell, H. F. and Scott, A. D. (1980), 'Costs of Learning abut the Environmental Damage of Mining Projects', *Economic Record,* 56, 36-53.

Cummings, R. G. and Mehr, A. F. (1977), 'Investment for Urban Infrastructure in Boom Towns', *Natural Resources Journal,* 17, 223-40.

Cummings, R. G. and Schulze, W. D. (1980), 'Optimal Investment Strategies for Boom Towns: A Theoretical Analysis', *American Economic Review,* 63, 374-85.

Garnaut, R. and Ross, A. D. (1975), 'Uncertainty, Risk Aversion and the Taxing of Natural Resource Projects', *Economic Journal,* 85, 272-87.

Levhari, D. and Liviatan, N. (1977), 'Notes on Hotelling's Economics of Exhaustible Resources', *Canadian Journal of Economics,* 10, 177-92.

Mackenzie, B. W. and Bilodeau, M. L. (1979), *Effects of Taxation on Base Metal Mining in Canada,* Centre for Resource Studies, Queen's University (Kingston, Ontario) pp. xviii + 190.

Paish, F. W. (1938), 'Causes of Changes in Gold Supply', *Economica,* 5, 379-409.

Saskatchewan Department of the Environment (1978), *The Cluff Lake Board of Inquiry, Final Report,* pp. xii + 429.

Schulze, W. D. (1974), 'The Optimal Use of Non-renewable Resources: The Theory of Extraction', *Journal of Environmental Economics and Management,* 1, 53-73.

Comment   Nancy Olewiler

The basic objective of their paper is to derive what the authors call a long-run supply curve for each of five uranium deposits located in Saskatchewan. My comments will focus on the interpretation and uses of this supply relationship, difficulties with the concept, and suggestions for alternative approaches. I will briefly present the key features of the paper, the theoretical model, and its application.

The model underlying the supply calculations is a formulation of the present value of a firm's profit from extracting and milling a fixed stock of ore. The firm's profits over its extraction horizon are given by Campbell and Wrean's equation (1),

$$\pi = \int_0^T e^{-rt} \{px - C(x) \cdot g(X)\}\, dt - K(x)$$

where the market price is exogenous and assumed constant over the extraction and milling period, because it is assumed that output from the mill in each period, x, is constant. The operating cost function, $C(x) \cdot g(X)$, depends on x at each t and X, which is cumulative extraction to that t. Both $C'(x)$ and $g'(X)$ are assumed to be positive. The cost function is assumed separable in x and X. $K(x)$ represents the capital costs, which are all incurred in the period prior to commencement of extraction.

It is important to note that x is mill output. The model is thus richer in descriptive detail than much of the existing literature. However, there may be some confusion resulting from equation (1) and the authors' discussion of their model in their second section because they frequently refer to x as the output from the mine. For example, on p. 291 they state: 'In our model we assume that the mine-owner chooses to exploit the mineral deposit at a constant rate', Because they later assume that it is the mill that operates at a constant rate, while the mine follows an extraction path that declines over time, I presume that all statements to constant output refer to that from the mill. They attempt to differentiate their work from others, but the comparisons made are some-what misleading because the traditional depletion models focus generally on the output from the mine—e.g., Hotelling (1931), Dasgupta and Heal (1979). Their assumption about mine output appears to be consistent with the traditional literature's results. Their analysis would be more revealing if the efficient extraction and milling paths were derived from the maximization problem. Assuming a path does not give us much economic insight into the extractive process. Their assumptions may indeed be the results obtained from the model, but one would like to see the formal analysis.[1]

The authors then sketch a solution to the model using nonlinear programming techniques and numerical methods to determine x and T, the maximum life of the mine/mill. Given different values of the market price, p, different x's are selected, and then T is computed as $\bar{X}/x$. If $xT > \bar{X}$, T is restricted to $\bar{X}/x$. Then for each (x, T), a present value calculation is made. The process is repeated for different values of p. The result is a grid of net present values for different p's and x's. In principle, there is only one output level for each p that is a maximum present value.[2] Holding x constant, present value of course rises with increases in p

The authors use the (p, x) grid to derive what are called long-run average and marginal cost curves, *LRAC* and *LRMC*. *LRAC* is defined as the break-even price of the output, *PAC*, for each x, where *PAC* is that unit price at which the net present value of the mine equals zero (equation (15) in their paper). *LRMC* is defined in equation (17) by the price of x at which the marginal *NPV* of revenues is equal to the marginal *NPV* of costs. *LRAC* is then given by the p at which $NPV = 0$ for each x (in each column) in the (p, x) grid, while *LRMC* is given by the x level where the *NPV* is at a maximum for each p (row) in the grid. The supply curve is then that portion of the *LRMC* curve that lies above *LRAC*. These cost curves are derived for five uranium deposits in Saskatchewan. The remainder of the paper then deals with the calculation of the (p, x) grid before and after resource taxation. I will consider these calculations later.

My comments will now focus on the supply curve postulated by the model. In particular, I will consider how these curves can be interpreted and what type of supply curves we might be interested in for policy analysis of depletable resource industries.

The *LRMC* curve derived by the paper shows the following. A market price is chosen at time 0, p_0, which is assumed to prevail over the extraction period of each mine. For each p_0, there will be a constant rate of milling $x(p_0)$ which maximizes the *PV* of the mine and for which $x \cdot T \leqslant \bar{X}$. The resulting supply curve could be called a planning or *ex ante* curve for each deposit. It shows how much ore would be milled if p_0 equals p_t for all t, given that capacity is equal to x. It of course says little about actual supply, which depends on the market equilibrium in each period.

Capacity puts an upper bound on extraction but, as noted before, there is no guarantee that mills will operate at capacity. In the extreme case, where p_t is constant at p_0 for ever, each firm's supply curve is a point at its capacity level, and industry supply is the sum over these capacities. So once capacity is installed, certain portions of the *LRMC* curve are no longer meaningful. Of course, if the price changes after production commences, the supply curves could be redefined. The *NPV* computation would then need to be redone at each t for the different p and new value of $\bar{X}_t$.

How can the *LRMC* curve be used? Its value is in an *ex ante* or planning phase of mineral supply. Suppose, for example, that the provincial and federal governments want to operate a uranium cartel. The break-even supply curves would then give the governments an idea of what uranium supply could be at different prices they set for the ore, assuming they know the total number of orebodies and all their characteristics. Alternatively, a government might be interested in the effects of different taxes and/or regulations on potential (but not producing) mines. For example, in the United States, the Bureau of Mines computes these break-even price supply curves for many minerals. They use them in making decisions about, for example, the allocation of public land among competing uses (mines versus forestry versus grazing), where they need to know at what price particular known deposits will be able to commence extraction.

Firms could use the supply curve in planning the development of new mines. Given some expection of the resource price path, the mine-owner could use the break-even price to determine the efficient level of capacity. In all of these examples, the break-even price curve is no longer very useful once the mine is operating, because no economic behaviour of the firm with respect to marginal decisions is modelled.

To see what the *ex ante* supply curve omits, I would like to look at the mineral supply process in greater detail. Why are we interested in curves for depletable resources, and what information do we want from them?

An economic supply curve for a reproducible good is a well defined concept in principle. One combines a vector of inputs to create a vector of outputs at each t. Time is not always a critical component of the analysis because the supply process can be repeated indefinitely. There are many ways of econometrically specifying a supply curve, derived from profit, production, or cost functions, with the usual qualifications and caveats. The supply process for depletable resources is more complex than that for a reproducible good, and there are some important distinctions between them. For a depletable resource firm operating in a competitive market, price no longer equals MC at the optimal extraction rate, but differs by the rental value of the resource. Production in any period depends not only on the current price and cost conditions, but on expected future prices, the rate of change in these prices, future costs, discount rates, and the remaining stock of ore. It might be more useful to think of mineral supply as a set of curves (or points) that depend on firms' expectations of future prices, etc., rather than as a unique curve for any t. Identification, in an econometric sense, of any of these curves is a non-trivial matter.

The supply process for a depletable natural resource also has four distinct but related stages: (1) acquisiton of resource-bearing land, (2) exploration for and discovery of new resource deposits. (3) development of productive capacity, and (4) extraction and processing. The concept of a unique supply curve thus ceases to be the well-defined notion it was with reproducible goods. Modelling any one of these activities, let alone all four simultaneously, is difficult. Econometrically, tricks such as using a recursive system, assuming the error terms are normally distributed and uncorrelated across equations and so on, generally cannot be employed. It is not too surprising that there are very few empirical studies of mineral supply that look at more than one phase in the process.

What most empirical studies of mineral supply do is either examine only one of the phases (e.g., Campbell and Wrean look at the third stage) or specify and estimate a reduced-form expression which incorporates variables from the different phases. The reduced-form expression may be derived from resource theory but more often is *ad hoc*. The formulation of supply will then affect the usefulness of the quantitative estimates derived. Most studies yield an estimate of the price elasticity of supply, a number useful for policy analysis. Elasticities are meaningful only if it is clear what is being measured, i.e., what the underlying model specification is. A study that examines only one part of the supply process yields an elasticity that ignores price-induced effects on supply from other phases of the process. The price will be treated as an exogenous variable, and the resulting elasticity estimate may be biased. In a reduced-form expression, the elasticity will reflect bits from all phases incorporated, without identifying the effects of each phase.

Supply curves used for public policy analysis must also incorporate the effects of government activity on the industry. Again, in an *ex ante* or planning supply analysis, one can introduce and alter policies to see their effects on non-producing mines.[3] But once the policies are already in effect and mines operating, identification of a mineral supply curve is difficult because government policies may shift both supply and demand as agents respond to the changed environment. This problem is often ignored or finessed in the supply literature by assuming, for example, that distortions affect only one curve, allowing the other to be identified. There is little theoretical justification for these approaches.

The purpose of these comments is not to discourage empirical work, but to identify difficulties encountered in estimating mineral supply and to caution about calling one phase in the process long-run supply. In addition, I would like briefly to note general difficulties encountered in doing empirical work on depletable resources. These include the paucity of data at the mine and/or firm level, jointness in production of many base metals, the difficulty of measuring inputs and outputs, and the non-existence of markets for some phases of the supply process. I want to emphasize that, when we do empirical work and try to solve the data and other problems, we should be building models derived from depletable resource theory that can take account of the different phases of mining. This does not mean that all models must be complex simultaneous equation systems, simply that the framework should allow for the addition of different phases when data become available. An alternative theoretical approach would be to specify a profit function given input costs and the output price, then derive and estimate simultaneously the associated supply and factor demand equations. The factor inputs would come from the previous mining phase which may be modelled explicitly when data permit. Work of this sort is being done by Uhler (chapter 9 above) and Lewis and Slade (1982).

I now will consider the remainder of the paper, and provide some specific comments and queries about the application of the model. First, I welcome the attempts made by the authors to introduce some of the technical peculiarities associated with mining into their model. The features of mining that

that make it interesting include the large amount of fixed capital involved, joint outputs, minimum and maximum constraints on production, possibilities of increasing returns to scale, and the different production processes (mining, milling, refining), to name a few.

In this section of their paper, the authors apply their model to five uranium deposits in Saskatchewan. The discussion centres on how to obtain the (p, x) grid defined before.

To compute the (p, x) grid, the authors must measure the *NPV* of the mine under different values of p and x. To do this, total costs must be calculated. The authors distinguish between mining, milling, and townsite activities, and specify both capital and operating cost functions for each activity. Valuation of input costs at the mill level presents a practical difficulty because the most important input, the ore extracted from the mine, is not sold in a market when the mine and mill are owned by the same company. As this appears to be the case for the uranium mines under consideration, some method of valuing the ore must be found. One method would be to find an operation for which mine and mill were owned by separate companies. There are a number of examples of this in other types of hard-rock mining. I believe that even in Saskatchewan uranium mines there is one company that has its ore milled by another (Eldorado Nuclear mills Cenex ore). One could then use the milling prices established for these transactions with suitable information about ore grades and other features to impute a 'minehead' price for the ore milled by the company's own mill. The advantage of this technique is that the minehead price will incorporate any resource rents accruing to the orebody assuming no monopsony power for the mill.

The authors take a different approach. They calculate the minehead price by subtracting from the value of each unit of the milled product the unit costs of milling. The minehead price thus includes resource rents from the orebody plus any rents or other distortions arising from the milling operation. As an accounting device this approach is acceptable, but one then cannot give a precise economic interpretation to the minehead price.

The authors then distinguish between the mining extraction rate and the milling rate. This is important in an open-pit mine where extraction produces ore and waste material, while milling produces ore. The amount of 'rock' produced in the mine thus exceeds the mill production. Cost functions are defined for rock extraction from the mine and ore production from the mill. There are also capital and operating cost functions for the townsite which must accompany new uranium mines being developed.

For the mine and mill, costs are described by the function $K = CZ^\alpha$ where K equals either total capital or unit operating costs, C and α are parameters, and Z is variously the mine's rate of production of rock, the mill's production of ore, or the size of the mining or milling labour force. I have some difficulty with these functions. First, it would be nice to see some explanation for the choice of functional form, especially since all cost functions have the same form. Second, C and α are not estimated but are obtained from a study done previously by Campbell and Scott (1980) on Australian uranium mines. I could not figure out how these parameter values were calculated in their paper. The townsite cost functions had a different form, and again the value of parameters for the functions came from the Australian study.

Before computing the (p, x) grid, the authors need a specific form for the cumulative cost component of the operating cost equation. This is where engineering and geological features enter the discussion. As my expertise in mining engineering is minimal, my comments are brief. The basic idea is that an open-pit mine looks in cross-section like a flower-pot with the ore lying in the centre of the pot (in a cylindrical shape) with waste material above it and surrounding it. To get at the ore, the waste must be removed by digging down the sides of the sloping pot to prevent collapse of the pit. As mining continues, proportionately more waste must be extracted to get the same amount of ore. Thus the marginal costs of mining ore shift with cumulative extraction. The formula for this process is given by the stripping ratio presented in equation (18) and n. 2 of their paper.

The depletion effect implied is that there is a mismatch between the mining and milling rates of production. Mills generally operate on a continuous basis year round and work best if they process a constant amount of rock per unit time. But because of the increasing extraction costs arising from cumulative extraction, the authors argue that the amount of ore mined will decrease over time. Therefore, to mill a constant amount of ore over the life of the mine, the rate of extraction from the mine must be large in the early periods of production, and the ore stock-piled for subsequent use by the mill. This is the basis for their assumptions about output made in their second section. This could well be the most efficient strategy for the firm, but I would prefer more formal analysis of the problem.

The set of federal and provincial taxes that existed at the time the paper was written are incorporated into the analysis by re-calculating the *NPV* of the mine net of taxes. In computing the taxes, all firms are assumed to own only one mine and to finance solely with equity. These assumptions do help to simplify the analysis, but they limit the applicability of the results. Most uranium firms are owned by large companies that have more than one deposit (and have other business activities), and that finance capital expenditures in many ways. A more detailed computation of the tax system might be desirable.

The findings of the study, the computation of the (p, x) grid for the five deposits, shows that the *LRMC* curves are positively sloped up to what looks like maximum capacity level. The after-tax curve generally lies to the right of the non-tax curve, indicating that taxation tends to increase the desired extraction rate for any price beyond what would be the case if no taxes existed. The curves for Rabbit Lake, a producing company of Gulf Minerals, are then used to compare predicted to actual output. The predicted values are too high, which the authors attribute to their assumption of risk neutrality. I would like to see some more discussion of this argument, as I am not sure what role risk plays in this analysis. One can also think of other reasons why actual output does not correspond to their curves. The *ex ante* supply curve modelled here does not take into account firm behaviour and market conditions, which can affect actual output once production commences (e.g., strikes, contractual arrangements, unanticipated cost changes, different price and interest rate expectations). The *LRMC* curves for all the deposits are then used to predict uranium supply over the next decade at an expected price of $40 per pound of U_3O_8. The forecast depends on their modelling of the supply process and the price assumption, which at this date looks somewhat optimistic.

NOTES

1. There has been some analysis of a capacity-constrained mine, e.g., Campbell (1980) and Olewiler (1982). These models generally yielded constant extraction paths for the *mine* over part of the extraction time period. They did not however discuss the mine and mill connection.
2. In examining the grids, one finds that the change in the net present value (*NPV*) arising from a change in x near the maximum *NPV* is very small. A fairly wide range of milling rates is thus compatible with the maximum *NPV*.
3. This is still a problem with this analysis because it ignores the impact of government activities on land acquisition and exploration for minerals.

REFERENCES

Campbell, H. F. (1980), 'The Effect of Capital Intensity on the Optimal Rate of Extraction of a Mineral Deposit', *Canadian Journal of Economics,* 13, 349–56.

Campbell, H. F. and Scott, A. D. (1980), 'Costs of Learning about the Environmental Damage of Mining Projects', *Economic Record,* 56, 152 (March), 36–53.

Dasgupta, P. S. and Heal, G. M. (1979), *Economic Theory and Exhaustible Resources,* Welwyn Garden City: Cambridge University Press.

Hotelling, H. (1931), 'The Economics of Exhaustible Resources', *Journal of Political Economy,* 39, 137–75.

Olewiler, N. (1982), 'Destructive Competition in the Extraction of Non-Renewable Natural Resources', unpublished paper.

Uhler, R. (1981), 'Oil Reserves Prices', Resources Paper no. 68, University of British Columbia.

11. Has the 'Economics of Exhaustible Resources' Advanced the Economics of Mining?

Paul G. Bradley

The phrase, 'the economics of exhaustible resources', belongs to Harold Hotelling. Hotelling's potent insight—the fundamental principle of the economics of exhaustible resources' (Solow, 1974, p. 3)—was revivified in the early 1970s when the prospect of running out of various natural resources became a topic of popular debate. It has served to fuel one of the major growth industries of economic scholarship over the past decade. There is no need here to survey the achievements of this effort.

The kernel of the Hotelling approach is the identification of a resource stock as a form of capital, which should therefore (at the margin) provide a return comparable to the yield on money capital. For example, since an exhaustible resource is by definition not growing, where it is assumed that quality is uniform and that the marginal cost of extraction is constant, efficient intertemporal allocation requires that the value of the resource in the ground appreciate at the rate of interest associated with money capital. Insightful though the concept of a resource as capital may be, when one examines the industries that produce the so-called exhaustible resources, it is clear that a number of other considerations intrude. Indeed, it becomes questionable whether the advances in the theory of exhaustible resources have contributed very much to our understanding of observed behaviour in the mining and petroleum industries.

While academics concerned with exhaustible resources have centred their analysis on resource stocks as a form of capital, mineral economists, and especially mining engineers, have been more concerned with the use of traditional man-made capital in the extractive industries. Petroleum and mineral production are notably capital-intensive. Investment decisions are conditioned by cost of capital, scale economies, and the risks imposed by future supply or demand shifts. These aspects of resource-output decisions have been neglected in the recent academic resource economics literature, where the distinction between short- and long-run analysis has been largely ignored.[1]

The tendency for economists to focus on resources as a form of capital may also help to explain another discrepancy between the assumptions found in the literature and actual industry circumstances. Minerals are often regarded as homogeneous; where variation in quality has been admitted, it has been portrayed as unfolding systematically through time. In reality, deposits of widely differing grades are usually being produced at any given time. The magnitude of differential rents is more in question than their existence. Quality trends over time, which depend on the set of producing units being considered, may be obscured as new deposits are discovered and old ones exhausted. Again a basic distinction—where, that of the firm or establishment as contrasted with the industry—is frequently glossed over or ignored in the theoretical literature.[2]

In the next two sections of this paper I will briefly describe some of the issues that are encountered in applied studies of the mineral industries. I will try to demonstrate that in the applied domain conventional approaches to cost and supply analysis are indispensable—indeed, that the search for time-varying Hotelling rents is at most an interesting sidelight. However, traditional cost and supply analysis must be adapted to take account of distinctive features of the extractive industries. The final section of the paper draws attention to several of these features and the attendant possibilities.

II

When a mine or petroleum reservoir is being developed, investment usually occurs in a concentrated initial dose, while operating costs commence with production and bear a continuing relation to output. The level of capacity chosen will depend on expectations about the future; if it proves to be either too large or too small the value of the resource owner's asset will be reduced. The capacity decision must be made in the face of two principal uncertainties: future demand (or price) and the size and quality of the resource deposit.

It is this last element that distinguishes the mine from the factory: the fact that output attributable to a development investment is ultimately limited by the nature of the resource. However, rather than focusing on this, we begin by analysing the output of a mine in light of similarities to manufacturing rather than differences. The significance of this is to direct attention to investment capital rather than resource capital.

The high capital intensity that is typical of production processes for fuel and non-fuel minerals has implications for both the short-run and long-run output behaviour of a mine. With regard to the former, it seems most likely that an operator will strive to maintain production at or near capacity—planned systematic reduction of output over time seems highly unlikely. Figure 11.1 incorporates the assumptions that lead to this result.

The short-run marginal cost (SMC) curve depicting extraction cost for the mine of figure 11.1 is essentially flat, though small steps are shown corresponding to shift differentials. This shape, rather than the textbook U-shape, is based on the assumption that for most in-place mining technologies capital and other inputs cannot be used in variable proportions; when fuel and labour inputs are reduced, equipment is idled. The other notable feature of the SMC curve in figure 11.1 is that it is low relative to minimum average cost, reflecting the predominance of capital costs.

For a mine, more is involved in the output decision than extraction cost. A ton of ore or barrel of crude oil not produced today is there tomorrow— the user cost interpretation of the Hotelling result. In figure 11.1 the shaded area depicts short-run user cost, the present value of proved reserves if their

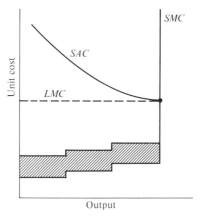

FIG. 11.1 Mine output, short-run cost curves. Shaded area depicts short-run user cost; *SMC*, short-run marginal cost; *SAL, IMC,*

production is deferred. The mine can therefore be expected to cease operation before price falls to the level of short-run marginal extraction cost. However, taking both short-run marginal extraction and user costs into account, as shown in figure 11.1, one is led to predict that output adjustments in response to minehead price will be made by discrete increments; if one-shift operation is not economical, the mine will be shut down. If these assumptions about extraction technology are realistic, there seems little likelihood of observing systematic, planned reductions in the output of a mine over time.

We next consider the circumstances of a mine in the long run. The size of a particular resource deposit, the 'resource constraint', is obviously significant in determining what capacity to install. Indeed, it is here that user cost has its most useful application.

To define a user cost pertinent to the capacity decision it is helpful to visualize the simplest case: the size of the deposit is known with certainty and the resource is homogeneous, so that output can be sustained at the level of installed capacity until exhaustion. More initial investment adds to cost, but the correspondingly quicker depletion means that the present value of output will be greater. In this constant-output, 'primal' case, the marginal condition for maximization of present value is

$$(P - C)a = \frac{dI}{dQ_0} + (P - C)Tv$$

where dI/dQ_0 = incremental investment per unit of capacity
    $(P - C)$ = net return after operating cost per unit mined
    T = the life of the mine
    a = the annuity factor, evaluated for T periods at the rate of interest r per period
    v = the discount factor, evaluated after T periods at the rate of interest r per period.

The benefit of incremental investment, is the present (annuity) value of the added unit of output for the life of the mine. The incremental cost comprises the extra investment outlay together with the long-run user cost. The latter, the term on the extreme right, is the present value to be obtained if the extra output (1 unit X T years) were instead produced when the deposit would otherwise be exhausted.

While output conditions for established mines do not appear to be significantly affected by short-run user cost considerations, we would certainly expect the capacity decision to be influenced by long-run user cost. Observed rates of use can be compared with calculated optimal ones to see if this is so— more particularly, if the postulate of present-value maximization is the appropriate one for explaining resource use by private developers.

There do not seem to be many studies in which economists have attempted to model specific examples of resource production with a view towards comparing computed optimal rates of use (by the criterion of maximum expected present value) with observed rates. Adelman and Jacoby (1979) note that, for a sample of high-cost oil fields, their estimated optimal rates of depletion are only slightly higher than those observed. They go on to point out, however, that typical capital–output ratios are much lower than in these selected examples. This would lead to forecasts of significantly more rapid rates of use, yet 'observed values of the depletion rate are not many times those calculated; in fact they are typically lower.' In an analysis of open-pit copper mining in British Columbia (Bradley, 1980), I calculated optimal rates of use which for the better deposits were substantially greater than those seen in practice. Campbell and Wrean, in chapter 10 above, derived rates that maximized the present value of uranium deposits, and found them to be much higher than those observed (except for one case where output was subject to government regulation). In the light of these examples, it is of interest to review factors that may explain the conservative, or conservationist, rates of use that distinguish practice from theory.

Most forms of taxation establish incentive for a producer to select a rate of depletion that is lower than the one that would maximize the social value of a resource deposit. Since profit-maximizing output rises in response to higher prices, other things equal, imposition of a royalty will depress the rate of resource use. Other tax effects may be less visible; for example, tax treatment of depreciation will typically exert a downward bias on capacity. These effects are illustrated in the analysis by Bradley, Helliwell, and Livernois (1981) of mining taxation in British Columbia.

While tax effects are a factor in explaining the bias towards low rates of resource use, the basic explanation is, I believe, to be traced to the required investment capital. Analyses of the optimal rate of use of *resources* capital usually employ very permissive assumptions about investment capital: it is available in perfectly elastic supply, and it enters into the production function without allowance for scale economies or diseconomies. In view of the high capital intensity of extractive industries we must examine more closely how considerations relating to investment capital condition the rate of resource use. We will look at scale effects presently, but first we turn to capital availability.

The postulate of present-value maximization is usually used in conjunction with the assumption that capital is available in perfectly elastic supply. This framework is natural for analyses where certainty is assumed. In reality, producers obviously face risks associated with changing future prices, unanticipated variation in estimated reserves or producing conditions, and greater exposure to taxation than is typical for manufacturing. It is necessary, therefore, to consider how actual circumstances dictate modification of present-value maximization as an investment decision standard.

When we examine the variation in present value with rate of resource use, one observation seems fairly general: present value is not highly sensitive to the extraction rate over a rather broad range surrounding the optimal point. This is illustrated in figure 11.2 for the case of a hypothetical petroleum reservoir. In this particular example, if output is set at only half the rate that maximizes present value (the life of the reservoir is doubled), the loss in present value is only about 5 per cent. Indeed, if the output is reduced to one-quarter of the maximizing rate, value only falls by about 20 per cent. This latter rate approximates the one that would be prescribed by the decision rule of maximizing the net present value *per dollar invested.* This rule, though not normally appealing, may set a reasonable lower bound to observed rate of use, while the

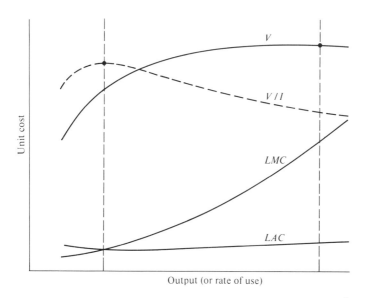

FIG. 11.2 Mine capacity, long-run cost curves. V = present value of reservoir; V/I = present value per dollar invested

maximum-present-value rule provides an upper bound. The salient point is that, with small and falling incremental return to additional investment, a risk-averse producer will probably opt to commit less capital and to operate at a lower rate than dictated by present value maximization.

The desirability of operating at a lower rate (lengthening the life of the mine) is strengthened by the irreversibility of most forms of mining investment. If forecasts of price and the nature of the mineral reserves do not prove unduly optimistic, the operator can expand capacity later.

The attractiveness of starting small receives further impetus because of the existence of other forms of risk beside those already mentioned. Increasingly, mining or petroleum development projects are situated in ecologically sensitive areas, for example, in the Arctic or on the continental shelves. They also may involve intrusion into unindustrialized areas, creating cultural and social problems for native peoples. Scott and Campbell (1979) have applied the term 'attenuation' to characterize the strategy of proceeding with mineral or petroleum development in small steps so as to gain 'learning-by-doing advantages' in dealing with ecological and human problems. The alternative may be a moratorium on development, exemplified in Canada by the recommendations of the Berger report.

Attenuated development must reduce the present value of receipts in most instances, since it is difficult to find documented rates of increase in real mineral values that exceed the social cost of capital. However, it seems likely that the crucial factor limiting the feasibility of attenuated resource development lies in the economies of scale to be obtained in the use of investment capital. This is not a subject area that has been traversed by many academic resource economists.

In our studies of copper mining in British Columbia, we related investment outlay to mining capacity and to milling capacity according to the type of formula widely used in engineering economics:

$$I = A \left(\frac{Q}{Q_0} \right)^k .$$

Values of the scale coefficient k were 0.85 and 0.60 for mining and milling, respectively. These are similar to values in process industries handling solids and fluids, respectively; they must seriously understate scale effects where access, product shipment facilities, and amenities must be developed. The degree to which attenuation strategies are practical (judged by the realized value of the resource) will probably hinge on scale economies associated with investment capital.

III

Discussion so far has been at the level of the establishment, that is, the exploitation of a particular ore body or petroleum reservoir. Homogeneity of the resource was assumed. However, even a single mine will typically contain varying grades of ore. Systematically taking first higher, then lower, grades of ore is not necessarily efficient unless nature has arranged them in that order of accessibility. The constraints imposed by the configuration of the deposit are particularly severe in open-pit mining (Bradley, 1980). In actual mining operations great attention is paid to obtaining the best ore as quickly as mining costs permit, but the configuration of the ore deposit is the most important factor in establishing quality variation over time.

If we now turn to the industry level of analysis, variation in resource quality becomes a critical consideration. Again, as in the earlier discussion of rate of use of a resource deposit, analysis based on the assumption of certainty yields interesting but not very applicable results. If exploration were cheap, so that we could 'inventory' reserve stocks, their exploitation could be ordered so that the differential rents would unfold smoothly through time: a resource would be used up when output from the last deposit was as costly as the best substitute. In reality, only a semblance of such ordering takes place. Differential rents at any point in time are an important aspect of the analysis of fuel and non-fuel mineral industries.

Differential rents appear even when the industry is defined over a relatively small geographical area. An example is provided in figure 11.3 which shows supply curves for open-pit copper mines in the Highland Valley region of British Columbia. The best two mines become profitable when copper prices yield a mine-site realization of 50 cents per pound. Two more become profitable at 75 cents per pound, while the fifth mine requires at least a dollar per pound.

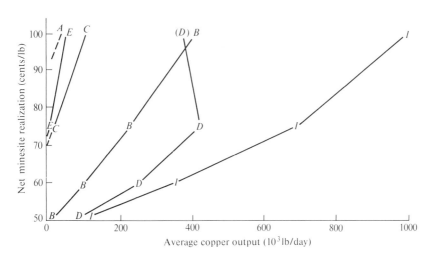

FIG. 11.3 Supply curves, individual mines and industry total. *A–E* are individual deposits, *I* is industry total. Output shown for each price is that which maximizes the present value of the mine to private investors, that is, the present value of after-tax returns. Points are in parentheses where maximum output constraint is binding. (*Source*: Bradley, 1980)

The presumption that differential rents are important is supported by the fact that, for both fuel and non-fuel minerals, physical parameters that are critical in determining production cost are observed to display wide variation across deposits. In many instances the lognormal distribution has been demonstrated to provide a tolerable description of this dispersion. The richness of ore is a principal determinant of hardrock mineral costs. For copper it has been held that the frequency of occurrence of ore bodies of a given grade can be described by the lognormal distribution (Singer, Cox, and Drew, 1975). For undergound coal mining, the critical cost-determining factor is seam thickness. The lognormal distribution has also been applied to this variable (Zimmerman, 1977). For petroleum there is an extensive literature in which the lognormal hypothesis is tested and applied to reservoir size.

Production costs are, of course, influenced by a variety of physical factors. The economics of working a particular deposit are governed by the extent to which these offset one another. Thus, a thin coal seam may be commercial if it is situated near the surface or can be drift-mined. Nevertheless, I suspect that the circumstances of figure 11.3 are the normal ones, with differential rents being significant.

Looking again at this figure, the price elasticity of supply can be attributed to output expansion at the extensive margin (additional mines) as well as at the intensive margin (within mines). That there is a significant extensive margin (another way of viewing differential rents) has obvious implications for policy, the most apparent being the attractiveness of intra-marginal resource rents as a tax base. That the extensive margin is significant underlies one observed feature of many mining industries: output expansion or contraction is borne by the marginal mines. The economic burden of cutbacks is therefore concentrated in particular communities or regions.

A vexing problem pertaining to resource use is explaining observed rates of exploration. Some writers have, with ample justification, stressed that the desire to pre-empt resources provides a strong bias towards excessive exploration effort, judged by the realized social value of the resource. Aside from this, what motivates exploration? Where pre-emption effects are not overriding, the value of a discovery is determined by comparison of its production costs against current and expected prices, in other words, the possibility of collecting differential rent. Inter-marginal rents that persist for long periods are observed; the possibility of finding the bonanza, the low-cost deposit, appears to be an important consideration in explaining exploration effort. The assumption that an industry moves systematically from low- to high-grade resources may be compelling from a very long-term vantage point, but provides doubtful foundations for a theory by which observed exploration rates might be explained.

IV

So far, a number of supply questions encountered in the extractive industries have been touched upon. Chief among these have been explaining observed rates of use (at the establishment level) and specifying supply curve character-istics (at the industry level). Related policy questions range from the broad issue of efficient use of resources to more specific issues such as tax policy, attenuation strategies, and employment stability. We might now consider what forms of economic analysis could be utilized in order to gain insight into these problems. In the opening paragraphs I noted that the central thrust of recent academic enquiry into the extractive industries has been in the style of Hotelling where the spotlight is turned on resource capital—specifically, allocation of stocks of various resources over time, given demand constraints and different forms of market organization. What alternative modes of analysis would shed light on some of the issues that loom large in applied work?

If man-made capital is an important consideration in the extractive industries, as argued in section II, then capacity costs and investment decision rules must be given a proper place in the analytical scheme. In dealing with capacity costs (operating costs present no problems), resource availability should enter the analysis as a constraint on the productivity of investment capital. By the time large capital expenditures are made—for example, mine shafts sunk or develop-ment wells drilled—the nature of the resource deposit is known to a fairly high degree of certainty. In cost theory terms, this resource constraint amounts to recognizing length of production run along with rate of output as jointly explaining unit cost.

This thinking is reminiscent of Armen Alchian's seminal article on cost analysis (1959). He argued that manufacturing costs have other basic deter-minants beside rate of output—in particular, total volume of output and the programmed delivery date. For manufacturing, the significance of the size of the production run has been recognized where product lines require large setup costs, but these circumstances have not warranted reformulation of cost measures. However, for firms producing exhaustible resources, the need to incorporate the volume element into cost analysis seems fundamental.

A method for including planned total output as an explanatory variable for cost has been discussed and employed elsewhere and need not be detailed here (Adelman, 1972; Adelman and Jacoby, 1979; Bradley, 1967). Average capacity cost is defined to be that realization which, when attained on every unit of planned output, will yield a cumulative present value equal to that of total capital expenditures. Thus the average cost measure is given by

$$AC = \frac{I}{PV(Q)}$$

where I = present value of capital expenditures $PV(Q)$ = present value of physical output. The corresponding marginal cost is

$$MC = \frac{\mathrm{d}I}{\mathrm{d}\{PV(Q)\}}$$

When capacity costs defined in this way are plotted against output, the resulting (long-run) curves can be expected to be U-shaped. To the left of AC_{min} declining costs reflect the predominance of economies of scale associated with man-made capital. To the right, rising costs indicate that such scale economies are dominated by the resource constraint, which requires that greater rates of output be associated with shorter production periods. The cost curves in figure 11.2 illustrate this behaviour; they were calculated based on reasonable assumptions describing a hypothetical petroleum reservoir.

Giving investment capital pride of place while not losing sight of resource constraints would be appropriate in the analysis of resource projects. It will be critical when examining the mega-projects currently being planned to produce and utilize petroleum resources in this country, especially when conflicts with non-economic interests make attenuation strategies appear attractive.

The mega-projects aside, decisions governing the use of extractive resources have traditionally been made by managers concerned with returns to private capital. Policy-makers concerned with the social value of fuel and non-fuel resources must reckon with private decisions made in response to the incentives established under various government leasing programmes and tax regimes. In recent work we compared two tax systems that have been imposed on the mining industry of British Columbia. When we considered their relative efficiency (a measure of the extent to which they distorted resource use from a present-value maximizing optimum) we found that differences were sometimes very substantial, depending upon the severity of tax rates. This type of comparison is illustrated in figure 11.4.

I fear that the assumption we relied upon in this work, that private decision-makers act to maximize present value, is inadequate. As already pointed out in section II, if the downside risk of exposure of large amounts of capital can be greatly reduced at modest cost to the expected value of a project, one can scarcely expect to observe rates of resource use as high as optimality (under certainty) would predict. In practice, uncertainty is typically dealt with by calculating project values (in present-value terms) conditional upon assumed future values for critical parameters, notably price. The capital investment decision is then based upon a subjective weighting by the decision-maker of the likelihood of various outcomes.

The needs of applied analysis would be served by studies of decision-making which would shed light on how industry risks are accounted for in the capital expenditure decision. The present thrust of resource theorists is to embellish the Hotelling theory of the mine with stochastic dynamic optimization. Whether the ultimate trickle-down will be helpful to applied economists is unclear. The emphasis, of course, remains on resource capital rather than investment capital.

When we turn from the mine (or establishment) level of analysis to the

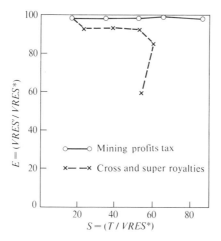

FIG. 11.4 Tax system efficiency *v*: total tax share of potential resource value. The efficiency measure, *E*, is the fraction of maximum attainable social value that is actually realized in the particular circumstances. The tax-share measure, *S*, is the fraction of maximum attainable social value that is taken by taxation. The comparisons are for a large open-pit copper mine in British Columbia, with the present and future net mine-site realization for copper assumed to be $0.75 per pound. (*Source*: Bradley, Helliwell and Livernois, 1981)

industry level, enormous problems emerge. If differential rents are important, as was insisted in the preceding section, industry analysis requires specification of supply curves. This poses severe practical problems. In some instances (the British Columbia copper industry is an example) it is feasible to try to assemble a supply curve by arraying estimates of cost and output for individual mines (Bradley, 1980). Another example of this type of modelling is provided by the paper by Campbell and Wrean in chapter 10 above.

Where the number of units is larger, it may be possible to aggregate deposits according to some specified rule—for example, petroleum reservoirs by field or by formation. A difficulty, if course, is that it is not clear that such categories as 'field' or 'formation' are valid groupings according to a production cost criterion. This is frequently taken as an article of faith, but it might better be dealt with as a testable hypothesis.

Over time, supply curves for a mineral industry are the resultant of offsetting forces—rightward shifts as new discoveries are made, leftward shifts as known deposits are depleted.[3] Given demand for the particular mineral, the position and slope of the supply curve evolves in accordance with the remaining resource base and the level of exploration effort. Examples of studies whose aim is to estimate the characteristics of the resource base are Uhler (1976) for crude oil and Zimmerman (1977) for coal. The crucial element of studies of this type is that the significant physical parameters that determine cost be identified and, further, that the values of these parameters be demonstrated to be distributed across deposits in some statistically regular fashion. The latter achievement makes it possible to map geological projections into economic ones.[4]

This paper has been concerned with identifying the kinds of analysis capable of yielding results that will improve our understanding of actual extractive industries—their viability, the tax base they provide, ways for modifying or mitigating their effects on natural or human environments, and structural factors that will influence market behaviour. Methods of analysis more sophisticated than those touched upon here will be called for, but I believe that economists would do well to begin by looking more closely at the extractive industries themselves. The marginal gain from taking more realistic account of the geological, engineering, and institutional characteristics of particular industries will be substantially greater that the marginal gain from further refinements in optimizing models, which continue to rely on unrealistic, 'stylized' assumptions.

ACKNOWLEDGEMENTS

Portions of this paper are drawn from an earlier working paper, 'Production of Depleting Resources: a Cost-Curve Approach', University of British Columbia Department of Economics, Resources Paper no. 41, 1979.

NOTES

1. P. J. Crabbé (1982) lists the assumptions that characterize the modern theory of the mine under certainty. With regard to investment capital inputs: 'Capital is assumed to be perfectly malleable and shiftable so that extraction capacity is never constrained.' This oversimplification has been addressed by more recent writers, including participants in this volume; see, for example, Campbell (1980) and Lasserre, chapter 6 above.
2. The Crabbé listing of assumptions that characterize the theory of the mine includes systematic depletion: 'Extraction and exploration are subject to a stock effect reflecting Ricardian decreasing returns, e.g., decline in the grade of the mineral, increasing difficulty of finding stocks, etc.'
3. This behaviour is detailed for the case of natural gas by Adelman (1962, pp. 15–23).
4. Forecasting based on this approach is perforce limited to the resource base of a region that is a geological entity. In this regard, the distinction between intensive and extensive margins emerges in exploration models; see Uhler (1975).

REFERENCES

Adelman, M. A. (1962), 'The Supply and Price of Natural Gas', *Journal of Industrial Economics,* supplement, Oxford: Basil Blackwell.
Adelman, M. A. (1972), *The World Petroleum Market,* Baltimore: The Johns Hopkins University Press.
Adelman, M. A. and Jacoby, H. D. (1979), 'Alternative Methods Oil Supply Forecasting', in R. S. Pindyck (ed.), *Advances in the Economics of Energy and Resources,* vol. 2, Greenwich, Conn.: JAI Press.

Alchian, A. (1959), 'Costs and Output', in M. Abramovitz and others (eds), *The Allocation of Economic Resources: Essays in Honor of B. F. Haley,* Stanford, Cal.: Stanford University Press.

Bradley, P. G. (1967), *The Economics of Crude Petroleum Production,* Amsterdam: North-Holland.

Bradley, P. G. (1980), 'Modelling Mining: Open-pit Copper Production in British Columbia', *Resources Policy,* March, 44–59.

Bradley, P. G., J. F. Helliwell, and Livernois, J. R. (1981), 'Efficient Taxation of Resource Income: the Case of Copper Mining in British Columbia', *Resources Policy,* September, 161–70.

Campbell, H. F. (1980), 'The Effect of Capital Intensity on the Optimal Rate of Extraction of a Mineral Deposit', *Canadian Journal of Economics,* 13, 349–56.

Campbell, H. F. and Wrean, D. L. (1982), 'Deriving the Long-run Supply Curve for a Competitive Mining Industry: the Case of Saskatchewan Uranium', presented at PNRE conference, 1982.

Crabbé, P. J. (1982), 'Sources and Types of Uncertainty, Information and Control in Stochastic Economic Models of Non-Renewable Resources', in G. Feichtinger (ed.), *Optimal Control Theory and Economic Applications,* Amsterdam: North-Holland.

Scott, A. and Campbell, H. (1979), 'Policies Towards Proposals for Large-scale Natural Resource Projects: Attenuation versus Postponement', *Resources Policy,* June, 113–40.

Singer, D. A., Cox, D. P. and Drew, L. J. (1975), 'Grade and Tonnage Relationships Among Copper Deposits', *Geological Survey Professional Paper 907A,* Washington: US Government Printing Office.

Solow, R. M. (1974), 'The Economics of Resources or the Resources of Economics', *American Economic Review,* 64, 1–14.

Uhler, R. S. (1975), 'Forecasting Petroleum Supply: Methods and Aggregation Bias', in D. Seastone and G. Linder (eds), *The Economics of Oil and Gas Self-Sufficiency in Canada,* University of Calgary.

Uhler, R. S. (1976), 'Costs and Supply in Petroleum Exploration: The Case of Alberta', *Canadian Journal of Economics,* 9, 72–90.

Zimmerman, M. B. (1977), 'Modelling Depletion in a Mineral Industry: The Case of Coal', *Bell Journal of Economics,* 8, 41–65.

Comment Gardner Brown, Jr

The major theme of Paul Bradley's paper is a simple one. The essential features underlying actual mining decisions differ so fundamentally from those derived from theoretical accounts that the latter greatly hinder our ability to characterize mining decisions empirically and to evaluate pressing public policy options. It is therefore a misallocation of intellectual resources to fiddle further at the margins of the simple optimizing models, investigating, for example, how the extraction path is altered if a parameter describing marginal variable cost is changed. The focus for research is, or should be, elsewhere, and Paul Bradley directs the reader to the key building block for the next wave of investigations on the extraction of non-renewable resources.

On the whole, I subscribe to Paul Bradley's theme, and there is evidence that some contemporary investigation is headed in the desired direction (viz. Pierre Lasserre's chapter 6 above). It is a pity that Paul ran out of space before turning his wise mind and mature intellect to set forth more promising ways of attacking the problems he raised.

Acknowledging the palpable fact that mines require large outlays for mine shafts, transport systems, and other fixed capital leads to the conclusion that the rate of extraction is roughly constant over time and is not tilted towards the present as the simple models suggest. Introducing scale economies and uncertainty about the size of the resource deposit and the future demand and supply makes the investment decision in non-natural resource capital even more interesting, Bradley believes.

One feasible way to understand the practical consequences of uncertainty may be to begin by incorporating into a model with fixed costs and scale economies the possibility that at some future date the demand for the resource might fall dramatically, or the value of the stock might depreciate suddenly, owing to the discovery of a substitute. Here the models of Dasgupta, Stiglitz, and others featuring arbitrage equations with chance shocks can be modified to include the initial capital requirement. The substantive point about these formulations is that introducing the assumption of an unfavourable event leads to the resource price rising at a rate faster than the discount rate but starting out at a lower initial value. The value is lower because a marginal unit today is worth less, when there is some chance it will be worth less in the future, compared with the alternative of no chance of worthlessness. A lower initial shadow value leads to a greater extraction rate earlier on, but this rule has to be modified by the fact that it takes higher initial investment to support the higher initial extraction rates.

In contrast to theory, the truth is that firms cannot always pick off the high-quality sites first. Sometimes the high-quality sites are found after extraction has begun from lower-quality sites. We also draw from a distribution of qualities, perhaps a lognormal one. Typically, a mixture of qualities is obtained; that is, the combination of qualities are locked together, particularly at early stages of production. The consequence of allowing for joint production (joint in quality) is to draw a sharp distinction between the efficiency consequences of a profit tax versus a royalty tax. This conclusion follows from the ambitious simulation studies of open-pit copper mines in British Columbia, that Bradley, Helliwell, and others have undertaken in recent years.

Bradley argues that observed rates of extraction, which are often lower than those obtained in the empirical models, follow not so much from an incentive to substitute the tax bite towards the future as from the magnitude and scale economies associated with the initial investment. Although output is greatly different, profit rates are not. Bradley's example involves a loss of present value of about 5 per cent when actual output is one-half the optimum. Surely this result depends critically on the facts of life, particularly the choice of discount rate and customary length of life of a mine. More explanation would help us to better understand these surprising results.

Turning to exploration, how would the location and rate of exploration be described if:

1. the size of discovery is a random variable?

2. the average quality of discovery is a random variable?
3. the qualities found cannot be unbundled?
4. a process such as smelting depends on average ore quality discovered whereas the marginal cost of extraction does not vary with ore quality?
5. initial unit capital costs fall with the size of discovery?

These are more realistic assumptions, and ought to be worked into next-generation models. If simple closed-form solutions do not exist, some researchers should turn to numerical solutions, not to different questions.

Bradley mentions pre-emption in passing as a reason for exploration. Another related motivation for exploration is to deter entry. When a firm or group of firms has regional (or broader) market power, it may use exploration to maintain its market advantage. Greater rates of exploration produce a greater stock of the resource. Rivals are deterred from entry not because access to ore has been denied—rivals may be pursuing alternative technologies—but because the owner (with market power) can drop price to ward off entry and sustain the price drop longer with greater stocks of resources. The origin of this argument is Spence (1977). The static case has been broadened to encompass non-renewable resources by Newberry (1978), Dasgupta (1980), and others.

The emphasis in this paper is on a single firm or a group of firms so small that their behaviour has no effect on price. This leads to the question of how to study a slice of a market in a way that is consistent with observed aggregate market behaviour through time. Needed, therefore, is greater analysis in which there is a market-clearing process. How do n firms behave? How does each pick initial capital outlay? How does the outcome vary with the number of firms? These questions suggest an attractive research programme.

There is, in my judgement, an error of commission and one of omission in this paper. The latter, mentioned earlier, is my wish that Bradley had told us not only what is wrong with what is being done, but also, more specifically, how it might be rectified. The second problem, if it exists, has to do with the explanation of a mine (firm) producing at a constant rate of extraction, as is mentioned in this paper. The assumptions in the paper are as follows.

1. The mine is too small for its rate of extraction (q) to affect unit price of extraction (P).
2. Investment (K_0) must be chosen initially. No additions to capital stock are permissible. There is no resale value for K_0.
3. A fixed amount (say, 1 unit) of capacity is required per unit of extraction.
4. There is a simple extraction cost function. The marginal cost of extraction is constant. In the model below, it reduces detail to assume that price is net of constant marginal extraction cost. The cost of initial capital is $\psi(K_0)$.

The current value Hamiltonian is

$$H = \{(p - \lambda)q - \psi(K_0) + \mu(K_0 - q)\}e^{-\ell t}$$

where ℓ = the discount rate, λ is the adjoint variable associated with the resource constant $\dot{S} = -q$, and μ is attached to the constraint that the extraction rates cannot exceed the level of capital.

$$\frac{\partial H}{\partial q} = P - \lambda - \mu = 0. \tag{1}$$

Extraction should be set equal to $q_t = q_{max} = K_0$. When $P - \lambda - \mu < 0, q = 0$. The result of a constant extraction rate does not depend on whether a large or small amount of initial capital, $\psi(K_0)$, is needed, or on whether there are economies of scale in initial capital, since positive and constant extraction is not dependent on K_0 in (1), although the rate of extraction is.

When the marginal cost of extraction is increasing in rate of extraction, there is an optimal capacity which creates a constraint on the rate of extraction for an initial interval of time. In a competitive economy capacity is added until the shadow value of the capacity constraint, summed over the duration of the constraint, equals the marginal cost of capacity.

Campbell shows that, under plausible assumptions, even when the marginal cost of extraction is not constant, the period during which the rate of extraction is constant can be quite a large fraction of a mine's total working life. The problem that remains is the extent to which economies of scale or high unit cost of capacities influence the length of the constant production run. As the marginal cost of capacity capital increases, it pays to substitute variable inputs and purchase lower-capacity capital. The capacity constraint will be binding for a longer period and the life of the mine will be extended. If economies of scale mean that the marginal cost of a unit of capacity is falling over some range, then one expects higher rates of output over a shorter duration and a shorter life of mine compared with a constant marginal cost of capacity.

The roles of economies of scale and high unit capital costs in the context of the mine are interesting to study in greater detail. It is a more interesting puzzle when there is uncertainty about future prices or extraction costs.

REFERENCES

Bradley, P. G. (1980), 'Modelling Mining: Open-pit Copper Production in British Columbia', *Resources Policy*, 6, 44–59.

Bradley, P. G., Helliwell, J. F., and Livernois, J. R. (1981), 'Efficient Taxation of Resource Income: The Case of Copper Mining in British Columbia', *Resources Policy*, 7, 161–70.

Campbell, H. F. (1980), 'The Effect of Capital Intensity on the Optimal Rate of Extraction of a Mineral Deposit', *Canadian Journal of Economy*, 13, 349–56.

Helliwell, J. F. (1978), 'Effects of Taxes and Royalties on Copper Mining Investment in British Columbia', *Resources Policy*, 4, 34–44.

Newbery, D. (1978), 'Sleeping Patents and Entry-deterring Inventions', unpublished paper, Churchill College, Cambridge University.

Spence, M. (1977), 'Entry, Investment and Oligopolistic Pricing', *Bell Journal of Economics,* 8, 534–44.

Stiglitz, J. and Dasgupta, P. (1980), 'Market Structure and Resource Extraction Under Uncertainty', Research Memorandum no. 262, Princeton University.

PART VI
IDEOLOGIES AND INSTITUTIONS

Introductory Note

Anthony Scott

In this Part are assembled four long papers or comments. These, going beyond the application of economics to natural resource questions, explore how society organizes itself to manage natural resources. Historically, social science has identified several grand schemes of social organization based on the need to deal with land and resources. The European feudal system, seen as a method comprehending military fiefs, property tenure, agricultural duties, and land incomes, is one of these. Another scheme would be the social systems of the ancient Middle East, centred on the allocation and husbanding of irrigation waters.

In this context, the system of common law property rights tenures could also be viewed as a social device, one that has evolved along with changing technology and increasing land scarcity to permit the market system to rationalize production. Still another would be an energy-centred economic system, using energy units as a unit of account, or even of exchange. In their studies of how this system works, scholars have found it useful to make comparisons with other systems of holding rights to use land and resources. Unfortunately, by choosing to contrast the well-developed system of agricultural land rights with the non-exclusive common law rights to pump irrigation water or catch ocean fish, scholars have lost the opportunity to compare like with like. Much more could be learned by comparing rights to farm land with other exclusive rights, such as those over trees or minerals.

Both comparisons are touched on here. Scott's paper distils a reconnaissance study that examines mineral and timber tenures in the common law, while Vernon Smith's comment extends his earlier conjectures about the decline of common-property hunting and collecting tenures. Scott attempts to conduct his analysis without the aid of the usual guiding principle of property analysis: that the evolution of tenure types always proceeds so as to increase economic efficiency. (This tradition, popularized by the Chicago–Los Angeles schools of law and economics, is hard to escape.) Smith also attempts some explanation of the processes by which resource property systems may have evolved and proposes some new systems.

To many, the paper by Berndt would be viewed as dealing with an even more fundamental question: the measure of value. The environmental revolution and the later energy crisis focused attention on an energy unit as the logical common denominator in the natural world. One group saw the transfer of energy among organisms in water and air bodies as the link that unified the ecology into a 'seamless web' where everything literally depended on everything else. The second group, basing themselves on the same thermodynamic laws as the first, originally considered energy units as the fundamental elements in a system of technocratic planning that might replace the market system and property altogether. Berndt's paper traces these ideas from their genesis with the influential Technocracy Inc. movement to their re-emergence among modern energy analysis, and criticizes the latter. Trudy Cameron suggests that it is possible to go too far in condemning modern 'energy analysts', and shows some sympathy with the engineers who propose it. She concludes that, while both factions have ventured strong and valid criticisms of the opposition's approach, each must concede that their own has some shortcoming for all the uses to which they wish to apply it.

12. From Technocracy to Net Energy Analysis: Engineers, Economists, and Recurring Energy Theories of Value

Ernst R. Berndt

INTRODUCTION

Pragmatically, a way to begin would be to set up a capability in government to budget according to flows of energy rather than money. Energy is the all-pervasive underlying currency of our society.

US Senator Mark Hatfield (1974, p. 6076)

In 1974 the Congress of the United States passed Public Law 93.577, the Federal Non-nuclear Energy Research and Development Act, in which it was stipulated that all prospective energy supply technologies considered for commercial application must be assessed and evaluated in terms of their 'potential for production of net energy'[1]—energy output minus the energy costs of producing that output. This is a rather interesting piece of legislation, for in effect it states that engineering-based net energy analysis should provide the criterion for evaluation of prospective commerical energy supply technologies, rather than conventional economic cost–benefit analysis, even when the latter is adjusted for externalities and market imperfections.

In response to the mandates of this legislation, net energy yields of geothermal, gasohol, and a variety of renewable and non-renewable energy supply technologies have been undertaken and published (see Gilliland, 1975; Chambers *et al.*, 1979; Hannon, 1980). Controversy among net energy analysts has arisen regarding whether net energy for nuclear power is positive or negative.[2] Net energy analysis has also enjoyed considerable publicity from the business press.[3]

One of the leading proponents of this legislation, Senator Mark Hatfield of Oregon, interpreted it as one step towards energy replacing money as a standard of value. Hatfield (1974, p. 6074) argued that 'Energy is the currency around which we should be basing our economic forecasts, not money supply . . . .' Hatfield's statement followed the much publicized proposal in 1973 by the engineer Bruce M. Hannon, who called for the adoption of an energy standard of value:

The adoption of a national—and consequently a personal—energy budget appears to be necessary. The annual budget would represent a portion—dictated by our value of the future—of the proven energy reserves. Individual allocations could be similar to that of our present economies, which reflect personal values, except that we would have to strive for the right to consume energy; the accrued currency would be regulated by the amount of energy budgeted for a given period. If less energy existed at the end of the period, then currency would have to be reduced proportionately during the next period; of course, an increase of currency flow would follow an abundance of energy. Recognition of the value of energy is equivalent to setting energy as the basis or standard of value. In doing so, society readmits itself into the natural system in which acknowledgement of energy's importance has never been lost. [Hannon, 1973, p. 153]

This recent call for the adoption of an energy standard of value is not, however, the first time such a proposal has been aired in the United States. About fifty years ago, in the midst of the Great Depression, *Harpers Magazine* published an article, 'Technology Smashes the Price System', by the industrial engineer Howard Scott, who stated that:

It is the fact that all forms of energy, of whatever sort, may be measured in units of ergs, joules or calories that is of the utmost importance. The solution of the social problems of our time depends upon the recognition of this fact. A dollar may be worth—in buying power—so much today and more or less tomorrow, but a unit of work or heat is the same in 1900, 1929, 1933, or the year 2000. [Scott, 1933, pp. 131–2]

Scott and the fascinating Technocracy Movement he founded proposed that dollars and money be replaced by energy certificates denominated in units such as ergs or joules, equivalent in total amount to the appropriate national net energy budget, which could then be divided equally among all members of the North American Continental Technate. The Technocrats argued that apolitical, rational engineers should be vested with authority to guide the nation's economic machine into a thermodynamically balanced load of production and consumption, thereby doing away with unemployment, debt, and social injustice.

The proposal to replace money with an energy standard of value is therefore a recurring phenomenon, and at least recently has enjoyed some political success. Professional economists, however, have been notably cool to the notion of an energy theory of value and to the idea that dollars should be replaced by ergs. Most economists believe that the allocation of scarce resources such as energy is the very issue that economic analysis deals with best of all. Although some economists might view net energy analysis as engineering-based encroachment on the territorial domain of time-honoured economic analysis, most economists tend not to take it seriously at all. After all, such energy analysis is essentially an energy theory of value, and why should one take seriously any movement that simply replaces Marx and the discredited labour theory of value with Carnot and thermodynamics? Energy is but one of many scarce inputs, and the beauty of the market price system is that it provides incentives for the combined wise use of all scarce inputs, not just energy.

But if the economic arguments against an energy theory of value are so compelling, why do such proposals appear again and again? While the answer to that question is not yet clear, in this paper I attempt to provide a better understanding of net energy analysis, Technocracy, and the reasoning underlying energy theories of value. I do this because I believe it well worth our while to understand paths rejected by economic analysis, and not just to comprehend those paths accepted and well-trodden. Moreover, it is useful to place current debates over net energy analysis within an historical perspective.

The plan of this paper is as follows. In the next section I provide an overview of net energy analysis and other recent variants on the energy theory of value. This is followed by a brief history of the fascinating Technocracy Movement, a review that by necessity will be considerably less than complete. In the fourth section I compare, contrast, and assess the technocracy and net energy analysis movements. Finally, I comment on the reasoning underlying recurring energy theories of value.

RECENT VARIANTS ON THE ENERGY
THEORY OF VALUE

. . . energy cannot be treated as just another input. Malcolm Slesser [1978, p. ix]

Although recent advocates of the energy theory of value are a heterogeneous group, almost all believe that energy is unique, all-pervasive, and critical. Energy is the most important input, certainly more important than labour. Not only has human labour been replaced by energy-driven machines, but man himself can be viewed simply as a machine transforming the calories of food into work, albeit in an inefficient manner.

The pervasiveness of energy has recently been emphasized by Jeremy Rifkin (1980, p. 241): 'Because everything is energy, and because energy is irrevocably moving along a one-way path from usable to non-usable forms, the Entropy Law provides the framework for all human activity.'[4] The pervasiveness of energy, along with its uniqueness, makes energy the ideal commodity for a standard and measure of value. Writing in a 1975 issue of *Science*, Martha Gilliland argued:

Since energy is the one commodity present in all processes, and since there is no substitute for it, using energy as the physical measure of environmental and social impacts, of material, capital, and manpower requirements, and of reserve quantities reduces the need to compare or add 'apples and oranges'. [Gilliland, 1975, p. 1051]

Moreover, the energy unit is potentially much more stable than the dollar, for the energy involved in work is an unambiguous and unchanging measure of what has been accomplished. According to ecologists Howard T. Odum and Elizabeth C. Odum (1976, pp. 58-9), money as a measure of value is rejected because externalities are not properly incorporated by the market pricing mechanism: 'Money is inadequate as a measure of value, since much of the valuable work upon which the biosphere depends is done by ecological systems, atmospheric systems, and geological systems that do not involve money.' Modern adherents of energy theories of value tend to view all goods and commodities as embodied or sequestered energy. Embodiment of energy, however, occurs in two different senses. First, much like Marx's labour theory of value, in which all commodities represent concealed labour, in the accounting sense commodities can be measured by the direct energy input into their production plus the indirect energy input embodied in capital, material, and other inputs.[5]

The second sense in which energy tends to be viewed as embodied or sequestered in materials is as thermodynamic potential. From the basic principles of physics and chemistry, it is known that materials have thermodynamic potential which changes as the materials pass through various states in productive processes, encountering heat energy and/or work.[6]

In principle, the sequestered energy of commodities could be measured using process analysis techniques, a procedure by which material and energy balances are described in great detail during each step of a specific physical transformation process. Process analysis is a classic tool of the industrial process engineer, particularly in the chemical process industries such as petrochemicals, aluminium, metallurgy, and iron and steel.[7] In the context of energy flows, three features of process analysis models are of particular interest.

1. All the numbers necessary to develop a complete energy flow balance of the process are available to the process engineer, or else can be estimated accurately from the principles of physics and chemistry. Indeed, maximum possible energy efficiency for the process can be calculated using the laws of thermodynamics.

2. The process engineer is myopic in the sense that he is not interested in what went on before his process inputs reached him, nor is he interested in what happens after his products and wastes leave his plant. The system boundaries of the process analysis model typically coincide with the particular industrial plant. Impacts on upstream or downstream energy flows that might be caused by changes made within the plant are not captured in the process analysis model.

3. The process analyst is typically not privy to how his energy balance compares with those of processes at other locations, which implies that he does not have complete knowledge of the whole industry. As a consequence, an accurate process analysis description for the industry as a whole is not in general attainable. In order for the detailed data and analyses of specific plant processes to be useful for broader industry-wide energy calculations, the specific process data of each plant would have to be made available to some central entity. David E. Gushee reports that, as of March 1976,

only one industry—iron and steel—has been able to develop such a central capability, at Arthur D. Little, Inc., in Cambridge, Mass. The data and mathematical model are held in tight secrecy to protect the proprietary individual company data, and not all the process units in the industry are represented although the majority (130 out of 139 plants of members of American Iron and Steel Institute, representing 99% of total AISI production) are. (Gushee, 1976, p. 7]

In summary, while process analysis models could be useful in assessing detailed changes in embodied or sequestered energy on a plant-by-plant basis, the inherent problems of narrow system boundaries and competitive isolation render them less accurate for broader issues such as calculating changes in embodied energy on an industry-wide basis. Hence their potential usefulness for implementing embodied energy pricing is limited. Moreover, not all processes are amenable to easy modelling and detailed physical description. Although manufacturing processes are most easily modelled, manufacturing processes in 1974 accounted for only about 25 per cent of the US gross national product, and about one-third of the nation's energy consumption (Myers and Nakamura, 1978, p. 4). For non-manufacturing processes such as agriculture, great difficulties are encountered when attempting to measure energy degradation accurately: 'Where the system is extremely complex, as in the growth of plants, or in human nutrition, we simply do not know enough to estimate the entropic contribution to free energy to better than one order of magnitude even when we can measure the energy [heat] contribution fairly accurately.'[8]

Undoubtedly, modelling and accurate measurement of energy degradation in sectors such as wholesale and retail trade, finance, insurance and real estate services, government, and government enterprises would be even more difficult; in 1974 these sectors together accounted for approximately 60 per cent of US gross national product.

Since data requirements at the industry-wide level are immense, and since the activities within a large number of industries are not easily amenable to detailed physical--chemical process analysis, it has been suggested that an alternative albeit less accurate procedure to model and account for energy flows would be to employ economic statistics found in input--output (I-O) tables.[9] I-O tables do not measure energy transfers, although figures on the dollar costs of fuel and electricity inputs are published. Nor do they indicate the functional end-use of energy inputs, such as feedstocks, process heat, space heat, or electric lighting. Hence with I-O data it is virtually impossible to model accurately changes in the quality of energy, or the extent of its degradation; the necessary process and functional end-use information is simply not available.

However, the important advantage of the I-O energy accounting framework over the process analysis models is that with I-O tables the system boundary is much larger. Not only can I-O analysis describe, for example, direct energy consumption in the motor car manufacturing sector, but it also includes 'first-round' indirect energy consumption in the iron and steel industry, plus 'second-round' indirect energy consumption in the mining of ores, and so forth. Indeed, indirect energy equals the limit of an infinite sum of such indirect items. The total direct plus indirect energy requirements for production of a commodity corresponds to a notion of the embodied or sequestered energy of a commodity; analysts often call this its *gross energy requirement*.

It should be noted clearly at this point that calculations of gross energy requirements using such I-O techniques are quite different from the embodied energy notions of thermodynamics. Instead of measuring energy degradation (depletion of free or available energy), for practical reasons of data availability and at times the sheer lack of scientific knowledge, practitioners of I-O gross energy analysis measure only the heat (enthalpy) attributes of energy.[10]

Considerable empirical work has been published which estimates gross energy requirements of certain commodities, based on the I-O tables. Bruce Hannon's (1972) pioneering study of container recycling is noteworthy in that it also attempts to assess income redistribution effects of rising energy prices by examining direct plus indirect energy expenditures. Additional examples of I-O studies include those of Robert Herendeen (1973), Hirst and Herendeen (1973), and Bullard and Herendeen (1975).

An additional development in energy accounting emerged from the simple observation that it takes energy to get energy. Concern over whether new energy technologies would produce less energy than they consume (directly plus indirectly) has led to the practice of *net energy analysis*:

Net energy analysis of an energy supply system involves identification and computation or measurement of the energy flows in a society that are needed to deliver energy in a particular form to a given point of use. These flows are then compared to the energy converted or conserved by the particular system under consideration. [Perry, Devine, and Reister, 1977, p. 1]

Martha Gilliland has proposed that the net energy ratio—energy output over direct plus indirect energy output—should be used to define an upper bound for fossil fuel reserve measurements. As Senator Hatfield and many others have stressed, current reserve estimates tend to be 'gross' rather than 'net' (see Gilliland, 1975, pp. 1053-4; Hatfield, 1974, p. 6074; and Odum, 1973).

Net energy analysis received wide public attention in the mid-1970s, when a debate took place concerning whether the net energy ratio for nuclear power was greater or less than unity.[11] More recently, in response to the mandates of federal legislation in the United States, net energy analysis has expanded to consider the net energy yields of other non-nuclear energy supply systems; see, for example, Gilliland (1975, p. 1053) for a study of geothermal, and Hannon (1980) for a comparison of a number of renewable and non-renewable resources. Net energy analyses of gasohol have reached widely divergent conclusions, owing, apparently, to different assumptions regarding systems boundaries and computational techniques (see, e.g., Chambers *et al.,* 1979, p. 795).

For purposes of calculating embodied energy and implementing energy theories of value, it is clear that gross energy requirement calculations would be more useful than the net energy analyses of energy supply systems. Suppose, however, that a nation determined it would maximize its net energy—the amount of energy remaining after the energy costs of finding, producing, upgrading, and delivering the energy have been paid. As has been shown succinctly by David A. Huettner (1976), the traditional competitive price mechanism would yield such a maximum net energy situation if and only if all products were priced solely on the basis of their gross (embodied) energy, i.e., only if a complete energy theory of value were implemented.[12]

This result highlights the important fact that notions of gross (embodied) energy requirements, net energy analysis, and an energy theory of value are very closely related. Indeed, it can be argued that net energy analysis makes no contribution at all unless it is motivated by an energy theory of value. Despite this logical problem, it should be pointed out that not all net energy analysts seek to identify themselves with an energy theory of value. Clark W. Bullard III, for example, states: 'While some practitioners of net energy analysis may subscribe to an energy theory of value, there is nothing about the quantitative methods proposed here that demand it' (1976, p. 381). At the International Federation of Institutes for Advanced Study (IFIAS) Workshop on Energy Analysis and Economics (1975), sensitivity regarding the association between net energy analysis and energy theory of value notions led workshop participants to conclude that 'The principal goal of energy analysis is the development of a portion of the precise physical description of the operation of real-world processes. This description does not supplant that of economic analysis, but supports and complements it and may provide new perspectives.' (p. 7). Specifically, participants in that workshop speculated that energy analysis might furnish signals of impending critical situations more quickly than the market, might require less time than economic analysis, would provide a more understandable specification of technological constraints than economic analysis, and would yield conclusions less sensitive to variations in prices. Participants also noted that the presence of externalities and market imperfections might render the market and economic analyses less useful and valuable for policy analysis. Some energy analysts compared net energy analyses of energy supply systems to environmental impact statements, since both introduce 'considerations that are not easily translated into economic terms' (Perry, Devine, and Reister, 1977, p. 3).

Critics of energy analysis, particularly economists, have of course pointed to the critical logical relationship between net energy analysis and energy theories of value. Moreover, after noting that energy analysis offers no assistance with the difficult problems of intertemporally allocating resources in finite supply, and that energy analysis faces aggregation problems similar to those encountered in economic analysis, Michael Webb and David Pearce (1975) state, 'Thus we must conclude that EA [energy analysis] as now formulated and practised does not have any use beyond that which is currently served by some other analytical technique' (p. 331).

In summary, recent advocates of the energy theory of value have cited the unique, pervasive, and critical features of energy, and have attempted to measure sequestered or embodied energy using the techniques of process analysis and net energy analysis. Hence embodied energy pricing would in principle be possible through use of such energy accounting procedures. However, it is a well-known analytical result in economic analysis that a competitive price mechanism will maximize net energy if and only if all products are priced solely on the basis of their relative gross embodied energy, i.e., if and only if a complete energy theory of value were implemented. This has created a serious problem for net energy analysis, for in effect it means that the notions of maximizing net energy and an energy theory of value are logically equivalent.[13]

TECHNOCRACY: A BRIEF HISTORICAL BACKGROUND[14]

Having briefly reviewed recent literature on measuring gross and net energy in order to implement energy theories of value, I now discuss earlier experiences with energy theories of value. Many of the themes underlying recent net energy analysis and energy theories of value were enunciated already half a century earlier by the Technocrats. Moreover, as we shall see, the gross energy requirement calculations undertaken by modern net energy analysts represent to some extent the fulfilment of dreams in the minds of these earlier advocates of an energy theory of value. To understand better the Technocracy Movement in the United States and Canada, it is useful to begin by reviewing the political, economic, and intellectual environment of the early twentieth century.

Much of the optimisim of progressive intellectuals in the first two decades of the twentieth century was grounded in the view that increasing industrialization and growth of the corporate form of organization could be directed rationally to bring about important social change in which injustice and class conflict would be abolished. Although progressives were a heterogeneous lot, one stream of progressive thought pointed clearly towards centralized, expert planning and administration. Disagreement arose as to whether government or the corporation was the appropriate institution for organizing the new society, but substantial consensus emerged that centralized planning would necessarily be guided by experts.

During this same period of time, a new generation of formally educated engineers began to appear, some of whom paralleled and interacted with the larger progressive movement. For example, Frederick W. Taylor and his scientific management disciples argued that the shift in factory and society from arbitrary power to apolitical, scientific administration would bring about the long-sought realization of social harmony (see Taylor, 1911). The central figures in such revolutionary change would of course be the professional technicians —industrial engineers, who bypassed traditional authority and operated out of planning departments, free from business and political interference, and who organized human affairs in harmony with natural laws.

Mobilization during the First World War provided further evidence to progressives and like-minded engineers in support of national planning, political non-partisanship, the separation of administration from business pressures and politics, and reliance on experts. As William Akin (1977) has noted, 'Mobilization directed by the wartime planning boards, staffed by nonpartisan experts, apparently balanced efficiency and the nation's well-being, planning and democracy. Was there any reason why such policies, if beneficial in war, should not be equally valuable during peacetime?' (p. 4).

One important theme of the progressive engineering movement was that engineers and technicians, not bankers and businessmen, were to be regarded as the sources of necessary expertise. Although initially unconnected with the progressive engineers, Thorstein Veblen effectively echoed these sentiments, particularly in *The Engineers and the Price System* (1921).[15] Like the engineers, Veblen honoured machine technology and mechanical rationality. To Veblen, engineers embodied ideal traits for the new social order: rationality, efficiency, scientific analysis, and workmanlike qualities. Business, however, was much different than industry. While industry was concerned with the common good, maximum production, peace, workmanship, efficiency, and matter-of-fact rationality, business was inextricably focused on pecuniary gain, the maximization of profits, waste, idle capacity, and coercion. According to Veblen, although businessmen were incapable of understanding the logic of technological progress, the engineer–technician fully understood and appreciated its rationality. Hence, to Veblen, control of industry must be transferred from businessmen to engineers.

Veblen began to explore the practical possibilities of organizing engineers for the revolution when he arrived at the New School for Social Research in New York in the autumn of 1919. The only engineer prominent in an informal discussion group centred at the New School was Howard Scott, a radical young man who sought, among many other plans, to form an organization of technicians, a 'technical alliance', to conduct an industrial survey of North America. Veblen became convinced that such a data-gathering project was the necessary first step toward engineers gathering control. This, he hoped, would 'bring the population to a reasonable understanding of what it is all about' (p. 150), and would provide engineers with data concerning energy resources, materials, manpower, and production—information that would enable them to determine objectively the most efficient and rational means of running industry.

Although little was known about Howard Scott's early life, he claimed to have been educated in Europe and to have had considerable experience as an industrial engineer. Flamboyant, lean, and 6ft 5in. tall, Scott lived in Greenwich Village and established himself 'as a kind of bohemian engineer' (Akin, 1977, p. 28). In 1920, as an outgrowth of his discussions with Veblen at the New School, Scott and some of his friends established a formal organization called the Technical Alliance, opened an office, and published an eight-page prospectus. The important research tasks of the Technical Alliance were to be accomplished by an extensive industrial survey of 'three-thousand leading commodities', which would chart changes over the past century in industry employment, productivity per employee, horsepower capacity, and horsepower used in production. A unique feature of the survey would be its attempt to measure production and waste in terms of horsepower or kilowatt-hours, rather than in the more conventional measures of labour expended or monetary costs.

The Technical Alliance lasted only about a year, breaking up in the spring of 1921 owing to financial difficulties and internal dissension. Members went their own ways, and only Scott remained, 'expounding his theories to anyone who would listen' (Elsner, 1967, p. 26). In the meantime, and into the early 1930s, Scott ran a floorwax business and preached to all who would listen that the price system would collapse imminently, that it must be replaced with a distribution system based on energy accounting, and that only technicians could provide the necessary technical expertise to manage such a system.[16]

In 1931 or early 1932, a young geophysicist named M. King Hubbert came from Chicago to be an instructor at Columbia University. Hubbert met Scott in New York, was most impressed by his ideas, and sought to give them a more firm scientific basis. According to Elsner (1967, p. 26), Hubbert 'paid Scott's back rent, moved in with him, and set about re-establishing something like the old Technical Alliance—an attempt that culminated in the Energy Survey of 1932'.

Apparently it is not clear yet precisely how Scott first met Walter Rautenstrauch, chairman of Columbia University's prestigious Department of Industrial Engineering. Rautenstrauch was an early advocate of the scientific management ideas developed by Frederick W. Taylor; he identified himself with the progressives' sense of social concern, and believed deeply that engineers should be responsible not only to their employers, but also to all of society. Although he was trained as a mechanical engineer with special interests in machine design and became a distinguished academic, Rautenstrauch felt that the university curriculum should be devoted more to specific problems of industrial research and industrial engineering, issues that in his view were not adequately dealt with at Columbia's School of Mines, Engineering and Chemistry. In 1916 Rautenstrauch persuaded Nicholas Butler, then president of Columbia University, to establish a Department of Industrial Engineering, the first such university department in the United States (Akin, 1977, pp. 46-51).

The depression convinced Rautenstrauch that the time had finally arrived when engineers must accept their social responsibilities and develop plans for solving the nation's crisis. To him, the malfunction of the socioeconomic mechanism was an engineering problem whose solution required technical expertise. Like most other such engineering problems, the first step was to assemble data to facilitate evaluation and to determine the feasibility of proposed solutions. Rautenstrauch quickly realized that he required a far more exhaustive industrial survey than could be accomplished by his students (Akin, 1977, pp. 56-60).

Initial contacts between Howard Scott and Walter Rautenstrauch proved to be mutually beneficial. In Scott, Rautenstrauch found an industrial engineer who shared a similar interest in an industrial survey, and who had in fact been at work on such a survey off and on for a decade. For Scott, contact with the distinguished Rautenstrauch provided renewed enthusiasm for the industrial survey. In summer of 1932 Rautenstrauch obtained permission to conduct a survey under the auspices of the Department of Industrial Engineering; he called it the Energy Survey of North America, and appointed Scott as director. A Committee on Technocracy—a research organization to conduct an empirical analysis of production and employment measured in terms of energy expended —was formed to supervise the project.[17] This committee included, among others, Rautenstrauch and M. King Hubbert. Funding was obtained on the dole from the Architects' Emergency Relief Committee of New York. Clearly, to Howard Scott, association with Columbia's prestigious Department of Industrial Engineering provided a much more credible public forum than the coffee-houses of Greenwich Village.

Although Rautenstrauch publicly announced formation of the Committee on Technocracy using cautious academic language, Howard Scott was considerably less restrained. Within weeks, he recorded a sensational interview with the *New York Times*. Scott told reporters that industrial engineers, of whom he was one, had been working for more than a decade on an analysis of the industrial and social system in the United States, measuring activity using energy consumption rather than dollars, since the latter was a 'rubber yardstick' (*New York Times*, 6 August 1932). Results of research indicated, according to Scott, that, because of the substitution of kilowatt-hours and machines for manhours, technological developments had been so violent that the whole economic mechanism had been thrown out of gear; even if a 1929 scale of operations were resumed in 1933, only 55 per cent of the workers thrown out of employment by the depression would be re-employed. The problem, according to Scott, was that production and consumption were no longer being balanced. Such a highly technical exercise could not be accomplished using elastic monetary units of measurement, but instead must be done using energy accounting and the technical principles of science.

Insisting that the industrial survey work of the past twelve years had been carried out quietly, 'without reference to the social, political or sentimental aspects of the problem', Scott defended his decision to make public the research findings in late 1932 because the researchers belived that violent collapse of the industrial system was inevitable and imminent unless engineering principles were applied:

The difference between this depression and those of the nineteenth century rests in the degree of speed at which the industrial system was traveling. The system of the past may be likened to a slow-moving oxcart which suffered a little damage in collision with a tree. The present highly mechanized system, however, by comparison resembles a high-speed racing car hurtling down a highway. When the car collides with an obstacle the resulting wreck is in proportion to the mass and velocity of the vehicle. In other words, the larger and more highly powered the industrial system, the more rigorously exacting must be its technical control in order to avert a wreck. [*New York Times*, 6 August 1932]

According to Scott, while orators might appeal to people and sway public opinion, they were impotent when it came to handling the vast mass of energy unleashed by modern science. Finally, concerning future research by the Committee on Technocracy, Scott indicated that a start had been made towards charting 3000 industries—roughly 150 had been completed to date; about

100 men would be employed at Columbia during the 1932–33 winter to finish the project.

So provocative and sensational an interview, backed as it seemed by the authority of the scientific method and the prestige of Columbia University, naturally created a great stir. Instantaneously, Scott became a celebrity, entertained by Wall Street barons and the nation's leading industrialists, sought after by the editors of *Time* and *Fortune* as well as by numerous other journalists. *Business Week* carried his portrait. Hordes of the curious descended on Columbia (Raymond, 1933, pp. 23–4).

Shortly thereafter *The New Outlook* published an article by Wayne Parrish, 'What is Technocracy?' which elaborated on Scott's interviews. According to Parrish, 'this civilization on the North American continent must be operated on a thermo-dynamically balanced load', and 'all social problems of North America today are technological' (Parrish, 1932, p. 17). Parrish concluded his article by stating: 'Technology has written "mene mene tekel upharsin" across the face of the price system' (p. 18).[18]

With such sensational interviews, prophesies of imminent disaster, and provocative magazine articles, Technocracy rapidly captured the attention and interest of the nation. The 23 January 1933 issue of *Time* (p. 28) devoted substantial space to the Technocrats, noting that in the previous week Technocracy had been cartooned (funniest: a technocratic hen laying an 'erg'); had been scorned by engineers ('Cleverest pseudo-scientific hoax yet perpetrated'— American Engineering Council); and economists ('Greenwich Village economics —University of Chicago); had made publishing houses scramble for interpretations; and had caused a store in Monrovia, California, to place a sign in its window, 'Pre-Technocracy Clearance Sale'. Cardinal Hayes of New York questioned the wisdom of Technocracy making public its preliminary research results. for 'it has introduced a disturbing element in an already sorely distressed world' (*New York Times*, 24 January 1933).

National leaders extensively discussed the theories of Scott and the Technocrats in articles and magazines. Liberal economist Paul H. Douglas summarized the Technocrats' energy theory of value as follows:

Commodities would be priced according to the amount of energy consumed in producing them. The sum total of prices would therefore be the number of millions of horsepower or kilowatt-hours of energy which had been expended. . . . The members of society would then be given energy cards, which would resemble suburban railway tickets, entitling them to purchase commodities with these energy quotations. As the purchase was made, the requisite number of energy units would be punched from or torn off the card. By the time the card was used up, the commodities would have passed into the hands of their final purchasers and the money units would also have disappeared from circulation. Here again, it is argued, consumption would balance production and depressions and unemployment would be avoided. [Douglas, 1933, pp. 59–60]

Douglas's final appraisal of Technocracy was a cautious one:

The Technocrats . . . underemphasize the great practical and theoretical difficulties which would be attendant upon the use of 'energy prices' . . . Particularly difficult would be the evaluation of services. How much energy, for example, would be involved in a surgical operation, the extraction of a tooth, the playing of a Beethoven concerto, the delivery of a lecture? . . . Technocracy is, therefore, as utopian as the theories of Owen and Fourier. . . . . it is necessary to combine the engineers with the labor movement before any real and fundamental change can be made. [p. 61]

Similar but even more sympathetic criticisms were voiced by Stuart Chase, a widely read economist and earlier disciple of Veblen:

Whenever a critic desires to refute any body of doctrine in this republic, he says, first, that it is inspired from Moscow; second, that it is against human nature. Technocracy, it appears, is both and immediately is endeared to me. At the same time I should like to know where the service trades fit in, and how a painting is to be measured in ergs. I can readily comprehend an energy system confining itself to physical things, like a water system confining itself to supplying the people of a given system with water. But as Technocracy's analysis stands, it accounts for only about half, or to be generous, two-thirds, of the present economic total. . . . I cannot, therefore, take my energy economics straight. [Chase, 1933, pp. 31–2]

Dr Karl T. Compton, president of the Massachusetts Institute of Technology, criticized technocracy for neglecting human factors in industrial management and for having given a misleading picture of the replacement of men by machinery. Compton believed instead that 'adequate sponges' could be found to 'sop up' any technological unemployment owing to increasing mechanization. The automobile and the radio were such new industries in the recent past, and 'new ideas of home building and air conditioning' might be similar new industries in the near future (quoted in Raymond, 1933, pp. 170-1).

Leaders of alternative radical movements in the early 1930s were notably less enthusiastic in their reactions. For example, Paul Blanshard pointed out that:

The amusing thing in the whole technocratic epidemic is that Socialists have been saying ninety-five percent of what the Technocrats say for a decade, and saying it better, but the American public has gone on believing that socialism has something to do with free love, anarchy, and the dividing up of all the world's wealth equally among workers and loafers. . . . Socialists must go on using the new stimulus to thought in Technocracy and pointing out how socialism has a program and a movement for economic reconstruction, whereas Technocracy has only a few significant footnotes. [Blanchard, 1933, pp. 188–9]

Norman Thomas, the 1932 Socialist candidate for President of the United States, described the Technocratic arguments as 'inadequate, though very illuminating' (Thomas, 1933, p. 10). A Marxist reviewer pointed out that 'What has popularized Technocracy is not the simple content, but the esoteric quality of science in which it is wrapped', then complained that 'the indebtedness of the Technocrats to Marx is everywhere patent and nowhere acknowledged', and finally concluded 'The Technocrats tinkle on a xylophone, while Marx played on a mighty organ (Mitchell, 1933, pp. 281, 283).[19]

A particularly slashing attack on Technocracy was authored by Virgil Jordan, an economic and social writer who called the Technocrats 'slide-rule Mussolinis'. Jordan rationalized the sudden popularity of Technocracy as follows:

While there is no justification in any facts that technocracy has assembled or in any of its speculations for any forecast of the future course of events in this or any other country, we are obviously eager to believe them at their face value because our faith in ourselves has been shaken. We just want to believe in Santa Claus, even though he is only a technocratic Kris Kringle. [Jordan, 1933, p. 69]

He then added that:

The technocratic trinity is the erg, the electron, and entropy. Energy is its jealous Jehovah. There is no God but the kiologram calorie and the engineer is his prophet. Its gospel is the second law of thermodynamics; the technocratic testament is written in statistical tables and charts and its catechism in differential equations. If Mr Scott is not precisely the Technocratic Christ, at least he is the engineering John the Baptist who has been living in the economic wilderness for forty years feeding on logarithmic locusts and wild-honey. [p. 66]

On a more serious vein, Jordan objected to Technocratic suggestions that their industrial survey was based on an hitherto-unanalysed microeconomic data base, and noted instead that 'they are based largely on familiar census data, with rough and ready estimates of such items as man-hours for which no accurate data are available at all, and there is nothing new in them to anyone who has any acquaintance with industrial statistics' (p. 67).

The most scathing critique, however, was that by Archibald MacLeish:

The infantile cowardice of our time which demands an external pattern, a non-human authority, has manufactured a new nurse. And that nurse is the Law of Physics. One mechanistic nipple replaces another. The economic determinism of Marx gives way to the scientific imperative of Mr Scott . . . All that is required of man in the Technocratic World is to submit to the laws of physics, measure all life by the common denominator of physical energy, discard all activities which are not susceptible of physical mensuration, and wait for the 'next most probable energy state'—the millenium. It is a picture shrewdly painted to appeal to American babbittry with its childish longing to believe in Science and Scientific Truths and Scientific Thinkers. But it is about as attractive to a man of human appetites as a patent antiseptic gargle. And about as nourishing. [MacLeish, 1933]

To Howard Scott, the most damaging publicity was the revelation uncovered by the New York *Herald Tribune* investigative journalist Allen Raymond, who discovered that, contrary to impressions held by Scott's research associates Walter Rautenstrauch, M. King Hubbert and others, 'Doctor' Scott had never earned an advanced academic degree.[20]

Within weeks, a somewhat embarrassed Rautenstrauch announced that Scott had been ousted as Director of the Energy Survey of North America, that the engineering research group at Columbia University with which the technocratic group had been associated had been 'formally taken over' by the Department of

Industrial Engineering and would 'hereafter be undertaken as a scholarly enterprise of the university which up to this time had merely been host to the technocracy group'. Scott responded by stating that 'My past does not matter as far as technocracy is concerned. The idea is bigger than any individual. The work will go on' (*New York Times,* 24 January 1933, p. 1).

The breakup of the committee appeared to many observers, especially the eastern press, to signal the end of Technocracy; the 'technocraze' was over, they believed. In fact, it was not over. Technocracy continued and indeed grew, albeit in a different form, particularly in the Midwest, the Far West and in western Canada. Specifically, by late 1932 and early 1933, Technocracy had become a widespread movement. Independent and uncoordinated technocratic organizations emerged spontaneously, articulating programmes that differed in many respects, but uniform in their view that power must be unequivocally vested in the engineers.

Now excluded from Columbia, in March 1933 Howard Scott and his associates formed a separate body incorporated as Technocracy, Inc. M. King Hubbert was named Director, Division of Education, and began writing a technocracy study course, intended to be the authoritative and definitive statement of technocracy doctrine and a text for guiding neophytes through technocratic theory.[21] Organizing activities of Technocracy, Inc. were directed by William Knight, an aeronautical engineer associated with an American subsidiary of a German aircraft company. The Technocracy, Inc. insignia, reproduced in figure 12.1, was called the monad and signified the Technocracy, Inc. concern with balance between production and distribution.

Under the direction of Knight, Technocracy, Inc. shifted toward a paramilitary organization. Howard Scott replaced his flamboyant, non-conformist Greenwich Village dress with Knight's new technocracy uniform: a tailored, double-breasted suit, gray shirt, and blue tie, with a monad insignia on the lapel. Akin (1977, p. 101) reports that one writer present at the time noted that 'all the Technocrats were saluting him (Scott) in public'.

Scott, Hubbert, and others continued to develop the Technocratic blueprints in greater detail, and Hubbert in particular maintained his empirical research activities on energy and mineral consumption, production, and employment. In 1937 Technocracy, Inc. released further details on its plan to replace money with energy certificates. Energy certificates would be issued, the total amount of which would 'represent the total amount of net energy converted in the making of goods and provision of services'. The aspect of energy to be measured was its ability to do work (availability), not its heat content.[22] Net energy was to be calculated as follows:

All operating, replacement, maintenance, and expansion costs (in energy) of the Continental complex, all costs of commerical services and provisions (such as local transportation, public health, and minimum housing space for each individual) are deducted before the net energy is arrived at. . . . The conversion of human energy does not enter into this calculation since it amounts to below two percent of the total consumer energy. [Technocracy, Inc. 1938, p. 12]

FIG. 12.1 The monad of Technocracy, Inc. (*Source*: Technocracy, Inc., 1975)

Distribution of energy certificates (an example of which is shown in figure 12.2) was socialistic—an equal part of the total net energy would be allocated to every adult above twenty-five years of age, and special allowances were envisaged for younger individuals. Debt would no longer exist. According to Technocracy, Inc.,

The certificate will be issued directly to the individual. It is non-transferable and non-negotiable, and therefore it cannot be stolen, lost, loaned, borrowed, or given away. It is non-cumulative, therefore cannot be saved; and it does not bear interest. It need not be spent but loses its validity after a designated time period. [Technocracy, Inc. 1938, p. 13]

When individuals purchased goods and services, certificates would be surrendered and perforated appropriately, thereby making record-keeping relatively straight-forward.

Because the engineers of technocracy sought to organize and direct economic activity within a geographical region nearly self-sufficient in resources and with a highly developed technology, the geographical boundaries of the Continental Technate were to include Canada, the United States, Mexico, and portions of

THE TECHNATE OF ⊙ NORTH AMERICA

DISTRIBUTION CERTIFICATE   180

William Smith   **1976-77**

9038·L·16794	8141	8·33···16·3	22···11
13090-23	205···21·05	H·76302	Z·97321
34·46···11·E·7·8			

The Distribution Certificate

IT IS   a Medium of Distribution
A Continental Accounting System
24 Hour Inventory
Identification and Record of Holder
Guarantee of Security

IT IS NOT   a Medium of Exchange
Subject to Fluctuation of 'Value'
Subject to Theft or Loss
Subject to Hoarding or Gambling
A Means to Wealth or Prestige
A Means of Creating Debt

FIG. 12.2 The proposed energy certificate. (*Source*: Technocracy, Inc., 1975)

South America to the north of the Amazon River basin (the geographical bound-aries of the Technate are shown in figure 12.3). An additional reason for this choice of boundaries was that to the Technocrats, hydrology was very important; a system of rivers and interconnecting canals was envisaged to provide abundant

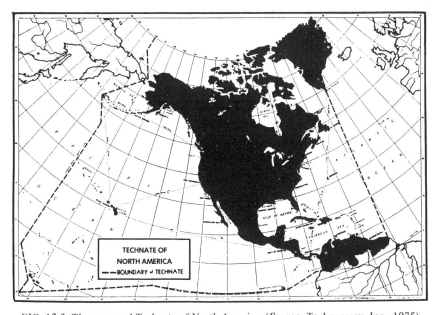

FIG. 12.3 The proposed Technate of North America. (*Source*: Technocracy, Inc., 1975)

hydroelectric power, low energy-cost water transportation of bulk commodities, and raised water tables in drier portions of the continent. Incidentally, Technocracy also proposed to limit population growth, prohibit immigration, and for reasons of efficiency permit only one language, a position that won considerable political support in western Canada (see Technocracy, Inc., 1975).

The Technocractic movement was still active in the late 1930s (both Technology, Inc. and the Continental Committee on Technocracy), and was marked by considerable local independence. Los Angeles, Denver, Washington state, and British Columbia had particularly active local organizations. Occasionally continental conventions were held. Interest in Technocracy, Inc. gradually waned, however, as the forecasted disasters failed to materialize, the New Deal gained popularity, and other radical third-party political movements allowed a restless people alternative direct and immediate political actions. The paramilitary and isolationist developments within Technocracy, Inc. resulted in statements by Howard Scott that leaders of Canada and the United States must be 'notified in no uncertain terms' not to become involved in the Second World War, and that 'Americans who conspire to make war off this Continent are guilty of Continental Treason' (as quoted in Elsner, 1967, pp. 142, 144). Later Scott announced that 'neither Canada nor the US could discuss war without permission of this organization'. In response to the perceived goal of technocracy to 'overthrow the government and constitution of this country by force', and because of Technocracy's opposition to conscription, on 21 June 1940 Canadian Prime Minister Mackenzie King announced in Parliament that an Order-in-Council had been issued which banned Technocracy, Inc. in that country.[23]

Scott's views mellowed little, if at all, in later years. To an audience at the University of British Columbia, he preached that one must choose either for or against Technocracy: 'If you don't make your decision now, if you hesitate and waver, after the manner of the intellectual liberal, you will have your decision made for you at the muzzle end of rifles in the hands of thirty-six million unemployed that there will be in the next depression' (quoted in Elsner, 1967, p. 198).

Technocracy, Inc. continued as an organization throughout the 1940s, 1950s and 1960s.[24] Howard Scott died in 1970, and was succeeded as Continental Director by John T. Spitler. Technocracy, Inc. is still active today, particularly in the West, where three magazines are published regularly: *The Technocrat*, in Long Beach, California; *The Northwest Technocrat*, in Seattle, Washington; and *Technocracy Digest*, in Vancouver, British Columbia.[25] Its continental headquarters reside in Savannah, Ohio. M. King Hubbert, well-known today as a petroleum geologist, retained an association with Technocracy until the late 1930s (see Hubbert, 1940, 1949). It is worth noting, incidentally, that Hubbert's much-publicized accurate prediction in 1956 that US annual oil production would peak somewhere around 1970 was based on his analysis of bell-shaped curves, a research procedure he initiated while serving as Director, Division of Education, at Technocracy, Inc. (see Hubbert, 1950, 1956, 1962, 1978, 1980). Although presently retired, Hubbert still maintains an active interest in issues addressed by the Technocrats in the 1930s (see Hubbert, 1963, 1974).

COMPARISON AND ASSESSMENT

There are obvious similarities between the fascinating Technocrats of the 1930s and recent adherents of energy value theories, even though the political and economic contexts differed dramatically. Some of the similarities and differences are worth examining in greater detail. I begin with similarities.

First, both Technocrats and energy analysts believe the authoritative laws of nature are not properly appreciated and respected in contemporary democratic and economic affairs, and that the possible consequences of continued lack of respect could be disastrous. This attitude tends to generate mistrust and occasionally contempt for democratic and market systems. In his 1931 *Harpers Magazine* article, Howard Scott, argued:

What does price mean in a country where 0.44 of a simple pound of coal can do the work that the average man can do in eight hours? It matters not a rap what men think, wish, or desire. We are face to face with a law of nature . . . There are no physical factors in existence which would prevent the efficient operation of this continent on an energy basis. The only thing that does prevent it is our devotion to a shibboleth-price; and it remains to be seen whether we shall pay for our devotion with our lives. [Scott, 1933, pp. 141, 142]

Similarly in 1977, net energy analyst Michael Common (1977) chimed that '. . . people's preferences cannot alter the laws of nature' (p. 146) and in 1978 science writer Malcolm Slesser (1978) added 'The price system does have one disadvantage. It is possible to conduct one's entire affairs without regard to the physical world' (p. 6).

Second, antipathy towards the price system extends to economists. Both Technocrats and net energy analysts have singled out economists as myopic apologists of the status quo who are unaware of the primacy of the laws of nature. According to Howard Scott:

It has been our great misfortune that in our disaster the only people that we have had to look to for guidance—now that distrust of the banking fraternity has become so widespread—have been the economists. These have ranged all the way from such stock market necromancers as Irving Fisher to the emotional popular economists who dream of a new state founded on a Russian model. Fundamentally the economists, Marxians, and all are as archaic as the bankers, for they are tied hand and foot to a conception of price. [Scott, 1933, p. 141]

In the *Technocracy Study Course* M. King Hubbert called economists apologists for businessmen; in particular, he singled out the 'professional apologists for our status quo' at the Brookings Institution (see Technocracy, Inc., 1934, pp. 99, 100). More recently, Howard T. Odum and Elizabeth C. Odum (1976) charged that 'the economists have not been educated in energetics and therefore have not understood the second law of energy and the fact that energy is not reused' (p. 226). Science writer Malcolm Slesser criticizes economists, since they 'tend to take technological progress for granted as if they could buy their way around the laws of thermodynamics' (1978, p. ix). Hence, antipathy towards economists is common both to Technocrats and to net energy analysts.

A third basic agreement among Technocrats and certain net energy analysts concerns the choice of prescription to replace the inadequate money price system: an energy standard. The Technocrats, it will be recalled, strongly advocated the notion that a central planning authority should issue energy certificates to individuals on an egalitarian basis. The reasoning underlying egalitarianism in technocracy is derived from the energy depravity of man—the energy degradation cost of maintaining a human being substantially exceeds his ability to repay. According to Hubbert,

> we can abandon the fiction that what one is to receive is in payment for what one has done, and recognize that what we are really doing is utilizing the bounty that nature has provided us. Under these circumstances we recognize that we all are getting something for nothing, and the simplest way of effecting distribution is on a basis of equality, especially so when it is considered that production can be set equal to the limit of our capacity to consume, commensurate with adequate conservation of our physical resources. [Hubbert, 1940, p. 28]

Similarly, in 1975 net energy analyst Bruce Hannon suggested that the government should distribute energy coupons to individuals. Hannon's notion was not as explicitly egalitarian: although the federal government would own energy resources and would sell individuals energy coupons (1975, p. 101) Hannon does not specify how purchasing power would be distributed.

Fourth, a principal agreement among the Technocrats and recent energy theory of value adherents is that energy and man-hours have been substituted as inputs. For example, the Technocrats reported in 1933 that 'technology has now advanced to a point where it has substituted energy for man-hours on an equal basis' (Arkwright, 1933, pp. 58-9), while in 1975 Bruce Hannon noted that 'in general, most United States industries are trading labor for energy— that is, becoming more energy-intensive and less labor-intensive' (Hannon, 1975, p. 145).

However, primarily because social and economic conditions varied dramatically in the 1930s and 1970s, some very important differences exist between the Technocrats and recent energy analysts. These differences are especially apparent in their analyses of unemployment. The Technocrats attributed unemployment to an 'under-consumptionist' condition, while net energy analysts cite it as being due to energy scarcity and an allocation problem. In particular, Scott and his fellow Technocrats viewed the extensive unemployment of the late 1930s as a result of automation and energy–labour substitutability. Believing that future energy supplies would be abundant and that more energy–labour substitutability was inevitable, they concluded that the problem facing North

America was to devise a measurement system of distribution for abundant goods and services to a people whose labour, sweat, and toil was no longer necessary. Once production was balanced with consumption through the use of energy accounting and energy certificates, sustained prosperity could emerge. Abundance and prosperity would be the norm. By contrast, the perceived energy scarcity, high energy prices, and substantial unemployment of the mid-1970s meant, to Bruce Hannon and his fellow net energy analysts, that energy conservation was the most important policy initiative. Because of energy–labour substitutability, either regulated or price-induced shifts in consumer demand away from energy-intensive goods would result in reduced unemployment. Moreover, since net energy analysts often noted that pollution was directly related to energy and heat consumption, less energy consumption implied potential beneficial environmental effects. Hence, in terms of principal emphasis, Technocrats viewed energy certificates as solving the problem of aggregate demand and overall *distribution,* while more recent adherents of energy theories of value view energy certificates as facilitating *allocation* between labour and increasingly scarce energy.

A second major difference between the Technocrats and recent energy theory of value adherents concerns their perception of the international environment. Technocracy presented itself in the United States during an isolationist period in US foreign policy when autarky seemed feasible. The Technocrats, for example, defined geographical borders of the North American Continental Technate in such a way that they believed energy self-sufficiency would be possible. Also, the Technocrats sought to prohibit immigration and to allow only the English language. By contrast, recent net energy analysts face a situation where energy and environmental problems appear inherently global in scope, and where self-sufficiency refers to the 'spaceship earth' rather than to any single country or continent.

A third difference between Technocrats and net energy analysts regards the concept of net energy. Although both used the term 'net energy', their notion of it differed significantly. To modern energy analysts, net energy is essentially the energy remaining for use outside an energy system after deducting all the energy embodied in the system and all the energy required by the system for operation and maintenance. To the Technocrats, however, net energy was a smaller number. It is the modern energy analyst's net energy figure, minus the energy consumption embodied in public provision of numerous services within that system, such as local transportation, public health, and minimum housing space.

Fourth, the political success of Technocracy was quite different from that of net energy analysis. Although the Technocratic Movement enjoyed a sudden rise to prominence in the 1930s, its proposals for government rule by technocrats and distribution via energy certificates never received extensive support. This is not surprising, for in a democracy it is inherently difficult to obtain widespread agreement with a notion of government by a selected elite, however knowledgeable they may be. Writing in 1933, Virgil Johnson stated that 'The people of these states may be in a pretty bad pickle, but they are probably not prepared to call in any men on horseback, even if these are all messiahs with an ME' (p. 69). But Al Smith (1932) reflecting on the presidency of Herbert Hoover, offered I think the definitive reason why Technocracy never gained hold as a political movement: 'As for substituting engineers for political leaders in running the country, I cannot refrain from mentioning the fact that we have just finished an era of government by engineers in Washington' (p. 12).

Modern adherents of an energy theory of value may never have been as organized politically as were the Technocrats, yet in 1974 net energy analysis was enthusiastically advocated by a respected US Senator and was successfully legislated into federal law. Today it is a mode of policy analysis common among engineers and technologists. In brief, net energy analysts appear to be more successful in policy analysis and influence than were their ancestors, the Technocrats. Reasons for this difference might include the facts that net energy analysts have not been as obviously elitist; they have adherents with professional credentials (the lack of which seems to have hurt Scott and the Technocrats); and they have had the support of many in the allied and better-organized environmental movements.

Finally, although there are various differences and similarities between them, net energy analysts have undertaken computations that can be viewed as a natural extension of technocratic thinking. Specifically, the gross energy requirement calculations of modern energy analysts can be viewed as the most ambitious attempt to date to fulfil Howard Scott's dream of completing an energy survey of North America. Such calculations yield estimates of the direct and indirect energy embodied in all goods and services, and thereby lay the groundwork for implementing an energy theory of value. Scott would likely have marvelled at the detailed 362-order input–output tables of the US economy and the even more disaggregated regional Canadian I–O tables, but even he would probably have been rather uneasy about the energy data. Recall that Scott and his fellow Technocrats sought to measure production costs on the basis of the degradation of energy quality, not on the basis of heat (enthalpy). Modern energy analysts might respond by saying that they agree with Scott's views, but data availability and at times lack of underlying scientific knowledge presently preclude implementation of complete economy-wide energy quality accounting.

CONCLUDING REMARKS

In the previous sections I have described recent variants on the energy theory of value (particularly net energy analysis), provided a brief history of the extremely interesting Technocratic Movement in the United States and Canada, and then compared and contrasted the technocratic and recent energy theories of value. The merits of doing any additional economic analysis of these energy theory of value movements here are to a great extent limited, since political associations such as technocracy and the allied net energy-environmental movements in large part reflect widespread frustrations, ideologies, and divergent group interests, rather than consistent economic arguments. Moreover, like many political movements, Technocracy was dominated by a highly visible leader, Howard Scott, and flavoured by his personality, rather than being led by the rules of logic and on the basis of intellectual foundations constructed with scholarly rigour. None the less, the idea of an energy theory of value has risen to prominence from time to time, and it seems appropriate to comment on why this phenomenon recurs.

Energy theories of value occur from time to time for a number of reasons. First, when the market pricing system is perceived to be functioning extremely poorly, alternative institutions will be discussed and considered. This certainly was the case in the 1930s, and to some extent again in the 1970s when energy shortages suddenly appeared. Moreover, the environmental movement so popular in the 1970s taught the public that the market pricing mechanism often failed to internalize important externalities such as pollution. Since in many industrial processes pollution is closely related to heat and energy consumption, it is understandable that discontent with excessive pollution could lead to a view that energy use is correlated with environmental damage, that much energy is 'wasted', and that consumption of scarce energy ought to be reduced considerably.

A second and closely related reason why energy theories of value may occur from time to time is that the layer of public belief in consumer sovereignty is, I suspect, in fact quite thin and can easily be pierced. From time to time the public has indicated its willingness to accept 'expert guidance' and regulations to protect innocent consumers from 'exploitation' by greedy and 'unprincipled' market participants. Public belief in the notion that consumption and production patterns of today's firms and consumers adequately provide for the welfare of future generations of consumers not yet born is certainly not strong. Mistrust in the ability of the pricing mechanism to allocate apparently finite energy sources over time may make more plausible an energy theory of value, particularly when energy sources are dominated by imperfectly competitive firms.

A third reason why energy theories of value recur is because the public well understands that there *is* something special about energy. However, these special features of energy do not, I believe, imply any need for an energy theory of value. Let me briefly consider three specious arguments offered in support of an energy theory of value. First, consider this argument: 'Energy is unique and natural as a measure of value, for it provides an unambiguous and unchanging measurement unit, namely, the measurement of physical work.' That the production and output of a nation's economy should be measured in terms of energy consumed and/or transformed is understandable; for if one is willing to view production as the completion of a task requiring work, then it may seem eminently reasonable to measure work the way physical scientists do, namely, in terms of the amount of energy degraded. In a number of industries (such as petrochemicals, aluminium, metallurgy, iron and steel, and electric utilities) it is possible to define tasks in a physical manner so that 'oputput' can be measured in terms of energy degraded or materials transformed. But many, indeed, an increasing number of activities in modern post-industrial economies, are not amenable to precise physical task definition and energy quality measurement. For example, the outputs of activities in wholesale and retail trade, consulting, finance, insurance and real estate, services, the government sector, the performing arts, and educational institutions are extremely important, are highly valued by society, but are not easily measured by energy degradation. In brief, while many tasks can be well defined in physical terms and can therefore be measured in work or energy units, the outputs of a large and growing number of activities in service-oriented economies are not amenable to accurate energy degradation measurement.

Now consider a second specious argument often offered in support of an energy theory of value: 'Since energy is homogenous, measurement of production based on an energy standard would avoid what Howard Scott called the "rubber yardstick" features of the conventional monetary pricing mechanism. Hence energy measurement would avoid "adding apples and oranges" ' (*New York Times*, 6 August 1932). This argument seems to be a premise of almost all net energy analysts, even those who may not subscribe to an energy theory of value. While it is of course the case that the b.t.u is a well defined physical unit and is homogeneous, it is quite a different matter to state that society is indifferent to a thousand b.t.u.'s of natural gas and a thousand b.t.u.'s of coal, i.e., that their value to society is identical. What is being confused here is the unit of measurement, which is homogeneous, and the phenomena being measured (values). Value is a multi-dimensional phenomenon. Attributes such as weight, cleanliness, safety, heat content, security of supply, amenability to storage, relative costs of conversion and co-operating end-use technology, and capacity to do useful work are all important; the various energy types (coal, crude oil, natural gas, electricity) differ in their attribute combinations, and so their value to society also varies. In terms of value, a b.t.u. of coal is not necessarily the same as a b.t.u. of crude oil or a b.t.u. of electricity. When energy analysts undertake to evaluate projects using the criterion of net energy, various energy types are aggregated using b.t.u. conversion rates; i.e., it is assumed that all b.t.u.'s are identical in value to society. Clearly, this is inappropriate. Problems of adding 'apples and oranges' or coal and crude oil would not be solved by changing from dollars to energy units.

A third argument in defence of an energy theory of value is more subtle: 'There are no substitutes for energy. Hence it is imperative that scarce energy stocks be valued and allocated on the basis of net energy content.' There are a number of problems and errors in such an argument. It is simply not the case that there are no substitutes for energy. The rate of energy degradation can be reduced in numerous ways, for example, by use of increased home insulation, more fuel-efficient motor cars, more energy-efficient appliances, replacement of conventional oil or gas home furnaces with heat pumps, and many others. While each of these examples of energy substitution involves increased use of physical capital equipment, which also embodies energy, undoubtedly it is the case that there are numerous possibilities for which the net impact on the rate of energy degradation is negative; i.e., energy–capital substitution possibilities are numerous. According to the Second Law of Thermodynamics, there are ultimate limits to the extent to which energy–capital substitutability can take place, but at the present time second law efficiency measures for many tasks are on the order of 10 to 15 per cent. These low second law efficiency measures partly reflect particular and somewhat inappropriate assumptions (for example, the absence of friction and the infinite passage of time), but they also indicate that a great deal of technological potential still exists for energy conservation.[26]

Although numerous technological opportunities exist for energy–capital substitutability, a substantial proportion of them may be unattainable for economic reasons. Other things being equal, energy-efficient appliances are more costly than the less energy-efficient models. Home insulation is not free. Many fuel-efficient motors require greater maintenance and fine tuning than the less fuel-efficient engines. Although driving 55 miles per hour consumes less fuel than at 65 miles per hour, slower driving exhausts a greater amount of scarce time. Solar panels require use of scarce and costly minerals and ores. Clearly, energy is not the only scarce input; capital, labour, minerals, and other material inputs are also scarce. According to economic analysis, value is determined both by demand and by production costs incurred through the combined wise use of all scarce inputs, not just energy. Hence, while in some sense energy may be an ultimate limiting factor, for the foreseeable future energy is but one of many scarce inputs. Indeed, other resources could be depleted long before energy exhaustion is approached.[27]

In summary, this third specious argument in support of an energy theory of value is attractive, for there is something special and unique regarding energy. However, such uniqueness does not imply any need for an energy theory of value. Many activities in our economy today are not amenable to accurate measurement in terms of energy degradation; problems of adding apples and oranges, or coal and natural gas, are not avoided by converting from dollars to energy units; and it is simply not the case that energy is non-substitutable.

There are other reasons why the public may from time to time become receptive to physical-science-based energy theories of value. One reason is that economic analysis is admittedly still rather vulnerable. It is no secret that real-world markets are quite different from the perfect markets typically envisaged by economic analysts. While recent econometric models represent great achievement and may be viewed by some as being enormously successful, significant problems still remain (see Thurow, 1981). Because of data availability and sheer size constraints, the econometrician, like the net energy analyst, faces difficult choices in relating the microeconomic process analysis data at the level of an individual firm or plant to macroeconomic phenomena such as national input–output coefficients, employment, output, and inflation. In economics, as in energy analysis, the bridge from micro to macro is somewhat precarious. Moreover, as is well-known by most engineering economists, econometric models are typically naive in their specification of environmental and technological constraints.[28] A great deal of work, jointly among physical scientists and economists, needs to be done in modelling more accurately and convincingly the physical and environmental constraints to economic activity. Even more important, perhaps, is the fact that, to both engineers and economists, factors affecting the complex and uncertain process of technological progress are still largely unknown.

Finally, when all is said and done, energy theory of value movements are likely to arise in a democratic society simply because individuals with strong convictions will have different sets of value, and from time to time these value judgements will concern the allocation of scarce energy resources over time. According to Nicholas Georgescu-Roegen,

All this calls for a radical change of the values everywhere. Only economists still put the cart before the horse by claiming that the growing turmoil of mankind can be eliminated if prices are right. The truth is that only if our values are right will prices also be so. We had to introduce progressive taxation, social security, and strict rules for forest exploitation, and now we struggle with anti-pollution laws precisely because the market mechanism by itself can never heal a wrong. [Georgescu-Roegen, 1978, p. xix]

ACKNOWLEDGEMENTS

Research supported by the Department of Energy, under Contract EX-76-A-01-2295 Task Order 67, is gratefully acknowledged, as is support for earlier research on this topic provided by the Social Science and Humanities Research Council of Canada and the MIT Center for Energy Policy Research. Discussions with participants of the Energy Policy Seminar at the MIT Center for Energy Policy Research are also gratefully acknowledged, as are the helpful comments of Morris Adelman, Donald Blake, Harrison Brown, Robert Evans, Bruce Hannon, Paul Heyne, M. King Hubbert, Ralph Huenemann, J. R. Norsworthy, Paul Samuelson, Anthony Scott, Kirk Smith, Peter Temin, and David Wood. Bibliographical assistance from librarians at the City of Calgary, New York University, MIT, City of Seattle, University of British Columbia and the City of Vancouver libraries is greatly appreciated.

NOTES

1. Federal Non-nuclear Energy Research and Development Act of 1974, Public Law 93-577, 93rd Congress of the United States, 31 December 1974, Section 5(a) (5).

2. For a review of this debate and for a reprint of some of the principal papers, see *Energy Accounting as a Policy Analysis Tool,* Serial CC, Subcommittee on Energy Research, Development and Demonstration of the Committee on Science and Technology, US House of Representatives, 94th Congress, Second Session, June 1976. Hereafter I will refer to this reprint of papers as *Energy Accounting Hearings,* and to pages within that document.
3. See, for example, *Business Week,* 'The New Math for Figuring Energy Cost', 8 June 1974, pp. 88-9, and the *Wall Street Journal,* 'Energy-Costly Energy is Wasting Resources; Some Analysts Worry', 3 May 1979, p. 1.
4. For a review of Rifkin's book, see Smith (1982).
5. For discussion of these approaches, see International Federation of Institutes for Advanced Study (1974, pp. 46-56); see also Costanza (1980, pp. 1219-24).
6. For further discussion, see Slesser (1978, chapter 2); Cozzi (1976, pp. 325-32); or Berndt (1978) and the references cited therein.
7. One of the best-known industrial process analysis models is that of Dow Chemical Company. For a discussion, see the article 'Balance of Power', the Wall Street Journal, 3 May 1979, p. 1. Note also that process models need not involve energy, but typically incorporate optimization subject to specific technological constraints.
8. International Federation of Institutes for Advanced Study (1974, p. 18); reprinted in *Energy Accounting Hearings,* p. 143.
9. The first I-O tables for the United States were published by Wassily Leontief (1941). Recently they have been published approximately every four or five years by the US Department of Commerce.
10. This statement does not necessarily hold, of course, when the system boundary is defined narrowly and excludes energy inputs embodied in agricultural products and in human labour. For an example of a study of gross energy degradation using relatively narrow system boundaries, see Berry and Fels (1973, pp. 11-17 and 58-60); See also International Federation of Institutes for Advanced Study (1974), p. 20.
11. For a review of this debate and for a reprint of some of the principal papers, see the *Energy Accounting Hearings.*
12. Huettner's argument is but a simple restatement of pricing under a labour theory of value.
13. For other recent critiques of net energy analysis, see Alessio (1981, pp. 61-74); Baumol and Wolff (1981), Huettner (1981, pp. 123-30); and Hyman (1979-1980, pp. 313-24).
14. For more complete historical studies of Technocracy, see Akin (1977); Elsner (1967); Raymond (1933); Schlesinger (1956, pp. 461-4 and the references on pp. 539-40).
15. Pages cited are from the 1963 edition published by Harcourt, Brace and World, New York (Harbinger Books).
16. Some of these views were also expressed in 1926 by the Nobel Laureate in chemistry, Federick Soddy. See Soddy (1926) and Wells (1914).
17. Although Scott popularized the word 'technocracy', its origin is unclear. Another engineer, William H. Smyth, earlier used the word in print; see Smyth (1919, pp. 208-12). Smyth's claim to originality was published in a letter to *The Nation,* 135, 646.
18. Rough translation: 'Your days are numbered.'
19. The Technocrats had taken great pains to distinguish themselves from other radical groups. Parrish (1932, p. 14), for example, spoke sharply: 'Our present system . . . is fit only for the same museum in which are housed the pathetically inadequate political and economic theories of Plato, Marx, and the great host of other diagnosticians and prophets who could not conceive of such a highly industrialized society as that in which we find ourselves today and Fascism, Communism and Socialism are likewise wholly inadequate to cope with our problem.'
20. Certain legends and stories concerning Scott's industrial engineering experience and athletic feats were also found by Raymond to be nothing but pure inventions. Other historical facts, cited by the Technocrats, were likewise called into question. See Raymond (1933, pp. 100-19, 149-59, 168-69); and Soule (1932, p. 178).
21. Copies of the fifth edition of the *Technocracy Study Course* (New York: Technocracy, Inc., 1940) can be found in many public libraries. The first edition was published in 1934.

22. In the *Technocracy Study Course* (Technocracy, Inc., 1934) the physical cost of production is explicitly defined as 'the energy degraded in the production of goods and services' (5th edn., p. 234).
23. This ban was lifted unconditionally on 15 October 1943. See Elsner (1967, pp. 142–5).
24. For a discussion of technocracy's activities during these decades, see Elsner (1967, chapters 9 and 10).
25. Articles in these magazines deal with classic issues. For example, the March/April/May 1979 issue of *The Technocrat* contain articles on 'Cleaner Coal Conversion' and 'Make Way for Social Change'; the April/May/June 1977 issue of *The Northwest Technocrat* has a front-page picture of a hydroelectric dam, a critique of recent US energy policy, and an article, 'A New Look at the Physical Trends', while the November/December 1978/January 1979 issue of *Technocracy Digest* contains a reprint of Howard Scott's classic *Harpers Magazine* article, 'Technology Smashes the Price System', an article, 'Producing an Abundance', plus several news items.
26. For further discussion of energy–capital substitutability and second law efficiency measures, see Berndt (1978), and Berry, Salamon and Heal (1978, pp. 125–37).
27. On this issue, see Huettner (1981, pp. 123–30).
28. On this, see Georgescu-Roegen (1979, pp. 1023–58), and the references cited therein; also see Berry, Salamon and Heal (1978, pp. 125–37), and Hertzmark (1981, pp. 75–88).

REFERENCES

Akin, William E. (1977), *Technocracy and the American Dream: The Technocratic Movement, 1900–1941,* Berkeley; University of California Press.

Alessio, Frank J. (1981), 'Energy Analysis and the Energy Theory of Value', *The Energy Journal,* 2, 61–74.

Arkwright, Frank (1933), *The ABC of Technocracy: Based on Authorized Material,* New York: Harper Brothers.

Baumol, William J. and Wolff, Edward (1981), 'Subsidies to New Energy Sources: Do They Add to Energy Stocks?' *Journal of Political Economy,* 89, 891–913.

Berndt, Ernst R. (1978), 'Aggregate Energy, Efficiency and Productivity Measurement', *Annual Review of Energy,* 3, 224–73.

Berry, R. Stephen and Fels, Margaret F. (173), 'The Energy Cost of Automobiles', *Science and Public Affairs,* 29, 11–17, 58–60; reprinted in *Energy Accounting Hearings, pp. 595–605.*

Berry, R. Stephen, Salamon, P., and Heal, Geoffrey (1978), 'On a Relation Between Economic and Thermodynamic Optima', *Resources and Energy,* 1, 125–37.

Blanshard, Paul (1933), 'The Gospel According to Technocracy', *The World Tomorrow,* 22 February 1933, pp. 188–9.

Bullard, Clark W. III (1976), 'Energy Costs and Benefits: Net Energy', *Energy Systems and Policy,* 1, 367–81.

Bullard, Clark W. III and Herendeen, Robert A. (1975), 'The Energy Costs of Goods and Services', *Energy Policy,* 3, 268–78; reprinted in *Energy Accounting Hearings,* pp. 651–61).

Business Week (1974), The New Math for Figuring Energy Costs', 8 June 1974, pp. 88–9.

Chambers, R. S., Herendeen, R. A., Joyce, J. J. and Penner, P. S. (1979), 'Gasohol: Does It or Doesn't It Produce Positive Net Energy?' *Science,* 16 November 1979, 789–95.

Chase, Stuart (1933), *Technocracy: An Interpretation,* New York: John Day.

Common, Michael (1977), 'The Economics of Energy Analysis Reconsidered', in John A. G. Thomas (ed.), *Energy Analysis,* Surrey IPC Science and Technology Press, pp. 140–7.

Costanza, Robert (1980), 'Embodied Energy and Economic Valuation', *Science,* 12 December 1980, 210, 1219–24.

Cottrell, Fred (1955), *Energy and Society*, New York: McGraw-Hill.

Cozzi, C. (1976), 'Thermodynamics and Energy Accounting in Industrial Processes', in US House of Representatives, *Energy Accounting as a Policy Analysis Tool*, June 1976, pp. 325-32.

Dorfman, Joseph (1966), *The Economic Mind in American Civilization, 1606-1865*, vol. II, New York: Augustus M. Kelley.

Douglas, Paul H. (1933), 'Technocracy', *The World Tomorrow*, 18 January 1933, 59-61.

Elsner, Henry, Jr (1967), *The Technocrats: Prophets of Automation*, Syracuse University Press.

Georgescu-Roegen, Nicholas (1976), *Energy and Economic Myths*, New York: Pergamon Press.

Georgescu-Roegen, Nicholas (1979), 'Energy Analysis and Economic Evaluation', *Southern Economic Journal*, 45, 1023-58.

Gilliland, Martha W. (1975), 'Energy Analysis and Public Policy', *Science*, 26 September 1975, 1051-56.

Gushee, David E. (1976), 'Introduction to Energy Accounting as a Policy Analysis Tool', in US House of Representatives, *Energy Accounting as a Policy Analysis Tool*, June 1976, pp. 3-13.

Hannon, Bruce M. (1972), 'System Energy and Recycling: A Study of the Container Industry', New York: American Society of Mechanical Engineers, 72-WA-ENER-3.

Hannon, Bruce M. (1973), 'An Energy Standard of Value in the Energy Crisis: Reality or Myth?' *Annals of the American Academy of Political and Social Science*, 410, 139-53.

Hannon, Bruce M. (1975), 'Energy Conservation and the Consumer', *Science*, 11 July 1975, 95-102.

Hannon, Bruce M. (1980), 'The Energy Cost of Energy', unpublished paper, Energy Research Group, University of Illinois at Urbana-Champagne (revised), June 1980.

Hatfield, Senator Mark (1974), 'Net Energy', *Congressional Record*, vol. 120, part 5, 11 March 1974, pp. 6053-76.

Herendeen, Robert A. (1973), 'Use of Input-Output Analysis to Determine the Energy Cost of Goods and Services', Document no. 69, Urbana, Illinois: Center for Advanced Computation, University of Illinois, 4 March 1973; reprinted with additional remarks in *Energy Accounting Hearings, pp. 101-10*.

Hertzmark, Donald I. (1981), 'Joint Energy and Economic Optimization: A Proposition', *The Energy Journal*, 2, 75-88.

Hirst, Eric and Herendeen, Robert A. (1973), 'Total Energy Demand for Automobiles', paper no. 730065 delivered at the International Automotive Engineering Congress, Society of Automotive Engineers, January 1973; reprinted in *Energy Accounting Hearings*, pp. 589-94.

Hubbert, M. King (1934), 'Future Ore Supply and Geophysical Prospectings', *Engineering and Mining Journal*, 135, 18-21.

Hubbert, M. King (1940), *Man-hours and Distribution*, New York: Technocracy, Inc.

Hubbert, M. King (1950), 'Energy from Fossil Fuels', *The Smithsonian Report for 1950*, Washington, DC, Publication 4032, pp. 255-72; also appears in condensed form in *Science*, 4 February 1949, 103-9.

Hubbert, M. King (1956), 'Nuclear Energy and the Fossil Fuels', *Drilling and Production Practice*, 1956, American Petroleum Institute, pp. 7-25.

Hubbert, M. King (1962), *Energy Resources: A Report to the Committee on Natural Resources of the National Academy of Sciences-(National Research Council, Washington*, DC: National Academy of Sciences-National Research Council, Publication no. 1000-D.)

Hubbert, M. King (1963), 'Are We Retrogressing in Science?' *Geological Society of America Bulletin*, 74, 365-78.

Hubbert, M. King (1974), 'Testimony on Relation Between Industrial Growth, the Interest Rate, and Inflation', US House of Representatives, 93rd Congress, Second Session, Hearings Before the Subcommittee on the Environment of the Committee on Interior and Insular Affairs, Serial no. 93-55, Washington, DC.

Hubbert, M. King (1978), 'US Petroleum Estimates, 1956-1978', *Annual Meeting Papers 1978*, Production Department, American Petroleum Institute, Dallas, pp. 0-1-0-58.

Hubbert, M. King (1980), 'Techniques of Prediction as Applied to the Production of Oil

and Gas', paper presented to Symposium on Oil and Gas Supply Modeling, US Department of Energy and National Bureau of Standards, 18–20 June 1980; processed.

Huettner, David A. (1976), 'Net Energy Analysis: An Economic Assessment', *Science*,
9 April 1976, 101–4.

Huettner, David A. (1981), 'Energy, Entropy, and Economic Analysis: Some New Directions', *The Energy Journal*, 2, 123–30.

Hyman, Eric L. (1979–80), 'Net Energy Analysis and the Theory of Value: Is It a New
Paradigm for a Planned Economic System?' *Journal of Environmental Systems*, 9,
313–24.

International Federation of Institutes for Advanced Study (1974), *Proceedings of the
Energy Analysis Workshop on Methodology and Conventions*, 25–30 August 1974,
Stockholm; reprinted in *Energy Accounting Hearings*, pp. 171–81.

International Federation of Institutes for Advanced Study (1975) *Proceedings of the
Workshop on Energy Analysis and Economics*, 22–27 June 1975, Lidingo, Sweden;
reprinted in *Energy Accounting Hearings*.

Jordan, Virgil (1933), 'Technocracy—Tempest on a Slide Rule', *Scribner's Magazine*,
93, 65–9.

Leontief, Wassily W. (1941), *The Structure of the American Economy, 1919, 1929: An
Application of Equilibrium Analysis*, Cambridge, Mass.: Harvard University Press.

MacLeish, Archibald (1933), 'Technocracy Speaks', *The Saturday Review of Literature*,
28 January 1933.

Mitchell, Broadus (1933), 'A Test of Technocrats', *The Virginia Quarterly Review*, April,
281–5.

Myers, John G. and Nakamura, Leonard (1978), *Saving Energy in Manufacturing: The
Post-Embargo Record*, Cambridge, Mass.: Ballinger.

New York Times, 6 August 1932, 21 January 1933, and 24 January 1933.

Odum, Howard T. (1973), 'Energy, Ecology, and Economics', *Ambio*, 2, 220–7; reprinted
in *Energy Accounting Hearings*, pp. 19–26.

Odum, Howard T. and Odum, Elisabeth C. (1976), *Energy Basis for Man and Nature*,
New York: McGraw-Hill.

Parrish, Wayne W. (1932), 'What is Technocracy?', *The New Outlook*, no. 166, November
1932, pp. 13–18.

Perry, A. M., Devine, W. D. and Reister, D. B. (1977), 'The Energy Cost of Energy: Guide-
lines for Net Energy Analysis of Energy Supply Systems', Oak Ridge, Tenn.: Oak Ridge
Associated Universities, ORAU/IEA(R)-77-14.

Raymond, Allen (1933), *What is Technocracy?* New York: Whittlesey House McGraw-
Hill.

Rifkin, Jeremy with Ted Howard (1980), *Entropy: A New York View*, New York: Viking
Press.

Schlesinger, Arthur M. Jr (1956), *The Age of Roosevelt: The Crisis of the Old Order, 1919–
1933*, Boston: Houghton-Mifflin; especially pp. 461–4 and associated references on
pp. 539–40.

Scott, Howard (1933), 'Technology Smashes the Price System', *Harpers Magazine*, 166,
129–42.

Slesser, Malcolm (1978), *Energy in the Economy*, New York: St Martin's Press.

Smith, Alfred E. (1932), 'The New Outlook', *New Outlook*, November, 9–12.

Smith, Kirk R. (1982), 'Review of Rifkin's "Entropy: A New World View" ', *Technological
Forecasting and Social Change*, 20, 369–72.

Smyth, William H. (1919), 'Technocracy: National Industrial Management', *Industrial
Management*, 57, 208–12.

Smyth, William H. (1932), 'Letter to the Editor', *The Nation*, 28 December 1932, 646.

Soddy, Frederick (1926), *Wealth, Virtual Wealth, and Debt: The Solution of the Economic Paradox*, New York: E. P. Dutton.

Soule, George (1932), 'Technocracy: Good Medicine or a Bedtime Story', *The New Republic*, 73, 178–80.

Taylor, Frederick Winslow (1911), *The Principles of Scientific Management*, New York:
Harper and Brothers.

Technocracy, Inc. (1934), *Technocracy Study Course*, New York (5th Edition, 1940).

Technocracy, Inc. (1938), *The Energy Certificate*, New York (12th printing 1963); adapted from an article in *Technocracy* magazine A-10, July 1937.

Technocracy, Inc. (1975), *Technocracy: Technological Social Design*, Savannah, Ohio.

Thomas, Norman (1933), 'Twenty-Five on Technocracy', *Common Sense*, 2 February 1933, 8–10.

Thurow, Lester (1981), 'The State of Economics', unpublished paper, Massachusetts Institute of Technology.

Time Magazine, 23 January 1933, 'Science' section.

United States House of Representatives, 94th Congress, 2nd Session, *Energy Accounting as a Policy Analysis Tool*, Serial CC Prepared for the Subcommittee on Science and Technology by the Environment and Natural Resources Division, Congressional Research Service, Library of Congress, June 1976.

Veblen, Thorstein (1921), *The Engineer and the Price System*, New York: B. W. Huebsch.

Wall Street Journal (1979), 'Balance of Power: Energy—Costly Energy is Wasting Resources, Some Analysts Worry', 3 May 1979, 1.

Webb, Michael and Pearce, David (1975), 'The Economics of Energy Analysis', *Energy Policy*, 3, 318–31; reprinted in *Energy Accounting Hearings*.

Wells, H. H. (1914), *The World Set Free*, Glasgow: Collings.

Comment   Anthony Scott

Ernest Berndt's paper picks *engineers* as the professional group who have sometimes advocated the b.t.u. value theory for economic analysis. But we should at the outset remember that still other disciplines than economics and engineering attempt to analyse the whole economic system. In the 1920s it was, indeed, engineers who produced an alternative model of production, and used it to prescribe not only a remedy for the Great Depression but also a new way of organizing exchange and distribution. Their successors are still with us, some still asserting the merits of their way of looking at the questions with which economics is concerned. In the interval, however, additional breeds of specialists have taken up the claim of energy analysis to supplant money as a numeraire and a measuring rod for opportunity costs. Only some of the new generation share a professional outlook with engineering: especially all those astronomers, earth scientists, and physicists who since 1930 have been drawn into using energy laws as tools of analysis for their own problems, or who have been drawn by the energy industries into entirely new practical questions involving the finding and use of coal, uranium, solar power, and user conservation.

But it would be wrong to assume, with C. P. Snow, that there are only two cultures. The new generation of analysts also includes those life-scientists who use energy transfer to study natural populations and their ecological interactions. This additional group includes such exotic figures as Donald Chant and Barry Commoner, talking the rudiments of a common language with the 'harder' technologists and scientists. Indeed, in many inter-disciplinary project-planning conversations these days, it is quite likely that economists are not even present. In brief, because project analysts trained in those other disciplines are to be found throughout government as well as in industry and academic

368 Institutions and Ideologies

life, the influence of energy analysis may be more pervasive than its champion-ship by engineers alone would indicate.

Has this change of disciplinary adherence to energy analysis affected the movement known as Technocracy, Inc? Berndt's discussion of the evolution of the economic thinking in the technocracy package suggests that energy analysis enthusiasm did not die with the technocracy organization after the Second World War; but there was little or no continuity among the individuals or organizations involved. As I have suggested, their disciplines were not even the same. Thus, Berndt's demonstration that the earlier and later policy ideas are in the same economic category may not by itself justify his identification of a continuous ideological stream.

Berndt does not go so far as to identify analytical method with an ideology, although the technocracy organizers would not have rejected that identification. I myself remember that when Canada banned the Technocracy, Inc., organization, which had been particularly vigorous around the west coast, there was little popular surprise or resentment. The movement had kept is visibility by becoming increasingly shrill and insistent, so that we younger people at least must have thought that it had clearly 'asked for' suppression. In other words, both Berndt's history and my recollection suggest that technocracy did make use of ideology in the sense defined by Anthony Downs and did aspire to be a social movement in the sense defined by interest group literature.

The message itself was Utopian. In looking forward to a cleaner and fuller life, it condemned ingredients of the present, which appeared to be preventing the continuance of some better former social situation. This particular stream of Utopianism has always been on the fringe of economics, and was taken very seriously by important orthodox economists. Consider William Godwin, who believed that there was inherent in mankind such generosity and inventiveness that plenty for all was potentially in easy reach. A few years later Saint-Simon argued that councils of doctors, technicians, and industrialists would be more likely to increase productive efficiency in France than those who then ran the French government. His views stimulated John Stuart Mill's writings on the same subject. Fifty years later, as Berndt mentions, Thorstein Veblen presented his two-stage view of human progress (reminding us of contractarians like Locke). At one time, he suggested, industry, technology, and trade had been entrusted to one class. But more recently these functions had become divided between 'businessmen' and 'engineers'. The former class had developed new pecuniary, predatory habits while the latter class had inherited the earlier job of making things and keeping them going. The former had invented such institutions or 'patterns' as nationalism and capitalism, while the latter had preserved 'instinct' of 'workmanship'. In short, society's fall from an earlier and better state had frustrated the potential that still existed to benefit economically from constructive and efficient behaviour.

That Howard Scott absorbed Veblen's Utopian message at the same time that he and Veblen discussed the more pragmatic industrial survey seems very likely. Scott's social movement would have needed more than the evidence of only two years of war to convince its recruits that technical competence and planning could permanently run a whole economy. It would have needed also the assurance (offered by writers like Saint-Simon, Marx, and Veblen) that in some golden era the engineers had successfully done so, later to have their role usurped by the business class.

Economic analysis of public choice can suggest questions about the survival of technocracy and its failure to catch on as a new religious sect making converts if not as a new party winning votes. Presumably what kept its members interested were the organizational, publishing, and missionary activities themselves. In this success they seem to have defied the lesson brought out in Olson's *Logic of Collective Action*: that costly collective action will be ephemeral unless it can be based on organizations to which its members adhere to obtain other benefits. (For example, trade unions, as a by-product of their industrial relations functions, play some low-marginal-cost political role.) It would be interesting to know what Berndt can tell us; how did technocracy sustain its membership and its labours when other non-political ideological groups collapsed by the middle 1930s? The religious movement explanation won't work. The Technocrats were not a religious sect confident of their own members' salvation if not of that of the rest of us. To supplant the market place they had to persuade all of us to consent to their revolution: they were the advocates.

Can we learn about technocracy's survival by considering its adherents? Berndt mentions engineers, and technocracy followed Veblen in identifying engineers as the chosen group. Engineers do share a common bond. Their training is arduous and their time at engineering school is an important experience. Many of them at least have a practical outdoor existence. Like their jobs, their training inculcates goal orientation, pragmatism, adaptability, and some scorn for theory and sentiment. It would not be surprising if all such persons felt that society had imposed certain responsibilities on them alone and that they were therefore the elements of a militia available to get society out of a jam by using methods familiar to it but foreign to business and government. But would such possible beliefs also lead them to incur the individual costs of investing in joining and supporting an organized movement? Mancur Olson's *Logic of Collective Action* leads us to predict that technocracy would soon wither away. What kept it going so long?

One answer available in economic analysis is that a 'social movement' needs what Benjamin Ward in 1969 called a sore-loser core of supporters. In a business-cycle trough opportunities slow down, thereby reducing the present value of human capital and lifetime income expectations. Experiencing this will lead many to attribute their plight to the social environment, if social entrepreneurs can offer an ideological explanation of what has gone wrong with the environment and offer remedy for it.

The Great Depression provided such an environment. Slumping capital spending left many trained engineers unemployed and without prospects. Their time to invest in participation became less costly. Their own perception of what had gone wrong was complementary to social–entrepreneurial explanations couched in the terms absorbed in engineering training. Their own experience of the helplessness of non-engineers to understand nature and industrial processes would incline them to accept the views of the entrepreneurs that the economy too needed an engineering approach. And their belief in organization and the indispensibility of data and numbers would incline them against the vagueness and emotion of social credit, EPIC, the Townsend Plan, and other soft alternative bourgeois platforms. Thus, the manpower ingredients for a real social movement were present, and the vigour of an emphasis on know-how, planning, and energy analysis survived into the Second World War and reappeared afterward.

But the movement was not transferred into the bureaucratic saddle or the political arena. It was not a 'movement' but was stuck on dead centre. The theory of public choice does not yet tell us what other conditions should have been satisfied. Why did technocracy not have the impetus of contemporary civil rights movements or of separatism and minority group nationalism? Many of these groups have survived even though they too have dispensed forming their own party.

Was it engineers' cultural disbelief in politics and politicians that prevented them from selling, or getting implemented, their ideas? Was it their lack of a geographical electoral base, and the resultant high information and organization costs? Was it that, with recovery from the Depression, their members were among the first to escape from the 'loser' category? Or was it that establishment economists, as Berndt shows, could easily discredit their theory of value?

Comment   Trudy A. Cameron

INTRODUCTION

Berndt's paper is primarily a history with which it is difficult to take issue. I will instead examine some of the conclusions he has drawn in his interpretation of this history. As a framework for my comments, I will draw on a useful analogy to the controversy over the appropriateness of 'net energy analysis' techniques. Along the way, I will offer a few irreverent observations on some of the seamier aspects of the debate.

AN ANALOGY

I think the most striking thing about the chronology of the debate about energy analysis and an energy theory of value is that it is more than vaguely reminiscent of the whole economic debate over the importance of money.

The early Quantity Theorists had a story about money (which was all but drowned out by the thunder of Keynesian economics); the Technocrats, in the 1920s and 1930s, had some ideas about the importance of energy. Technocracy's popularity waned over the middle of the century, until a number of separate groups of researchers 'rediscovered the wheel', with great fanfare, in the early 1970s. In a flurry of controversy between 1973 and 1977 (not surprisingly, coincident with the awakening of the collective energy consciousness), attitudes about the importance of energy suddenly diverged quite dramatically. Starting from the fairly unanimous interim opinion that 'energy *doesn't* matter', there arose a vocal faction insisting that '*only* energy matters'. After numerous scuffles, we seem to have arrived at a somewhat tenuous agreement that 'energy *also* matters', although many economists still insist on appending '. . . maybe'. By substituting the word 'money' wherever 'energy' appears, you could have the now-standard textbook chronology of the evolution of the Monetarist-Keynesian debate.

THE CONDUCT OF THE DEBATE

The sad thing about the debate over the appropriateness of net energy analysis is that it seems to have added considerably to the animosity between engineers and economists. Anyone doing applied economics in the field of energy has encountered the quagmire of misunderstanding between the two disciplines. Problems encountered during interactions over this issue stem from the same source as past problems: the divergence between the economist's objective of functional simplicity in modelling, and the engineer's imperative of attention to detail. What has made this particular controversy especially bitter seems to have been the early tactics of the debate.

The opening salvo in the debate arose during a brief sortie into the economics camp by Martha Gilliland (a civil engineering professor at Norman, Oklahoma). Despite previous rumblings, the debate did not hit the popular press until Gilliland's article appeared in *Science* in 1975. Fortunately for us spectators, Gilliland's article (1) was fraught with inconsistencies, (2) was 'wide open on the economics flank', and (best of all) (3) lent itself *admirably* to misinterpretation. The battle lines were drawn.

Many of the ensuing skirmishes were conducted in much the same fashion as some of the grubbier episodes in the Monetarist-Keynesian debate. The strategy seems to have been much like this (for *both* sides):

Step 1: *select* some slip of the tongue, or overly zealous conclusion, on the part of someone in the enemy camp (note that this need not be someone in the upper echelons);

Step 2: *cast* this claim or issue as one of the fundamental tenets of the opposition;

Step 3: *heap* upon this notion as much ridicule as your sense of academic propriety will allow; and then, finally,

Step 4: *retreat* to your serious research and wait for the countervailing attack.

Harry Johnson (1971, p. 31), in his discussion of the Monetarist–Keynesian debate, also describes 'techniques of scholarly chicanery used to promote a revolution or a counter-revolution in economic theory'. The consequence of these strategies during the 1975–6 zenith of the net energy analysis issue was a maximization of the polarity between economists and engineers.

'UNGRANTED NON–EMPIRICAL ASSUMPTIONS'

Now, what of Berndt's analysis? I would be not too rash in accusing him of being an economist, so, not surprisingly, *his* history of the movement may show a slight predilection for the decisive victories of the economic counter-attack. On reading his summary, one is left with the feeling that the truth will out, and exclusive net energy analysis has been successfully discredited, at least in the minds of the cognoscenti. I assert, however, that the 'debunking' was by no means conclusive as the dust settled on the mid-1970s controversy.

Thomas S. Kuhn (1970), in his writings on scientific revolutions, points out that 'the proponents of competing paradigms are always at least slightly at cross-purposes. Neither side will grant all the non-empirical assumptions that the other needs in order to make its case.' He further concludes that the 'most fundamental aspect of the incommensurability of competing paradigms [is that the proponents of each one] . . . practice their trades in different worlds'. Kuhn's observations are particularly relevant to the controversy at hand. There are a number of irreconcilable differences between the attitudes of economists and engineers pertaining to net energy analysis. Steering clear of the cheap shots, I would like to emphasize five persistent, fundamentally divisive, issues hampering the resolution of this debate.

The first issue concerns the *relevant* boundaries for a productive system. At the economists' extreme, the 'firm' is the relevant boundary, with net inputs to production defined to be the usual components of value added—labour, capital, resources, and energy—each viewed as being completely separable. Criticisms levelled at this definition emphasize the inadequacy of such partial equilibrium analysis, and especially its insufficient recognition of externalities. At the engineering extreme, the ideal boundary for global productive activity should be the upper stratosphere, with the only net input being solar insolation. From the economists' point of view this represents general equilibrium analysis carried into the realm of the absurd. The typical criticism is that this approach would require overwhelming quantities of unnecessary details. It is attractive in principle, but intractable in practice.

The second issue concerns the *relevant* time-frame for analysis. Economists have sometimes posed resource use as a one-period optimization problem, with no attention to inter-generational equity. With such a short-run focus, there is the assurance of extensive substitution possibilities between energy and other inputs. Such an approach has justifiably drawn fire for being too myopic. In the other corner, engineering energy analysts have argued that stocks of fossil fuels and uranium are fixed and incident solar energy is of relatively low quality and enters at a fixed rate, so therefore the supply of energy is essentially fixed. We *need* energy to perform any productive activity; *ergo*, there are no substitutes for energy over the extremely long run. The ready response to this logic is that, over any *sane* time-horizon, of course there are substitutes for energy.

The third issue is the unresolvable question, Whose measuring stick is 'least bad'? Economists argue that the problems of inflation and market imperfections and the unquantifiable aspects of externalities do not invalidate the use of the price system. Critics rebut that, even so, dollars are *not* homogeneous. On the other hand, engineers argue that, while it is difficult to attribute figures for embodied energy to service industries, government activity, and labour in general, these little problems do not invalidate the use of an energy accounting system. Other critics respond by pointing out that b.t.u.'s are not homogeneous either. (As an aside, it should be noted that neither camp seems actually to have expended much effort defending the shortcomings of its own measure, but was very quick to point up the inadequacies of the other. Authors such as Gerald Leach (1975) and Michael Common (1977) have entered pleas for humility all around.)

There is then the fourth question at issue: Who is better qualified to be the arbiter of the social objective function? The more narrow-minded economists advocate GNP maximization. Critics worry about other objectives, such as national welfare, externalities, and intertemporal trade-offs. Some engineering analysts recommend a different extreme: minimize the use of energy (or maximize conservation). The standard criticism of this suggestion is that energy chauvinism is unjustified because energy is not the only scarce resource. (Note that, when cornered, both sides eventually emphasized the positive, as opposed to the normative, aspects of their respective forms of analysis. At the bottom line, both seem to abdicate responsibility for normative judgements about the objective function and limit themselves to clarifying society's *constraints*.)

The fifth and last major issue is the argument over whether the undertaking of net energy analysis is tantamount to adopting an energy theory of value. Economists will unfailingly point out that 'we refuted single-factor theories of value years ago'. The engineering rebuttal is an insistence that an energy theory of value is not implied by net energy analysis, which will continue to elicit the economists' inevitable counterpoint: so what *is* the purpose of net energy analysis?

Now, it is rarely possible to end an argument merely by asserting that it is over. Economists Michael Webb and David Pearce (1975) seem to have felt they had closed the case when they concluded that net energy analysis served no useful purpose; it was, at best, a 'technique searching for a function'. A trio of questions must follow. Is this a fair condemnation, coming from an ecomist? How *does* much of the empirical work in the field of applied econometrics evolve? Does the tractable problem always emerge *before* the solution technique is developed?

SCYLLA AND CHARYBDIS: A CHOICE CRITERION

In comparing economic and net energy analyses, we must also assess the usefulness of 'economic' versus 'energy' information. I am worried about the tendency for economists to self-protectively conclude that net energy analysis adds little to a decision process, and is at best redundant. (Heaven knows, we would not want energy analysts to get a foothold in the business of information provision.) But maximum information should be a prerequisite for any policy decision. For this reason, the policy-maker should *not* turn the energy analyst away from his door. The crunch comes, however, when the energy analyst asks for funding to generate the information. A suitable criterion for judging net energy analysis versus economic analysis might be something like 'the relative social welfare return (in correctness of policy decisions) per dollar invested in information collection', or 'per b.t.u. invested in data collection'! Now we have to decide who will measure the costs and benefits used in assessing the relative performance of the two types of information. A curious circularity emerges. Given the shortcomings in both types of measurement, I have to concur with Berndt's eventual conclusion that the debate on net energy analysis (and energy theories of value) is not dead, but merely dormant.

HAVE THERE BEEN BENEFITS?

In closing, I would like to draw again on the Monetarist–Keynesian analogy. As in that famous debate, one is left with the suspicion that, although neither side has emerged triumphant, each should probably concede that useful ideas have emerged. Harry Johnson's summary of the 'Monetarist counter-revolution' could usefully be paraphrased in the context of Berndt's 'net energy analysis counter-revolution':

If we are lucky, we shall be forced as a result of the counter-revolution to be more conscious of [energy] influences on the economy and more careful in our assessment of their importance. If we are unlucky, we shall have to go through a post-counter-revolution, as the price of further progress on the [energy] side of our science.

REFERENCES

Common, Michael (1977), 'The Economics of Energy Analysis Reconsidered', in John A. G. Thomas (ed.), *Energy Analysis,* Surrey, IPC Science and Technology Press, pp. 140–7.
Gilliland, Martha W. (1975), 'Energy Analysis and Public Policy', *Science,* 26 September, 189, 1051–6.

Kuhn, Thomas S. (1970), *The Structure of Scientific Revolutions* (2nd ed.), University of Chicago Press.

Johnson, Harry G. (1971), 'Revolution and Counterrevolution in Economics', *Encounter,* 36, 23–33.

Leach, Gerald (1975), 'Net Energy Analysis—Is It Any Use?' *Energy Policy,* 3, 332–44.

Webb, Michael and Pearce, David (1975), 'The Economics of Energy Analysis', *Energy Policy,* 3, 318–31.

13. Property Rights: Developing the Characteristics of Interests in Natural Resources

Anthony Scott and James Johnson

INTRODUCTION

The interests of users of natural resources under the common law can be described in a number of different ways: these can be regarded as the characteristics of a standard type of resource tenure. For example, one characteristic is duration of tenure. This tends to distinguish two types of tenure, in that leases are typically limited to a certain term of years, while freeholds or 'Crown grants' are unlimited. In this paper I shall also consider other characteristics and the types of resource tenure that have them: standard tenures, under the common law.

Property rights in resources are articles of commerce. They are bought and sold in the market place. The behaviour of participants in this market are familiar subjects of economic enquiry in such fields as agriculture and urban economics, and in finance to the extent it deals with instruments such as mortgages. It is natural for economists to regard property rights as assets or commodities like any other, having both quantity and quality dimensions—for example, an amount of land of a particular location or fertility. It is also natural to identify this quality dimension with the characteristics of the right to the land. This approach can be deceptive.

It is true that the demander can shop around for combinations of quality, quantity, and tenure. But the supplier is not as free as a manufacturer to vary his product to meet demand. Its features are fixed in two respects. First, as classical economists noted, being largely a gift of nature and the original powers of the soil, its physical attributes cannot be varied. Second, the characteristics of the tenure are fixed by the common law of property, a social institution external to the market-place. Thus, although market forces can change the value of various combinations of physical quality and legal characteristics embodied in title to a parcel of land, it is not obvious that market forces can change the combination itself.

This paper addresses an economic aspect of this matter: the analysis of changes in the characteristics of standard tenures in natural resources. Its theme is that, although the market for parcels of land does not shape the bundle of rights (the characteristics) that constitute a standard property right, the contents of the bundle can be explained by the working of a different 'market': the market for changes in resource tenure characteristics.

The paper is part of a longer study of natural resource property rights. Another part, not presented here, considers the changes in the standard bundle resulting from new statutes concerning the law of private property and also the terms for the disposal of public lands. The main thrust of the whole work, however, is that such government intervention has been less important in bundling property rights than the working of convention and custom. This idea brings my approach close to that of many anthropologists, whose work on 'property' as a social institution deals mostly with property in land. Dealing with primitive and isolated peoples, they have tended to identify the property system as one of the chief dimensions differentiating one society from another. Their detailed research has been influential outside anthropology proper, and various contemporary economists cited here have used anthropological material to buttress their arguments about real (landed) property rights. Among them are Vernon Smith (1975), Harold Demsetz (1967), J. C. McManus (1972), and Gary D. Libecap (1978a and b).

It is more difficult to define the relationship between my approach and that of the new 'contractarians'. These are economists who emphasize the element of coercion involved in the rules of political society, allowing governments to tax, redistribute, borrow, and spend. They liken individuals' consent to these governmental actions to the presence of a social contract, explored in the seventeenth and eighteenth centuries but abandoned by Hume, Smith, and most later economists. While this contractarian literature deals mostly with the state and its constitution, to a certain extent it deals also with private property as a second institution made possible by the contract (i.e. by implicit, continuing, social consent). Indeed, writers interested in the law of minerals and mining (particularly Umbeck 1977, and Libecap, 1978a and b) have gone farther. They have shown that the process by which certain standard property rights were negotiated and decreed involved an actual historical social compact.

In this concern with process they have gone well beyond the generality of the group of economists, lawyers, and economic historians concerned with real property rights. This central group is usually silent on the means by which the characteristics or attributes of bundles of rights were promulgated. It is not interested in process. Instead, it uses formal economic reasoning about stylized historical situations to show that a particular characteristic might be expected to lead to an inefficient allocation of land, labour, and capital, or to discourage the introduction of a new technique. It infers that the resulting distortion, if removed, would lead to a significant gain in social product. Demsetz (1967) and North and Thomas (1973), for example, show how changing economic values of inputs or outputs have made the removal of particular legal barriers socially profitable. However, the actual process of removal is barely hinted at by North and his co-author. The reader is left to believe that it can have been profitable only because the social gain would accrue to certain individuals, individuals having influence enough to achieve consent to a change in standard property rights. I refer to such implicit theorizing, in which North is in the company of such eminent experts as R. A. Posner, H. Demsetz, and R. H. Coase, as the product of the 'it-must-have-been' school of explanation of the development of property rights.

This paper takes the opposite tack. It is not assumed that changes in the characteristics of property rights have been socially valuable, or were predictable from changes in potential social product. The explanatory model offered is more partial, more micro, in its pretensions. The common law is enough to try to understand. The contention here is that the special characteristics of mineral rights have evolved in response to the special characteristics of the users of alluvial and hard-rock minerals, and of the economic and technical problems special to their industry. The evolution has taken place through the courts, where precedents have gradually changed the recognized characteristics of 'standard' bundles of rights.

CHARACTERISTICS

What are the 'new characteristics' of resource property? We have defined resource 'property' as a bundle of rights and obligations exercisable through time. The bundle belongs to a person, but is attached to a unit of land or resource. In the common law it is called 'real' property, as opposed to 'personal' (or 'moveable') property. In themselves, without the aid of other branches of law or statutory provisions, the property bundle includes rights of exclusion, enforcement, and transferability.

Terminology appears to be very permissive in this field. Rights over real estate are referred to, with the same general meaning as in this paper, as tenures, interests, claims, privileges, titles, or entitlements, although a lawyer would make some clear distinctions among them. The conveyance (deed, transfer, disposal, or sale), on the other hand, defines how an interest is acquired or released; but it must be admitted that deed, instrument, licence, lease, claim, and even sale are to be found used in either sense. A contract (agreement) sets out the arrangements and promises that lead to the transfer of the parcel or property.

From the point of view of the economics of law and property, an interest in land should be examined for evidence about the extent to which it gives the user of land (occupant, tenant, grantee) a right to exclude others. To understand this, consider the ownership of a personal asset, such as a car or appliance. When one person sells it to another, the new owner feels he is entitled to enjoy it exclusively. But his power to enforce this exclusion of others to prevent their using, claiming, or taking (say) his car is not inherent in his ownership claim and is not a part of the civil law. To rid his car of use by other persons he may be forced to appeal to the police and to criminal law. The contract by which he acquired the car does not in itself give him robust rights against third persons. Indeed, most jurisdictions have a large amount of statutory motor-vehicle, motorway, insurance, and criminal law to handle this situation.

Land law is different. A grantee of a freehold property, for example, acquires not only the right of transferability (which also applies to most personal property) but also the rights to exclude and rights to enforce the exclusion of third parties.

The grantees of other interests in land, such as leases, automatically have these rights also, to an extent transferred by the grantor or by customary standard interest in common law.

In the common law (and probably in other systems of property) there are other characteristics of interests in land and in natural resources. We examine them below. Together, they are a way of characterizing the 'bundle' of rights making up a standard interest. The bundle contains rights to do certain things, and obligations as well: to pay the grantor, maintain the assets, and pay taxes. It is customary in economic literature to write as though the presence of these characteristics combines to contribute to the 'completeness' of the occupant's right. This is a helpful idea, but it can be misleading. First, almost any interest must have both positive and negative elements in the bundle: both rights and obligations. Thus, an interest could be both thin and 'complete'. Second, land and resources, when they are scarce, are subject to multiple use. For example, on the same site the original landowners may have granted interests in underground minerals, surface minerals, water, soil, or residential location. Use of these rights may proceed simultaneously. Instruments conveying these rights can hardly be described as 'complete'. Instead, each grantee must abide by obligations to prevent interference with other users. (Note in this example that the users need not be occupiers and that uses may also follow one another sequentially. Thus, a miner or logger may be required to make provision for a subsequent farmer. This is also multiple use of a site.)

Without going through the logic of how each characteristic or feature is stated in a document conveying a bundle of rights, it is fairly obvious that the following seven must be stated or understood.

1. *Degrees of exclusivity*. In practice, this usually means the extent of use of the same space by others, and when.
2. *Degree of right to enforce exclusive use*. Against whom can a grantee enforce (through invoking the law) his use of a resource? Under most tenures, against everyone. (Indeed, the grantee may in practice be under an obligation to protect not only himself but also the grantor; for example, the document may require the tenant to fence, to prosecute trespassers, and generally to protect the landlord's interest by, for example, paying taxes, voting, and observing local sanitary and pollution rules.)
3. *Transferability to others*, including divisibility of a holder's bundle of rights among different users.

Although some forms of resource tenure convey a transferability that is indirect and costly, and therefore incomplete, most do include full rights of exclusion and enforcement. Indeed, tenures that lack the three general characteristics are not very interesting, in law or in economics. Tenures that do possess them may well become 'standardized', clamped by custom and legal precedent into agreed combinations of them and of the remaining four specific characteristics, listed below.

4. *Area.* The property's boundaries, location, and shape.
5. *Use.* The precise manner and amount of use to be made of the property; the amount of each kind of material to be removed; the condition that the property is to be kept in, or must be in at the termination of the occupancy.
6. *Duration and timing.* The date at which the rights and obligations come into effect; the period or periods during which they are valid; the manner of their termination, renewal, relinquishment, or abandonment.
7. *Payment.* Provisions about initial and periodic rentals; work obligations and other payments in kind; piece rates, profit sharing royalties.

In brief, a person having an interest in land will have rights concerning these seven characteristics. The first three may be implicit, depending on which standard interest he has. The remaining four will be explicit, reflecting an understanding between the grantee and the grantor (or their successors) about each of the four matters described.

There are other ways the characteristics might have been classified. In particular, resource policy discussions would suggest that we describe tenures by their economic features, such as risk-sharing; encouragement of multiple use; and flexibility over time. These features are not so much characteristics as criteria. The consequences of other characteristics, they are already inherent in the seven-fold classification suggested above. For example, the extent of risk-sharing is the consequence of the manner of payment and the provisions concerning timing. The extent of multiple use arises from the extent of exclusivity granted to each use or user, over space and over time. Flexibility is a matter of the interaction of the provisions about timing, duration, and renewal.

Most dimensions of the characteristics of a resource-use tenure emerge from contractual negotiations between grantors and grantees before the use is begun. The procedure and results of the agreement are susceptible to the ordinary economic analysis of bargaining. Countless bundles of rights are in unchallenged existence, and many are successfully negotiated and transferred every day. Litigation is rare, either between the two parties or by third persons. Economic analysis of real estate bargaining is familiar and straightforward, and almost all economic analysis justifiably presupposes secure and costless tenure.

It is obvious that, for a particular interest in a particular resource parcel, the contents of the bundle of rights may require minute specification. Such specification, requiring information, clarity of expression, and subsequent monitoring by grantor and grantee, can be costly. These costs can be reduced by developing standard terminology for the various rights, and standard combinations of rights. Words like 'use', 'enjoyment', and 'access', for example, may acquire a finely detailed significance when applied to a particular kind of resource or material, and with cumulative precedent this significance may become generally recognized.

Bundles of rights and obligations may be packaged into standard property forms, understood without the need for repeated explanation and bargaining. While such standardization may create new problems for private parties, demanding ingenuity in fashioning bundles according to their particular needs, it offers in return general acceptance and recognition of labelled groupings of interests, such as 'freehold' or 'leasehold' tenure.

Every system of property rights has its own range of standard bundles. The common law is extensive, having developed from feudal and even earlier social tenure arrangements. The standard interests have distinguishing features which, to guarantee general recognition, amount to requirements. So long as these are met, the parties can deal with ancillary characteristic rights obligations by agreement.

It follows that the common law range of standard property rights is a blend of rigidity and flexibility. The rigidity is encountered in the basic requirements that have to be satisfied to deal in the prescribed range of interests; whereas the flexibility is derived from the opportunity to tailor rights to particular needs in that overall framework.

It is, therefore, important to list the distinguishing features of so many of those interests as are relevant to resource management questions. The following description adds some detail to the information collected in the table 13.1 (for which we are deeply indebted to Michael Crommelin).

1. *Freehold* (fee simple). This interest in land is, with minor exceptions, identifiable by its two distinguishing characteristics: indefinite duration, and the absence of continuing obligations to the party from whom the interest is derived. As such, the freehold (estate in fee simple) approaches absolute ownership (falling short in the theoretical sense only in that the Crown always retains a position of overlord, and in the practical sense in that the Crown may, as with one type of Crown-granted forest land, impose a perpetual royalty, similar to the older quit-rents on freehold agricultural land). However, the exercise of fee simple rights is subject to the general law in two major respects. First, the common law places restrictions upon such rights in order to reconcile potential conflicts (the externalities problem). For example, to the extent that exercise of rights impinges upon another person's property, that exercise may be curtailed by the law of nuisance. Second, the legislature may always interfere with the exercise of any property rights including freehold rights by statutory means, such as pollution, ownership, and zoning regulation; taxation; expropriation; and registration. Subject to these, this interest can be subdivided and transferred.

2. *Leasehold.* The feature that distinguishes leasehold from freehold rights is certainty of duration: rights are exercisable for a stated term of years rather than an uncertain period. The feature that distinguishes leasehold from the more limited interests listed below is the requirement of exclusive possession. As long as these features are present, the parties may determine further rights

TABLE 13.1
Property rights in land

Category property	Legal characteristics				
	Scope of rights	Exclusion	Degree of enforcement	Transferability	Duration
Freehold (fee simple)	Unlimited (subject to general law)	Complete	Against grantor and third parties	Complete	Unlimited
Leasehold	Unlimited (subject to waste and agreement)	Complete	Against grantor and third parties	Subject to agreement	Certain duration term of years
Profit	Resource production	Limited (to activity)	Against grantor and third parties	Subject to agreement	As per agreement
Easement	Passage	Limited (to activity)	Against grantor and third parties	Complete	Unlimited or certain term of years
Licence	Entry	None	None	None	At will of grantor

and obligations by agreement. For example, the doctrine of waste suggests that a lessee must return the land at the end of his term in a condition similar to that prevailing at the beginning of the term, subject to reasonable wear and tear. This doctrine normally prevents the opening of new mines by the lessee. However, the doctrine of waste is negotiable, and the parties are free to reach an agreement allowing the lessee to conduct mining operations.

3. *Profit à prendre and easement.* Both profits and easements involve rights that may be acquired over the land of another. They do not, for example, allow exclusive possession but rather a limited entry for a specified purpose. The main characteristic of a profit is the right to take something (forming part of the land) off another person's land. Timber-cutting, hunting, fishing, and mining are all activities comprehended by profits. There is no requirement regarding duration—it can be freehold or leasehold, and the parties are free to fix the appropriate period.

4. *Licence.* The main feature of a licence is permission given by the occupier of land to do something that would otherwise amount to a trespass. A simple example is permission to enter land to take a walk, enjoy the view, or play a game. In common law a licence does not permit the taking away of anything forming part of the land. The law regarding licences is presently undergoing development. Whereas it used to be accepted that a licence continued only as long as a grantor wished (that is, the licence was revocable at will), there is now some doubt in cases where the licence has been granted by contract. Furthermore, there are a few examples of licences being enforceable directly against parties other than the grantor, although the status of these examples remains in doubt.

A number of points need to be made concerning the above classification. As mentioned earlier, the categories are not exhaustive; only those interests relevant to resource management issues have been considered. Next, the labels attributed by private parties to interests dealt with by them are not determinative of the nature of the interests. In a famous case decided in 1957, the Supreme Court of Canada held that a petroleum and natural gas lease entered into by private parties, despite the name and language employed in the documentation, conveyed a profit à prendre. Similar confusion frequently surrounds the use of 'licence'.

This may seem clear enough. But along the shallow margins of the deep sea of property rights all is in ferment. Characteristics of a right to use a resource that may have seemed reasonably clear when conveyed may turn out to have several meanings when applied in new circumstances. For example, there may be difficulty in agreeing what an agreed boundary means when newly discovered sub-surface minerals are to be removed, or when water flowing across several bounded areas becomes valuable. These difficulties may lead to new negotiations, perhaps to conflict or litigation, and eventually to the emergence of new standard descriptions and terminology for describing the bundle of rights under the new circumstances, capable of standing up to future challenges to interests in property. Additionally, standardized bundles of property rights, previously easily understood and enforced, may turn out in new locations to permit resource utilization only with difficulty or at increased cost. For example, consider a grantor's intention to permit multiple use of his forest. He may find that a right to dispose of timber-cutting rights separately from other rights is not part of the bundle in his standardized freehold tenure, and so would not be enforceable against a third party to whom he transferred his remaining interests. Thus, transferability of his bundle is less easy or more costly than if there were a recognized freehold right from which timber rights had been stripped.

Such a problem is not the result of careless contractual arrangements. Those could be cleared up between the parties, perhaps with the help of the courts. Rather, they arise as unexpected barriers to a use or enjoyment of the resource not contemplated when the resource was acquired or the interest in resources standardized. Any of three kinds of change may have been responsible. First, the tenure may have been standard or customary for such a resource, but turn out not to be fully applicable to a new region or climate (a riparian water right would be a good example). Furthermore, new technology, demand, or value may indicate some mode of use not previously understood between the two main parties, or by third parties. Finally, as major population or macroeconomic events or feudal or seignorial social rights, were changing, familial stipulations about performance of other obligation may be rejected without any obvious means for establishing a renewed relationship between the resource user, the grantor, and others. In most of these circumstances the legal problem is not so much to arrive at a new understanding between the original parties as to devise a deal or tenure that is valid against encroachment or challenge from others, and is transferable. No suitable enforceable definition of rights known to the law (understood by and applicable against people who are not parties to the original agreement) may be available.

To conclude. We have examined the characteristics of various standard tenures in land. These are best-known, and most important, examples of property as a bundle of rights and obligations. There are other standard tenures, although they are not always regarded as such. One is the oil lease, a profit à prendre that has evolved on private lands in North America; a second, more difficult to fit into the mould presented here, is the riparian right to water; a third is a mineral lease or right. Where these rights have not been supplanted by statutory forms of tenure, they are understood by third parties to convey an 'exclusive' right to use a resource in a specific way in a certain period to varying extents, exclusive and enforceable against third parties. The difficulty of enforcing a riparian water right (to withdraw or consume water) against third parties is well known. Enforcement is possible, but is costly when the identity and number of persons who may be reducing the grantee's rightful flow of water is unknown. These information costs are in themselves enough to make water users in dry climates despair of the riparian system (to drive them to drink!).

Transferability and divisibility are not characteristics of all forms of common law tenure. For example, although there must not be total restraint on transferability, a leaseholder cannot necessarily sell his leasehold to a third party. It is an obvious rule that a grantor cannot dispose of a larger bundle of rights in land than he owns: a pipeline company cannot relinquish an easement it owns by selling the underlying land, which it does not own, although it can sell the pipeline and the easement with it to another company. It is a less obvious rule that a seller cannot unreasonably limit his buyer's freedom to sell to a third party. If a freehold seller does attempt to restrict his grantee's freedom, the courts may strike out the restriction. Even for leases and profits à prendre total restraints are invalid. Thus, to take a hypothetical example, a municipality that held lands upstream of its waterworks to protect the watershed from siltation could not 'sell' them stripped of the timber rights. That is, it could not limit the buyer to a bundle of land uses that did not include forestry, for the courts would not recognize this inconsistency with the standard bundle of rights known as fee simple (freehold) tenure. The municipality would have to improvise: perhaps to attach a negative or restrictive covenant to the fee simple, or instead to license the prospective buyer only to graze cattle (or play cricket) on municipal watershed lands. If it had recourse to licensing, or granted a lease in this way, it could both specify in the licence or lease how the user was to treat the trees and whether the user might convey his limited entitlement to another occupant.

It is interesting to note that, as we understand the common law, mineral rights are different from timber rights. The right to cut timber can be held as a profit à prendre, similar to, say, an oil lease. But the feasibility of vertically dividing the pyramid of land 'from the centre of the earth to the heavens' into strata makes it possible to convey or grant a layer in *all* forms of tenure. Thus a surface owner can strip the mineral rights from his surface rights. Both can then be transferred separately by sale or otherwise to third and further parties. The courts in accepting this divisibility also developed a body of law to give the mineral owner rights of surface access and the surface owner rights of protection against undue harm to his farming or residential activities and property. This invocation of the three-dimensionality of land has enabled the common law to accommodate the mining industry. The forest products industry has not yet won a special concept for timber property (perhaps such as might have been drawn from the forest economics distinctions between 'site' and 'soil').

THE MOTIVES FOR LEGAL ACTION

It is not usual for economists to consider the activity of engaged landowners in litigation, so a little explanation may be helpful.

In this section we develop the demand side of the market in new characteristics of resource property rights. The simple idea is that, if the standard bundle of property rights becomes unsuitable and costly for a resource user, he will be driven to seek a way out. His search will, among other results, suggest litigation. This is the demand side of the mechanism. (We shall trace the supply side below.) Then the litigation, if successful, may contribute to a flow of decisions and judgements having similar implications. These implications may amount to a modification in the content of a standard bundle of property rights.

Notice that, although this final result would be the provision of a new public good, the motive of the litigant is less ambitious. Davis and North suggest that he should be regarded as an innovator, acting purposively (1971, pp. 39–63). My model does not require that he be thus assumed to seek a change in an interest's standard definitions or contents, but merely that he seek a release from one or more onerous characteristics of this interest. Thus, his role and behaviour in the legal process are analogous with that of the isolated demander of a good in a competitive market who unwittingly, by single actions or responses, contributes to a market's determination of price and output.

The holder of a resource may find his tenure insecure or inadequate for the profitable uses he has in mind. As the grantee in a previous transfer, he may be in a dispute with the grantor or with third parties. Examples of disputes involving surface rights (similar to environmental, waste disposal, and pollution disputes) are to be found in Coase (1960). Comparable disputes could arise concerning separated mineral rights, access to rivers and lakes, ground water, fisheries, and logging.

The active party need not be the occupant: a dispute may arise because the original grantor is dissatisfied with the grantee's performance, or seeks to recover the property or to be paid for it. Another source of litigation is a third person, questioning the contents or interpretation of a grantee's bundle of rights in relation to the common law.

The motive I impute to such persons is the maximization of profit or utility arising from resource use and marketing, subject to conventional production functions and to market prices of all inputs and outputs. Ordinary profit-seeking behaviour leads them to acquire, hold, and dispose of property, not only for production, but also for speculation and for tax reasons. Imperfect or insecure title to some use of land, often written about as 'preventing' resource development, should more generally be thought of as a source of loss—that is, lost profit. The losses arise because, while a resource user may be able to exploit a site efficiently, he may be forced by characteristics of his title to spend more on compensating or buying off an objector to his use, on building fences or similar boundary markers, on relevant transactions-cost activities such as obtaining information, monitoring, and bargaining, or on meeting some 'onerous' specification about timing or duration. The amount of the expected loss (whether front-end or annual) can be regarded as a measure of his willingness to pay to avoid it. It is, in other words, a determinant of his derived demand for an improved title. As the list of adjustment activities suggests, their relative costs will vary from place to place and time to time. Consequently, the attractiveness of litigation as yet another adjustment will depend on external events.

Litigation is therefore an alternative front-end investment in security of investment along with fence-mending, and of course bargaining and out-of-court settlement. Litigation may be only a threat, to spur along discussions. On the other hand, as 'litigious' communities demonstrate, it may be inexpensive enough in relation to other recourses to justify early and frequent trips to the lawyer's office and to the courts.

More generally, the potential litigant will have in mind a combination of actions to make the best of the structure of interests and rights held by him and others. How much he invests in litigation depends on the characteristics of a 'security' production function and on the prices of all the inputs that might be combined to produce the useful amount of this intermediate input operation.

It is interesting to consider whether we would expect potential litigants to cause the courts to be as busy with cases dealing with interests in minerals and timber as they have been through the centuries with cases dealing with other uses of land. Of course, we would first have to adjust the comparison for the fact that the demand for mineral properties has been much greater in the last two centuries than in the whole earlier history of mankind; and that in most countries infinitely more people are employed by, and greater product emerges from, farming than from mining and logging. Conversations with lawyers to whom I have put this question suggest that the high costs of obtaining raw materials and the high values of ore and trees when they make their way to the world's markets, make many of the property right obstacles to obtaining tolerable tenure of secondary importance. Consequently, rather than litigate when property problems arise, mining and wood product enterprises will settle out of court, buy out the opposition, or mount a campaign for statutory change (not discussed in this paper). Consequently, while there may indeed be a good deal of mining litigation concerning the rights of investors, prospectors, banks, and tax collectors, there will be fewer cases concerning mineral property rights than would be suggested by a reading of agricultural history.

This expectation is confirmed by considering alluvial and placer mining. These are activities in which imperfections or flows in rights to small claims and tracts may be a source not of mere lost profit, but of the whole opportunity to mine. Here the industry's concern with law and property is overwhelming. One reason is that in new 'mining camps' the inherited system of mineral law will be inappropriate to the needs of a new mineral rush. The new miners will be familiar with the mining law used or worked out in the last place they mined. Charles Howard Shinn, one of many writers who traces mining law from Cornwall, Thuringia, Iowa, Mexico, and Lousiana via California to Australia, Transvaal, British Columbia, the Yukon, Chile, and Colombia, notes the common demands of hundreds of new miners and their impatience with local systems of leasing or ownership. The playing-out of a field sent them off with new experience to meet the ill-prepared authorities in the next gold rush jurisdiction. Unlike investors in capital-intensive undergound workings, these people had a high willingness to pay for security, for there were few substitutes for a clear system of mining rights. Where there were courts, there was gold mining litigation.

Jurisdictional differences will not be the only source of legal activity. Variation in topography and mineralogy between mining areas will lead to disputes and a demand for clarification of rights. This source of dissatisfaction with old property systems can be illustrated by the movement of gold and silver mining from underground operations in the Old World, to river basin operations in the New World, back to deep mining in the 1890s and the 1930s. It can also be illustrated by the displacement of the common law and civil law systems of water rights, such as riparian rights, by the appropriated water rights now found in western North America. But minerals are the best example, for the exhaustion of old deposits endlessly drives miners to new ores in new jurisdictions.

It is revealing to list the ways in which exhaustibility may explain the difference between agriculture and mining litigation. First, as already discussed, exploration and development can bring to light new property right problems. Second, even the events attendant on exhaustion, such as abandonment and subsidence, can give rise to property conflicts. Third, the rate of technical progress embodied in new capital is higher because old capital is abandoned 'prematurely' when resources peter out. This more rapid change of technique, often biased, leads to demand for different property bundle characteristics to accommodate new demands for access, economics of scale, infrastructure, water, air, light, waste disposal, or changes in the timing of activities.

Fourth, resource users will have a greater knowledge of possible alternative property rights, owing to their career mobility among legal systems, and so may be quicker to protest their inadequacy or insecurity encountered in a new jurisdiction.

To conclude, we may consider the effect of shocks on the demand for litigation. This is derived from the demand for the resource output. Consequently, anything that reduces the costs of discovery, development, operation, treatment, transport, or infrastructure, or postpones their timing; anything that increases final demand or advances its timing; and anything that biases the technology in use towards a changed demand for space or reserves will induce a general attempt to adjust the property-rights bundle of characteristics, and (depending on the cost of alternative means of adjustment) an increase in dispute settlement and litigation.

SUPPLY OF NEW CHARACTERISTICS

In this section we turn from the demand for litigation to the supply of new property right characteristics. As pointed out in the previous section, a potential litigant is not necessarily demanding a general change in the definition of a standard interest in resource property. He wishes, usually, only to obtain legal sanction for what he is doing or intends to do. Winning a case in the courts is one of his recourses, the one to be considered further here.

We may attribute to operators whose property right security is threatened, and who decide to meet the law head on, three modes of response. In each mode they will meet actors who will, at some cost, attempt to help them. First, through bargaining they can attempt to come to agreement with those whose claimed rights conflict with theirs. More formally, they can settle independently of a legal ruling, on the advice of lawyers, mediators, or arbitrators. These routes are said to be used far more frequently than litigation. Important as they may be, we must leave them aside because they do not obviously lead to legal precedents or recorded *obiter dicta* that might be added to the accretion of decisions that may eventually lead to an accepted redefinition of a standard property right. At the very most, settlements out of court may gradually change local customs, and these customs may eventually be taken into account in decisions.

A second route open to those who attempt to meet the law head-on is to get the law changed. Charles Shinn, John Nef, and other writers maintain that mining camp law outside the main fabric of organized society has been the source of most established mineral law from medieval times to the present. Umbeck (1977, 1981a and b), building on this history and on the theory of the social contract, sees it as responsible for the initial distribution of mineral property and for setting up courts for its subsequent enforcement and amendment. I will not discuss the appeal to government here, simply noting that the attractiveness of litigation depends on the availability of courts, themselves created by actors such as politicians and bureaucrats. New courts of equity, appeal courts, and just a greater number of courts of the old type have all improved the effectiveness of legal action as a recourse when property security is threatened.

The third route is to undertake litigation, getting response from actors in the legal system: lawyers and judges. We shall assume that lawyers are the voices of their clients, adding to the cost of litigation but essentially well instructed and loyal agents. Juries are nowadays rare in property actions and we may concentrate on judges. It is they who supply or provide the variable in which we are interested: changes in the characteristics of resource property rights.

We may first consider two arguments that the behaviour of judges in response to litigation does not matter. The best-known view is that of Richard Posner. Posner avoids a theory of legal decision by arguing that the drift of property law, like that of most other legal subjects dealt with in his textbook, is towards greater efficiency in the allocation of resources (Posner, 1972, 1979a; Landes and Posner, 1979). This argument seems to parallel the Hicks-Kaldor doctrine: judges will tend to decisions that, by increasing the social product, make it possible for winners to over-compensate losers. In other places the argument stems from the Coase–Calabresi doctrine: judges will tend to set precedents that, by reducing subsequent transaction and litigation costs, will enable subsequent parties to come to agreement on the best use of wealth. Posner's prediction of an 'efficient' outcome has inspired other writers to attempt to specify a process that leads to his results. We have found Rubin and Priest helpful (Priest, 1977; Rubin 1976).

Priest and Rubin suggest the following. Judicial bias does not matter; what matters is the selection of cases to go to court. There will be less reason to litigate when the property right central to a dispute is efficient. If the right is already efficient, then what will be at issue between the parties will be merely of a distributive nature; the pie cannot be made any larger, by definition of the word 'efficient'. But if the right is capable of improvement, then in some of the cases in dispute one of the parties will stand to gain from winning. Consequently, his case will be 'selected' to be taken into court. Even if litigation costs for this and all cases are high, the cases that are concerned with an increase in the size of the pie will tend to be selected. This suggests why judicial bias does not matter. If judges were biased against what amounted to a reform of an inefficient right, the worst they could do would be to prolong the life of that right. If enough cases are brought before them, they will eventually make a finding the other way, and through cumulative precedent the reform will be underway. This is an ingenious argument, but at a later stage we shall suggest that it is simply an assertion.

Lawyers in practice and in law schools are fascinated by judges, and their biases, and there is an opposition literature to the automaton theory just described. This is because they are interested in the outcome of particular cases in which they are involved, not in statistical averages or tendencies to efficiency. Judges are regarded as actors whose utility functions are like other men's, but whose means of obtaining utility are constrained by the unique positions to which they have been appointed. We will mention two or three views of the outcome of these constraints (see Michelman, 1977–8; Dworkin, 1980).

It goes without saying that most lawyers start from the same view as that held by Smith and Bentham. Judges are people who have been put in a position where they cannot gain from acting in a way that differs substantially from what litigants would regard as neutrality and objectivity. They are often, or usually, paid well enough to remove from them the temptations of corruption, sometimes much more than is required for this. Appointment to the bench is an honour, and good judging adds to the honour and prestige of the incumbent. Furthermore, promotion to higher courts depends among other things on success as judged by senior members of the bench and the bar, people who know which judges are capable of rendering swift, clear, and fair judgments.

With this as a starting point, lawyers have attempted to distinguish among judges with respect to their views on the matters on which they must give decisions. This is a promising idea, but it seems not to have lead to many useful predictions. For example, the general belief that judgements reflect the attitudes of the social classes from which judges are recruited, while suggestive, is essentially unverifiable. It merely indicates that judges will be jealous of the institutions, laws, and tradition which they respect. To put it another way, the fact that judges are and were conservative and suspicious, or unresponsive to ideas that could lead to reform of land tenure, is something like a shift variable in the supply of decisions. We have to ask what it is that changed their mind.

This question has been answered by those who feel that judges are aware of the effect of their decisions on other cases by saying that judges will shrink from finding for a litigant if the finding will 'open the floodgates' to further cases. Indeed, this may indicate that judges who are receptive to an argument or plea will nevertheless search for a solution that will change the body of property law as little as possible. In higher courts this refuge takes the form of finding for a deserving litigant on grounds that cannot easily be used by later litigants. This judicial respect for the status quo, and unwillingness to make a finding that will have an impact on a large number of people who are not appearing before the court, may explain not only the inertia in the common law, but also the fact that, when changes do eventually suceed, they may lead to the very rapid crumbling of widespread legal beliefs and the necessity of large-scale adjustments among enterprises.

All this suggests that we are not going to be able to explain large shifts in the supply of judgments favourable to changes in the characteristics of land tenures. Some shifts come from changes in ideas, some from changes in the selection of cases that are put to judges. These appear to be largely exogenous to the supply and demand situation.

We are left with price. The price or unit value that explained the amount of litigation demanded is the unit cost of litigation, relevant to the unit cost of other methods of obtaining security in land tenure. Can this variable also affect the supply of favourable judgments?

We suggest that in some circumstances it can. The supply of judgments depends on the amount of judging that goes on. This, in turn, depends on the stock of judges, and their alternative opportunities along with judging define the stock of legally trained persons. The history of British Columbia's gold rush and the history of Nevada's Comstock lode recounted by Libecap (1978b) both suggest that the work accomplished by the bench is greatest when lawyers are well-paid and relatively scarce. During the Cariboo gold rush, for example, Governor Douglas appointed lay magistrates and judges even when there were few qualified barristers to appear before them.

Such observations can be fortified by a rather *ad hoc* model of an isolated labour market. Assume that legislatures keep judicial salaries slightly above the average level of practising lawyers' incomes. Many legislators are lawyers and they are unlikely to agree to judicial salaries being much higher than their own incomes. When legal incomes are low, able lawyers may not be willing to become judges because they can earn some target income by strenuous practice, but not by being on the bench. When incomes are higher, however, able lawyers will be attracted by the non-financial aspects of being judges. It is however difficult to extend this model to a more open market. Instead of having a fixed stock of suitable lawyers, we may assume that the stock is added to by the immigration of lawyers trained elsewhere (and, more slowly, by the training of more lawyers). When litigation increases, lawyers' incomes will rise, including judicial incomes. Newly attracted lawyers will then become available to the bench from outside, and the capacity of the bench to deal with the litigation will increase. Although these considerations do not tell the whole story, it does seem reasonable to postulate that the amount of judicial activity supplied varies positively with the cost of legal services (legal incomes).

Demand confronts supply in this market as follows. We start with profit-maximizing property users. When technology, final demand, or transport change, those who use natural resources increase their demand for property. Because of diminishing returns on old parcels and sites, and because of exhaustion of old deposits and timber stands, these users move on to new locations, new types of natural resource, and into new legal jurisdictions. These events lead to conflicts between people who have different understandings about what can be done under given standard resource rights, and these conflicts lead to attempts to get around the obstacles by a number of recourses, one of which is litigation.

In a jurisdiction in which natural resources have in this manner come into intensified use or demand, the number of disagreements referred to the courts will increase, and this will appear as a shift in demand for changes in the characteristics of standard natural resource tenures. This demand will be (negatively) elastic with respect to the unit cost of litigation likely to change the characteristics of tenures. The supply of these changes will depend on the capacity of the judicial system to give decisions: the more decisions, the more changes in standard tenures. The supply function will be more or less elastic with respect to the unit cost of litigation, mostly lawyers' salaries. The shift in demand will increase the amount supplied. Therefore, the time rate at which standard tenures are reformed in response to resource users' profit opportunities will increase.

We have cited Posner, Landes, Priest, and Rubin to record the view in the literature of the economics of law that this responsiveness is also 'efficient', in that the new tenures developed will improve the allocation of resources. This opinion seems to me to be unreasonably optimistic. It is possible to imagine decisions and precedent 'reforming' tenures by cumulatively adding sought-after features that increase social costs and distort resource allocations; that is, because litigation is inspired by individual cases and opportunities, its success may reshape standard tenures in a way desired by no one. Responsiveness to stimuli is likely, but efficient responsiveness remains to be proved.

RESULT: NEW CHARACTERISTICS OF OIL LEASES

It is tempting to believe that at one time the common law dealt only with feudal agricultural tenures, and with those in towns. The literature suggests, on rather scant evidence, that the important mining districts had special jurisdictional arrangements, in which the Crown conceded personal political and juridical liberties not conceded to those under common law. Let us assume that it was so.

Because minerals played out, these special arrangements did not last and did not cast their shadows into the future. No one is interested in an old mineral tenure when the tin, iron, or coal is gone. Consequently, during the Industrial Revolution many mineral deposits were opened up on existing properties held under common law. To stylize a complicated and fragmented series of situations, let us assume that the problems facing the mining industry and its grantors was the lack of a mineral lease such as might be expected to evolve from the emerging rural leasehold tenure. Private landholders attempted to transfer surface and underground rights without government regulation or participation. (We are not discussing Crown mineral rights.)

We are helped to understand the modern private oil lease as differentiated from its ancestor the older mineral right by reference to J. B. Ballem's *Oil and Gas Lease in Canada* (1973). The legal characteristics of this lease are similar to those also in private lands in the United States. This instrument is the result of a blending process, combining elements of agricultural leasehold with elements of the profit à prendre. Some elements were discarded, as well. For example, the doctrine of waste, suggesting that the owner must regain his parcel in the condition in which he granted it, is obviously useless for a mineral or oil lease. On the other hand, leasehold tenure has evolved considerably since tenants had to co-operate in the use of common lands, while oil companies in North America customarily have to live with others drilling into the same reservoir. Furthermore, farm land is not necessarily exhaustible, but oil fields certainly are.

Relying on Ballem and a knowledge of oil fields, we have attempted to explain the characteristics of the standard oil lease as it is now recognized by the industry and in the courts from the physical and economic characteristics of oil field drilling and operation, that is, from its obvious differences from agriculture. These differences are shown in the first column of table 13.2. In the next two columns are listed some presumed characteristics of the typical grantor, a farmer who originally owns the mineral rights, and the grantee, an oil company, which seeks to acquire them in the course of an oil play. The standard lease is a printed document available in pads from stationers and brandished by oil company landmen who once rode and now drive from farm to farm. They and the farmers constitute a market in oil drilling and development rights, which is assumed to be competitive. The farmers are active in using the soil, have access to an imperfect capital market, and must incur transactions costs to acquire information, to bargain, and to monitor the deals made. Individual

TABLE 13.2

Explaining the main characteristics of oil and gas leases

Characteristics of oil and gas transaction	Motive of grantors	Motive of companies (grantees)	Result for oil and gas lease characteristics
1. Heterogeneity (scale) of resources included in fee simple title	Wish to retain surface rights, dispose of others	Do not wish to acquire farming rights	Separation of mineral rights
2. Borrowing, lending, and discounting rates unequal among each other and two parties	Wish certain pattern of payments over time; probably prefer early payment	Unable to finance all properties acquired at once; probably prefer postponed payment	Compromise blend of initial and spaced-out payments
3. Common property	Fear company will not capture full share of oil in pool	Desire to keep down expense of drilling but unprofitability of acquiring major share of suspected field	Drilling depth, off-setting, and time and spacing specifically provided for

4. Uncertainty (buyer's risk)	N/A	Unwillingness to carry entire risk	Payment includes initial bonus plus a royalty linked to discovery and production
5. Uncertainty (seller's risk)	Fear company will not act as agent but will speculate on land rather than drilling and producing	N/A	Exploration-and-production requirement or cash payment penalty
6. Uncertainty (unequal knowledge, familiarity with law)	Suspicion of land man, no access to legal or geological advice	Fear of loss of acreage to rivals	Standard, printed lease
7. Ultimate exhaustibility	Now-or-never nature of transaction	N/A	Standard, 'safe' lease form

farms are believed to be smaller than the horizontal area occupied by the oil reservoir.

When the play opens the reservoir is not delineated. The companies' agents acquire leases in advance of exploration and production. Farmers lease or sell mineral rights because they do not wish to enter the oil industry themselves. Both parties wish to bargain concerning an instrument that will protect them; that will be transferable; that can be adapted to subsequent arrangements arising from the special problems of access, and of making the best of common property such as unitization and secondary recovery. In this connection, both sellers and buyers understand that the common law of capture indicates the desirability of a lease that is standard, familiar, and gives rapid secure conveyance of rights.

The final column of the table contains provisions to be found in this printed standard instrument, which have struck me as of special interest. My contribution is in having linked these provisions and characteristics to the items in the first column, which are assumed to be exogeneous features of oil and of the industry, via the behavioural characteristics summarized in the second and third columns. The features of the industry that seem to have survived a screening-out process of features that were not needed to explain characteristics of the standard oil lease were: common property; joint production (i.e., the products of the farm and of the reservoir); risk, uncertainty, and lack of information; imperfect capital markets for the farmer; exhaustibility of the reservoir.

Perhaps the chief triumph for the system in evolving this instrument for a resource that cannot in North America be owned exlusively is that it has produced a tenure that is easily transferable and in a special sense divisible over time and space.

The farmer at least retains more or less exclusive rights to the surface, subject to the company's exclusive right to drill (if not exclusive right to the oil in place), and to the company's right of reasonable access.

It is interesting to note that exhaustibility does not appear to be a vital explanatory characteristic. This contention can be tested by imagining that the oil were not exhaustible, but, like a widow's cruse, flowed for ever after discovery of a common pool. The *ultimate* recovery from each well can be imagined to be infinite, although the rate of recovery may depend on the amounts recovered through other wells. So far as I can see, on these imagined facts, the bundle of rights would be the same as if the oil were exhaustible. This surprising discovery provokes me to two additional hypotheses. (1) An infinite flow is like a replenished flow; and this explains why an oil lease and a right to replenished underground water are very much the same. (2) This also explains why, in a famous 1921 case in Texas oil tenure, problems could be resolved on the basis of an incorrect understanding by the court that underground oil was similar to a migratory bird or to wildlife.

Furthermore, table 13.2 suggests that risk aversion is not a particularly important explanation of the characteristics of an oil lease. For example, if we knew farmers were really risk-averse, it would be possible to explain the characteristics of an oil lease on the basis of the first three features listed in the table. It seems to be that royalties are paid because farmers like a gamble. However, it must be agreed that uncertainty, or rather the costs arising from poor information, can be avoided by agreeing to pay for oil rights with a per-barrel royalty. This may explain why all mineral rights have much the same payment features.

In any case, there is a logical problem in using as a tenure explanation the difference between the risk averseness of companies and of farmers. It is an identification problem. Why do oil companies not seek to bear all the risk? It may be that, the standard oil lease now being everywhere available, companies have passed from the hands of the original risk prone entrepreneurs to those widows and orphans who value the protection offered by the risk-sharing pro-visions of the lease. In other words, investors may not press for the standard lease to include a royalty provision, but the availability of the standard lease may select the investors. We cannot disentangle this possible circularity with the evidence available.

To summarize this exercise, we have suggested that in the oil industry the participants have, by litigation and custom, reformed the traditional common law agriculture leasehold tenure. The standard oil lease is now capable of dealing with the problems of surface land use, common property, and uncertainty that are special features of oil exploration and development. By becoming adapted to these problems it has become (separately from surface rights) within the financial and industrial sector of the economy, bankable and susceptible to special tax treatment.

At the same time, this part should not be interpreted as an unqualified paeon of praise for the evolution of common law rights. The path of litigation need not always lead to a successful form of resource tenure. For example, the heterogeneity of timber rights seems to have defied efforts to provide a special instrument adapted to transactions in growing trees. Growing trees may be sold with the land, or as a profit, and perhaps as personal property. But we believe there is not anywhere in the common law a distinct 'timber lease' in-strument, analogous to a mineral right or oil lease.

Furthermore, the evolving common law can lead resource users into hopeless dead-ends. Exploiters of the so-called common properties—wild animals, ocean fisheries, and rivers—have acquired freedoms and rights under a rule of capture that seem beyond the evolutionary powers of litigation to withdraw.

It is difficult to imagine disputes and judgements between vessels in over-fished waters developing a sea fishery catch quota, or in watersheds hammering out ex-clusive rights to water supplies. We would expect instead to find what we do find: courts affirming non-exclusive 'freedom to fish' in tidal waters, and 'riparian rights' in streams. New property institutions have had to be deliberately invented in the past hundred years and to be installed by statute. It may be that jurispru-dence can now adapt and polish these statutory systems, but, unlike the private oil lease and a similar groundwater right, they are not 'spontaneous' inventions.

CONCLUSION

In this paper I have offered a model that applies economic reasoning to the explanation of property rights in natural resources. The discussion has been limited to the standard rights that have evolved in the system of common law. Other rights, devised by governments by statute or for the disposition of public lands, will be discussed in another paper.

I have attempted to avoid the trap that has paralysed the economics-of-law literature on real property rights, the trap of 'efficiency'. Writers have started with the presumption that rights in land are efficient, or they have endeavoured to show that the legal process makes the rights system even more efficient. While this preoccupation may be justified by what is eventually discovered, I feel that it is premature as basis for a research agenda. The economics of law as a field has not yet enough understanding of *how* institutions are created (and abandoned) to be able to assert that they are efficient (compared to what?) or that they are becoming more so (at what rate?).

I have attempted to sketch the change of resource property rights as the outcome of a market-like process. Elements of the economics-of-law literature have been alloyed into the supply and demand blades of the scissors, especially into the supply or cost side of the process. On the demand side, I have argued that, because litigation is an investment made by individual users of resources as an alternative to other ways of reducing their losses or increasing their profits, we should attempt to understand the events (shocks) that induce increased legal activity.

I have argued that the mineral industry provides many illustrations of these shocks. This industry shifts men from worked-out ores in old mining regions to new regions, bringing with them experience with property rights and tenures found suitable in other legal jurisdictions and an impatience with, or disrespect for, unsuitable or unhelpful institutions. Expanding on this argument, I have speculated that the fact of exhaustibility is perhaps sufficient (though not necessary) to explain the uniqueness of the environment of this industry and the rapid evolution of its institutions, including property rights that differ from the parent model.

Finally, I examined the system of private oil leases (a system of leasing not evolved by statute). This proves to be interesting in itself, but the examination does not serve either to confirm or deny the validity of the preceding supply and demand model of legal process. There are two exceptions. First, it turns out that the personal or class characteristics of the parties who presumably shaped the oil lease (farmers and companies) do not explain the characteristics of the lease that was evolved to expedite oil property transfers. One obtains as much illumination from assuming that both parties are farmers, oil companies, intermediaries, or speculators. Because economists make much of risk aversion and access to markets, this tentative finding is somewhat surprising. But it is consistent with my model, in which I did not give any importance to the personal or social characteristics of the actors in the process. The second exception has to do with exhaustibility. Because (1) my model has suggested that exhaustion explains the rate at which mineral tenure systems evolve and (2) oil fields were very exhaustible in the old days, one would expect to find that there are characteristics of the oil lease not found in the farm lease that can be linked to exhaustibility. Not so. It is clear that, in further research and rumination, it will be necessary to think again about the comparison of different systems of tenure and the explanation of observed differences by the 'physical' characteristics of the industry with which they are associated.

REFERENCES

Alchian, Armen A. (1977), *Economic Forces at Work*, Indianapolis: Liberty Press.

Alchian, Armen A. and Demsetz, Harold (1973), 'The Property Rights Paradigm', *Journal of Economic History*, 33, 16–27.

Ault, David E. and Rulman, Gilbert L. (1979), 'The Development of Individual Rights to Property in Tribal Africa', *Journal of Law and Economics*, 22, 163–82.

Baden, John, Stroup, Richard, and Thorman, Walter (1981), 'Myths, Admonitions and Rationality: The American Indian as a Resource Manager', *Economic Inquiry*, 19, 132–43.

Ballem, John Bishop (1973), *The Oil and Gas Lease in Canada*, University of Toronto Press.

Barringer, D. M. and Adams, J. S. (1897), *The Law of Mines and Mining in the U.S.*, Boston: Little Brown.

Bassleman, Fred. P. (1975), 'Property Rights in Land: New Statutory Approaches', *Natural Resources Journal*, 681–93.

Beaglehole, Ernest (1968), 'Property', *International Encyclopedia of the Social Sciences*, New York: Macmillan.

Breen, D. H. (1981), 'Anglo-American Rivalry and the Evolution of Canadian Petroleum Policy to 1930', *Canadian Historical Review*, 62, 282–303.

Buchanan, James M. (1975), *The Limits of Liberty*, University of Chicago Press.

Buchanan, James M. (1977), *Freedom in Constitutional Contract*, Texas A & M University Press.

Burroughs, Peter (1967), *Britain and Australia 1831–55*, Oxford: Clarendon Press.

Cail, Robert E. (1974), *Land, Man, and the Law: The Disposal of Crown Lands in British Columbia, 1891–1913*, Vancouver: UBC Press.

Campbell, R. S., Pearse, P. H., Scott, A. D., and Uzelac, M. (1974), 'Water Management in Ontario An Economic Evaluation of Public Policy', *Osgoode Hall Law Journal*, 12, 475–526.

Cheung, Steven N. (1969), 'Transaction Costs, Risk Aversion, and the Choice of Contractual Arrangements', *Journal of Law and Economics*, 13, 23–42.

Cheung, Steven N. (1970), 'The Structure of a Contract and the Theory of a Non-Exclusive Resource', *Journal of Law and Economics*, 13, 49–70.

Christy, Francis T. Jr (1975), 'Property Rights in the World Ocean', *Natural Resources Journal*, 695–712.

Ciriacy-Wantrup, S. V. and Bishop, R. C. (1975), 'Common Property as a Concept in Natural Resources Journal, *713–25.*

Clawson, Marion (1957), *The Federal Lands*, Lincoln: University of Nebraska Press.

Coase, R. H. (1960), 'The Problem of Social Cost', *Journal of Law and Economics*, 3, 1–44.

Crabbé, Philippe (1979), 'Analyse économique de la règlementation de l'exploration dans la Loi des Mines du Quebec', paper presented to the Congrès de l'ACFAS, Montreal, May 1979.

Crain, W. Mark and Zardkoohi, Asghar (1978), 'Test of Property-rights Theory of the Firm: Water Utilities in the US', *Journal of Law and Economics*, 21, 396–408.

Crommelin, Michael and Thompson, Andrew R. (eds) (1974), *Mineral Leasing as an Instrument of Public Policy*, Vancouver: UBC Press.

Crommelin, M., Pearse, P. H., and Scott, A. D. (1978), 'Management of Oil and Gas Resources in Alberta: An Economic Evaluation of Public Policy', *Natural Resources Journal*, 18, 337–89.

Crowe, Arthur Fleming (1930), *Mines and Mining Laws of BC*, Calgary: Burroughs & Company.

Currie, J. M. (1981), *The Economic Theory of Agricultural Land Tenure*, Cambridge University Press.

Dalton, George (1977), 'Economic Anthropology', *American Behavioural Science*, 20, 5.

Davis, Lance E. and North, Douglas C. (1971), *Institutional Change and American Economic Growth*, Cambridge University Press.

De Alessi, Louis (1980), 'The Economics of Property Rights: A Review of the Evidence', *Research in Law and Economics*, 2, 1–42.

Dean, E. (1966), *The Supply Responses of African Farmers: Theory and Measurement in Malawi*, Amsterdam: North-Holland.

Demsetz, Harold (1967), 'Toward a Theory of Property Rights', *American Economic Review*, 57, 347–59.

Denman, D. R. (1958), *Origins of Ownership*, London: Allen and Unwin.

Dewsnap, R. L. and Jensen, D. W. (1973), *A Summary Digest of State Water Laws*, Arlington, Va.: National Water Commission.

Dick, Trevor J. O. (1900), 'Property Rights, Forest Wealth, and Canadian Economic Growth', unpublished paper.

Driver, M. (1969), *Indians of North America* (2nd ed.), University of Chicago Press.

Dworkin, Ronald M. (1980), 'Is Wealth a Value?' *Journal of Legal Studies, 9, 191–226.*

Ely, Northcutt (1964), 'Mineral Titles and Concessions', in *Economics of the Mineral Industries*, York, Pa.: Maple Press.

Farb, Peter (1968), *Man's Rise to Civilization as Shown by the Indians of North America from Primeval Times to the Coming of the Industrial State*, New York: Dutton.

Feeny, David (1980), 'The March of the Rational Peasant? Competing Hypotheses of Collective Action', McMaster University Working Paper no. 80-18.

Fernow, Bernhard E. (1902), *Economics of Forestry* (3rd ed.), New York: Thomas Y. Crowell & Company.

Fernow, Bernhard E. (1911), *History of Forestry*, Toronto: University of Toronto Press.

Fredlund, Melvin C. (1976), 'Wolves, Chimps and Demsetz', *Economic Inquiry*, 14, 279–90.

Friedman, David (1979), 'Private Creation and Enforcement of Law: A Historical Case', *Journal of Legal Studies*, 8, 399–415.

Furubotn, E. and Pejovich, S. (1972), 'Property Rights and Economic Theory: A Survey of Recent Literature', *Journal of Economic Literature*, 10, 1137–62.

Furubotn, E. and Pejovich, S. (1974), *The Economics of Property Rights*, Cambridge, Mass.: Ballinger.

Gaffney, Mason (1968), 'Economic Aspects of Water Resources Policy', paper delivered at colloquium at Pennsylvania State University, June.

Gates, Paul W. (1968), *History of Public Land Law Development*, Washington: Public Land Law Review Commission.

Gide, Charles and Rist, Charles (1959), *History of Economic Doctrines from the Time of the Physiocrats to the Present Day*, London: Harrap.

Goodman, John C. (1978), 'An Economic Theory of the Evolution of Common Law', *Journal of Legal Studies*, 7, 393–406.

Gordon, H. Scott (1976), 'The New Contractarians', *Journal of Political Economy*, 84, 573–89.

Gould, G. (1979), *State Water Laws in the West: Implications for Energy Development*, Los Alamos Scientific Laboratory Informal Report no. AL-7588-MS.

Gray, Lewis C. (1933), *History of Agriculture in the Southern U. S. to 1862*, Washington: Carnegie Institute.

Griffith, J. A. G. (1977), *The Politics of the Judiciary*, Manchester University Press.

Harris, Marshall (1953), *Origin of the Land Tenure System in the U.S.*, Ames: Iowa State College Press.

Herskovits, Melville J. (1940), *Economic Anthropology: The Economic Life of Primitive Peoples,* New York: W. W. Norton.

Hibbard, Benjamin Horace (1924), *A History of the Public Land Policies,* New York: Macmillan.

Hirschman, Albert O. (1977), *The Passions and the Interests,* Princeton University Press.

Hochman, Harold M. (1976), *The Urban Economy,* New York: W. W. Norton.

Hogbin, H. Ian (1934), *Law and Order in Polynesia,* London: Christophers.

Hutchins, Wells A (1942), *Selected Problems in the Law of Water Rights in the West,* Washington, DC.: US Department of Agriculture.

Hutchins, Wells A. (1971), *Water Rights Laws in the Nineteen Western States,* Washington, DC: Department of Agriculture.

Ise, John (1920), *The US Forest Policy,* New Haven, Con.: Yale University Press.

John Muir Institute (1980), *Western Water Institutions in a Changing Environment,* 2 vols, Napa: John Muir Institute.

Johnson, Ronald and Micha Gisser, (1981), 'The Definition of a Surface Water Right and Transferability', *Journal of Law and Economics,* 24, 273–88.

Kaufman, Alvin (1976), 'Mineral Disposal Systems', in *Economics of the Mineral Industries,* New York: AIME.

Kronman, Anthony T. (1900), 'Wealth Maximization as a Normative Principle', *Journal of Legal Studies,* 9, 227–42.

Knight, F. H. (1921), *Risk, Uncertainty and Profit,* New York: Houghton, Mifflin.

Knight, F. H. (1924), 'Some Fallacies in the Interpretation of Social Cost', *Quarterly Journal of Economics,* 38, 582–606.

Landes, William and Posner Richard (1978), 'Salvers, Finders, Good Samaritans, and Other Rescuers: An Economic Study of Law and Altruism', *Journal of Legal Studies,* 7, 83–128.

Landes, William and Posner, Richard (1979), 'Adjudication as a Private Good', *Journal of Legal Studies,* 8, 235–84.

Lang, Andrew G. and Crommelin, Michael (1979), *Australian Mining and Petroleum Laws: An Introduction,* Sydney: Butterworths.

Laslet, Peter (ed.) (1965), *John Locke: Two Treatises of Government* (Mentor edn), New York: New American Library.

Lawson, F. H. (1958), *Introduction to the Law of Property,* Oxford: Clarendon Press.

Leistritz, Larry F. and Voelker, Stanley L. (1975), 'Coal Resource Ownership: Patterns, Problems, and Suggested Solutions', *Natural Resources Journal,* 643–62.

Lewis, George Randall (1907), *The Stannaries—A Study of the English Tin Miner,* Cambridge, Mass.: Harvard University Press.

Libecap, Gary D. (1978a), 'Economic Variables and the Development of the Law: The Case of Western Mineral Rights', *Journal of Economic History,* 38, 338–62.

Libecap, Gary D. (1978b), *The Evolution of Private Mineral Rights,* New York: Arno Press.

Libecap, Gary and Johnson, Ronald (1979), 'Legislating Commons: The Navajo Tribal Council and the Navajo Range', unpublished paper, University of New Mexico.

Malinowski, Bronisla (1926), *Crime and Custom in Savage Society,* New York: Harcourt Brace.

McDonald, Stephen L. (1979), *Leasing of Federal Lands for Fossil Fuel Production,* Baltimore: Johns Hopkins University Press Resources for the Future.

McManus, John C. (1972), 'An Economic Analysis of Indian Behavior in the North American Fur Trade', *Journal of Economic History,* 32, 36–53.

McPherson, C. B. (1962), *The Political Theory of Possessive Individualism: Hobbes to Locke,* Oxford University Press.

Megarry, R. E. and Wade, H. W. R. (1958), *The Law of Real Property,* London: Stevens.

Michelman, Frank I. (1977-8), 'Political Markets and Community Self-Determination Judicial Models of Local Government Legitimacy', *Indiana Law Journal,* 53, 144–206.

Michelman, Frank I. (1979), 'A Comment on Some Uses and Abuses of Economics in Law', *University of Chicago Law Review,* 46, 207–315.

Milliman, J. W. (1959), 'Water Law and Private Decision-Making: A Critique', *Journal of Law and Economics*, 2, 41-63.

Moloney, D. G. and Pearse, P. H. (1979), 'Quantitative Rights as an Instrument for Regulating Commercial Fisheries', *Journal of the Fisheries Research Board Canada*, 36, 859-66.

Nef, John (1964), *The Conquest of the Material World*, University of Chicago Press.

Nisbet, John, (1909), *Our Forest and Woodlands*, London: J. M. Dent.

North, Douglass (1977), 'The New Economic History After Twenty Years', *American Behavioral Scientist*, 21, 187-200.

North, Douglass C., and Thomas, Robert Paul (1973), *The Rise of the Western World: A New Economic History*, Cambridge University Press.

Pearse, P. H. (ed.) (1979), 'Symposium on Policies for Economic Rationalization of Commercial Fisheries', *Journal of the Fisheries Board of Canada*, 36.

Pearse, P. H. (1980), 'Property Rights and the Regulation of Commercial Fisheries', *Journal of Business Administration*, 11, 185-207.

Pejovich, Svetozar (1971), 'Towards a General Theory of Property Rights', *Zeitschrift fur Nationalokonomie*, 31, 141-55.

Pejovich, Svetozar (1972), 'Towards an Economic Theory of the Creation and Specification of Property Rights', *Review of Social Economy*, 30, 309-25.

Polanyi, Karl (1957), *The Great Transformation: The Political and Economic Origins of Our Time*, Boston: Beacon Press.

Posner, Richard A. (1972), *Economic Analysis of Law*, Toronto: Little, Brown.

Posner, Richard A. (1979), 'Some Uses and Abuses of Economics in Law', *University of Chicago Law Review*, 46, 281-315.

Posner, Richard A. (1979b), 'Utilitarianism, Economics and Legal Theory, *Journal of Legal Studies*, 8, 103-140.

Posner, Richard A. (1980a), 'A Theory of Primitive Society, with Special Reference to Primitive Law., *Journal of Law and Economics*, April, 1-54.

Priest, George L. (1977), 'The Common Law Process and the Selection of Efficient Rules', *Journal of Legal Studies*, 6, 66-82.

Pritchard, M. F. Lloyd (ed.) (1968), *Collected Works of Edward Gibbon Wakefield*, London: Collins.

Pryor, Frederic L. (1972), 'Property Institutions and Economic Development: Some Empirical Tests', in *Economic Development and Cultural Change*, 406-37.

Pryor, Frederic L. (1977), 'The Origins of the Economy': *A Comparative Study of Distribution in Primitive and Peasant Economy*, New York: Academic Press.

Radosevich, George E. (1978), *Western Water Laws and Irrigation Return Flow*, US Environmental Protection Agency, Environmental Protection Technology Series Report no. 600/2-78-180.

Randall, Alan (1975), 'Property Rights and Social Microeconomics', *Natural Resources Journal*, October 1975, 729-47.

Rawls, John (1971), *A Theory of Justice*, Cambridge, Mass.: Harvard University Press.

Reid, Joseph (1977), 'The Theory of Share Tenancy Revisited—Again', *Journal of Political Economy*, 85, 402-7.

Robbins, Roy M. (1962), *Our Landed Heritage—The Public Domain, 1776-1936*, Lincoln: University of Nebraska Press.

Rubin, Paul H. (1976), 'Why is the Common Law Efficient?' *Journal of Legal Studies*, 6, 51-63.

Russell, Clifford S. (ed.) (1979), *Collective Decision-Making*, Johns Hopkins University Press Resources for the Future.

Sadie, J. L. (1960), 'The Social Anthropology of Economic Underdevelopment', *Economic Journal*, 70, 294.

Sax, Joseph L. (1974), *Water Law, Planning and Policy*, New York: Bobbs-Merrill Company.

Scheiber, Harry (1973), 'Property Law, Expropriation, and Resource Allocation by Government: The United States, 1789-1910', *Journal of Economic History*, 33, 232-51.

Schlatter, Richard (1973), *Private Property—the History of an Idea*, New York: Russell & Russell.

Scott, A. D. (1976), 'The Cost of Compulsory Log Trading', in William McKillop and W. Head, (eds), *Timber Policy Issues in British Columbia*, Vancouver, UBC Press.

Shinn, Charles Howard (1965), *Mining Camps—A Study in American Frontier Government*, New York: Harper & Row first published 1884.

Smith, Vernon L. (1975), 'The Primitive Hunter Culture, Pleistocene Extinction, and the Rise of Agriculture', *Journal of Political Economy*, 83, 727-55.

Stjernquist, Per (1973), *Laws in the Forest*, Lund.

Stroup, Richard and Baden, John (1979), 'Property Rights and Natural Resource Management', *Literature of Liberty*, 5-41.

Symposium on Law and Economics (1979), *Journal of Legal Studies*, 8.

Symposium on Natural Resource Property Rights (1975), *Natural Resources Journal*, 4 October.

Thompson, A. R. (1964), 'Basic Contrasts Between Petroleum Land Policies of Canada and the US', *University of Colorado Law Review*, 36, 187-221.

Thompson, Andrew (1973), 'Natural Resources and the Ecosytem: Is Ten Years the Future?' *Canadian Bar Review*, May.

Tober, J. (1973), 'The Allocation of Wildlife Resources in the US 1850-1900', unpublished dissertation.

Trelease, Frank J. (1974), *Cases and Materials on Water Law* (2nd ed.), St Paul, Minn.: West Publishing.

Umbeck, John (1977), 'The California Gold Rush: A Study of Emerging Property Rights', *Explorations in Economic History*, 14, 197-226.

Umbeck, John (1981a), 'Might Makes Rights: A Theory of the Formation and Initial Distribution of Property Rights', *Economic Inquiry*, 19, 38-59.

Umbeck, John (1981b), *A Theory of Property Rights with application to the California Gold Rush*, Iowa State University Press.

Vaughn, Karen Iversen (1980), *John Locke: Economist and Social Scientist*, University of Chicago Press.

Veljanovski, Cente, G. (1981), 'Wealth Maximization, Law and Ethics—On the Limits of Economic Efficiency', *International Review of Law and Economics*, 1, 5-28.

Wihlborg, Clas and Wijkman, Per (1981), 'Outer Space Resources in Efficient and Equitable Use: New Frontiers for Old Principles', *Journal of Law and Economics*, 24, 23-43.

Wittfogel, Karl A. (1957), *Oriental Despotism: A Comparative Study of Total Power*, New Haven, Conn.: Yale University Press.

Winch, D. N. (1965), *Classical Political Economy and the Colonies*, London, Cambridge, Mass.: Harvard University Press.

Wunderlich, Gene (1979), 'Landownership: A Status of Facts', *Natural Resource Journal*, 97-118.

Yedelman, M. (1964), *Africans on the Land: Economic Problems of African Agricultural Development in Southern, Central and East Africa*, Cambridge, Mass.: Harvard University Press.

Comment   Vernon L. Smith

Anthony Scott and James Johnson have provided a thorough treatment of the history, evolution, and economic evaluation of property rights, particularly as they relate to natural resources. This is a valuable paper from which I have learned much, and which is certain to be a useful reference to the growing number of us whose interests in exchange have led us increasingly to the study of the property right systems that support exchange. All of us now know, in a way that we did not know—or at least did not adequately appreciate—twenty years ago (before the contributions of Coase, Alchian, Demsetz, Chueng, Buchanan, and others) that exchange and property rights are inseparable social phenomena.

AN INTERPRETIVE HISTORY OF THE DEVELOPMENT
OF MAN

Some distinguishing characteristics of man

As a means of providing some perspective on the development of property rights, I would like to begin with a proposed list of five characteristics that define what it means to be human: the use of (1) language, (2) tools, (3) organization, (4) property rights, and (5) exchange. I want to suggest that in this list only the phenomenon of exchange is unique to man (unless one chooses to count certain forms of symbiosis as 'exchange'). Countless species employ some form of elementary language. A monkey will pick up a stick to reach a banana (but the monkey's tool is natural resource—not manufactured—capital). Wolves have an elaborate non-market social organization and property right system. This social system serves wolves as co-operative hunters, but also provides a means of controlling wolf mating and population (Woolpy, 1968). Although we might disagree as to the extent and depth to which these five characteristics are unique to the human species, we would not, I think, disagree that the simultaneous conjunction and interdependence of these characteristics is surely unique to man.

Modern man as a creature of the Agricultural Revolution

The archaeological record shows that man, as a species distinguishable from other animals, has been in existence on earth for at least a million years. During almost the whole of this period he has lived as a hunter–gatherer. Then—by comparison, suddenly—a mere 10,000 years ago, men began growing crops, husbanding domesticated animals, and living in villages. Although in many cultures man's diet continued to be supplemented by hunting, this form of production greatly diminished in importance. The record suggests that this development occurred independently, and at different times, in widely separated geographical areas. In the scientific study of man and the development of culture it is difficult to exaggerate the importance of the Agricultural Revolution (North and Thomas, 1977, call it the First Economic Revolution). Once man became a farmer and herder, living in settled communities, we have the pre-conditions for a much more sophisticated development of man's unique combination of characteristics; the possibility of greatly enlarged production surpluses, the emergence of the state, and ultimately the Industrial, or Second Economic, Revolution. *Everything that we are today flows from an event that occurred only in the last 14 minutes of man's 'day' on earth.* As economists, it might have a humbling effect to realize that the economic study of man has been confined to the last 20 seconds of this 'day'.

Pleistocene extinctions and the rise of agriculture

Why did men abandon hunting–gathering for agriculture?

The Pleistocene Epoch dates from about 2 million years ago, and is characterized by at least four great cycles of glaciation. The late Pleistocene is characterized by an unprecedented wave of large animal extinctions. Martin (1967) suggests the loss of over 200 genera world-wide, including some 80 late Pleistocene extinct animals in North America (such as the mammoth, mastodon, camel, horse, and ground sloth). Unlike previous worldwide extinctions that had affected marine life, plants, and the smaller animals, the late Pleistocene extinctions struck disproportionately the larger herbivores and their dependent carnivores and scavengers. Martin (1967) has argued that the world-wide pattern of these extinctions correlates with the chronology of prehistoric man's spread and development as a big game hunter, beginning in Africa more than 40,000 years ago (with the loss of some 50 genera), spreading through Eurasia, and (coinciding with the late arrival of man) culminating in North America within the last 10,000 years and in New Zealand and Madagascar only in the last 1000 years. Martin maintains that climatic change alone cannot account for this pattern; nor can it explain the survival of these great megafauna through similar climatic changes after previous periods of glaciation.

Whether these extinctions were due to 'overkill' or climatic change, or some combination of factors, I think a good case can be made that the loss of the favoured easy prey substantially increased the opportunity cost of hunting and gathering compared with agriculture (Smith, 1975; North and Thomas, 1977). Hunting had brought knowledge of animals; gathering had brought knowledge of seeds and eggs; extinction brought a change in relative costs. Under these conditions it was but a short step for mankind to plant for harvest, and to husband the turkey, the auroch, and other more docile game that had been previously hunted.

One wonders, in this interpretation, what would have happened to the subsequent history of man if he had learned the principle of 'efficient' sustained yield harvesting of the mammoth! Would lack of necessity indefinitely have postponed the Agricultural and Industrial Revolutions? It is thoughts like these that give me much pause in arguing for efficiency as the 'obvious' criterion for choosing between social states.

The hypothesis that the First Economic Revolution was due to a dramatic shift in the productivity of labour in agriculture relative to hunting—gathering is underscored by the fact that this shift was not once-and-for-all. Thus, in North America the re-introduction of the horse by the Spanish, only 8000 years after *Equus* had become extinct throughout the Americas, had a profound effect on most of the plains Indian tribes. The so-called 'fighting' Cheyenne and Arapahoe in the northern plains abandoned their villages, pottery arts, and horticulture to become nomadic bison hunters (Smith, 1975, pp. 734-5). By the sixteenth and seventeenth centuries, for these tribes agriculture simply could no longer compete with the manifold increase in the bison harvest made possible by a technology that combined the horse with the bow. On the other hand, the Pawnee retained the growing of maize when they turned to bison hunting while the Apache adapted the horse to a pre-existing bison hunting culture. But nomadism increased, so that the first European settlers on the plains, seeing the great tepee encampments, were witnessing a technologically transformed native American.

Property rights and exchange in hunter cultures

A good working hypothesis is that property rights and exchange predate the Agricultural Revolution. The evidence is in the many hunter–gatherer cultures that have been studied in the last hundred years. These cultures, with widely differing languages and located in regions scattered throughout the world, have exhibited highly developed social organization, property rights, and exchange systems. Heizer (1955) (see also Gordon, 1954, pp. 134–5) cites private ownership of land such as fishing and hunting grounds, nut trees, and grass seed areas as common. For the Karok (Kroeber and Barrett, 1960), owning the right to fish a particular stretch of river was independent of who owned the land along the river, and the right was transferable by inheritance or sale. The right to hunt sea lions on a particular rock could be transferred by inheritance or sale. Peter Freuchen (1961), who lived among the Eskimo at the turn of this century, describes the social organization, trading behaviour, and other aspects of life among these prehistoric hunting–fishing people. His discussion of crime and punishment in this stateless society is consistent with the hypothesis that well developed property right systems exist among hunter cultures, and may be of ancient origin. That such property rights were incentive-based, and could involve non-market rules of allocation, is illustrated in the Eskimo hunting party when the prey was the dangerous polar bear. The allocation rule was that the upper half of the bear's skin, prized for its long mane hairs and used to border women's boots, was awarded to the individual who was the first to fix his spear in the bear (Freuchen, 1961, p. 53). One must marvel at this early incentive compatible property right solution to what must have been a serious free-rider problem and potential 'tragedy of the commons'.

Property rights and exchange without the state?

How is it possible for exchange and property right systems to flourish without the enforcement power of the state as we have come to know it? The reason, I think, is that property right systems are far more self-policing than we give them credit for being. Specialization and exchange can develop without a state-like enforcement system because of the incentives created by a continuing trade relationship. If I grow corn, you grow pinto beans, and we exchange our surpluses, I have a stake in protecting your property right in beans and you have a stake in protecting my property right in corn. If I play the game of 'steal', instead of the game of 'trade', that will end the prospect of our having a trading relationship tomorrow. This arrangement must have been lost and rediscovered many times in prehistory before it came to be 'remembered' in cultural traditions as a survival principle. The fable of the goose that laid the golden eggs is an example of the many oral traditions emphasizing the long-run costs of impulsive and impatient consumption. It is possible that such principles came to be 'remembered' by genetic selection among early men, including the principle that the reciprocal relationships of trade create mutual dependence on the supporting property right institution. I am reminded of Jonathan Hughes's (1982) account of the seasonal closing of the Alaska cannery where he worked in the summer of 1952. The half-Eskimo winter watchman was removing the locks and chains from various items. When asked why, he replied that locks were not needed now that the Christians were gone. Transients everywhere pose a different problem of property right enforcement than do those who perceive themselves as being in permanent commerce with each other. I would offer the hypothesis that what was most significant about the Agricultural Revolution was the simple fact that transients became a smaller and less significant proportion of the population. This would allow experimentation with new property right systems to proceed on a more self-enforcing basis. Once the value of new property right systems was established from experience, it might then be easy for men to see the worth of more formal legal recognition of such rights.

This self-policing property of the pricing system is in no way a characteristic only of primitive societies. All modern pricing systems depend upon the fact that contracts rarely have to be enforced. I have used the same stockbroker in Indianapolis for ten years—a man I met only recently for the first time. He has executed countless orders for me, all given verbally over the telephone. Occasional 'errors' have all been corrected without contest. Our contractual agreements are never written, but always honoured. Business everywhere would be seriously crippled if more than an insignificant fraction of contracts had to be policed. North (1981, chapter 5) recognizes this when he emphasizes the importance of ideology to a theory of the state, where 'ideology' is the name given to the belief system that engenders individual restraint in abiding by the rules of the exchange game. In a world in which crime pays, the fact that there are not more criminals is a rationalist mystery as deep as the fact that so many people vote. Yet when there is a mini-doomsday problem, following a tornado, flood, or earthquake, not even the full police power of the state (e.g., National Guard patrols) is able to contain looting by otherwise law-abiding citizens.

The pricing system as a 'spontaneous' social invention

When left to their own devices, people all over the world, at different times and under different circumstances, have invented pricing systems and whatever supporting property right institutions were required for exchange. The invention of a pricing system is comparable to the invention of a language in terms of (1) its importance in history, (2) the method of discovery, (3) the phenomenon of multiple independent discoveries, and (4) its indestructability. Without exchange it is difficult to imagine an Agricultural Revolution, and without markets it is certainly impossible to imagine an Industrial Revolution. Like language (as noted by Hayek), a pricing system is invented not by one mind, but by thousands, perhaps millions, of minds over countless generations of trial-and-error filtering, combined with an ancestral memory for those arrangements that work 'best'. Like language, it survives war, pestilence, plagues, and the mercantilist repression of early monarchs and contemporary democracies; it survives police state repression in command economies like the Polish and Russian in the form of favours, bribes, barter, commodity money, and underground exchange. To my knowledge, no primitive society has ever been observed that did not have an exchange and property right system. Although it is a cultural invention, simultaneously it is what makes culture possible. I doubt that there is any way of stating what we mean by a cultural revolution (whether agricultural or industrial) without describing the accompanying developments in exchange and property rights, and the resulting new surplus that changed the way people lived.

MODERN PROPERTY RIGHTS AS A SOCIAL INVENTION

I read Scott and Johnson's insightful history and analysis of the common law development of land tenure and natural resource rights as a grand case history in what it means to say that nobody invented the pricing system or its supporting property right institutions; everybody did, in the sense that each land use interest had a part in influencing the balance struck by the adaptive common law definition of land use rights. *Precedent* is the mechanism by which the system remembers those arrangements that seem best. Variation in land use tenure across time, technological characteristics, and degree of uncertainty, all reflect opportunity cost as expressed in the negotiations of affected parties. The result is an institution that can properly be called rational, but no one could or did sit down at a drawing board to design it. This institution, which culminates in instruments such as the oil lease, represents a blend of forces and bits of information from many individuals, each of whom in negotiating in his own interest promoted the production of a public good 'which was no part of his intention', and on which all of us now 'free-ride'.

The common law can be interpreted as a formalization of the many voluntary associations in which men, in their individual and collective interests, have banded together to create and enforce a property right institution. In the territory of California before an appropriate body of law and its enforcement was in existence, the mining district contract was created out of the voluntary association of miners (Umbeck, 1982). This is an instance in which a stateless society invented a contractual institution tailored to the technology, physiography, and sociology of the mining camp. This institution assigned and enforced rights to mineral property. The invention was not instantaneous but was one that evolved and adapted in response to changing cost–benefit circumstances and perhaps to the discovery of dominating contractual rules. Thus, voluntary agreement to accept restrictions on the sale of mining claims is explained by Umbeck in terms of the need to maintain a group large enough to yield low-cost enforcement. But this characteristic of early mining camp contracts was relaxed at a later date to allow sale to outsiders only. Hence, the original contract provision can be interpreted as a mistake; i.e., it restricted freedom of exchange more than was necessary to maintain group size. Under this scenario, the original rule was dominated by the new policy of allowing sales to outsiders—so might describe one of the many filtering mechanisms that cumulatively improve institutions. Another such mechanism is the balancing of benefits and costs in the original agreement, whereby miners voluntarily restrict their rights to sell claims in return for a viable enforcement system. It is no different today with the many 'neighbourhood watch' groups formed across the country in response to the rising burglary rate with which the police apparatus of the state is unable to cope. Apparently, the information cost of centralized crime control cannot compete with a decentralized voluntary contract among neighbours to rotate the watch.

Anderson and Hill (1979) have summarized the great variety of voluntary organizations that characterized the nineteenth-century American West, which experienced an influx of settlers before there existed any government enforcement of property rights. These case studies include land clubs, formed to enforce the claims of squatters to public land, and cattlemen's associations, formed to protect grazing rights and to protect cattle from being stolen, or 'rustled'. The Wagon Train was perhaps the most colourful association formed for the protection of those on the move into the new territories of the West.

The oil lease, which is a standard printed document sold over the counter of any well-stocked stationer, is an excellent example of a property right system embodied in a single multi-dimensional instrument that has been created partly out of whole cloth and partly by reforming 'the traditional agriculture leasehold tenure', Scott and Johnson's analysis and attempt to explain the characteristics of the oil lease is one of the most stimulating parts of the paper. Since this lease is a 'new' instrument, i.e., created in only the last hundred years, I wonder if it would not be feasible to trace the historical sequence in which these characteristics were added to the 'standard instrument' (if this was the case) at different times, in different regions, under different conditions. In this way one would seek a test, *à la* Umbeck (1982), of Scott's supply and demand hypothesis of property right formation. I would suggest that Scott and Johnson's model of the oil lease may explain the absence in the common law of a distinct 'timber lease' instrument. Perhaps such an instrument cannot be purchased from your friendly local stationer because of the absence, in table 13.2 of characteristics 6 and 7 in timber land; that is, grantor and grantee both know where the timber is located.

It is one thing to argue that the common law created property rights that responded to the supply and demand for such rights, but it is quite another matter to infer that such rights promoted efficiency. Just as it is not clear that the state can tell the difference between property right systems that may promote efficiency (the oil lease, the property deed, mineral deed rights) and property right systems that appear to be highly inefficient (the entitlements of the Department of Energy, the monopoly licensing of everything from taxi-cabs and cable television to common carrier truckers), so also did the common law produce undifferentiated controls over all manner of business activities. Thus Hughes, while emphasizing that 'in the ancient English tenure of free and common socage lay the seed of American capitalism as it would be in the future, a powerful right of private ownership of land and natural resources' (Hughes, 1977, p. 13), also notes that, throughout nineteenth-century contin-ental expansion, 'all business activity remained in the grip of common law, even where there were no specific statutes in the new states . . . the specific non-market controls of the colonies, controls over business in terms of number, entry, price and quality, continued in the original states' (pp. 78-9). Scholars have hardly begun the task of sorting out those property right elements that have enhanced and those that have hindered growth and efficiency, let alone identified their historical origins or development.

AN INTERPRETATION OF THE HISTORY OF OIL IN TERMS OF THE SEARCH FOR PROPERTY RIGHT INSTITUTIONS

In this section I am going to present a scenario in which the major events in the history of 'big oil' are interpreted in terms of the 'market's' repeated attempt to satisfy a strong demand for an incentive-compatible property right institution. Since factual and counterfactual documentation is incomplete, I claim only to proffer a hypothesis. The key geological fact is that the oil reservoir is a common property resource.

1. The scene opens with the discovery of oil in 1859 in Titusville, Pennsyl-vania, by the drifter and ex-railroad conductor, 'Colonel' Drake. The Colonel's well pumped 25 barrels a day into a market that paid $20 per barrel.[1] (I let the reader guess what that barrel would be worth at today's prices.) 'When the oil word leaked out, northwestern Pennsylvania was overrun with business-men, speculators, misfits, horse dealers, drillers, bankers, and just plain hell-raisers' (Armentano, 1981). Get the picture: a common property resource worth $20 per barrel so near the surface that it was leaking into various north-western Pennsylvania creeks. There is no possibility here, as in the California gold rush, for the creation of 'mining districts' in which surface right claims can be used to define property rights that are appropriately incentive-compatible. A different innovation is required.

2. Enter now an army of wildcat drillers. The average wellhead price of crude is reported by Andrews (1889, p. 145) for the years 1876-81 as shown in the table below. Twenty-two years after its discovery, Pennsylvania oil is selling for 3 per cent of its 1859 price.

Year	Crude price at wells (cents/gallon)
1876	5.988 ($1.90/barrel)
1877	5.684
1878	2.761
1879	2.098
1880	2.240
1881	2.029 ($0.63/barrel)

3. In January 1882, 'out of the witchery of the Standard Oil interest' (Andrews, 1889, p. 149), the Standard Oil Trust was formed—probably the most significant event in the early history of the anti-trust movement, but possibly far more significant to the hypothesis that the demand for property right institutions is derived from the increase in the gains from exchange that are created by such institutions. The 'trust' associated with the late nineteenth-century period of the 'robber barons' was apparently itself an outgrowth of an old common-law tradition (Armentano, 1981, p. 66). Subsequently, the price of crude evolved as follows (Andrews, 1889, p. 145):

Year	Crude price at wells (cents/gallon)
1882	1.873
1883	2.519
1884	1.993
1885	2.106
1886	1.696
1887	1.587

4. With this further erosion in crude prices, resource economists will appreciate the significance of the following event.

[On] November 1, 1887, the Standard Oil authorities made a stipulation with the Producer's Protective Association of the oil fields, by which five million barrels of oil belonging to the Standard were set apart for the benefit of the Association, upon its engaging to curtail the production of crude oil at least 17,500 barrels a day. . . . If at the end of the year the production proved to have been lessened by the aforesaid amount, the Producers were to get all that this oil sold for above sixty-two cents a barrel, storage, fire losses, and insurance being first subtracted. To make good its part of the writing, the Producers' Association entered into a covenant with the Well-drillers' Union, agreeing to pay them the profits over sixty-two cents a barrel on one million barrels of oil and part profits on another million, in return for their promise to desist from drilling and cleaning wells throughout the oil field, thus actually rewarding a very large number of men for lying idle. . . . After the date of this agreement, the average reduction was 25,000 barrels a day. Perhaps to the extent of 7000 barrels it was due to natural shrinkage, but the rest was in consequence of the shut-down. [Andrews, 1889, pp. 146-7]

It is claimed by Andrews (1889, p. 122) that 'not a few' of the many trust combines 'have come to nothing'. Those 'without effect' and with 'not the slightest ability to harm' include the rubber, Kentucky distillers, nail, glucose, and lead trusts. Furthermore, of the four then most conspicuous trusts (Sugar, Cotton Oil, Distillers and Cattle-feeders, and Standard Oil), 'the Standard Oil Trust is the most renowned as well as the most solid and successful of the quartette' (Andrews, 1889, pp. 128–30).

Questions:

A. Is it true, indeed, that the Standard Oil Trust was the most successful of all these early trust combines?
B. If so, was this difference due not just to successful price rigging (and rent extraction from consumers), but to a property right solution (incentive payments to the drillers), to the deadweight loss caused by the 'tragedy of the commons?'
C. Is there any difference in incentive effects between Standard Oil bribes to well-drillers and an externality tax on drilling? As I read Andrew's report, the Standard Oil Trust anticipated the resource economist's solution to the commons problem by three-quarters of a century.

The point of this argument is *not* that, contrary to the conventional wisdom, trusts are really secret purveyors of unmitigated social good. The point I want to make is that the trust is an instance in which individual agents (apparently voluntarily) experiment with a new institution in an attempt to improve their lot. Is the Standard Oil Trust, an example of how, in this process, surplus-increasing property right arrangements may be discovered? To the extent that the trust monopolized oil it reduced the gains from exchange, but to the extent that its contract with the producers, and indirectly with the drillers, eliminated waste in the commons it increased these gains. Since it is claimed by many that price-rigging cartels are unstable, would the experiment eventually have filtered out the monopoly element while retaining some form of the internalized commons? Never mind that the members of the Standard Oil Trust (and the economists of the day) may have been incapable of understanding this difference —money was money to those nine Standard Oil trustees; I am speculating about how man may promote the discovery of property rights institutions that are 'no part of his intention'. The process was cut short by the Sherman Antitrust Act (1890), so that all we have left is what was recorded before Sherman started 'contaminating' the experiment.

5. The next event in this chronology is the unitization movement in the 1920s and 1930s. This required society (the courts) to discover that oil 'conservation', in common pools, was separable from production restrictions designed to achieve monopoly prices. In view of the mixed record of success with both private and state arrangements to control rule-of-capture production from Oklahoma and Texas oil fields (Libecap and Wiggins, 1982), it seems unlikely that the Standard Oil Trust would have been successful in the long run. However, to my knowledge the Trust's experiment with direct, privately contracted, incentive payments to reduce production and drilling represents the

first and last attempt to use such a mechanism. Also significant in this chronology is the success of the oil industry in getting the oil depletion allowance accepted as a special deduction from taxable income. This provided a subsidized increase in the after-tax return to drilling and production which to some unknown extent tended to offset whatever rationality unitization may have brought to reservoir management. Hence, the industry continued to be plagued by 'price wars'.

6. The end of the Second World War brought the emergence of the international oil companies: Exxon, Mobil, Socal, Texaco, Gulf, British Petroleum, and Shell, followed in the 1950s and 1960s by an expansion abroad by the large American domestic companies such as Amoco, Phillips, and Continental, and 'independents' such as Getty, Hunt, and Occidental. By far the most significant element in this development was a subtle new property right failure which brought rule-of-capture in the development of foreign oil: the international oil companies controlled the production and marketing of oil from the Persian Gulf countries, but these companies had *no ownership claim on the reserves*. They owned all the oil they could place on tankers, after paying royalties to the oil-exporting companies, but they had no secure property right in the reserve stock. Consequently, unrecovered oil had zero value to the oil companies, recovered oil had a value determined by its market price, and the resulting 'doomsday' incentive was to flood world markets with oil from these foreign sources.

7. The years 1959-60 brought two significant events. (1) In response to intense lobbying by the small independent domestic crude oil producers, President Eisenhower imposed mandatory import quotas on foreign crude oil in 1959.[2] (2) The Organization of Petroleum Exporting Countries (OPEC) was formed in 1960. The first event was the direct result of the flood of imported oil caused by the property right failures recounted above; the second event is significant because it would ultimately, so I shall argue, correct this property right failure. The waste of premature recovery constituted the high opportunity cost of a property right system that separated the right to the stock from the right to recovered flows.

8. Persian Gulf oil selling for $2.22 per barrel in 1947 was down to $1.10 per barrel in 1969. Then came the decade of the 1970s in which OPEC succeeded in taking over the production and marketing decisions previously controlled by the international oil companies. As noted by Mancke (1981, p. 121), 'As the 1970s progressed the oil-exporting countries increasingly chose to supply for themselves the general contractor services previously provided by the International oil companies.' Persian Gulf oil selling for $1.10 per barrel in 1969 was bringing $30-$36 per barrel in 1980. As resource economists are aware, the recovery decision is determined by the condition $P - V = C'(q)$, where P is the market price of a barrel of recovered oil, V is the value imputed to a barrel of reserves, and $C'(q)$ is the marginal recovery cost of a barrel of oil. In 1969 and earlier, $V = 0$ to the companies making the production decision

and for whom there was *no property right* in tomorrow's oil. By 1980, the production decision was being made by those who owned the reserves, and *V* was now determined by the price expected to prevail for tomorrow's oil. This demand for a property rights model predicts a dramatic decrease in output and increase in crude oil prices in the decade of the 1970s. None of us knows whether OPEC, as a price-rigging cartel, had any effect on this price increase. But we do know that each member of OPEC had an independent competitive market incentive to lower output.[3]

CAN WE CONSCIOUSLY DESIGN NEW AND BETTER PROPERTY RIGHT SYSTEMS?

Based on my interpretation of the origin and process of property right forma-tion, I am sceptical about whether, as professionals, any of us as yet knows and understands enough about our subject matter to allow an affirmative answer to this question. I also believe that we have made much progress in the last two decades in our understanding of the problem of incentive compatibility in institutions; but in the longer view of this instant in history such a belief may be a delusion. What we lack is the knowledge that comes from practice, from trying, failing, and learning from the results. It is one thing to articulate an *ex post* property right interpretation of the mining district, the oil lease, or the fact that the individual members of OPEC combined the right to un-recovered oil with the right to recovered oil in the early 1970s; it is quite another to design *ex ante* property right institutions that will operate in the way that we claim that these 'natural experiments' have operated. For one thing, our claims and interpretations may be wrong; for another, we may not permit our designs to be reshaped by the opportunity cost challenges that operate in less structured environments.

In spite of these disclaimers and words of caution, for purposes of debate I am going to propose some property right instruments and institutions designed to privatize various common property stock, stock-flow, flow, and public land resources.

Rights to water and fisheries stocks

The city of Tucson and its surrounding urban, agricultural, and mining estab-lishments obtain all of their water from deep wells into the Tucson basin. It is pure water, if a little hard, and normally requires no chlorine additive. Anyone with a surface right to land has been free to sink a straw into this huge natural aquifer and pump water to the surface. Consequently, people who are otherwise good neighbours living in the Tucson basin are constantly poaching on each other's water supply. The city and surrounding county water authorities charge only for the cost of drilling, pumping, distributing, and 'managing' this water system. The water is free, and swimming pools abound along with grass lawns in a middle- to high-desert climate.

This aquifer is estimated to contain 20–40 million acre-feet of recoverable water. The natural recharge rate, according to 1975 estimates, is about 75,000 acre-feet per year, and the consumption rate is about triple this amount— 225,000 acre-feet per year (Barr and Pingry, 1976). My proposal, which somewhat simplifies an earlier proposal (Smith, 1977) is as follows.

1. Let the County of Pima issue 30 million 'shares' or deed certificates, each representing a claim on one acre-foot of water. These water deeds could be issued partly in proportion to the surface area held by all landowners, and partly in proportion to each water-user's base-period consumption rate. The idea is to recognize 'squatters' rights' to water; i.e., the value of all current land in Pima County reflects the implicit right to draw on underground water supplies. Deeds could be issued in denominations of 1, 5, 10, 100, or fractional acre-feet of water.

2. Any part of the rights conveyed by these deeds could be bought, sold, assigned, or bequeathed by contracts separable from contracts for the transfer of real property, except perhaps for any prior real estate deed provisions which restrict or define the water rights of current deeds to land.

3. All water deed transfers would be recorded in county records in the same manner as transfers of real property have been recorded in the past. The idea is to utilize to the extent possible any existing institutional procedures that have stood the test of time.

4. All contract prices would be negotiable, advertisable, and publishable, and thereby would assist the development of an ongoing market in these deeds.

5. At regularly spaced fixed intervals (one, two, or five years), depending on the consequent cost, the total recharge of water over the previous such interval would be estimated and a fractional stock dividend on the outstanding deed certificates would be issued in an amount equal to this recharge. In the event that the original water stock estimates were later found to be too high by better measurement methods, one could simply introduce a 'stock split' (or reverse split) to adjust the outstanding deed claims to the actual water stock.[4]

6. All water use would be metered on farms, ranches and mines, etc., as is now done for residential users. Each user would be billed monthly in dollars for the cost of this water management system (including pumping and distribution cost, where appropriate, as in the city), and monthly in deed certificates to be surrendered for all water consumed.

In this system, the price of water must reflect continuously the updated estimated supply of water in the aquifer, as well as the marginal benefits to all users. Residents with swimming pools and grass lawns might find it preferable to drain the pools, plant native cactus, and sell their unneeded deeds. Cotton farmers might find that the value of their water deeds was greater in the market for water than in the market for cotton. Mining companies might operate more profitably by using reclaimed water and selling their excess water deeds. Any new resident moving to the city, or any new industry, would have to satisfy their needs for water by buying deed certificates in the open market.

The above property right system would also apply to any fishery in which it was feasible to estimate the stock and meter the catch. Fishermen would have deeds to live fish that would be surrendered as live fish became landed fish. Fishermen could use any non-interfering technology they pleased—hooks, nets, traps—so long as monitoring the stock and metering the catch are practicable and not too costly. Regular positive (or negative) stock dividends would be declared to adjust the outstanding stock of certificates for variations in the natural growth rate in the biomass of fish.[5] There would be a continuous market in certificates corresponding to the estimated stock of fish.

Marketable catch quota systems have been proposed and analysed by Pearse (1981) and by Scott and Neher (1981). These proposals differ fundamentally from the institution that I am suggesting. They would create property rights in landed fish, while my proposal creates property rights in live fish. The difference is like that between night and day. Marketable catch quotas, or a 'system of usufructuary rights' (Scott and Neher, 1981, p. 41), modifies the regulation of fisheries by using the market, rather than a regulatory bureaucracy, to allocate the annual total catch quota. But these quotas would still be regulated, that is, determined centrally. My proposal would abolish all fisheries' regulatory agencies as now constituted. In its place one would institute deed certificates to live fish, by species. Just as one needs a county clerk's office (a government agency) to record and keep track of transfers of deeds to real property, or an American Kennel Club (a private agency) to record births and track transfers of AKC-registered Alaskan Malamutes, so one would need an agency to monitor individual landings by species and require payment of an equivalent poundage of surrendered certificates. Since enforcement may require police and gunboats, the appropriate agency might be governmental, e.g. the Coast Guard, but this is not a foregone conclusion.[6] Unless the counterfeiting of certificates or, if computerized, electronic fraud were to be a problem, I see no absolute necessity for the agency to serve a registrar function, but this is an open question.[7] The crucial requirements of my proposal are that (1) the catch be monitored, and (2) certificate claims to live fish be surrendered in 'payment' for the catch. Less crucial, but important, is the need for a periodic ballpark estimate of the stock of fish. Good estimates of the stock would be helpful, but all markets are well practised in dealing with uncertainty.

No one needs to decide in each year, month, or week how many pounds of halibut, salmon, or king crab are to be harvested. Individuals would be free to catch as few or as many fish as they please, by any method that does not violate the rights of others. The constraint, of course, on each individual will be the market for landings together with the going market price of live, unharvested, fish (certificates). If salmon certificates are trading at $3 per pound, it will not be necessary to tell fishermen how much to reduce their catch if salmon landings are fetching $2.75 per pound. Nor will it be necessary to raise the catch quota when certificates are trading at $1 per pound and the canneries are paying $2.50 per pound. Under my proposal, fishermen would be 'regulated' by the spread between the market for current fish landings and the market for certificate claims to live fish (which will reflect the future value of harvested fish). In effect, each fisherman becomes 'sole owner' in the sense of Gordon (1954), and Scott (1955), depending upon that fisherman's free choice of a portfolio of certificates. If I am the sole owner of Great Slave Lake, then I own a portfolio of live fish represented by whatever uncertain stock of fish is in Great Slave Lake. If instead I own a portfolio of live fish certificates, subject to uncertain fluctuations (certificate 'dividends' and reverse splits) which reflect changes in the periodic estimates of the fish population, my situation is substantively the same as if I were a sole owner of Great Slave Lake. The fact that stocks are uncertain should produce *less* of a problem for the certificate holders than for the sole owner of a fishery, since certificates are finely divided while fisheries are indivisible in the absence of unit property right claims. Hence, each fisherman's ownership claims to fish can be adjusted divisibly to his attitude towards risk.

As a further means of reducing uncertainty through markets, it would be desirable to encourage the development of an options market in certificates by species. Thus, a salmon fisherman confronted with four species in the same waters, and being unsure as to which species, in what amounts, will fill his nets, can buy options on all the species, exercise those options needed to pay for his catch, and sell those options that are unused. This would require much less capital than to carry a portfolio of certificates in all four species.

It should be noted that the certificate system would convert the open access fishery into a property right system analogous to that for range cattle in the American West. Domesticated cattle are descended from the auroch—once widely hunted throughout Europe in open-access hunting grounds. In the western territories of the United States, cattle were first introduced in open unfenced ranges before state and/or federal law existed. The property right system took the form of cattle branding, with property rights enforced by cattlemen's associations, who sometimes hired professional gunmen (Anderson and Hill, 1979). Live fish certificates are, in effect, like branded range cattle, but with interchangeable brands. With the growth in agriculture, the resulting externality conflict between crops and cattle, and the invention of barbed wire, an inferior property right system—branding—yielded to a superior system— enclosure. But for a time (and, on low-productivity ranges, even today) branded range cattle provided the property right system that was essential to the support of cattle markets.

Water resource flows

Where water use is from a flow source—a creek, river, or canal—deed certificates would be perpetuities, e.g., a right to one acre-foot of water per year. As water is consumed certificates would not be surrendered; it would be necessary only to verify that a user's portfolio of perpetuities matched his/her consumption for the year with any deficit covered by open market purchase and any surplus being freely saleable. As with fishing rights among the Karok, owning deed perpetuities for water along a river would be independent of who owned the land provided that easement access titles were clear.

Creating rights in public lands: the combinatorial auction

Elsewhere (Smith, 1982) I have discussed criteria for the divestiture of public lands, and have advanced a proposal for divestiture designed to satisfy these criteria. This section will not attempt to do more than summarize that discussion.

From its inception to the present day, some of the Republic's bitterest political battles have been fought over rights to public land: conflicting rights to land by squatters, Indians, and the holders of land warrants and scrip (issued to finance the War of Independence, the War of 1812, the Mexican War, and various Indian wars) were a preoccupation of all levels of government well into the nineteenth century. The Homestead and Morrill Acts were culminations of long political contests. Forty years of mega-dam-building by the Bureau of Reclamation climaxed with the Sierra Club's successful defeat of the Bureau's proposal to flood Marble Canyon and Grand Canyon behind two great dams. Today the Sage Brush rebellion resumes the eighteenth- and nineteenth-century political cry for increased private access to public land.

Over the past two decades there has been an accelerating scholarly (see the citations in Smith, 1982), as well as political, criticism of government steward-ship of the public lands. Environmentalists, ranchers, lumbering interests, and oil companies all complain of the policies or lack of appropriate policy in the Forest Service, the Park Service, and the Bureau of Land Management. The Bureau of Reclamation, together with the Army Engineers, have undoubtedly produced much ecosystem 'damage' behind water inpoundments that are of doubtful net economic benefit. Recent decades have also been characterized by the increased direct participation of private conservation organizations in the acquisition of land to be managed for preservation purposes (for example, the National Audubon Society, Ducks Unlimited, Nature Conservancy, and Save the Redwoods League: see the Appendix to Anderson, Baden and Stroup, 1982).

The following proposal would seek to de-politicize the management of the public lands through a divestiture procedure that would create private property rights in all public land. Its principle features are as follows.

1. All public land would be divested over some stated period, say between twenty and forty years.

2. All such lands would be partitioned into unit tracts which could vary in size, depending on certain classifications of the land.

3. Corresponding to each tract would be a set of distinct separable elemental deed rights appropriate for each tract: mineral, oil and gas, water, grazing, timber, recreational use, wilderness use, and surface or other rights not otherwise specified. Certain land use restrictive covenants could be written permanently into a deed in special areas; e.g., public parks such as Grand Canyon could have

surface rights permanently restricted to recreational or wilderness use. Owners of subsurface rights could be enjoined from exercising such rights without the consent of the owner of surface rights.

4. Once divested, these tract deed rights would be transferable, individually or in any combination, by bequest, sale, assignment, lease, and so on.

5. Any individual with a documented historical claim to rights defined by one or more of these deeds—BLM grazing permits might qualify as an example—would be assigned these 'squatters' rights', with any payments now required by the individual being paid to the new owner of the surface rights.

6. All these elemental tract deed rights would be assembled into blocks, and at regular intervals over the divestiture period, one of these blocks would be advertised for sale in a sealed-bid auction.

7. Bids would *not be denominated in money*; they would be denominated in public land share certificates. These certificates would be issued, all at once, well in advance of the first auction, and would be redeemable only for land at auction. For example, each US citizen might be granted ten certificates with some 2 billion shares initially outstanding. These certificates would be freely bought and sold, assigned, or bequeathed over the divesture period. To facilitate exchange, certificate shares could be listed on all stock and commodity exchanges, with the exchanges free to create futures or options markets in shares. This allows all citizens to share in the wealth created by divestiture without the necessity of owning land.

8. The auction procedure for the divestiture of each block of land would use a 'combinatorial' sealed-bid auction (Rassenti, Smith, and Bulfin, 1982); i.e., each bidder would be free to bid on any right or any combination of rights for any tract or any combination of tracts. The winning bidders would be determined by a computer program that would select those bids (combinations of rights) that yielded the largest certificate value for the entire block. This procedure permits elementary property rights in land to be allocated to those package combinations that are most highly valued by society through the market.

NOTES

1. The incredibly high price of petroleum in 1859 was due to its exclusive use as a medicine, lubricant, and a source of kerosene (lamp or stove oil), which could be distilled from crude petroleum. But the term 'kerosene' appears to be of more recent origin. Historically, it was called 'coal oil' because it was distilled from coal—a source economically competitive with whale oil for lamps. Shale was another early source of lamp oil. Before 1859, since the price was right, the market had no difficulty sustaining oil production from coal and shale. The Titusville strike wiped out production from these sources, and many manufacturers of coal oil either went out of business or converted to petroleum refining.
2. Tony Scott, in commenting on an earlier draft of this paper, asks: 'Since these [oil import

420   *Institutions and Ideologies*

quotas] worked against the rents of the Middle Eastern governments, as well as against the foreign profits of the major oil companies, do you suggest that, symmetrically with the Trust, the *system* of quotas was a means of instituting limited rights to the Arabian commons? More on this would be interesting.' Actually, I meant only to report that by 1959 the impact on domestic US oil prices of my hypothesized rule-of-capture recovery in the Middle East was so severe that it led to the indicated political response. But the point is correct—it is symmetrical with what the Trust attempted to accomplish. To the extent that the United States was the primary consumer of Middle Eastern oil, the import quota became, in effect, a production quota on Middle Eastern oil, and hence an indirect attempt to solve the property rights problem. An optimal quota system is just the mathematical dual of an optimal tax (or bribe) system for internalizing the social costs of the commons. This interpretation is also symmetric with my discussion of the Trust in that domestic producers, it can be supposed, were just trying to arrest the decline in crude prices, and Esienhower was just responding to a powerful constituency. None of the principals would have seen themselves as solving an Arabian property rights problem! This led to import quotas that indeed can be interpreted as a crude, indirect 'means of instituting limited rights to the Arabian commons'. The solution was of course exceedingly crude, since what was needed was not an overall quota but a quota on each Arabian source of petroleum which was equal to what a sole owner would find it profitable to produce in a world in which *each reservoir* is controlled by a sole owner with a secure property right. Essentially, all indirect solutions (quotas, taxes on production, bribes not to overproduce) must simulate the competing sole owner solution—the property rights solution we all learned originally from the path-breaking work of Scott (1955). Gordon (1954) had earlier emphasized that the over-fishing problem was due to the failure of each fisherman to have a secure property right in each fishing ground. I might add that the *right* quota system would not have 'worked against the rents on middle eastern governments'. With optimal quotas providing surrogate sole owner rights, these rents would not be dissipated by rule-of-capture entry.
3. Phil Neher pointed out to me at the conference that the failure of OPEC to develop a quota system among its members is consistent with this property rights interpretation.
4. A simpler procedure, which would be equivalent to certificate dividends, or splits, would simply be to change the redemption terms for certificates. Thus, if new estimates of the stock of ground water (or of fish in open access fisheries) are lowered, then one simply increases the redemption exchange rate—say 1.1 certificates per acre-foot of water (or per pound of fish) harvested. Any scheme that maintains equality between the floating stock of certificate claims and the estimated real stock of the resource would be satisfactory.
5. See n. 4.
6. The fact that our knee-jerk reaction is always to assume that the government is the appropriate agent to enforce property rights does not make it valid; counter-examples abound; e.g., the cattlemen's associations in the West, and the American Kennel Club. Since there are international conflicts over fishing grounds, perhaps one would not want privately hired gunmen squaring off in 'High Noon' confrontation with Russian trawlers.
7. To facilitate an ongoing market for certificates, by species, they could be listed for trading on the commodity and/or stock exchanges, in which case a stock registrar would be needed, but private agencies (banks) could do this as they now do for corporate securities.

REFERENCES

Anderson, Terry, Baden, John, and Stroup, Richard (1982), 'Report to the Department of Interior on Innovative Resource Management Strategies', Montana State University, February 1982.

Anderson, Terry, and Hill, P. J. (1979), 'An American Experiment in Anarcho-Capitalism: The *Not* So Wild, Wild West', *Journal of Libertarian Studies,* 3, 9–29.

Andrews, E. B. (1889), 'Trusts According to Official Investigations', *Quarterly Journal of Economics,* January, 117–52.

Armentano, D. T. (1981), 'The Petroleum Industry: A Historical Study in Power', *The Cato Journal,* 1, 53–85.

Barr, James and Pingry, David (1976), 'Rational Water Pricing in the Tucson Basin', *Arizona Review,* 25, 1–12.

Freuchen, Peter (1961), *Book of the Eskimos,* Cleveland: World Publishing.

Gordon, Scott (1954), 'The Economic Theory of a Common-property Resource: the Fishery', *Journal of Political Economy,* 62, 124–42.

Heizer, Robert (1955), *Primitive Man as an Ecological Factor,* Krober Anthropological Society Papers no. 13. Berkeley: University of California Press.

Hughes, Jonathan (1977), *The Governmental Habit,* New York: Basic Books.

Hughes, Jonathan (1982), 'The Great Strike at Nushagak Station, 1951: Institutional Gridlock', *Journal of Economic History,* 42, 1–20.

Kroeber, A. L. and Barrett, S. A. (1960), *Fishing Among the Indians of Northern California, Anthropological Records,* vol. 21, no. 1. Berkeley: University of California Press.

Libecap, Gary D. and Wiggins, Steven N. (1982), 'Contracting by Heterogeneous Firms and Government Regulation of Crude Oil Production', Department of Economics, Texas A & M University.

Mancke, Richard B. (1981), 'Competition and Monopoly in World Oil Markets: The Role of the International Oil Companies', *The Cato Journal,* 1, 107–27.

Martin, Paul (1967), 'Prehistoric Overkill', in P. S. Martin and H. E. Wright, Jr (eds), *Pleistocene Extinctions,* New Haven, Conn.: Yale University Press.

North, Douglas (1981), *Structure and Change in Economic History,* New York: W. W. Norton.

North, Douglas and Thomas, Robert (1977), 'The First Economic Revolution', *Economic History Review,* 30, 229–41.

Pearse, Peter H. (1981), *Conflict and Opportunity. Toward a New Policy for Canada's Pacific Fisheries,* Vancouver: Commission on Pacific Fisheries Policy.

Rassenti, Steven, Smith, Vernon L., and Bulfin, Robert (1982), 'A Combinatorial Auction Mechanism for Airport Time Slot Allocation', *Bell Journal of Economics,* 13, 2, 402–17.

Scott, Anthony, (1955), 'The Fishery: The Objectives of Sole Ownership', *Journal of Political Economy,* 63, 116–24.

Scott, Anthony and Neher, Philip A. (eds) (1981), *The Public Regulation of Commercial Fisheries in Canada,* Economic Council of Canada.

Smith, Vernon L. (1975), 'The Primitive Hunter Culture, Pleistocene Extinction, and the Rise of Agriculture', *Journal of Political Economy,* 83, 727–55.

Smith, Vernon L. (1977), 'Water Deeds: A Proposed Solution to the Water Valuation Problems', *Arizona Review,* 26, 7–10.

Smith, Vernon L. (1982), 'On Divestiture and the Creation of Property Rights in Public Land', *The Cato Journal,* 3.

Umbeck, John (1982), *A Theoretical and Empirical Investigation into the Formation of Property Rights,* Iowa City: University of Iowa Press.

Woolpy, Jerome H. (1968), 'The Social Organization of Wolves', *Natural History,* 77, 46–55.

List of Contributors

Ernst R. BERNDT
 The Sloan School, Massachusetts Institute of Technology, Cambridge, Massachusetts, 02139

Paul G. BRADLEY
 Department of Economics, University of British Columbia, Vancouver, BC, V6T 1Y2.

Paul M. BOOTHE
 International Department, Bank of Canada, Ottawa, Ontario, K1A 0G9

Gardner BROWN, Jr
 Department of Economics, University of Washington, Seattle, Washington 98195

Trudy A. CAMERON
 Department of Economics, University of British Columbia, Vancouver, BC, V6T 1Y2

Harry F. CAMPBELL
 Department of Economics, University of British Columbia, Vancouver, BC, V6T 1Y2.

Colin W. CLARK
 Department of Mathematics, University of British Columbia, Vancouver, BC, V6T 1Y2.

Anthony CHARLES
 Department of Mathematics, University of British Columbia, Vancouver, BC, V6T 1Y2.

Partha DASGUPTA
 Department of Economics, London School of Economics and Political Science, Houghton Street, London WC2A 2AE

Mukesh ESWARAN
 Department of Economics, University of British Columbia, Vancouver, BC, V6T 1Y2

and

Institute for Policy Analysis, University of Toronto, Ontario, M5S 1A1.

Ardo HANSSON
Department of Economics, University of British Columbia, Vancouver, BC, V6T 1Y2
and
Harvard University, Cambridge, Massachusetts 02138

James P. JOHNSON
Ministry of Energy, Mines and Petroleum Resources, Province of British Columbia, Victoria, BC, V8V 1X4

Lawrence R. KLEIN
Department of Economics, University of Pennsylvania, Philadelphia, 19104

Pierre LASSERRE
Département de sciences économiques, Université de Montréal, Montréal, Quebec, H3C 3J7

Tracy R. LEWIS
Department of Economics, University of British Columbia, Vancouver, BC, V6T 1Y2.

Michael MARGOLICK
Department of Economics, University of British Columbia, Vancouver, BC, V6T 1Y2
and
Margolick & Associates, Vancouver, British Columbia

Robert N. McRAE
Department of Economics, University of Calgary, Alberta, T2N 1N4.

Gordon R. MUNRO
Department of Economics, University of British Columbia, Vancouver, BC, V6T 1Y2

Philip A. NEHER
Department of Economics, University of British Columbia, Vancouver, BC, V6T 1Y2

Nancy OLEWILER
Department of Economics, Queen's University, Kingston, Ontario, K7L 3N6

Tim PADMORE
Department of Economics, University of British Columbia, Vancouver, BC, V6T 1Y2
and
The Vancouver Sun, Vancouver, British Columbia

Robert S. PINDYCK
The Sloan School, Massachusetts Institute of Technology, Cambridge, Massachusetts 02139

Andre PLOUDRE
Department of Economics, University of British Columbia, Vancouver, BC, V6T 1Y2

Reg PLUMMER
Department of Economics, University of British Columbia, Vancouver, BC, V6T 1Y2

William SCHWORM
Department of Economics, University of British Columbia, Vancouver, BC, V6T 1Y2

Anthony SCOTT
Department of Economics, University of British Columbia, Vancouver, BC, V6T 1Y2

Margaret SLADE
Department of Economics, University of British Columbia, Vancouver, BC, V6T 1Y2

V. Kerry SMITH
Department of Economics, University of North Carolina, Chapel Hill, North Carolina, 27514

Daniel F. SPULBER
Department of Economics and Institute for Marine and Coastal Studies, University of Southern California, University Park, Los Angeles, California 90007

Russell S. UHLER
Department of Economics, University of British Columbia, Vancouver, BC, V6T 1Y2

G. Campbell WATKINS
    DataMetrics Limited, 604–1414 8th Street SW, Calgary, Alberta, T2R 1J6
    and
    University of Calgary, Alberta T2N 1N4

Douglas L. WREAN
    Ministry of Energy, Mines and Petroleum Resources, Province of British
    Columbia, Victoria, BC V8V 1X4.

Programme in Natural Resource Economics
Department of Economics,
University of British Columbia

RESOURCES DISCUSSION SERIES

Resource paper

No. 1   Crommelin, Michael, Pearse, Peter H. and Scott, Anthony (1978), 'Management of Oil and Gas Resources in Alberta: An Economic Evaluation of Public Policy', *Natural Resources Journal*, 18, 337-89.

No. 2   Clark, Colin W. and Munro, Grodon R. (1978), 'Renewable Resources and Extinction: The Consequences of Irreversibility', *Journal of Environmental Economics and Management*, 5, 198-205.

No. 3   Wilen, James E. (1976), 'Common Property Resources and the Dynamics of Overexploitation: The Case of the North Pacific Fur Seal', unpublished paper.

No. 4   Neher, Philip A. (1968), 'The Pure Theory of Muggery', *American Economic Review*, 68, 438-43.

No. 5   Helliwell, John F. (1978), 'Effects of Taxes and Royalties on Copper Mining Investment in British Columbia', *Resources Policy*, 4, 35-44.

No. 6   Helliwell, John F. (1977), 'Arctic Pipelines in the Context of Canadian Energy Requirements', *Canadian Public Policy—Analyse de Politiques* 3, 344-54; different versions published in *Financial Times*, Canada, 1977, and in Canadian Arctic Resources Committee's *Northern Perspectives*, 5, 1-4.

No. 7   Helliwell, John F, with Duncan, B. C. E., Hendricks, K. McRae, R. N., May, G. and Williams D. B. C. (1979), 'An Integrated Simulation Approach to the Analysis of Canadian Energy Policies', in P. Nemtz (ed.), *Energy Policy: The Global Challenge*, 283-93; also in a special issue of *Journal of Business Administration*, 10, 1-2.

No. 8   Clark, Colin, W., Clark, Frank H., and Munro, Gordon R. (1979), 'The Optimal Management of Renewable Resource Stocks: Problems of Irreversible Investment', *Econometrica* 47, 25-47.

No. 9   Campbell, Harry F. (1977), 'The Evaluation of Open-pit Mining Projects', unpublished paper.

No. 10   Eswaren, Mukesh, and Wilen, James E. (1977), 'Expectations and Adjustment in Open Access Resource Use', unpublished paper.

No. 11   Berndt, Ernst R. (1977), 'Tax Policy, Energy Demand and Economic Growth', unpublished paper.

No. 12   Osler, Sanford L. (1977), 'An Application of Marginal Cost Pricing Principles to BC Hydro', unpublished paper.

No. 13   Heaps Terry, and Neher, Philip A. (1979), 'The Economics of Forestry when the Rate of Harvest is Constrained', *Journal of Environmental Economics and Management,* 6, 297-319.

No. 14 Uhler, Russell S. (1977), 'The Rate of Petroleum Exploration and Extraction', unpublished paper.

No. 15 Bradley, Paul G. and Scott, Anthony (1977), 'Coastal Oil Spills: Alternative Courses for Canadian Policy', unpublished paper.

No. 16 Berndt, E. R. and Wood, David O. (1979), 'Engineering and Econometric Approaches to Energy Conservation and Capital Formation: a Reconciliation', *American Economic Review,* 69, 342-54.

No. 17 Jones, R. A., Pearse, P. H., and Scott, A. D. (1980), 'Joint Project Selection Considerations for Cooperation among Independent Jurisdictions', published as 'Conditions for Cooperation on Joint projects by Independent Jurisdictions', *Canadian Journal of Economics,* 13, 231-44.

No. 18 Munro, Gordon R. (1979), 'The Optimal Management of Transboundary Renewable Resources', *Canadian Journal of Economics,* 12, 355-76.

No. 19 Helliwell, John F., and Cox, Alan J. (1979), 'Wood Wastes as an Energy Source for the BC Pulp and Paper Industry: Economic Implications and Institutional Barriers', in P. Nemetz (ed.), *Energy Policy: The Global Challenge,* pp. 245-61; also in *Journal of Business Administration,* 10, 1-2.

No. 20 Cox, Alan J. (1978), 'An Economic Evaluation of the Use of Wood Wastes to Generate Heat and Electricity at Pulp and Paper Mills in British Columbia', unpublished paper.

No. 21 Cox, Alan J. and Helliwell, John F. (1980), 'Economic Modelling of Energy Supply from Burning Wood Wastes at BC Pulp and Paper Mills', In W. T. Ziemba *et al.* (eds), *Energy Policy Modelling: US and Canadian Experiences,* Hingham, Mass.: Martinus Nijhoff, 1, 159-74.

No. 22 Cox, Alan J. and Helliwell, John F. (1980), 'Electricity Pricing and Electricity Supply: The Influence of Utility Pricing on Electricity Production by Pulp and Paper Mills', *Resources and Energy,* 2, 51-74.

No. 23 Uhler, R. S. (1978), 'Least-squares Regression Estimates of the Schaefer Production Model: Some Monte Carlo Simulation Results', unpublished paper.

No. 24 Campbell, Harry (1980), 'The Effect of Capital Intensity on the Optimal Rate of Extraction of a Mineral Deposit', *Canadian Journal of Economics,* 13, 349-56.

No. 25 Berndt, Ernst R. (1978), 'Aggregate Energy, Efficiency, and Productivity Measurement', *Annual Review of Energy,* 3, 226-73.

No. 26 Campbell, Harry and Scott, Anthony (1979), 'Postponement vs. Attenuation: An Analysis of Two Strategies for Predicting and Mitigating the Environmental Damage of Large-Scale Uranium Mining Projects',

Resources Policy, 5, 113-40, and *Economic Record* (1980), 36-53.

No. 27   Helliwell, John F., with Hendricks, K. and Williams D. B. C. (1980), 'Canadian Perspectives on the Alaska Highway Pipeline: Modelling the Alternatives', in W. T. Ziemba *et al.* (eds), *Energy Policy Modeling: US and Canadian Experiences,* 2, 279-317.

No. 28   Berndt, Ernst R. (1978), 'Aggregate Energy, Efficiency, and Productivity Measurement', *Annual Review of Energy,* 3, 226-73.

No. 29   Neher, Philip A. (1978), 'Rent-A-Rig', unpublished paper.

No. 30   Berndt, Ernst R. and Morrison, C. J. (1979), 'Income Redistribution and Employment Effects of Rising Energy Prices', *Resources and Energy,* 2, 131-50.

No. 31   Bradley, Paul G. (1980), 'Modelling Mining: Open Pit Copper Production in British Columbia', *Resources Policy,* 6, 44-59.

No. 32   Panayotou, Theodore (1979), 'The Copper Cartel and Canada: Likelihood and Implications of OPEC-type Strategies', unpublished paper.

No. 33   Morey, Edward R. (1979), 'The Demand for Site-specific Recreational Activities: A Characteristics Approach', unpublished paper.

No. 34   Clark, Colin W. and Munro, Gordon R. (1980), 'Fisheries and the Processing Sector: Some Implications for Management Policy', *Bell Journal of Economics,* 11, 603-16.
         Munro, Gordon R. (1982), 'Bilateral Monopoly in Fisheries and Optimal Management Policy', in L. J. Mirman and D. F. Spulber (eds), *Essays in the Economics of Renewable Resources,* Amsterdam: North-Holland, 187-202.

No. 35   Helliwell, John F., and Cox, A. J. (1978), 'Simulation Analysis of Energy Production in the BC Pulp and Paper Industry', in M. B. Carver and M. H. Hamza (eds), *Simulation, Modelling, and Decision in Energy Systems,* Anaheim and Calgary: ACTA Press, 314-19. Proceedings of a conference, Montreal.

No. 36   Larmour, Peter (1979), 'The Concept of Rent in 19th-Century Economic Thought: Ricardo, Mill, Marx, Wolras, and Marshall', unpublished paper.

No. 37   LeMarquand, David and Scott, Anthony (1980), 'Canada's International Environmental Relations', in O. P. Dwivedi (ed.), *Resources and the Environment,* Toronto: McClelland & Steward.

No. 38   Berndt, E. R. and Morrison, C. J. (1979), 'Energy, Capital and Productivity', chapter 9 in Joy Dunkerley (ed.), *International Energy Strategies; Proceedings of the 1979 IAEE/RFF Conference,* Cambridge, Mass.: Oelgeschlaeger, Gunn and Hain, Inc., 79-99.

No. 39   Berndt, E. R., Cox A. J., and Pearse, P. H. (1979), 'Estimation of Logging Costs and Timber Supply Curves from Forestry Inventory Data', *The Forestry Chronicle,* August, 144-7.

No. 40   Clark, Colin W. (1980), 'Towards a Predictive Model for The Economic

Regulation of Commercial Fisheries', *Canadian Journal of Fisheries and Aquatic Sciences,* 37, 1111-29.

No. 41   Bradley, Paul G. (1979), 'Production of Depleting Resources: A Cost-Curve Approach', unpublished paper.

No. 42   Pearse, Peter H. (1979), 'Property Rights and the Regulation of Commercial Fisheries', unpublished paper.

No. 43   Muller, R. A. (1979), 'On the Use of the Restricted Profit Function in Industrial Economics: With an Application to the Canadian Pulp and Paper Industry', unpublished paper.

No. 44   Loose, Verne W. (1979), 'A Bioeconomic Commercial Pacific Salmon Fisher Model', unpublished paper.

No. 45   Crabbe, Phillipe J. (1979), 'The Contribution of L. C. Gray to the Economic Theory of Exhaustible Natural Resources', unpublished paper.

No. 46   Panayotou, Theodore (1979), 'Predicting Ultimate Mineral Resources: An Extended "Tonnage-Grade" Model with an Application to Copper in Zambia', unpublished paper.

No. 47   Helliwell, John F. (1980), 'Taxation and Energy Policy', *Report of Proceedings of the 31st Tax Conference,* Toronto: Canadian Tax Foundation, 7-20.

No. 48   Helliwell, John F., (1980), 'The Distribution of Energy Revenues within Canada: Functional or Factional Federalism?', UBC Resource paper.

No. 49   Berndt, E. R., Morrison, J. and Watkins, G. C. (1981), 'Dynamic Models of Energy Demand: an Assessment and Comparison', chapter 12 in E. R. Berndt and B. C. Field (eds), *Modeling and Measuring Natural Resource Substitution,* Cambridge, Mass.: MIT Press, 259-89.

No. 50   Lewis, Tracy, and Neher, Philip (1980), 'Consistent and Revised Plans for Natural Resources Use', chapter 3 of L. J. Mirman and D. F. Spulber, *Essays in the Economics of Renewable Resources,* Amsterdam: North-Holland.

No. 51   Berndt, E. R. (1980), 'Energy Price Increases and the Productivity Slowdown in United States Manufacturing', in *The Decline in Productivity Growth,* Boston: Federal Reserve Bank of Boston Conference Series, no. 22, 60-80.

No. 52   Scott, Anthony (1980), 'Divided Jurisdiction over Natural Resource Revenues', Royal Society of Canada *Transactions,* 18, 203-22.

No. 53   Livernois, John R. (1980), 'Summary Evaluation of Northeast Coal Development in BC', unpublished paper.

No. 54   Helliwell, John F., (1981), 'Using Canadian Oil and Gas Revenues in the 1980's: Provincial and Federal Perspectives', in Barker, T. and Brailovsky, V. (eds), *Oil or Industry? Energy Industrialisation and Economic Policy in Canada, Mexico, the Netherlands and the United Kingdom,* London: Academic Press.

No. 55   Eswaren, Mukesh, and Lewis, Tracy R. (1980), 'A Note on Market Structure and the Search for Exhaustible Resources', *Economic Letters,* 75-80.

No. 56   Helliwell, John F. and Margolick, Michael (1983), 'Some Hard Economics of Soft Energy: Optimal Electricity Generation in Pulp and Paper Mills with Seasonal Steam Requirements', in *Global Econometrics: Essays in honour of L. R. Klein,* (edited by Hickman, Lau, and Adams).

No. 57   Helliwell, John F. (1980), 'The Stagflationary Effects of Higher Energy Prices in an Open Economy', *Canadian Public Policy—Aanlyse de Politiques,* 7, Supplement, 155-64.

No. 58   Helliwell, John F., Bradley, Paul, and Livernois, John (1981), 'Efficient Taxation of Resource Income: The Case of Copper Mining in British Columbia', *Resources Policy,* 7, (3).

No. 59   Diewert, Erwin W. and Lewis, Tracy (1981), 'The Comparative Dynamics of Efficient Programmes of Capital Accumulation and Resource Depletion', in W. Eichorn (ed.), *Economic Theory of Natural Resources,* 301-27, Springer Verlag.

No. 60   Lewis, Tracy R. and Schmalensee, Richard (1981), 'Optimal Use of Renewable Resources with Nonconvexities in Production', chapter in L. Mirman and D. Spulber (eds), *Essays in the Economics of Renewable Resources,* Amsterdam: North-Holland.

No. 61   Salant, Stephan, Eswaran, Mukesh, and Lewis, Tracy R. (1981), 'The Length of Optimal Extraction Programs When Depletion Affects Extraction, unpublished paper.

No. 62   Lewis, Tracy R. (1981, 'Sufficient Conditions for Extracting Least Cost Resources First', *Econometrica,* (July 1982), 1081-4.

No. 63   Eswaren, Mukesh and Lewis, Tracy R. (1981), 'Production from Differentiated Exhaustible Resources in Oligopolistic Markets', unpublished paper.

No. 64   Hansson, Ardo (1981), 'An Economic Analysis of Methanol Production by Wood-Using Techniques in British Columbia', unpublished paper.

No. 65   Margolick, Michael, Hansson, Ardo, and Helliwell, J. F. (1981), 'Competing Energy Uses for Wood Wastes in British Columbia', unpublished paper.

No. 66   Uhler, Russell S. (1981), 'Oil Reserves Prices', unpublished paper.

No. 67   Eswaren, Mukesh, Lewis, T. R. and Heaps, T. (1981), 'On the Nonexistence of Competitive Equilibria in Exhaustible Resource Markets' *Journal of Political Economy,* Feb. 1983, 154-68.

No. 68   Neher, Philip (1981), 'Rent-a-Rig', unpublished paper.

No. 69   Margolick, Michael, and Helliwell, John F. (1981), 'Electricity Generation from Wood Waste in BC', unpublished paper.

No. 70   Margolick, Michael, Charles, Anthony, and Helliwell, John F. (1981), 'The Value of Information to Electricity Investment Planners', unpublished paper.

No. 71   Munro, Gordon R. (1981), 'Fisheries, Extended Jurisdiction, and the Economics of Common Property Resources', *Canadian Journal of Economics,* 15, 405-25.

No. 72   Flaaten, Ola (1981), 'Resource Allocation and Share Systems in Fish Harvesting Firms', unpublished paper.

No. 73   Slade, Margaret (1981), 'Dominant-firm Pricing and Byproduct Supply: the Structure of the US Molybdenum Industry', unpublished paper.

No. 74   Uhler, Russell (1982), 'The Supply of Natural Gas Reserves in Alberta', chapter 9 above.

No. 75   McKelvey, Robert (1982), 'Economic Regulation of Targeting Behavior in a Multispecies Fishery', unpublished paper.

No. 76   Gallini, N., Lewis, Tracy, and Ware, R. (1983), 'Monopoly Pricing of an Exhaustible Resource with Lagged Entry', *Canadian Journal of Economics,* Aug. 1983, 429-56.

No. 77   Eswaren, M. and Lewis, Tracy (1983), 'Evolution of Market Structure in a Dominant Firm Model with Exhaustible Resources', chapter 8 above.

No. 78   Bernard, J. T., Bridges, G. E. and Scott, A. D. (1982), 'An Evaluation of Potential Ricardian Hydroelectric Rents', unpublished paper.

No. 79   Flaaten, Ola (1982), 'The Optimal Harvesting of a Natural Resource with Seasonal Growth', unpublished paper.

No. 80   Slade, Margaret E. (1982), 'Measures of Market Power in Extractive Industries: the legacy of US v. General Dynamics', unpublished paper.

No. 81   Slade, Margaret E. (1982), 'Taxation of Nonrenewable Resources: A Production-Function Approach', unpublished paper.

No. 82   Hansson, Ardo H. (1982), 'Modelling the Possibilities for Economic Use of Alternative Motor Fuels', unpublished paper.

No. 83   Slade, Margaret E. (1982), 'Tax Policy and the Supply of Exhaustible Resources: Theory and Practice', unpublished paper.

No. 84   Lewis, T. and Cowans, J. (1982), 'The Great Fish War: A Cooperative Solution', unpublished paper.

No. 85   Charles, Anthony (1982), 'Optimal Fisheries Investment: Comparative Dynamics for a Deterministic Seasonal Fishery', unpublished paper.

No. 86   Charles, Anthony (1982), 'Optimal Fisheries Investment Under Uncertainty', unpublished paper.

Author Index

Subject Index

absorption prices , 28-9, 56
adjustment costs *see* costs
Agricultural Revolution, 404-6, 407
Alsands, 55-7
amenity benefits, 96, 130-9
arbitrage equations, 330
attenuated resource development, 322, 326

CANDIDE, 86
capacity, 293, 319-22, 325, 332
  fishing, 113-15
  taxes and, 320
  uncertainty and, 318
capacity choice, 318-22
capacity constraint, 328n
capacity costs, 325-6, 332
capacity use, 27, 29
capital, availability of, 321-2
  durability of, 180, 192
  extraction and, 174, 176-202, 328n,
    330, 332
  interest rate and, 187-200
  investment, 317-32
  malleable, 177, 182, 188-92, 197,
    199-200, 328n
  non-malleable, 95, 105-9, 171, 180,
    182-3, 197-8, 262
  resources as, 91, 94, 104, 317-18,
    325-8
  resource use and, 321-2
  supply price, 24
capital costs, capacity choice and, 293
cartels, 242-59
  property rights and, 410, 412-14, 420n
coal, 37, 324, 327
coal oil, 419
common law, property rights and, 376-99
common property, 394, 396
  fisheries, 95, 99-100, 102
conservation, 139, 218
copper, 320, 322-3, 324, 327
cost curves, models of, 299-302, 311
  mining, 318-19, 331-3
crude oil *see also* energy, oil
  prices, 35, 37-9, 262, 264, 327

delayed investment, 112, 268-72, 281, 288
  excess capacity and, 269-70
  models of, 269-72
  prices and, 270-3
  reserves appreciation and, 275-8
democratic exploitation of natural resources,
  96, 130-52

depletion rate, mining and, 320-2, 327-8n
differential rents, 317, 323-4, 327
discovery *see also* exploration
  forecasting, 328n
  models of, 263, 265, 272-4, 284-7
  oil leases and, 395
  pre-emptive, 242-59
  price changes and, 263-4, 267-78,
    281-4
  supply curves, and, 324, 327
  uncertainty and, 243, 257
Dutch disease, 58

easement, 382-3, 385
electricity, 34-7
energy *see also* natural gas, oil
  certificates, 351-2
  demand equations, 18
  economic rents and, 37
  MACE 17-89
  prices, 17-18, 27-30, 34-7, 81, 85,
    87-8
  production, 18, 26-7, 37-41
  supply, 37-41
  taxes, 35-41
  theories of value, 337-75
  use, 18, 22-3, 81, 87
Energy Resources Conservation Board, 270,
  282
Energy Survey of North America, 346, 350-1
environment, 99, 120, 139, 322
excess capacity, 95, 105-6, 171-2
  delayed investment, 269-70
excess supply, mining, 135
exchange, 403-4, 406-8
exhaustible resources *see also* energy,
  mining, natural gas, oil, uranium
  empirical analysis of, 261-333
  extraction of, 174-201
  market structure of, 242-59
  theoretical analysis of, 173-259
exploration, 37-9, *see also* discovery
  differential rents and, 323-4
  gas leases and, 395
  models of, 261-332
  pre-emptive, 175, 242-59, 331
  price changes and, 263
  property rights and, 388, 395-7
  royalties and, 217-20
  supply curves and, 327
extraction, capital and, 174, 176-202,
  244-5, 328, 330, 332
  exploration and, 236